D1481361

# HORIZONTAL-SPAN
# BUILDING STRUCTURES

## WOLFGANG SCHUELLER

Professor of Architecture and Building Construction
Virginia Polytechnic Institute and State University

A Wiley-Interscience Publication

JOHN WILEY & SONS

New York · Chichester · Brisbane · Toronto · Singapore

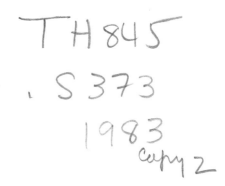
Copyright © 1983 by John Wiley & Sons, Inc.

All rights reserved. Published simultaneously in Canada.

Reproduction or translation of any part of this work
beyond that permitted by Section 107 or 108 of the
1976 United States Copyright Act without the permission
of the copyright owner is unlawful. Requests for
permission or further information should be addressed to
the Permissions Department, John Wiley & Sons, Inc.

*Library of Congress Cataloging in Publication Data:*

Schueller, Wolfgang, 1934–
  Horizontal-span building structures.

  "A Wiley-Interscience publication."
  Bibliography: p.
  Includes index.
  1. Structural engineering.  2. Building.  3. Space
frame structures.  I. Title.

| L.C. call no. | Dewey Classification no. | L.C. card no. |
|---|---|---|
| TH845.S373 | 690′.21    82-4841 | |
| ISBN 0-471-86756-X | AACR2 | |

Printed in the United States of America

10  9  8  7  6  5  4  3  2  1

*To Ria and Uschi*

# PREFACE

In this book a wealth of horizontal-span building structures ranging from small to large-span systems, from single to multibay structures, from rigid to flexible construction, and from skeleton to surface structures is presented in an ordered manner. The structures may be of modular or plastic character, they may be exposed and an integral part of the building design, or they may be hidden behind nonstructural elements to serve solely as support. The various structure types are organized according to their form and behavior. Their development in an historical context is briefly reviewed to give some frame of reference and an appreciation for continuity.

A special asset of this text lies in the inclusion of the new construction methods such as space frames, folded plates, shells, prestressed net roofs, tents, and pneumatic structures, which have developed in the second half of this century. For the first time these systems have been made accessible, in this comparative approach, to a broader group of professionals. This treatment of surface structures should be of real assistance to architects, engineers, contractors, and other building officials whose specialties lie elsewhere. An introduction to new lightweight materials for soft shells and to novel construction techniques, together with the visualization of the continuum of geometry and the spatial force flow along various surface forms, are all features which enrich and strengthen the expertise of the building designer.

This book grew out of not only the need to organize and discuss the behavior of the various building structure types in a systematic manner, but also to bring the field of structural engineering closer to architecture; that is, to make structure an integral part of architecture and to recognize it as the anatomy or one of the essential ordering systems of buildings.

Currently, there is a lack of communication, particularly on the college level, between structure, construction, and architectural design. In courses on structures the structural element, together with its loading, is usually already isolated from its context so that primary emphasis can be placed on the various analytical methods of solution. In contrast, this book emphasizes the setting up of the problems based on actual buildings; loads, member shapes, and boundary conditions are derived from the layout of a structure, from construction methods, and from detailing and appearance requirements. The student may have to resolve a complex continuous system into several basic ones so that the structural elements can be evaluated and proportioned quickly. By deriving the mathematical and behavioral concepts of mechanics from an actual building, the student can better understand the purpose and logic of structure, and be helped to perceive how it functions and how it affects the building form. Furthermore, and most importantly, it teaches students to see mathematics as an efficient means of communication rather than an end in itself. Through this approach the student will develop a sense for behavior and thus will gain confidence in dealing with structure.

The presentation of actual buildings will help designers explore the three-dimensional order of structure as well as to visualize the force flow and spatial interaction of structural elements. Architects will perceive the order of structure and learn to control the interplay of material and nonmaterial spaces during the design stage. Similarly, structural engineers will be able to translate the behavior of building elements into abstract images, with which they are already familiar from other structure courses.

The treatment of structures is broadened and enriched by relating it partially to the traditionally separated fields of construction systems, structural analysis and design, materials, geometry, graphical analysis and presentation, and history. Nearly equal emphasis has been placed on the descriptive, analytical, and graphical investigation of the topics. The visual portion of the book is essential to the education of the building designer; more than 2000 graphical images will prove this point.

The need for more extensive education in the actual building of buildings becomes quite urgent after the recent failures of several long-span structures. Among the more publicized examples are: the Hartford Civic Center Coliseum in Hartford, Connecticut (1978); the auditorium of the C. W. Post Center of Long Island University, Greenvale, New York (1978); the Crosby Kemper Jr. Memorial Arena, Kansas City, Missouri (1979); the Rosemont Horizon Arena, Rosemont, Illinois (1979); and the Congress Hall, West Berlin, Germany (1980).

Charles Lewis wrote in the *New York Times* on August 31, 1981:

> There is a serious crisis in the structural design of America's long-span, column-free buildings, and considering the frightening number of collapses and near collapses in recent years, perhaps our desire for attractive, open-space buildings has exceeded our ability to design and construct them safely.
>
> It is not a question of technology but of slumping on-the-job competence that victimizes an innocent public. For several reasons, far too many architects and structural engineers in this country—at our peril—are guilty of negligence.
>
> What happened at the Hyatt Regency in Kansas City last July has been happening all too frequently in recent years throughout the nation. . . .

There is a danger that the public will become worried and slowly lose confidence in the expertise of the building professionals. The American Institute of Architects, quite aware of this situation, formed a committee to review the technology of buildings with large, column-free interior spaces. In 1981, the results of its investigation were published in the report "Towards Safer Long-Span Buildings." Recommended among several other considerations is that course material for architecture and engineering schools should be developed stressing topics appropriate to long-span buildings.

Colleges that teach the design of buildings must also be concerned with physical reality; it is not enough to investigate some isolated issues only. Furthermore, this physical reality may easily get lost in formal or mathematical abstractions, which may develop into such intricate systems that they become ends in themselves. Although the computer is a necessary tool, the complete reliance of the designer on its answers may result in the loss of feeling for the behavior of structure and thus the designer's capability of independent checking. It can only be hoped that the approach used in this book will aid the designer to further develop the sense of structural behavior and knowledge about horizontal-span structures, as well as to bridge the gap between various fields of building design and construction, thus helping to reduce the risk of building failures.

This book is intended as a text for structure courses in the fields of architecture, building technology, and the branch of civil engineering concentrating on building construction. One of the most important purposes is to interpret the structural behavior of the elements within various building forms by using a minimum of mathematics, while estimating the preliminary member sizes with reasonable accuracy. The mathematics is deliberately kept at a basic level so that the primary emphasis on behavioral aspects is not hidden behind complex analytical processes. Throughout the book, however, the reasons for any of the simplifications are explained; the process of design is never reduced to merely plugging into ready-made formulas. The discipline of thought as established by the engineering sciences over a long period of time is an important portion in the designers education.

The student will never truly comprehend the complexity of structural behavior by just reading descriptive material and/or listening to fascinating lectures. He or she must actually solve problems in order to really learn the subject matter and to find out what is not understood. To support this goal, emphasis is placed on analytical exercises; more than 370 problems are given, nearly all of which are solved in the *Solutions Manual*. Eventually, the student will have developed that certain feeling which brings the building structure alive because suddenly he perceives himself as being the structure and thus experiencing the pain of stress concentrations and the distortions of his bones.

This text does not replace books on the precise analysis and design of structural components or on construction. It is assumed that the reader has taken elementary courses in the fields of statics as well as the design of steel, concrete, and timber; however, some of these important basic topics are reviewed in Chapter 1.

The descriptions of the many building cases should help students to expand their ability to communicate and talk about structure, as well as to relate abstract principles to physical reality; they must understand that structure does not just happen on a mathematical level. The more than 360 building cases were selected solely to exemplify structural concepts and to develop a feeling for structure and form rather than to support specific architectural styles or structural acrobatics.

This book is organized as follows. Basic concepts required for the structural design of buildings are reviewed in Chapter 1; the nature of loading, material characteristics, member response, foundation systems, and the principle of prestressing are discussed. Structural systems, the nature of the horizontal and vertical building planes, as well as stability considerations are investigated in Chapter 2. In Chapter 3 flexible linear elements (cables) are studied, and in Chapter 4 rigid linear enclosure units such as portal frames, A-frames, arches, and multibay systems are analyzed.

The second part of the book deals with surface structures. Space frames and folded plate structures are introduced in Chapters 5 and 6. General concepts of bent surface structures, covered in Chapter 7, are then investigated in more detail with respect to application to rigid shells in Chapter 8 and soft shells in Chapter 9.

Should the book be used for a one-semester course to introduce structure systems, then Chapters 1–4 should be covered, with the possible exception of certain topics which may have already been discussed in another course or which may be treated on a qualitative level only. This portion of the book basically covers general structural concepts and the behavior of linear structural components. The student of structures should be familiar at least with most of the quantitative approaches in Chapters 2 and 4 with the possible exception of arches. The second portion of the book relating to surface structures can be investigated in another more advanced course. Obviously, there are all kinds of course organizations possible, but this text is adaptable to the teacher's educational goals.

It should be helpful for the student to select as a project one or more building cases to study graphically and analytically the layout and behavior of a particular structure in more detail. Most of the figure references in the back of the book will provide the necessary background information for a conceptual investigation.

This book can be used not only as a text for courses in structures, but also as a reference for design studios and classes in construction. The book will be extremely helpful to the young engineer, who for the first time is faced with the reality of a building. The comparative presentation of the many building cases together with the references should be an asset to the architectural and structural designer in practice.

The subjects in this book are obviously dealt with only on an introductory level. However, it is hoped that the process presented here not only will familiarize the designer with the wealth of horizontal-span building structures but also will develop critical thinking and initiate enough curiosity for further studies and strengthen the creative response to the design and construction of buildings. This book should provide another bridge for the communication and understanding of the various professionals involved with the building of buildings.

WOLFGANG SCHUELLER

*Syracuse, New York*
*May 1982*

# ACKNOWLEDGMENTS

My sincere gratitude to that small but dedicated group of students of the School of Architecture at Syracuse University, who have faithfully developed under my direction many of the graphical presentations in my elective structure courses. The students who have been involved more substantially over a period of several years and to whom I am deeply indebted are: Edward E. Asfour, David G. Beilman, Diana Chen-See, John M. Currie, Jeffrey Elghanayan, Read Ferguson, Alejandro A. Firpi, David G. Fisk, Michael T. Gunn, Dennis N. Hertlein, David Holmes, Kenneth Kerly, Jeffrey T. Malter, Stephen W. Lu, Paul S. Pizzo, Donald Pulfer, Juan de Dias Salas-Canevaro, Jody Schornstein, Scott K. Van Sweringen, Warren K. Wake, Ronald C. Weston, Anthony Whaley, William W. Worcester, Li Tiene, Carl R. Tucker, and Michael Unger.

I also thank those other students, whose names I have not mentioned, but who also have been involved in the preparation of the drawings and who have supported me through their critical and constructive thinking in writing this book.

I am grateful to Warren K. Wake for doing the computer graphics, which was programmed in Digital Effects' VISIONS/APL, on an IBM 370 computer and plotted on a Calcomp 936 plotter.

Greatly appreciated is the help of my assistants Michael J. Costantin, Michael T. Gunn, Dennis N. Hertlein, Michael H. Konopka, Joe Lomonaco, Jeffrey T. Malter, and Ronald C. Weston, who drew many of the illustrations, checked the mathematics, and typed some of the manuscript. Their commitment and positive attitude was of stimulating support to me.

The spirit and approach of this book could not have been possible without the contributions of the many architects and engineers, whose design of buildings or whose mathematical interpretation of structural behavior has given a basis to this text. These individuals are too numerous to identify here, but they are given credit in the references and list of illustrations.

Particularly, I am indebted to Mario Salvadori of Columbia University, who has done pioneering work by helping to define structures as a part of architectural education in this country.

Finally, I thank the publisher's editorial and production staff for their sincere support.

W. S.

# CONTENTS

# 1 INTRODUCTION AND REVIEW

To some this chapter may be a review and to others an introduction to the basic concepts of structural design. At the beginning is an investigation of a wide range of loading cases to which a building may be subjected and which it must be able to resist. How the various load types are generated is shown, as well as the code requirements that must be satisfied. The common materials and their mechanical properties, which are the basis for structural behavior, are studied. The properties of the major structural materials—concrete, masonry, steel, and timber—are compared with the properties of other materials and then evaluated.

In the section on structural members (Fig. 1.1) a classification of structure elements and connection systems is presented along with a summary of design formulas for the sizing of beams and columns in reinforced concrete, steel, and timber. The design formulas are taken from the respective codes; some of them are simplified versions to allow for the fast approximations rather than for the precise final design of members.

Because of the special nature of foundations they are treated separately in a special section. The complex features of the material soil are discussed and the various foundation systems are introduced along with their loading conditions.

Finally, the principle of prestressing in architecture is introduced. Examples are taken from many different building and member types; some simple prestressed concrete beams are designed.

## 1.1 LOADS

A structure enclosing space must be strong enough to resist the many types of physical forces imposed upon it. The magnitude and direction of these forces vary with the material, type of structural system, purpose of the building, and the locality. The most obvious loads are due to gravity action as caused by the weight of the building, snow, and occupancy. Lateral forces are exerted upon the structure by wind and earthquakes, as well as earth and hydrostatic pressure. While the lateral forces tend to slide and rotate the building block and the wind attempts to lift up the roof, gravity in contrast will counteract and stabilize the structure. The loads may be permanent, such as the dead load, or

1

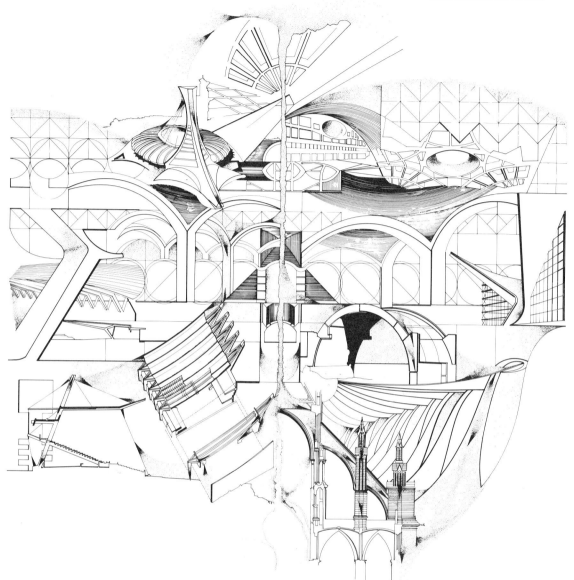

**Fig. 1.1** The lateral thrust.

temporary such as the live load. The duration of the live load is of importance especially for deflection considerations (e.g., creep). Live loads may be *static* or *dynamic*. While the everchanging occupancy loads are in general static since they do not change rapidly, gusty winds, depending upon the stiffness and mass of the building, may have to be considered dynamic. The dynamic loads may be cyclic, as due to the vibrations caused by a machine, or random, such as the impact loads due to an explosion. Loads may be distributed as point, line, or surface loads.

Forces may be induced deliberately as in prestressing, or involuntarily, as residual stresses due to the production and fabrication process; they also may be locked into members when the material is prevented from responding to changes in temperature and humidity, and when the material cannot creep, as caused by constant loading.

Some loads are time-independent such as the dead load while others are time-dependent; for instance, the shrinkage of concrete in its early stage of hardening occurs at a decreasing rate. Most loads, whether geophysical or man-made (Fig. 1.2) are extremely complex, and care must be taken by the designer to properly predict their action. The following discussion of the various loads should only be considered introductory—as needed for preliminary design purposes. For a precise description of loads, the appropriate state or local construction codes as well as one of the four model codes listed below should be consulted:

- *Southern Standard Building Code* (SSBC)
- *The Basic Building Code* (BOCA)
- *The Uniform Building Code* (ICBO)
- *The National Building Code* (NATIONAL)

The model codes become law when adopted by the state or city. In the absence of any governing code the best reference for building loads is

- American National Standards Institute (ANSI)—*Minimum Design Loads in Buildings and Other Structures*

The designer must always keep in mind that the information given in codes is only for minimum loading and may be inadequate for special loading conditions.

**Dead Loads**

The dead load of a structure consists of the weights of all the permanent components of a building such as walls, floors, mechanical and electrical systems, etc. The weights of some typical materials are shown in Table 1.1 and are further discussed in the sections on materials.

At the initial design stage the dead weight of the structural element must be estimated. The best procedure is to follow the force flow starting at the roof level. The live loads are supported by the decking which carries them, together with its own weight, to the beams or joists from where these loads and the additional beam weights are transferred to the main beams (trusses, girders, etc.) which, in turn, transmit the accumulated loads to the columns or walls.

At the different design stages the estimated loads (i.e., member sizes) should be checked and adjustments should be made so that errors do not accumulate. In order to facilitate the estimate of the dead weight for the preliminary design of the structural elements, approximate weights per square foot of various construction materials are given in Table 1.1. Only typical values for rigid construction systems are shown. Weights for flexible structures are discussed later.

The roof structure weights (Table 1.1) consisting of the primary bending elements obviously increase with span, though not in a linear manner. Since the various structural

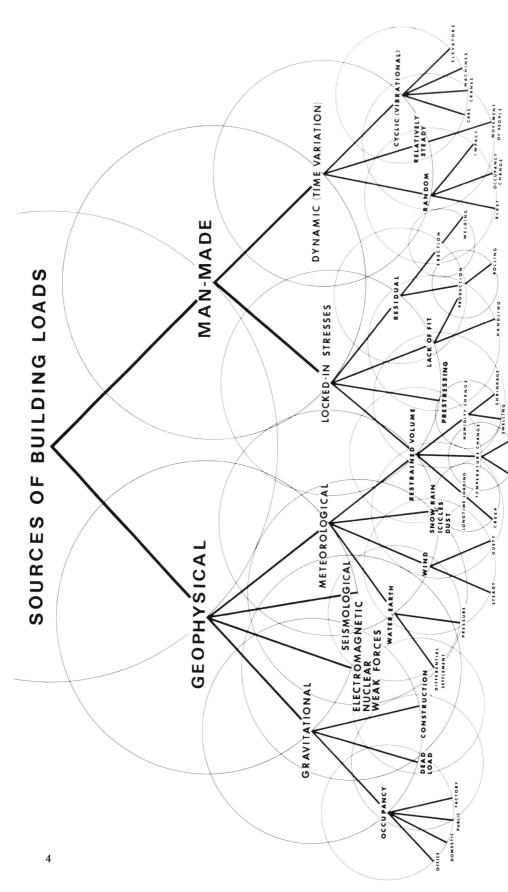

Fig. 1.2  Sources of building loads.

Table 1.1   Approximate Weight per Square Foot of Various Construction Materials

**Roofs**

Primary bending members
(beams together with trusses)

| | | |
|---|---|---|
| span: | 40 ft | 4 – 8 psf |
| | 100 ft | 9 –12 psf |
| | 150 ft | 12 –16 psf |
| | 200 ft | 15 –20 psf |
| | 300 ft | 21 –28 psf |
| | 400 ft | 27 –36 psf |

| | |
|---|---|
| Beams (joists) separate | 2 – 4.5 psf |
| Trusses (separate) 40 ft span | 2 – 3.5 psf |
| Roof bracing | 0.5– 1.5 psf |
| 2–4-in. solid timber decking | 3 –11 psf |
| Nonwood decking per inch | 2 – 7 psf |
| Concrete floor per inch | 8.5–12.5 psf |
| Hollow-core concrete planks 6-in. thick | 43 –50 psf |
| Metal deck | 1 – 3 psf |
| Three-ply roofing | 1 psf |
| Three- to five-ply and gravel | 5.5– 6.5 psf |
| Lightweight fill or insulation | 0.2– 2 psf |
| Clay tile | 10 –20 psf |
| Cement asbestos shingles ($\cong \frac{3}{4}$ in.) | 4 psf |
| Asphalt shingles ($\cong \frac{1}{4}$ in.) | 2 psf |
| Hollow-core concrete planks with 2-in. topping | 68 –75 psf |

**Ceilings**

| | |
|---|---|
| Lath and plaster ceiling | 5 –10 psf |
| Acoustical tile or suspended wood furring strips | 3 psf |

**Walls**

| | |
|---|---|
| Brick, unplastered, 8-in. thick | 80 psf |
| Hollow concrete block (light-heavy) 8 in. | 24 –55 psf |
| Gypsum or cement on wood or metal lath | 8 –10 psf |
| Steel or wood studs, two layers $\frac{1}{2}$-in. gypsum board each side | 9 psf |
| Metal lath and studs | 18 psf |
| 3–6-in. gypsum tile | 10 –18 psf |
| 3–6-in. clay tile | 17 –28 psf |
| Plaster, 1-in. thick | 10 psf |
| Wood paneling, 1-in. | 2.5 psf |
| Windows, glass, frame, and sash | 8 psf |

systems are economical for certain span ranges only, bending systems may be replaced by shell systems where the profile provides axial force resistance.

Although the prediction of the dead loads is much more precise compared to the other loading types, there are still sources of error. Often the detailing of nonstructural elements (ducts, pipes, ceiling systems, curtain walls, etc.) may not yet be known and their weights have to be estimated while the structural design is already partially finished.

The unit weights as given by producers or codes may not be consistent with the actual weights, and the nominal member sizes may vary from the actual sizes, especially for cast-in-place reinforced concrete construction.

### Live or Occupancy Loads

In contrast to dead loads, occupancy loads are variable; they change over time in magnitude and location. They are temporary or semipermanent loads such as caused by people, furniture, supplies, mechanical equipment, movable partition walls, and similar items—whatever is not considered under dead load. The typical loads shown below, determined statistically and empirically by building codes, tend to be conservative, although there may be extraordinary situations, such as a change of occupancy, where higher safety factors are warranted.

Most live loads are regarded as uniformly distributed, although there may be occasions where load concentrations due to heavy weights like safes and machines have to be considered.

In continuous structures live loads must be arranged in such a manner so that the structural components may be designed for the maximum stress conditions. Some typical minimum live loads, which include furniture, etc., are found in Table 1.2. Special concentrated live loads are given by codes for garages, stair treads, railings, etc.

**Table 1.2  Approximate Weight per Square Foot of Typical Minimum Live Loads**

| | |
|---|---|
| Dwellings | 20– 40 psf |
| Classrooms | 40 psf |
| Public corridors | 60–100 psf |
| Assembly halls | 60–100 psf |
| Dining rooms | 100 psf |
| Dance halls | 100 psf |
| Offices | 60– 80 psf |
| Manufacturing | 125 psf |
| Storage warehouses | 125–250 psf |
| Stores | 75–125 psf |

The probability of full live loading decreases as the area that a member supports increases. In addition, the probability is small that all spaces are fully loaded simultaneously. Therefore, building codes allow a reduction of live loads of 100 psf or less if the member is supporting at least 150 ft$^2$, except for places of public assembly. The reduction $R$ should not exceed 0.08% for each square foot of area supported; $R$ should neither exceed 60% nor exceed the value obtained from the following formula:

$$R = 23.1\left(1 + \frac{D}{L}\right) \leqslant 60\% \qquad (1.1)$$

where

$R$ = reduction, in percent

$D$ = dead load (psf)

$L$ = live load (psf)

Roof live loads will not be reduced. Also, no reduction is made to live loads above 100 psf except for columns, where a 20% reduction is permitted.

**Example 1.1** Determine the live load reduction for floor beam $B_1$ in Fig. 2.131 assuming a dead load of 60 psf and a live load of 40 psf.

The beam supports an area of

$$A = 10(24) = 240 \text{ ft}^2 \geqslant 150 \text{ ft}^2$$

Since the live load is less than 100 psf and the area the beam is supporting is in excess of 150 ft$^2$, live load reduction is permitted:

$$R_1 = 0.08A = 0.08(240) = 19.2\%$$

$$R_2 = 23.1\left(1 + \frac{D}{L}\right)$$

$$= 23.1\left(1 + \frac{60}{40}\right) = 57.75\%$$

$$R_3 = \qquad\qquad = 60\%$$

The minimum reduction of 19.2% controls. Hence the design live load may be reduced to

$$L_r = 40 - 0.192(40) = 0.808(40) = 32.32 \text{ psf}$$

### Snow, Rain, Ice, and Minimum Roof Live Loads

The distribution of maximum ground snow loads (in psf) in the United States as recorded by the U.S. Weather Bureau is shown in Fig. 1.3. The snow load map indicates values that range from 80 psf in the Northeast to 5 psf in the South. Special values must be used for the mountain regions where certain localities record snow loads of up to 300 psf.

One inch of snow weighs approximately 0.5-1 psf in correspondence to the moisture content.

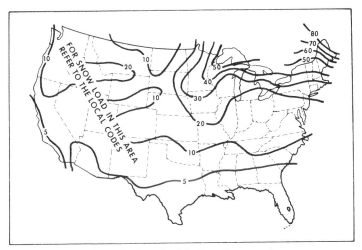

Fig. 1.3  Snow load (psf) on the ground.

The magnitude of roof snow loads depends on the geometry of the roof, its exposure, its insulation, and the direction of the wind. In most cases the roof snow loads are lighter than the ground snow loads. The snow slides off singly pitched or curved roofs; the wind blows the loose snow off flat roofs, and some of the snow melts and evaporates due to heat loss through the roof skin. However, there are occasions where the snow accumulates, as in the valleys of multiple folds, the lower levels of multilevel roofs, or at roof projections and parapet walls; for these cases heavier loads must be considered. Furthermore, asymmetrical loading conditions may arise as a result of drifting.

Some codes allow a reduction factor of 0.8 to convert ground snow load to roof snow load for a roof slope of up to 30°, and for a height-to span ratio of less than 1/10 for curved roofs; beyond slopes of 70° snow loading may be neglected. For the leeward slope, however, the snow loads must be increased if the roof inclination on the windward side is greater than 20° and $h/L$ for curved roofs is greater than 1/10. For special exposure conditions the weight of the roof snow loads must be adjusted.

Because of the unpredictable character of snow accumulations local codes often require the use of the ground snow loads for roof snow loads applied on the horizontal roof projection. This rather conservative approach will be used in this book for the preliminary design of the ordinary single buildings with no special exposure conditions. The snow loads are assumed to have a duration of two months.

Water loads may become important if the roof is not properly drained, that is, it may not have sufficient slope or drains may clog. For instance, a flexible flat roof may deflect over time (e.g., creep, sag) and lose its initial slope. Rain with a weight of 5.20 psf/in. of depth will collect and form standing pools, thereby deflecting the roof further and, in turn, gathering more water. This process is called ponding and may result in the collapse of the roof. Should the water freeze and be prevented from expanding, large lateral pressures are exerted upon its boundaries. The situation is worsened when snow is added to the ice; the sequence of snowing, melting, and freezing without proper drainage causes heavy loading.

One must also consider the heavy loads of icicles which may form on protruding roof elements and the formation of ice surfaces on open structures which may attract wind forces.

A minimum roof live load of 20 psf on the horizontal projection is required by most codes for flat, pitched, and curved roofs to allow for construction loads. Some codes permit a reduction of this load depending upon the slope of the roof and the contributory area of the member.

### Soil and Hydrostatic Pressures

Structures below ground must resist lateral and vertical loads due to earth and, possibly, hydrostatic pressure when also submerged in groundwater. For further discussion refer to Section 1.4, Foundation Systems.

### Loads Due to Restrained Volume Change and Similar Causes

Materials change in volume due to the effects of creep, shrinkage, and daily and seasonal temperature variations. Should the structure be restrained, or continuous and indeterminate, then its members are prevented from freely moving, and stresses are induced. Similar conditions occur due to settling of a support or through poor fit, if a member that is too long is forced into the desired position.

Some of these hidden forces can be eliminated by providing expansion joints and hinges to release the potential movement, which in turn results in a less rigid structure that may not be appropriate for other direct load action (see also Fig. 2.27).

In the following example the large effect of temperature change is exemplified.

**Example 1.2** Consider a steel beam ($A$36) with a span of $L = 20$ ft to be installed at 40°F and to be fixed between its boundaries. Determine the thermal stresses at 120°F considering only a mean beam temperature (i.e., axial action only).

The linear coefficient of expansion $\alpha$ and the modulus of elasticity $E$ are taken from Table 1.3:

$$\alpha = 6.5 \times 10^{-6} \text{ in./in./}°F \qquad E = 29000 \text{ ksi}$$

First, the beam is considered to expand freely

$$\Delta L = \alpha(\Delta T)L \tag{1.2}$$

$$= 6.5(10)^{-6}(120-40)20(12) = 0.125 \text{ in.}$$

Now the force or compression stress is found which is needed to bring the member back to its original length

$$\Delta L = \frac{PL}{AE} = \frac{fL}{E} \tag{1.3}$$

$$0.125 = f\frac{20(12)}{29000}$$

$$f = 15.10 \text{ ksi}$$

Or, in general terms

$$\alpha(\Delta T)L = \frac{fL}{E}$$

$$f = \alpha(\Delta T)E \tag{1.4}$$

$$= 6.5(10)^{-6}(80)29000 = 15.08 \text{ ksi}$$

The thermal compressive stresses are quite large in comparison to the allowable stress of $F_c = 0.6 F_y = 22$ ksi, not even considering buckling.

Note that the temperature stresses are independent of the size and length of the beam, and are only a function of temperature change and material.

### Wind Loads

Wind forces are among the most violent sources of destruction in nature. It is extremely difficult to predict their complex behavior since they are not constant and static like dead load, but are dynamic and fluctuate in an unpredictable manner not only in magnitude but also in direction. Wind behavior is influenced by the topography (open, wooded,

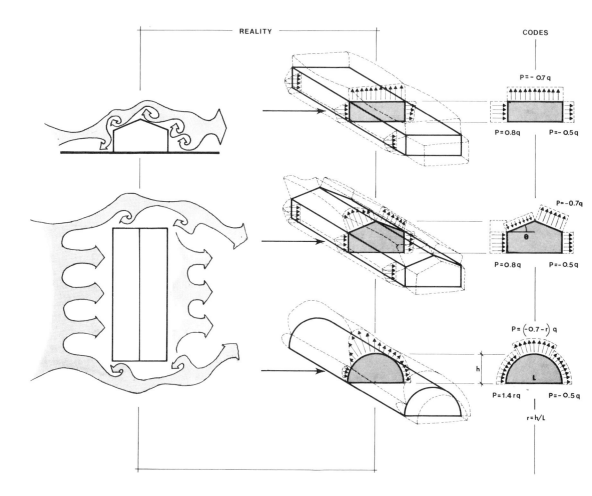

**Fig. 1.4** Wind pressure distribution and pressure coefficients.

rolling, hilly, urban, vegetation, roughness, etc.), the building type (shape, size, height, texture, flexibility, degree of tightness, openness, etc.), and the nature of the airflow (air density, direction, velocity, degree of steadiness, etc.)

Since the behavior of an airstream is harder to visualize than the flow of water, imagine a simple solid object submerged in flowing water rather than in an airstream in a wind tunnel. This simple object placed perpendicular to the current may have various forms such as a flat plate, a round cylinder, or an airfoil. Each of these shapes generates a different complex flow pattern. It is obvious that the streamlined tear-drop shape, ignoring its surface friction, provides the least resistance to the original flow pattern; examples are aircraft wings, the bodies of some birds, and fishes. Nature provides in the body profile of the dolphin a convincing statement of the efficiency of form relative to the least resistance in water. Consider now ordinary building shapes, as those given in Fig. 1.4, to be submerged. When the stream passes the obstruction its behavior is drastically altered; it is deflected and then rejoins the original flow pattern behind the object. The degree of disturbance of the original flow pattern that is the crowding of the streamlines indicate the increased speed and the corresponding intensity of load action. The flowing water exerts pressure upon the front side and suction on all other sides, that is drag forces in the direction of flow and, like airplane wings, lift forces perpendicular to it. Turbulence is generated at abrupt changes of geometry as is the case in the vicinity of the building corners and ridges.

The ordinary structures of rectangular plan with flat, gabled, and arched roofs in Fig. 1.4 are considered long enough so that the typical wind distribution along the long faces is not disturbed by the airflow around the corners and edges where large local suctions with updrafts are found.

The following evaluation of the wind pressure is primarily based on the *Timber Construction Manual* (reference 69). The approximate magnitude of the wind pressure is derived by treating the wind as a perfect fluid for which the dynamic or velocity pressure $q$ (psf) normal to its flow as based on a standard mass density $m$ of the air at $15°C$ at sea level and a wind velocity $V$ (mph) is given by

$$q = \tfrac{1}{2} mV^2 = 0.00256 \, V^2 \tag{1.5}$$

Thus the wind loads are proportional to the square of the magnitude of the instantaneous wind velocity that is the wind speed.

This ideal velocity pressure is transformed into an effective pressure $q_h$ taking into account the terrain, height at which it acts, and wind fluctuations

$$q_h = 0.00256 \, V_h^2 G_F \tag{1.6}$$

where

$$V_h = V_{30}\left(\frac{h}{30}\right)^{\frac{1}{x}}$$

This effective dynamic pressure is converted into an equivalent static pressure $p_e$ (psf) acting externally and perpendicular to the surface of a solid airtight building by multiplying it by the external pressure or drag coefficient $C_{pe}$, often called the shape factor:

$$p_e = C_{pe}q_h = 0.00256 \, C_{pe} \, V_h^2 \, G_F \tag{1.7}$$

The wind velocity $V_h$ (mph) generally increases with height $h$ and depends on exposure conditions and roughness of the surrounding terrain, which is taken into account by the exponent $x$. Designers often assume $x = 7$ for an open flat terrain with minimal obstructions. In the context of this book, primarily low building types are investigated, hence, letting the design height $h = 30$ ft yields a basic wind velocity $V_h = V_{30} = V$. This velocity represents a standard one as established from weather station data. A distribution of maximum wind velocities in miles per hour in the United States at 30 ft above ground occurring only once in 50 years is shown in Fig. 1.5. Note the maximum wind velocities range from 60 to 110 mph with most inland areas in the range 70–80 mph.

The wind pressure is not steady, it is time-dependent. That is, the wind velocity pressure fluctuates rather than being constant and its behavior depends on how the structure responds to these fluctuations. The gust factor $G_F$ takes this dynamic feature of the airflow into account. A gust factor of 1.3 is recommended for gusts of relatively short duration acting on narrow structures. Since most of the low buildings designed in this book are relatively wide and stiff, the dynamic amplification can be considered small, unlike that for tall, slender buildings. The gust factor can be ignored and the application

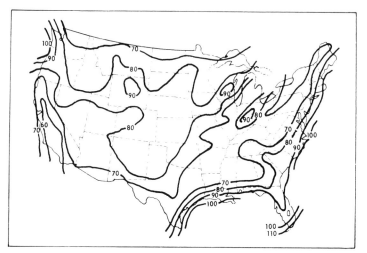

Fig. 1.5   Minimum wind velocity (mph) at 30 ft above ground.

of the equivalent static loading can be considered reasonable. Hence the expression for the effective velocity pressure reduces to the one for an ideal gas, yielding an external wind pressure of

$$p_e = C_{pe}q_h = 0.00256\, C_{pe}V^2 \qquad (1.8)$$

where $p_e$ = external equivalent static pressure (psf); $C_{pe}$ = drag coefficient (pressure coefficient, shape factor); $q_h$ = effective velocity pressure (psf); and $V$ = basic velocity (mph).

Shape factors for various ordinary building types can be found in the major building codes. Typical values are given in Fig. 1.4 for common, relatively long building shapes with rectangular plan layouts.

The wind pressure on a box-type solid building causes pressure on the windward wall with $C_{pe}$ = 0.8 and suction upon the leeward wall with $C_{pe}$ = -0.5 as well as suction along the roof. The total lateral force the building must resist is due to the combined action of pressure and suction $C_{pe}$ = 1.3 which is assumed to act entirely on the windward face. Substituting this combined force action into Eq. (1.8) yields

$$p_e = 0.00256\, C_{pe}\, V^2 \qquad (1.8)$$

$$= 0.00256(0.8 + 0.5)V^2$$

$$p_e = 0.00333\, V^2 \qquad (1.9)$$

Using a wind velocity of $V$ = 77.5 mph results in a minimum wind pressure of 20 psf upon walls of low buildings which can be considered typical for most parts of the inland United States

$$p_e = 0.00333(77.5)^2 = 20 \text{ psf}$$

The lateral wind pressure upon the walls of a long gabled building is the same as for the box type building (Fig. 1.4). The wind pressure distribution on the windward slope depends on the angle of inclination of the roof. As the slope of the roof increases the suction changes into pressure. This change occurs roughly at $\theta = 30°$ depending on the height to width ratio of the building, while the leeward slope remains under suction with $C_{pe} = -0.7$. Shape factors for the windward slope may be used for preliminary design purposes:

$$\theta \leqslant 20° \quad C_{pe} = -0.7$$
$$\theta = 30° \quad C_{pe} = 0$$
$$\theta \geqslant 60° \quad C_{pe} = 0.6$$

Suction coefficients for roof slopes between 20° and 30° and pressure coefficients between 30° and 60° may be found by linear interpolation.

Light roofs are most vulnerable to wind suction especially when the effect of internal pressure is added. The possible uplift must be prevented by adequate anchorage of the roof.

In the context of this book the uniform wind pressure is considered on the vertical projection of the roof (i.e., uniform wall pressure is continued up to the top of the building) which is conservative for the design of the primary structure at least up to a roof slope of 7/12 ($\theta \cong 30°$) or a pitch of 7/24. However, for the sizing of the purlins and the roof deck, suction and pressure normal to the roof should be used.

The wind pressure distribution along arched or cylindrical roof forms is quite complex and depends, among other criteria, on the height-to-width ratio of the structure. Its distribution as simplified by codes is shown in Fig. 1.4 where radial pressure appears on the windward side while maximum suction perpendicular to the surface occurs at the crown.

As for gabled buildings, a uniform wind pressure on the vertical projection of the structure is also assumed for the preliminary design of rigid arch structures.

Special shape coefficients must be applied to other structures like unusual building shapes, open cantilevered structures (e.g., grandstands), buildings with partial or no exterior walls (e.g., parking garages, recreation shelters), cable structures, trussed or solid towers, bridges, multistory structures, etc. Local pressure factors must be used for certain building portions like ridges, overhanging eaves, cornices, corners, etc., to take into account the higher local wind pressure.

The wind pressure distribution for flexible buildings, as for pneumatic and tent structures, is even more complex than for rigid ones since they deform under load and change their shape thereby influencing the wind action. They may flutter and vibrate so that dynamic loading must be included. This topic is discussed further in Chapter 9, Soft Shell Structures.

The wind pressure distribution for large-scale special structures must be obtained from model testing in a wind tunnel. The magnitude of the pressure coefficients reflects the efficiency of the building shape with respect to wind action; streamlined buildings have the smaller coefficients.

Until now only external wind pressures as based on airtight solid buildings have been considered. In reality buildings are not solid, there is always leakage through joints, cracks, and vents. Doors and windows may be open or portions of a wall may have large openings. When the openings are in the windward side, the internal pressure will be positive and will approach the external pressure value as the wall openings increase. Openings in the leeward face will cause internal suction.

The internal wind pressure is determined like the external one by multiplying the wind velocity pressure, which does not include the gust factor, by the internal pressure coefficient

$$p_i = C_{pi} \, q \qquad\qquad (1.10)$$

The following internal pressure coefficients are assumed to be uniform on all internal surfaces due to the balloon-like effect, and may be used:

■ For the condition of no openings but some permeability of all walls and roof

$$C_{pi} = \pm 0.3$$

■ Where the wall contains more than 30% of window and door area, consider the building as open-sided and the internal pressure equal to the external one on the windward side, while the internal pressure on the leeward side is slightly larger:

  windward side:  $C_{pi} = +0.8$   (pressure)
  leeward side and parallel side:  $C_{pi} = -0.6$   (suction)

■ Use linear interpolation between the limits for smaller percentage of wall openings.

A building element must be capable of resisting the pressure difference between its two opposite faces. The algebraic sum of external and internal pressures considering both as positive (i.e., compressive), yields

$$p = p_e - p_i = q(C_{pe} - C_{pi}) \qquad\qquad (1.11)$$

The resultant lateral pressure an entire building (e.g., frame) must resist in most cases is only caused by external pressure, since the internal pressure acting with the same magnitude upon each opposite wall tends to self-balance. However, secondary members such as purlins, girts, wall and roof panels, glazing, anchorage, and so on must be designed for the different load combinations due to external and internal pressure.

**Example 1.3**  The lateral wind pressure on a one-story box-type building was determined for the given wind direction as 20 psf [Eq. (1.9)]. Find the internal wind pressure by assuming 20% potential openings in the windward and leeward walls. Then determine the resultant pressures due to external and internal pressures required for the design of the secondary structural elements in the roof and wall planes. The internal pressure coefficients with no openings are ±0.3 and for more than 30% openings are +0.8 (windward side) and -0.6 (leeward side).

By linear interpolation, for openings on the windward side

$$\frac{0.8 - 0.3}{30} = \frac{C_{pi} - 0.3}{20}$$

$$C_{pi} = 0.63$$

while for openings on the leeward side

$$\frac{-0.6 - (0.3)}{30} = \frac{C_{pi} - (-0.3)}{20}$$

$$C_{pi} = -0.5$$

The velocity pressure is

$$q = 0.00256 \ V^2 \tag{1.5}$$
$$= 0.00256(77.5)^2 = 15.38 \ \text{psf}$$

The resultant uplift upon the roof skin is

$$p = q(C_{pe} - C_{pi})$$
$$= 15.38[-0.7 - (+0.63)]$$
$$= 15.38(-1.33) = -20.46 \ \text{psf}$$

The resultant pressure upon the wall panels on the windward side with openings closed on this side, but opened on the leeward side is

$$p = q(C_{pe} - C_{pi})$$
$$= 15.38[0.8 - (-0.5)]$$
$$= 15.38(1.3) = 20 \ \text{psf}$$

The resultant pressure upon the wall panels on the leeward side with openings closed on this side, but opened on the windward side is

$$p = q(C_{pe} - C_{pi})$$
$$= 15.38[-0.5 - (+0.63)]$$
$$= 15.38(-1.13) = - 17.33 \ \text{psf}$$

The wind does not necessarily act uniform and perpendicular to the walls as is assumed. Its nonuniform distribution will cause asymmetrical action with respect to the center of rigidity of the structure and thus will generate torsion and twist the building. Wind forces from different directions must be considered in the design of buildings.

Wind action upon ordinary low rigid buildings rarely controls the design of the primary structure as is exemplified later in this book. However, it will influence the sizing of the secondary structural elements.

The information on extreme winds as provided by building codes must be used with caution since local meteorological and topographic features may require higher values. Furthermore, wind maps do not show tornado winds, since building regulations do not require taking them into account in the design. If a building is located in a tornado-prone area and not designed to withstand it because of economic reasons, a protective shelter should be incorporated into the design.

Tornadoes are among the most devastating forces in nature. In the United States they mostly appear between the Rocky and Appalachian Mountains with a tangential wind velocity of possibly as high as 500 mph within the tornado tunnel. Buildings designed for the 200-mph range should generally be safe 95% of the time and this design should also be safe for severe hurricanes. The impact of flying debris should also be taken into account. While tornadoes only act over a relatively small area (about 3 square miles) hurricanes affect many thousand square miles and thus are much more destructive. Hurricanes occur in the United States primarily along the Atlantic coastal zones. They not only cause damage because of the high wind velocity but also because of the waves (erosion) and rainfall (flooding). The maximum winds appear close to the eye of the hurricane. Typical design values for strong hurricanes are 150 mph and 90 mph for average ones. The radius of curvature of the rotating winds of hurricanes is so large that their path may be considered straight.

## Seismic Loads

Earthquakes are among the most awesome natural forces. They occur suddenly, without warning, and within 10–20 s can turn cities into wastelands, make islands disappear, and give birth to new land and lakes. Building designers in the United States often automatically relate earthquakes to California; they do not realize that the earthquakes of Charleston, South Carolina (1886) and of New Madrid, Missouri, near Memphis (1811, 1812) were more severe than the one in San Francisco (1906), and that more than a third of the U.S. population lives in areas of high to moderate seismic risk. Not only the large Western cities of Los Angeles and San Francisco, but also metropolitan areas of Buffalo, Providence, Boston, Charleston, Memphis, St. Louis, Salt Lake City, Seattle, and Anchorage are regions prone to major earthquakes. Building designers must be acquainted with the effect of quakes so they can make buildings earthquake resistant and safeguard life.

According to the theory of plate tectonics, the earth crust consists of separate plates, which float upon the earth's molten interior. Each of the plates moves (creeps) a few inches every year. At points of convergence the plates want to slide past each other, as, for instance, along the San Andreas fault where the northwestward moving Pacific plate and the North American plate move in the same direction but at a different rate. If the plates are prevented from doing so at certain locations by friction or by being locked into each other, elastic strain is stored and accumulates until the forces can no longer be resisted by the material. When the capacity is exceeded, sudden rupture and slippage occur. This abrupt release of strain energy results in complex vibrations propagating in high speeds from the source (focus, hypocenter) in all directions through the earth and along its surface, reaching a building at different time periods with different velocities, from different directions. The faster primary wave ($P$-wave) compresses the earth in front and moves building foundations back and forth in the direction of travel, thereby identifying itself as a push–pull wave. The slower, secondary seismic wave moves the building foundations up and down and at right angles to the $P$-wave showing the characteristics of a shear wave ($S$-wave). In addition to these primary body waves, there is the family of surface waves.

Most earthquakes are generated along the plate boundaries, as was just discussed, however few occur at faults within plates as is the case in the East and Midwest United States.

The primary effects of earthquakes causing possible building damage are:

- Ground rupture in the fault zone.
- Ground failure due to land slides, where ground displaces horizontally and/or vertically without ground rupture, mud slides, avalanches, ground settlement, and shaking, resulting in loss of bearing capacity as due to liquefaction, where saturated granular soil is transformed from a solid state into a liquefied state due to porewater pressure causing the soil to behave like quicksand.
- Tsunamis, which are sea waves generated by the sudden displacement of land at the ocean bottom.
- Ground shaking: its effect is influenced by the magnitude of energy released, the location of the focus, its duration, and site and building characteristics.

Among the secondary and often more critical effects of earthquakes are fire, disease, explosion, flooding, and disruption of economic and social life.

Earthquakes are classified either according to the magnitude of energy they release or according to their intensity, that is destructiveness. The Richter Scale (Charles F. Richter, 1935) is a measure of the energy released at the focus. It ranges from 3 to 9 as based on the logarithmic scale, where each unit increase reflects an increase of about 32 times more energy. Comparing the energy release of the Hiroshima atom bomb with about 6.4 on the Richter Scale with the 1964 Alaska earthquake of 8.4, shows that about 1000 (i.e., 32 × 32) times more energy was freed by the earthquake. The largest known earthquake is 8.9 (Colombia, 1906). Earthquakes above 6 on the Richter Scale are considered severe, while the ones between 4 and 5 are considered moderate. The Richter Scale does not concern itself with the effect of the earthquake. An earthquake of the Richter magnitude 6 may be far more destructive when it hits a densely populated region directly, than one of magnitude 8 with its focus far away from inhabited areas.

The Modified Mercalli Intensity Scale (MMI), as initially developed by Guiseppe Mercalli (1850–1914), is of a subjective nature, it describes the degree of damage as based on 12 intensity divisions. The Seismic Risk Map (Fig. 1.6) is used by the Uniform Building Code and correlated with the MMI Scale.

The remaining discussion of earthquake-resistant building design will be concerned only with ground shaking as the source of damage. The structural design for earthquake forces, because of their random character, cannot be considered as an exact engineering science; some engineers even claim it more of an art. The design is based on assumptions rather than on precise data; the prediction of the ground motion together with the response of the building riding on the earth along three directions may be impossible to determine accurately.

For the sake of simplicity, visualize the complex, random ground vibrations to be known horizontal movements travelling back and forth. Ignored are the vertical displacements, since the building is already designed for gravity in this direction. As the earth abruptly accelerates horizontally in one direction, taking the building foundations along, but leaving the portion of the building above the ground behind, it causes lateral inertia forces to act (Fig. 1.7a). This phenomenon is similar to the one experienced by a person

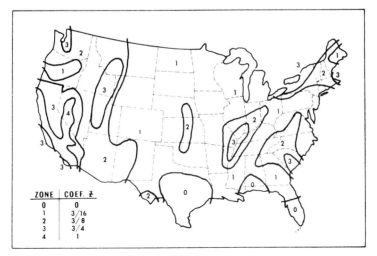

| ZONE | COEF. $Z$ |
|------|-----------|
| 0 | 0 |
| 1 | 3/16 |
| 2 | 3/8 |
| 3 | 3/4 |
| 4 | 1 |

Fig. 1.6  Seismic zone map.

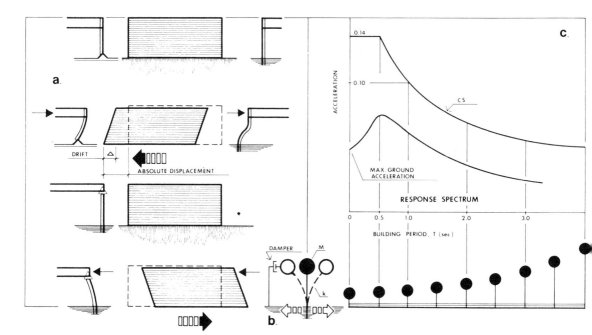

**Fig. 1.7**   Response of various structures to seismic action and spectrum response graph.

travelling in a car which suddenly increases its speed, or the vertical inertia force experienced when an elevator abruptly rises. One may conclude that the shaking of the building back and forth causes lateral inertia forces to be set up throughout the structure.

Should the building be rigid (infinitely stiff), then according to Newton's second law of motion, the lateral force $(F)$ is equal to the mass $(M)$ of the building multiplied by the acceleration $(a)$ it experiences

$$F = Ma \qquad (a)$$

The mass is equal to the building weight $(W)$ divided by the acceleration of gravity $(g = 32 \text{ ft/s}^2)$

$$F = W\frac{a}{g} = WC \qquad (b)$$

Letting $C = a/g$ results in the ground acceleration $a$ expressed as a percentage of $g$: $a = C(g)$. For example, a ground acceleration of $0.2g$ is equal to $0.2(32) = 6.4 \text{ ft/s}^2$, or the lateral inertia force is 20% of the weight of the rigid building.

The ground acceleration during earthquakes is measured by strong-motion accelerographs.

A building is never infinitely stiff, as was assumed; not only the building mass, but also its stiffness must be taken into account in order to evaluate the magnitude of the lateral force action.

One-story buildings displace laterally under elastic action in a specific manner, as is shown for various types of frames and a shear wall structure in Fig. 1.7a. These structures are called single degree of freedom systems, where the mass of the building $M$ can be visualized as lumped together at a single point, the roof level (Fig. 1.7b). If the seismic motion is assumed harmonic with a circular period of vibration of $w = 2\pi/T$ and if damping is neglected, then it can be shown that the time it takes for this ideal building to go through one full cycle of one back and forth free motion, also called the natural period $T$, is given by

$$T = 2\pi \sqrt{\frac{M}{k}} \qquad \text{(seconds)} \qquad (1.12)$$

The equation expresses the fact that the period of a one-story building is not only dependent on its mass, but also on the stiffness of the lateral force resisting structural elements as reflected by the stiffness factor $k = 1/\Delta$, which is the inverse of the deflection at the top due to a unit horizontal load (see the section, Stiffness Considerations in Chapter 4).

To evaluate the effect of the building stiffness upon the lateral inertia force or building acceleration, consider several one-story buildings of decreasing stiffness, shown as inverted pendulums in Fig. 1.7c (bottom), where the taller columns represent the higher flexibility. An average damping value, as provided by the internal friction and all the building materials, is included. Damping is an important property of the building, since it dissipates vibration and decreases the amplification of the ground motion. The structure is assumed to behave linearly. But keep in mind that this may not be realistic, and that the material should be allowed to be stressed beyond its elastic limit resulting in a nonlinear response with permanent deformations.

The "single degree of freedom buildings" (Fig. 1.7c) are shaken back and forth under a simulated ground acceleration which is based on the maximum one experienced as obtained from an actual or simulated earthquake accelerogram. If the maximum response (i.e., acceleration, absolute displacement, or lateral inertia force) of each of the buildings is plotted, a so-called response spectrum is formed for the given seismic movement. The following important characteristics can be derived from the diagram. For an infinitely stiff structure with the period $T = 0$ (i.e., no lateral displacement; $k = \infty$), the acceleration of the building is equal to that of the ground. As the structure becomes less rigid and its natural period increases to about $T = 0.5$ s, it reaches a lateral acceleration much larger than the one of the ground. This is the state where the natural period of the building tends to coincide with the typical ground motion, theoretically resulting in resonance (infinite large forces) if there would be no damping present. Beyond this location, as the building becomes more and more flexible and its period increases, its acceleration decreases and eventually becomes less than the ground acceleration.

One may conclude that flexible buildings with long periods of vibration attract less lateral force than stiff buildings with short periods of vibration. Most low-rise structures such as shells, space frames, and box buildings are stiff compared to high-rise buildings, though long-span rigid frames and suspension structures are quite flexible. The response of high-rise buildings is much more complex, not only are they more vulnerable to longer periods of vibration approaching their own periods (i.e., resonance), but also they are multi-degree-of-freedom systems with many possible modes or patterns of vibration. However, for high-rise buildings also, the first mode as exemplified with the pendulum still may contribute the largest influence.

The principle of the response spectrum is used by the major building codes. Its shape as approximated by the Uniform Building Code (UBC 1976) is shown in Fig. 1.7c (top), and defined mathematically by the expression $C$ multiplied by the soil factor $S = 1.5$.

The factor $C$, already identified in Eq. (b), accounts for the building acceleration as has just been discussed

$$C = \frac{1}{15\sqrt{T}} \leqslant 0.12 \tag{1.13}$$

The actual natural period $T$ of the fundamental mode of vibration of the building can only be found when it is designed. The code provides as an approximation the following empirical expression.

$$T = \frac{0.05h}{\sqrt{D}} \quad \text{(seconds)} \tag{1.14a}$$

where $h$ = height of structure (ft) and $D$ = building dimension parallel to applied force (ft).

Should the building structure consist of only ductile frames, then the code permits as approximation a period of 0.1 s per floor ($N$)

$$T = 0.1\,N \tag{1.14b}$$

Hence, a single story rigid, ductile frame has a period of $T = 0.1$ s and a seismic coefficient of $C = 0.12$.

The total lateral force, or the so-called base shear, as given by Eq. (b) is further corrected by the Uniform Building Code by taking the following additional factors into account:

- The location of the building ($Z$)
- The type of structure ($K$)
- Geology of site ($S$)
- Importance of building ($I$)

Hence, the effect of seismic ground shaking is presented by UBC (1976) as an equivalent total, lateral, static force $V$

$$V = Z\,I\,K\,C\,S\,W \tag{1.15}$$

where

$V$ = total lateral seismic force acting on the building

$Z$ = zone factor as identified for different earthquake zones in the United States (Fig. 1.6) as 3/16, 3/8, 3/4, 1

$I$ = importance factor based on occupancy
  = 1.5 for essential facilities as hospitals, fire and police stations
  = 1.25 where primary occupancy is for assembly use of more than 300 persons in one room
  = 1.00 all others

$K$ = framing coefficient, taking into account the effect of the structural system. The benefit of ductile frames allowing damping of vibration like shock absorbers, by local yielding of the structure, results in lower factors as compared to rigid shear wall structures which do not have the ability to absorb energy and thus have a factor nearly twice as high.

    = 0.67 for moment resisting, ductile frame structures

    = 1.33 for box (shear walls and braced frames) structures

    = 0.80 for structures consisting of a combination of the above

    = 1.00 for all other structure types

$C$ = seismic coefficient [Eq. (1.13)]. Low-rise buildings tend to have a low period of vibration with a relative high acceleration and large inertia force.

$S$ = numerical coefficient, taking into account the amplification of the seismic waves due to the site's geophysical properties. Seismic intensity seems to increase from hard ground, to gravel, to sand, to clay; low-rise, rigid buildings, however, seem to perform better on softer ground.

    = 1.5 if site conditions are not known. Note: $CS$ need not exceed 0.14

$W$ = total weight of the building including partitions; the normal human live load and snow loads up to 30 psf are not included. But warehouses shall have 25% of the floor live load included in the weight.

Since the probability is small that high-speed winds occur at the same time as a major earthquake, building codes do not require to design buildings for simultaneous action, hence, structures are designed for either wind or seismic action. The Uniform Building Code requires buildings to withstand minor earthquakes with no damage, but to resist major earthquakes without collapse yet allowing for some structural and nonstructural damage.

One can draw the following conclusions from the base shear formula. Heavy buildings attract more force than light ones. Increase of stiffness for the sake of reduction of deflections and vibrations also result in larger inertia forces, hence a rigid frame, not too flexible, is preferred to a braced frame or shear wall structure. The mass of a building should be selected so that it yields a period different from the one of the ground motion in order to prevent the building response from being amplified. The centroid of mass should not deviate from the centroid of the lateral force resisting system also called the centroid of rigidity (see Fig. 2.21) as to prevent torsion; if possible, a building should have two axes of symmetry. The UBC, however, requires the shear resisting structural elements to be capable of resisting a torsional moment assumed to be equivalent to the story shear acting with an eccentricity of not less than 5% of the maximum building dimension at that level. It is apparent that irregular and odd building shapes (Figs. 2.27, parts 1–3) will be subject to major torsional stresses. In such buildings not only the stiffness, but also the mass is not evenly distributed, resulting in lateral inertia forces of different magnitude causing torsion. It may be more efficient to separate irregular buildings at junction points, so that they can behave as regular building blocks. A building with several supports has a higher redundancy than one only supported by two cores which is much more vulnerable to failure.

The Uniform Building Code further specifies that parts or portions of structures and their anchorages shall be designed for lateral forces $F_p$, proportional to their weight and function in accordance with the following formula.

$$F_p = Z I C_p W_p \qquad (1.16)$$

where $W_p$ = weight of the part being considered: $C_p$ = 0.3 for walls; $C_p$ = 0.8 cantilever parapet; for other values refer to UBC.

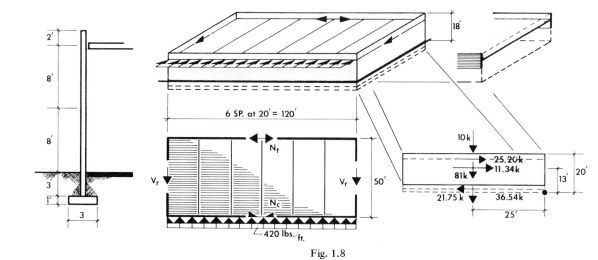

Fig. 1.8

**Example 1.4** A one-story industrial building located in seismic zone 3 is investigated for lateral force action; its dimensions are shown in Fig. 1.8. The structure is of the box type with 8-in. exterior masonry walls which act as shear walls to resist the lateral forces. The roof structure consists of wood framing with joists supported on girders which, in turn, are resting on the long walls.

The layout of the vertical structure is simplified by arranging it symmetrically about both major axes and ignoring the effect of wall openings for doors and windows that may not be symmetrically placed. There is assumed to be no eccentricity between the center of mass and the center of rigidity which would cause torsion (see discussion in Chapter 2).

The loads are as follows

| | |
|---|---|
| felt, three ply with gravel | 5.5 psf |
| $\frac{1}{2}$-in. plywood sheathing | 1.5 psf |
| joists and bridging estimated as: | 3.0 psf |
| insulation, lights, and misc. | 5.0 psf |
| suspended ceiling | 5.0 psf |
| roof framing | 20.0 psf |
| girders estimated as | 4.0 psf |
| roof weight | 24.0 psf |
| live load | 20.0 psf |
| average load for 8-in. masonry walls and pilasters | 90.0 psf |
| wind load | 20.0 psf |

First, the entire building is checked for wind and seismic forces before the individual structural elements are investigated. Here, only lateral force action perpendicular to the long walls is checked. The shear due to force action from the other direction is easily taken by the long walls to which the roof diaphragm is connected by shear connectors.

The equivalent static seismic load acting laterally on the building is

$$V = Z I K C S W \qquad (1.15)$$

where $Z = 0.75$, $I = 1.0$, $K = 1.33$, and $CS = 0.14$,

$$V = 0.75(1.0)1.33(0.14)W = 0.14\ W$$

The weight of the structure causing lateral seismic action upon the roof diaphragm is due to the roof itself and the wall portion consisting of the parapet and one-half of the height between floor and roof. It is conservatively assumed that there are no openings in this upper portion of the wall

$$W_R = 24(50 \times 1) + 90(10 \times 1)2 = 3000\ \text{lb/ft}$$

Thus the seismic load at the roof level is

$$V_R = 0.14\ W = 0.14(3000) = 420\ \text{lb/ft}$$

The resulting wind pressure at this level is equal to

$$P_W = 20(10 \times 1) = 200\ \text{lb/ft} < 420\ \text{lb/ft}$$

The seismic force clearly controls the structural design.

The roof acts as a deep beam similar to a plate girder placed horizontally, and transfers the lateral seismic load to the two short vertical shear walls. The total shear these walls each must support is

$$V_{WR} = 0.420\ \frac{120}{2} = 25.20\ \text{k}$$

Considering this shear to be distributed along the wall evenly yields the following shear per foot of wall

$$p = \frac{25200}{50} = 504\ \text{lb/ft}$$

Anchorage must be provided so that this shear can be transferred from the roof plane to the wall.

The axial chord forces (Fig. 1.8) at midlength of the long walls as caused by the bending of the roof diaphragm is discussed in Chapter 2 (Problem 2.10). The additional shear due to the torsional effect, as required by the 5% of the long building dimension to be placed off center, is small and can be neglected (see Problem 2.9).

To obtain the shear, which must be transferred from the cross-wall to the foundation, the seismic shear due to the weight of the wall above the floor has to be included. The weight of the cross-wall above the ground is

$$W_W = 0.090(18 \times 50) = 81\ \text{k}$$

The wall weight causes a lateral seismic force at the centroid of the wall (Fig. 1.8) having a magnitude of

$$V_W = 0.14\ W = 0.14\ (81) = 11.34\ \text{k}$$

The total shear to be resisted between wall and foundation (Fig. 1.8) is

$$V_{tot} = 25.20 + 11.34 = 36.54\ \text{k}$$

Assuming a uniform distribution of this force yields

$$p_{tot} = \frac{36540}{50} = 730.8 \text{ lb/ft}$$

This force causes a shear stress of

$$v = \frac{p}{A} = \frac{730.8}{8(12)} = 7.61 \text{ psi}$$

The shear stress is small and carried by friction and steel dowels.

The lateral sliding of the building can be evaluated approximately by using a coefficient of friction between the footing and ground of $\mu = 0.55$ for coarse grained soil without silt.

The total weight acting upon the wall is due to a portion of the roof load, the weight of the wall, and the weight of the foundation.

| | |
|---|---|
| The roof load is: | $W_{R'} = 0.020(10 \times 50) = 10 \text{ k}$ |
| The foundation weight is: | $W_F = 0.145(3 \times 1 \times 50) = 21.75 \text{ k}$ |
| The total weight is: | $W_{tot} = 10 + 81 + 21.75 = 112.75 \text{ k}$ |

The safety factor against sliding is

$$SF = \frac{\mu W_{tot}}{V_{tot}} = \frac{0.55(112.75)}{36.54} = 1.7 > 1.5$$

The wall is satisfactory against sliding even when neglecting the passive earth pressure at the building ends, the increase of weight due to the soil overburden, and the partial resistance provided by the long walls at the corner areas.

The shear wall must also be checked for overturning. The acting moment due to the seismic action is

$$M_{act} = 25.20(20) + 11.34(13) = 651.42 \text{ ft-k}$$

The potential reacting moment due to the dead load acting on the wall (Fig. 1.8) is

$$M_{react} = 112.75 (25) = 2818.75 \text{ ft-k}$$

The safety factor against overturning is

$$SF = \frac{M_{react}}{M_{act}} = \frac{2818.75}{651.42} = 4.33 > 1.5$$

The wall is clearly safe against overturning.

Finally the lateral load for which the wall must be designed is determined. The uniform lateral seismic load acting perpendicular to the masonry wall and causing the panel to bend, is

$$F_p = Z I C_p W_p \qquad (1.16)$$

where $Z = 0.75, I = 1.00, C_p = 0.3, w_p = 90 \text{ psf}$

$$F_p = 0.75(1)0.3(90) = 20.25 \text{ psf}$$

Note the seismic load is only slightly larger than the wind pressure of 20 psf. One may conclude that for lighter walls wind will control the design of the wall panel for this specific seismic zone.


### Dynamic Loads

In contrast to dead loads, which are stationary and fixed in magnitude, direction, and location, live loads are movable. Live loads are considered static if they are applied slowly, as in the case of occupancy loads, but dynamic when they are applied abruptly or change rapidly; dynamic action causes larger loads than a comparative static action. The effect of wind upon a structure not only depends on the variation of the wind pressure, but also on the natural period of the structure which, in turn, is a function of its stiffness and mass. If the period of the building is significantly shorter than the period of the load, then the load can be considered static. This is the case for ordinary low buildings which are relatively stiff and have a natural period of less than 0.3 s as compared to the time variation of wind in typical intervals of 4–5 s or possibly short gusts of 1–2 s. However, for a slender structure such as a relative flexible multistory frame building with a period of more than 2 s, or a horizontal suspension structure of a 6-s period, dynamic loads must be considered, since the periods of the load and structure are dangerously close to each other and may result in resonant loading that is a steady increase of lateral deformations finally causing collapse. Because of the complexity of a dynamic analysis codes allow an empirical, equivalent static approach for ordinary conditions. This has already been discussed for seismic and wind loading, where dynamic magnification factors were applied. Codes also provide factors for common dynamic loading conditions as caused by impact and vibration. When moving loads such as cars, trains, cranes, elevators, etc., change their speed (accelerate, decelerate), they cause an impact upon the supporting structure which results in longitudinal forces in the direction of movement, or centrifugal forces upon curved structures in a radial direction. For instance, codes require an impact factor of 2 for an elevator; hence, an elevator suddenly stopping is assumed to double its effective weight.

Vibration loads, as generated by machinery, cause the stresses and deformations of the supporting structure to increase. These loads become critical when their periods are on the order of the period of the structure and thus approach resonance. Resonant loads build up the amplitude of oscillations of the structure and lead to failure for undamped conditions. Codes take this type of cyclic load action into account by requiring live loads to be increased, as for example for a traveling crane by 25% in addition to the longitudinal force action due to the impact loading.

Other dynamic loads such as wave loads are of hydrodynamic nature, or of random nature such as blast loads caused by explosions inside or outside the building; sonic booms are blast loads on a smaller scale.


### The Effect of Load Duration

Wood has the particular ability to carry substantially greater loads for a short period of time. As live loads are not permanent, their duration of action is a critical factor in determining the member load capacity. Allowable working stresses are assigned on the basis of normal loading of a cumulative duration of approximately 10 years. The allowable stresses may be increased for following shorter loading conditions by:

- 15% for snow, which is considered to act over a two months period
- 25% for construction loads which are considered to be of 7-day duration
- 33% for wind or seismic action assumed of only 1-day duration
- 100% for impact loading

## Load Combinations

Many of the loads just discussed may act simultaneously and should be combined if they are superimposable. One must keep in mind, however, that the given loads are maximum. For instance, the probability of a wind with a 50-year recurrence interval occurring at the same time as an earthquake, where most damage is done in a period of 30–60 s, is extremely small and negligible. Similarly, for most roof structures, the probability of maximum snow acting together with maximum wind is small, since 70 mph winds will blow at least part of the snow off the roof. To take conditions like that into account, codes allow an increase of allowable stresses or a reduction of loads for certain load combinations. For example, where dead load, $D$, acts together with live load, $L$, and wind load, $W$, the allowable stresses can be increased by 33% or the loads reduced by 25%. This is equivalent to multiplying the loads by a load combination probability factor of 0.75.

According to the National Building Code, the following load combinations must be checked to determine the maximum stresses:

$$
\begin{array}{r}
D \\
D + L \\
D + (W \text{ or } E) \\
D + T \\
\hline
[D + L + (W \text{ or } E)]\ 0.75 \\
(D + L + T)\ 0.75 \\
[D + (W \text{ or } E) + T]\ 0.75 \\
\hline
[D + L + (W \text{ or } E) + T]\ 0.66
\end{array}
\qquad (1.17)
$$

where $D$ = dead load, prestress forces; $L$ = live load, snow load, earth and hydrostatic pressure, dynamic loads; $W$ = wind load; $E$ = earthquake load; and $T$ = loads due to temperature and moisture changes, and due to shrinkage, creep, and settlement.

## Ultimate Strength Loads

In the elastic or working stress theory, members are designed as based on the material behavior in the elastic range. The service loads cause stresses which must be kept below the allowable ones. The permissible stresses are specified by codes as a fraction of the yield stress as, for example, for steel beams with $F_b = 0.66\,F_y$, or as a fraction of the crushing strength of the material such as $F_b = 0.45 f_c'$ for reinforced concrete beams, or as a fraction of the buckling load for slender columns. Timber, masonry, and mostly steel structures are designed for elastic behavior.

The strength design is based on the largest load, called the ultimate load, that the structure carries safely before it fails. Failure in steel structures is reached when a sufficient number of plastic hinges have formed causing the structure to collapse. A reinforced concrete member fails when the concrete has reached its ultimate strength of $0.85 f_c'$ and the steel its yield point $F_y$.

The ultimate load causing failure is equal to the service load $Q$ multiplied by the load factors $\gamma$. They reflect the safety against failure; larger factors are assigned to the live loads than to the dead load, thus identifying the more unpredictable character of the live loads. The load factors for reinforced concrete, structural steel and steel cables are given below. The factor of 1.7 is comparable to the safety factor $1/1.7 \approx 0.6$ defining the allowable elastic stresses in steel (e.g., $F_t = 0.6 F_y$).

According to the *AISC Specification for the Design, Fabrication, and Erection of Structural Steel for Buildings,* the steel strength as based on plastic design shall not be less than that required to support

$$1.7(L + D) \tag{1.18}$$

$$1.3[D + L + (W \text{ or } E)]$$

According to the *AISI Steel Cable Manual* (reference 166), the effective design breaking strength of the cable shall be at least equal to the largest value produced by the following typical cable tension conditions, where the prestress force is denoted by $P$

$$2.2(D + P)$$

$$2.2(D + L + P)$$

$$2[D + L + P + (W \text{ or } E)] \tag{1.19}$$

$$2(D + P + (W \text{ or } E))$$

According to the *ACI Building Code for Reinforced Concrete* (ACI-318-77) the required strength $U$ to resist the following typical ultimate load combinations should be at least equal to the calculated strength which is equal to the theoretical strength (resistance) $R$ multiplied by the capacity reduction factor $\phi$.

$$U = \Sigma \gamma_1 Q_1 \leqslant \phi R \tag{1.20}$$

$$U = 1.4D + 1.7L$$

$$U = 0.75(1.4D + 1.7L + 1.7(W \text{ or } E))$$

$$U = 0.9D + 1.3(W \text{ or } E)$$

$$U = 1.4(D + T)$$

where for several situations the capacity reduction factors are:

| | |
|---|---|
| flexure and axial tension in reinforced concrete | $\phi = 0.90$ |
| shear, torsion, bond and anchorage | $\phi = 0.85$ |
| axial compression for tied columns and bearing on concrete | $\phi = 0.70$ |
| flexure in plain concrete | $\phi = 0.65$ |

## Problems

**1.1** A low-rise gabled building of rectangular plan form has a roof slope of 1/3 and is located in southern Wisconsin. Investigate the wind pressures the overall primary structure (i.e., frame) and the secondary structural elements in the wall and roof planes must resist for a wind direction perpendicular to the long front walls. Assume the potential wall openings on the windward as well as leeward sides as 15% each.

**1.2** Can you think of a primary structure system for a single-story building, which may have to be designed for the combined action of external and internal wind pressure?

**1.3** Determine the wind pressure distribution for a box-type, single-story long building caused by a tornado. Assume a wind velocity of 250 mph, with all doors and windows closed. When the tornado passes over the building, it causes a lower outside pressure than inside the house for a short time, resulting in a uniform internal pressure attempting to burst outward. Consider the pressure drop as 0.1 atm = 212 psf.

**1.4** Determine the live load reduction for the floor beams in Fig. 2.13f, considering a live and dead load of 60 psf each.

**1.5** Find the thermal stresses for the beam in Example 1.2 at a temperature of $-30°F$ and compare them with the allowable stresses.

**1.6** Determine the maximum spacing of vertical expansion joints for a facade brick wall. Use 1-in. joints with a sealant which has a maximum allowable strain of 50%. The wall is built at a temperature of $35°F$; consider a maximum future summer temperature of $115°F$. The coefficient of expansion for the brick wall in the horizontal direction is $3.4 \times 10^{-6}$ in./in./$°F$ and the factor for moisture expansion is roughly equal to 0.0002 in./in.

**1.7** What would happen in the reinforced concrete, if the coefficients of thermal expansion of steel and concrete are not approximately the same?

**1.8** Redesign the building in Example 1.4 by using prestressed precast double Tee concrete members as the roof structure and as wall panels. The roof dead load is 70 psf and the wall panels weigh 75 psf. Consider the foundations and wall openings to be the same as in Example 1.4.

**1.9** Redesign the building in Example 1.4 as a wood structure with a stud wall of 20 psf and the roof dead load remaining the same.

## 1.2  GENERAL MATERIAL PROPERTIES

To define all of the properties of building material is extremely difficult. They include mechanical, chemical (composition, corrosion, reactivity, etc.), and physical (acoustical, electrical, magnetic, optical, thermal, etc.), characteristics. The mechanical properties are of great interest to the structural designer since they relate to the response of the material to loading as expressed in strength and deformation, and hence are briefly discussed here.

Not all materials exhibit the same response in every direction of loading; the materials which do have that feature are called *isotropic* (metals, plastic film, coated fabrics, rubber membranes, etc.). Materials which do not have identical properties in all directions are called *anisotropic* (masonry, wood, some plastics, woven/gridded fabrics, etc.). Most materials, on a microscopic scale, show different properties from point to point and hence are nonhomogeneous; however, on a macroscopic scale they can be considered *homogeneous*. *Composite* materials such as reinforced concrete, plaster board, plywood, and reinforced plastics obviously do not have monolithic qualities.

Structural members are not perfectly rigid bodies as is assumed in statics; they deform under loads. The most simple deformation is caused by axial force action. Visualize that a linear member is tested axially up to its failure in either tension or compression. Its response to tension as expressed by the elongation $\Delta L$ is recorded with the corresponding load $P$. The resulting diagram is called the stress–strain curve. The stress is plotted along the ordinate and is equal to the axial force divided by the original cross-sectional area $A$ of the member

$$f = \frac{P}{A}$$

The ultimate strength of the member corresponds to the highest point on the curve (Fig. 1.9).

The strain is plotted along the abscissa and is equal to the axial deformation $\Delta L$ divided by the original length $L$ of the member,

$$\epsilon = \frac{\Delta L}{L} \tag{1.21}$$

The maximum strains at the point of rupture vary extensively. The tensile strains of the metals in Fig. 1.9 range from a maximum for carbon steel to a minimum for cast iron.

The majority of materials show stress–strain diagrams for compression and shear resembling the ones for tension, particularly for the elastic range. The moduli of elasticity in tension and compression are equal for many materials.

The material properties are derived from a simple test specimen, thereby neglecting that the properties vary with time, temperature, and methods of testing, as well as the fact that real members are subject to two- three-dimensional stresses. Only short-time loading is considered, but materials like concrete, masonry, wood, etc., exhibit *time-dependent* features.

The stress–strain curves for different materials vary widely as is shown in Fig. 1.9. The basic mechanical material properties are derived from these curves. All but the concrete curves, are based on tension tests.

There seem to be three different types of curves:

- A continuous curve as for cast iron and concrete
- A straight line as for plexiglass
- A straight line abruptly or gradually changing into a curve as for steel and aluminum

Other curve types such as those for organic materials are not shown.

The stress–strain diagrams are defined by two distinct regions: the *elastic* and *inelastic* areas. When a member is loaded in the elastic range and then unloaded, the element returns to its original position like a rubber band. This is not the case for a member loaded

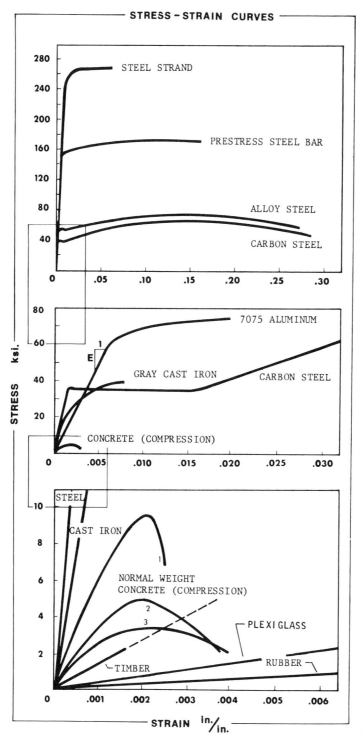

Fig. 1.9 Stress-strain curves.

into the inelastic region. When this member returns, it will have a permanent deformation. The range of the elastic strain is small in comparison to the inelastic strain. Materials which pass through large deformations before failing such as steel and aluminum are called *ductile,* while materials with relatively little deformation at failure, such as cast iron, concrete, and glass, are called *brittle.* Brittle materials do not yield, they fail suddenly without warning; they are inherently the strongest material but also most vulnerable to failure because of their lack of ductility.

In brittle material at points of overstress, cracks form and propagate, and then suddenly fail. In ductile materials, at points of stress concentration, the material yields locally and forces the surrounding material to take over, that is, the stresses are redistributed. Ductile material can absorb much more punishment and gives adequate warning of impending collapse by showing extensive plastic deformations. Some ductile materials become brittle at very low temperatures, such as steel at –30°F.

All materials are elastic to a certain degree, but not all show deformations proportional to loading, that is there are linearly and nonlinearly elastic materials. Ductile materials like some metals, and brittle materials such as glass and plexiglass, show a linear stress–strain relationship in the elastic range. Robert Hooke (1635-1703) found that deflection is proportional to load. Based on Hooke's Law, Thomas Young (1773-1829) recognized that the ratio of stress to strain is constant. Today this constant is called Young's modulus, the modulus of elasticity, or the elastic modulus $E$. It represents the slope of the stress–strain curve in the elastic range and is a measure of the material stiffness

$$E = \frac{f}{\epsilon} \tag{1.22}$$

Substituting the expressions for strain and stress into this equation yields

$$E = \frac{f}{\epsilon} = \frac{f(L)}{\Delta L} = \frac{PL}{A \Delta L}$$

Rearranging the terms gives the familiar expression for the axial deformation of a linear member of length $L$ and cross-sectional area $A$,

$$\Delta L = \frac{PL}{AE} \tag{1.23}$$

The various stress–strain curves in Fig. 1.9 show distinctly different slopes in the elastic range. A material with a steeper slope or larger modulus of elasticity will deform much less than a material with a less steep slope and a small $E$ assuming the same force action, cross-sectional area, and member length.

For the measure of stiffness $E$ of nonlinearly elastic brittle materials (e.g., concrete and cast iron) respective codes should be consulted. According to *ACI 318-77,* the modulus of elasticity for normal weight concrete $E_c$ and a concrete strength of $f_c'$ (in psi) may be taken as

$$E_c = 57000 \sqrt{f_c'} \tag{1.24}$$

While $E$ for steels is constant and independent of strength, for concrete it is a variable with the heavier and stronger concrete being stiffer. For lightweight concrete the elastic modulus is generally 20-50% lower than for normal weight concrete. Also, for wood the modulus of elasticity varies according to grade and species.

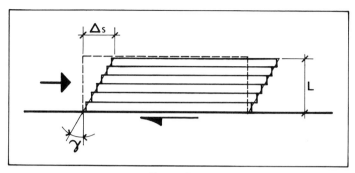

Fig. 1.10

The transition from the elastic to the inelastic range is not clearly defined by some materials (e.g., concrete, cast iron). For these materials the elastic limit, that is, the location where permanent deformations occur when the load is taken away, must be determined. Notice that some brittle materials such as glass have a nearly linear stress–strain curve up to fracture! For many materials the elastic limit is equal to the proportional limit and for all practical purposes may be considered equal to the location of the yield point. Beyond this point, stress and strain are no longer proportional to each other; the strain increases much more rapidly than the stress. Many steels demonstrate a perfect distinction between the different behavioral ranges of the stress–strain curve. The straight line relationship of the elastic range clearly changes to the horizontal plateau of the plastic range, where only the strain increases without an increase of stress, before it changes to the strain-hardening range. Steel strands, prestress wire, and aluminum do not exhibit a sharply defined yield point, as is characteristic of mild steels, and are also much less ductile.

For mild steels the plastic range may be 8–20 times greater than the elastic range.

Strains are induced not only in the direction of the force action ($\epsilon_L$) but also in the two mutually perpendicular directions. This effect was evaluated by S.D Poisson (1781–1840) and is known as Poisson's ratio

$$\nu = -\frac{\epsilon_t}{\epsilon_L} \qquad (1.25)$$

For most metals it is in the range 0.25–0.35. For structural steel $\nu = 0.3$ may be assumed. For concrete it varies from about 0.11 for high-strength concrete to 0.21 for low-strength concrete. For concrete shells Poisson's ratio may be assumed equal to zero.

In contrast to axial forces which change the length of a structural element, shear forces tend to deform the shape of a body as is shown in Fig. 1.10 for, say, a typical low wall. Visualize the wall to consist of thin layers which under translational force action slide with respect to each other, resulting in a maximum shear deflection of $\Delta_s$ at the top. The average shear strain $\gamma$ is defined by the angular change of the originally perpendicular horizontal and vertical faces as measured in radians

$$\tan \gamma \cong \gamma = \frac{\Delta_s}{L} \qquad (c)$$

According to Hooke's Law, the shear modulus $G$ measures the elastic shear stiffness. It represents the slope of the shear stress $(f_v)$–strain diagram in the elastic range

$$G = \frac{f_v}{\gamma} = \frac{VL}{A\Delta_s} \qquad\qquad (d)$$

The lateral shear deformation can now be given in terms of the shear $V$ acting along the shear area $A$, the shear modulus of the material $G$, and the height of the element $L$

$$\Delta_s = \frac{VL}{AG} \qquad\qquad (1.26)$$

The shear modulus can be expressed for isotropic materials in terms of the modulus of elasticity and Poisson's ratio

$$G = \frac{E}{2(1+\nu)} \qquad\qquad (1.27)$$

Construction materials are classified according to their nature or according to their function. Their function is identified by their usage and their purpose (e.g., structural versus nonstructural). The nature of materials is organized as metallic (cast iron, steels, alloys, etc.), nonmetallic (stones, gravel, asbestos, glass, etc.), ceramic products (concrete, cement, brick, tile, etc.), chemical products (gypsum, paints, lubricants, etc.), polymers (thermoplastic and thermosetting materials, etc.), wood, natural fibers (cotton, flax, silk, etc.), cellulosic products (paper, cardboard, felt, etc.), and other miscellaneous materials.

These materials, in turn, are selected according to their suitability. Some typical performance criteria are strength, flexibility, weight, durability, dimensional stability, workability, machinability, compatibility, availability, cost, toughness, hardness (i.e., resistance to penetration), resistance to fire or heat, sound resistance, weather proofing, ease of jointing and handling, response to biological damage and other chemical attack, ease of maintenance, and many other criteria.

Various materials are shown in Table 1.3. The reader is familiar with most of the common construction materials with the possible exception of plastics. Plastics derive their name from the fact that at some stage they are plastic and can be formed into the desired shape; most are derived from petroleum. The two important groups of plastic materials in the building construction field are foams and composites. Foams are mostly used as insulation material, but also in shell construction and as structural components in sandwich panels. The plastic in composites serves as matrix and continuous phase to bond the reinforcing glass-fibers together. The two distinct classes of plastics are *thermoplastics* (e.g., nylon, acrylic, vinyl) which can be softened by heat many times, and *thermosets* (e.g., polyester, epoxy, polyurethane, phenolic) which are in the plastic stage only once and then harden irreversibly. Reinforced thermosetting plastics find general use in structures, while thermoplastics because of their low modulus of elasticity and low melting point are less suitable as reinforced plastics. The most common of all reinforced plastics in construction industry are the glass-fiber reinforced polyester (GRP) composites, while thermoplastics are often used without reinforcement (e.g., translucent acrylic domes, pipes). For the discussion of further characteristics of plastics refer to Sections 8.1 and 9.1.

The primary mechanical and physical material characteristics, in this context, as re-

Table 1.3   Material Properties

| | UNIT WEIGHT | ULT. STRENGTH ksi | | MODULUS OF ELASTICITY | COEFFICIENT OF THERMAL EXPANS. |
|---|---|---|---|---|---|
| | pcf | COMPR. | TENS. | $10^3$ ksi | $10^{-6}$ in./in./°F |
| STEEL: | | | | | |
| CARBON STEEL | 490 | 58 | 58 | 29 | 6.5 |
| ALLOY STEEL | 490 | 60–115 | 60–115 | 29 | |
| STEEL TUBING | | 45–70 | 45–70 | 29 | |
| STEEL SHEET | | | 55–85 | 29 | |
| REINFORCING BARS | | | 70–90 | 29 | |
| PRESTRESS BARS | | | 160 | 26 | |
| PRESTRESS STRAND | | | 270 | 28 | |
| CABLE STRAND | | | 220 | 24 | |
| WIRE ROPE | | | 150 | 20 | |
| STAINLESS STEEL (AISI 301) | 501 | | 105 | 28 | 9.4 |
| CAST IRON | 450 | | 30 | 15 | 5.9 |
| SHEET COPPER | 556 | | 36 | 17 | 9.8 |
| ALUMINUM (1100 – H14) | 169 | | 18 | 10 | 13.1 |
| ALUMINUM ALLOY (7075-T6) | 175 | | 76 | 10.4 | 13.1 |
| LEAD | 710 | | 2.5 | | 15.9 |
| TITANIUM | 282 | | 80–145 | 15.5 | 5.4 |
| TUNGSTEN WIRE | 1204 | | 500 | 53 | 2.4 |
| FILAMENT: | | | | | |
| BORON FIBERS | 164 | | 500 | 70 | |
| GLASS FIBERS | 156 | | 650 | 12.6 | |
| GRAPHITE FIBERS | 109 | | 390 | 60 | |
| ALUMINA WHISKERS | | | 3000 | 62 | |
| PLASTICS: | | | | | |
| UNDIRECTIONAL COMPOSITES | | | | | |
| GLASS/EPOXY | 112 | 90 | 160 | 5.7 | |
| GRAPHITE/EPOXY | 93 | 165 | 204 | 30.1 | |
| GLASS/POLYESTER PANEL | 100 | | 15.5 | 1.25 | 17.5 |
| ACRYLIC SHEET (e.g. PLEXIGLASS DOME) | 72 | 17 | 10 | 0.4 | 41 |
| GLASS FIBER REINF. CEMENT PAN. | 105 | 7–11 | 1.2–1.6 | 1.5 | 7 |
| CONCRETE | 145 | 3–9 | 0.3–0.5 | 3.2–5.5 | 5.5 |
| NATURAL STONE | | | | | |
| GRANITE | 162 | 10–40 | 0.6–1.0 | 5.7–9.6 | 4.5 |
| LIMESTONE | 144 | 4–10 | 0.3–0.7 | 3.0–5.4 | 2.7 |
| WINDOW GLASS (SILICATE) | 156 | | 4 | 7–13 | 5 |
| TIMBER | 21–51 | 1.5–10 | 4–20 | 0.7–2.0 | 2 |
| OTHER MATERIALS: | | | | | |
| BONE | | | 20 | 4 | |
| COTTON | 93 | | 42–125 | | |
| DIAMOND | 220 | | | 130 | 0.67 |
| FLAX | 93 | | 100 | | |
| GOLD LILY | | | 28 | 3.6 | |
| PAPYRUS | | | 29 | 1.9 | |
| LEATHER | 59 | | 6 | | |
| RUBBER | 59 | | | 0.001 | |
| SILK | 84 | | 45–83 | 14.5 | |
| SPIDER'S THREAD | | | 35 | | |
| WOOL | 80 | | ·17–28 | 4.7 | |

| | UNIT WEIGHT | APPROX. ALLOWABLE STRESSES (ksi) | | | MODULUS OF ELASTICITY | COEF. OF EXPANSION $10^{-6}$ |
|---|---|---|---|---|---|---|
| | pcf | TENS. | COMPR. | SHEAR | $10^3$ ksi | in./in./°F |
| CARBON STEEL | 490 | 22 | 22 | 14.5 | 29 | 6.5 |
| TIMBER | 34 | 1 | 1 | 0.09 | 1.7 | 2.1 |
| BRICK MASONRY | 120 | 0.02 | 0.4 | 0.03 | 2.0 | 3.4 |
| NORMAL WEIGHT CONCRETE | 145 | 0.1 | 2 | 0.07 | 3.7 | 5.5 |
| LIME STONE | 144 | 0.06 | 0.4 | 0.17 | 4.2 | 2.7 |
| SOILS (FOUNDATIONS): | | | | | | |
| SOFT CLAY | | | 0.02 | | | |
| FINE SAND | | | 0.03 | | | |
| LOOSE GRAVEL | | | 0.06 | | | |
| HARD SPAN | | | 0.14 | | | |
| SEDIMENTARY ROCK | | | 0.2 | | | |
| FOLIATED ROCK | | | 0.6 | | | |
| BED ROCK | | | 1.4 | | | |

lated to the building structure are weight, strength, stiffness, and to a certain degree the effects due to temperature change. These properties are shown and compared for various materials in Table 1.3.

As the scale of a building enlarges, its weight increases faster than the live loads it is supporting. For instance, as a building gets higher, its weight grows with the volume ($ft^3$), while the live load only increases with the area ($ft^2$). It is quite obvious then that material weight is an important consideration. Ideally a minimum weight should support a maximum live load, ignoring economic factors and problems related to minimum weight structures. There are occasions, however, when weight is a desired feature, as for reasons of stability.

As can be seen in Table 1.3 for typical structural building materials, the weights range from the very dense steel with 490 pcf to about 35 pcf for the weight of timber; steel is about 14 times heavier than timber, 5 times denser than plastics, and roughly 3 times heavier than aluminum and concrete. Since timber is so light, large sections can be assembled and relatively easily handled. It is obvious that the comparison of the material densities must include the effect of strength and stiffness (as discussed later).

The elastic modulus determines how stiff or flexible a material is, assuming that the cross-section of a member does not change for the various materials. In comparing the stiffness of the typical structural building materials one finds that steel is about 3 times stiffer than aluminum, about 10 times more than concrete, and roughly 30 times stiffer than wood. In long-span beam structures where the beam size is a function of the allowable deflection and where the superimposed loads are much larger than the dead load, steel may be a better choice, since aluminum, for instance, deforms about three times as much as a steel beam. In cases where the live load is small in comparison to the dead load, as for long-span roof structures, the light timber and aluminum may offer certain advantages.

In building construction the structural use of aluminum is for cladding systems, formwork for concrete, stud walls, and frames, as well as for space frames and geodesic domes, where the short members form a rigid spatial grid structure. Care must be taken that aluminum is separated from dissimilar materials by painting or insulation. Electrostatic corrosion is caused by moisture when aluminum is in permanent contact with certain other metals, and chemical attack may occur when it is in contact with porous materials like wood and fiberboard that may absorb water, or when it is in contact with wet alkaline materials such as mortar, plaster and concrete.

The comparison of member stiffness for different materials is based on the elastic modulus and short-term force action. However, one must keep in mind that certain materials like concrete, masonry, timber, and plastics deform in time, that is, creep under long-term loading.

The tensile strength for common building materials ranges from the high strength of steel and some composites to the low strength of timber. The allowable stress for steel is about 22 times higher than for timber. The tensile strength of pure aluminum is relatively low, but the strength of aluminum alloys is in the range of alloy steels. It is apparent that materials like concrete, stone, and masonry are not tensile materials; they must be reinforced to resist tension.

Plastic is moderately strong but lacks stiffness. To increase its structural properties it must be reinforced with stronger and stiffer material such as fibers to form a fiber-reinforced composite. The fibers which are finer than human hair can be of inorganic nature (e.g., glass, steel, asbestos, carbon, boron) or organic nature (e.g., natural such as cotton, jute and sisal, or synthetic such as polyester). The most common fibers in the building construction industry are glass fibers. Fibers are larger and weaker than whiskers; they are thin needle crystals which can be grown from most substances. Whiskers may be up to 2 $\mu$m thick and possibly inches long; they are the strongest material (Table 1.3). In the late 1920s in England, A.A. Griffith showed that thread-like forms of material are by far stronger than the bulk in which material is generally used; this is especially true for brittle materials. According to Griffith's Law, for the fibers of brittle material the strength is inversely proportional to the diameter. Hence, the strength of the fibers increases as they get thinner. It makes sense that when the fiber material is used in bulk form, imperfections enter; *the strength of the whole is not equal to the strength of the sum of its parts.* Fibers cannot be structurally used by themselves; they may form cables or fabrics, or they may be embedded in a matrix material to form a composite. Glass-fiber reinforcement in plastics appears as chopped strand, chopped strandmat, roving or cloths. In other words, the fibers may be placed in the plastics in a random manner, or woven and possibly placed in several layers. Since the stiffness of fiber-reinforced plastics is still moderate, it is advantageous to use inherently stiff geometrical shapes like shells, folded and polyhedral structures, inflatable structures, and sandwich construction made up entirely of laminae or layers in which the stiffer material is placed along the outer faces.

The compressive strength is closely related to slenderness considerations and buckling criteria, that is, it is a function of the geometry and type of the structure. The relationship between tensile and compressive strength of materials is interesting. While steel is about equally strong in tension and compression, wood is 2-3 times stronger in tension, and concrete is 10-20 times stronger in compression.

A comparison of the coefficients of expansion for the various materials shows that aluminum expands or contracts twice as much as steel, while plexiglass changes in length 20 times more than timber and about 6 times more than steel. It clearly indicates that care must be taken to allow for the large dimensional change of plexiglass at its boundaries. For reinforced plastics the expansion approaches that of steel.

To evaluate one aspect of structural efficiency, material weight must be related to its strength and stiffness. First, the length or rupture length $L_u$ for the material is derived. The ultimate stress $f_u$ of a suspended bar carrying its own maximum weight $W_u = \gamma(V_u) = \gamma A L_u$ is

$$f_u = \frac{W_u}{A} = \frac{\gamma A L_u}{A} = \gamma L_u$$

or

$$L_u = \frac{f_u}{\gamma} \qquad \left(\frac{\text{lb ft}^3\ 12^2 \text{in.}^2}{\text{in.}^2\ \text{lb ft}^2}\right)$$

$$L_u = \frac{f_u(12)^2}{\gamma} \qquad (\text{ft})$$

$$L_u = 0.0273\frac{f_u}{\gamma} \qquad (\text{miles})$$

$$(1.28)$$

The rupture length is a constant. The strength-to-weight ratio $f_u/\gamma$ is called the *specific strength.* Similarly, the elastic modulus-to-weight ratio $E/\gamma$ is called the *specific elasticity.*

As the strength of a material increases and its weight decreases, its rupture length or specific strength increases. The strength-to-density ratio for typical steel and aluminum is about the same while the one for timber is approximately twice as much, which shows the advantage of wood. Some synthetic cables have an ultimate length while under short-term loading of roughly three times greater than steel cable strand; the rupture length for cotton fibers as used in tent construction is in the same range. Concrete has a low strength-to-weight ratio and is most effective when used in long-span roof structures in shell construction, and prestressed concrete—resulting in a reduction of its high dead-to-live load ratio. High strength-to-weight structures are essential for mobile structures (e.g., car bodies, space vehicles, aircraft) where lightweight materials such as aluminum alloys, titanium, and reinforced plastics are essential. Keep in mind that the effect of high strength-to-density ratios results in smaller member sizes for framed structures which, in turn, may cause instability problems.

The elastic modulus-to-weight ratios of the typical steel and aluminum are in the same range, while the ratios for timber is about a third less. The specific elasticity of the steel cable strand and the synthetic cable (glass–epoxy) are approximately the same. Though reinforced plastic has a high strength-to-weight ratio, it also has a relatively low specific elasticity and therefore is used in the building construction industry mostly for geometrically stiff spatial forms.

## Problems

**1.10** What effect does material have on the deflection of beams? How does the deflection of beams made of steel, cast iron, aluminum, and timber compare if the beam is part of a lightweight structure where the superimposed loads are large in comparison to the dead load? Consider the beam inertia as constant.

**1.11** Repeat Problem 1.10, but consider the beam inertia as a variable and leave the beam depth constant; in other words, evaluate the beam deflection as a function of the elastic flexibility $EI$.

**1.12** To evaluate strength properties of different tensile materials, determine the ultimate length, or rupture length, of the following materials: carbon steel, timber, aluminum, steel cable strand, steel wire rope, glass–epoxy cables, graphite-epoxy cables, boron fibers, alumina whiskers, cotton, and silk. Assume the material to be of constant cross-section and to hang vertically, so that it is stressed in tension by its own weight and fails in rupture.

**1.13** Investigate the materials in Problem 1.12, but now consider deflection as a criterion. Evaluate the deformation in terms of the specific elasticity $E/\gamma$. Derive this expression and compare the results.

**1.14** Determine the structural efficiency of some materials such as: carbon steel, aluminum, plexiglass, concrete, limestone, window glass, and timber. Consider the specific strength and the specific elasticity; draw your conclusions.

**1.15** For a given superimposed load, two beams, one of steel and the other of aluminum, will have the same inertia if the two materials have the same strength. According to Problem 1.13, aluminum and steel have approximately the same specific elasticity. Does this mean that the two beams deform by the same amount?

**1.16** Study the range of the following material characteristics: density, tensile strength, elastic flexibility, ductility, and expansion-contraction due to temperature change. Draw your own conclusions.

**1.17** To visualize the thermal properties of materials, consider an element of 100 in. length to pass through a temperature differential of 100°F. Compare the following materials: steel, aluminum, tungsten, concrete, limestone, brick masonry, window glass, plexiglass, and timber.

**1.18** Compare the compatibility of the composite action of a reinforced concrete member 10 ft long for a temperature change of 100°F. Compare the concrete with steel and aluminum bars.

**1.19** How much supporting area is required for a given compression load considering the following materials: carbon steel, timber, brick masonry, concrete, limestone, soft clay, loose gravel, sedimentary rock, and bed rock. Express the required area in terms of steel area.

**1.20** How much more ductile is a mild steel as compared to a normal strength concrete?

**1.21** A steel pipe 8 Std column is filled with concrete and supports an axial load of 250 k. What are the stresses in the concrete and the steel? Neglect buckling.

## 1.3  STRUCTURAL MEMBERS

It is the purpose of this section to briefly introduce and define rigid structure systems from a geometrical point of view, to review the procedures for the preliminary design of beams and columns in steel, timber, and reinforced concrete, and to review basic concepts of connection design.

### Structure Systems

From a purely geometrical point of view, the basic structural building components can be classified as:

- Straight line elements (beams, columns)
- Folded and curved line elements (frames, arches)
- Surfaces to which loads are applied mainly in a perpendicular fashion (slabs)
- Surfaces upon which the loads act primarily parallel, that is within the surface (plates, walls)
- Curved surfaces (shells)

The use of these basic structural components for roofs of surface character or of spatial envelope forms is exemplified in Fig. 1.11. This simple organization will provide a frame of reference for the more detailed discussion of the individual systems during the rest of the book.

The architect in the early design stage must make structural decisions without the help of the engineer, must determine the layout of the solid building elements defining the spaces, proportion the members and thereby possibly influence the aesthetics of the building. Even if the visual image of the building is derived from other proportional orders or

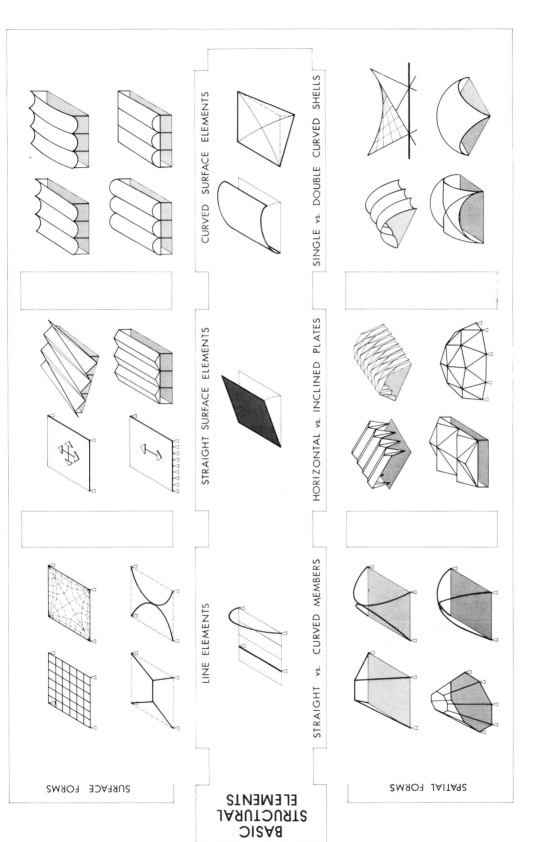

**Fig. 1.11** Introduction to rigid, horizontal-span structure systems.

39

subjective opinions, that is design theories which do not include structures in their vocabulary, the architect who intends to build must have a sense of scale and purpose of structure, that is, the physical reality of the building independent of stylistic trends. It is impossible to build a body without the knowledge of the anatomy of the bone structure supporting its organs—the structure is a necessity!

To give a design idea a sense of physical reality in the conceptual design stage, empirical structural design aids are necessary so that member sizes can be estimated without the help of rigorous mathematical investigations. Rules of thumb have been developed over time from experience, keeping in mind that member proportions may not be controlled by structural requirements, but by dimensional (clearance, structural detail, story height, formwork, etc.), environmental, and aesthetic considerations.

Typical empirical design aids as expressed in span-to-depth ratios for horizontal-span roof structures (or for lightly loaded floor structures such as for residential usage) are presented in Fig. 1.12. The systems are classified according to their span ranges in decking, shallow beams, deep beams, and envelope-type structures. Some typical ratios for common structural elements are:

decking:                    one-way concrete slab

$$\frac{L}{t} = 35 \quad \text{or} \quad t \approx \frac{L}{3} \quad \text{(where } L \text{ is in feet and depth } t \text{ in inches)}$$

shallow beams:              average ratio for floor beams

$$\frac{L}{t} = 24 \quad \text{or} \quad t = \frac{L}{2} \quad (L \text{ in feet, } t \text{ in inches)}$$

deep beams:                 trusses

$$\frac{L}{t} = 10 \quad \text{or} \quad t = L \quad (L \text{ in feet, } t \text{ in inches)}$$

envelope systems:           refer to respective sections in this book for
                            more detailed discussion of rules of thumb.

The preliminary sizes of columns as expressed by the ratio of their unbraced length to the least thickness are in the range of 5–25. Typical values for lightly loaded, relatively short columns to multistory columns may be roughly estimated as

in timber and steel:     24–10
concrete:                15–5

Each of the structural systems in Fig. 1.12 is applicable just for a certain scale range only. One must keep in mind that proportions which are derived from behavioral considerations do not remain constant! Galileo Galilei (1638) was the first to demonstrate the effect of scale in nature, particularly the relationships of surface-to-volume and weight. Later many other scientists like D'Arcy Thompson (1917) became fascinated by the same phenomenon. The impact of scale upon structure and form is quite apparent from nature, where, for instance, the slenderness of the wheat stalk (height-to-diameter) is around 500, while it is only about 15 for the tallest trees—clearly illustrating that proportions are not con-

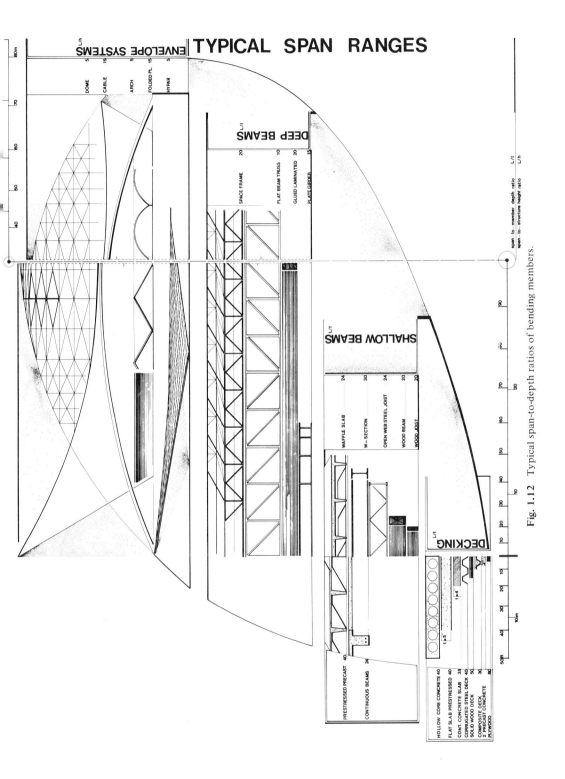

# TYPICAL SPAN RANGES

**ENVELOPE SYSTEMS**

DOME
CABLE
ARCH
FOLDED PL.
HYPAR

**DEEP BEAMS**

SPACE FRAME
FLAT BEAM TRUSS
GLUED LAMINATED
PLATE GIRDER

**SHALLOW BEAMS**

WAFFLE SLAB
W–SECTION
OPEN WEB STEEL JOIST
WOOD BEAM
WOOD JOIST

PRESTRESSED PRECAST
CONTINUOUS BEAMS

**DECKING**

HOLLOW CORE CONCRETE
FLAT SLAB PRESTRESSED
CONT. CONCRETE SLAB
CORRUGATED STEEL DECK
SOLID WOOD DECK
COMPOSITE DECK
2 PRECAST CONCRETE
PLYWOOD

span- to- member depth ratio    L/t
span- to- structure height ratio    L/h

Fig. 1.12  Typical span-to-depth ratios of bending members.

41

stant but change. Another, even more convincing example is the fact that animal skeletons become much bulkier with an increase of size as reflected by the change from the tiny ant to the delicate gazelle and finally to the massive rhinoceros and elephant. In other words, while an ant can support a multiple of its own weight, it could not even carry itself if its size were proportionally increased to the size of an elephant, since the weight increases with the cube while the supporting area only increases with the square as the linear dimensions are enlarged. Thus the dimensions are not in linear relationship to each other, the weight increases much faster than the corresponding cross-sectional area. Hence, either the proportions of the ant's skeleton would have to be changed or the material to be made lighter, or the strength and stiffness of the bones increased; obviously, the same principle applies also to a building of any shape!

For structures, it is impossible to clearly identify in which range, exactly, specific structure systems constitute an optimum solution, since several concepts are competing with each other and may all be efficient, and the selection is not necessarily based on structural considerations of efficiency.

The systems in Fig. 1.12 are rigid and subject to buckling and bending. As the span increases, these structures gain weight very rapidly so that they must be replaced at a certain point by lightweight cable structures. The characteristics of tension systems are discussed in other parts of this book.

The systems in Fig. 1.12 are presented only for preliminary design purposes; they should not be taken as recipes out of a cookbook—structures cannot just be plugged into the spatial organization as kind of an afterthought. The various beam-column examples in Fig. 1.13 attempt to correct this impression. Here the designers have convincingly expressed structure as architecture, and have articulated a clarity reflecting their own orders whether based on modularity, kits of elements, craftsmanship, machine-like high-precision technology, construction process, integrity of materials, logical disciplined simplicity, economy and function, biological or historical forms, minimal shapes, and so forth. Whatever the reason for the various forms, all of them are an integral part of the total design and are proof that the designer is in full control of the structure, and independent of time and fashion.

## Beams

Various beam types in an architectural context have been described in Fig. 1.13. Beams are distinguished in shape, that is in cross-section and elevation, material, and support conditions. They may be part of a repetitive grid, such as joists, or they may constitute individual members; they may support a floor structure or span a stadium; they may form a stair, a bridge, or an entire building.

From a structural point of view, typical beams may be organized as shallow beams, deep beams, wall beams, and shell beams (Fig. 1.14).

The direction, location, and nature of the loads as well as the member shape and curvature determine how the beam will respond to the force action, as is indicated in the center portion of Fig. 1.15. In this context it is assumed that the beam material obeys Hook's law, and that a linear distribution of stresses across the member depth holds true. For wall beams other design criteria must be developed. Only curved beams of shallow cross-section that makes them only slightly curved (e.g., arches) can be treated as straight beams

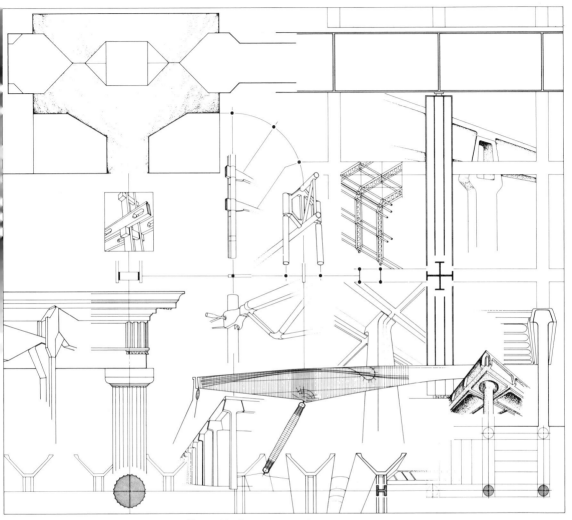

**Fig. 1.13** Beam versus column.

using linear bending stress distribution. Further, it is assumed that the beam will act only in bending and not in torsion, hence there will be no unsymmetrical flexure. This condition of symmetrical bending occurs for doubly symmetrical shapes, such as rectangular and W shapes, when the static loads are applied through the centroid of their cross-section, which is typical for most cases in building construction.

Beams, in general, must be checked for the primary structural determinants of bending, shear, deflection, and stability.

The largest bending stresses appear along the top and bottom faces of the beam, while the largest shear stress mostly occurs at the neutral axis, where the flexural stress is zero. The geometry of the I section is in direct response to this stress distribution, where the flanges primarily resist bending and the web resists the shear. While in shallow beams flexural stresses are generated by rotation of the entire section, in deep beams (girders, trusses) the bending capacity of the web may be neglected; hence, one may assume that

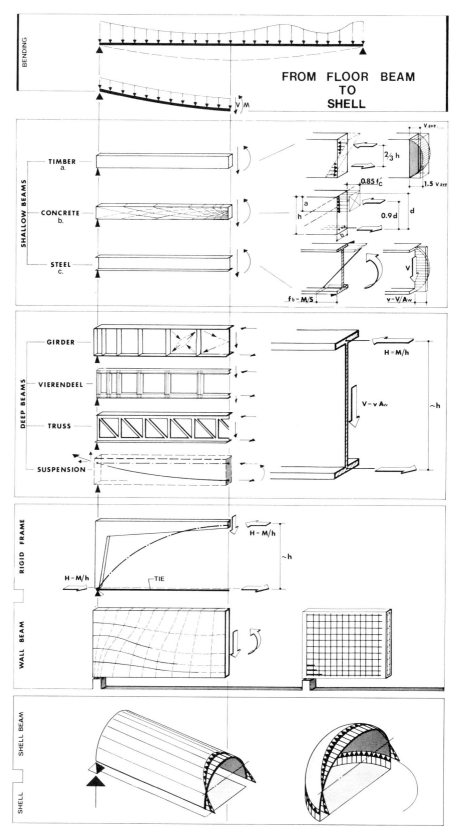

Fig. 1.14   Bending member types.

the moment is resolved into an internal couple of horizontal forces resisted by the flanges, thus causing mainly direct stresses (Fig. 1.14)

$$M = H(h)$$

Hence, each of the flanges must resist an axial force of

$$\pm H = \frac{M}{h} \tag{1.29}$$

This condition is even more apparent for the arch or cable (Fig. 1.14), where the internal force couple consists of the compressive force carried by the arch at the crown, and the tension force resisted by the tie at the base. Similarly, one may visualize the moment for a shallow beam to be resolved into a couple represented by the resultants of the flexural stress diagram. For instance, for a rectangular beam section the distance between the internal resultants is $0.67h$, while for a round section it is only $0.59h$; but for a W section it can be approximated as $0.9h$, clearly demonstrating the efficiency of the section.

When the solid cross-section of the member is transformed from a linear into a spatial-linear shape, such as the shell beam in Fig. 1.14, then the geometry of the section is effectively used, since the rotation is resolved into direct longitudinal axial forces; rather than rotating the solid material, the entire section is rotated thus allowing the thin shell solution. Even more efficient from a force flow point of view is the dome shell. Here the moment is transformed into direct forces which balance each other along the three-dimensional surface geometry. This dome is a true shell—not a beam anymore; its space geometry is most effectively used to transform rotation into the so-called membrane action.

The moment increases rapidly with the square of the span ($L^2$), thus the required member depth $h$ (i.e., lever arm of resisting internal forces) must also correspondingly increase, so that the stresses remain within the allowable range. The additional influence of deflection, member strength, and geometry are discussed throughout this text.

The design of concrete members is derived from the ultimate behavior while the design of steel and timber is based on elastic theory, which will be reviewed first.

The maximum elastic bending stresses for a straight symmetrical shallow beam section are equal to the moment $M$ at the given location divided by the section modulus $S$ at that location; they must be less than the allowable stress $F_b$

$$f_b = \frac{Mc}{I} = \frac{M}{S} \leqslant F_b \tag{1.30}$$

where $c = h/2$, and $I$ = moment of inertia. Hence, the required beam section is

$$S \geqslant \frac{M}{F_b} \tag{1.31}$$

The section modulus can be selected from the Tables A6 to A8 or other references (e.g., steel and timber construction manuals).

The allowable bending stress for compact, hot-rolled steel members is $F_b = 0.66F_y$, and $F_b = 0.75F_y$ for doubly symmetrical I and H shapes bent about their minor axes. The

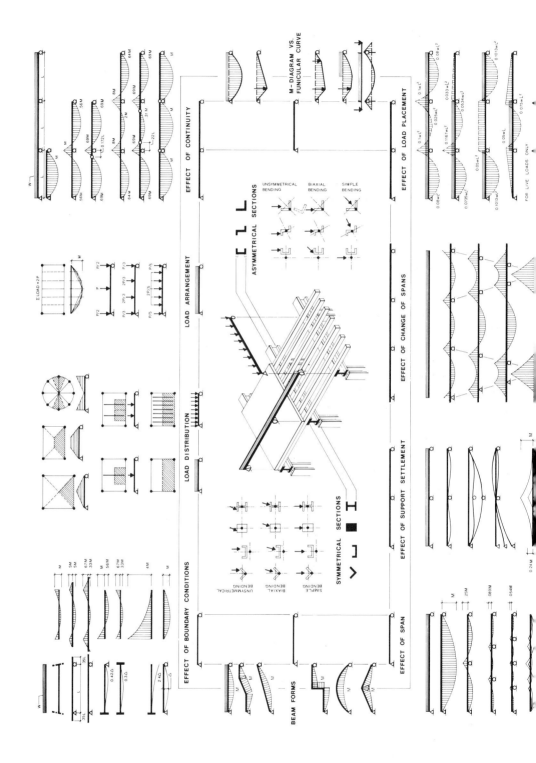

EFFECT OF CONTINUITY

M-DIAGRAM VS. FUNICULAR CURVE

EFFECT OF LOAD PLACEMENT

FOR LIVE LOADS ONLY

LOAD ARRANGEMENT

UNSYMMETRICAL BENDING

BIAXIAL BENDING

SIMPLE BENDING

ASYMMETRICAL SECTIONS

EFFECT OF CHANGE OF SPANS

LOAD DISTRIBUTION

EFFECT OF SUPPORT SETTLEMENT

SYMMETRICAL SECTIONS

SIMPLE BENDING

BIAXIAL BENDING

UNSYMMETRICAL BENDING

EFFECT OF BOUNDARY CONDITIONS

EFFECT OF SPAN

BEAM FORMS

46

allowable bending stresses do not have to be reduced as long as the beam is laterally stable and its compression portion is prevented from buckling. Wood beams with a typical width-to-depth ratio of 1/3 or 1/4 should be laterally braced at least at their ends. For steel beams the theoretical yield stress $F_y'$ (see Table A8) at which the flange becomes unstable should be larger than the yield stress $F_y$. Further, the unsupported length of the compression flange $L_b$ should be less than $L_c$ (see Table A8). Should $L_b$ be larger than $L_c$ but less than $L_u$, or should $F_y'$ be less than $F_y$, then the section is considered partially compact and the allowable bending stress may be taken as $F_b = 0.6F_y$. Box-like beam sections have a larger resistance to torsional-flexural buckling than open beam forms like W sections.

For the preliminary design of timber members the allowable stresses are not corrected to take into account either the effect of beam depth and beam shape or the effect of beam curvature and load duration.

Biaxial bending may occur such as for the pitched roof in Fig. 1.16. Here the roof skin is assumed to prevent the twisting $P(e)$ of the purlins ($e = 0$). The maximum stresses are found by superimposition of the bending stresses about the $x$ and $y$ axes, and appear at the extreme top (1) and bottom (2) corners of a purlin at its midspan

$$\pm f_{b\ max} = f_{b\ max_x} + f_{b\ max_y} \leqslant F_b \tag{1.32}$$

For the condition where the allowable bending stresses about the two principal axes are different, the following relationship holds true

$$\left(\frac{f_{b\ max}}{F_b}\right)_x + \left(\frac{f_{b\ max}}{F_b}\right)_y \leqslant 1 \tag{1.33}$$

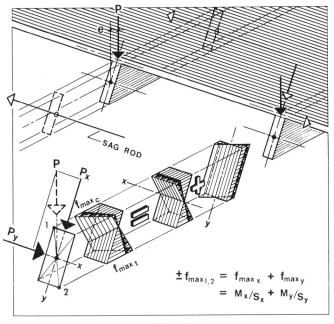

Fig. 1.16

Should the purlins of the pitched roof be channel sections, which have a low bending capacity about their web axis, then sag rods may be used to reduce the span length and thus the moments in this direction. Biaxial bending in the purlins can be prevented by resolving the force on top of it into components $P_x$ and $P_y$ and by letting the roof skin act as a diaphragm (deep beam), which transfers the force component $P_y$ directly to the frames, thus leaving only $P_x$ to be resisted by the purlin in simple bending.

For light framing (e.g., residential) light-gauge steel members are often used. They are cold-formed by bending thin sheets into the desired member shapes. Quite common in building construction is the light-gauge steel deck (or siding) which is produced as a shallow type ($1\frac{1}{2}$ in.) for roofs with a maximum span of about 10 ft. In floor construction the corrugated steel deck is generally used in composite action with lightweight concrete; here the shallow deck spans about 15 ft, whereas the deeper type (3 in.) has a larger capacity. For the design of cold-formed structural steel members refer to the respective manufacturers' catalogs and, if necessary, to the specifications published by AISI.

The shear stress in steel beams may be assumed to be uniformly distributed across the web area $A_w$ of W sections (Fig. 1.14c)

$$f_v = \frac{V}{A_w} \leqslant F_v = 0.40 F_y \tag{1.34}$$

For solid rectangular wood beams the maximum horizontal shear stress occurs at the neutral axis at the supports and is 50% larger than the average shear stress $V/A$ (Fig. 1.14a)

$$f_v = 1.5 \frac{V}{A} \leqslant F_v \tag{1.35}$$

For larger span conditions deflection controls the design of beams. The allowable immediate deflection values shown in Table 1.4 may be applied.

Additionally, in concrete design, long-term deflection due to sustained loads must be considered. Another elastic property which must be checked in concrete design is the width of the cracks, especially when higher-strength reinforcing steels are employed.

The preliminary depth $h$ or $t$ for bending members of normal weight concrete and Grade 60 reinforcement can be selected from Table 1.5 as based on avoiding deflection computations; the reduction of the minimum thickness for lesser steel grades may be conservatively neglected (e.g., 20% for Grade 40 steel). Typical economical proportions of beam width to beam height are in the range $b/h = 1/2.5$-$1/3$.

**Table 1.4   Allowable Immediate Deflection Values**

|                               | $LL$    | $DL + LL$ |
| ----------------------------- | ------- | --------- |
| Roofs                         |         |           |
| Industrial                    | $L/180$ | $L/120$   |
| Other building types          |         |           |
| Without plaster ceilings      | $L/240$ | $L/180$   |
| With plaster ceilings         | $L/360$ | $L/240$   |
| Floors                        |         |           |
| Ordinary conditions           | $L/360$ | $L/240$   |

Table 1.5  Minimum Thickness of Nonprestressed Beams or One-Way Slabs Unless Deflections are Computed

| Member | Minimum Thickness $h$ | | | |
| | Simply Supported | One End Continuous | Both Ends Continuous | Cantilevers |
|---|---|---|---|---|
| Solid one-way slabs | $L/20$ | $L/24$ | $L/28$ | $L/10$ |
| Beams or joist slabs | $L/16$ | $L/18.5$ | $L/21$ | $L/8$ |

A more precise prediction of the beam depth can be derived from the shear conditions. The actual nominal, average ultimate shear stress should be less than the allowable one. For the case of a typical amount of shear reinforcing, a shear stress of $v_u = 5\sqrt{f_c'}$ is assumed, that is $v_u - v_c = 3\sqrt{f_c'}$, where the shear capacity of the concrete is $v_c = 2\sqrt{f_c'}$

$$v_u = \frac{V_u}{\phi bd} \leqslant 5\sqrt{f_c'} \qquad (1.36)$$

Using these values: capacity reduction factor $\phi = 0.85$, $d \approx 2.7b$, and $f_c' = 4000$ psi, yields the following simple relationship for the member depth

$$d = \frac{\sqrt{V_u}}{10} \qquad (1.37)$$

where $V_u$ is in pounds and $d$ in inches.

The distance $d$ from the compression face to the centroid of the steel reinforcement can be approximately related to the member thickness $h$ for interior exposure conditions, as

beams–single layer: $\qquad h = d + 2.5$ in.
beams–double layer: $\qquad h = d + 3.5$ in.
joists and two-way slabs: $\qquad h = d + 1.5$ in.
one-way slabs: $\qquad h = d + 1.0$ in.

The approximate tension reinforcing for under-reinforced bending members can be found by balancing the ultimate moment $M_u$ with the steel reinforcement (Fig. 1.14b)

$$M_u = \phi A_s f_y(z)$$

or

$$A_s = \frac{M_u}{\phi f_y(z)} \qquad (e)$$

The lever arm length $z$ between the resultant internal forces varies. For a typical steel ratio $p = A_s/bd = p_{max}/2 = 0.014$, that is an amount of steel of about 1.4% of the cross-sectional area of the concrete beam, Grade 50 steel and 4000 psi concrete, the following value for $z$ can be derived from the equilibrium of the internal forces:

$$\Sigma F_x = 0 = A_s f_y - 0.85 f_c'(a)b$$

or

$$a = \frac{A_s f_y}{0.85 f_c' b} = \text{depth of rectangular stress block} \qquad (1.38)$$

but

$$p = \frac{A_s}{bd} = 0.014, \qquad A_s = 0.014bd$$

$$\frac{f_y}{f_c'} = \frac{50}{4}$$

$$a \approx 0.2d$$

or

$$z = d - \frac{a}{2} = 0.9d \qquad (f)$$

Substituting this expression for $z$, together with $\phi = 0.9$, into Eq. (e) yields approximately

$$A_s = \frac{M_u}{0.8 f_y d} \qquad (1.39)$$

This equation for reinforcing is satisfactory for quick estimation purposes as long as the steel ratio is less than about 0.014. Though this expression was derived for rectangular beam sections, it may also apply for the positive moment regions of T sections with large compressive capacity, where the neutral axis lies within the flange (e.g., slab). For one-way slabs as for T beams the typical steel ratio is in the range of $p = 0.005$.

The minimum reinforcing for concrete beams, for $f_y$ in psi, should be

$$A_{s\,\text{min}} = \frac{200}{f_y}(bd) \qquad (1.40)$$

For minimum reinforcement of concrete slabs refer to Eqs. (8.4), (8.5). The size of a plain concrete member without any reinforcing (e.g., a footing) depends on the tensile capacity of the concrete. The required section modulus $S$ for a member in bending for normal weight concrete can be found from the familiar expression

$$f_{tu} = \frac{M_u}{\phi S} \leqslant 5\sqrt{f_c'} \qquad (1.41)$$

where

$$\phi = 0.65$$

$$S \geqslant \frac{M_u}{3.25\sqrt{f_c'}}$$

The nature of beam behavior is reviewed in Fig. 1.15 and in Problems 1.22-1.36. The effect of the following criteria is investigated.

- Boundary conditions: simple beams, continuous beams, fixed beams, cantilever beams, etc.
- Support location: repetitive versus variable spans for continuous beams
- Type of loading: static versus dynamic loads, direction and location of loads
- Load distribution: the effect of floor structure layout
- Live load placement for indeterminate and cantilever beams
- Moment diagrams versus funicular lines
- Beam forms in elevation: straight, curved, tapered
- Beam forms in section: rectangular, round, hollow, solid, composite, etc.
- Beam material and stiffness
- Type of bending: simple, biaxial and unsymmetrical bending
- Support settlement
- Methods of analysis and construction: simple spans versus continuous spans versus composite action—elastic design with moment redistribution versus plastic or ultimate design

Obviously, all of these criteria do interact, but their individual study, on a comparative basis, provides an awareness of certain design implications. For example, the rapid increase of bending moments with an increase of span becomes quite apparent from the superimposed moment diagrams of the "effect of span" (Fig. 1.15); the addition of a support at midspan reduces the moment by 75%! While the bending moment only increases with the square of the span, $L^2$, ignoring the increase in beam weight, the deflection does so with the span to the fourth power, $L^4$, clearly indicating that with increase of span, deflection becomes more critical. On the other hand, with decrease of the beam slenderness ($L/h$), that is with decrease of span and/or increase of beam depth, the effect of shear must be taken into account. Deflections in the elastic range are independent of material strength and are only a function of the stiffness $EI$, while shear and bending are dependent on the material strength; bending is also a function of the beam inertia $I$, and shear a function of the cross-sectional area $A$.

Another important conclusion which can be drawn from Fig. 1.15 is that continuous beams much more effectively distribute the moments, especially when the cantilever principle is applied. Although continuous beams are heavier than the respective cantilever beams, they have the advantage because of their continuity, of being stiffer, which is an important consideration when high strength materials are employed.

Other conclusions can easily be derived from Fig. 1.15 by the reader.

## Problems

1.22 A beam spans 20 ft and carries a load of 1 k/ft; select the most economical W section ($A36$) for the cases in Fig. 1.17a-e, j-l as based on bending criteria. Assume the compression flange to be laterally supported. Study what effect the change of support (i.e., boundary) has on the design of the beam.

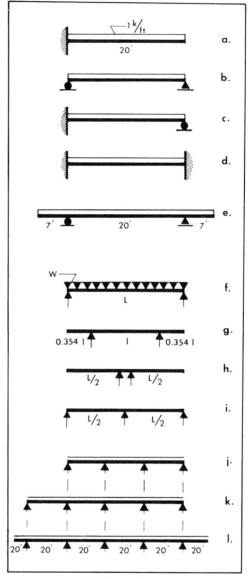

Fig. 1.17

**1.23** Design the beam (Fig. 1.17b) using Southern Pine with an allowable bending stress $F_b$ = 1265 psi and a modulus of elasticity $E$ = 1400 ksi.

**1.24** Do a preliminary design of the beam (Fig. 1.17b) using 4000 psi concrete and Grade 40 steel. Assume live and dead loads to be equal to each other.

**1.25** Determine the deflections for the beams illustrated in Fig. 1.17a and b based on the beams selected in Problem 1.22. Are the beams still satisfactory if the allowable deflection is assumed as $L/180$?

**1.26** Does the deflection control the design of the beams in Problems 1.23 and 1.24 if the allowable deflection for the timber beam is $L/240$?

**1.27**  Reduce the span of a beam by placing a column at midspan. By how much can the beam section be decreased if bending controls?

**1.28**  Determine the approximate size of a continuous beam with three equal spans of 15 ft. The beam carries a live load of 0.4 k/ft and a dead load of 0.2 k/ft. Use Southern Pine with the following properties in bending and shear: $F_b$ = 1300 psi, $F_v$ = 95 psi. The modulus of elasticity is $E$ = 1500 ksi. The live load deflection should not exceed $L/240$ and the total load deflection should not exceed $L/180$. Consider the critical load arrangement for the live load!

**1.29**  Which of the four beams in Fig. 1.17f–i, bridging the same space, yields the most economical section? Reason! Show moment diagrams of all cases superimposed on top of each other and drawn to scale. Express critical moments in terms of the maximum moment of the single span beam.

**1.30**  Since the maximum moments of cases (f) and (h) in Fig. 1.17 are the same, are then the beams of constant size also identical? Reason by first considering timber and then reinforced concrete.

**1.31**  Show the various live load arrangements for the beam in Fig. 1.17g. Assume uniform load action and consider that bending controls.

**1.32**  Is it reasonable to replace a continuous beam carrying a constant uniform load by an assemblage of fixed beams for approximate analysis purposes?

**1.33**  (a) Determine the preliminary size of a continuous beam with two equal spans of 15 ft and carrying a load of 1 k/ft. Use $A36$ steel. Assume that the beam is laterally supported.

(b) Is the beam still all right if the outer support starts settling? Evaluate the moment conditions by following the movement of the support.

(c) Determine the change in beam section if the central support settles $\frac{1}{2}$ in.

(d) Discuss what happens to the beam as the central support continues to settle.

**1.34**  Determine the size of an $A36$ W section spanning 40 ft and carrying a load of 1 k/ft. Assume the compression flange to be laterally supported. Investigate the following methods of design: simple beam, simple beam composite action with concrete, fixed elastic beam, fixed plastic beam, and fixed plastic composite beam. This is only a rough preliminary design estimate.

**1.35**  What is meant by simple bending? Consider the shape of the beam and the direction of the load.

**1.36**  Think about the effect that the following criteria have upon the design of a beam: boundary conditions, span, material, scale, beam cross-section, load placement, settlement, and moment redistribution.

### Columns and Beam Columns

Compression columns are not always necessarily the standard rectangular, solid sections as in concrete and timber construction, nor the W sections as used in steel; many variations in cross-section and elevation are possible as exemplified in Fig. 1.18. In cast-in-place concrete the formwork allows the building of any desired shape, as for instance

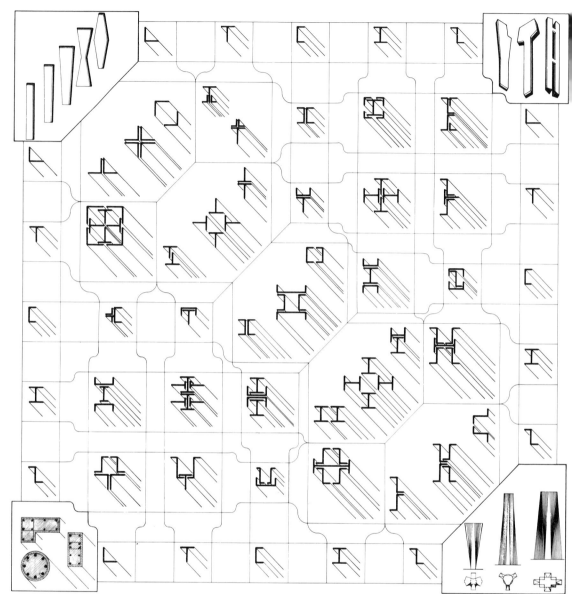

**Fig. 1.18** Columns.

expressed by the branching principle, as do prefab systems where members can be combined in infinitely many ways. However, one must keep in mind that the column as a
whole and its thin parts locally must resist buckling, that is the bending which is caused
by purely concentric force action.

The cross-section of a column may be varied and may decrease towards zero-moment
locations at midheight or top and/or bottom in $x$ or $y$ directions. On the other hand, the
column cross-section may be enlarged at midheight to strengthen its buckling resistance at
this critical location.

Some of the many possibilities for various column forms in steel are investigated in
Fig. 1.18; these forms are not necessarily based on structural considerations of efficiency

but may be determined by other requirements. They range from single members, such as ordinary pipe or rolled W sections and cover-plated columns, to the multiple member built-up systems composed of angles, tees, channels, or W sections.

These multiple members are generally arranged in an open cruciform or closed tubular fashion so as to yield the same buckling resistance about both major axes. However, the context of the column may require other arrangements of the elements. The vertical multiple column components may be connected into one unit by employing continuous or perforated cover plates, or by batten plates or diagonal lacing. A column concentrically loaded by an axial force $P$ causes a uniform stress. The tensile stress, on the effective net member area $A_e$, is

$$f_t = \frac{P}{A_e} \leqslant F_t \tag{1.42}$$

The compressive stress is

$$f_a = \frac{P}{A} \leqslant F_a \tag{1.43}$$

The allowable axial stress $F_a$ is not constant, it is dependent on the column slenderness.

Only for short sturdy columns, or for columns which are prevented from buckling, is the allowable compressive stress constant and based on the material strength, such as, for example, $F_a = 0.6F_y$ for structural steel. Long, slender columns fail in elastic buckling as Euler already determined in 1757. He showed that the critical stress at buckling is dependent on the modulus of elasticity $E$ and the column slenderness $KL/r$

$$f_{cr} = \frac{\pi^2 E}{(KL/r)^2} \tag{g}$$

This formula reflects the fact that with increase of slenderness the buckling stress decreases in proportion to the square of the column length as well as depends on the bending stiffness $I = Ar^2$ and the material stiffness $E$. The term $KL$ is the effective column length or the distance between the inflection points. Hence the stiffness factor $K$ measures the amount of restraint at the boundaries (degree of fixity at top and bottom). The range of $K$ factors for various typical building conditions is given in Fig. 1.19.

The problem lies in defining the degree of column end restraint and the effect of sidesway. For instance, for the case where a simple two-hinge portal frame is laterally braced the $K$ factor is 0.7 if the girder is rigid, but it is 1.0 if the girder is flexible and does not provide any restraint to the column (Fig. 1.19 bottom). The real condition, however, will fall between these extreme cases. Should the frame not be braced, then it may be quite unstable depending on the flexibility of the girder ($2 \leqslant K < \infty$). The selection of the $K$ factors is discussed further in the context of the problems.

Columns are rather slender in buildings which are laterally braced and where the floors/roof prevent their rotation. Usually wood columns are considered pin-end and braced against lateral sway ($K = 1$). For a safety factor of SF = 2.73, Euler's formula (g) yields an allowable axial stress, for solid wood columns, of

$$F_a = \frac{\pi^2 E}{2.73(L/r)^2} = \frac{3.62E}{(L/r)^2} \leqslant F_{c\parallel} \tag{1.44}$$

where $L/r \leqslant 173$.

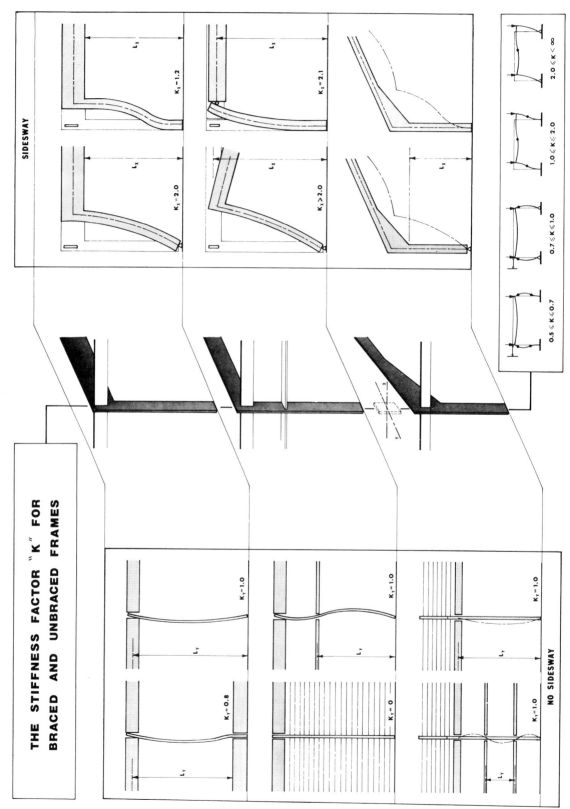

Fig. 1.19

For rectangular column sections with $r = \sqrt{I/A} = \sqrt{d^2/12}$, the allowable axial stress is

$$F_a = \frac{0.3E}{(L/d)^2} \leqslant F_{c\parallel} \tag{1.45}$$

where $L/d \leqslant 50$. The slenderness $L/d$ must be checked for both column axes to determine the critical one. The allowable compressive stress as based on buckling obviously can only control when it is smaller than the allowable unit stress parallel to the grain $F_{c\parallel}$, which is derived from the material strength.

In steel design Euler's formula becomes

$$F_a = \frac{\pi^2 E}{1.92\,(KL/r)^2} \tag{h}$$

This formula is only applicable for slender columns (e.g., bracing, truss members), where buckling appears in the elastic range,

$$\frac{KL}{r} \geqslant 126 \text{ for } A36$$

However, typical building columns in steel are not slender as Euler had assumed; they have already partially yielded when they buckle. A complex formula for the allowable axial stress has been derived by AISC as based on inelastic buckling.

Allowable stress values for $A36$ steel, as function of the slenderness ratio $KL/r$ for short, intermediate and long columns, are reproduced from the *Manual of Steel Construction* in Table A 9.

Rarely do columns solely support axial forces (Fig. 1.20). In most instances they also must resist the bending caused by transverse loading (wind, earthquake), continuous boundary conditions, or minor bending effects due to eccentric axial force application (beam connections, etc.). This combined action causes a direct stress $f_a$ and a flexural stress $f_b$ for bending about one axis only; for symmetrical sections it is equal to

$$f = f_a \pm f_b = \frac{P}{A} \pm \frac{M}{S} \leqslant F \tag{1.46}$$

For different allowable stresses in axial action and bending this expression becomes

$$\frac{f_a}{F_a} \pm \frac{f_b}{F_b} \leqslant 1 \tag{1.47}$$

It can be shown that this interaction equation is reflective of the beam column behavior for the condition of low axial stresses; according to AISC this is the case when $f_a/F_a \leqslant 0.15$. Most low-rise buildings discussed in this book are primarily bending systems, so that this simple interaction equation is applicable.

Should the axial stress be in the range of the flexural stress, then the axial force does magnify the moment, and causes additional column rotation. For this condition the simple interaction equation can only be used for preliminary estimation purposes. Here

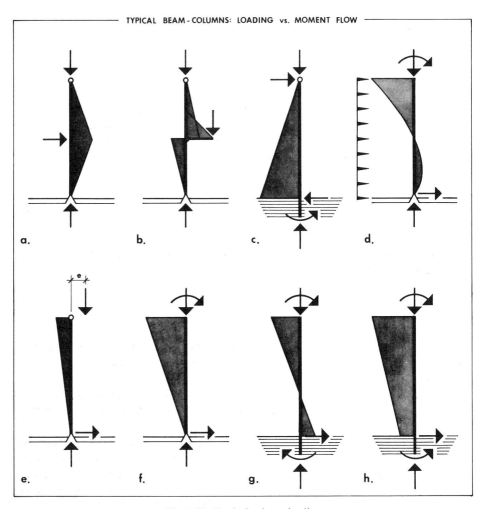

**Fig. 1.20** Typical column loading.

it is helpful to conservatively assume that $F_b = F_a$, so that Eq. (1.47) for maximum compression becomes

$$f_a + f_b \leqslant F_a$$

$$\frac{P}{A} + \frac{M}{S} \leqslant \frac{P_{\text{all}}}{A}$$

$$P + \frac{A}{S} M \leqslant P_{\text{all}} \tag{i}$$

The ratio of $A/S$ is called the bending factor $B$, $(B_x = A/S_x)$. As can be seen from Eq. (i), it transforms the moment into an equivalent axial force $P'$

$$P + P' = P + BM \tag{1.48}$$

Now, the column tables in the *AISC Manual* can be conveniently used. It can be shown that this approach usually overestimates the member size. Therefore not the required section, but the next lower one may be selected as a trial section.

The maximum ultimate design load capacity $P_u$ for short, tied concrete columns with a minimum load eccentricity is

$$P_u = \phi(0.80) \left[ 0.85 f_c'(A_g - A_{st}) + f_y A_{st} \right] \tag{1.49}$$

The column size $A_g$ can be approximated from this expression using the 1% minimum longitudinal reinforcement $A_{st}$, so that the section will be big enough, and larger moments, as obtained from exact analysis, can be resisted by additional reinforcing

$$P_{min} = \frac{A_{st}}{A_g} = 0.01$$

or

$$A_{st} = 0.01 A_g \qquad \phi = 0.7$$

By substituting these values into Eq. (1.49), the preliminary column size is

$$A_g = \frac{P_u}{0.47 f_c' + 0.0056 f_y} \tag{1.50}$$

Most cast-in-place concrete columns are usually relatively stocky and much stiffer than W steel sections. For ordinary height conditions and normal strength concrete, the effect of slenderness considerations is minor, especially when the columns are laterally braced, and can be neglected for preliminary design purposes. Should buckling have an effect, then it can be taken care of in the final design by magnifying the moment which must be resisted by additional longitudinal reinforcement as was mentioned before.

## Problems

**1.37**  A $W8 \times 67$ ($A36$) is used as a warehouse column. The bottom clip angle connection is equivalent to a pin connection in each direction. Deep plate girders frame into the web thereby fixing the weak axis of the column at the top; small bracing beams are clipped to the flanges and cause a pinned condition about the strong axis (Fig. 1.21a). Determine the capacity of the column; assume that the column does not sway.

**1.38**  A tubular steel column is 20-ft long and has to support an axial load of 50 k (Fig. 1.21b). The column can be considered hinged at the lower end and fixed by the deep trusses at the top. The building does not sway. Select circular structural tubing ($A36$).

**1.39**  Design a rectangular structural tubular column to carry an axial load of 40 k (Fig. 1.21c). The column is 20-ft long; it is pin-connected at its ends and fully braced by a masonry curtain wall about its weak axis. Assume that the column does not sway; $F_y = 46$ ksi.

**1.40**  A stud wall carries a load of 2 k/ft. What is the spacing of $2 \times 4$'s (i.e., 12, 16, or 24 in.)? The wall is finished on both sides (Fig. 1.21d). Use Hem-fir No. 2 with $F_c = 850$ psi, $E = 1400$ ksi.

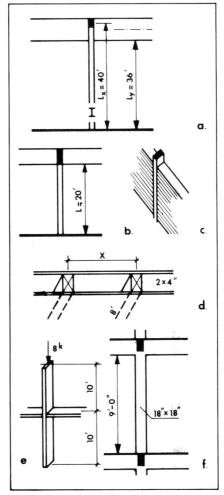

Fig. 1.21

**1.41** Determine the column size for an axial load of 7700 lb. The rectangular column is 20 ft long and braced about its weak axis at midheight (Fig. 1.21e). Use Douglas fir south No. 1 posts with $F_c$ = 875 psi and $E$ = 1200 ksi.

**1.42** Find the axial capacity of a 18 × 18 in. concrete column 9 ft high (Fig. 1.21f). The column is reinforced with 4 #11 bars; the concrete capacity is 4000 psi and Grade 60 steel is being used. Only minimum moments are assumed to act. Check if slenderness reduces the column capacity.

## Connections

The general function of joints is discussed in more detail in Chapter 2; here only the one characteristic of joint performance, that of stress resistance, is briefly reviewed. Individual structural members must be connected so that forces can flow from one component to the other. There are many different connection types resulting from joining a multitude of member shapes and sizes. They not only depend on the material, member shapes, and degree of continuity (strength) required, but also on detail considerations (e.g., number and inclination of members), fireproofing, geometric fit, handling and erection, service conditions, cost of installation, fabrication precision, construction expertise, appearance, and so on. A joint should allow for correction in dimensional variations and should be assembled easily. The connection type influences the behavior of the joined members; its capacity should be at least equal to those of the members.

Typical structural building details for steel, timber, and precast concrete are standardized and can be obtained from manuals published by the respective industries (e.g., AISC, AITC, PCI). Some common connection systems are shown in Fig. 1.22.

There are many ways of organizing connection systems; here the brief review is approached as based on the following criteria.

1  *Location of joint* (Fig. 1.22): Joints for typical skeleton or bearing wall construction appear in the horizontal floor planes and the vertical supporting planes.
   (a)  Collinear connections: column-to-column, beam-to-beam, wall-to-wall, slab-to-slab, etc.
   (b)  Planar, 90° connections: beam-to-beam, beam-to-column, slab-to-wall, slab-to-beam, wall-to-beam, wall-to-foundation, etc.
   (c)  Other angular connections: truss connections, etc.

In steel frame construction one may distinguish basically between beam connections, base plates, and connections for axial systems.

2  *Connection methods*
   (a)  Single-plane joints without connector plates: butt, scarf, finger, key, and other interlocking joints as well as monolithic joints, such as for cast-in-place concrete (wet joints) and masonry.
   (b)  Single-plane joints with connector plates: gusset plates, seating angles and web angles in steel construction, and metal hangers, framing anchors, metal straps and steel or wood plates in timber construction.
   (c)  Lap joints—single and multiple laps.

Most connection methods of larger scale in component construction employ some type of fastener system.

3  *Fastener types*
   (a)  Steel: rivets, bolts (unfinished and high-strength), pins, fusion welding, forging, etc.
   (b)  Timber: nails and spikes, staples, screws, bolts, adhesives and glues, connectors (e.g., split rings, shear plates, spike grids, sheet-metal nail plates).
   (c)  Precast concrete: prestress cables, lapped reinforcing bars, metal studs, inserts, anchored steel shapes, etc.
   (d)  Masonry: mortar (mixtures of lime or cement with sand and water), wire ties, steel reinforcing, etc.

From a structural point of view only a single pin provides a true point connection with no rotational resistance but, on the other hand, it also generates high stress concentrations. A weld reflects a line connection while an adhesive provides a surface connection over the entire bonded contact area thus clearly resisting rotation. The action of a group of individual fasteners may be considered as a system of point actions, while realizing that the density and pattern of arrangement as well as

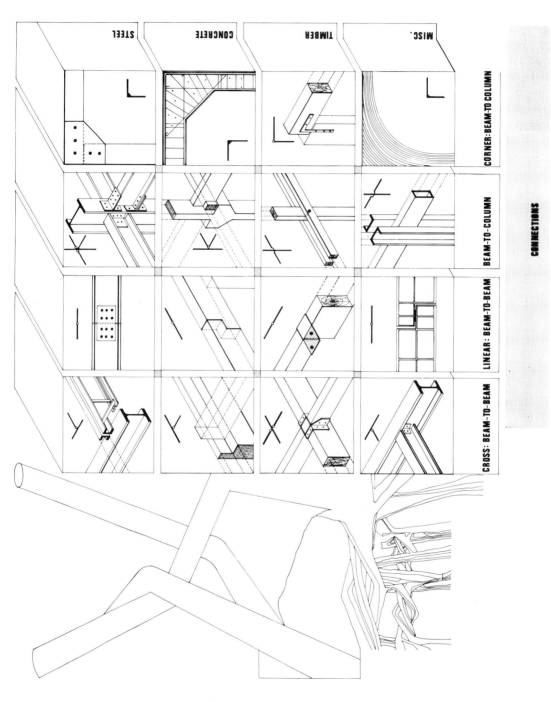

Fig. 1.22 Connections.

CONNECTIONS

STEEL | CONCRETE | TIMBER | MISC.

CORNER: BEAM-TO-COLUMN | BEAM-TO-COLUMN | LINEAR: BEAM-TO-BEAM | CROSS: BEAM-TO-BEAM

62

the character of the material and fasteners influence the nature of the force flow
across the joint.

4  *Structural behavior:* According to the type of forces which must be transferred
across the joint, one may distinguish between the following connection systems.

    (a)    *Simple connections,* also called hinged, pin or flexible connections, allow-
ing free rotation. Typical examples are the beam-to-beam cases in Fig.
1.22.

        (1)    *Shear connections* (or bearing-type): the load transmission
causes the fasteners to be in shear and bearing; it may only
cause direct shear and, in addition, torsion.

        (2)    *Friction-type connections:* High-strength bolts are prestressed
and thus clamp joining plates together so that forces are transmitted in friction rather than by the connectors in shear or
bearing.

        (3)    *Tension connections:* the loads cause the fasteners to be in
tension.

        (4)    *Compression-type connections:* typical examples are column-
to-foundation (bearing plates), column-to-column, wall-to-
wall, etc.

        (5)    *Combined shear and tension connections.*

    (b)    *Moment connections,* also called continuous or rigid connections. As the
name suggests, in addition to direct forces, rotation is transmitted. In semirigid connections, the moment capacity is only a fraction of the full restraint. Moment connections are typical for rigid frame construction (see
also continuous portal knee connections in Fig. 1.22).

In general, it is reasonable to assume that the shear is transferred along the web
faces of bending members, while rotation is carried along the flange faces.

## 1.4  FOUNDATION SYSTEMS

Foundations are usually made of concrete, and are necessary to transfer forces from the
building structure to the ground if the building is not directly founded on solid rock. The
capacity of the soil is generally much less than that of the structural materials (Table 1.3),
thus at the junction where columns and walls meet the soil, transitional structures with a
wider base may be required; the resulting spread footings have a similar purpose as base
plates for columns, though they must, in addition, limit settlement, particularly differential settlements of the various vertical support elements.

Should the footings be relatively close to each other, or should the soil be weak, then
individual footings can be combined, or all the footings can be joined to form a raft
foundation allowing the entire building somehow to float on the earth.

For the condition where the strength of the upper soil strata is not sufficient to support the building, deep foundations rather than the shallow spread footings may be necessary. Here bearing piles or caissons transfer the loads to the bedrock or a firm soil layer
below. However, should these strata be too far below the ground surface, then shallow
foundations together with friction piles may have to be employed.

Special foundation systems such as retaining walls and sheet piling (Fig. 1.26) are required for support of vertical earth banks and the loads on top of them.

This brief introduction to foundation systems calls attention to the necessity for investigation of the subsurface conditions and soil stratification, so that the appropriate foundations can be selected. Soil engineers must determine the strength and settlement characteristics as well as other criteria pertinent to the design of foundations. Often only confirmatory soil explorations are required, especially in urban areas where the geology is known and subsurface maps are available, and the performance of adjacent buildings can be evaluated. In more detailed investigations borings are usually used to determine the soil profile along with the soil and groundwater conditions. The spacing and depth of borings depends on the complexity of the site and the type of building. The testing of the soil samples obtained from the borings yields the important material properties like shear strength, compressibility, and permeability. Should there be no soft layers below the footing, the usual depth of investigation is up to twice the width of the largest footing, since the stress at that level is only about 10% of that directly beneath the footing.

Common foundation systems are shown in Fig. 1.23. They may be classified as shallow and deep foundations. As the name suggests, shallow foundations transfer loads in bearing close to the ground surface. They may be further subdivided into spread footings and mat foundations. While most footings support single columns and walls, combined footings carry two or more columns, which are either so close to each other that their individual footings would overlap, or where a column is too close to the property line and would cause large rotation on a single foundation. When single footings are linked by a beam, or beams, rather than by a continuous slab, they are called strap or cantilever footings.

For poor soil conditions an entire building may be placed on a mat or raft foundation. Here the upward acting soil pressure is in balance with the downward column and/or wall loads. The foundation can be visualized as an inverted floor structure using identical framing systems.

In the case of extremely poor soils, high groundwater level, and in order to minimize settlements, the entire building substructure may be considered a cellular rigid foundation. The building is floating similar to a ship, when the weight of the excavated earth is approximately equal to the weight of the building, thus keeping settlements to a minimum (see also Archimedes principle, Fig. 1.27).

Deep foundations are used when adequate soil capacity is not available close to the surface and loads have to be transferred to firm layers substantially below the ground level. Deep foundations are basically columns. When of small diameter they are called piles, when of large diameter they are called caissons. Caissons can have any type of cross-section, but are at least 3 ft in diameter to allow for inspection; they are hollow and usually are excavated inside. Piles are driven, drilled, or placed (cast) into prebored excavations. They are made of treated timber, steel, cast-in-place or precast prestressed concrete, or they may be composite systems. Piles can act in endbearing and/or skin friction. Whether a single building column is supported by only two piles, or whether a group of columns (walls) is supported by a cluster of piles, a concrete cap is always necessary to distribute the loads from the superstructure to the piles. Where pile groups are subject to lateral forces and to avoid bending of piles, it may be advantageous to employ batter piles; typical batters vary from 1/12 to 5/12.

In seismic areas the individual spread and pile foundations may have to be tied together by so-called bracing struts so that the entire building foundation can act as a unit in sharing the load resistance. Special foundations are sometimes required, as for the

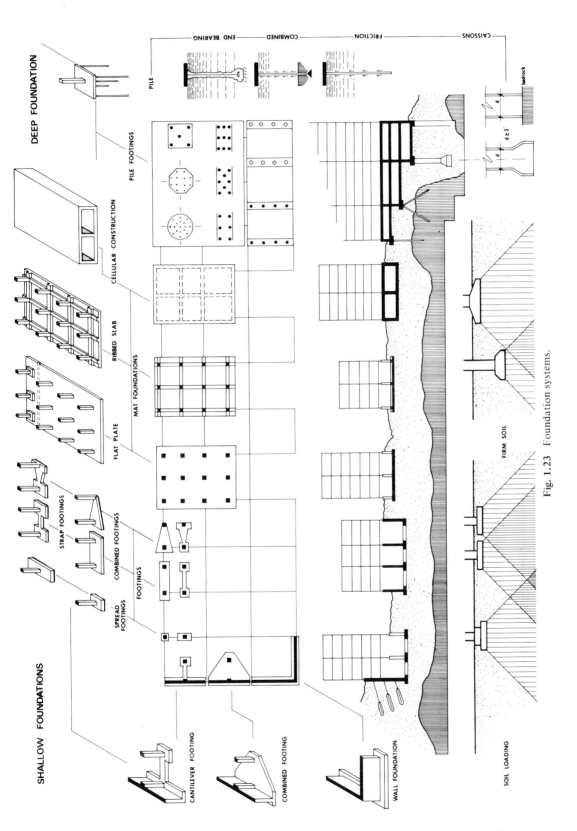

Fig. 1.23 Foundation systems.

65

building that cuts into the hill (Fig. 1.23). One solution may have been to let the building act as a cellular retaining wall in order to transfer the lateral earth pressure to the foundations. Another approach could have been a reinforced soil wall, where the earth is stabilized by some reinforcement technique. The solution shown employs tensile anchors or tiebacks to support the embankment.

It is quite apparent that for low bearing soils the structural layout should be uniformly arranged with many supports and hence many small foundations, so that the loads are distributed over a large area. Buildings with only few core supports and large foundations require firm soils.

Foundations for low-rise residential buildings of not more than two stories are usually selected and sized as based on empirical methods and rules of thumb, since the loads in comparison to the bearing capacity of the soil are small. The typical foundation systems are:

- Bearing walls with footings for buildings with basements
- Foundation walls or beam on pier (column, pilaster) foundations for buildings with crawl spaces
- Concrete slabs on ground and grade beams, which in turn may be supported on spread or pile foundations

The popularity of underground structures as energy savers is rising rapidly. They are not subject to the wide temperature fluctuations; the earth is an almost perfect insulator with respect to the daily temperature changes and even for seasonal changes the earth temperature is relatively stable and constant.

In contrast to conventional houses, earth-sheltered residences (Fig. 1.24) must not only support an extensive earth weight on top of their roofs, yielding a high dead load of the structure as well as large foundations, but must also withstand lateral earth and possibly groundwater pressures.

These lateral pressures may become critical when they do not balance each other and tend to move the building as indicated for some cases in Fig. 1.24. Here the lateral forces must be transmitted to the foundations and then into the ground. To reduce and control the magnitude of the lateral earth pressure, fully drained sand and gravel backfill should be used to prevent the possible swelling of clay and any loading due to frost.

The heavy, relatively constant loads upon underground buildings may make funicular (curvilinear) structures much more appropriate and effective.

### Bearing Pressure Versus Footing Size

The base size of a column or wall footing, or the base width of a retaining wall, depends on the allowable bearing capacity of the soil $q_a$, provided that a settlement investigation has been made. The allowable bearing pressure should obviously be equal to or greater than the actual contact pressure caused by the external loading. For the evaluation of the bearing capacity of the soil, refer to the respective literature on soil mechanics. Building codes give allowable (working) bearing pressures for specific soils, which can be used for preliminary estimation purposes. Some of the typical allowable bearing values are: 3 ksf for medium density soft clay, 4 ksf for fine loose sand and 8 ksf for loose gravel or compact coarse sand (Table 1.3).

The distribution of the contact pressure between the soil and the bottom face of the

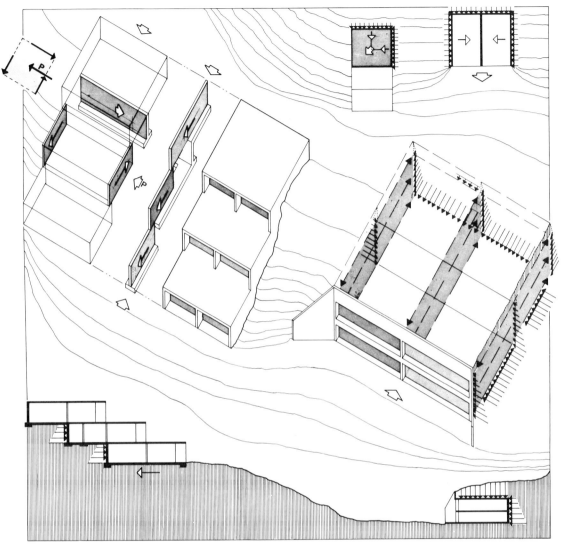

Fig. 1.24

foundation is rather complex. It is not only dependent on the type of force action but, also on the stiffness of the foundation, and on the stiffness of the ground as well.

A centrically loaded footing is assumed to cause a uniformly distributed soil pressure. This assumption is based on a rigid foundation which does not deflect and thus does not influence the pressure distribution; it is further based on truly elastic soil behavior, resulting in a straight-line pressure distribution. In reality, the soil is not an elastic, homogeneous material, and uniform force action does not generate a uniform response in the soil. The rigid foundation is supported at points which have deformed the least. These points of maximum pressure are underneath the column for cohesionless soils such as sand and gravel, and along the footing's outer edges for cohesive soils such as saturated clay (Fig. 1. 25a). For most practical purposes, a uniform distribution of contact pressure can be assumed.

A footing can be loaded either concentrically or eccentrically. Should the line of action of the force resultant $P$ of all the loads acting on the foundation pass through the centroid of the base area $A$ of the footing, then there is no rotation and the contact pressure is uniformly distributed. The average contact pressure $q$ is

$$q = \frac{P}{A} \leqslant q_a \qquad (1.51)$$

The minimum required base area of the footing is

$$A = \frac{P}{q_a} \qquad (1.52)$$

where $P$ consists of all the vertical loads acting at the footing base, which includes the building loads, foundation weight, and the soil surcharge on top of the foundation.

Should the resultant of the superimposed loads not coincide with the centroid of the footing base area, the footing is loaded eccentrically and rotation is generated. This condition may be caused by placing the force resultant $P$ out of line with the footing's center, or by applying an external moment which is transferred through the continuous juncture of column or wall and foundation to the ground as shown in Fig. 1.25g.

The distance between the resultant of the loads (the resultant of the pressure diagram) and the center of the base area is the eccentricity $e$. In the case where an external moment $M$ is transferred to the ground, the moment can be replaced by a normal load acting eccentric with respect to the centroid of the contact area of the footing

$$M = P(e) \qquad e = \frac{M}{P} \qquad (1.53)$$

The equivalent eccentricity $e$ is equal to the ratio of moment to normal force. Should the eccentricity be zero, the moment is zero and the footing is concentrically loaded.

For a footing eccentrically loaded about one axis, the soil contact pressure is no longer uniform. The maximum contact pressure $q_{max}$ appears along the foundation edges where the translational pressure $P/A$ and rotational pressure $M/S$ are added, while the minimum pressure appears at the opposite edge of the foundation where the tension due to rotation decreases the direct compression (Fig. 1. 25b-d)

$$q_{\substack{max \\ min}} = \frac{P}{A} \pm \frac{M}{S} \qquad (j)$$

For a rectangular footing with a contact area of $A = Lb$, a section modulus of $S = bL^2/6 = AL/6$, and a moment of $M = P(e)$, Eq. (j) can be simplified to read:

$$q_{\substack{max \\ min}} = \frac{P}{A}\left(1 \pm \frac{6e}{L}\right) \qquad (1.54)$$

This equation can only be used if there is no tensile stress, which cannot be transferred from foundation to soil. The maximum eccentricity of the normal force not causing any tension can be easily determined for a rectangular footing from Eq. (1.54)

$$q_{min} = 0 = \frac{P}{A}\left(1 - \frac{6e}{L}\right)$$

$$e = \frac{L}{6} \qquad (1.55)$$

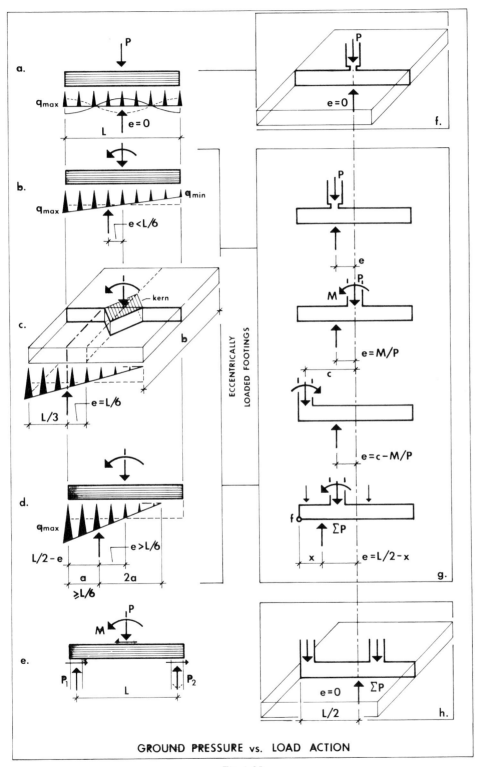

a.

$q_{max}$    L    $e=0$

P

b.

$q_{max}$    $q_{min}$    $e<L/6$

c.

kern    b    $e=L/6$    L/3

d.

$q_{max}$    $e>L/6$    L/2−e    a    2a    ≥L/6

e.

M    P    $P_1$    L    $P_2$

f.

P    $e=0$

ECCENTRICALLY LOADED FOOTINGS

g.

P    e

M    P    $e=M/P$

c    $e=c-M/P$

f    ΣP    x    $e=L/2-x$

h.

$e=0$    ΣP    L/2

GROUND PRESSURE vs. LOAD ACTION

Fig. 1.25

The same result is obtained from the location of the resultant force for a triangular pressure distribution (Fig. 1.25c) which acts at $L/3$ measured from $q_{max}$, or $L/6$ measured from the centroidal axis.

One may conclude that the eccentricity $e$ should be less than one-sixth of the footing width $L$ if no tensile stresses are to appear. In general, the load should be applied in the middle third of the base area, which is called the kern (Fig. 125b). Should the resultant normal force be acting outside the kern, tensile stresses occur. The equation for the maximum compressive stresses under this condition is derived from Fig. 1.25d

$$\Sigma F_y = 0 = P - q_{max} \frac{3a}{2} b$$

$$q_{max} = \frac{2P}{3ba} = \frac{2P}{3b(L/2 - e)}$$

$$q_{max} = \frac{P}{A} \frac{4L}{3L - 6e}$$

(1.56)

Note that when $e > L/2$ the footing is unstable. However, since a safety factor of 1.5 against overturning must be maintained, $e$ must always be less than or equal to $L/3$, or $a \geqslant L/6$ [see Example 1.7 and Eq. (2.3)].

Should bending occur about both axes of the base area, an approach similar to that applied previously is used to derive the following equations, which assume no tensile stresses

$$q = \frac{P}{A} \pm \frac{M_L}{S_L} \pm \frac{M_b}{S_b}$$

(1.57)

or for a rectangular footing $e_L \leqslant L/6$, $e_b \leqslant b/6$

$$q = \frac{P}{A} \left(1 \pm \frac{6e_L}{L} \pm \frac{6e_b}{b}\right)$$

(1.58)

For footings of nonrectangular shape, more laborious procedures which are beyond the scope of this introductory discussion are necessary.

In the case where the footing is to be supported by piles, the pile forces can be determined approximately by statics, by assuming the piles to be elastic and to be hinged to the rigid foundation (Fig. 1.25e). Taking moments about the pile force $P$, and summing up the forces, yields:

$$\Sigma M_{P1} = 0 = P(L/2) - M - P_2(L) \qquad P_2 = \frac{P}{2} - \frac{M}{L}$$

$$\Sigma F_y = 0 \qquad\qquad\qquad\qquad P_1 = \frac{P}{2} + \frac{M}{L}$$

Horizontal forces are transferred to the soil either by friction between the footing and the soil, by passive soil pressure, or by using a key to anchor the foundation to the ground. Piles may resist horizontal forces in an axial manner (battered piles) and/or in shear and bending (vertical long piles).

**Example 1.5**  A single column footing carries an axial load of $P = 100$ k, which is assumed to include the footing weight and soil overburden. The allowable soil pressure is 4 ksf. The footing length $L$ is determined for a constant footing width of $b = 5$ ft, for the following different loading conditions

(a) no rotation, $e = 0$: The required footing size is

$$A = \frac{P}{q_a} \tag{1.52}$$

$$5L = \frac{100}{4} \qquad L = 5 \text{ ft}$$

Try a 5 × 5 ft footing.

(b) $M = 100$ ft-k: The equivalent eccentric location of the normal force is

$$e = \frac{M}{P} = \frac{100}{100} = 1 \text{ ft}$$

Assuming no tensile stresses and using Eq. 1.54 yields a minimum footing length of

$$q_{max} = \frac{P}{A}\left(1 + \frac{6e}{L}\right) \tag{1.54}$$

$$4 = \frac{100}{5L}\left(1 + \frac{6(1)}{L}\right)$$

$$L^2 - 5L - 30 = 0$$

$$L = \frac{5}{2} \pm \sqrt{\left(\frac{5}{2}\right)^2 + 30}$$

$$L = 8.52 \text{ ft}$$

Checking the assumption that there are no tensile stresses

$$\frac{L}{6} = \frac{8.52}{6} = 1.42 \text{ ft} > 1 \text{ ft}$$

No tensile stresses are present. Try an 8 ft 7 in. × 5 ft footing.

(c) The tension stresses are exactly equal to zero:

$$q_{min} = 0 \quad \text{or} \quad e = \frac{L}{6}$$

$$q_{max} = \frac{P}{A}(1 + 6e/L)$$

$$= \frac{P}{A}(1 + 6L/6L)$$

$$q_{max} = \frac{2P}{A}$$

$$4 = \frac{2(100)}{5L}$$

$$L = 10 \text{ ft}$$

Try a 10 × 5 ft footing. The equivalent moment acting upon the footing is

$$M = P(e) = 100\left(\frac{10}{6}\right) = 166.67 \text{ ft-k}$$

(d) $M = 200$ ft-k: The equivalent eccentric location of the normal force is

$$e = \frac{M}{P} = \frac{200}{100} = 2 \text{ ft}$$

Assuming that tensile stresses will be present, as based on the result of (c), since $M$ = 200 ft-k > 166.67 ft-k:

$$q_{max} = \frac{2P}{3ba} \tag{1.56}$$

where $a = L/2 - e = L/2 - 2$

$$4 = \frac{2(100)}{3(5)(L/2 - 2)} \qquad L = 10.66 \text{ ft}$$

Checking the assumption that there is tensile action present independent of (c)

$$\frac{L}{6} = \frac{10.6}{6} = 1.78 \text{ ft} < 2.00 \text{ ft}$$

Therefore tension is present. Try a 10 ft 8 in. × 5 ft footing.

   In general, eccentrically loaded footings should only be placed on compacted soils, because on loose soils settling will cause additional rotation, together with an increase of bearing pressure. Therefore, only concentrically loaded footings should be used on compressible soils, where settlement is more likely to be uniform. For low soil bearing capacities, or where the exterior building column or wall is close to the property line, single footings may have to be combined. A footing carrying two or more columns or walls is generally designed so that it causes a uniformly distributed soil pressure (Fig. 1.25h).

### Earth and Hydrostatic Pressure—Retaining Walls

Basement walls, exterior walls of underground structures (tunnels and other earth-sheltered buildings), or retaining walls must resist lateral earth pressure as well as additional pressure due to other types of loading. Basement walls carry lateral earth pressure as vertical slabs (beams) supported by the floor framing at the basement level and upper floor level(s). The axial forces in the floor structure are, in turn, either resisted by shear walls or balanced by the lateral earth pressure coming from the opposite side of the building.

Retaining walls, on the other hand, are freestanding. Their stability depends on their own weight and/or the weight of the soil on top of the footing. Typical retaining walls are shown in Fig. 1.26. The most common types are:

- Gravity wall—made of plain concrete, stability depends on its weight, no tension forces are in the wall.
- Cantilever wall (T and L shaped)—consists of three projecting elements (wall or stem, heel, and toe) each of which acts as a cantilever. Stability depends on the weight of the wall and backfill, and on the strength of the projections in bending.
- Counterfort and buttress walls—counterforts (in tension) and buttresses (in compression), spaced at regular intervals, support the wall (stem) and footing which act as continuous horizontal slabs.

The magnitude and direction of the lateral earth pressure depends on many variables, such as the type of backfill (cohesionless versus cohesive), its unit weight, degree of saturation, drainage, compaction, the angle of internal friction (for cohesionless soils), groundwater level, frost line, the slope of the ground surface behind the wall, and loads on the ground surface. The precise evaluation of the lateral soil pressure is beyond the scope of this text, and the reader is referred to books on soil mechanics and foundation engineering.

Here, only granular soils, which are generally used as backfill, are considered; cohesive soils, such as clays or silts and organic soils should be avoided because of the large lateral pressures they exert.

The Rankine theory is used to develop an approximate expression for the magnitude of lateral earth pressure, and to transform it into an equivalent fluid pressure by assuming zero pressure at the top and maximum at the base, yielding a triangular load action (Fig. 1.26).

Visualize the wall to move slightly in the horizontal direction, thereby causing a wedge of the backfill material to separate from the rest of the soil, which, by sliding downwards, causes an active lateral pressure on the wall. The magnitude of the lateral earth pressure at a distance $y$ from the free surface is

$$p_y = k_a wy \tag{k}$$

Or the maximum unit soil pressure at the base (Fig. 1.26) is

$$p_a = k_a wh \tag{l}$$

In this expression the lateral pressure $w(h)$ of a true fluid is corrected by the coefficient of active earth pressure $k_a$ which takes into account the fact that the lateral pressure of the soil due to cohesion and friction cannot be equal to the vertical pressure of the unit weight $w \times h$, as is the case for a true fluid.

The coefficient of active earth pressure is a function of the angle of internal friction $\phi$ and, according to Rankine, for a horizontal grade surface, $k_a$ can be expressed as:

$$k_a = \tan^2 \left( 45 - \frac{\phi}{2} \right) \tag{m}$$

For approximation purposes, a medium dense granular soil may be assumed as backfill which has a unit weight of about 100 pcf and an angle of internal friction of $\phi = 32°$.

**Fig. 1.26** Retaining walls.

$h$

$M_{max}$

D>h to 1.5h (i.e. firm to loose)

active pressure

$P_a h$

$P_a (h+D)$

$P_p D$

passive pressure

CANTILEVERED

$M_{max}$

HINGED

$M_{max}$

ANCHORED

SEMI-FIXED

SHEETPILING

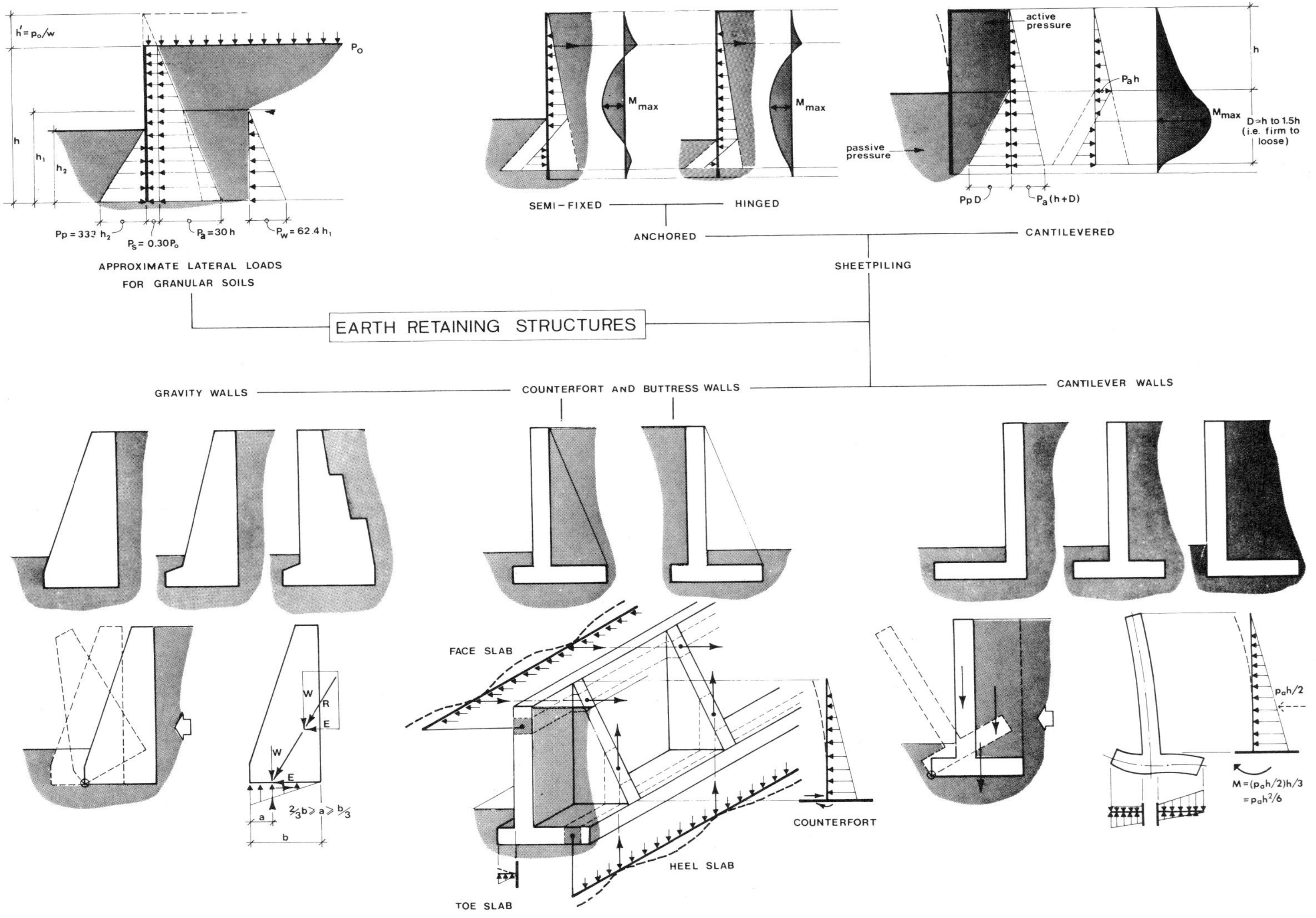

EARTH RETAINING STRUCTURES

$P_o$

$P_w = 62.4 h_1$

$P_a = 30 h$

$P_s = 0.30 P_o$

$P_p = 33.3 h_2$

APPROXIMATE LATERAL LOADS FOR GRANULAR SOILS

$h' = p_o/w$

$h_1$

$h_2$

$h$

CANTILEVER WALLS

$P_a h/2$

$M = (p_a h/2) h/3$
$= P_a h^2/6$

COUNTERFORT AND BUTTRESS WALLS

COUNTERFORT

HEEL SLAB

FACE SLAB

TOE SLAB

**Fig. 1.26** Retaining walls.

GRAVITY WALLS

W

R

E

W

E

a

b

$\frac{2}{3}b > a > \frac{b}{3}$

Substituting these values into Eq. (m) gives $k_a \cong 0.30$. The maximum pressure at the base for this condition from Eq. (l) is

$$p_a = k_a wh = 0.30(100)h = 30h \qquad (1.59)$$

Hence, the lateral active earth pressure may be approximated by using an equivalent fluid pressure of 30 pcf.

Approximate equivalent fluid pressures of other dry soils with level-grade backfill are:

| | |
|---|---|
| clean sand and gravel as derived above | 30 pcf |
| silty fine sands and clayey sands and gravels, stiff residual silts and clays | 45 pcf |
| soft clay, silty clay, organic soil and clay | 100 pcf |
| medium to stiff clay | 120 pcf |

As the soil expands, causing an active lateral pressure, it may encounter the resistance of backfill on the opposite side of the wall. This resisting soil contracts and provides a so-called passive earth pressure $p_p$. The passive earth pressure is always larger than the active one. For the given soil conditions it can be shown that the coefficient of passive earth pressure $k_p$ is the inverse of the coefficient of active earth pressure $k_a$. Hence the maximum passive earth pressure at the base of the wall (Fig. 1.26) can be shown as equal to

$$p_p = k_p wh_2 = \frac{wh_2}{k_a} = \frac{100(h_2)}{0.30} = 333h_2$$

Hence, the lateral passive earth pressure may be approximated by using an equivalent fluid pressure of 333 pcf.

Additional pressure that must be resisted by the wall may be caused by loads acting on top of the backfill due to people, cars, slabs, and buildings. These loads are called surcharge, and may be approximated by uniform strip, line, or point loads. The lateral pressure $p_s$ due to a uniform surcharge $p_0$ may be approximated by transforming it into an equivalent height $h'$ of earth backfill. The equivalent height of the soil is assumed to be equal to the surcharge divided by the weight of the soil $w$

$$h' = \frac{p_0}{w} \qquad (n)$$

From Fig. 1.26 the following simple relationship can be derived:

$$\frac{h'}{p_s} = \frac{h}{p_a} \quad \text{or} \quad p_s = \frac{p_a(h')}{h} \qquad (o)$$

Substituting Eqs. (n) and (1.59) into (o) yields the approximate equivalent lateral pressure

$$p_s = \frac{k_a wh}{h} \frac{p_0}{w} = k_a p_0 \qquad (1.60)$$

Notice that the horizontal pressure due to surcharge is constant along the wall. For the assumed noncohesive soil conditions (Fig. 1.26) it is

$$p_s = 0.30 p_0 \qquad (1.61)$$

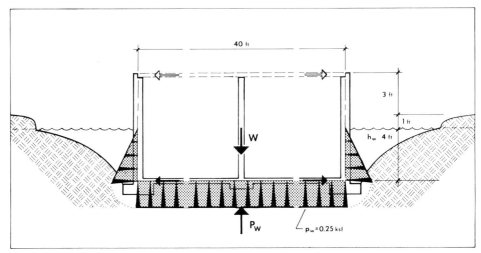

Fig. 1.27

Lateral pressure may also be caused by ice thrust from frozen ground. The voids of fine-grained soils contain water which, when subjected to freezing, expands in volume; provision for proper drainage of the backfill helps to alleviate this problem. The swelling pressure as caused by water absorption in clayey soils can be prevented by replacing it with a granular, noncohesive backfill material.

In cases where groundwater is present, a lateral pressure is caused by the unit weight of water, 62.4 pcf,

$$p_w = wh_1 = 62.4h_1 \tag{1.62}$$

Due to the hydrostatic pressure the weight of the soil below the water level is reduced, as the buoyant weight of the soil is equal to its normal dry weight reduced by the weight of the water it has displaced. It is conservative for approximation purposes to neglect the buoyant weight of the soil by considering the dry weight. Often, as a first approach, an equivalent fluid pressure of 75 pcf for the combined action of the noncohesive soil and water may be used. Keep in mind that proper drainage behind the wall, and weep holes through the vertical stem may reduce or eliminate the water pressure.

**Example 1.6** The phenomenon of buoyancy can be exemplified by evaluating the effect of sudden flooding during the construction of a watertight residential basement. The water table rises up to 4 ft above the basement floor level, or 1 ft below ground surface. The building basement is $40 \times 60$ ft$^2$ in plan; for other information about the building layout refer to Fig. 1.27. Assume a weight of 100 psf for exterior walls, 60 psf for the interior wall, and 80 psf for the basement slab.

The approximate weight of the basement at the stage of flooding is

$$W = 2[8(60 + 40)]0.100 + 8(60)0.060 + 40(60)0.080 = 380.80 \text{ k}$$

The maximum lateral hydrostatic unit pressure at the base of the wall is equal to the uniform uplift pressure of

$$p_w = wh = \frac{62.4(4)}{1000} = 0.25 \text{ ksf}$$

The total uplift force caused by the unit pressure across the whole basement floor area is

$$P_w = 0.25(60)40 = 600 \text{ k}$$

The same buoyant force is obtained by using the Archimedes principle which states that a body wholly or partly immersed in a fluid is buoyed up with a force equal to the weight of the fluid displaced by the body. For the given condition, the volume of the displaced water is

$$V = 60(40)4 = 9600 \text{ ft}^3$$

The weight of the displaced water is

$$P_w = wV = \frac{9600(62.4)}{1000} = 599.04 \text{ k}$$

The uplift force is larger than the basement weight. The building will be lifted to a level at which it will float like a ship; at that level the buoyant force will be equal to the basement weight.

This problem could have been eliminated by using a drain and pump operation to keep the water away from the building. However, this method only works if the soil has a low permeability; for high-permeability soil the pumps will not be able to keep up with the inflow of water.

**Example 1.7** Investigate the earth pressure against the cantilever wall in Fig. 1.28. Check the stability of the retaining wall and the foundation, which are resisting a granular backfill 20 ft high and a surcharge of 200 psf. The weight of the backfill is 100 pcf and of the concrete 145 pcf. The allowable soil pressure is given as 5 ksf.

The vertical loads due to the weight of the stem ($P_3$), the weight of the base ($P_2$), and the weight of the soil on top of the heel including the surcharge ($P_1$), ignoring the soil above the toe, per foot of wall are

$$
\begin{aligned}
P_1 &= 0.100(18)8(1) + 0.200(8)1 & &= 16.00 \text{ k} \\
P_2 &= 0.145[2(12)1] & &= 3.48 \text{ k} \\
P_3 &= 0.145[18(1)1 + 18(1)\tfrac{1}{2}] = 2.61 + 1.31 &= 3.92 \text{ k} \\
\hline
P_T & & &= 23.40 \text{ k}
\end{aligned}
$$

The maximum equivalent active liquid pressure $p_a$ at the base of the foundation is

$$p_a = 30h = 30(20) = 600 \text{ psf} \qquad (1.59)$$

The uniform lateral horizontal pressure $p_s$ due to the surcharge $p_0 = 200$ psf is equal to

$$p_s = 0.3p_0 = 0.3(200) = 60 \text{ psf} \qquad (1.61)$$

The passive earth pressure is conservatively neglected. With respect to the stability of the wall the surcharge live load must be considered, since its lateral action constitutes a critical condition though its vertical action is beneficial as a stabilizing element.

The horizontal load resultants due to backfill ($H_2$) and surcharge ($H_1$) are:

$$H_2 = \frac{600(20/2)}{1000} = 6.00 \text{ k}$$

$$
\begin{aligned}
H_1 &= \frac{60(20)}{1000} = 1.20 \text{ k} \\
\hline
H_T & \qquad\qquad 7.20 \text{ k}
\end{aligned}
$$

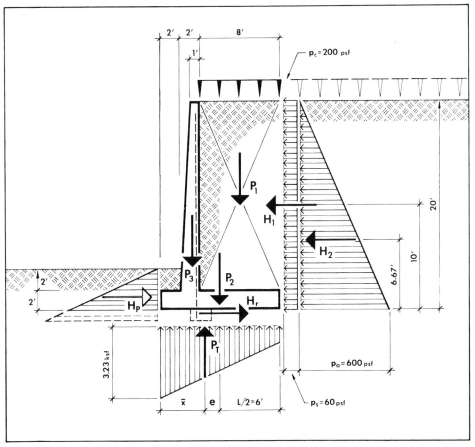

Fig. 1.28

The lateral loads tend to rotate the wall about its toe. This overturning moment is

$$M_0 = 1.20(10) + 6.00(6.67) = 52.02 \text{ ft-k}$$

The vertical loads are attempting to resist the overturning. The resisting moment is equal to:

$$M_r = 16.00(8) + 3.48(6) + 2.61(3.5) + 1.31(2.67) = 161.51 \text{ ft-k}$$

To have adequate safety, the stabilizing moment should be at least 50% larger than the acting moment for granular soils. For cohesive backfill, the resisting moment should be at least double as large as the overturning moment.

$$\text{SF} = \frac{M_r}{M_0} = \frac{161.51}{52.02} = 3.11 > 1.5 \tag{1.63}$$

The proportions of the retaining wall are adequate with respect to tilting.

The lateral pressure does not only cause rotation, but also translational movement. The resistance to sliding is provided by the friction and/or adhesion between the base and the soil, if one conservatively neglects the passive earth pressure. The magnitude of the horizontal resisting force $H_r$ can be approximated by using the coefficient of friction $\mu$. It can be shown that the maximum frictional force which can be developed is proportional to all the normal forces $P_T$ between the two surfaces. The ratio of $H_r/P_T$ is defined by the static coefficient of friction. Hence the resisting frictional force can be expressed as:

$$H_r = \mu P_T \tag{1.64}$$

For approximation purposes the following coefficients of friction may be used:

| | |
|---|---|
| Silt: | 0.35 |
| Coarse-grained soil with silt: | 0.45 |
| Coarse-grained soil without silt: | 0.55 |
| Sound rock with rough surface: | 0.60 |

For this exercise a coefficient of friction $\mu = 0.55$ is assumed. The total resisting friction is:

$$H_r = \mu P_T = 0.55(23.40) = 12.87 \text{ k}$$

The safety factor against sliding should be at least 1.5, that is, the horizontal resistance $H_r$ should be at least 50% greater than the horizontal force action

$$SF = \frac{H_r}{H_T} = \frac{12.87}{7.2} = 1.79 > 1.5 \quad \text{(O.K.)}$$

The retaining wall proportions are also satisfactory with respect to sliding especially since the passive earth pressure was neglected. Should that not have been the case, then either the wall base could have been widened, or a key could have been formed under the base of the footing to increase the passive earth resistance.

Finally, the proportions of the foundation have to be checked so that the vertical contact pressure between soil and bottom face of the base slab is less than the allowable bearing capacity of the soil. The rotational equilibrium of all the forces about the toe in Fig. 1.28 yields the location $\bar{x}$ of the resultant of the bearing pressure, which is equal in magnitude to the sum of all the vertical forces $\Sigma P_i = P_T$ (see also Fig. 1.25g)

$$\sum M_F = 0 = \sum_{i=1}^{n} P_i x_i - \sum_{i=1}^{n} H_i y_i - \sum_{i=1}^{n} P_i(\bar{x}) = M_r - M_0 - P_T(\bar{x})$$

Notice that the magnitudes of the resisting moment $M_r$ and acting moment $M_0$ have already been determined. Hence the location of the resultant soil pressure force is

$$\bar{x} = \frac{M_r - M_0}{P_T} = \frac{161.51 - 52.02}{23.40} = 4.68 \text{ ft} \tag{1.65}$$

The eccentricity $e$ as measured from the center of the base area is

$$e = \frac{L}{2} - \bar{x} = \frac{12}{2} - 4.68 = 1.32 \text{ ft} < \frac{L}{6} = \frac{12}{6} = 2 \text{ ft}$$

The resultant force is acting within the kern or middle third of the base area, which shows that there will be no tensile stresses. The maximum soil pressure at the toe for this case can be determined from Eq. (1.54).

$$q_{max} = \frac{P}{A}\left(1 + \frac{6e}{L}\right) = \frac{23.40}{12(1)}\left(1 + \frac{6(1.32)}{12}\right)$$

$$= 3.24 \text{ ksf} \ll 5 \text{ ksf} \quad (\text{O.K.})$$

The allowable soil pressure is larger than the actual maximum contact pressure. Now, the assumed thickness of the stem and base (heel and toe) must be checked for the shear forces and moments that they will have to withstand.

**Example 1.8** The masonry basement wall in Fig. 1.29a must support a granular backfill with an equivalent fluid weight of 30 pcf. Determine the maximum moment the wall must resist.

The wall carries the lateral earth pressure as a simple one-way slab supported axially by the basement and first story floors, respectively.

The maximum pressure at the bottom of the wall is

$$P_a = 30h = 30(9) = 270 \text{ psf/ft of wall}$$

The resultant of the triangular load is

$$H = \frac{0.270(9)}{2} = 1.22 \text{ k/ft}$$

It can be found from any beam table that the maximum moment for this triangular loading case is equal to

$$M_{max} = 0.1283 \, Hh = 0.1283 \, (1.22)9 = 1.41 \text{ ft-k/ft of wall}$$

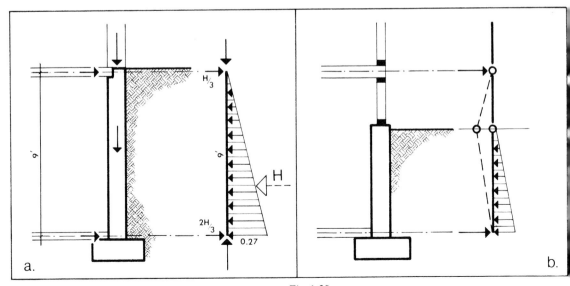

a.                                                                    b.

Fig. 1.29

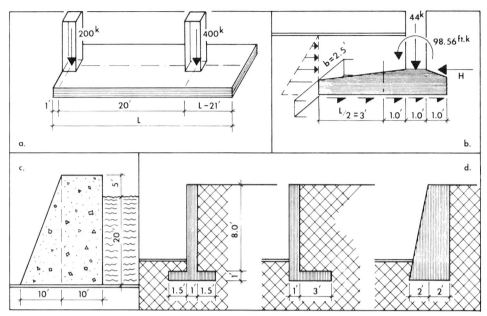

Fig. 1.30

In this example the surcharge loads were considered insignificant. However, should a street, for instance, be close to the wall, special surface loads must be taken into account.

The wall in Fig. 1.29b is not supported by the first floor slab, hence it cannot span vertically, assuming it not to be designed as a cantilever wall; this wall must act as a horizontal slab supported by the cross walls!

## Problems

**1.43** Determine the width $b$ of a rectangular footing with a length $L = 5.40$ ft so that it can support a concentric axial load of $P = 50$ k and a moment of (a) $M = 0$, (b) $M = 22.5$ ft-k, (c) $M = 45$ ft-k, (d) $M = 77.5$ ft-k. The allowable net soil pressure is 4 ksf for the given sandy soil conditions; the footing weight is considered already deducted from the soil capacity.

**1.44** Determine the size of the multiple column footing, or in this case, a combined footing supporting two columns as shown in Fig 1.30a, so that it does not rotate and uniform earth pressure is generated. Assume a net allowable soil pressure of 4 ksf.

**1.45** Determine if the rectangular footing size shown in Fig. 1.30b is satisfactory for the given loading conditions (as taken from Problem 4.9e). The lateral thrust $H$ due to gravity loading is carried by a horizontal tie rod connecting the column bases of the frame, the lateral thrust due to the lateral wind forces is assumed to be taken by the passive soil resistance and frictional resistance along the base. Assume an allowable net soil pressure of 5500 psf. Further, find the magnitude of the critical moment along the face of the column for which the footing should be designed.

**1.46** Determine the height of the water level at which the building of Example 1.6 will float. What would you do to prevent the lifting of the building?

**1.47** Determine the maximum stem moment for the cantilever retaining wall of Example 1.7. Show where to place the reinforcing in the wall.

**1.48** A concrete dam of the dimensions shown in Fig. 1.30c must support a water depth of 20 ft. Determine if the resultant force lies within the central third of the base (kern) so that seepage under the dam may not be a problem.

**1.49** For the retaining walls shown in Fig. 1.30d, consider the lateral earth action as an equivalent liquid pressure of 30 pcf. The soil is assumed to weigh 100 pcf and the concrete 145 pcf. The soil-bearing capacity is 5 ksf. The coefficient of friction between concrete and soil is assumed as 0.4. Passive earth pressure may be neglected. Investigate overturning, sliding, and maximum soil pressure for each retaining wall. Further, show the primary reinforcing for the retaining walls given and also for a counterfort wall.

**1.50** Determine the maximum moment the wall in Fig. 1.29a must resist, if in addition to the backfill it also must support a surcharge load on the ground of 100 psf.

**1.51** Determine the maximum moment for the basement wall in Example 1.8, if the groundwater level rises to 6 ft from the ground surface. Neglect conservatively the buoyant weight of the earth below the water table.

**1.52** Determine the maximum moment for the basement wall in Example 1.8, if only part of the wall is in the ground. Consider the height of the backfill as 5 ft.


## 1.5  INTRODUCTION TO PRESTRESSING

A structure is prestressed if it is resisting internal forces without any external load action ignoring its own weight. The prestress forces induced under a controlled process cause stresses which oppose and reduce the critical stresses due to external loading, thereby resulting in a more economical internal force distribution and an increase of the structure's capacity.

The principle of prestressing is not new. An example in nature is the growth of the tree that causes the outer fibrous layer of the trunk to be highly stressed in tension while most of the solid sapwood and the central heartwood are in compression. Other examples with which we are familiar are found in the iron bands over wooden wheels which were heat-shrunk and the iron rings around wooden barrels which were tensioned. Today prestressing, willingly or unwillingly is applied to all kinds of materials and structural elements. Undesired residual stresses are locked into steel members due to uneven cooling after hot-rolling; they are also generated by uneven cooling due to welding or due to bending of cold-formed shapes from flat-rolled steel. On the other hand, glass may be prestressed deliberately by thermal or chemical tempering. High-strength bolts are pretensioned to such a level that the loads are transferred in friction along the contact surfaces. Prestressing is used to stabilize earth formations and sides of excavations to eliminate inside bracing. High-strength steel plates may be welded to the flanges of beams which are bent with the help of jacks. When released, moments are induced in these beams and the plates are put into tension. A similar result is obtained by cambering the beam or placing a prestressed cable at the bottom face of a simply supported beam, for instance, which will cause the member to bend upwards (Fig. 1.31g). Under its own weight the beam may then be in a horizontal position resulting in a deflection only due to live loading. An additional strut support may be added to this beam at center span by using a pretensioned cable; this structure is called a King-post trussed beam (Fig. 1.31 g). Prestressing may be achieved through shortening cable members with a turn buckle or by forcing members which are too long into place, or by tightening tie rods at the base of a frame. The characteristics of concrete to shrink can be used beneficially as a prestress agent by simply preventing the movement by adjoining structures.

Flexible structures must be prestressed so that they are stable. This can be done by air pressure as for pneumatic structures or by directly tensioning double curvature anticlastic surfaces as for tent structures.

Rigid structures strong in tension and compression, such as steel or timber systems, may be prestressed to reduce the deflection of long-span bending members and increase the buckling capacity of slender compression members resulting in a reduction of weight and increase of stiffness. Rigid structures weak in tension but strong in compression like masonry and concrete are prestressed so that the compression induced cancels the tension due to external loading. In the past this was achieved through increase of weight. The vaulting in gothic cathedrals was kept in compression by an intricate system of buttresses and pinnacles. The 16-story Monadnock Building (1891) in Chicago required massive walls at its base to overcome the tensile stresses due to wind action.

Today the predominant application of prestressing is in the concrete construction. Because of the weakness of the material to resist tension, cables are placed along the tension flow of a member. When prestressed, these cables induce compression in the surrounding concrete and thereby prevent the section from cracking if the member is fully prestressed. In ordinary reinforced concrete beams, only the cross-sectional area above the neutral axis is effective in resisting bending, while the rest below (i.e., cracked portion) is just a dead weight burden. When fully prestressed, the beam is uncracked and its entire cross-section is available in resisting external loads, which in turn results in an increase in strength and stiffness or reduction of weight and thus in material savings. Though prestressed concrete is more expensive than conventional reinforced concrete due to higher costs of the stronger materials, the necessary accessories and operations, the qualified labor and the initial financial investments, the higher costs may still be offset by the speed of construction of precast units, the required larger member span with low dead-to-live load ratio, reduction of building height because of less floor depth, and the prefabrication of complex structural shapes and assemblages under high quality control.

The modern development of prestressed concrete is closely associated with the French engineer Eugene Freyssinet (1879-1962) in the first half of the 20th century. He recognized that the prestressed member shortens due to shrinkage and creep resulting in a loss of prestress, which he found can be reduced by applying much higher prestress forces; the large tension forces, in turn, require high strength steel and concrete. Some other engineers who made important early contributions to the practical application of prestressed concrete are: Gustave Magnel of Belgium, Y. Guyon of France, and R. Morandi of Italy as well as Franz Dischinger, Ulrich Finsterwalder, E. Hoyer, and Fritz Leonhardt of Germany. The rapid application of prestressed concrete started after World War II when steel was in short supply. T. Y. Lin of the University of California at Berkeley has distinguished himself since the early 1950s in making prestressed concrete a recognized and widely used method of construction in the United States. The first major prestressed concrete bridge

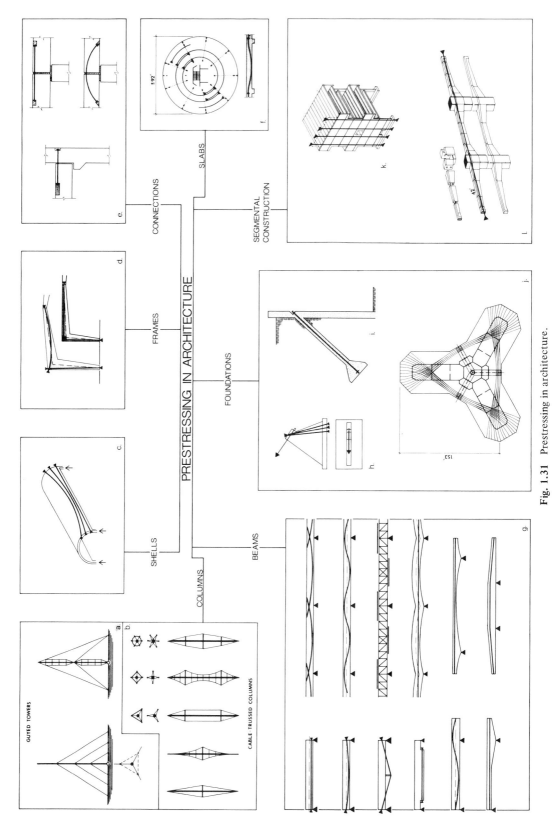

**Fig. 1.31** Prestressing in architecture.

84

in the United States was the Walnut Lane Bridge in Philadelphia built in 1949, while the world's first prestressed concrete highrise building was the Diamond Head Apartments built in 1956 in Honolulu, Hawaii.

While the design of ordinary reinforced concrete is generally based on strength (ultimate) design, fully prestressed concrete members may be proportioned on the basis of linear elastic behavior, since prestressing is used to improve the member performance at service level and since the concrete is uncracked and steel and concrete are stressed at a relatively low level.

Two primary tensioning methods are used in concrete construction: mechanical prestressing using jacks and chemical prestressing using expansive cements. Another tensioning method, though commercially not available, is based on electrical prestressing, where tendons are lengthened by heating them.

The most common method is the mechanical one, which uses either pre- or posttensioning. Pretensioning is usually associated with precast concrete produced in manufacturing plants. Tendons anchored to the forms or abutments outside the forms are tensioned before the concrete is cast. When the concrete has reached enough strength, the tendons are cut but prevented from returning to their original length by the concrete to which they are bonded, thus placing the surrounding concrete into compression.

Post-tensioning of tendons is done by hydraulic jacks after the concrete has hardened by inserting the wire or rods in the metal or plastic conduits, which were placed in the forms before the concrete was poured. The concrete element carries the compression in bearing through special anchoring devices at the end faces rather than through bond as in pretensioning; however, end blocks must spread the concentrated prestress forces over the whole beam section. Since there is no bond between tendons and concrete, tension can be applied at different stages. Post-tensioning techniques can be used on site with the member in place or for prefab concrete in a precast plant. It is usually applied to longspan structures and segmental construction.

Chemically prestressed concrete was originated with the commercial development of expansive cements by the French engineer H. Lossier in the late 1930s. In the United States, Alexander Klein, at the University of California at Berkeley, reported in 1958 on a new compound anhydrous calcium sulfoaluminate, which together with portland cement in concrete causes an expansion of the concrete during the early stage of hydration. When the concrete attempts to expand it is placed into compression because it is prevented from moving either by adjoining structures, subgrade friction, or the reinforcement. Expansive cement concretes are classified according to the level of prestress as:

- Shrinkage-compensating (25–100 psi)
- Self-stressing (150–500 psi)

Chemical prestressing has been successfully applied to large scale prefabricated units in box construction; it has been used in composite floor structures, where chemically prestressed precast corrugated plates served as formwork for cast in place shrinkage-compensating concrete; it has been applied to surface elements like walls, slabs, plates, and shells to prevent the development of shrinkage cracks.

There are three kinds of prestressing steel: high-strength strand, wires, and bars. The typical steel for pretensioned concrete is high-strength strand usually uncoated seven-wire stress relieved strand with an ultimate breaking strength of at least 250 and 270 ksi depending on the grade. Sizes are available from 0.25–0.60 in. diameter. Round wires are mostly used in post-tensioned concrete; their minimum tensile strength ranges from 235 to 250 ksi. They are available in four diameters (0.192, 0.196, 0.250, and 0.276 in.). Alloy steel bars are produced with a minimum ultimate strength of 145 and 160 ksi; they are available in diameters from $\frac{1}{2}$ to $1\frac{3}{8}$ in. or from #4 to #11 bars as based on designations for standard reinforcing bars.

There are hundreds of patented post-tensioning systems; they distinguish themselves by the method of anchoring, type of stressing tendon, and the grouting which is necessary to protect the steel from rust.

Prestressed concrete responds to forces instantaneously but in addition has the undesirable property of showing time-dependent characteristics such as creep which causes the member to shorten and results in loss of prestress as was mentioned before. To overcome this loss, large prestress forces are necessary requiring high strength concrete to support these forces. The concrete capacities are in the range from 4000 to 5000 psi and from 6000 to 10000 psi for precast concrete. Prestressing is applied to normal weight (145 pcf) as well as light weight (130–85 pcf) concretes.

There is no limit to the application of the prestress principle in the building construction field. It has been applied to individual members like piles, utility poles, railroad ties, and pavements, as well as to the large-scale building such as parking structures, residential construction, grandstands, vessels, storage tanks, water towers, ocean structures, ships, bridges, long-span and high-rise buildings just to name some examples. Prestress tendons are not only arranged along linear members and surfaces, but also may be placed in a multidirectional fashion.

### Application of the Prestress Principle to Various Structure Systems

Some typical applications of the prestress principle to architecturally designed elements or buildings are shown in Figs. 1.31 and 1.32. These examples will now be briefly discussed.

### Beams

Typical layouts of prestress cables are shown in Fig. 1.31g. As can be seen, tendons may be placed within the beam as for prestressed concrete or outside the beam as for a steel section. They may consist of short pieces, overlapping tendons, or continuous cables. Prestressing can be applied to any beam types such as W steel sections, concrete beams of any shape, or trusses. Cables can be arranged in a linear, draped, or curved manner. For the condition where the cable is straight and located at the centroidal axes of the beam section, the prestress force $P$ only causes uniform axial stresses along the beam.

$$f_c = \frac{P}{A_g} \tag{1.66}$$

When the tendon is placed with an eccentricity $e$ away from the centroidal $x$ axis but still located on the centroidal $y$ axis, additional bending stresses due to $M = P(e)$ are generated on this symetrical section (Fig. 1.33a)

$$f = \frac{P}{A_g} \pm \frac{P(e)}{S_x} \tag{1.67}$$

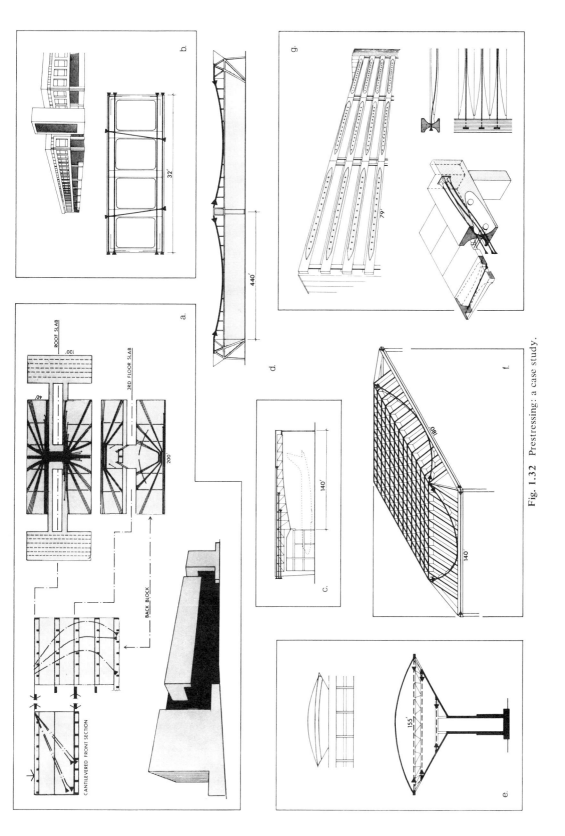

Fig. 1.32 Prestressing: a case study.

The magnitude of the compressive stresses due to full prestressing is such that it only allows a small amount of tensile stresses due to the superimposed gravity loading to develop so that the concrete does not crack.

While the tendon profile in post-tensioned concrete beams of constant cross-section may be curved and follow the tensile stress flow by responding as a suspended cable to the gravity loading (see Example 1.9), the tendon profile in pretensioned beams cannot do so because of the process of fabrication. The straight tendons must be held down at certain points, hence yield a draped profile. However, this shortcoming can be corrected by using arched, tapered, or haunched member forms with straight cables, yielding a similar result as curved tendons in straight members.

### Slabs

In slab construction prestressing has been used for one-way and two-way solid and joist slabs. One-way slabs can be visualized as consisting of parallel slab strips or 1-ft wide beams. The rather flexible flat plates are especially suitable for post-tensioning to obtain a wider column spacing, less floor depth, and a watertight roof deck. The two-way structural steel girder grid of the National Gallery in Berlin, Germany (Fig. 5.19g) was cambered at the center and the four cantilevered corners to counteract deflection. This cambering has a similar effect to the prestressing. The thickness of a circular slab with the curved tendon layout shown in Fig. 1.31f, was reduced by 33% through circular prestressing resulting in overall economy because of reduction in weight. The y shaped cellular foundation slab of the CN Tower in Toronto (Fig. 1.31j) with the triangular tendon layout was prestressed to keep it crack-free.

### Towers and Columns

In cable-trussed columns (Fig. 1.31b) used for tent structures, the long slender compression member is laterally braced by intermediate struts or tensile elements which, in turn, are held in place by prestressed cables. The critical buckling length of the slender column is reduced to the distance between the struts and/or tensile bracing. The areas of the guys are part of the column cross-section and since they are a substantial distance away from the centroidal axis, yield a large moment of inertia which lessens the significance of buckling. The guyed cables can be placed in several planes and are supported by open or closed ring strut systems. The composite action of the cable-trussed column can be compared with the central spine and ribs of the human body resisting compression while the muscles carrying the tension. Tall antenna structures (Fig. 1.31a) are guyed at intermediate levels with an initial tension high enough to insure the cable on the leeward side to stay in tension under maximum wind pressure. The critical buckling length of the mast is the distance between the cable supports. Similarly, the masts of sailing ships are prestressed and laterally supported by the rigging.

It is useful to prestress precast concrete columns which are subject to severe climatic conditions as well as to cracking during handling, transportation, and erection and which must resist bending so that the entire cross-section can be used to resist rotation and reduce lateral sway. Since prestressing increases the column stiffness, the buckling capacity of the slender column is also increased.

Prestressing has been applied to tall concrete towers used for water storage, rotating restaurants and broadcast facilities. The world's tallest free-standing structure is the 1815 ft high CN Tower in Toronto which is fully prestressed. The 144 tendons in the cantilevering tower shaft were post-tensioned by a force of about 1000 tons so that no tensile stresses occur in the concrete under normal loading conditions.

## Walls

Precast, prestressed wall panels are made from a variety of shapes ranging from flat solid to ribbed panels of small and large scale; they range from plain interior concrete walls to perforated or framed facade panels. For instance, limestone facade panels have been post-tensioned to allow them to overcome their low tensile capacity and to span the distance between the column supports.

## Frames

The prestress tendons in frames (Fig. 1.31d) follow the tensile force flow as caused by the governing gravity loading case as is further discussed for the load-balancing method of analysis in Example 1.10.

## Segmental Construction

Prefab concrete sections are produced and possibly prestressed in temporary or permanent precasting plants. There is no limit set to the potential member shape. Typical standardized pretensioned sections as mass-produced by the precast concrete industry are hollow-core slabs, single and double T's for floors and roofs, as well as inverted T, L, and I shapes and box sections as supporting beams. Precast elements may be used in combination with conventional construction or may be the building blocks of a fully prefabricated building system. The structural elements are assembled on the site and tied together through post-tensioning to form a rigid monolithic whole; the segments are supported by frictional forces between the contact surfaces as generated by the prestress forces. The continuity between the precast members can be established and moments transferred by post-tensioned short tendons (Fig. 1.31e); long tendons provide better continuity. The interlocking of the prefab boxes for Habitat 67 in Montreal into a complex aggregate was made possible by post-tensioning the units together with continuous cables.

The ICO Building System (Fig. 1.31k) developed by Sepp Firnkas of Boston consists of pretensioned floor panels and precast wall panels vertically post-tensioned. The spandrel beams of the Gulf Life Building in Jacksonville, Florida (Fig. 1.31l) that cantilever 42 ft, consist of precast concrete segments strung together with post-tensioning cables. Another example are the 70-ft concrete I-beams of the Trade Group Office building in Canberra, Australia (Fig. 1.32g), which are post-tensioned and support the T-beam floor units that are also post-tensioned as the exposed ends of the tendons along the webs of the girders indicate.

## Shells and Folded Plates

Though the stress level in shells is generally low, post-tensioning is advantageous for stabilizing the shape as well as to avoid shrinkage and tensile cracks especially where watertightness is essential. To avoid the cracking of the shell, it may be prestressed along the principal tensile stress trajectories. Shell beams (Fig. 1.31c) can be prestressed to increase their span capacity, or the cantilevering portion of a hyperbolic paraboloid (see Fig. 8.29d) may be tensioned along its suspended curvature to reduce the deflection. Precast concrete panels may be laid on top of a network of post-tensioning tendons, as for example the 10 × 10 ft mesh for the 380-ft circular saddle roof of the Arizona State Fair Coliseum in Phoenix (1965), which are then prestressed to form a continuous shell surface. The tension rings of concrete domes that resist the lateral thrust due to gravity, are in general prestressed. An example is the Toronto City Hall (Fig. 1.32e), where the tension ring along the edge of the dome and the two perimeter beams in the upper portion of the truncated cone are post-tensioned. Ring beams are prestressed in a natural way, when instead of a dome a suspended membrane or prestressed anticlastic net are being used. The prestressing of the shells can also occur at the foundation level, where the ties may be pretensioned thus, in addition, possibly eliminating the abutments.

### Trusses

Around the turn of this century it was not unusual to use iron rods beneath wrought iron bridge trusses to apply an upward curvature. Steel rods along the upper chord of the 140-ft cantilever steel truss of the United Airlines Hangar at Chicago's O'Hare International Airport (Fig. 1.32c) are prestressed. The result was 20% less steel as compared to a conventional truss construction. In the Rock Island parking structure (Fig. 1.32b), 11 ft 10 in. high precast Vierendeel trusses span 32 ft between the columns supporting the roof and second floor at the top and bottom chords, respectively. The trusses had to be post-tensioned horizontally and vertically in the precaster's yard because of height limitations due to clearance requirements under bridges and weight considerations for reduction of transportation costs.

### Suspended Concrete Hangers and Arches

The tension columns or hangers along the facade of a high-rise building supporting the floors can be made from prestressed concrete. The concrete is prestressed so that no tensile cracks form under full loading and the member extension due to live loading is kept to a minimum. The loads of the truncated rectangular pyramidal dome of the Baltimore Convention Center (Fig. 1.32f) are carried by post-tensioned suspended concrete arches located in the four inclined dome faces where they are transferred to the corner columns. The perimeter tie beams along the base of the sloped sides are also post-tensioned. A Lufthansa hangar at the Frankfurt Airport in Germany (Fig. 1.32d), employs twin suspended roofs, each spanning 440 ft. The roof consists of prestressed lightweight concrete strips 34.50-ft wide and 3.38-in. thick, supported by a transverse prestressed concrete box girder at midlength and trussed abutments at the ends. Other types of prestressed tension members are tension rings for dome structures and tie beams for frames and shells.

### Foundations

Retaining walls or sheet pile walls, as needed for excavation, may have to be anchored by prestressed tie backs directly into the rock or by post-tensioned concrete piles deep in the soil (Fig. 1.31i). Foundation concrete piles of the bearing and friction type are often prestressed to increase their bending capacity. The slot and wedge type foundations used for the anchorage of the guy cables for the Olympic membrane roof in Munich are prestressed along the tensile force flow (Fig. 1.31h).

*Building Block*

The potential application of the prestress principle is exemplified by the multidirectional layout of the post-tensioning system of the Tax Court building in Washington, D.C. (Fig. 1.32a), where the curvilinear cable pattern follows the tensile force flow. The cantilevered building box located centrally above the entrance is anchored with post-tensioning tendons to the four-story building block at its rear. The cables run in the vertical planes along the parallel shear walls. While some tendons continue in the walls to the base of the anchor block, others run into the top and third floor slabs of the cantilevered and anchor blocks. Additional post-tensioning cables are located in the roof and third-floor slabs.

## Design of Prestressed Concrete Beams

To develop some understanding for the behavior of prestressed flexural members, a simple beam is investigated in the following examples first as based on allowable stresses and then as based on load balancing.

**Example 1.9** Simply supported, cast-in-place concrete beams are spaced 18-ft apart and support 6-in. deep hollow-core slabs weighing 43 psf in addition to the 10 psf for the superimposed or service dead load and the 40 psf live loading (Fig. 1.33d). The $20 \times 36$ in. beams are post-tensioned with parabolic draped tendons, which are located at midspan 7 in. above the bottom surface of the beam. Use 5000 psi normal weight concrete with a compressive strength of $f'_{ci} = 4000$ psi at the time of tensioning and use Grade 160 pre-

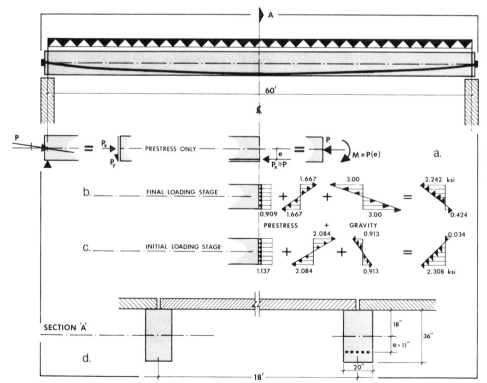

Fig. 1.33 Allowable stress method of analysis.

stress tendons. Determine the approximate magnitude of the post-tensioning force at the critical location at midspan and find the number and diameter of bars required. Check if the selected cross-section is satisfactory.

The beam must carry the following loads:

| | | |
|---|---|---|
| beam weight | $w_0 = 0.145(36 \times 20)/12^2 = 0.73$ k/ft | |
| service dead load: | $w_s = 18(43 + 10)/1000 \quad = 0.95$ k/ft | |
| | $w_D =$ | $= 1.68$ k/ft |
| live load | $w_L = 18(40)/1000$ | $= 0.72$ k/ft |
| | $w_T =$ | $= 2.40$ k/ft |

The moments at midspan as caused by the various loads are:

$$M_0 = 0.73(60)^2/8 = 328.50 \text{ ft-k}$$
$$M_S = 0.95(60)^2/8 = 427.50 \text{ ft-k}$$
$$M_D = \qquad\qquad\; = 756.00 \text{ ft-k}$$
$$M_L = 0.72(60)^2/8 = 324.00 \text{ ft-k}$$
$$M_T = \qquad\qquad\quad 1080.00 \text{ ft-k}$$

The beam will be fully prestressed so that the concrete itself can carry the maximum tensile stresses. This condition is quite different from a partially prestressed beam with a cracked section, where additional tensile reinforcing must be provided. Since for this case the concrete beam is assumed not to crack under loading, its entire section is effective and thus can be treated as any other homogeneous beam. The effect of steel (i.e., transformation of reinforcing bars into equivalent concrete) can be neglected for all practical purposes and the gross concrete area $A_g$ may be used for bonded and unbonded conditions.

The gross concrete area of the beam is

$$A_g = bh = 36(20) = 720 \text{ in.}^2$$

The moment inertia of the section about its centroidal $x$ axis is

$$I_x = \frac{bh^3}{12} = \frac{20(36)^3}{12} = 77760 \text{ in.}^4$$

The corresponding section modulus is

$$S_x = \frac{bh^2}{6} = \frac{I_x}{h/2} = \frac{77760}{18} = 4320 \text{ in.}^3$$

At least two loading stages are critical for the preliminary design: the initial stage with the beam bending upward as caused by the prestress force and the final stage where the beam deflects downward as governed by the full gravity loading.

In general, the final loading stage controls the magnitude of the prestress force. At this stage the tensile stresses in the bottom fibers at midspan are maximum and must be below the permissible ones. Furthermore, the concrete has reached its full strength, however there has been a loss of the initial prestress force $P_i$ due to creep because of sustained compression, shrinkage due to drying and elastic shortening of the concrete, as well as relaxation (creep), frictional resistance between tendon and concrete during tensioning, and slippage of steel. It is beyond the purpose of this discussion to deal with the complex behavior of prestress loss. Often, a 20% reduction of the initial prestress force $P_i$ is considered reasonable for the preliminary design. Hence the final prestress force is

$$P = 0.8\,P_i \qquad (1.68)$$

The magnitude of the prestress force is estimated from the critical tensile stresses due to full loading

$$f_t = \frac{P}{A_g} + \frac{P(e)}{S_x} - \frac{M_T}{S_x} \leqslant -6\sqrt{f_c'} \qquad (1.69)$$

$$= \frac{P}{720} + \frac{P(11)}{4320} - \frac{1080(12)}{4320} = \frac{-6\sqrt{5000}}{1000} = -0.424$$

$$= \frac{P}{720} + \frac{11P}{4320} = -0.424 + 3.00 = 2.576$$

$$P = 654.60 \text{ k}$$

The initial prestress force before losses is

$$P_i = \frac{P}{0.8} = \frac{654.60}{0.8} = 818.26 \text{ k}$$

The maximum compressive stresses in the top fibers as generated by this prestress force and the full gravity loading are

$$f_c = \frac{P}{A_g} - \frac{P(e)}{S_x} + \frac{M_T}{S_x} \leqslant 0.45\,f_c' \qquad (1.70)$$

$$= \frac{654.60}{720} - \frac{654.60(11)}{4320} + \frac{1080(12)}{4320}$$

$$= 0.909 - 1.667 + 3.00 = 2.242 \text{ ksi} < 0.45(5) = 2.25 \text{ ksi}$$

The beam cross-section must also be checked for the initial loading stage, where the prestress force and especially its location determine the maximum rotation which causes the beam to bend upward being counteracted only by its own weight.

First the tensile stresses in the top fibers are checked.

$$f_{ti} = \frac{P_i}{A_g} - \frac{P_i(e)}{S_x} + \frac{M_0}{S_x} \leqslant -3\sqrt{f_{ci}'} \qquad (1.71)$$

$$= \frac{818.26}{720} - \frac{818.26(11)}{4320} + \frac{328.5(12)}{4320}$$

$$= 1.137 - 2.084 + 0.913 = -0.034 \leqslant \frac{-3\sqrt{4000}}{1000} = -0.19 \text{ ksi}$$

Checking the maximum compressive stresses at the bottom face, yields

$$f_{ci} = \frac{P_i}{A_g} + \frac{P_i(e)}{S_x} - \frac{M_0}{S_x} \leqslant 0.6 f'_{ci} \tag{1.72}$$

$$= 1.137 + 2.084 - 0.913 = 2.308 \text{ ksi} \leqslant 0.6(4) = 2.40 \text{ ksi}$$

Note the actual maximum tensile and compressive stresses are barely below the allowable ones at the initial loading stage! One may conclude that the beam section and the magnitude of the prestress force as well as its sag are satisfactory. Keep in mind that this section does not necessarily constitute the most economical solution. At the support the prestress cable applies axial stresses while the shear stresses counteract the shear due to gravity loading. The amount of prestressing steel needed depends on the allowable tensile stress which, in turn, is based on the stage directly after prestress transfer or tendon anchorage and is equal to 70% of the ultimate steel strength $f_{pu}$

$$f_t = \frac{P_i}{A_s} \leqslant 0.7 f_{pu} \tag{1.73}$$

$$A_s = \frac{P_i}{0.7 f_{pu}} = \frac{818.26}{0.7(160)} = 7.31 \text{ in.}^2$$

try 5 #11, Grade 160 deformed prestressing bars, $A_s = 7.81$ in.$^2$

The web reinforcement to resist the shear is found in a similar fashion as for conventional reinforced concrete. But, one should keep in mind that the vertical component of the draped or curved prestress tendon acts upwards hereby reducing the shear due to gravity action.

**Example 1.10** Another approach may be used to investigate the prestressed beam of the previous example.

Visualize the parabolic prestressed tendon to be tensioned with such a magnitude that it generates a uniform upward force exactly equal to the uniform downward gravity load. The result is a net zero load and pure constant compression along the beam (Fig. 1.34a). This approach is called the load-balancing method of analysis. The cable profile corre-

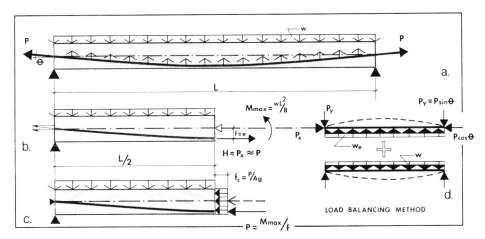

Fig. 1.34   Load balancing method of analysis.

sponds to the arrangement of the applied loads so that it generates equivalent forces acting opposite to the applied ones. In other words, the cable forces produce a moment diagram exactly opposite to the one caused by the applied loads which were chosen to be balanced. In this example, the uniform loads generate a moment which varies parabolically, hence the chosen cable profile is also parabolic. This flat parabolic draped tendon or compressed concrete arch represents the funicular shape of the uniform loading and thus responds in pure axial action.

The designer must determine the portion of the applied load to be balanced by the prestress force. Often the dead load and one-half of the live loading are assumed to be balanced for the condition where the live load is high in comparison to the dead load. In this example the live load constitutes a relatively small percentage of the total load only. Therefore, the beam weight and two-thirds of the superimposed dead load only will be balanced. The moment caused by this load is resisted by the cable force times its sag $f$ at the point of investigation. At midspan of the beam this relationship (Fig. 1.34b) is

$$H(f) = \frac{wL^2}{8} \tag{p}$$

Since the cable is rather shallow, one may assume that the cable tension $P$ is constant and equal to the lateral thrust $H$ (see also the discussion of parabolic cable in Chapter 3). Hence the required prestress force after losses and letting the sag $f$ equal to the eccentricity $e$, is equal to

$$P = H = \frac{wL^2}{8e} \tag{1.74}$$

$$= \frac{[0.73 + 0.67(0.95)]\,60^2}{8(11/12)} = 670.83 \text{ k}$$

The initial prestress force is

$$P_i = \frac{P}{0.8} = \frac{670.83}{0.8} = 838.54 \text{ k}$$

Only uniform compressive stresses are generated by the prestress force due to the balance of the loads (Fig. 1.34c)

$$f_c = \frac{P}{A_g} = \frac{670.83}{720} = 0.932 \text{ ksi}$$

Under full loading, additional bending stresses due to the rest of the loads which are not balanced, must be resisted by the beam

$$\pm f_b = \frac{M}{S} = \frac{[324.00 + 0.33(427.50)]\,12}{4320} = 1.292 \text{ ksi}$$

The maximum combined compression stresses at the top face of the beam are

$$f_{top} = 0.932 + 1.292 = 2.224 \text{ ksi} \leqslant 0.45\,f_c' = 0.45(5) = 2.25 \text{ ksi}$$

The tensile stresses at the bottom face for this loading case are

$$f_{bot} = 0.932 - 1.292 = -0.36 \text{ ksi} \leqslant -6\sqrt{f_c'} = -0.424 \text{ ksi}$$

At the initial loading stage the beam must resist the prestress force and its own weight (see Problem 1.53).

**Example 1.11** The effect of prestressing upon the immediate deflection at the initial loading stage can be derived from the load-balancing method

$$\frac{w_e L^2}{8} = P_i(e)$$

Hence the equivalent load (Fig. 1.34d) is equal to

$$w_e = \frac{8 P_i e}{L^2} \tag{1.75}$$

Placing this expression into the familiar maximum deflection formula for a simply supported beam loaded with uniform loads, yields an upward deformation at midspan of

$$-\Delta_{pi} = \frac{5 w L^4}{384 EI} = \frac{5 P_i e L^2}{48 EI} \tag{1.76}$$

Hence, the initial critical deflection due to member weight and prestress force is equal to

$$\Delta_i = -\Delta_{pi} + \Delta_0$$

$$\Delta_i = \frac{5 L^2}{48 EI} \left( -P_i(e) + \frac{w_0 L^2}{8} \right) \tag{1.77}$$

If the beam is fully prestressed, then it may be considered uncracked and the moment of inertia of the gross concrete section can be used. The effect of long-term deflection, especially due to concrete creep, is beyond the scope of this introductory discussion.

Only a simple rectangular beam was investigated, however, one has to keep in mind that this section, from a material efficiency point of view, is uneconomical for long spans. For this range box sections as well as symmetrical and asymmetrical I and T shapes with thin webs and flanges are generally being used. These sections provide large internal lever arms as measured from the centroid of the steel to the resultant compression force. T-beams with their high compressive capacity concentrated in the flanges are suitable for cases where the live load is small in comparison to the beam weight as is the condition for large span roof structures. On the other hand, inverted T sections are more appropriate where live loads are high as compared to the dead load.

## Problems

**1.53** Check the stresses for the beam in Example 1.10 at the initial loading stage.

**1.54** Determine the immediate deflection at the initial loading stage for the beam in Example 1.10.

**1.55** Investigate conceptually the behavior of the beam in Example 1.9 for the condition where the tendon is extended straight from midspan to the support (i.e., straight cable profile).

**1.56** Determine the approximate live load capacity of a standard reinforced concrete beam with a steel ratio of $p = 0.18 f_c'/F_y$ and the same dimensions as the prestressed beam in Example 1.9 ($f_c' = 5000$ psi, $F_y = 50$ ksi). Compare the results.

**1.57** A roof structure consists of parallel prestressed standard PCI T-beams (8 ST 36) with a span of 90 ft. The flange width of a typical section is 8 ft. 0 in. and the depth is 36 in. with the location of the centroidal axis at 9.99 in. measured from the top face of the beam. The cross-sectional area is $A_g = 570$ in.,$^2$ the moment of inertia is $I_{xg} = 68917$ in.$^4$. The normal weight concrete (150 pcf) has a strength of $f'_c = 5000$ psi and $f'_{ci} = 3500$ psi. Use Grade 270 standard cable ($f_{pu} = 270$ ksi). Consider 6 psf superimposed dead load and 20 psf live load. Determine the required number of tendons, if their location at midspan is at 4 in. from the bottom of the beam.

**1.58** A rectangular concrete beam of the type shown in Fig. 1.34 is prestressed so that no tensile stresses appear. Because of this simplifying assumption the effect of pre-stress loss may be ignored. Assume a maximum cable eccentricity (sag) of $e = 0.3h$ and a depth-to-span ratio of 20; consider only the final loading condition. Find the prestress force and the uniform load the beam can support.

**1.59** Check the results obtained in Problem 1.58 by using the data of Example 1.9 for fast approximation purposes.

# 2 BASIC STRUCTURAL DESIGN CONCEPTS

Geometrical patterns as a basis for the organization of building structures, as well as an awareness of visual order and visual thinking, are introduced briefly in this chapter. Basic concepts of building stability and load distribution are discussed. The flow of gravity forces along the horizontal building planes and the flow of lateral forces along the vertical building planes are also investigated. Common structural systems including floor structures are introduced. Finally, the purpose of the building joint is studied briefly.

## 2.1 PATTERNS AND MODULAR COORDINATION

The form of a building is in response to a rather complex interplay of design generators caused by functional, behavioral, political, economic, and aesthetic forces.

Its geometry is defined by its enclosed spaces (e.g., rooms) and by the shapes of its solid components (walls, doors, etc.), all in an ordered relationship to each other. This interdependence of solid and void is described in planar views by horizontal and vertical sections, each one with its own formal organization. The resulting patterns establish a visual order in themselves. It is the recognition, or rather appreciation of this visual order which is so important for the further discussion in this book. It is not possible to develop a formula for the objective understanding of this organization, but only a certain sensitivity, since its two dimensions can only describe the geometrical result, while the process of creation and change, that is the higher dimension, can only be interpreted and seen in the behavioral context.

Some of the infinitely possible patterns related to this investigation are shown in Fig. 2.1. They range, at one end, from the regular surface subdivisions that occur on tiled floors and wall paper, and that have been systematically explored by the Islamic art, to the other end of a complex, ever-changing organism, the city.

The regular linear grids can be replaced by curvilinear ones as expressed so powerfully by the late Baroque architects or as revived by the modern architects Paolo Portoghesi and Vittorio Gigliotti with their overlapping circles as space organizers. The nature of curvilinear patterns is further investigated in Fig. 2.2, where the geometries of various buildings are superimposed in such a manner as to balance the lateral thrust of the arched forms and to express the effect of weightlessness as well as the dynamics of continuity.

Fig. 2.1 Patterns.

99

This dynamics of movement is experienced in the structure of the wood grain as its growth responds to stress flow and is affected by the interference of knots and notches (Fig. 2.1) resembling the contours of the earth or the wind pressure distribution along a building surface.

Also, the photoelastic diagram of the simple beam reacting to two single loads exposes similar phenomena of stress concentrations at the loads, while the equally spaced lines in the center portion indicate the linear stress distribution. Similar behavioral patterns are experienced by the effects of an island in a river, which interferes with the natural flow of the current by pushing aside the stream lines and causing turbulences, or as experienced around a hole in a member that is under tension.

The emergence of form out of force flow is expressed by the slab rib pattern following the isostatic lines of the principal bending moments as based on isotropic plate behavior. This interplay of force and form is often called tectonics, and is experienced so convincingly in the architecture of the Gothic cathedrals.

Finally, the pattern that is derived from a proportional system in search of absolute harmony and a universal eternal order seems to be in exact opposition to the sudden random pattern caused by a gunshot wound or explosion, as seen in the crack pattern of window glass.

A building is a cellular aggregate of spaces which must be dimensionally coordinated so that it can be built. This dimensional network forms patterns of a certain order. The key to understanding that order lies in the nature of mathematical figures which shall be reviewed briefly.

Most interesting to the field of construction are the regular polygons with identical edge lengths and the same angles, reflecting basic considerations of economy. There exists an infinite number of regular polygons ranging from the simple ones, to the more complex star-shaped and other compound forms. Within this context, the simple regular polygons are of more interest. They may be organized according to the number of sides they have as: the equilateral triangle, the square, the pentagon, the hexagon, the heptagon, the octagon, the nonagon, the decagon, and finally approaching the circle with the increase in the number of edges. This transition from the regular triangle to the circle also reflects the transition from the longest perimeter necessary to enclose a given area to the least perimeter in the case of the circle.

The regular polygons are symmetrical with respect to the folding line (mirror or bilateral symmetry) and rotation (point symmetry). A square, for example, has four lines of symmetry, that is, when folded about any one of these lines both portions match exactly. The circle is the most symmetrical of all geometrical figures; every corner of regular polygons lies on the circle (see Fig. 3.8).

The perfect regularity of the simple polygons can be relaxed by either allowing unequal angles with still equal sides, called semiregular polygons (e.g., rhombus) or allowing only equal angles (e.g., rectangle).

The simplest planar networks (grids, lattices, tiles, nets, mosaics, tessellations, etc.) are derived from the regular polygons. There are only three regular polygons that can fill a surface just by themselves. They are the triangle, hexagon, and square; the grids which they form are called the three regular equipartitions.

The eight semiregular equipartitions (Fig. 2.1) are made up of two and three regular polygons, with the same ones meeting at each vertex, however, the different polygons do not form equal angles any more. In addition to the three regular suface grids, the semiregular polygons of the rhombus and pentagon can each also fill a surface.

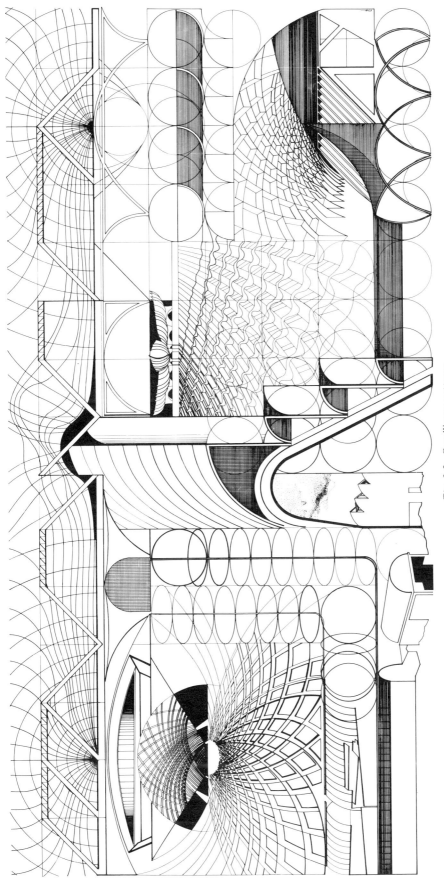

Fig. 2.2  Curvilinear patterns.

Relaxing the regularity of lattices results in an infinite number of patterns; random arrangements can be developed with the regular polygons. Further, there exists an infinite number of grids that are comprised of identical polygons of unequal-sided figures (e.g., rectangle, rectangular triangle, parallelogram, trapezoid).

The layout of a building is coordinated with a dimensional grid that is derived from its modularity (Fig. 2.3). The basic building module is a frame of reference, a unit mesurement which attempts to encompass, in a purely geometrical fashion, all the building modules, that is all the requirements of its components (production, transportation, size, position, performance, etc.) and construction process (planning, installation, communication, tolerances, etc.).

In systems building the degree of complexity of the modular coordination is quite high since it not only responds to standardization necessary for mass production, but also provides the rules and framework for the interaction of design, manufacturing, and construction as represented by the various building professionals.

The layout of most buildings is coordinated by a repetitive rectangular network in the horizontal and vertical directions as explained visually in Fig. 2.3; obviously, any other dimensional lattices can be used if the arrangement of the building components so requires. Visualize the typical building to be subdivided by a cubic spatial network of reference lines as derived from the international basic module of 100 mm ($\approx$ 4 in.). The typical grids of organization for a building are:

- The basic modular grid or the multimodule as a multiple of the basic module
- The planning grid
- The structural grid, shown as dash-dotted line

For example, a multimodule of 2 or 4 ft is usually used in home building as developed around the manufacturing of building materials, in particular the standard panel size of 4 $\times$ 8 ft and the production of joists in increments of 2 ft. This modular grid is a multiple of the reference grid of 4 in.

Similarly, the Japanese employed for the design of their traditional houses the Tatami, a straw mat of 3 $\times$ 6 ft size, as the module from which the building grew.

From a mathematical point of view these networks represent simple arithmetic or geometric sequences. In geometric sequences each term is found by multiplying the previous number by a given number $a$ such as

$$1, 2, 4, 8, 16, \ldots$$

Each building element is a rectangle with each of its dimensions being a multiple of the basic module of 100 mm (or 4 in.). The resulting proportions of the rectangles consist always of the ratios of whole numbers (1:1, 1:2, 1:3, 1:4, 2:3, 3:4, etc.) as shown in Fig. 2.3.

Proportions have always been one of the most essential elements of visual order and an important consideration of aesthetics. They have been systematically researched in the Renaissance and well-documented by the architects Alberti and Palladio. But also the Gothic builders have expressed the secrets of dimensional interrelationships in the cathedrals. Already the Greek mathematicians developed rational models as seen in the mathematical regularities of proportions to explain harmony and beauty as an absolute, universal order. They considered the ratios based on rational numbers to reflect a

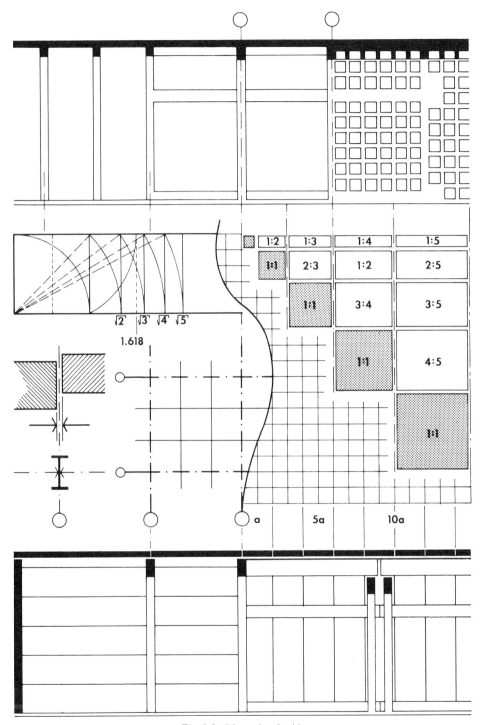

Fig. 2.3 Dimensional grids.

static symmetry, while the ratio of irrational numbers (e.g., $1:\sqrt{2}, 1:\sqrt{3}, 1:(1+\sqrt{5})/2 = 1:1.618$) to be of dynamic symmetry. The root or dynamic rectangles (Fig. 2.3) played an important part in Greek art and architecture in the search for expressing the mystery of order and unity. Pythagoras and Euclid found especially pleasing the rectangle with the ratio of $1/1.618$ (often approximated as $3/5$), which they called the rectangle of the Divine Section, also known as the Golden Rectangle. This magic ratio of the Golden Mean not only occurs in the creation of art, architecture, music, literature and other design forms, but also in nature, in the form of the logarithmic or golden spiral, especially abundant in the field of botany defining growth patterns. It probably was already familiar to the Egyptians as suggested by the proportions of the Pyramid of Gizeh. This mystic number has preoccupied the minds of scholars from Vitruvius to Leonardo da Vinci, Dürer, Kepler, Bernoulli, and recently Le Corbusier.

The golden mean may also be derived from the Fibonacci series, which had so much influence upon modern architecture. Fibonacci invented his famous sequence of numbers in the early thirteenth century. In this series, each number is equal to the sum of the two preceding numbers starting with a pair of initially chosen numbers, for example 3 and 5, resulting in

$$3, 5, 8, 13, 21, 34, 55, 89, \ldots$$

By dividing any of the Fibonacci numbers by the next higher number yields the golden mean, though the early small numbers in the sequence only approximate the magic ratio.

Le Corbusier derived his proportional system the "Modulor," for the dimensional coordination of the building, by subdividing the human body, assumed to be 2.26 m to the finger tips of the raised arm, first into two basic parts of 0.86 m from the feet to the hanging arm and $2.26 - 0.86 = 1.40$ for the upper portion as based on the golden section. With these consecutive numbers of 0.86 and 1.40 he constructed his "Blue Series" upward and downward according to the Fibonacci series.

Whatever the basis is for the derivation of the dimensional network, be it from the simple geometric series or the more complex harmonic series, the modularity is essential for the construction process, though it may not necessarily be expressed by the appearance of the building. On the other hand it can be the design generating determinant as exemplified by Walter Netsch's "field theory," where interlocking lattices reflect the dynamic interplay of various behavioral systems (e.g., Fig. 4.63k). Or, going even one step further, the building module may be a prefabricated room unit. In this case, the cells are assembled and stacked adjacent to and on top of each other, as in Moshe Safdie's Habitat in Montreal.

## 2.2  STRUCTURAL PATTERNS

The structural grid coordinates the location and dimensions of every structural element in the building (Fig. 2.3). The regularity of the grid allows for a standardized construction process and makes it easier to control and reduce sources of errors.

Investigated first are the patterns formed by the structural fabric. Distinguished are the floor/roof framing of the horizontal building planes, and the walls, frames, and stairs of the vertical support structure.

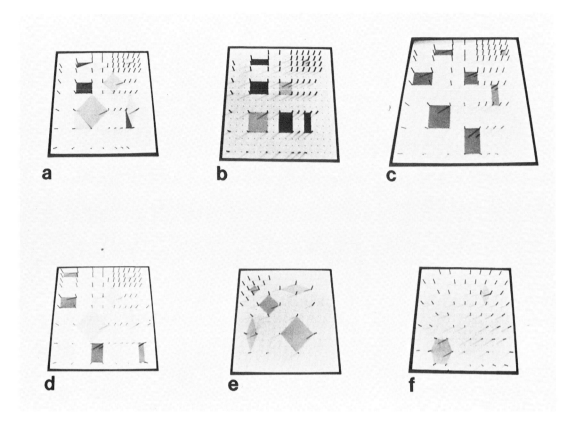

Fig. 2.4 Support structure system.

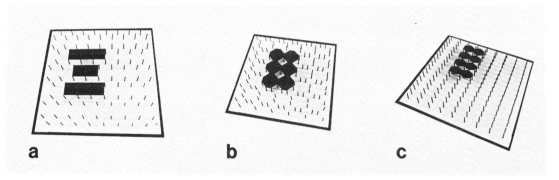

Fig. 2.5 Support structure systems.

## Vertical Support Structures

There are an infinite number of structural layouts possible as developed from a given basic modular grid, as is suggested in Figs. 2.4 and 2.5. In this case just columns are used as support systems. They can be arranged on the basic coordinating net in a manner yielding spaces of varying proportions in parallel and diagonal directions; they may be widely or closely spaced. It should be apparent that there is variety within repetition since even

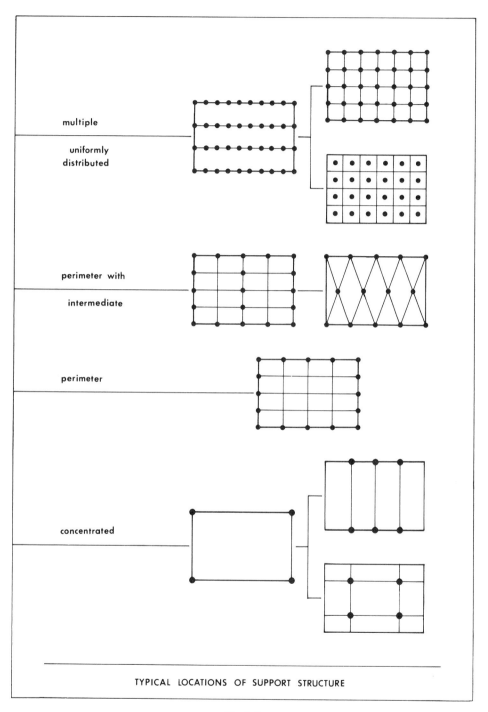

TYPICAL LOCATIONS OF SUPPORT STRUCTURE

Fig. 2.6

the nonuniform and seemingly irregular patterns are all derived from the basic organizational grid.

The structure layout must respond to the functional organization of the building, where the columns and walls may help to separate and reinforce the spaces to allow for different activities. Various arrangements of vertical support structures for a typical rectangular building unit are compared in Fig. 2.6; a similar approach could be taken for buildings of other basic forms. The essential distinction is between multibay structures of one- and two-directional character and single unit, long-span structures, where columns only appear along the perimeter to allow for unobstructed interior space. The typical patterns established by the various column layouts are quite apparent from Fig. 2.6.

A similar study is done in Fig. 2.7 for a multicell rectangular building as derived from a basic grid by using different column-wall arrangements. Here the formal transition from a column system laterally stabilized by three walls (a) to a pure wall structure (p) is presented. The wall components have various shapes ranging from linear and open compound forms (e.g. L, J, H, and T) to closed cores. They may be combined and arranged to result in the patterns of Fig. 2.7.

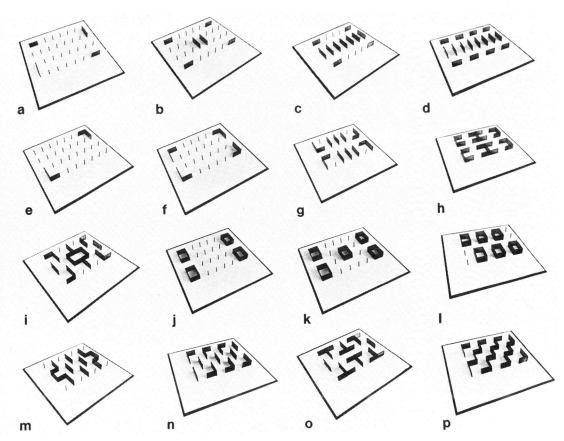

Fig. 2.7   From skeleton to wall structure.

### Floor and Flat Roof Structures

Beams can connect the same uniform column grid in many ways, in order to support a one-way floor structure (Fig. 2.8). Some typical beam framing patterns are: one-directional (a), one-directional changing into the opposite direction along the diagonal (c), and spiral-like.

When the columns are connected directly to the slab units rather than the beams, then again several patterns can be developed (Fig. 2.9). The column-slab kits may be organized according to the structure type as an umbrella unit, a two-leg table, or a four-leg table arranged either along the basic or diagonal grid.

The basic floor or flat roof framing systems, as derived from the direction of their beam layout, are identified in Fig. 2.10. They are arranged in parallel, radially, or diagonally, in one-, two-, or multiple-directions. Since the roof live loads are generally low, the roof framing should only be equated to the floor framework supporting light loads as for residential usage. Other roof forms, not flat but of various spatial profiles, are discussed throughout this volume.

The building shape, the type as well as location of the support structure, the scale of span and loading, and the functional requirements all influence the selection of the appropriate framing system. There is no magic formula for choosing a floor structure, each

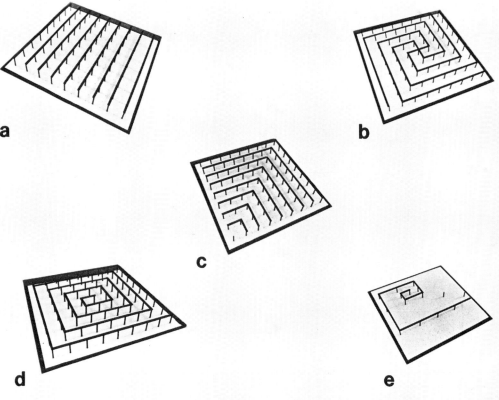

**Fig. 2.8** Beam framing patterns.

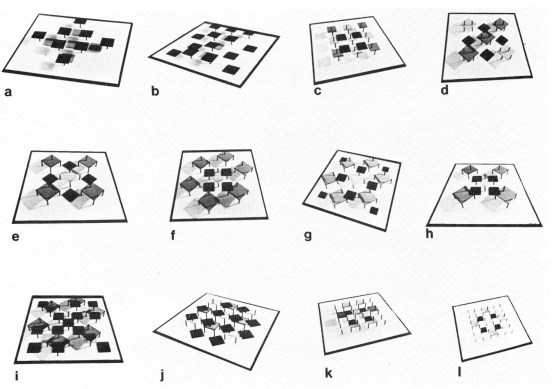

**Fig. 2.9** Column-panel systems.

building has its own unique conditions relating to site, functional needs, support of equipment, openings, labor practices, fire-proofing, underfloor ductwork, electrical conduit distribution, sprinkler systems, suspended ceiling, light fixtures, adaptability to future changes, the consideration of less weight for deeper floor framing versus shallower but heavier floors yielding less overall building height, the designer's experience and prejudice, etc.

The roof structure must not only provide the necessary strength to support itself and any superimposed loads, but must also control the climate, that is the flow of heat, sound, water, air, and water vapor; in addition it must have a certain degree of fire resistance. As for the floor structure, it may have to accommodate electrical, plumbing, heating, air conditioning, and sprinkler systems; it must adapt to the attachment of the ceiling or other finishing materials.

Flat roofs should have a slight slope of $\frac{1}{4}/12$, that is, a pitch of about 1% to have proper drainage. To prevent the penetration of water, most flat roofs use a waterproof membrane of built-up or elastomeric roofing or sheet metal attached to the deck, while steeply pitched roofs may apply shingles (e.g., asbestos-cement, asphalt, metal, wood), clay tiles, or roofing slate. The roof may have to be insulated against heat loss and gain (e.g. blanket, rigid board, foamed-in-place); a vapor barrier may have to be provided at the underside of the insulation, possibly together with vents.

Common flat roof and floor frameworks are shown conceptually at the bottom of

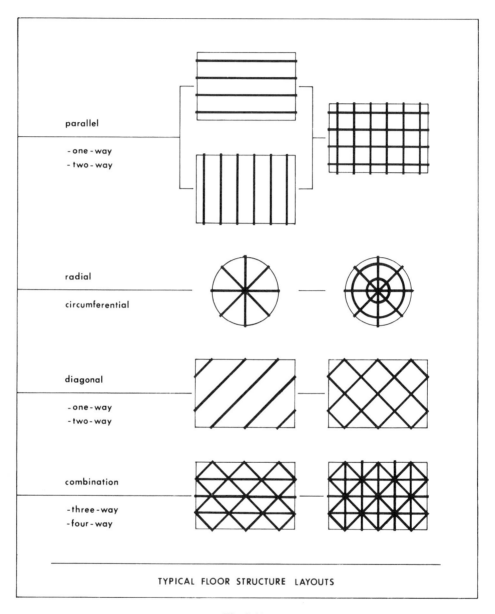

Fig. 2.10

Fig. 2.11; for typical span ranges the reader may refer to Fig. 1.12. The surface skin (i.e., deck or slab) may be a one-way or two-way structure. It is either directly supported on the primary structural members (walls, columns, primary beams, Fig. 2.13a–c), or it rests on secondary filler beams or joists (i.e., bay subframing, Fig. 2.13d–f). The skin may just be sitting on the framework or it may be a composite part of it, such as cast-in-place concrete, stressed-skin panelized systems, or composite construction between concrete slab, corrugated steel deck and steel beams.

Some of the familiar structural skins are:

- Structural decks on joists or beams (plywood sheathing, corrugated steel deck, precast concrete planks, gypsum deck, solid wood deck, etc.)
- One-way solid concrete slab on primary beams or walls (4-10) in. thick, 12-20 ft typical span range)
- Precast hollow-core concrete slabs (6-12 in. thick, 20-50 ft span range)
- Composite $1\frac{1}{2}$ in. steel deck concrete slab (12-15 ft span range)
- Concrete joist slabs (6-20 in. thick, 15-50 ft typical span range)
- Precast prestressed concrete single and double Tees (12-36 in. deep, 30-100 ft span range)
- Two-way concrete flat plate (5-14 in. thick, up to 35 ft span)
- Two-way concrete waffle slab (17-29 in. thick, 25-60 ft span range)

The span range of concrete slabs can be extended by prestressing.

Some of the important characteristics of floor structures are further investigated in Fig. 2.11. They deal with the following aspects on a purely visual and introductory level:

1  The effect of various types and positions of support systems upon different slab forms as caused by uniform loading and expressed in load distribution, floor framing systems, and floor openings.
2  The solid slab behavior under uniform loading as effected by the support conditions and reflected by crackline patterns derived from the yield line theory and principal moment contours as based on elastic behavior. Nervi's isostatic rib slabs are derived from the principal moment flow; they also can be seen as the contour lines of conical tent structures (see Fig. 9.19), realizing the similar relationship between cable response and loading as well as the shape of the corresponding moment diagram (Fig. 1.15).
3  Typical framing patterns for repetitive multibay floor systems
4  Steel reinforcing layout patterns

Buildings with complex, irregular plan shapes (e.g., Fig. 2.27.1a-g) are organized by the structural grid into basic units of mostly rectangular or other polygonal forms. As mentioned before, these basic building units may require long-span floors/roofs that are only supported along their perimeter or they may be further subdivided into smaller bays yielding shorter span floor framing systems (Fig. 2.6). Common frameworks for such bays are shown in Figs. 2.13 and 2.14; a typical rectangular bay may have to be subdivided by secondary or filler beams as for cases (d)-(f) and (i) in Fig. 2.13 or the examples of Fig. 2.14. Various floor framing layouts for the same building are compared in Fig. 2.15. Heavy equipment should be directly supported by a beam(s) and placed as close as possible to the supports to reduce the bending and deflection.

Before further exploring the nature of the floor structures in Fig. 2.13, a typical framework with a stair opening is investigated in Fig. 2.12a. The floor deck (concrete slab, deck, joists, etc.) spans in the short direction perpendicular to the parallel beams, that are 8 ft apart, as indicated by the arrows. Visualize the deck to act between the

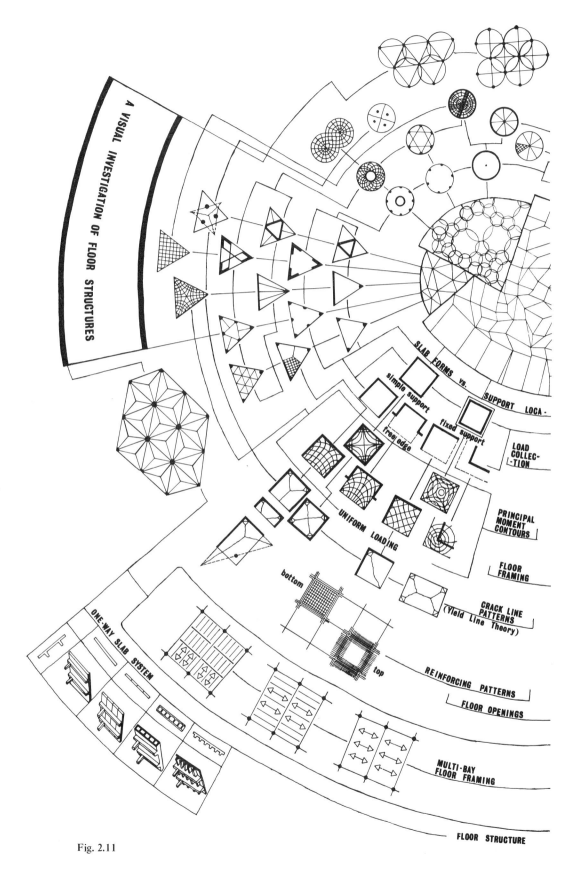

Fig. 2.11

112

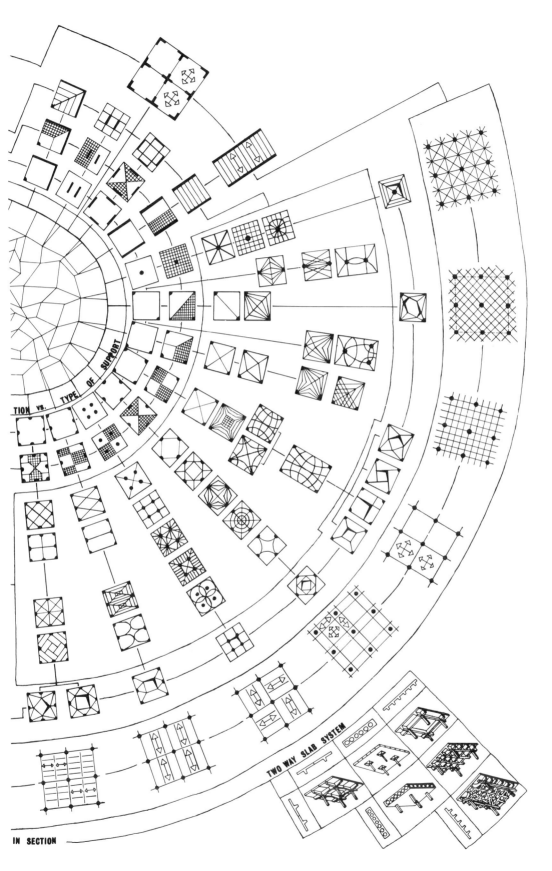

TION vs. TYPE OF SUPPORT

IN SECTION

TWO WAY SLAB SYSTEM

113

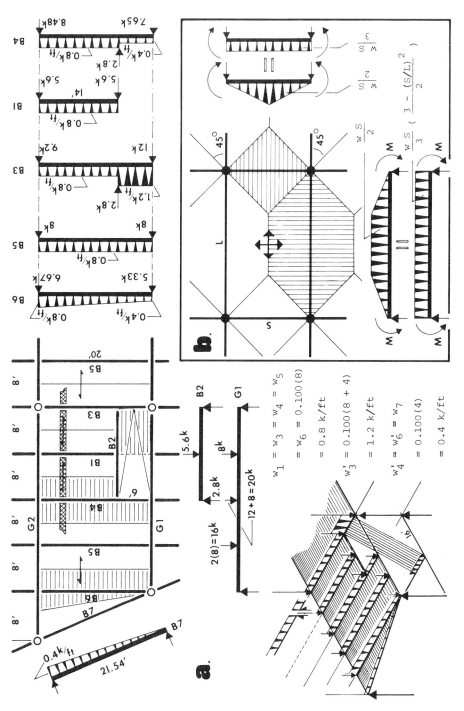

Fig. 2.12

beams as parallel, 1-ft wide, simply supported beam panels or as joists spaced 1 ft apart which transfer one-half of the deck loads to the respective supporting beams. The contributing floor area each beam must support is shaded and identified in Fig. 2.12a; it is subdivided into parallel load strips that cause a uniform line load on the parallel beams. However, beam $B7$ is positioned on an angle and hence will have to carry a triangular tributary area. The loading diagrams with numerical values are given for the various beams in Fig. 2.12a, as based on a hypothetical load of 100 psf including the beam weights; this load is also used for the stair area, but is assumed on the horizontal projection of the opening (see Chapter 4.3, The Simply Supported Inclined Beam).

Beam $B1$ is supported by beam $B2$ framing the opening; its reaction causes single loads on $B2$ and $G2$. Beam $B2$, in turn, rests on beams $B3$ and $B4$; its reactions are equal to the single loads acting on these two beams. Since most of the beams are supported by the interior girders, their reactions cause single load action on the girders as indicated for $G1$, where the beam reactions from the other side are assumed to be equal to the ones for $B5$; the girder weight is ignored.

The effects of various structural design criteria on the floor framing are studied in Fig. 2.13 and numerically evaluated in the homework. They include the following considerations:

- The effect of span direction [(a), (b), (k), (m), (n), (s)]
- The effect of bay proportion [(b), (c)]
- The effect of cantilever beam construction [(t)]
- The effect of beam spacing [(d), (e), (f), and Fig. 2.14]
- The effect of framing floor openings for stairs, elevators or other vertical shafts [(g), (h)]
- The effect of column layout [(k), (n), (u)]
- The effect of cantilevering [(l), (j)]
- The effect of a slanted corner [(o)]
- The effect of scale [(p)]
- The effect of corner or intersecting building units [(q)]
- The effect of a partition wall or other heavy load layout [(r)]

For all practical purposes one-way span action may be assumed for a rectangular slab having the proportions of 1:2 or greater, even if it is also supported along the short sides. On the other hand, it is quite apparent that a square concrete slab with the proportions of 1:1 and properly reinforced in both directions will span two ways and carry an equal load to each of the four supporting beams.

In general, for a rectangular, two-way structure the loads may be considered to be distributed in the two perpendicular directions to the supporting beams according to the tributary areas formed by the intersection of 45° lines extending from the columns as shown in Fig. 2.12b.

The bending moments for the indeterminate continuous beams may be approximated by an equivalent uniform load per lineal foot as given in Fig. 2.12b and derived in Problem 2.6. The approximate behavior of the two-way slab will be investigated in Fig. 5.18 and the respective discussion.

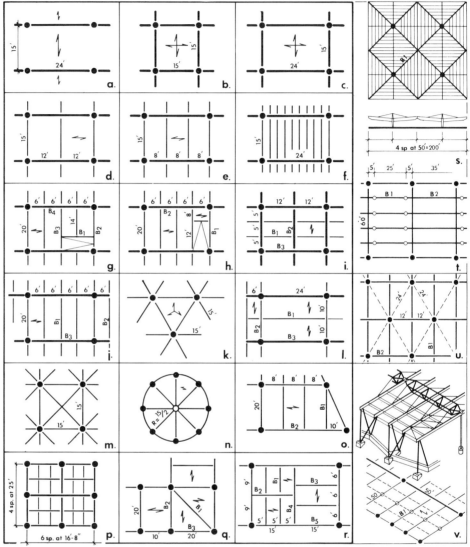

Fig. 2.13

## Problems

**2.1** For the typical floor or roof framing systems of Fig. 2.13 with the exception of cases (g)–(j), (l), and (r)–(v) determine the maximum moment of the primary beams (not filler beams); consider the beams to be simply supported. Use a uniform live and dead load of 100 psf which includes the weight of the beam.

**2.2** For the framing plans of cases (g)–(j), (l), and (r)–(v) of Fig. 2.13 determine the size of the simply supported beams as indicated. Assume a floor and stair loading of 100 psf which includes the beam weight; consider the stair span equal to the length of the stair well opening. Use A36 steel. For this preliminary design, bending is

assumed to control and the compression flange is considered to be laterally supported by the floor structure.

**2.3**   Determine the placement of the filler beams for a typical structural bay (Fig. 2.14a)
to yield the most economical section for beam $AB$ that is, find the smallest possible
moment in the beam by comparing the following filler beam spacings: 2, 3, 4, 5
equal spacings, and 1 ft on center.

**2.4**   Determine the most economical open-web steel joist to span the typical interior
bay (Fig. 2.14b). Use $A$36 steel, $L J$ series. Assume a dead load of 50 psf and a live
load of 80 psf. Neglect the change in dead load as the joist spacing changes.

**2.5**   Compare the floor structure in Fig. 2.14c, where the joists are spaced at 5 ft and
span the long direction, with the case where the joists span the short direction and
are also 5 ft apart (e.g., Fig. 2.14a and b). Use the same gravity loading as for Problem 2.4. Which of the two framing systems is the lighter one? Select $LJ$–joists and
beam sizes.

**2.6**   Derive the equivalent uniform loads for the short beam as well as the long beam due
to the uniform loads $w$ on a two-way slab (Fig. 2.12b). Do not include the weight
of the beam.

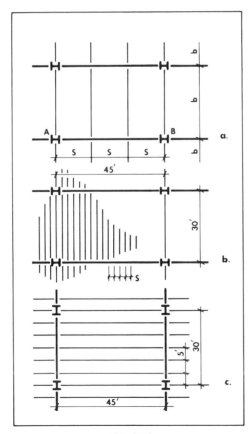

Fig. 2.14

## Structure Systems in Residential Construction

Among the earliest European methods of house construction were the polebeam, the braced pole and the log cabin in timber, as well as the stone wall structure. In the Middle Ages the timber-framed (Fachwerk) houses developed in central Europe with each region establishing its own style of framing pattern. Many of these houses are quite beautiful and seem to convey such a romantic notion and idyllic atmosphere.

The common structure systems are introduced and compared in this section to help to develop a first understanding for the more detailed investigation of the individual systems in the following portion of the book. The structure systems are presented by using residential construction as example. As small-scale buildings, they are often not engineered, or only partially so and may be designed empirically according to the accepted practice of conventional framing techniques.

Since the spatial requirements of homes are clearly defined and rather standardized in the housing field, the bearing wall principle is most frequently used, because the walls not only carry the loads, but also act as partitions between the various spaces. The bearing walls may be concrete, masonry (brick, concrete block, stone), metal/wood stud walls, or any combination. In the United States, most low-rise homes employ light-frame wood construction as based on platform framing, where the joist floors extend to the outside of the exterior building walls and provide a platform upon which the one-story high stud walls are placed. The traditional balloon framing is still to be found in use for split-level houses, where the floor joists are nailed directly to the sides of the wall studs which are continuous over the full building height. It is customary to space the studs of bearing walls (normally 2 × 4's) at 16 in. on center.

Nearly all of the cases in Fig. 2.15 are custom designs and not typical examples for home construction, however, they do exemplify the organization of structure systems. Some of the structural concepts like the bearing wall and modular box systems are typical for the housing field and are not dealt with any further since the emphasis in this book is on more open-ended, multipurpose, and long-span building types.

The various arrangements of the bearing walls in Fig. 2.15 express distinctly different features. The wall may form a protective boxlike enclosure such as the building (a) appears to be. The walls may be arranged in a parallel manner and be tied together by the roof platforms (b), thus creating linear, open-ended tubular spaces which seem to draw nature into the building. Quite in contrast to this is the geometrical, more organic wall pattern of (c), which resembles the continuous meandering flow similar to a river winding around islands (cores) in response to the topography.

The lightness and strength of the steel frame seems to be so perfectly expressed in Mies van der Rohe's famous Farnsworth house (d). Rather than emphasizing the beam-column principle, Mies articulated the cantilevering roof and floor planes by letting them float effortlessly between the four columns located on each of the long facades. This dynamic effect is amplified by the bare minimum amount of steel material needed for vertical support and by the glass skin between the horizontal slabs.

The modular skeleton structure of case (e) seems to be of the exact opposite spirit, and not only because of its different planar order. Here the post-beam idea articulates an organic quality of stability by letting the flow of gravity directly continue to the ground in a very static manner. The hinged timber frame is laterally braced by the solid in-fill panels.

The pole construction offers an advantage for difficult sloping sides or where the first

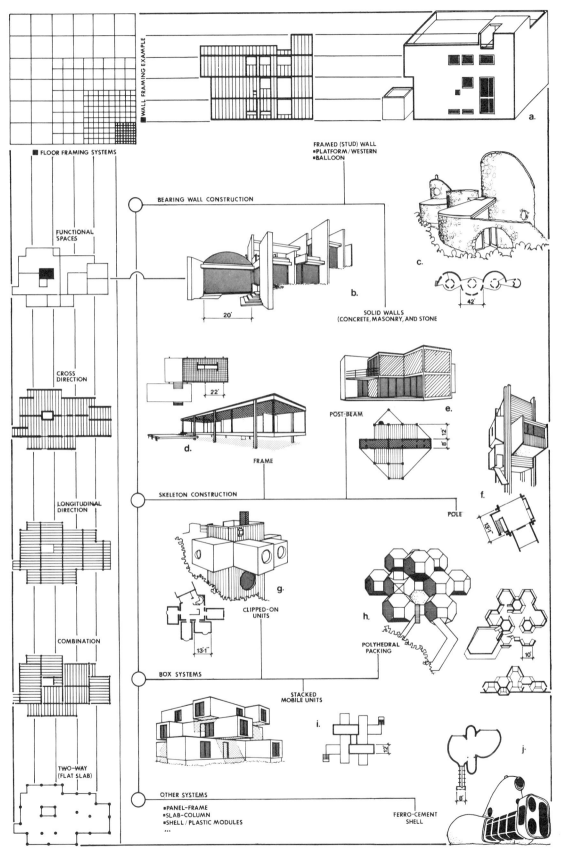

■ FLOOR FRAMING SYSTEMS

■ WALL FRAMING EXAMPLE

FUNCTIONAL SPACES

CROSS DIRECTION

LONGITUDINAL DIRECTION

COMBINATION

TWO-WAY (FLAT SLAB)

BEARING WALL CONSTRUCTION

FRAMED (STUD) WALL
■ PLATFORM / WESTERN
■ BALLOON

SOLID WALLS
(CONCRETE, MASONRY, AND STONE

a.

b.

c.

20'

42'

d.

FRAME

22'

POST-BEAM

e.

8' 12'

f.

13'-1"

SKELETON CONSTRUCTION

POLE

g.

CLIPPED-ON UNITS

h.

POLYHEDRAL PACKING

10'

13'-1"

BOX SYSTEMS

STACKED MOBILE UNITS

i.

12'

j.

OTHER SYSTEMS
■ PANEL-FRAME
■ SLAB-COLUMN
■ SHELL / PLASTIC MODULES
...

FERRO-CEMENT SHELL

8'

Fig. 2.15  Structure systems in residential construction.

floor must be raised because of flooding or other functional requirements. The poles of the building in (f) are tied together by the floor platforms and the walls. In case (i) independent lightweight steel modules, as derived from the assembly-line procedures of the mobile-home manufacturers, are stacked in alternate directions around a central utility shaft. In case (g), the steel capsules are simply cantilevered out from the concrete core.

The structural principle of case (h) is based on stacking and clustering self, all-space filling truncated octahedra. Often space frames or paperboard structures are associated with polyhedral forms. The strength is derived from the continuous double curvature of the folded surface which allows a thin shell of a low-modulus of elasticity, such as corrugated paperboard coated on both sides with glass-reinforced polyester resin, to be used.

The ferrocement shell (j), as familiar from boat construction, consists of a 6-in. network of $\frac{3}{8}$-in. steel rods to which are applied four layers of chicken wire on each side and three layers of cement mortar.

Obviously, infinitely more composite structural geometries can be derived by combining the principles of the basic systems.

## 2.3  THE LATERAL FORCE RESISTING STRUCTURE

For a building to be stable, the horizontal roof and floor structures must be able to transfer the lateral forces due to wind, earthquake, moving cranes, etc., to the vertical structural planes. These vertical lateral force resisting structures may be, as identified in Fig. 2.16a, individual column elements, planar systems, or spatial core-type units. Individual members are only stable if they are fixed to the ground, and act as vertical cantilevers in resisting lateral loads. Should the columns be hinged to the base, then they must be supported by additional elements. Planar stability of a typical pin-jointed rectangular frame may be achieved by one of the following methods:

- Fixing at least one of the columns to the ground, for post-beam systems
- Using diagonal bracing (i.e., braced frames)
- Making at least one of the beam-column connections rigid (i.e., frames)
- Using infill panels for the frames or using walls (solid or stressed skin)
- Using a combination of any of the above methods

Some vertical support structures only carry gravity loads. They are not stable by themselves, but are prevented from collapsing because of stable elements elsewhere in the building (Fig. 2.16b).

As the lateral wind forces strike the building facade, the curtain panels are assumed to act similar to one-way slabs arranged vertically. They transfer the loads to the foundations and the roof level, from where, in turn, they are distributed to the lateral force-resisting structural systems. The force flow or force distribution depends on the location of the lateral force-carrying structures and the rigidity of the roof and floor structures. Possible locations of the vertical stable structures are shown in Fig. 2.16b. The horizontal roof framing is trussed to indicate its ability to act as a horizontal beam and to transfer the lateral forces.

In the case where the vertical bents are relatively close to each other and each one resists the lateral forces in its own plane, the load distribution is just a function of the
tributary facade area, since the edge beams carry the forces directly to the vertical bents;
the roof framing is primarily a gravity supporting structure. When the lateral force-
resisting elements are spaced rather far apart, the whole roof framing system must act as a
large girder to resist lateral deformation, and to transmit the loads to the respective vertical stable bents.

The behavior of the roof under lateral loading depends on its structure. Trussed roof
framing and concrete slabs are relatively rigid in comparison with some of the thin skin
constructions, which are quite flexible. In the flexible skin-framed structures the roof
sheathing or decking acts as a diaphragm, when properly fastened with shear connectors
to the purlins and perimeter members so that shear can be transferred. A diaphragm can
be visualized as the thin web of the large roof girder, mentioned above, primarily resisting
shear, while the boundary members (edge beams or walls) perpendicular to the load
action act as the girder flanges by carrying the moments in axial action. A typical flexible
diaphragm action is shown in Fig. 2.17. The roof skin transfers the shear to the vertical
braced frames. The maximum shear the roof web must carry is

$$V = \frac{pS}{2}$$

The maximum moment is resisted by the longitudinal edge members in compression and
tension

$$M_{\max} = \frac{pS^2}{8} = N_T(L) = N_C(L)$$

Hence, the boundary members must carry the following axial compression and tension
forces, respectively,

$$N_T = N_C = \frac{pS^2}{8L}$$

Obviously, the mathematical interpretation of the roof behavior under lateral loads is
an oversimplification, since the degree of flexibility or rigidity is highly indeterminate.

To stiffen the roof structure, bracing may be provided. In addition, true truss action
may be necessary for the distribution of the loads to the respective bents. Bracing effectively resists the racking of the roof especially under lateral loads from a direction other
than parallel or perpendicular to the building, that is, torsional stiffness for the roof plane
must be provided. Bracing may also be needed during the construction stage. It consists,
generally, of single steel angles or rods capable of acting in tension only, although they
will carry compression if they are prestressed. They are usually arranged in crossing pairs
so that if racking puts one of the elements into compression (which it is incapable of resisting), its complement will resist the racking by being placed in tension. In the case of
deep roof beams, the bracing may be located along the upper or lower chord planes, or
the planes may be linked, forming a kind of space truss. Bracing may also be necessary to
prevent the lateral buckling of the entire roof plane and to keep the filler beams in place

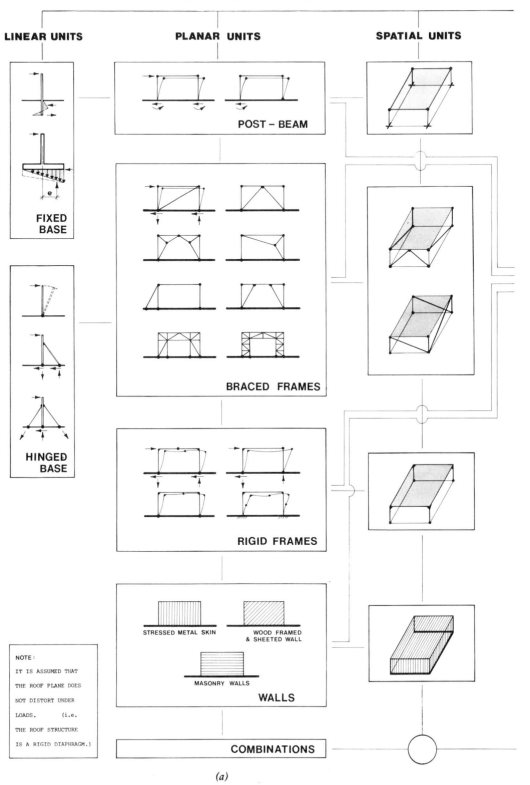

(a)

Fig. 2.16 Stability of basic vertical structural building units.

**SYMMETRICAL ARRANGEMENT**

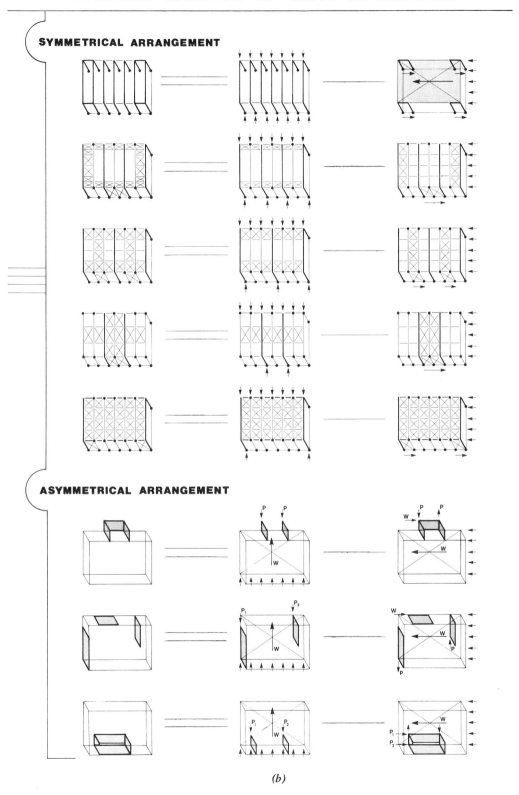

**ASYMMETRICAL ARRANGEMENT**

(b)

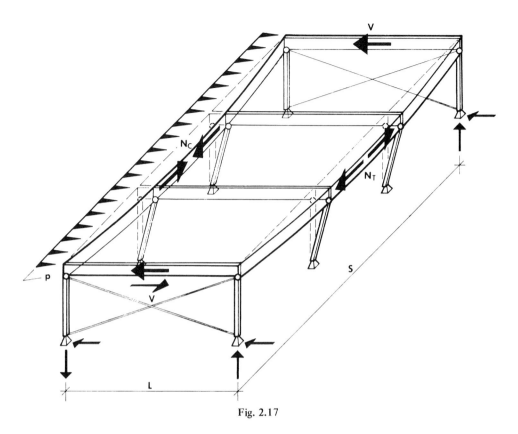

Fig. 2.17

so they give the proper lateral support to the compression flange when the major beam bends (Fig. 2.18).

The specific arrangement of the bracing depends on the position of the lateral force resisting elements, the required stiffness of the roof structure, and the magnitude of the force flow. Various layouts of trusses as function of their supporting bents are shown in Fig. 2.16b. The reader can easily follow the flow of forces from roof level to foundations as caused by lateral loading along the major building axes.

The lateral force-resisting structures may be arranged in a symmetrical or asymmetrical manner (Fig. 2.16b). For the symmetrical case, they will only carry direct forces as caused by translation. For the asymmetrical case, additional forces due to rotation (torsion) are generated. In the following discussion, the magnitude of the loads that the lateral force-resisting elements carry is investigated. First, only symmetrical cases are studied.

For closely spaced, parallel, stable vertical support structures, the lateral load distribution is known, being just a function of the tributary facade area. However, the load distribution is quite indeterminate if the rigid bents or shear walls are spaced rather far apart, since now the force distribution depends on the rigidities of the roof diaphragm and the supporting structure. Though there is no such thing as an infinitely rigid or flexible diaphragm, the concepts are still useful for developing some understanding about lateral force flow. Concrete slabs and some types of steel deck are considered to be rigid diaphragms which are assumed to distribute the horizontal forces to the vertical supporting structures in proportion to their relative rigidity $R$ for shear walls or their relative stiffness

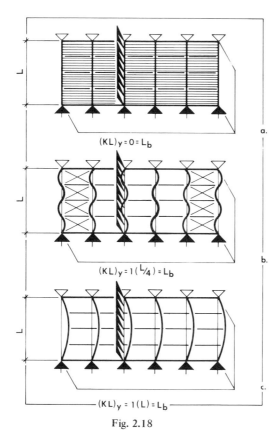

$(KL)_y = 0 = L_b$

a.

$(KL)_y = 1(^L/_4) = L_b$

b.

$(KL)_y = 1(L) = L_b$

c.

Fig. 2.18

$k$ for frames. These concepts of rigidity–flexibility are further discussed and developed in Chapter 4, Stiffness Considerations.

For a building with four equally stiff shear walls (or equivalent frames) each wall carries the same force (Fig. 2.19a). In case b, the interior walls only provide one-half the rigidity of the exterior walls (i.e., the wall thickness is the same, but the interior walls have only one-half the length). In this case the total wind pressure must be distributed in proportion to the wall rigidities. The total rigidity is

$$\Sigma R = 2\left(R + \frac{R}{2}\right) = 3R$$

Hence each of the exterior walls carries $120(R/3R) = 40$ k, or one-third of the total load, while each of the interior walls resists $120(0.5R/3R) = 20$ k, or one-sixth of the total load.

Roofs with diagonal wood or plywood sheathing, or with some types of steel deck, are considered to be flexible diaphragms. They are so much more flexible in comparison to the lateral force-supporting systems that the supporting structures are considered to be rigid. The behavior of the flexible diaphragm may be visualized as simply supported, discontinuous deep beams sitting on unyielding supports. Thus, the loads can be distributed as based on the tributary area. For the case in Fig. 2.19c, note that the smaller interior walls carry double the force as the longer exterior walls, because their tributary areas are

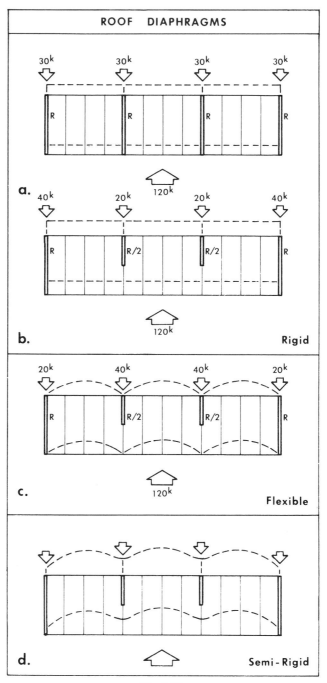

Fig. 2.19

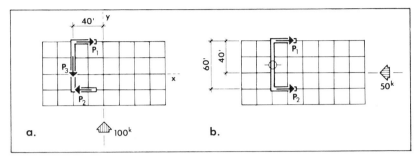

Fig. 2.20

twice as large as the ones for the exterior walls; the capacity of the walls is not considered since they are assumed infinitely rigid.

The behavior of semiflexible or semirigid diaphragms is highly indeterminate. They are assumed to distribute the loads like a continuous beam, supported on flexible supports (Fig. 2.19d). Should flexible diaphragm roofs be used on irregular plans such as L or T shapes, then the plan must be subdivided into rectangular diaphragms by introducing proper boundary members called drag struts. These drag struts control the incompatibility of stresses and deflections along the intersection of the rectangular plan units.

If the lateral force-resisting structures are arranged in an asymmetrical fashion [Fig. 2.16b (bottom)], then in addition to translation (i.e., direct shear), rotation (i.e., torsional shear) is generated.

The solution for the distribution of the lateral forces to the asymmetrically arranged shear walls can be approached by distinguishing between determinate and indeterminate systems as based on the following simplifying assumptions.

- Consider the roof as a rigid diaphragm. Flexible diaphragms are considered incapable of transmitting rotational forces.
- Neglect the bending stiffness of the walls about their weak axis.
- Consider intersecting walls as separate units. There is no shear flow around the corners.
- Consider the shear forces along the wall to be constant.
- Neglect the effect of columns in resisting lateral forces.

Hence, according to these assumptions, as based on statics, a minimum of three shear walls or other types of lateral force-resisting planar systems is necessary to stabilize a building against force action from any direction; the arrangement of the walls should neither be parallel nor concurrent according to the laws of statics.

The analysis of buildings stabilized by three shear walls is determinate. For the condition shown in (Fig. 2.20a and b) a total wind force of 100 k acting perpendicular to the long facade of the building in Fig. 2.20a. must be resisted by the forces $P_1$, $P_2$, and $P_3$. Remember that the wall assemblage is not considered as a single channel-shaped unit but as three individual, independent elements.

Taking moments about the intersection of the unknown forces $P_1$ and $P_3$ yields the unknown wall force $P_2$

$$\Sigma M = 0 = 100(40) - P_2(60), \quad P_2 = 66.67 \text{ k}$$

Equilibrium in the $x$ direction results in

$$\Sigma F_x = 0 = 66.67 - P_1, \qquad P_1 = 66.67 \text{ k}$$

Equilibrium in the $y$ direction results in

$$\Sigma F_y = 0 = P_3 - 100, \qquad P_3 = 100 \text{ k}$$

For the case where the lateral force resultant of 50 k acts perpendicular to the short facade (Fig. 2.20b), the force $P_3$ along the long core wall is zero, because

$$\Sigma F_y = 0 = P_3$$

Rotational equilibrium about force $P_1$ yields

$$\Sigma M = 50(40) - P_2(60), \qquad P_2 = 33.33 \text{ k}$$

Equilibrium in the $x$ direction results in:

$$\Sigma F_x = 0 = 33.33 + P_1 - 50, \qquad P_1 = 16.67 \text{ k}$$

For the condition of more than three shear walls which are neither parallel nor concurrent, the analysis is indeterminate; hence, additional information must be obtained.

But first, the special cases of tubular cores with circular and square cross-sections are investigated (Fig. 2.21). The resultant total lateral force due to the wind pressure acts at the center of the facade, or the resultant seismic force acts through the center of the building mass. Since the load center does not coincide with the center of rigidity, that is, the location of the resultant force resisting structure, then in addition to translation, rotation is generated. This torsion about the core is clearly expressed in Fig. 2.21! Again, when the special conditions of symmetry do not exist, besides mere translational movement, torsion is created. The eccentric core in Fig. 2.21 must support a translational force of 100 k and a moment of 100(60) = 6000 ft-k.

Only for the circular core (Fig. 2.21c) are the torsional stresses uniform, assuming the core not to be weakened by openings so that it can be considered a truly closed unit. The torsional shear capacity is equal to the unit shear stress $f_{vt}$ multiplied by the cross-sectional wall area $A = (2\pi R)t$.

$$\Sigma F = f_{vt} A = f_{vt} (2\pi R)t$$

The moment is equal to the forces acting tangentially along the core.

$$M = \Sigma FR = f_{vt}(2\pi R)Rt = f_{vt}(2\pi R^2)t \tag{a}$$

Or, expressed in terms of torsional shear stress

$$f_{vt} = \frac{M}{2\pi R^2 t} = \frac{M}{RA} \tag{b}$$

The direct shear stress is not constant as the torsional one, but it can be shown that for practical purposes, where the walls are thin in comparison to the core diameter, its maximum value at the neutral axis is twice the mean value. Thus the combined stresses due to translational and rotational shear must be less than the allowable shear stress $F_v$.

$$f_{v\,\text{max}} = \frac{2P}{A} + \frac{M}{RA} \leqslant F_v \tag{2.1}$$

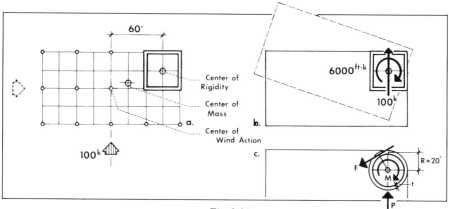

Fig. 2.21

Or, expressed as the maximum shear force per unit length of wall,

$$F = f_{v\ max}(A) = f_{v\ max}(t \times 1) = \frac{2P + M/R}{2\pi R} \tag{2.2}$$

For the given example (Fig. 2.21) the maximum shear force is about

$$F_{max} = \frac{2(100) + 6000/20}{2\pi(20)} = 3.98 \text{ k/ft}$$

In the square, tubular core the torsional forces are not constant, this being true only for the circular core. For this condition the simplifying assumptions for asymmetrically arranged shear walls can be applied again. The core seems to be an indeterminate structure since there are four unknown wall forces but only three static equilibrium equations. In this specific case, however, the solution is determinate according to the previous assumptions because the walls are of equal length and thickness, and are arranged to form a square tube. The symmetry of the tube provides the additional information of equal force resistance against torsion. The direct force of 100 k is equally shared by the walls parallel to the force action (Fig. 2.22a), while the moment is resisted by the two parallel wall systems (Fig. 2.22b) which each provide a force couple

$$6000 = 2(P)40$$

Hence, the forces in the walls due to torsion are:

$$P = \frac{6000}{2(40)} = 75 \text{ k}$$

The same result is obtained by taking moments about any of the wall intersection points.

$$\Sigma M = 6000 - P(40) - P(40) = 0, \quad P = 75 \text{ k}$$

The largest force acts along the wall for which the forces due to translation and rotation add in superimposition (Fig. 2.22c)

$$P_{max} = 50 + 75 = 125 \text{ k}$$

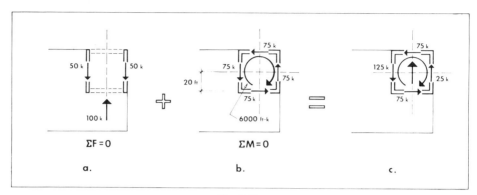

Fig. 2.22

However, should the core not be square but rectangular (Fig. 2.23), then further information with respect to the distribution of the torsion is required. It may be assumed that the
torsional shear stress distribution along a thin walled tube is constant, hence the wall
forces for equally thick walls of the same material can be considered proportional to the
wall lengths

$$\frac{P_L}{80} = \frac{P_S}{40} \quad \text{or} \quad P_S = \frac{P_L}{2}$$

Now the forces in the walls due to rotation can be found. The moment is resisted by the
wall couples:

$$6000 = 0.5\, P_L\, (80) + P_L\, (40)$$

$$P_L = 75 \text{ k}$$

$$P_S = 0.5\, P_L = 37.5 \text{ k}$$

The largest force due to translation and rotation is still equal to

$$P_{max} = 50 + 75 = 125 \text{ k}$$

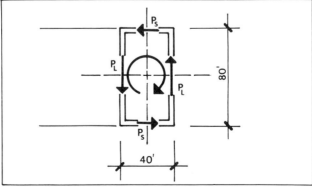

Fig. 2.23

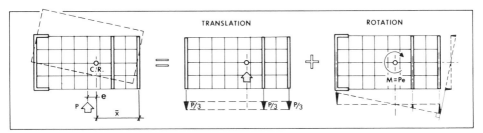

**Fig. 2.24**

For the general condition of an asymmetrical arrangement of more than three shear walls, the location of the center of rigidity is not known and must first be found. Also, the term of shear center is often being used; it describes quite well the fact that a resultant force acting through it does not generate torsion (see also center portion of Fig. 1.15). The magnitude of the torsional forces in the walls can be assumed proportional to their distance from the shear center (i.e., center of rigidity in Fig. 2.24) taking into account the relative wall rigidities, which in this case are for low-rise buildings assumed to be controlled by shear rather than flexure. These assumptions may be used for approximation purposes; they are based on perfect, rigid diaphragm action.

The centroid of rigidity for the building in Fig. 2.24 can be found by taking moments with the wall areas, say about the centroidal axis of the right wall $A_3$ assuming that all the walls have the same strength (i.e., same material)

$$A_{total}(\bar{x}) = A_1(8) + A_2(2)$$

where

$$A_{total} = A_1 + A_2 + A_3$$

Since the wall areas for this specific case are all the same, $A_1 = A_2 = A_3 = A$, the equation above reduces to the simple expression: $3A(\bar{x}) = A(8) + A(2)$, or

$$3\bar{x} = 8 + 2$$

or

$$\bar{x} = 3.33 \text{ units}$$

Or the eccentricity $e$ is equal to $e = 4 - 3.33 = 0.67$ units. Now enough information is available to determine the forces each wall must resist as caused by translation and rotation.

Once the magnitude of the lateral forces for each shear wall component is known, the walls or frames must be checked for stability by taking into account sufficient reserve strength. Codes usually require the lateral force-resisting structures to have a capacity against overturning and sliding of at least 50% larger than the lateral force action.

The lateral force $P$ (Fig. 2.25a) causes the structure to rotate about the edge on the leeward side at the horizontal plane under consideration: $M_{act} = Ph$. This overturning moment is resisted by the weight $W$ of the lateral force-resisting structure above the level under investigation as well as the capacity of the material and the anchorage establishing the continuity with the structure below. Considering conservatively that only the weight

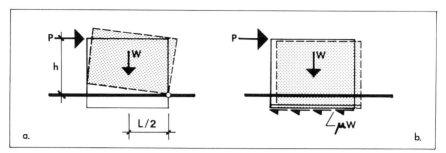

Fig. 2.25

counteracts, results in the following reacting moment: $M_{\text{react}} = W(L/2)$. The ratio of the reacting moment to the acting moment should be at least equal to 1.5

$$\text{SF} = \frac{M_{\text{react}}}{M_{\text{act}}} = \frac{W(L/2)}{Ph} \geqslant 1.5 \qquad (2.3)$$

The lateral forces also tend to slide the building horizontally (Fig. 2.25b). This translational movement is resisted by the friction between the surfaces as well as by the shear capacity of the anchors and possibly by the passive soil pressure. The frictional resistance, say between foundations and soil, is a function of the weight of the structure and the coefficient of friction $\mu$. Considering only this friction to resist the lateral force action, then the ratio of the potential lateral resistance to the lateral force action should be at least 1.5

$$\text{SF} = \frac{\mu W}{P} \geqslant 1.5 \qquad (2.4)$$

The reader may refer to Example 1.4 for application of the principles of stability to an actual building.

Codes also require checking roofs, especially with slopes less than $20°$, for wind suction. The uplift due to wind (or hydrostatic head) must be resisted by the dead load acting directly as well as through anchors; these combined resisting forces shall be not less than 1.25 times the uplift force.

## Problems

2.7  Determine the approximate magnitude of the forces the shear walls in Fig. 2.26 cases a–f, must resist. Assume a constant wind pressure of 20 psf to act against the 25 ft high facade walls. First evaluate the wall reactions to the wind action parallel to the short direction of the building and then the reactions to the wind action parallel to the long side. The square grid in Fig. 2.26 represents a dimensional network of 25 × 25 ft. Assume rigid diaphragm action and neglect the columns in resisting any lateral forces. The wall thicknesses are constant. Consider the curtain to carry one-half of the pressure to the roof plane.

2.8  Determine the approximate magnitude of the forces in the shear walls of cases a and c in Fig. 2.26 assuming flexible roof diaphragm action. The loading is the same as for Problem 2.7.

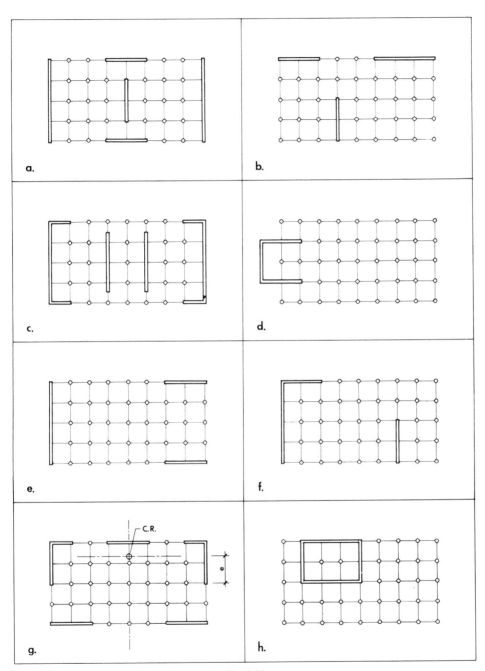

Fig. 2.26

**2.9**   Determine the magnitude of the additional shear forces in the cross walls at the roof level due to torsion using the 5% minimum eccentricity (UBC) for the building in Example 1.4.

**2.10**  Consider the roof diaphragm of the building in Example 1.4 to be flexible. Determine the axial chord forces due to bending of the roof and cover the tension in the masonry walls with reinforcing bars ($F_t$ = 20 ksi). Think about the connection of the roof plane to the walls.

**2.11**  Determine the approximate magnitude of the forces the walls in case (d) Fig. 2.26 would have to resist if the core is closed and forms a square tube. For further information refer to Problem 2.7. Also find the maximum shear stresses for the 8-in. thick walls.

**2.12**  Replace the square tube in Problem 2.11 with a circular one of the same diameter. Determine the approximate magnitude of the critical shear stresses in the 8-in. walls.

**2.13**  Determine the approximate magnitude of the forces along the walls of case (h), Fig. 2.26. For the loading conditions refer to Problem 2.7.

**2.14**  Investigate case (g) of Fig. 2.26 for the same loading conditions as in Problem 2.7. Consider only the wall resistance parallel to the force action.

**2.15**  Investigate case (g) of Fig. 2.26, but without considering the front facade walls.


## 2.4   THE BUILDING JOINT

The traditional methods of construction are being replaced more and more by automated operations which includes the assembly of prefabricated components that place increasing importance on building joints and jointing. At the junction of every building component occurs a joint (disregarding the joints within the prefinished components). The joint type is dependent on the location and position of the adjacent members. The components may be closely fitted or a gap may be left between them deliberately. This gap may have to be sealed by familiar materials such as bedding, caulking and glazing compounds, putties, mastics, or gaskets. The members at a joint may either stay clear of each other or they may be interlocked in some fashion. Similarly on a large scale, joints may separate or partially separate (i.e., allowing certain movements) entire building blocks that have different mass and stiffness characteristics; here the joints are usually formed between double members (e.g., beams and columns) or at the ends of cantilevered members. A joint may have to satisfy any of the following performance requirements: *environmental control:* sealing (moisture, wind, dirt, sound, insects, etc.); *dimensional control* (component and construction tolerances); *functional control* (maintenance, replacement, etc.); *movement control* (sliding, rotation, etc.); *structural control* (for load bearing connections see Section 1.3).

The joints may be designed as so-called "open joints" to allow for more movement and less precision in the fitting of members (i.e., larger dimensional tolerances). In closed joints the gap between the components is simply closed by a weatherproofing seal of mastics or gaskets. Whatever the joint type, the width of the joint and the sealant must respond to the performance criteria; the sealants must be sufficiently elastic to permit the movement between the elements.

It is not the purpose of this discussion to study and classify the seemingly endless number of joint systems that have been established by the various traditional building trades or that are developing presently from the new technologies, nor to teach joint detailing, but rather to concentrate on expansion joints and to examine the sources and nature of movement for the building components as exemplified by the examples in Fig. 2.27. For the discussion on the structural performance of joints the reader may refer to the section on connections in Chapter 1.4.

The principal causes for the movement of individual components or entire building sections are *changes in material volume, earth settlement,* and *direct force action.* Whatever the source is for the displacement of the members, if they should be held back from free movement additional forces will be induced into the component itself as well as the adjacent members preventing the free deformation.

### Changes in Material Volume (Fig. 2.27, Part 4)

As has been discussed in Section 1.2 (Table 1.3), all materials more or less expand or contract as a result of a change in temperature. Some materials, such as brick and timber, swell and shrink with variations in moisture content. Other materials, like concrete and concrete masonry, go through the chemical process of drying shrinkage as caused by air-drying during the early months of construction. The same materials also creep and shorten under sustained loading.

One should keep in mind that the building dimensions are based on the particular temperature and humidity during the erection stage and possibly the moisture content of the component, as for timber. The exterior skin of buildings is in direct contact with the weather and therefore must react to any changes in temperature and humidity. Allowance for the differential movement between the curtain/panels/windows and supporting structure must be made. Should the structure be exposed along the facade or the exterior skin be poorly insulated, then differential movements with respect to the interior members, which stay within a relatively controlled environment, are generated; in other words, exterior walls or frames move differently than the interior structures. But, even the exterior structure does not displace evenly since the south side walls and roofs are subject to larger temperature differentials than the shaded building parts. As a result of higher temperature variations in the upper building portion, intermediate expansion joints may have to be placed there (1g).

Proper joints must be provided between the different materials that comprise the facade and have dissimilar expansion features [(4a), (4e)] as well as at offsets and wall junctions of long masonry walls.

It has been shown in Eq. (1.2) that the amount of displacement of a linear element increases directly with the length. For instance, the long masonry wall [(4c), (4d)] tends to contract due to thermal and moisture changes as well as movement of the roof, but is restrained from doing so at its base by the frictional resistance along the contact surface with the foundation which does not have to face temperature and humidity fluctuations. Tensile stresses will gradually build up in the wall and may cause cracks to relieve the stresses. To absorb some of the horizontal movement, vertical expansion joints must be provided to reduce the wall length and thus to keep the stresses within their allowable limits (see Problem 1.6).

Similarly, horizontal expansion joints control vertical movement, for example under shelf angles, which may be attached to a concrete spandrel beam and support a masonry

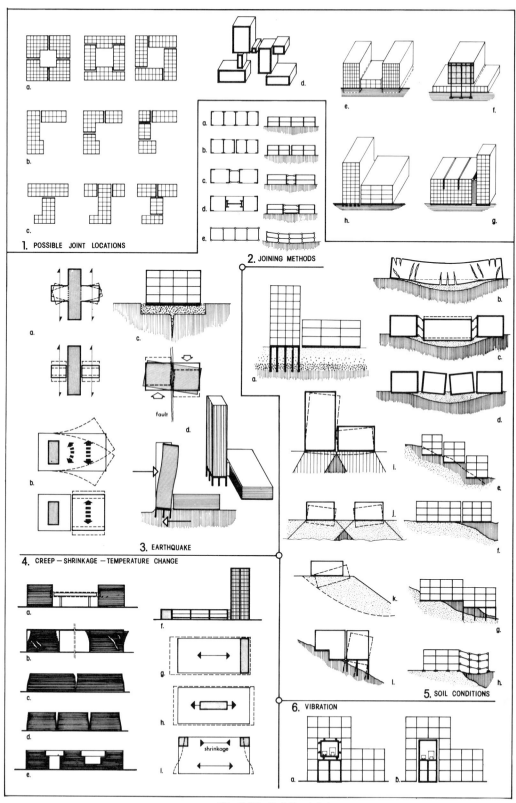

1. POSSIBLE JOINT LOCATIONS

2. JOINING METHODS

3. EARTHQUAKE

4. CREEP — SHRINKAGE — TEMPERATURE CHANGE

5. SOIL CONDITIONS

6. VIBRATION

fault

shrinkage

Fig. 2.27 Building joints.

curtain wall. Here the expansion of the curtain wall due to temperature and moisture in-crease as well as the contraction of the concrete frame as caused by its elastic response to loading, creep, and possibly shrinkage must be superimposed.

In concrete or concrete masonry walls, *control joints* with reduced restraints may be provided to control the location of cracking due to the drying shrinkage during the first months. Concrete roof slabs are very vulnerable to excessive movement, especially when poorly insulated or when the insulation is on the inside. The length of the slab should be limited and slip planes provided between the slab and supporting vertical structure, other-wise free horizontal movement is prevented and lateral deflection is generated in the verti-cal structure which is particularly critical for stiff masonry walls with their low modulus of elasticity.

Considering the extraordinary situation of a fire, the expansion of large floor areas may become particularly critical, and wider or an increased number of expansion joints or fire barriers may have to be introduced.

Should the lateral forces on a building not be resisted in a uniform manner, but by concentrated stiff core structures, then the location of the core within the building is an important consideration [(4g), (4h), (4l)] .

Uniform lateral displacement occurs for the condition where the core is symmetrically arranged at the center of the building (h), while only one-directional movement will appear when the core is located eccentrically at the outer end (g). This lateral deflection may cause large stresses in the facade masonry curtain if not taken into account and properly controlled.

During construction the entire building is exposed and vulnerable to temperature changes. This is especially true for long-span roof structures, when the erection of the roof members takes a long time and goes through different seasons. For this condition, temporary joints may be required to equalize temperature effects.


### Earth Settlements (Fig. 2.27, Part 5)

Earth settlements can be caused by soil consolidation, shear failure of soil, change of groundwater table (e.g., sinkhole), shrinkage and swelling (e.g., clay), collapse (failure of sewer, mine, cave, etc.), expansion (frost depth), landslides [unstable slopes(k)] , chemical attacks, and by many other factors.

A long flat building with uniformly distributed loads sitting on compressible soils deflects in a concave manner (b), while it may respond in a convex form if the primary support structures and foundations are placed eccentrically. It will be advantageous to subdivide the long building, including foundations, into small blocks separated by expan-sion joints or hinged bays (b), (c).

Differential settlements are also generated when the same building block sits on differ-ent soils (f), on sloping sites (e), (g), or is unevenly loaded (j) and, in addition, uses dif-ferent foundation types. On sloping sites the tendency of the upper soil layers to slide downward, as initiated by the building weight, may be avoided by anchoring the outer building unit with deep foundations to the lower soil strata (l). Tall, slender buildings tend to tilt under differential settlement (i), as for example, when the ground below is unevenly loaded by an adjacent building. The effect of settlements can be reduced by re-placing the indeterminate stiffer continuous structure with the determinate more flexible hinged structure (h).

The examples in Fig. 2.27, part 5 show how the joints control the settlement movement so that potential stresses are reduced to a minimum.

### Displacements Due to Direct Force Action

Each structural element in a building may bend and deform axially under force action. The horizontal floor framing deflects vertically under gravity loading while the vertical structural building planes sway laterally under wind and seismic action. The recent development of increased strength of the major structural materials has resulted in a decrease of rigidity and hence an increase of member deflection.

The dead loading causes a permanently deformed state to the structural members if they are not cambered as in the case of beams. When nonstructural systems like partitions or cladding are placed beneath beams, enough clearance space must be chosen so that during future live load deflections the beams are not touching these components and imposing loads upon them which may cause the material to crack. Similar reasoning may be applied to the rather stiff plaster ceilings, which may form cracks when the beams to which they are directly attached are too flexible. Special care must be taken in handling the large deflections of cantilevers as well as the considerable extensions of cable structures.

On the larger scale of entire building blocks, stiffer units deflect less than flexible ones employing different structure systems. The same situation of differential movement occurs between building sections of dissimilar mass distribution, slenderness, and load distribution as visually expressed by the various geometrical structural patterns in (1d)–(1g), as based on the same material strength. The differential vertical, horizontal, and rotational movements between the building units should be controlled by joints so the building blocks are separated and can behave independently; keep in mind that each unit has its own structure or otherwise adjacent units must support each other, which in turn requires special structural joints (2d).

Similar reasoning can be applied from a visual point of view where the nonalignment of the structural grids requires some type of rigid or flexible transition system. Some of the possible joining methods are identified in (2a)–(e). They range from a continuous structure (a), the structure with only one joint at midlength (b), to the structure with a soft, hinged bay that acts as a large scale joint (c), (d), and finally the flexible hinged structure capable of adjusting to any differential motion.

Vibrational movements as caused by oscillating machinery, escalators, cars, and other equipment should be isolated either by separating the structure that supports the source (6b) or by damping the movement with special joints so that the vibration is not transmitted to other building parts (6a). Damping devices may also be used to control the oscillations caused by gusty winds.

Seismic joints (Fig. 2.27, part 3) control the lateral building sway as initiated by the ground movement, by separating building masses so that they can behave independently. For instance the shallow wings of a building with an irregular plan shape (3a) may tend to move in different directions while the deep, and hence stiffer, central portion may hardly displace. These torsional as well as translational movements will cause large stresses at the junction of the wings to the central portion. In general, buildings with irregular configurations due to different mass or stiffness distribution should be separated as is indicated for examples (1a)–(1g).

Torsion is also generated in the regular building with an eccentric core (3b), since the center of mass (i.e., location of resultant seismic force) does not coincide with the center of rigidity. The clearance gap between the tall flexible building and the much stiffer adjacent low building (3d) must be wide enough so that they are not touching each other.

For the extraordinary condition where a building is constructed across a fault, its rupture may be prevented by tying the building together with a mat foundation and letting it float on a sand cushion (3c). This cushion is similar to a joint in that it allows the structure to rotate and possibly slide under the differential movement along the fault line.

One may conclude that whatever the main purpose of an expansion joint is, be it for the control of temperature and moisture, creep and shrinkage, settlements, seismic or dynamic loading, or any other reason, the following criteria should be considered.

- Long buildings should be subdivided into units realizing that the joints are spaced closer for stiffer than for flexible buildings.
- Buildings with compound or irregular plan shapes should be separated into units as indicated in (1a)-(1c).
- Buildings consisting of different blocks of high- and low-rise sections, each with its own structural system, should be separated at their junction.

# 3 SUSPENDED CABLE STRUCTURES

The principle of suspension as reflected in tent construction, ship sails, and suspension bridges, has been known for thousands of years. Suspension bridges can be considered the true forerunners of the present day cable structures. The Chinese Emperor Ming (65 A.D.) supposedly built a 200-ft iron chain cable bridge. Suspension bridges were quite common for a long time in China, India, Africa, and South America; vines, bamboo, hemp, birch, cane, twisted lianas, and similar materials were used for construction. The first major cable suspension bridge in the western world is credited to James Finley (Jacob's Creek Bridge, Pennsylvania, 1801). John A. Roebling is considered by many the inventor of the modern long-span suspension bridge as demonstrated by the 1595-ft Brooklyn Bridge where he employed a secondary cable system to counteract flutter. The bridge was finished in 1883 by his son Washington Roebling.

The longest suspension bridge in the world is currently England's Humber Bridge with a 4626-ft main span, 366 ft longer than New York City's Verrazano-Narrows Bridge (1964). A suspension bridge of approximately 11,000 ft span is proposed between Sicily and the Italian mainland. A high-voltage transmission line spans 16,000 ft across the Sogne Fjord in Norway.

The Russian engineer V. G. Shookhov is usually regarded as the first modern designer to apply the suspension principle to building construction for the pavilions at the All-Russian Exhibition in Nijny-Novgorod (1896). The real evolution of cable structures, however, was initiated in 1953 with Mathew Nowicki's State Fair Arena at Raleigh, North Carolina (see Chapter 9).

## 3.1 GENERAL PRINCIPLES

The cable is inherently flexible and form active, thus it can only carry tensile forces. Because of the absence of bending, buckling, and due to the high strength of cable material, the cables are rather light. A single cable must adjust its suspended form to the respective loading condition so that it can respond in tension. The cable takes familiar geometrical forms such as polygonal, parabolic, elliptical, and circular shapes (Fig. 3.1a) called funicular tension lines which are discussed in more detail in later sections. It is quite apparent

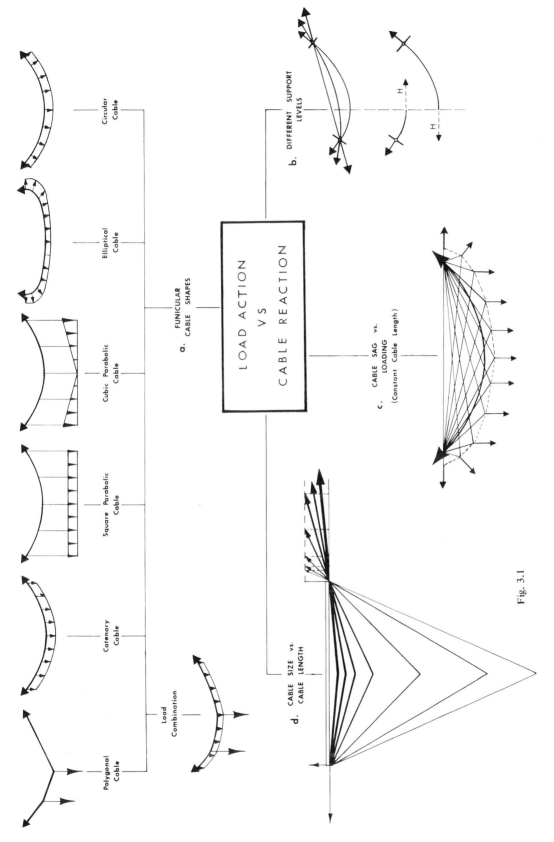

Circular Cable

Elliptical Cable

Cubic Parabolic Cable

Square Parabolic Cable

Catenary Cable

Polygonal Cable

Load Combination

**a.** FUNICULAR CABLE SHAPES

LOAD ACTION
VS
CABLE REACTION

**b.** DIFFERENT SUPPORT LEVELS

**c.** CABLE SAG vs. LOADING (Constant Cable Length)

**d.** CABLE SIZE vs. CABLE LENGTH

Fig. 3.1

from Fig. 3.1d that for constant vertical reactions the lateral thrust components increase as the cable sag decreases. Hence the cable size increases with the reduction of cable length and cable sag. However, as the cable length increases, so does its weight. It is shown in Problem 3.11 that an optimum sag-to-span ratio is considered in the range of 1/10 to 1/20 for buildings and 1/8 to 1/12 for suspension bridges. For a sag-to-span ratio larger than 0.2, high boundary support structures have to be designed which may not be economical. When the sag-to-span ratio becomes too flat, the axial cable forces are so high that elastic deformations cannot be ignored anymore. As a single load moves along a cable (Fig. 3.1c) from midspan towards the support, the sag decreases, hence the cable force and size increases. Notice that the sag is less for the cable under uniform loading.

Due to the lack of stiffness a cable roof must be stabilized against formal instability so that it does not adjust its shape every time the loads change and thus can also absorb the uplift as caused by the wind. Furthermore, the flexibility and lightness of the roof makes it vulnerable to gusty winds which tend to oscillate it requiring special stabilization so that the movement is dampened, as will be discussed later in this chapter.

Various methods for stabilizing a cable roof against formal instability, but not necessarily against dynamic force action so that the roof may be assumed to behave statically for preliminary design purposes, are shown in Fig. 3.2. They are:

1  Dead weight sitting on top or suspended below the roof, where the permanent dead load should be substantially larger than the asymmetrical live loads to prevent asymmetrical deformations.

2  Rigid members acting as beams/arches that provide stiffness.

3  Rigid surfaces behaving as inverted shells/vaults; they may be prestressed by preloading the cables.

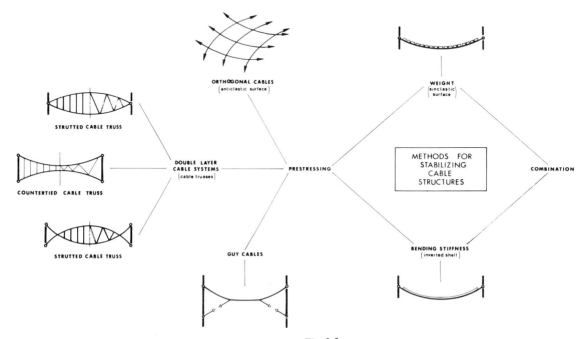

Fig. 3.2

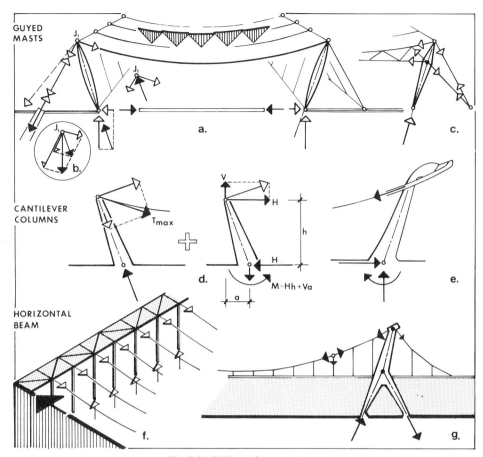

**Fig. 3.3** Cable anchorage systems.

4 Secondary cables prestressing the main cables so that the cables always remain in tension.

    (a)    The secondary cable is placed perpendicular/diagonally to the primary cable to form an anticlastic net surface.

    (b)    The secondary cable is in plane with the main cable to form cable trusses; this principle can be extended to spatial tensegrity structures.

    (c)    The main cable is guyed to other structures.

Cable roofs not only challenge the designer with respect to their flexible and lightweight character but also with respect to the problem of anchoring the tension forces to the bearing boundaries. Some typical solutions for suspended cables arranged in a parallel fashion are shown in Fig. 3.3. They are:

- Guyed masts (a), (c)
- Cantilever columns (d), (e), legged columns (g), A-frames, towers, or other boundary structures responding in bending
- Vertical columns together with horizontal edge beams which must be laterally supported (e), (f)

- Inclined, vertical cylindrically curved walls
- Form responsive boundary shapes

By inclining the guyed masts (a), the magnitude of the forces in the columns and the diagonal guys is reduced (b) which is especially important because the tensile forces that the ground anchors must resist are decreased. When the pendulum-type columns are placed vertically, they do not resist any lateral thrust and leave this entirely to the guy cables requiring, in turn, an extensive tensile foundation (see Fig. 9.4). Further, the magnitude of the tension in the guys decreases by making them less steep.

For the case where no diagonal guys are used the columns must act as a vertical can-

### Table 3.1  Steel Cable Properties

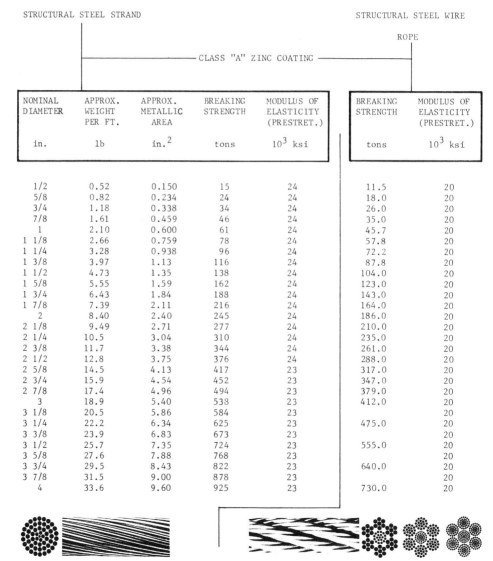

| STRUCTURAL STEEL STRAND | | | | | STRUCTURAL STEEL WIRE ROPE | |
|---|---|---|---|---|---|---|
| CLASS "A" ZINC COATING | | | | | | |
| NOMINAL DIAMETER | APPROX. WEIGHT PER FT. | APPROX. METALLIC AREA | BREAKING STRENGTH | MODULUS OF ELASTICITY (PRESTRET.) | BREAKING STRENGTH | MODULUS OF ELASTICITY (PRESTRET.) |
| in. | lb | in.$^2$ | tons | $10^3$ ksi | tons | $10^3$ ksi |
| 1/2 | 0.52 | 0.150 | 15 | 24 | 11.5 | 20 |
| 5/8 | 0.82 | 0.234 | 24 | 24 | 18.0 | 20 |
| 3/4 | 1.18 | 0.338 | 34 | 24 | 26.0 | 20 |
| 7/8 | 1.61 | 0.459 | 46 | 24 | 35.0 | 20 |
| 1 | 2.10 | 0.600 | 61 | 24 | 45.7 | 20 |
| 1 1/8 | 2.66 | 0.759 | 78 | 24 | 57.8 | 20 |
| 1 1/4 | 3.28 | 0.938 | 96 | 24 | 72.2 | 20 |
| 1 3/8 | 3.97 | 1.13 | 116 | 24 | 87.8 | 20 |
| 1 1/2 | 4.73 | 1.35 | 138 | 24 | 104.0 | 20 |
| 1 5/8 | 5.55 | 1.59 | 162 | 24 | 123.0 | 20 |
| 1 3/4 | 6.43 | 1.84 | 188 | 24 | 143.0 | 20 |
| 1 7/8 | 7.39 | 2.11 | 216 | 24 | 164.0 | 20 |
| 2 | 8.40 | 2.40 | 245 | 24 | 186.0 | 20 |
| 2 1/8 | 9.49 | 2.71 | 277 | 24 | 210.0 | 20 |
| 2 1/4 | 10.5 | 3.04 | 310 | 24 | 235.0 | 20 |
| 2 3/8 | 11.7 | 3.38 | 344 | 24 | 261.0 | 20 |
| 2 1/2 | 12.8 | 3.75 | 376 | 24 | 288.0 | 20 |
| 2 5/8 | 14.5 | 4.13 | 417 | 23 | 317.0 | 20 |
| 2 3/4 | 15.9 | 4.54 | 452 | 23 | 347.0 | 20 |
| 2 7/8 | 17.4 | 4.96 | 494 | 23 | 379.0 | 20 |
| 3 | 18.9 | 5.40 | 538 | 23 | 412.0 | 20 |
| 3 1/8 | 20.5 | 5.86 | 584 | 23 | | 20 |
| 3 1/4 | 22.2 | 6.34 | 625 | 23 | 475.0 | 20 |
| 3 3/8 | 23.9 | 6.83 | 673 | 23 | | 20 |
| 3 1/2 | 25.7 | 7.35 | 724 | 23 | 555.0 | 20 |
| 3 5/8 | 27.6 | 7.88 | 768 | 23 | | 20 |
| 3 3/4 | 29.5 | 8.43 | 822 | 23 | 640.0 | 20 |
| 3 7/8 | 31.5 | 9.00 | 878 | 23 | | 20 |
| 4 | 33.6 | 9.60 | 925 | 23 | 730.0 | 20 |

tilever to resist the lateral thrust (d), (e); the columns are now primarily bending members and require large foundations to resist the overturning moment. The lateral thrust must be carried directly by the soil or may be balanced by a horizontal compression strut (a), (e) as for the Stadthalle in Bremen (Fig. 1.1).

No tensile anchors are needed if closed boundary ring arches which resist the lateral forces in a self-balancing manner are employed. For example, circular compression rings are used for radial cable layouts, while other ring forms respond to other cable patterns (see Fig. 3.8 and Fig. 9.4) so that they will behave as funicular arches under symmetrical loading conditions.

Complex boundary support forms may evolve out of anticlastic surface structures as is further discussed in Chapter 9. (The reader may also refer to Fig. 1.1 where the phenomenon of lateral thrust is studied, and Fig. 4.48 for the discussion of arch forms.)

Little formwork is necessary for the erection of suspended cable roofs. Since a long span roof is about as easily erected as a short span roof, the economy of construction increases for longer spans by offsetting the larger costs of fittings and abutment systems.

There are two types of cables (usually in steel): strand and wire rope (Table 3.1). Wires are laid helically around a center wire to produce a strand, while ropes are formed by strands laid helically around a core. The minimum ultimate tensile strength of the cables is in the range 200–220 ksi depending on the coating class. The strand has more metallic area than a rope of the same diameter, hence is stronger and stiffer. Notice, the effective elastic modulus for cables is less than for other structural steels. The moduli of elasticity in Table 3.1 are based on the assumption that the constructional stretch has been removed through prestretching. The capacity of cables is approximately five times higher than for normal structural steels, while the material costs may only be about twice as high, resulting in savings if the structure is large enough so that other additional costs are reduced. Three coating weights are available to meet the range of corrosion resistance requirements. Class A represents the least weight coating for less corrosive atmospheres. Since ropes are more flexible than strands, they are easier to handle and can be used for smaller radii of curvature.

The cables support the roof cladding which consists of roofing, deck, insulation, and possibly framing depending on the capacity of the deck. Some typical roof cladding systems are discussed in Chapter 9 (see Fig. 9.2). The magnitude of the weight of the suspension roof is a function of the roof skin and the type of stabilization used. It ranges from 9 to 31 psf for the case study examples discussed in the following section.

## 3.2  ORGANIZATION OF CABLE STRUCTURES

Cable structures may be organized as shown in Table 3.2. The primary classification is according to the action of the cable as an individual, isolated member; as an assemblage of cables forming a surface structure; or as a three-dimensional net structure.

Structures employing individual tensile members as primary supports are called line-supported systems or *cable-supported structures*. A system of cables may form a surface by directly supporting the roof skin as is typical for cable roof structures. Here one may distinguish between two groups: *membrane skin structures* such as tents and pneumatic skins, and *cable structures*. Cable structures are further subdivided into linear and surface cable systems.

**Table 3.2**

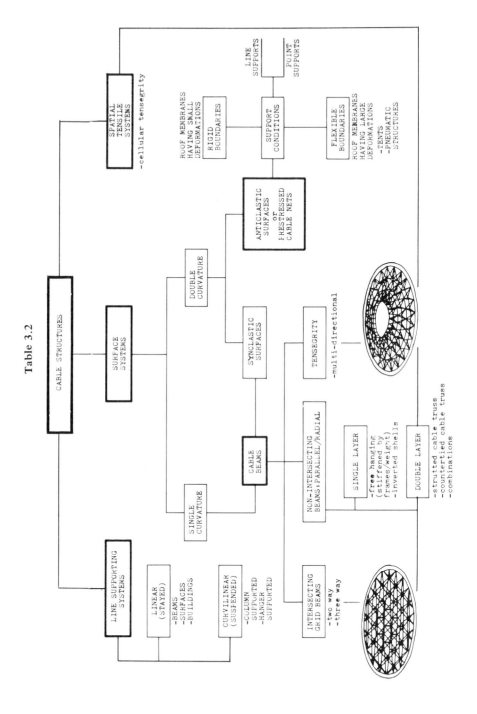

CABLE STRUCTURES

- LINE SUPPORTING SYSTEMS
  - LINEAR (STAYED)
    - –BEAMS
    - –SURFACES
    - –BUILDINGS
  - CURVILINEAR (SUSPENDED)
    - –COLUMN SUPPORTED
    - –HANGER SUPPORTED
- SURFACE SYSTEMS
  - SINGLE CURVATURE
    - CABLE BEAMS
      - INTERSECTING GRID BEAMS
        - –two way
        - –three way
      - NON-INTERSECTING BEAMS: PARALLEL/RADIAL
        - SINGLE LAYER
          - –free hanging (stiffened by frames/weight)
          - –inverted shells
        - DOUBLE LAYER
          - –strutted cable truss
          - –countertied cable truss
          - –combinations
  - DOUBLE CURVATURE
    - SYNCLASTIC SURFACES
      - TENSEGRITY
        - –multi-directional
    - ANTICLASTIC SURFACES or PRESTRESSED CABLE NETS
      - ROOF MEMBRANES HAVING SMALL DEFORMATIONS
        - RIGID BOUNDARIES
      - SUPPORT CONDITIONS
        - LINE SUPPORTS
        - POINT SUPPORTS
      - ROOF MEMBRANES HAVING LARGE DEFORMATIONS
        - FLEXIBLE BOUNDARIES
          - –TENTS
          - –PNEUMATIC STRUCTURES
- SPATIAL TENSILE SYSTEMS
  - –cellular tensegrity

Linear cable systems in the context of this book are called cable beams because their layout is similar to the one-directional beam framing and because a cable (simply suspended or a cable truss) can be analyzed as an isolated member. The typical cable arrangement for single curvature roofs (e.g., cylindrical) is parallel while for double curvature, synclastic surfaces (e.g., inverted dome) it is radial.

Surface cable systems may be formed by semirigid hanging tensile membranes (e.g., polygonal dishes) and prestressed cable nets as found in anticlastic roof structures.

Three-dimensional surface structures as generated by intersecting cable trusses or by the multidirectional tensegrity principle, where the floating individual compression members are not touching each other and are held in place by the continuous tension cables. Surface cable systems and membrane skin structures are treated as soft shells and are discussed in Chapter 9. In this chapter only cable-supported structures and cable structures using simple suspended cables and cable trusses (i.e., cable beams) are investigated.

## Cable-Stayed Structures (Fig. 3.4)

In cable-supported structures cables act as tensile columns or suspended members to support structural components such as beams, surfaces, and building volumes. The linear cable may also be an integral part of a structural system (e.g., king-post truss).

Cable-stayed bridges exemplify clearly the principle of supporting a beam with inclined tensile members. The origins of the concept are old, although it was not until the last two decades that the principle was reborn with beautiful steel cable-stayed bridges in Germany and the concrete-stayed bridges by the Italian Riccardo Morandi. The cable arrangement for multiple cable systems may be fan-shaped, where all the cables lead to the top of a tower, or may be harp-shaped with the diagonal tensile members running parallel; the cable pattern for the Bonn Bridge (k) falls somewhere between. While the Bonn Bridge is supported by a large number of stay cables in one vertical plane carrying a central hollow box girder, the Severin Bridge in Cologne (see Fig. 4.31b) has fewer cables which spread from the top of the A-frame tower to the edges of the roadway deck in a double oblique fashion. The suspended floors of case (h) resemble the stayed bridge principle greatly. A similar approach is applied to the Olympic Ice Arena in Squaw Valley (i), where the two cantilevering roof portions (i.e., tapered box plate girders) are cable supported from tapered steel masts arranged in parallel bents.

The top floor and one level of inclined seating of the racetrack grandstand for the New Jersey Sports and Exposition Complex (g) are hung from a cantilevering truss which, in turn, is suspended from a mast and anchored to the back of the building. The decking type for cable stayed cantilever roof structures may have to be based on the minimum weight requirements that will resist uplift due to wind and reduce flutter. The horizontal thrust component of the cable force is carried by the roof beam in compression which must also carry relatively high bending moments due to gravity loading. In the case of extremely high winds the beams may resist part of the uplift in cantilever bending, requiring the beams to be moment connected to the post.

The roof of the Juan Ramon Loubriel Stadium (Fig. 1.1) is tied down to prevent uplift. Its structure shows an imaginative treatment of the suspension principle applied to a grandstand building. The eliptically shaped roof of the Pan American Terminal at the Kennedy Airport, New York (j) consists of main radially arranged steel girders. Each cantilevering girder is seated on a column at the facade near midspan and supported by cables

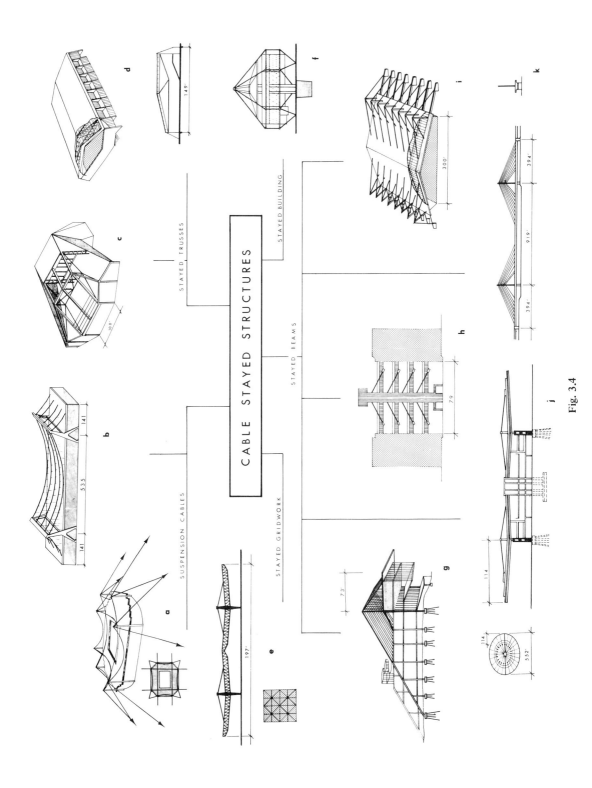

Fig. 3.4

resembling the king-post truss system as well as by inner vertical tension columns at the central core which resist the upward thrust due to the gravity cantilever action. The roof of the printing plant in Tapiola, Finland (see Fig. 4.63b) consists of umbrella-like units. The roof framing is hung from eight prestressed concrete ties which are supported by central hollow core towers. In 1927, Buckminster Fuller proposed the hexagonal, mast-hung, cable supported Dymaxion House (f) for mass production.

For the auditorium roof of the Robin Hood Dell Amphitheater in Philadelphia (c) an intricate system of two-way king-post trusses was used, resulting in a roof framing weight of only 9.5 psf as compared to 13 psf for a conventional truss layout. The appearance of the papermill at Mantua, Italy (b), is clearly that of a suspension bridge. The steel trussed roof framing covering the enormous clear span of 817 ft is hung from four suspended cables. Nervi's mastery of balancing the thrust forces is convincingly expressed by the backwards leaning concrete support towers (Fig. 3.3g).

## Cable Beam Structures (Fig. 3.5)

Suspended cable roofs are organized according to whether the cable arrangement is parallel or radial, and also according to whether it is a single or double layer system. The spans of the roof structures range from about 150–450 ft.

The powerful pull of the suspended roof of the Dulles International Airport at Chantilly, Virginia (a), completed in 1962, is perfectly counteracted by the giant outward sloping concrete columns (Fig. 3.2d). The roof is a cable-supported, post-tensioned inverted vault. This solution of a rigid arched surface was considered necessary to eliminate vertical oscillations of the single-layer cable system. The dead load of the roof structure, about 31 psf, is quite high as compared to double-layer cable roofs. The suspended, prestressed lightweight concrete roof strips of the hangar in Frankfurt, Germany, completed in 1970 (Fig. 1.32d) span the enormous distance of 440 ft!

The fan-shaped plan of the multispan suspended roof of the John Deere Building in Timonium, Maryland (b) in principle is a singly curved vault surface similar to Dulles Airport. Continuous prestressed cables span across three bays and are supported by ridge beams which in turn sit on pendulum-type columns; auxiliary straight cables above the roof were used to keep the columns upright. Only on one side are the cables tied to an edge beam supported by buttresses, while on the other side the cables are gathered and tied directly to earth anchors as is done for tent structures. The powerful shapes of the huge concrete ties of the City Center in Bremen, Germany (Fig. 1.1), respond dramatically to the post-tensioned suspended roof.

To stabilize the 308-ft diameter suspended dish roof for the Municipal Stadium at Montevideo, Uruguay (1957) without increase of weight, the engineer Leonel Viera developed the ingenious method of prestressing the cables by placing ballast on the 2-in. thick precast concrete panels which were clipped to the cables and then grouting the radial and circumferential joints. When the cement mortar had hardened the ballast was removed hereby precompressing the concrete dish into a monolithic stiff surface. The roof of the Villita Assembly Hall, San Antonio, Texas (h), is based on the same construction principle but supports in addition the trussed ceiling frames that hang from the $\frac{11}{16}$-in. diameter cables. The central roof portion consists of an inner ring and an outer tension ring connected by radial trusses resembling a bicycle wheel.

The single-layer roof cables ($2\frac{3}{16}$-in. diameter) of the Oakland-Almeda County Coli-

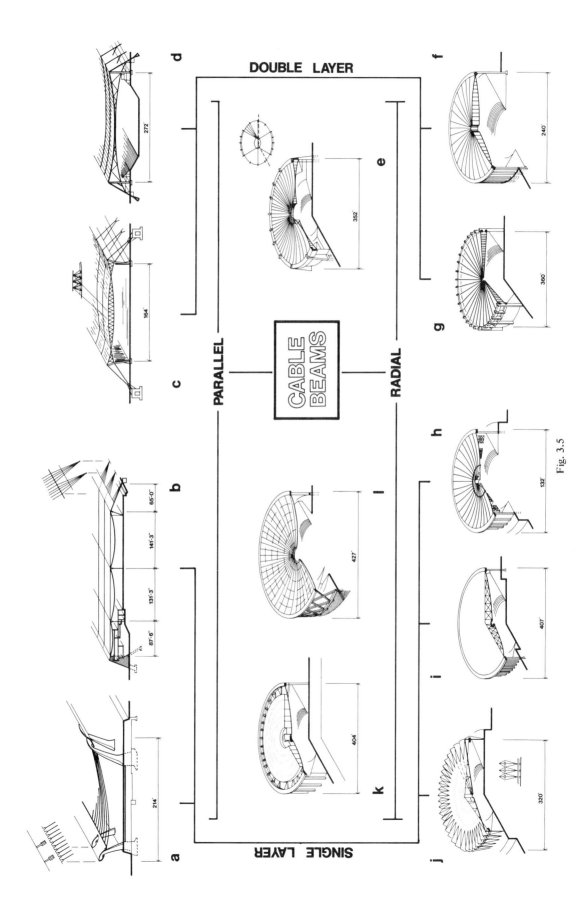

DOUBLE LAYER

PARALLEL

RADIAL

CABLE BEAMS

SINGLE LAYER

a — 214'

b — 87'-6" 131'-3" 141'-3" 65'-0"

c — 164'

d — 272'

e — 352'

f — 240'

g — 360'

h — 132'

i — 407'

j — 320'

k — 404'

l — 427'

Fig. 3.5

seum in California (l) are stabilized by precast concrete I sections which have a longitudinal slot in the bottom flange to fit over the cable and match the drape. In addition, the suspended roof is weighed down by the 260 ft-diameter steel frame penthouse containing the mechanical and electrical equipment. The X columns along the perimeter form a cylindrical trussed wall to effectively resist wind and seismic forces.

The circular suspended roof of Madison Square Garden in New York (k) is prevented from vibrating by the weight of the mechanical equipment housed in a two-story steel-framed structure on top of the $3\frac{3}{4}$-in. diameter cables. The dead load of the roof is equal to 15 psf and the dead load of the equipment is 36 psf. The main structural elements of the conventionally framed structure are five concentric ring trusses which distribute the loads equally and provide lateral stability. Similarly, the suspended cable roof (3-in. diameter cables) of the stadium at Inglewood, California (i) is stabilized by a trussed roof frame. The roof dead load is 30 psf.

The roof of the Hampton Roads Coliseum in Virginia (j) is prevented from fluttering by three concentric steel trusses atop of 2-in. diameter suspended cables as well as by the folded extensions of the wall along the roof perimeter.

Double-layer cable roof structures consist of linear or spatial (c) cable trusses. The dual-cable layers may be tied and/or strutted together (Fig. 3.2). This type of construction is self-damping as is discussed later; it results in a lightweight roof structure such as the 9 psf roof of the Ice Stadium Johanneshov in Stockholm, Sweden (d). The lens-shaped roof of the Utica Memorial Auditorium in Utica, New York (f) completed in 1959, looks like a bicycle wheel. Here the primary lower cable (2-in. diameter) is stabilized by the upper one ($1\frac{5}{8}$-in. diameter). The dead load of the roof structure is only 14 psf. The suspended roof of the Arena in Salt Lake City (g) resembles two dishes placed back-to-back. In this case, the lower cable ($1\frac{5}{8}$-in. diameter) stabilizes the upper, main cable ($2\frac{3}{8}$-in. diameter).

The drainage of cylindrical surfaces is easily achieved by sloping the roof in the longitudinal direction, that is, perpendicular to the curvature. Bowl-shaped roofs, however, collect the water at the center in tanks from which the water must be pumped back up to drain lines at the periphery wall. In the event of a catastrophic storm the overflow from the pooling area is dumped into the arena. Since cables are subject to large deformations due to loading and temperature change, watertightness becomes an important design consideration.

## 3.3 INTRODUCTION TO CABLE ANALYSIS

The following investigation of cable behavior can only be considered as a basis for preliminary design. The effect of changes in cable geometry due to deflection upon the location and direction of applied forces is neglected; large deflection theory should be used rather than the familiar small deflection theory of rigid structures. Since the suspended cable changes its shape under different types of loading, the superposition method is no longer valid. It is assumed that the cable is stabilized, that is, it does not flutter under dynamic loads such as wind, earthquake, or other external forces that cause vibration. In this investigation only static loads are considered. Before studying some typical cable roof structures with specific loading characteristics, it is helpful to identify the cable behavior as related to general loading conditions. Since cable geometry is a function of load action, it is discussed together with the different types of cable roof structures.

Visualize an arbitrary vertical load acting on a horizontal plane to be supported by a suspended cable with reactions at different heights (Fig. 3.6a). The location of the resultant $W$ of this load is assumed to be at the distance $x_1$ from support $B$. Translational equilibrium requires that the horizontal reaction forces $A_h$ and $B_h$ have to balance each other. Further, the free-body (Fig. 3.6e) shows that the horizontal component of the cable force $T_x$ is also equal to the horizontal reaction. One may conclude that for vertical loading the horizontal force component $H$ does not vary along the cable: it is a constant,

$$A_h = B_h = T_{xh} = H \tag{3.1}$$

The vertical reactions at $A$ and $B$ are found by taking moments about supports $B$ and $A$:

$$\Sigma M_B = 0 = A_v(L) - W(x_1) + H(h)$$

$$A_v = \frac{Wx_1}{L} - \frac{Hh}{L} = A'_v - \frac{Hh}{L}$$

$$B_v = \frac{W(L - x_1)}{L} + \frac{Hh}{L} = B'_v + \frac{Hh}{L} \tag{3.2}$$

Where $A'_v$ and $B'_v$ are the reactions for a horizontally supported cable carrying the same loads as the inclined cable. For a short suspended inclined cable with a small sag (see dashed line in Fig. 3.6a) the vertical reaction at support $A$ is acting downward and will be equal to

$$A_v = \frac{Hh}{L} - A'_v$$

$$B_v = \frac{Hh}{L} + B'_v \tag{3.3}$$

The slope of the cable curvature at the reactions is proportional to the reaction forces

$$\tan \theta_A = \frac{A_v}{H} \qquad \tan \theta_B = \frac{B_v}{H} \tag{3.4}$$

The maximum tensile force in the cable appears at one of the reactions. Assuming it to be at the upper support and using Pythagoras' theorem, the following relationship between force components may be set up

$$T_B^2 = B_v^2 + H^2$$
$$T_B^2 = (H \tan \theta_B)^2 + H^2$$

Hence the maximum cable force is

$$T_{max} = H\sqrt{1 + \tan^2 \theta_{max}} = \frac{H}{\cos \theta_{max}} \tag{3.5}$$

Figure 3.1d clearly shows that as the cable length or the cable slope $\tan \theta$ at the reactions decreases, the tensile force increases and becomes infinitely large when the cable is a straight line. At this stage, the cable is obviously no longer suspended. It either has to be prestressed or replaced by a rigid beam, and bending stiffness must be provided.

The magnitude of the force flow along the cable is best understood by first visualizing

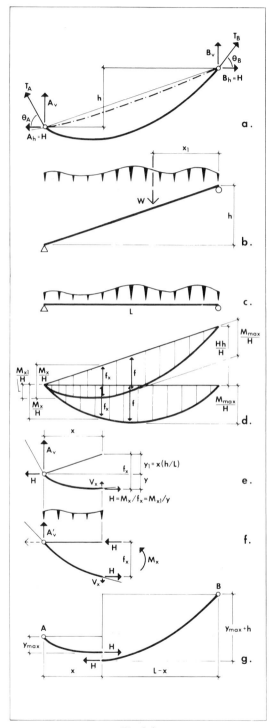

Fig. 3.6

the loads supported by an inclined beam. It is shown in the discussion of simply supported inclined beams that the moment flow along its length is equal to the moment flow for an equivalent beam on the horizontal projection carrying the same loading. (Fig. 3.6b and c). This fact simplifies calculations considerably. In a rigid beam the moments are resisted by bending stiffness, while a flexible cable system uses its geometry to carry the rotation in pure tension. The beam moment $M_x$ at any point along the cable is resisted by a force couple separated by the distance $f_x$, called the cable sag. This force couple consists of the horizontal components of the cable force at the reaction and the point to be investigated (Fig. 3.6f)

$$M_x = H f_x \qquad (3.6a)$$

The same result is obtained by considering that the moments along the flexible cable must be zero

$$\Sigma M_x = 0 = H(f_x) - M_x$$

$$M_x = H(f_x) \qquad f_x = \frac{M_x}{H} \qquad (3.6b)$$

The cable sag $f_x$ is directly proportional to the moment diagram because the force $H$ is a constant. The curve of a suspended inclined cable is equal to the moment diagram, divided through $H$ of a linear inclined beam replacing the cable. Keep in mind that for any location the moment $M_x$ that is the sag $f_x$ of the inclined beam is equal to $M_x$ or $f_x$ for the horizontal beam.

The horizontal force component $H$ can be found from any known geometrical condition. At whatever location the sag of the cable is given, the beam moment can be determined and thus the force $H$ can be found. From Fig. 3.6e,

$$H(y) = M_{x1}$$

from Fig. 3.6e,f,

$$H(f_x) = M_x$$

In general,

$$H = \frac{M_x}{f_x} = \frac{M_{x1}}{y} \qquad (3.7)$$

For a suspended cable with supports at the same level, the sag $f_x$ is equal to the cable shape $y$ at a given location. In most cases, the maximum sag-to-span ratio $f/L = n$ for a cable structure is given. For cable roofs the typical ratios are in the range from $1/10$ to $1/20$. The largest sag appears at the location of the maximum beam moment. Hence, the horizontal force $H$ can easily be found since the maximum beam moment and its location are known (Fig. 3.6d)

$$H = \frac{M_{max}}{f} \qquad (3.8)$$

For the inclined cable structure the maximum cable sag $f$ is the same as for the projected horizontal cable system (Fig. 3.6d). However, the low points of the two structures do not occur at the same position.

Should the low point $y_{max}$ be given for the inclined cable for the purpose of clearance requirements, slightly more tedious mathematical operations are necessary, since the location of the low point has to be found. Hence, there are two unknown conditions: the location $x$ of the low point and the magnitude of the horizontal force $H$. The two unknowns can be solved by setting up the rotational equilibrium for the left and right free-bodies in Fig. 3.6g

$$\Sigma M_A = H(y_{max}) \qquad \Sigma M_B = H(y_{max} + h)$$

where $\Sigma M_A$ and $\Sigma M_B$ are the moments caused by the loading in their respective free bodies. The cable force $T_x$ at any point along the cable is:

$$T_x = \frac{H}{\cos \theta_x} = \frac{V_x}{\sin \theta_x} = H\sqrt{1 + \tan^2 \theta_x} \qquad (3.9)$$

In general, the maximum cable force at one of the reactions is only of interest since it is one of the determinants for the design of the cable.

**The Polygonal Cable**

The suspended cable assumes the shape of a polygon under the action of point loads. The cable portions between the location of the concentrated loads have no curvature, assuming that the tension forces in the cable are by far larger than the effect of the cable weight which would cause a curvilinear cable response (see discussion of the catenary cable).

**Example 3.1** The behavior of a suspension cable with a sag ratio n = 1:10 is investigated for a simple, symmetrical loading condition. Assume the cable to carry two single loads of 20 k each. For the geometry of the structure refer to Fig. 3.7a. Because of symmetry of loading and support, each of the vertical reactions carries one-half of the total load

$$A_v = B_v = W = 20 \text{ k}$$

The horizontal reaction forces or minimum cable force may be found from Eq. (3.8)

$$A_h = B_h = H = \frac{M_{max}}{f} = \frac{WL}{3f} = \frac{20(100)}{3(10)} = 66.67 \text{ k}$$

The maximum cable slope at the reactions is:

$$\tan \theta_A = \frac{A_v}{H} = \frac{3f}{L} = 3n = 0.3 \qquad (3.4)$$

Thus, the maximum tensile force according to Eq. (3.5) is

$$T_{max} = H\sqrt{1 + \tan^2 \theta_{max}} = 66.67\sqrt{1 + 0.3^2} = 69.61 \text{ k}$$

or

$$T_{max} = \frac{H}{\cos \theta_A} = \frac{66.67}{0.958} = 69.61 \text{ k}$$

The maximum ultimate tensile capacity required [Eq. (1.19)] is

$$T_{u \, max} = LF(T_{max}) = 2.2(69.61) = 153.14 \text{ k}$$

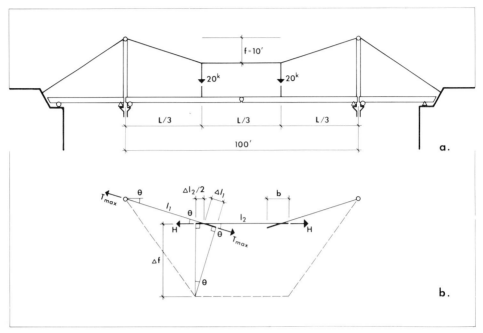

**Fig. 3.7**

Select $1\frac{1}{8}$ in. diameter single-strand class $A$ coating (see Table 3.1)

$$A = 0.759 \text{ in.}^2 \qquad E = 24{,}000 \text{ ksi}$$

The cable length is obtained by adding up the lengths of the straight and inclined portions:

$$l = \frac{100}{3} + 2\sqrt{10^2 + \left(\frac{100}{3}\right)^2} = 102.94 \text{ ft}$$

Notice that the cable is only about 3% longer than the horizontal distance between supports. To find the cable elongation due to the loading, visualize the cable to be disassembled into three segments (Fig. 3.7b). Each segment deforms under its axial load in a linear manner.

$$\Delta l_1 = \frac{T_{\max}(l_1)}{AE} = \frac{69.61\sqrt{10^2 + (100/3)^2}}{0.759(24000)} = 0.133 \text{ ft}$$

$$\Delta l_2/2 = \frac{H(L/3)}{2AE} = \frac{66.67(33.33)}{2(0.759)24000} = 0.061 \text{ ft}$$

The total cable elongation is

$$\Delta l = (0.133 + 0.061)2 = 0.388 \text{ ft}$$

The linearly deformed cables are reassembled. The horizontal center portion moves vertically downward. Its elongated endpoints intersect with the new endpoints of the inclined sections which are rotated about their respective reactions. Because of the small scale of the sag increase, the inclined portion is assumed to be rotated along a straight line; this assumption simplifies the calculations considerably. The increase in sag is solved as follows (refer to Fig. 3.7b):

$$\Delta f = \frac{b}{\tan \theta} = \frac{b}{0.3} \tag{a}$$

$$\cos \theta = \frac{0.133}{b - 0.061} = 0.958 \tag{b}$$

Solving the two equations with the two unknowns $b$ and $f$ yields an increase of cable sag:

$$\Delta f = 0.666 \text{ ft}$$

A general expression for the increase in cable sag may be developed from Eqs. (a) and (b):

$$\Delta f(\tan \theta) = \frac{\Delta l_1}{\cos \theta} + \frac{\Delta l_2}{2}$$

but

$$\tan \theta = \frac{f}{L/3} \qquad \cos \theta = \frac{L/3}{l_1}$$

$$f(\Delta f) = l_1(\Delta l_1) + \frac{(L/3)\Delta l_2}{2}$$

Assuming the length of the inclined cable portion to be equal to the length of its horizontal projection: $l_1 \approx L/3$

$$\Delta f = \frac{\Delta l_1 + \Delta l_2/2}{3n}$$

but

$$\Delta l = 2 \left( \Delta l_1 + \frac{\Delta l_2}{2} \right)$$

$$\Delta f = \frac{\Delta l}{6n} \tag{3.10}$$

Using this approximate equation for the given exercise

$$\Delta f \simeq \frac{0.388}{6(0.1)} = 0.647 \text{ ft}$$

There is only about 3% difference between the approximation and the more accurate solution. The actual cable sag is approximately 10.666 ft. This larger sag results, however, in smaller cable forces which in turn decrease the amount of the sag. The true solution can be obtained by an iterative process.

In situations where single forces of the same magnitude act in a radial manner, the funicular shape of the cable is a regular, closed polygon (Fig. 3.8). Visualize the central tension ring of a round, dish-shaped suspension roof or the outside tension ring of a dome structure. The radial forces $P$ are spaced at regular intervals, that is, the roof is subdivided into $m$ parts

$$\theta = \frac{360}{m}$$

The constant cable force is determined from the free-body in Fig. 3.8 by summing up the horizontal forces

$$\Sigma F_x = 0 = P - 2 \left[ T \cos \left( 90 - \frac{\theta}{2} \right) \right]$$

$$T = \frac{P}{2 \cos (90 - \theta/2)} \tag{3.11}$$

### The Circular Cable

In the discussion of single forces acting in a radial fashion on a closed cable, it was discovered that as the spacing of the concentrated loads becomes closer, approaching uniform radial force action, the funicular response of the cable becomes more circular in shape (Fig. 3.8). Visualize a circular cable to resist a radial uniform pressure $p$ as caused by the action of a fluid, such as the air pressure of a pneumatic structure. Cut the circular cable to form a semicircle or a circular segment where the lateral thrust forces balance (see Fig. 7.7d). Now the uniform pressure $p$ also acts perpendicular to the imaginary base line of

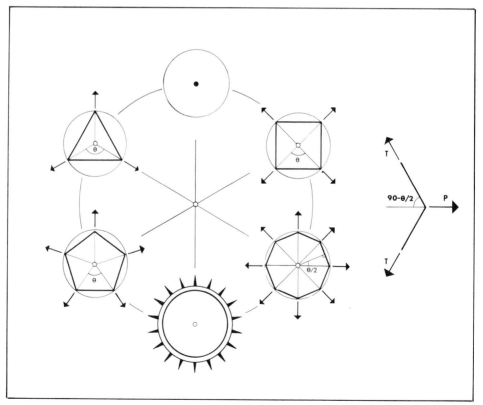

**Fig. 3.8**  Funicular tension rings.

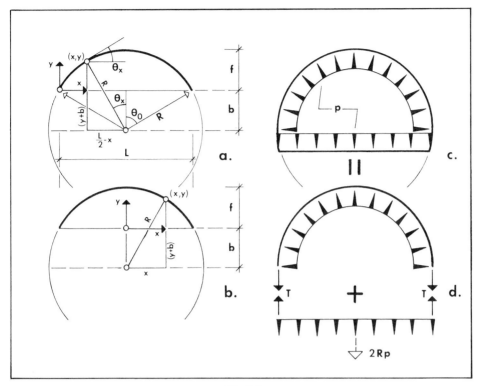

Fig. 3.9

the semicircle (Fig. 3.9c). This pressure may be considered to be a resultant or balancing pressure equal to $2Rp$. In reality, the uniform base pressure is nonexistent but is provided by the resisting forces in the cable (Fig. 3.9d)

$$2T = 2Rp$$

$$T = pR \qquad (3.12)$$

Thus, for constant radial pressure $p$, the cable forces $T$ are proportional to the radius of curvature of the cable. Since the radius of a circle is constant, the cable forces must be constant. The circular cable length $l$ is derived from Fig. 3.9a as follows

$$\sin \theta_0 = \frac{L/2}{R}$$

$$\theta_0 = \arcsin\left(\frac{L}{2R}\right) \qquad (3.13)$$

$$\frac{2\theta}{360} = \frac{l}{2\pi R}$$

$$l = \pi R\left(\frac{\theta^\circ}{90^\circ}\right) \qquad (3.14)$$

The elongation of the cable with cross-sectional area $A$ and modulus of elasticity $E$ due to the constant axial force $T$ is

$$\Delta l = \frac{TL}{AE} = \frac{pRl}{AE} = \frac{p\pi R^2}{AE}\left(\frac{\theta_0^0}{90^\circ}\right) \tag{3.15}$$

The increase in the radius of curvature may be approximated from Eq. (3.14) as

$$\Delta l \simeq \pi \Delta R\left(\frac{\theta^\circ}{90^\circ}\right)$$

$$\Delta R \simeq \left(\frac{\Delta l}{\pi}\right)\left(\frac{90^\circ}{\theta^\circ}\right)$$

and substitute Eq. (3.15)

$$\Delta R \cong \frac{pR^2}{AE} \tag{3.16}$$

By placing the origin of the coordinate system at the cable support, the shape of the circle may be defined as follows (Fig. 3.9a):

$$R^2 = (y + b)^2 + \left(\frac{L}{2} - x\right)^2$$

$$y = -b + \sqrt{R^2 - \left(\frac{L}{2} - x\right)^2} \tag{3.17}$$

The slope is

$$\tan \theta_x = \frac{dy}{dx} = \frac{L/2 - x}{\sqrt{R^2 - (L/2 - x)^2}} \tag{3.18}$$

For a given span $L$ and sag $f$ the radius of curvature $R$ is:

$$R^2 = \left(\frac{L}{2}\right)^2 + b^2 \qquad b = R - f$$

$$R = \frac{L^2 + 4f^2}{8f} \tag{3.19}$$

For a semicircle with $b = 0$, $L/2 = R$, and $f = R$, the shape of the circle is defined as:

$$y = \sqrt{2Rx - x^2} \tag{3.20}$$

The slope of the curvature for the semicircular cable is

$$\tan \theta_x = \frac{dy}{dx} = \frac{R - x}{\sqrt{2Rx - x^2}} = \frac{R - x}{y} \tag{3.21}$$

Sometimes it may be more convenient to place the origin of the coordinate system at the midspan (Fig. 3.9b). Now the shape of the circle is defined to be

$$R^2 = (y + b)^2 + x^2$$
$$y = -b + \sqrt{R^2 - x^2} \tag{3.22}$$

For the semicircle, $b = 0$:

$$\text{shape:} \quad y = \sqrt{R^2 - x^2} \tag{3.23}$$

$$\text{slope:} \quad \tan \theta_x = \frac{dy}{dx} = \frac{-x}{\sqrt{R^2 - x^2}} = -\frac{x}{y} \tag{3.24}$$

### The Catenary Cable

A cable carrying a uniform load along its length such as its own weight assumes the shape of a catenary. It can be shown that for small sag-to-span ratios (i.e., $n \leqslant 1/10$) the geometry of a catenary and a parabola are practically the same. Since the equations defining a parabola are much simpler than the ones for a catenary, parabolic equations are generally used, that is, the loads are assumed to act uniformly along the span rather than along the cable.

### The Parabolic Cable

Assume a cable to carry a uniform load along the horizontal span, such as for a suspension bridge or a flat, single-curvature cable roof spanning a rectangular plan.

*The Suspended Cable with Supports at the Same Elevation* (Fig. 3.10)

The following primary cable characteristics are derived:

■ *Cable Forces*

The vertical reactions are

$$A_v = B_v = \frac{wL}{2} \tag{3.25}$$

The horizontal reactions or minimum cable force is found from Eq. (3.8)

$$A_h = B_h = H = \frac{M_{\text{max}}}{f} = \frac{wL^2}{8f} \tag{3.26}$$

The maximum cable slope from Eq. (3.4)

$$\tan \theta = \frac{A_v}{H} = \frac{4f}{L} = 4n \tag{3.27}$$

The maximum cable force according to Eq. (3.5) is

$$T_{\text{max}} = \frac{H}{\cos \theta_A} = \frac{A_v}{\sin \theta_A} = H\sqrt{1 + \tan^2 \theta_{\text{max}}} = H\sqrt{1 + 16n^2} \tag{3.28}$$

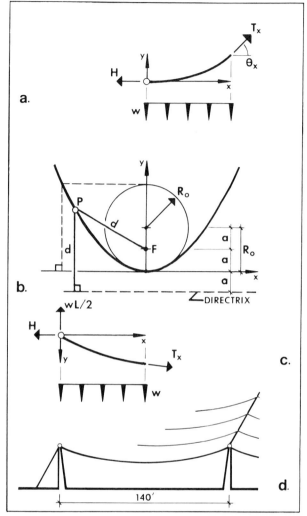

Fig. 3.10

■ *Cable Geometry*

A free-body portion of a cable is shown in Fig. 3.10a. The origin of the coordinate system is placed at the lowest point of the cable, where the cable slope is zero. Rotational equilibrium about $T_x$ yields:

$$\Sigma M_x = 0 = H(y) - wx\left(\frac{x}{2}\right) \qquad H = \frac{wL^2}{8f}$$

$$y = \frac{wx^2}{2H} = 4f\left(\frac{x}{L}\right)^2 \qquad (c)$$

This is the equation for the parabola with its apex at the intersection of the coordinate axes. The general mathematical equation for this condition is

$$y = \frac{x^2}{4a} \tag{d}$$

Mathematically a parabola is defined as a locus of a point moving in a plane so that its distance $d$ from a fixed line called directrix is always equal to its distance from a fixed point $F$ called focus not on the line. In Eq. (d) the coefficient $a$ (Fig. 3.10b) determines the shape that is the flatness of the parabola. For the uniform loading case the coefficient $a$ can be derived from Eqs. (c) and (d) as follows:

$$\frac{1}{4a} = \frac{w}{2H} = \frac{4f}{L^2}$$

$$R_0 = \frac{1}{k_0} = 2a = \frac{H}{w} = \frac{L^2}{8f} \tag{3.29}$$

Where $R_0$ is the radius of curvature at the apex and $k_0$ is the curvature at that point (Fig. 3.10b). Hence, the general equation for the uniform loading with the coordinate system at the cable low point is:

$$y = \frac{x^2}{2R_0} = \frac{k_0 x^2}{2} = \frac{wx^2}{2H} = 4f\left(\frac{x}{L}\right)^2 \tag{3.30}$$

The slope of the curvature $\tan\theta_x$ is easily found by taking the derivative of $y$ with respect to $x$

$$\tan\theta_x = \frac{dy}{dx} = \frac{x}{R_0} = xk_0 = \frac{wx}{H} = \frac{8fx}{L^2} \tag{3.31}$$

At the supports, where $x = \pm L/2$ and $y = f$, the slope is

$$\tan\theta = \frac{\pm 4f}{L} = \pm 4n \tag{3.27}$$

This result was already derived by using the ratio of vertical to horizontal reaction forces.

Sometimes it is helpful to express the geometry of the parabola by placing the origin of the coordinate system at one of the reactions (Fig. 3.10c). Rotational equilibrium about a point located at a distance $x$ from the support yields

$$\Sigma M_x = 0 = \frac{wL(x)}{2} - \frac{wL^2(y)}{8f} - wx\left(\frac{x}{2}\right)$$

The equation of the parabola is

$$y = \frac{4f(Lx - x^2)}{L^2} = 4f\left[\frac{x}{L} - \left(\frac{x}{L}\right)^2\right] \tag{3.32}$$

The slope is:

$$\tan\theta_x = \frac{dy}{dx} = \frac{4f(L - 2x)}{L^2} \tag{3.33}$$

■ *Cable Length*

The cable length is obtained by integrating the differential length $dl$ along the cable (see Problem 3.15)

$$l = 2 \int_0^{L/2} dl = 2 \int_0^{L/2} \sqrt{1 + \left(\frac{dy}{dx}\right)^2} \; dx$$

where the slope $dy/dx = 8fx/L^2$

$$l = L\left(1 + \frac{8}{3}n^2 - \frac{32}{5}n^4 + \dots\right) \simeq L\left(1 + \frac{8n^2}{3}\right) \tag{3.34}$$

■ *Cable Elongation*

The increase (or decrease) in cable length due to change in temperature is:

$$\Delta l = \alpha l \Delta T \cong \alpha \Delta T\left(1 + \frac{8n^2}{3}\right) \tag{3.35}$$

The elastic stretch for a linear cable of length $L$ and cross-sectional area $A$ responding to a constant force $T$ is

$$\Delta L = \frac{TL}{AE} \tag{1.23}$$

However, along the parabolic cable the tensile force $T_x$ varies. The total change in length of the cable is equal to the summation of the elongations of the differential length $dl$ as caused by $T_x$ (see Problem 3.15)

$$\Delta l = 2 \int_0^{L/2} \frac{T_x}{AE} \, dl = \frac{2H}{AE} \int_0^{L/2} \frac{dl}{dx} \, dl$$

but $T_x/dl = H/dx$

$$\Delta l = \frac{2H}{AE} \int_0^{L/2} \left(\frac{dl}{dx}\right)^2 dx = \frac{2H}{AE} \int_0^{L/2} \left[1 + \left(\frac{dy}{dx}\right)^2\right] dx$$

The increase in cable length due to elastic stretch is:

$$\Delta l = \frac{HL}{AE}\left(1 + \frac{16}{3}n^2\right) \tag{3.36}$$

■ *Increase in Cable Sag*

The approximate increase in cable sag may be obtained by taking the derivative of the cable length $l$ with respect to cable sag $f_x$

$$\frac{dl}{df} = \left(\frac{d}{df}\right)L\left(1 + \frac{8}{3}n^2\right) = \frac{d}{df}\left(L + \frac{8f^2}{3L}\right) = \frac{16f}{3L} = \frac{16n}{3}$$

Considering $dl/df$ as a finite quantity yields as approximate increase of cable sag

$$\Delta f \simeq \frac{3\Delta l}{16n} \tag{3.37}$$

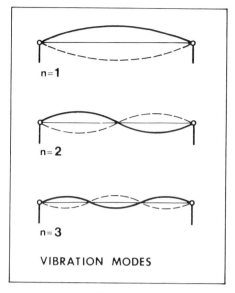

Fig. 3.11

■ *Dynamic Behavior*

The suspended roof is very vulnerable to aerodynamic instability; as a flexible system it tends to have a high period close to the one of the wind. The collapse of the Tacoma bridge in 1940 is the best known example of the significance of this dynamic force action.

It can be shown that the dynamic response or period $P$ of a single undamped cable with a mass $m = w/g$ uniformly distributed can be approximately determined as

$$P_n = \frac{2L}{n} \sqrt{\frac{w/g}{T}} \qquad (3.38)$$

where $g = 32.2$ ft/s$^2$ is the acceleration due to gravity and $n = 1, 2, 3, \ldots, \infty$. Since the amplitudes of the modes of vibration (i.e., deflections) decrease with the number of waves (Fig. 3.11) it is reasonable to consider only the first few ones. The first mode of vibration ($n = 1$) is called the fundamental mode or the natural period of the cable; it represents the time in seconds for one up-and-down movement. For the special condition where only the uniform dead load causes the tension (i.e., no prestressing as in a double-layer system) and letting $T = H$ [see Eq. (3.26)], Eq. (3.38) can be further simplified to

$$P_n = \frac{2}{n} \sqrt{\frac{8f}{g}} \qquad \text{(s)} \qquad (3.39)$$

One may conclude that the period $P_n$ [note in Eq. (1.12) the period is called $T$] is independent of the loading, in other words the increase in weight cannot stabilize the roof aerodynamically. Only the mode of vibration and the cable sag influence the period, which should not be in the vicinity of the period of the exciting force to prevent resonant loading ($P_n/P_e \neq 1$). Suspended roofs are stabilized neither by weight nor much by stiffness, but primarily through the use of prestressed double cable systems (Figs. 3.2 and 3.16) against vibrational force action.

**Example 3.2** A typical cable of a single-layer suspension roof (Fig. 3.10d) is investigated for preliminary design purposes. The cables are spaced on 6 ft. centers and span 140 ft. The maximum sag-to-span ratio is 1/15. Dead and live loads are 20 and 30 psf, respectively; they are assumed to act on the horizontal roof projection. Temperature change is 50°F.

The maximum cable sag is

$$\frac{f}{L} = \frac{1}{15} \qquad\qquad f = \frac{140}{15} = 9.33 \text{ ft}$$

The uniform load that a typical interior cable must support

$$w = 6(0.020 + 0.030) = 0.3 \text{ k/ft}$$

The minimum horizontal cable force is

$$H = \frac{wL^2}{8f} = \frac{0.3(140)^2}{8(9.33)} = 78.78 \text{ k}$$

The maximum cable slope is

$$\tan \theta_A = 4n = \frac{4}{15} = 0.267$$

The maximum cable force is

$$T_{max} = H\sqrt{1 + 16n^2} = 78.78\sqrt{1 + 16\left(\frac{1}{15}\right)^2} = 81.53 \text{ k}$$

or

$$T_{max} = \frac{H}{\cos \theta} = \frac{78.78}{0.966} = 81.53 \text{ k}$$

Notice that there is only about 3.5% difference between the largest and smallest tensile force; the difference decreases as the cable profile becomes smaller. The ultimate tensile strength required is

$$T_u = \text{LF}(T) = 2.2(81.53) = 179.37 \text{ k}$$

Try $1\frac{1}{4}$-in. diameter single-strand class $A$ coating (see Table 3.1).

$$A = 0.938 \text{ in.}^2 \qquad T_u = 192 \text{ k} \qquad E = 24,000 \text{ ksi}$$

The equation defining the cable shape from Eq. (3.30) is:

$$y = \frac{wx^2}{2H} = \frac{0.3x^2}{2(78.78)} = \frac{x^2}{525.2}$$

For instance, for the cable displacement 30 ft from the support or 40 ft from midspan

$$x = 40 \text{ ft} \qquad\qquad y = \frac{40^2}{525.2} = 3.05 \text{ ft}$$

or, 9.33 – 3.05 = 6.28 ft measured from the horizontal chord connecting the two supports. The same result is obtained by using Eq. (3.32).

$$y = 4f\left[\frac{x}{L} - \left(\frac{x}{L}\right)^2\right] = 4(9.33)\left[\frac{30}{140} - \left(\frac{30}{140}\right)^2\right] = 6.28 \text{ ft}$$

The approximate cable length for one span from Eq. (3.34) is:

$$l \approx L\left(1 + \frac{8n^2}{3}\right) = 140\left[1 + \frac{8}{3}\left(\frac{1}{15}\right)^2\right] = 141.66 \text{ ft}$$

Note that there is only about 1% difference between the cable length and its span.
    The cable elongation due to the tensile action from Eq. (3.36) is

$$\Delta l = \frac{HL}{AE}\left(1 + \frac{16n^2}{3}\right) = \frac{78.78(140)}{0.938(24\,000)}\left[1 + \frac{16}{3}\left(\frac{1}{15}\right)^2\right] = 0.50 \text{ ft}$$

The cable elongation due to temperature increase from Eq. (3.35) is

$$\Delta l_t = \alpha \Delta Tl = 6.5 \times 10^{-6}(50)(141.66) = 0.05 \text{ ft}$$

Note that the influence of temperature at this scale is relatively small. Should there be a decrease in temperature the cable will shorten and reduce the sag, thus increasing the maximum cable force. The approximate increase in cable sag due to elongation from Eq. (3.37) is

$$\Delta f \approx \frac{3\Delta l}{16n} = \frac{3}{16}(0.5 + 0.05)15 = 1.55 \text{ ft}$$

This increase in sag is about $(1.55/9.33)(100\%) = 16.61\%$ of the maximum sag, which clearly shows the large deflection character of the cable structure.
    The increase in sag due to the superimposed live loads neglecting the correction for temperature is

$$\Delta f_{LL} = 1.55\,\frac{30}{50} = 0.93 \text{ ft}$$

$$\frac{\Delta f_{LL}}{L} = \frac{0.93}{140} = \frac{1}{151}$$

which is quite high in comparison to $L/360$! Taking into account the increase in sag and assuming, for this approximate approach, that the sag is proportional to the maximum tensile force, yields the corrected maximum tensile force

$$T_{max} = 81.53\,\frac{9.33}{9.33 + 1.55} = 69.92 \text{ k}$$

As the sag increases the maximum tensile force decreases. However, for a smaller maximum cable force there also will be less sag. Hence, the maximum force will be somewhere between 81.53 and 69.22 k. The natural period of the cable is

$$P_n = \frac{2}{n}\sqrt{\frac{8f}{g}} \tag{3.39}$$

$$P_l = \frac{2}{1}\sqrt{\frac{8(9.33)}{32.2}} = 3.05 \text{ s}$$

This value is less than a typical wind period in the range of 4–5 s, but still its proximity indicates that the magnification of the forces due to the dynamic action must be considered.

### The Inclined Cable

■ *Cable Forces* (Fig. 3.12a)

The horizontal reaction forces or the minimum cable force are obtained by using Eq. (3.8)

$$A_h = B_h = \frac{M_{max}}{f} = \frac{wL^2}{8f} \tag{3.40}$$

The vertical reaction forces are obtained from Eq. (3.2)

$$A_v = A_v' - \frac{Hh}{L} = \frac{wL}{2} - \frac{Hh}{L}$$

$$B_v = B_v' + \frac{Hh}{L} = \frac{wL}{2} + \frac{Hh}{L} \tag{3.41}$$

The maximum cable slope at support $B$, using Eq. (3.4)

$$\tan \theta_B = \frac{B_v}{H} = \frac{wL}{2H} + \frac{h}{L} = 4n + \frac{h}{L} \tag{3.42}$$

The maximum cable force according to Eq. (3.5) is

$$T_B = T_{max} = H\sqrt{1 + \tan^2 \theta_B} = H \sqrt{1 + \left(4n + \frac{h}{L}\right)^2} \tag{3.43}$$

■ *Cable Geometry* (Fig. 3.12b)

The origin of the coordinate system is located at the upper support. The vertical distance to the cable at a horizontal distance $x$ is

$$y = y_1 + y_2$$

The vertical displacement $y_1$ is equal to the sag at that location for a cable with supports at the same level, as discussed in Introduction to Cable Analysis. The vertical distance $y_2$ is linearly related to the height $h$

$$\frac{y_2}{h} = \frac{x}{L} \quad \text{or} \quad y_2 = \frac{xh}{L}$$

Hence, the equation for the parabola is

$$y = y_1 + y_2 = 4f \left[ \frac{x}{L} - \left(\frac{x}{L}\right)^2 \right] + h\frac{x}{L} \tag{3.44}$$

Should the origin of the coordinate system be at the lower support, the equation for the parabola becomes

$$y = y_1 - y_2 = 4f\left[\frac{x}{L} - \left(\frac{x}{L}\right)^2\right] - h\frac{x}{L} \tag{3.45}$$

The cable slope is found by taking the derivative of $y$ with respect to $x$

$$\tan\theta_x = \frac{dy}{dx} = \frac{4f}{L^2}(L - 2x) + \frac{h}{L} \tag{3.46}$$

The slope of the cable curvature at the supports is

$$x = 0 \quad \tan\theta_B = \frac{h}{L} + \frac{4f}{L} = \frac{h}{L} + 4n$$

$$\tag{3.47}$$

$$x = L \quad \tan\theta_A = \frac{h}{L} - \frac{4f}{L} = \frac{h}{L} - 4n$$

For the special case where the cable curvature at the lower support is zero, the following relationship between maximum cable sag and difference in support elevation can be derived:

$$\tan\theta_A = 0 = \frac{h}{L} - 4n \qquad\qquad f = \frac{h}{4} \tag{3.48}$$

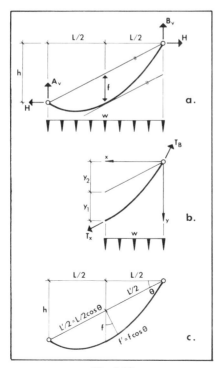

Fig. 3.12

Should the lower support be at the ground, then the maximum cable sag should not be larger than a quarter of the height $h$ in order for the cable to clear the surface. In general, the location where the slope of the curvature is zero or where the cable sag has its low point, is

$$x = ?: \quad \tan \theta_x = \frac{dy}{dx} = 0 = \frac{4f}{L^2}(L - 2x) + \frac{h}{L}$$

$$x = \frac{L}{2}\left(1 + \frac{h}{4f}\right) \tag{3.49}$$

Hence, the low point of the cable appears as given in Eq. (3.49) keeping in mind that the origin of the coordinate system is at the upper support.

The slope of the curvature at midspan is

$$x = \frac{L}{2} \qquad \tan \theta_{L/2} = 4f\left(\frac{1}{L} - \frac{1}{L}\right) + \frac{h}{L} = \frac{h}{L} \tag{3.50}$$

The slope of the curvature at midspan is parallel to the chord connecting the supports. This phenomenon was already discussed in the section Introduction to Cable Analysis.

■ *Cable Length (Fig. 3.12c)*

For small sags it is considered accurate enough to derive the length of the inclined cable from the cable length for a parabolic cable with supports at the same levels. According to Eq. (3.34) the cable length is

$$l \simeq L'\left[1 + \frac{8}{3}(n')^2\right]$$

where

$$n' = \frac{f'}{L'} = \frac{f \cos \theta}{L/\cos \theta} = n \cos^2 \theta$$

Hence, the approximate cable length for the inclined cable is

$$l \simeq \frac{L}{\cos \theta}\left(1 + \frac{8}{3}n^2 \cos^4 \theta\right) \tag{3.51}$$

■ *Cable Elongation*

The cable elongation is obtained in a manner similar to that used for the cable with supports at an equal level (see Problem 3.16). The increase in cable length as caused by the tensile forces is

$$\Delta l = \frac{HL}{AE}\left[1 + \frac{16n^2}{3} + \left(\frac{h}{L}\right)^2\right] \tag{3.52}$$

The increase in cable length as caused by temperature increase is

$$\Delta l_t = \frac{\alpha \Delta T}{\cos \theta} \left( 1 + \frac{8}{3} n^2 \cos^4 \theta \right) \tag{3.53}$$

### The Cubic Parabolic Cable

A cable carrying a linearly increasing continuous load along its horizontal base, such as a triangular- or trapezoidal-shaped load, takes the funicular form of a cubic parabola. The following common loading cases are investigated

*Case A*

The cables of a round suspension roof are arranged in a radial manner. Each cable carries the typical triangular loading shown in Fig. 3.13a, assuming uniform load action on the

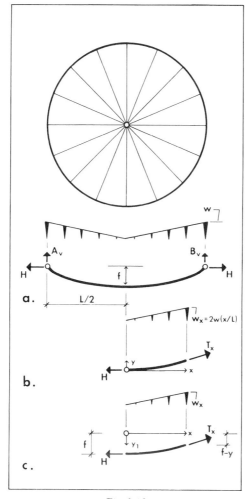

Fig. 3.13

roof. This assumption neglects the central tension ring causing single loads, and the weight of the cable being distributed uniformly along the length of the cable. The reactions are

$$A_v = B_v = \frac{wL}{4} \tag{3.54}$$

$$H = \frac{M_{max}}{f} = \frac{wL^2}{24f} \tag{3.55}$$

The maximum cable slope at the reactions is

$$\tan \theta_A = \frac{A_v}{H} = 6n \tag{3.56a}$$

The maximum cable force at the support is

$$T_{max} = \frac{H}{\cos \theta_A} = H\sqrt{1 + \tan^2 \theta_A} = H\sqrt{1 + 36n^2} \tag{3.57}$$

Placing the origin of the coordinate system at the low point of the cable (Fig. 3.13b), the equation for the cable shape can be derived as follows:

$$\Sigma M_x = 0 = H(y) - \frac{w_x(x)}{2} \frac{x}{3}$$

but

$$w_x = 2w\left(\frac{x}{2}\right)$$

$$H(y) = \frac{wx^3}{3L}$$

$$y = 8f\left(\frac{x}{L}\right)^3 \tag{3.58}$$

The slope of the curvature at any distance $x$ from the low point of the sag is

$$\tan \theta_x = \frac{dy}{dx} = \frac{24fx^2}{L^3} = 24n\left(\frac{x}{L}\right)^2 \tag{3.59}$$

The slope of the cable at the support at $x = L/2$ is

$$\tan \theta_B = 24n(\tfrac{1}{2})^2 = 6n \tag{3.56b}$$

The equation for the parabola may also be given by placing the origin of the coordinate system as shown in Fig. 3.13c

$$y_1 = f - y = f\left[1 - 8\left(\frac{x}{L}\right)^3\right] \tag{3.60}$$

The cable length is derived in a similar manner as for the square parabolic cable.

$$l = 2 \int_0^{L/2} dl = 2 \int_0^{L/2} \sqrt{1 + \left(\frac{dy}{dx}\right)^2}\ dx$$

$$l = L\left(1 + \frac{18}{5} n^2 - 18n^4\right) \tag{3.61}$$

For the derivation of the preceding expression refer to Problem 3.24. The change in cable length as caused by elongation due to loading is

$$\Delta l = 2 \int_0^{L/2} \frac{Tx}{AE} \, dl = \frac{2H}{AE} \int_0^{L/2} \left[1 + \left(\frac{dy}{dx}\right)^2\right] dx$$

$$\Delta l = \frac{HL}{AE}\left(1 + \frac{36}{5} n^2\right) \tag{3.62}$$

For the derivation of the formula for elastic stretching refer to Problem 3.24.

*Case B*

Assume the superimposed loads such as snow and mechanical/electrical equipment to be concentrated at the central roof portion of the round suspension roof of Case A, as shown in Fig. 3.14a. The reactions are

$$A_v = B_v = \frac{wL}{4} \tag{3.63}$$

$$H = \frac{M_{max}}{f} = \frac{wL^2}{12f} \tag{3.64}$$

The maximum cable slope at the reactions is

$$\tan \theta_A = \frac{A_v}{H} = 3n \tag{3.65}$$

The maximum cable force is

$$T_{max} = \frac{H}{\cos \theta_A} = H\sqrt{1 + \tan^2 \theta_A} = H\sqrt{1 + 9n^2} \tag{3.66}$$

The equation for the cable shape is derived as based on the location of the origin of the coordinate system as shown in Fig. 3.14b

$$\Sigma M_x = 0 = \frac{wL}{4}(x) - H(y) - \frac{w_x(x)\, x}{2}\frac{x}{3}$$

$$H(y) = \frac{wLx}{4} - \frac{wx^3}{6L}$$

$$y = f\left[3\frac{x}{L} - 4\left(\frac{x}{L}\right)^3\right] \tag{3.67}$$

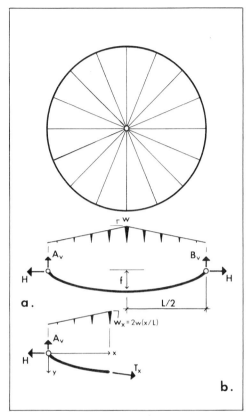

Fig. 3.14

As a rough first approximation for the cable length of any type of loading, the equation for the cable length of the square parabola may be used.

*Case C*

The cables for a tent-like structure are radially arranged and supported by a central column (Fig. 3.15). The tent has to be prestressed so its surface does not flutter under the varied types of loading. By prestretching the radial cables, tension forces are induced in the ring cables, thus putting the whole cable net in tension. The magnitude of the prestress forces depends on, among other considerations, the superimposed loads which should not cause the cables to slack. The design of a typical suspended cable is a function of the prestress force and the additional tension caused by the other loading cases. Here, only the triangular gravity loading case (Fig. 3.15) is investigated. The vertical reactions are found by taking moments about the supports

$$\Sigma M_B = 0 = A_v(L) + \frac{wL}{2} \frac{2L}{3} - H(h)$$

$$A_v = \frac{Hh}{L} - \frac{wL}{3} \tag{3.68}$$

$$\Sigma M_A = 0 = B_v(L) - \frac{wL}{2}\frac{L}{3} - H(h)$$

$$B_v = \frac{Hh}{L} + \frac{wL}{6} \tag{3.69}$$

The horizontal reaction or cable force is

$$H = \frac{M_{max}}{f} = \frac{0.064wL^4}{f} \tag{3.70}$$

Now the maximum cable force can be found by checking resultant forces at both supports (see Problem 3.25). The approximate cable length for any type of loading may be found with the following equation:

$$l \simeq L\left[1 + \frac{8}{3}n^2 + \left(\frac{h}{L}\right)^2\right] \tag{3.71}$$

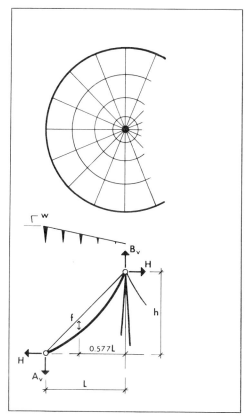

Fig. 3.15

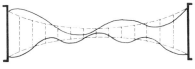

Fig. 3.16

### The Dual-Cable Beam

Visualize a single suspended cable, the primary cable, to be stabilized by a secondary arched cable. This secondary cable can be placed on top of the primary cable by employing compression struts, thus forming a lens-shaped beam; or it can be located below the primary cable by connecting the two with tension ties. The use of this dual-cable approach not only causes the single, flexible cable to be more stable with regard to fluttering, but also results in higher strength and stiffness. The cable beam is highly indeterminate from a force flow point of view; it obviously cannot be considered a rigid beam with a linear behavior in the elastic range; in addition, the effect of large deflections cannot be neglected. Even for equal vertical displacement of the top and bottom cables, the compressive force in the arched cable is not linearly related to the tension force in the suspended cable at a given section. The sharing of the loads between the cables, that is finding the proportion of the load carried by each cable, is an extremely difficult problem. It is surely overly conservative to assume all the loads to be supported by the suspended cable, while the secondary cable's only function is to damp the vibration of the primary cable. Lev Zetlin has shown that the oscillating of a single cable can be successfully dampened by using a secondary cable (reference 151). Each of the cables always takes a different geometric configuration under dynamic loading, thus one cable counteracts the movement of the other (Fig. 3.16). Furthermore, it is apparent from Eq. (3.38) that the fundamental period in the primary cable is substantially reduced due to the additional large prestress force, while the weight is only increased slightly. In the following example the approximate behavior of a cable beam is investigated. Linearly related behavior of the cables is assumed, which in general is not true. The preliminary sizing of the cables is based on strength only, neglecting the effect of deformation and dynamic loading.

**Example 3.3** A stadium is covered by cable trusses spaced parallel at 17 ft on center. The trusses span 272 ft. The cable trusses are either strutted or countertied (Fig. 3.17). Sag and rise of the cables are each 14 ft. The following typical loads are used: 9 psf dead load, 20 psf live load, a uniform wind suction of 8 psf, and an equivalent uniform prestress load of 15 psf. The wind loads are obviously not acting as given. However, the assumed uniform action makes it possible to consider the wind as a possible design determinant for this preliminary investigation. A typical interior cable beam must support the following loads:

$$
\begin{aligned}
\text{dead load:} \quad & w_D = 0.009(17) = 0.15 \text{ k/ft} \\
\text{live load:} \quad & w_L = 0.020(17) = 0.34 \text{ k/ft} \\
\text{wind load:} \quad & q = 0.008(17) = 0.14 \text{ k/ft} \\
\text{prestress load:} \quad & p = 0.015(17) = 0.26 \text{ k/ft}
\end{aligned}
$$

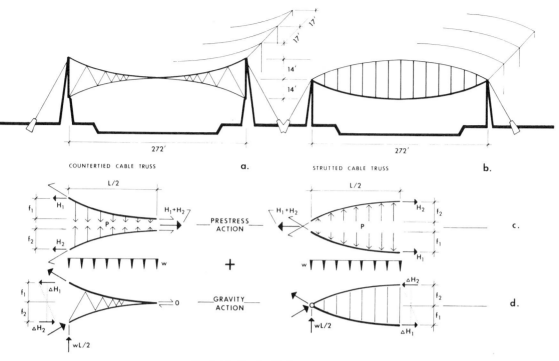

Fig. 3.17 Dual-cable beams.

Using the uniform force action along the cable beam neglects the effect of the concentrated action of the struts or ties causing single loads. The single loads, in turn, generate a polygonal cable form, rather than a parabolic curvature as is assumed in this analysis for both cables. Visualize the web members to consist of a continuous membrane causing uniform force distribution.

In the first loading stage, prestress forces are induced into the beam structure. The initial tension (i.e., prestress force minus compression due to cable weight) in the arched cable should always be larger than the compression forces that are induced by the superimposed loads due to the roofing deck and live load; this is to prevent the convex cable and the web members from becoming slack. The degree of prestressing, however, is not only dependent on this one loading condition, but also on the allowable deflection and the damping of vibrations. Investigating the prestress case first (Fig. 3.16c), it can be shown that for a cable sag-to-cable rise ratio that is not equal to one, the tension forces in the cables are not equal to each other, thus leading to different natural periods of vibration whose oscillating frequencies tend to cancel out rather than reinforce one another. Rotational equilibrium as based on linear behavior of a rigid system yields the cable tension forces:

$$H_1(f_1) = H_2(f_2) = \frac{pL^2}{8}$$

$$H_1 = \frac{pL^2}{8f_1} \qquad H_2 = \frac{pL^2}{8f_2} \tag{3.72}$$

$$\frac{H_1}{H_2} = \frac{f_2}{f_1} \tag{3.73}$$

177

The ratio of the tension forces in the cables is equal to the inverse of the sag (rise) ratio. In this approach the effect of cable size upon the magnitude of the cable forces is neglected. For this specific problem the cable forces in the upper and lower cable are equal to each other because the sag and rise are the same:

$$f_1 = f_2 = 14 \text{ ft}$$

$$H_1 = H_2 = H = \frac{pL^2}{8f} = \frac{0.26(272)^2}{8(14)} = 171.75 \text{ k}$$

It is assumed that the external loads are shared equally between the two cables because of their identical geometry. It is further assumed that the cable sizes are approximately equal to each other so that each cable carries one-half of the superimposed loads (i.e., the loads applied after prestressing the truss). On the other hand, should the size of the primary load-carrying cable be much larger, then all of the superimposed loads have to be assumed to be carried by the suspended primary cable. The change in tension in the two cables is

$$\Delta H = \frac{(w/2)L^2}{8f} = \frac{wL^2}{16f}$$

The same result is obtained by balancing the external moment with the force couple provided by the cables

$$\Delta H(2f) = \frac{wL^2}{8}$$

$$\Delta H = \frac{wL^2}{16f} \tag{3.74}$$

Should the cable curvatures be different, distribute the load to each cable in proportion to the inverse of their respective sag or rise

$$\frac{w_1}{f_2} = \frac{w_2}{f_1} = \frac{w}{f_1 + f_2} \tag{3.75}$$

For the specific example with $f_1 = f_2$

$$w_1 = w_2 = \frac{w}{2}$$

The change in tension is

$$\Delta H = \frac{wL^2}{16f} = \frac{w(272)^2}{16(14)} = 330.29w$$

The change in tension for the different loading cases is as follows:

$$
\begin{array}{lll}
\text{dead load:} & \Delta H_D = 330.29(0.15) = 49.54 \text{ k} \\
\text{live load:} & \Delta H_L = 330.29(0.34) = 112.30 \text{ k} \\
\text{wind load:} & \Delta H_W = -330.29(0.14) = -46.24 \text{ k}
\end{array}
$$

Notice that the change in tension due to dead load is actually only caused by the superimposed dead load which should not include the weight of the truss as is assumed for this approximation. Since the sag ratio for the given cable structure is rather small the minimum cable force $H$ can be considered equal to the maximum tension force $T_{max}$ as shown below. The maximum cable slope is

$$\tan \theta = 4h = 4\left(\frac{14}{272}\right) = 0.21$$

The maximum tension force is

$$T_{max} = H \sqrt{1 + \tan^2\theta} = H \sqrt{1 + 0.21^2} = 1.02H$$

This small difference between the tension forces is considered unimportant in comparison to the other rough approximations which were taken. First, the arched or convex cable is checked for slacking under any loading. The governing loading case is due to full gravity action

$$T_{min_2} = 171.75 - 49.54 - 112.30 = 9.91 \text{ k} \geqslant 0$$

There will be no slack (i.e., there will be no compression).

Several loading cases have to be checked to determine the critical ones for the design of the cables. For the design of the arched cable it is assumed that the loading case of initial tension, dead load, and wind suction controls

$$T_{max_2} = 171.75 - 49.54 + 46.24 = 168.45 \text{ k}$$
$$T_u = \text{LF} (T_{max}) = 2.2(168.45) = 336.90 \text{ k}$$

Try $1\frac{3}{4}$ in. diameter steel strand class A coating

$$A = 1.84 \text{ in.}^2 \qquad T_u = 376 \text{ k}$$

The critical loading case for the design of the primary cable is the increase of the initial tension due to full gravity action

$$T_{max_1} = 171.45 + 49.54 + 112.30 = 333.59 \text{ k}$$
$$T_u = \text{LF} (T_{max}) = 2.2(333.59) = 733.90 \text{ k}$$

Try $2\frac{1}{2}$ in. diameter steel strand class A coating

$$A = 3.75 \text{ in.}^2 \qquad T_u = 752 \text{ k}$$

Note that the primary cable has about twice as much area as the secondary cable which means that the superimposed loads should have been distributed to the cables approximately in proportion to these cable areas, that is, about 2/3 to the primary cable and 1/3 to the secondary cable. This, in turn will yield a larger primary cable size. The size of the secondary cable will not be influenced that much by the different distribution of the superimposed loads, because its most important size-determining factor is the magnitude of the original prestress force.

## Problems

3.1   The single-cantilevered roof for a hangar is cable supported. Masts are spaced 30 ft apart and carry pairs of steel strands which support steel girders upon which the purlins rest. The weight of the roof is 14 psf, just enough to counteract the uplift due to wind; the snow load is 30 psf. Only uniform gravity loading is considered for this preliminary design. For the building geometry refer to Fig. 3.18a.

(a) Determine the cable size by considering only the front roof portion; verify that the steeper cable for the back will be larger. Neglect the cable extension.

(b) Determine the cable extension and the vertical displacement of the beam support.

(c) Discuss how you would proceed in designing the steel girder.

(d) What is the major problem in a single-cantilever structure? Compare it to the double-cantilever structure in the next problem.

**3.2** For the cable supported double-cantilevered hangar (Fig. 3.18b) determine the cable sizes. The cables support the steel girders set at 25.5-ft intervals. Assume a roof dead load of 15 psf and a live load of 40 psf.

**3.3** For cases (d) – (f) in Fig. 3.18 determine the reactions, cable forces, cable shape, cable length, increase of cable length, and increase of cable sag.

**3.4** Determine the approximate cable size for a single-strut trussed beam (king-post truss). Neglect the elastic deformations of the cable. For the geometry of the truss refer to Fig. 3.18c, with $L = 40$ ft, $f = 4$ ft, and $w = 4$ k/ft. Discuss the design of the beam.

**3.5** What can you say about the maximum cable force and cable sag as a single load moves from midspan (Fig. 3.18d) to the quarter span?

**3.6** Why should case (f) (Fig. 3.18) not be solved by using the superposition method?

**3.7** What difference does it make in cable size for case (d), if the sag is increased from 10% of the span to 20% of the span?

**3.8** Assume a cable of a given length to carry different types of loads. How does the sag change for cases (d), (f), and (g)?

**3.9** For the cable shown in Fig. 3.18g, with $L = 100$ ft, $f = 10$ ft, and carrying a load of $w = 100$ lb/ft, determine the size, geometry, sag at 20 ft from the support, slope, length, elongation and increase in sag.

**3.10** Decrease the sag in Problem 3.9 to $f = 1$ ft. What impact does this change of sag-to-span ratio to $n = 0.01$ have on the design and analysis?

**3.11** Determine for case (g) with $w = 1$ k/ft (Problem 3.9), which sag-to-span ratio yields the most economical solution as based on cable weight. Plot sag-to-span ratios: 0.05, 0.1, 0.15, 0.2, and 0.3 against the cable weight. Neglect elastic deformations for this approximate approach.

**3.12** The length of the cable in Problem 3.9 was determined for a temperature of $50°F$. Find the change in the unstressed length of the cable and the change in sag at a temperature of $110°F$. The coefficient of linear expansion is $\alpha = 0.0000065$ in./in./$°F$. Draw your conclusions.

**3.13** A prestretched or trampoline-like cable roof is used rather than the suspended one of Problem 3.9. The cables are pretensioned each to 350 k to stiffen the roof against fluttering and to reduce the deflection due to gravity loading. Determine the

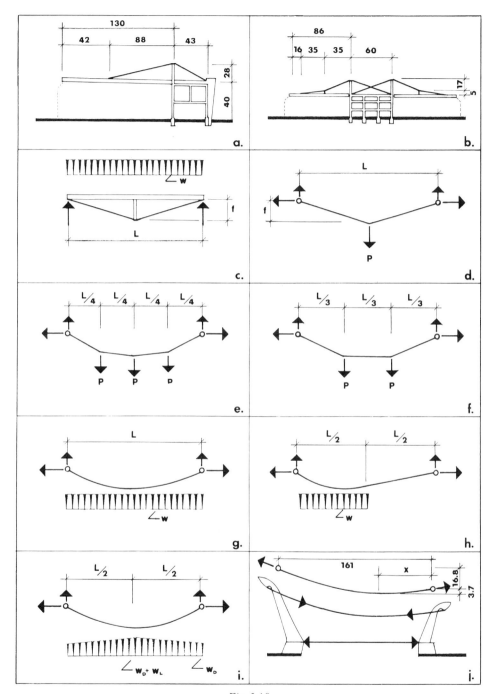

Fig. 3.18

approximate displacement of the cable at centerspan. Assume that the magnitude of the prestress force is hardly changed by the superimposed external loads.

**3.14** The single-layer suspension roof for a rectangular building with the parallel cables spaced 5 ft apart, spans 240 ft and has a maximum sag-to-span ratio of $n = 1/12$. The roof must support a dead load of 20 psf and a live load of 30 psf assumed to act on the horizontal roof projection. Determine the cable size, cable geometry, cable sag at $L/4$, cable slope at $L/4$, cable length, increase in cable length and cable sag; assume a temperature difference of 50°F. Ignore dynamic considerations.

**3.15** Derive in more detail the length [Eq. (3.34)] and elastic elongation [Eq. (3.36)] for a cable with supports at the same level.

**3.16** Derive the expression for the elongation of the inclined cable [Eq. (3.52)] carrying a uniform load on its horizontal projection.

**3.17** For the roof structure shown in Fig. 3.18j, determine the size of a typical interior cable spaced at 10 ft on center. The cable size is based on the construction stage where the roof acts as a true suspension structure supporting only the dead load of 33 psf due to the precast concrete panels and concrete ribs and ceiling. In the final stage, the roof does not act as a true suspension system since the concrete ribs along the cables together with the concrete slab form a suspended ribbed shell which due to its stiffness controls deflection and the danger of flutter.

**3.18** A dome spans 138 ft. It is supported by eight ribs which exert a lateral thrust of 1706 k at the base (see dome of S. Maria Del Fiore in Florence, Italy). Determine the size and number of cables to resist this thrust.

**3.19** For case (h) (Fig. 3.18) determine the location of the low point of the cable, the maximum cable force, and the equation defining the geometry of the cable.

**3.20** Consider the snow load in Problem 3.14 to be zero at the edges but twice as much at the center (i.e., 60 psf). Does this new loading condition change the design of the cable?

**3.21** A round stadium roof with a span of 420 ft is supported by radially arranged cables. The single layer of cables is weighed by precast I-sections to stabilize the roof against flutter. The cables are spaced at 3.75° intervals, framing outward from a 45 ft diameter tension ring in the center, to a compression ring that rests on 32 pairs of X columns. Assume a total load of 50 psf to act on the horizontal projection of the roof. For this approximate solution neglect the 45 ft center opening (i.e., line load) and continue the surface loading. Determine the cable size, cable shape, vertical displacement of cable at 100 ft from the support, cable length, and cable elongation. Assume a sag-to-span ratio of $n = 0.1$.

**3.22** Using the horizontal cable force found in Problem 3.21, determine the approximate size of the central 45 ft tension cable by assuming the cable forces to act as a uniform radial load $p$.

**3.23** Assume the cable roof of Problem 3.21 has to carry an additional steel-framed penthouse to house the mechanical and electrical equipment. Consider the weight to be equivalent to a single load of 10 k per cable to act at the centerspan. Find the cable size.

**3.24** Derive for the cable carrying a triangular load as in Problem 3.21, the cable length [Eq. (3.61)] and the cable elongation [Eq. (3.62)].

**3.25** Determine the maximum cable force for the inclined tent cable carrying a triangular load (Fig. 3.15).

**3.26** Consider the triangular load (Fig. 3.15) to act on a cable having its supports at the same elevation. Derive the equations for the maximum cable force and cable shape.

**3.27** How much does the bottom cable have to be spread, approximately, to introduce the initial prestress force in Example 3.3 for a lens-shaped cable truss?

**3.28** Determine the approximate deflection of the cable truss in Problem 3.27. Assume conservatively the deflection of the bottom cable to be equal to the deformation of the whole truss (i.e., neglect the effect of the top cable).

**3.29** A prestretched flat horizontal roof is designed for very high prestress forces, as to allow only a small sag and to reduce fluttering. Investigate this circular roof of 120-ft diameter to be prestressed for 600 lb/ft and permit a maximum sag of 10 ft. Neglect the small amount of additional tension due to the superimposed loading and ignore any cable extensions. First assume the flat roof to be built of radially arranged cables and then of a surface membrane. Determine the loads which can be carried.

**3.30** A flat roof consists of a series of parallel cables pairs arranged 2 ft on centers horizontally and $1\frac{1}{2}$-ft apart vertically. The cables are pretensioned and strung between concrete abutments 200-ft apart. A maximum deformation of only 10 in. is permitted for the 15 psf dead load and the 20 psf live load. Determine the approximate cable sizes.

# 4 SINGLE-STORY SKELETON STRUCTURES

As the name suggests, skeleton structures are composed mainly of line elements, that is beams and columns (struts, ties, etc.). They can be classified into two basic groups:

- Frames that have some rigid joints and thus continuity, so that loads can be resisted primarily in bending.
- Trusses that consist of individual members which are hinged to each other and generally form triangles. The predominant response of the members to loading is in axial action.

Obviously, the frame and truss concepts can be used in combination with each other.

The skeleton principle can be employed for single- or multibay systems. In this chapter only one-way skeletons are investigated; two-way and spatial systems are discussed in other portions of the book.

## 4.1 THE FRAME

Some of the typical basic frame forms which will be discussed are shown in Fig. 4.1. The geometrical frame characteristics are identified through transition from a triangular to a rectangular, to an arched shape, thereby suggesting the infinite possibilities of basic unit shapes. These frames can be arranged in a parallel, radial, or any other fashion to form a building envelope.

The frame forms can also be derived in direct response to the primary loading. Visualize a cable to react to given loads. In order to resist forces in pure tension, it must adjust its shape to form a so-called funicular line; some common funicular shapes have already been shown in Fig. 3.1. When this funicular cable is made rigid and rotated to a standing position, it acts as an arch in pure compression.

The comparison of the ideal funicular form, also called pressure line, with the real frame (Fig. 4.2) helps to identify the formal efficiency from a force flow point of view, since the difference between the forms is equivalent to rotation (i.e., eccentricity of axial force with respect to funicular line).

184

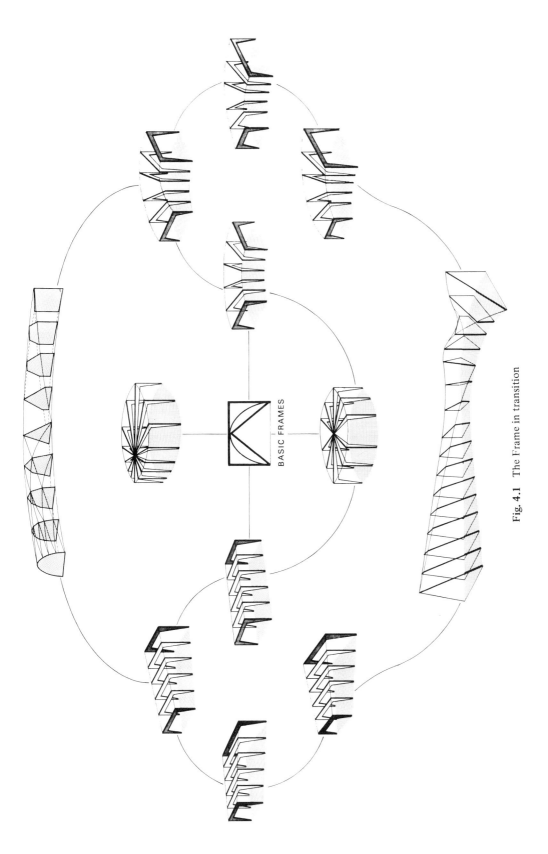

BASIC FRAMES

Fig. 4.1   The Frame in transition

185

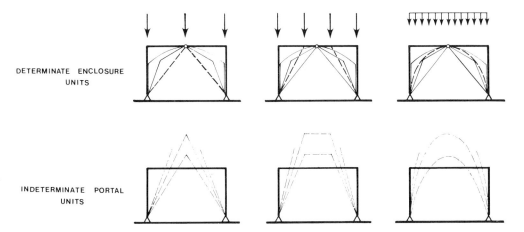

Length of funicular shape as a function of relative stiffness of column and beam

**Fig. 4.2** The deviation of enclosure units from funicular shape

The rectangular frame differs quite a bit in shape from the parabolic funicular line for the typical uniform loading condition, clearly expressing the dominant character of bending. On the other hand, the pressure line for the arch may fall within the kern of the section (e.g., central third for rectangular cross-section), with moments so small as to not cause any tension; this feature is important for materials of weak tensile capacity, such as masonry.

The nature of the basic frame unit is further investigated in Fig. 4.3. Here the following characteristics are identified: material, member structure (solid, trussed, etc.), member form (constant versus variable cross-section), member kit (l, L, T, I, etc.), and details. Further, different ways for placing hinges, that is, simple field connections not transferring any moments, are studied in Fig. 4.4.

### Behavioral Considerations

A planar structure can be at rest only if there is no translational or rotational movement present, as clearly reflected by the following three equations of equilibrium:

$$\Sigma F_x = 0 \qquad \Sigma F_y = 0 \qquad \Sigma M_z = 0$$

Remember, other alternate equation sets are possible.

These conditions of equilibrium do not apply only to the external conditions of a member or member assemblage (beam, column, frame, truss, entire building, etc.), that is, the equilibrium between the external loading and the reactions of the respective nondeformable, perfectly rigid members, but also to the internal force flow along the member, now taking into account its behavioral elastic properties. The nature of the internal force flow at a given location is found by cutting the member; at any cut not more than three force components occur.

The behavior of the overall structure (of adequate strength) depends not only on how

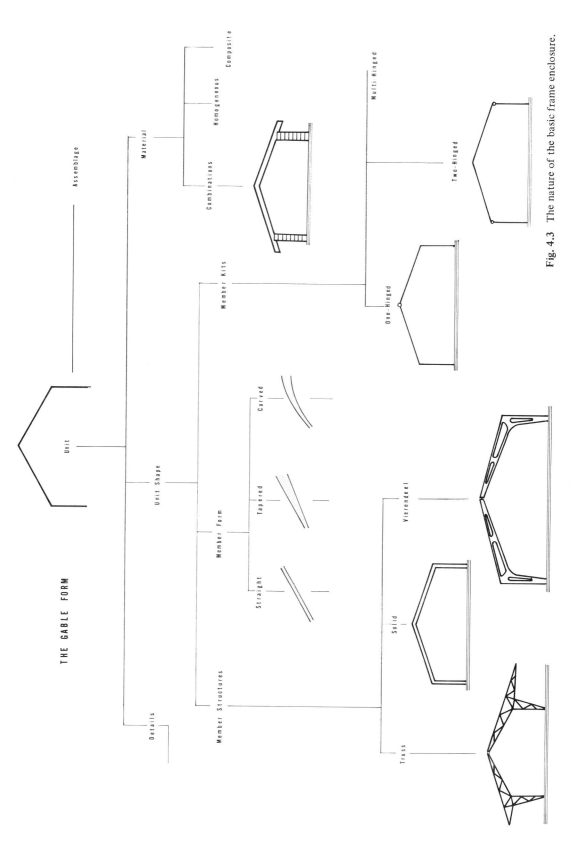

Fig. 4.3  The nature of the basic frame enclosure.

THE GABLE FORM

Details

Unit

Assemblage

Unit Shape

Member Structures

Member Form

Member Kits

Material

Straight

Tapered

Curved

Solid

Vierendeel

Truss

One-Hinged

Two-Hinged

Multi Hinged

Combinations

Homogeneous

Composite

187

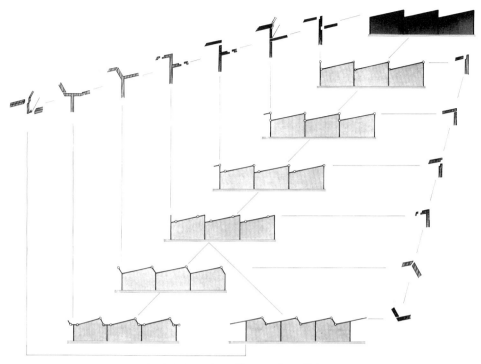

**Fig. 4.4** Location of beam-column linkages.

it is supported, but also on how its members are arranged and connected to each other. For instance, the various types of rectangular frames in the top portion of Fig. 4.5 demonstrate clearly unstable conditions.

The first frame is externally unstable because only two roller supports are provided; the two vertical reaction forces are not sufficient and cannot prevent horizontal movement. Equilibrium of planar, nonparallel, nonconcurrent force systems requires at least three reactive conditions. But the reactions should be placed so that they are neither concurrent nor parallel, since otherwise the structure would be geometrically unstable. The other frames in Fig. 4.5 are internally, rather than externally, unstable, either due to missing members or because of too many hinged connections. A structure which is unstable does not necessarily collapse, since it may reach a state of equilibrium after it has moved.

When the external and/or internal conditions of the structure are such that the three equations of equilibrium are not sufficient for the solution of the force flow, then additional equations are necessary, and the structure is called indeterminate. Hence, planar structures are only statically determinate if the three equations of equilibrium can solve for the magnitude of the internal and external forces due to any type of loading. It should be obvious that a structure must be stable, whether the method of analysis is determinate or indeterminate.

The degree of indeterminacy may be found by making the structure statically determinate and stable by removing supports and/or cutting members. The number of force-resisting conditions taken away is equal to the degree of indeterminacy or redundancy so named after the number of forces which are not needed to insure static equilibrium. For instance, the continuous rigid frame [Fig. 4.5 (bottom)] can be made determinate by cutting the beam, thus forming two independent, cantilevering, determinate tree units.

Three restraints have been removed: the normal, shear, and moment resistance. Hence the structure is three times indeterminate or has three redundants. Redundancy is an important phenomenon because it allows the force flow to take an alternate path if the structure should be failing at a certain location, thus not necessarily resulting in a progressive total collapse of the building.

The process of determining the possible redundancy and stability of a structure can be formalized as follows. The unknown forces in a planar frame of $(m)$ members are the shear $(V)$, the axial force $(N)$, and the moment $(M)$ for each member, as well as the support reaction components $(r)$

$$\text{unknown conditions:} \quad 3m + r \tag{a}$$

Each rigid joint $(j)$ is capable of transferring translational and rotational forces and thus furnishes three equations of equilibrium $(3j)$. However, in a frame members are not necessarily all connected with moment resisting joints; some may be pinned to each other, or internal hinges may appear along members. These special conditions $(c)$ release some of the unknown internal forces

$$\text{known conditions} \quad 3j + c \tag{b}$$

One may conclude that if the number of unknown conditions is equal to the number of known conditions, only then is the structure determinate and stable

$$3m + r = 3j + c \tag{4.1a}$$

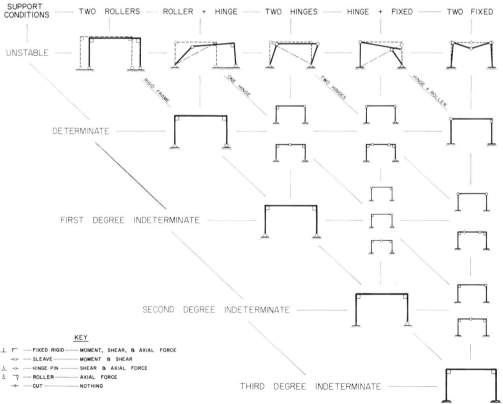

Fig. 4.5

The structure is unstable if

$$3m + r < 3j + c \qquad (4.1b)$$

The structure is indeterminate if

$$3m + r > 3j + c \qquad (4.1c)$$

The condition of the three-hinge portal frame (Fig. 4.5) can be evaluated as follows, realizing that a pin support prevents horizontal and vertical movement ($r = 2$) and that the hinge in the beam releases one unknown, the moment ($c = 1$):

$$
\begin{aligned}
3m + r &= 3(3) + (2 + 2) = 13 \\
3j \;\; + c &= 3(4) + 1 \qquad\;\; = 13 \\
\hline
13 &= 13
\end{aligned}
$$

The frame is determinate and stable.

The degree of indeterminacy for the continuous frame with a hinged joint can be determined as follows. A fixed-end support provides resistance to horizontal, vertical, and rotational movement ($r = 3$). In general, a pinned joint with $n$ members framing into it can be visualized as consisting of $n - 1$ members with hinged ends

$$
\begin{aligned}
3m + r &= 3(3) + (3 + 3) = 15 \\
3j \;\; + c &= 3(4) + 1 \qquad\;\; = 13 \\
\hline
15 &> 13
\end{aligned}
$$

The frame is twice indeterminate.

Although this comparison of known and unknown conditions is necessary, it is not sufficient with respect to stability of framed structures. For further discussion of this topic, the reader may refer to Review of Truss Characteristics and Section 5.2.

A structure with redundant members or support conditions is stronger and stiffer; it is less vulnerable to collapse, if some of the members should be failing. Redundancy is a particularly important consideration for long-span structures, which cannot rely on adjacent structures for support as short-span structures do; they are extremely vulnerable not to localized but total building collapse as so clearly exemplified by the failure of the Hartford Civic Center Coliseum in 1978. Statically determinate structures, on the other hand, can absorb material changes and movements (shrinkage, creep, temperature and moisture changes, settlement, lack of fit, etc.) without causing additional stresses.

In order to design a member, the internal force flow along that member must be known so that its minimum required size can be found which will be capable of responding to the maximum internal stresses with an appropriate safety margin. The internal force flow is determined by cutting the structural element that is under investigation. The member portions to the left or to the right of the section are called free bodies. Typical free-bodies are shown in Fig. 4.6.

The internal forces which occur at the point of section represent the equivalent internal actions and identify the minimum required material resistance to shear, axial action, and rotation; they are determined from equilibrium with external loads and reactions of the respective free-body.

It is helpful to derive general expressions for the magnitude of the internal forces as based on the typical loading conditions given in Fig. 4.6. For example, the following

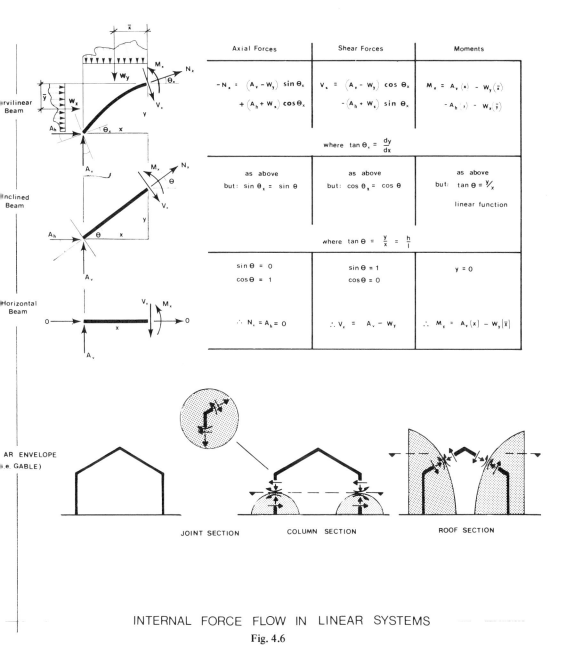

INTERNAL  FORCE  FLOW  IN  LINEAR  SYSTEMS

**Fig. 4.6**

equation for the shear $V_x$ can be derived from the arch free-body by summing all the forces parallel to $V_x$

$$\Sigma F_y = 0 = A_v \cos \theta_x - A_h \sin \theta_x - W_z \sin \theta_x - W_y \cos \theta_x - V_x$$
$$V_x = (A_v - W_y) \cos \theta_x - (A_h + W_z) \sin \theta_x$$

The other equations for $N_x$ and $M_x$ in Fig. 4.6 can be derived in a similar manner. The same equations can also be obtained from the free-bodies of the right structure portion rather than the left; for this condition only the shear equation will be negative.

The following conventions are used in plotting the force flow along the frame members:

- The moments are shown along the tension side of the members.
- The compression forces are shown along the exterior faces of single-unit enclosure systems.
- The positive shear (defined by the direction of the shear forces in the free-bodies) is also shown along the exterior faces.

One should keep in mind that slight inaccuracies are introduced by replacing the actual structure with an idealized model, the so-called line diagrams. For example, a wall does not provide just a single load reaction to a beam sitting on it; along the contact area of beam and wall a bearing pressure is generated, the resultant of which can be visualized as the reaction. Rarely does a simply supported beam rest on a roller and pin, as is assumed; for example, a joist may sit on opposite masonry walls of exactly the same nature.


## Design Considerations

As will be shown in the Example section, the primary design determinant for the proportioning of the beams and columns of typical single-story frames is bending due to gravity action, rather similar to the behavior of continuous beams; that is quite in contrast to high-rise buildings where axial action is obviously an important consideration. The axial compression in addition to bending, especially in the columns, is rather small but still significant enough to be considered in the preliminary design; however, the simple interaction equation (1.47) needs only to be considered.

The spacing of parallel frames is in the range from 16 to 20 ft and up to 40 ft, depending on the building type. The purlins span the distance between the frames and support the deck or sheathing. For pitched roofs it is assumed that the force component parallel to the roof plane is transferred by the roof skin in diaphragm action to the frames, so that the purlins neither have to twist nor to bend about their weak axis (Fig. 1.16).

To prevent sidesway buckling of the columns about their weak axes, as well as to resist lateral force action perpendicular to the frames, shear walls or diagonal bracing in certain bays along the facade are provided. Further, depending on the stiffness of the roof diaphragm, bracing may have to be added along the roof plane to prevent lateral buckling of the frame beams (Fig. 2.18) which should be determined solely by the spacing of the purlins.

Most frames are pin-connected to their foundation, realizing that for normal soil conditions (no rock) the footings probably will rotate anyway and thus form equivalent hinges independent of the degree of fixity between the columns and their foundations. The lateral thrust, especially for frames with small height-to-span ratios, is so large that it must be resisted by tie rods between the column bases rather than directly by the soil.

The loads can be selected by referring to Chapter 1.1; reasonable preliminary dead loads can be estimated from Table 1.1. Typical load distributions for a simple building envelope are shown in Fig. 4.7. The placement of the gravity loading depends on the spacing of the roof joists (purlins, beams, etc.) that span the distance between the frames. It has been shown in the discussion of floor framing systems in Chapter 2 that the beam

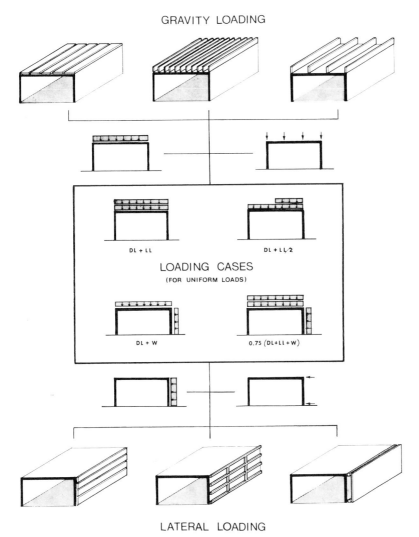

GRAVITY LOADING

LOADING CASES
(FOR UNIFORM LOADS)

DL + LL          DL + LL/2

DL + W          0.75 (DL+Ll+W)

LATERAL LOADING

**Fig. 4.7** Load distribution for portal frames.

spacing has hardly any influence on the magnitude of the moment that acts on the supporting frame beam, but only on the shear distribution which for preliminary investigations may be considered as not critical. Hence, for preliminary purposes, gravity loading can be considered uniformly distributed. Similar reasoning can be applied to the lateral force action which the building curtain transfers to the frames, keeping in mind that direct uniform pressure upon the column will cause larger bending moments in the column (Problems 4.1p–r).

Only the primary critical load arrangements and combinations are given in Fig. 4.7 and are studied further in the context of the design problems. Usually, for single-story frames of small height-to-width ratio (but not for fixed post-beam systems), lateral forces do not have to be considered, since they, in combination with other loads, do not control the design of the primary structural frame units.

**Problems**

**4.0**   Investigate the frames in Fig. 4.67f–l with respect to stability and redundancy.

## 4.2  PORTAL FRAMES

It is impossible to define exactly the concept of the beam-column/wall system; the examples in Fig. 4.8 can only suggest the many different possibilities, in this case just for single-span units. The beam may be part of a repetitive system of beams, as will be demonstrated by the cases in Fig. 4.64, and may be hidden between the roofing and ceiling, or it may be an individual, more isolated member; it may also be exposed thus expressing its purpose as structure. The beam may just sit on its supports and be hinged to them, or it may form a continuous frame together with the column(s).

Only the more common basic frame types in Fig. 4.9 will be investigated in detail in the following section. While the geometry of these support structures is symmetrical, live loading will introduce conditions of asymmetry. Some typical asymmetrical frames are identified in Fig. 4.8 and are studied as homework problems.

With an increase of span, the simply supported concept becomes less efficient because of the rapid increase in moment and deflection, that is, increase in dead weight. The magnitude of the bending stresses is very much reduced by the cantilever-type of construction as the graphical analysis in Fig. 4.10 explains. The maximum moment in the double cantilever beam is only 17% of that for the simply supported case for the given arrangement of supports and loading! Similarly, the large field moment of the simply supported beam can be decreased by introducing continuity between beam and column, thus causing indeterminacy and thereby transferring part of the field moment to the beam-column intersection; these frame characteristics are discussed in more detail later in this section.

Some typical long-span post-beam building structures are shown in Fig. 4.11, all examples requiring column-free interior space. In his famous Crown Hall (a), Mies van der Rohe has articulated the power and beauty of the post-beam structure by exposing the lightness of the steel skeleton as contrasted by the glass surface. The roof platform is suspended from the welded plate girders, which are 60 ft apart and, together with the columns, form continuous portal frames.

The roofs of cases (c), (e), and (f) also hang from exposed primary beam systems. Because of the enormous span of 324 ft, the rigid bents of case (f) formed by tubular, triangular space trusses (27 ft deep, spaced 153 ft on center) were necessary, thus giving wind resistance in the transverse as well as longitudinal directions. The separation of the bents from the roof substructure allows for the independent movement of the exposed trusses.

The 17-ft deep triangular steel-pipe trusses of case (c) are simply supported on laced double steel columns that form a frame to resist the wind. For this case, the double truss members are on top, where the compression occurs. In case (e), the space trusses are arranged in a radial manner to support the step pyramid-like dome structure below.

The major portion of the roof of case (h) is supported by parallel, tapering steel trusses (10–14 ft deep) spaced at 44 ft on center that are simply supported on twin-column pylons. These pylons form trussed frames to resist wind in the transverse direction.

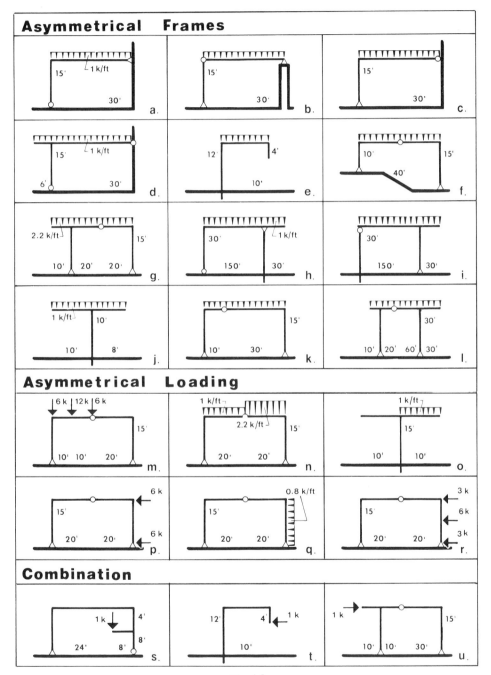

Fig. 4.8

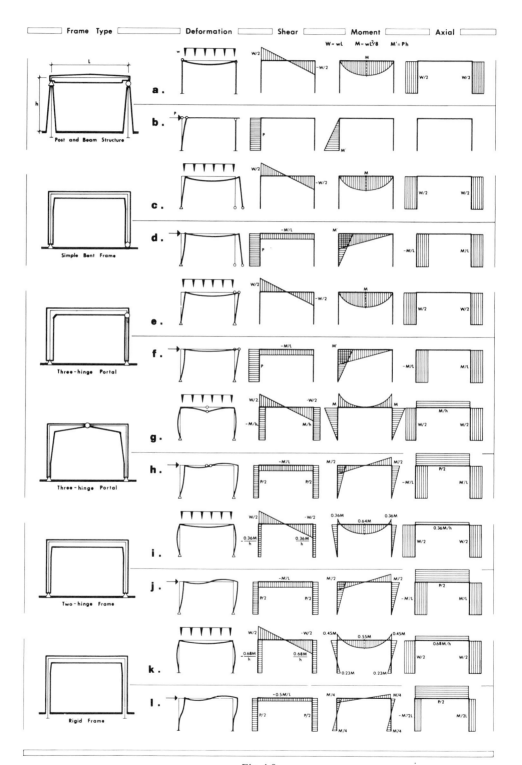

Fig. 4.9

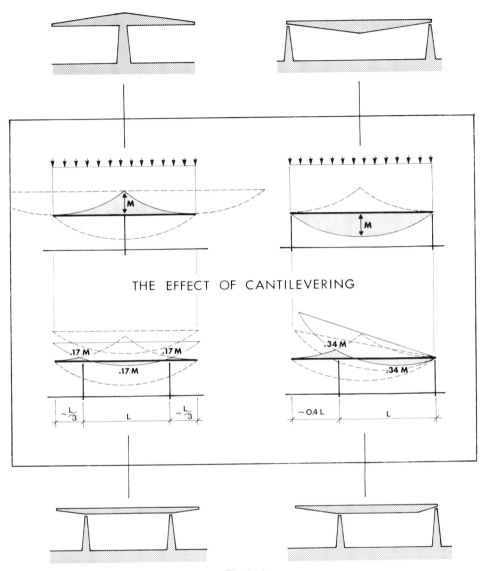

Fig. 4.10

The primary structural elements of the roof structure of case (g) are the two 15-ft deep trusses that rest on the 5-ft diameter concrete columns. In the other direction, plate girders support the inclined walls which are also used to resist the wind in the transverse direction. The wind in the longitudinal direction is carried by the triangular units formed by the stepped seating, the end walls, and the floor slab.

In case (d), sets of post-tensioned concrete portal frames intersect to form a two-way frame structure. They not only support the roof, but also the cantilevering exterior concrete wall girders and the interior balcony that is hung from them.

The four primary roof steel girders of case (b) are supported by ten inclined Y-shaped concrete columns, which, in turn, form a ring system of interlocking portal frames following the plan of the elongated hexagon.

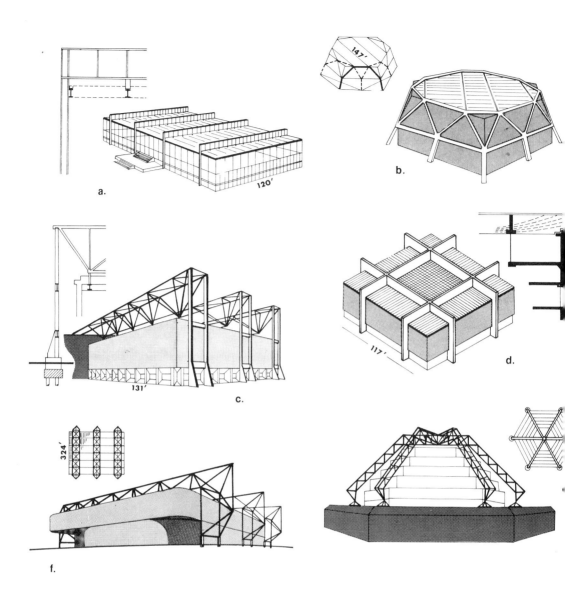

a.

b.

c.

d.

f.

## LONGSPAN PORTALS

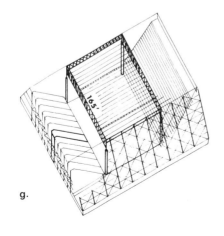

g.

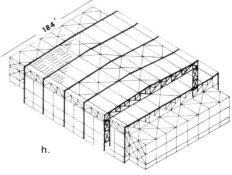

h.

Fig. 4.11

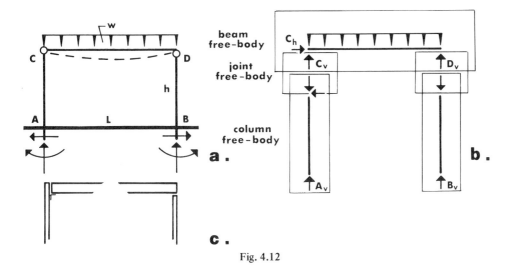

Fig. 4.12

## Determinate Frames

### *The Post-Beam Frame*

The internal force flow along the beam and columns is determined by considering first gravity loading and then lateral force action.

■ *Uniform Gravity Loading*

First separate the members, that is, the beam from the columns, as shown in Fig. 4.12b. The free-body of the beam shows that at the roller support $D$ only a reacting force perpendicular to the beam (parallel to the column) can be provided, while at the pin support $C$ both a horizontal and a vertical reaction can be accommodated. Obviously, without the potential to resist horizontal forces the beam is unstable and moves freely under lateral force action, assuming that it is not stabilized by other building parts.

In this case, no lateral force resistance is needed, since the loads act perpendicularly to the member, thus

$$\Sigma H = 0 = C_h$$

It can be concluded that the beam is a typical simply supported bending member carrying a uniform load; the shear and moment flow for this case should be quite familar

$$M_{max} = M_{L/2} = \frac{wL^2}{8} \qquad V_C = -V_D = \frac{wL}{2}$$

With respect to the column free-bodies it is clear that the beam reactions cause only axial force action in the columns. For instance, in column $AC$:

$$\Sigma V = 0 = C_v - A_v \qquad C_v = A_v$$

$$\Sigma H = 0 = A_h$$

$$\Sigma M = 0 = M_A$$

Notice that for this loading case the fixed column-to-ground connections provide only axial force resistance, although they are capable of resisting lateral and bending forces as well.

The internal force flow along the post-beam structure is shown in Fig. 4.9a.

■ *Lateral Loading*

Separating the beam from the columns, one notices in Fig. 4.13b that all of the horizontal force is carried by the column located at the side of the force action. In this case the beam cannot transfer horizontal forces to the far column because the roller connection cannot transmit any lateral force action.

The free-body of the column clearly shows a vertical cantilever beam supporting a single point load at its free end. The force flow of this case is also well known, and is shown in Fig. 4.9b.

$$\Sigma H = 0 = P - A_h \qquad A_h = P$$
$$M_A = M_{max} = Ph$$

Obviously, it would be more efficient for both columns to share the lateral force response. This can be accomplished by replacing the right-hand roller support with a pin connection similar to the one on the left side. Assuming that both columns are the same size, one can also assume that the load is shared equally by both, as shown in Figs. 4.13c and d.

The post-beam structure is now once indeterminate with respect to gravity loading, because free horizontal movement of the beam is restrained by the hinge connections at both ends. This restraint will create moments in the columns when the beam is subject to gravity loading (refer to the discussion of indeterminate portal frames, Example 4.2).

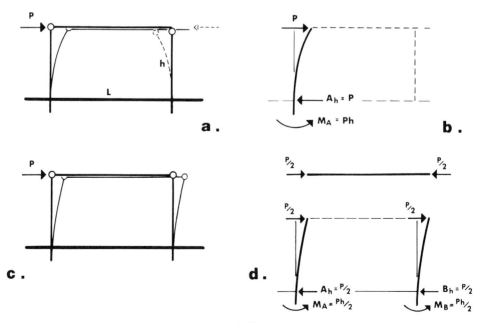

Fig. 4.13

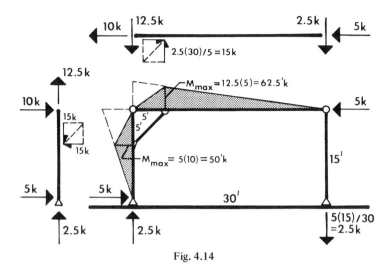

**Fig. 4.14**

However, for approximation purposes these relatively small column moments may be neglected.

### The Post-Beam Frame with Hinged Base

The simple four-hinge frame is unstable in its own plane (Fig. 4.5). But, if this frame is laterally supported by the roof or truss within the roof plane which, in turn, is carried by rigid bents or shear walls, then the four-hinge frame is stable; it is only used to resist gravity loads. This frame can also be stabilized by a diagonal corner brace as shown in Fig. 4.14. With respect to uniform gravity loading this frame can be treated like case 4.9e, that is like a simply supported beam.

**Example 4.1**   Check the solution given in Fig. 4.14 for lateral force action. In addition, investigate the axial force flow along the members.

### The Simple Bent Frame

■ *Uniform Loading (Fig. 4.15)*

First the frame reactions are determined. Since there is no lateral force action, the potential of pin support $A$ to resist horizontal forces is not used, and $A_h = 0$. Due to the symmetry of uniform gravity loading, each vertical reaction equals one-half of the total load

$$A_h = 0 \qquad A_v = B_v = \frac{wL}{2}$$

The columns carry only axial forces and thus do not cause any bending in the beam, which means that the beam is equivalent to a simply supported bending member even though it is continuously connected to the columns! This statement can be made because the roller support $B$ allows for free lateral movement. The force flow along the frame is

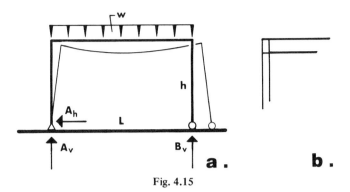

Fig. 4.15

shown in Fig. 4.9c, and is analogous to the post-beam case; the deformation, however, is quite different.

■ *Lateral Loading*

The reactions are determined by means of the freebodies illustrated in Fig. 4.16a. The force $P$ is fully resisted by $A_h$

$$\Sigma H = 0 = P - A_h \qquad A_h = P$$

The rotational equilibrium equation about point $A$ yields

$$\Sigma M_A = 0 = P(h) - B_y(L) \qquad B_y = \frac{Ph}{L}$$

Summing up the vertical forces

$$\Sigma V = 0 = B_y - A_y \qquad B_y = A_y = \frac{Ph}{L}$$

Thus, the two vertical reactions form a couple or resisting moment against the rotation caused by the lateral load.

The force flow within the frame is found by first examining the left-hand column free-body (Fig. 4.16b). The axial and shear forces along the column are constant, while the moment increases with the distance from point A, reaching its maximum at the top of the column

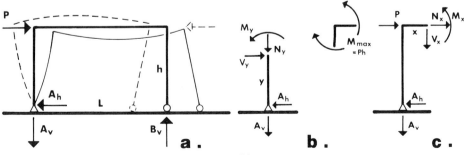

Fig. 4.16

$$\Sigma V = 0 = A_v + N_y \qquad N_y = -A_v = \frac{Ph}{L}$$

$$\Sigma H = 0 = A_h - V_y \qquad V_y = A_h = P$$

$$\Sigma M_y = 0 = A_h(y) - M_y \qquad M_y = A_h(y)$$

$$y = h \qquad M_h = M_{max} = A_h(h) = Ph$$

The column at the far side carries an axial force only, that is equal to the reaction $B_y$.

From Fig. 4.16c, the forces in the beam are derived

$$\Sigma V = 0 = A_v + V_x \qquad V_x = -A_v = \frac{Ph}{L}$$

$$\Sigma H = 0 = A_h - P - N_x \qquad A_h = P \qquad N_x = 0$$

$$\Sigma M_x = 0 = A_v(x) - A_h(h) + M_x$$

$$M_x = Ph - \frac{Phx}{L} = Ph\left(1 - \frac{x}{L}\right)$$

$$x = L \qquad M_L = 0$$

At the intersection of the beam and the right-hand column, the moment in the beam is zero; note also that the column does not transfer any rotation to the beam.

$$x = 0 \qquad M_0 = M_{max} = Ph$$

The moment in the beam at point $C$ ($x = 0$) is the same as the moment at the top of column $AC$ ($y = h$), the beam moment has to be in equilibrium with the column moment at joint $C$. For the force flow along the frame refer to Fig. 4.9d.

### The Three-Hinge Portal Frame

■ *Uniform Gravity Loading (Fig. 4.17)*

Due to symmetry of loading and frame geometry the gravity loads are split evenly between each column

$$A_v = B_v = \frac{wL}{2}$$

To determine the horizontal reactions free-body $b$ is used. Note that the hinge only transfers shear and axial forces. Vertical equilibrium shows that $V_C = 0$. Taking moments around point $A$ while realizing that the horizontal forces must balance each other, yields

$$\Sigma M_A = 0 = \frac{wL}{2}\left(\frac{L}{4}\right) + N_C(h)$$

$$-N_C = A_h = \frac{wL^2}{8h}$$

The response of the frame may also be interpreted by comparing the geometry of the frame to the funicular shape (Fig. 4.2).

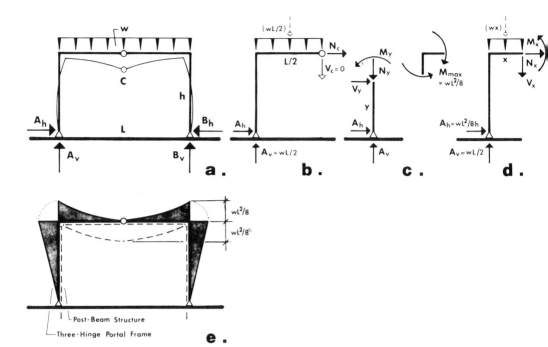

Fig. 4.17

The acting moment at midspan, as caused by gravity loading, is

$$M_{act} = \frac{wL^2}{8}$$

The resisting moment as provided by the frame geometry, that is, the horizontal reaction forces that prohibit lateral displacement of the frame, is

$$M_{res} = A_h(h) = B_h(h)$$

The two moments must counterbalance each other:

$$M_{act} = M_{res}$$

Therefore

$$A_h = B_h = \left(\frac{1}{h}\right)\frac{wL^2}{8} = \frac{wL^2}{8h}$$

From the column free-body $c$, the force flow along the column is derived. Horizontal and vertical equilibrium show that the axial and shear forces along the column are constant while the moment increases linearly with height and is maximum at the top of the column

$$\Sigma v = 0: \qquad N_y = A_v = \frac{wL}{2}$$

$$\Sigma H = 0: \qquad -V_y = A_h = \frac{wL^2}{8h}$$

$$\Sigma M_y = 0: \qquad M_y = -A_h(y) = -\frac{(y/h)wL^2}{8}$$

$$y = h: \qquad M_h = M_{max} = -A_h(h) = -\frac{wL^2}{8}$$

Note that the moment acts in a direction opposite to the one assumed in the free-body diagram, and causes tension along the outside of the columns.

The force flow along the beam is derived from the free-body Fig. 4.17d. Horizontal equilibrium shows that the axial force in the beam is constant.

$$\Sigma H = 0 = \frac{wL^2}{8h} + N_x$$

$$N_x = \frac{-wL^2}{8h} \qquad \text{(negative tension force)}$$

$$N_x = \frac{wL^2}{8h} \qquad \text{(compression force)}$$

The shear force flow is the same as that observed in a simply supported beam under the same uniform gravity loading

$$\Sigma V = 0 = \frac{wL}{2} - wx - V_x \qquad V_x = w\left(\frac{L}{2} - x\right)$$

The moment along the length of the beam varies as shown in the following equilibrium equation:

$$\Sigma M_x = 0 = \frac{wL}{2}x - \frac{wL^2}{8h}h - wx\frac{x}{2} - M_x$$

$$M_x = \frac{wLx}{2} - \frac{wx^2}{2} - \frac{wL^2}{8}$$

$$x = 0: \qquad M_0 = M_{max} = -\frac{wL^2}{8}$$

$$x = \frac{L}{2}: \qquad M_{L/2} = 0$$

Obviously, the moment at the end of the beam ($x = 0$) has to be equal to the moment at the top of the column ($y = h$) because the moments at the corners must be in equilibrium. For the response of the frame to its loading refer to Fig. 4.9g.

In Fig. 4.17e, it is shown that the moment diagram for the post-beam structure is "lifted up" so that the maximum moment $wL^2/8$ appears at the ends of the beam rather than at midspan. From the point of view of gravity loading, one may conclude that the three-hinged frame is less efficient than the post-beam structure. The columns must carry beam moments as well as axial forces. It is assumed that strength, not stiffness, is the basis of the design. Keep in mind, also, that the cost of a continuous beam-column connection is much greater than that of a simple hinged connection.

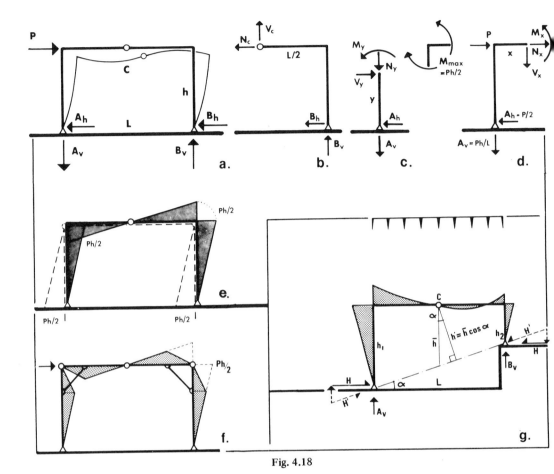

**Fig. 4.18**

■ *Lateral Loading (Fig. 4.24)*

The vertical reactions are found by taking moments about point A

$$\Sigma M_A = 0 = B_y(L) - P(h) \qquad B_y = \frac{Ph}{L}$$

Vertical equilibrium yields

$$\Sigma V = 0 = B_y - A_y \qquad B_y = A_y = \frac{Ph}{L}$$

The horizontal reaction forces are determined from the free-body Fig. 4.18b

$$\Sigma M_c = 0 = B_y(L/2) - B_h(h) \qquad B_h = \frac{P}{2}$$

$$\Sigma H = 0 = P - A_h - B_h \qquad A_h = \frac{P}{2}$$

The forces along the column are obtained from the column free-body Fig. 4.18c

$$\Sigma V = 0 = \frac{Ph}{L} + N_y \qquad N_y = \frac{-Ph}{L} \quad \text{(negative compression)}$$

$$N_y = \frac{Ph}{L} \quad \text{(tension)}$$

$$\Sigma H = 0 = \frac{P}{2} - V_y \qquad V_y = \frac{P}{2}$$

$$\Sigma M_y = 0 = \frac{P}{2} y - M_y \qquad M_y = \frac{Py}{2}$$

$$y = h \qquad M_h = M_{max} = \frac{Ph}{2}$$

The forces in the right-hand column are derived in a similar manner. Its axial force, however, is compression and not tension.

For the derivation of the forces along the beam see Fig. 4.18d

$$\Sigma V = 0 = \frac{Ph}{L} + V_x \qquad V_x = \frac{-Ph}{L}$$

$$\Sigma H = 0 = P - \frac{P}{2} + N_x \qquad N_x = \frac{-P}{2} \quad \text{(negative tension)}$$

$$N_x = \frac{P}{2} \quad \text{(compression)}$$

$$\Sigma M_x = 0 = \frac{Ph}{L} x - \frac{P}{2} h + M_x \qquad M_x = \frac{Ph}{2} - \frac{Phx}{L}$$

$$M_0 = M_{max} = \frac{Ph}{2} \qquad M_{L/2} = 0$$

For the response of the frame to the lateral loading refer to Fig. 4.9h. The moment flow for the hinged frame with the diagonal corner bracing in Fig. 4.18f can be derived in a similar fashion.

Again, comparing the three-hinge portal with the post-beam structure (Fig. 4.18e) one notices that in one case the maximum moment is carried at the beam-column intersection while in the other case it is resisted at the column-foundation intersection. From a lateral loading point of view the post-beam structure is less efficient because of the large foundation necessary to transmit the rotation to the ground.

When the frame supports are not at the same level as for the case in Fig. 4.18g, then the horizontal thrust forces will influence the magnitude of the vertical reaction forces. The usual procedure of taking moments about one of the reactions and the beam hinge yields two equations with two unknowns. Another interesting approach for the solution of the reactions in the example of Fig. 4.18g is as follows:

$$\Sigma H = 0: \qquad A_h = B_h = H \quad \text{or} \quad A_h' = B_h' = H'$$

$$\Sigma M_c = 0: \qquad H'(\bar{h} \cos \alpha) = \frac{wL^2}{8}$$

where $\bar{h} = (h_1 + h_2)/2$
Hence

$$H = H' \cos \alpha = \frac{wL^2/8}{\bar{h}}$$

Note that this result for the magnitude of the thrust has already been derived in Eq. (3.8). Now, with the known thrust forces the vertical reaction forces can be found by taking moments about the supports.

## Indeterminate Portal Frames

Only typical rectangular bents are investigated. When a portal frame is pinned to its base, the frame is once indeterminate. However, if it is fixed so that rotation is transferred to the foundation, it is three times indeterminate. Besides the three equations of static equilibrium, other methods of analysis must be developed in order to determine the magnitude of the force flow along these frames. Here, the deflected shape of the frame under controlling loading conditions yields the approximate location of the inflection points of the curves which, in turn, gives additional information so that the frame analysis is made determinate. The response of the frame to uniform gravity loading and lateral force action is investigated in the following section.

In general, uniform force action along the beam portion of a frame may be considered as the controlling loading case for a preliminary investigation of gravity action. For this condition, frames can be unfolded and treated as three-span continuous beams as shown in Fig. 4.19. Because of symmetry of loading and frame geometry, the small effect of beam-column joint displacement is ignored. It can easily be shown that the moment diagram for the continuous determinate three-span beam with a hinge at midpoint of the center span is the same as for the three-hinge portal.

The two-hinge frame is once indeterminate, hence one more equation (in addition to the three static equilibrium equations) is needed for finding the force flow. In this case the "Three-Moment Theorem" is used to determine the support moment $M_S$ so that the beam can be solved by simple statics. For the three-span continuous beam, with a uniform loading on the central span (Fig. 4.19), and constant beam and column inertias, the three-moment equation takes the form

$$M_A \left( \frac{h}{I_C} \right) + 2M_S \left( \frac{h}{I_C} + \frac{L}{I_B} \right) + M_S \left( \frac{L}{I_B} \right) = \frac{-wL^2}{4} \frac{L}{I_B}$$

Because of the hinged boundary conditions the support moments are zero ($M_A = 0$), so that the equation further simplifies to:

$$M_S \left( \frac{2h}{I_C} + \frac{2L}{I_B} + \frac{L}{I_B} \right) = \frac{-wL^2}{4} \frac{L}{I_B}$$

$$M_S = -\frac{wL^2}{12} \left( \frac{1}{1 + \frac{2}{3}(I_B/L)(h/I_C)} \right) \qquad (4.2)$$

This expression clearly shows that the magnitude of the support moment $M_S$ is dependent on the stiffness of beam ($I_B/L$) and column ($I_C/h$). As the column stiffness decreases the

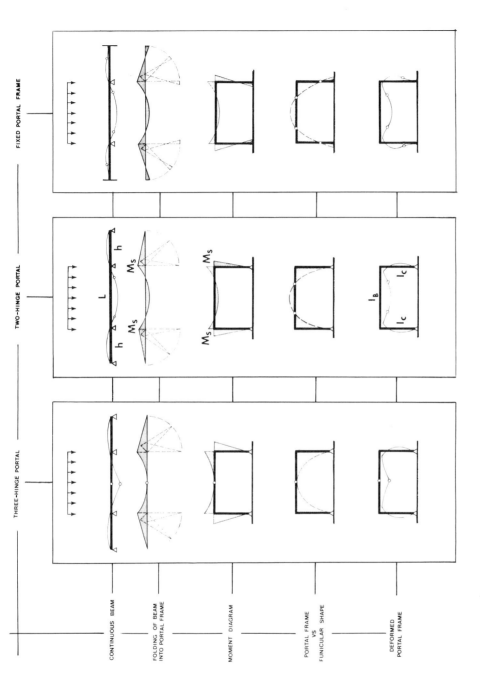

THE EFFECT OF CONTINUITY

Fig. 4.19

209

support moment $M_s$ approaches zero or the beam approaches simply supported conditions. On the other hand, as the column stiffness increases the beam approaches fixed beam conditions with a boundary moment of $M_S = -w^2/12$. The effect of the stiffness of beam and column upon moment flow, or the transition from a simply supported beam to a fixed beam is described in the top portion of Fig. 4.20 for a frame with fixed base conditions.

It is reasonable to assume for approximation purposes that the beam and columns have equal stiffness, or

$$\frac{I_B}{L} \frac{h}{I_C} = 1$$

Hence, the support moment for this condition is

$$M_S = 0.05wL^2$$

This, in turn, yields a maximum field moment at midspan of

$$M_{\max} = 0.125wL^2 - 0.05wL^2 = 0.075\ wL^2$$

The inflection points are located at $0.11L$ measured from each column. In general, for typical stiffness conditions the location of the inflection points are between $0.10L$ and $0.12L$. In this context, inflection points are assumed at $0.1L$, yielding larger beam sizes for preliminary design purposes.

It is not only the stiffness of the members that influences the location of the inflection points, but also the type of loading. For instance, for the case of a single, vertical load acting at midspan of the two-hinge frame, it can be shown that inflection points form at $0.15L$ for equal beam and column stiffnesses.

If the hinged support conditions of the rectangular bent are replaced by fixed ones, then not only are additional inflection points introduced in the columns, but also the location of the zero-moment points in the beam are influenced. It can be shown that the equation for the moment $M_S$ at beam-column intersection is equal to Eq. (4.2) if the factor of $\frac{2}{3}$ in the denominator is replaced by a factor of $\frac{1}{2}$. It can be further shown that the support moments at the fixed base are equal to $-M_S/2$, causing inflection points in the columns at $h/3$ measured from the base. For equal column and beam stiffnesses, the points of zero moment in the beam are at $0.13L$ as measured from the columns. (For further discussion refer to Fig. 4.23.)

Under lateral force action (Fig. 4.18a) the two-hinged portal deflects by forming an inflection point at beam midspan, assuming equal column sizes and the beam to be capable of acting as an axial member.

If the pinned ends of the bent are fixed, additional inflection points will form in the columns. The location of these points of contraflexure depends on the relative stiffnesses of columns and beam as indicated in the bottom portion of Fig. 4.20. For deep girders, which do not allow any rotation, inflection points will be at $0.5h$. For flexible beams, which are unable to resist rotation, the zero-moment point moves to the beam-column intersection, that is, the column behaves as a vertical cantilever. For equal stiffnesses of beam and columns the point of contraflexure is at $0.57h$. For typical frames the inflection point is in the range $0.5$–$0.6h$ measured from the base. In this text, the location is assumed at $0.5h$.

The approximate approach just presented ignores the additional secondary moments

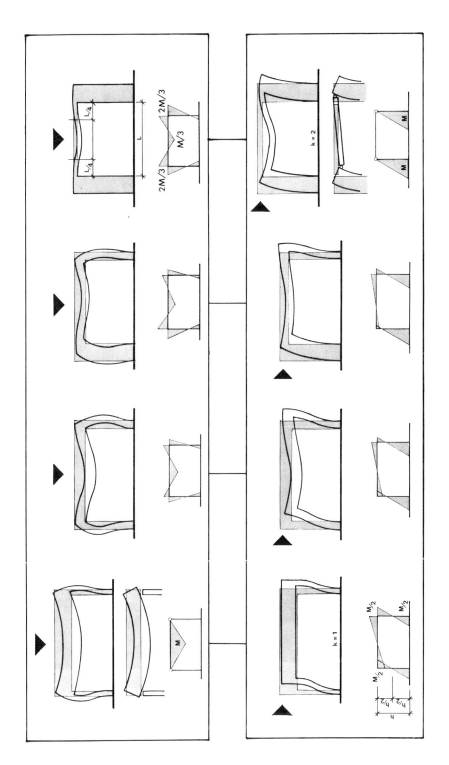

PORTAL FRAME BEHAVIOR AS A FUNCTION OF RELATIVE RIGIDITY OF BEAM TO COLUMN

Fig. 4.20

211

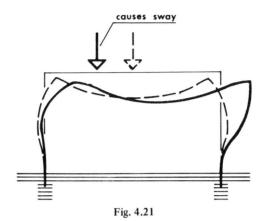

**Fig. 4.21**

due to the first-order displacements. Under unsymmetrical vertical loading (Fig. 4.21) or the combination of symmetrical vertical and lateral loads the frames displace laterally in an effect referred to as sidesway. Obviously these displacements cause additional bending which cannot be neglected in an exact engineering analysis. This also clearly indicates that the superposition of critical values due to lateral forces and symmetrical vertical loading as presented here, can only be approximate, since the combined force action of the cases generates a new condition, that is, the sum of the individual actions is not equal to the combined action.

### The Two-Hinge Portal Frame: An Approximate Solution

■ *Uniform Gravity Loading (Fig. 4.22)*

The vertical reactions are each equal to one-half of the total, symmetrically arranged load

$$A_v = B_v = \frac{wL}{2}$$

The frame is separated into three free bodies at the assumed inflection points of its deformation curvature. One may visualize these points as being imaginary hinges that divide the system into a simple beam supported at each end by an L-shaped column, as shown in Fig. 4.22b and c. The horizontal reactions are found from free body $b$ by taking moments about the inflection point.

$$\Sigma M_C = 0 = A_h(h) - \frac{wL}{2}(0.1L) + w(0.1L)\frac{0.1L}{2}$$

$$A_h = \frac{0.045wL^2}{h}$$

$$\Sigma H = 0: \qquad A_h = B_h$$

The force flow along the columns is determined in exactly the same manner as for the three-hinge portal frame. The maximum moment at the top of the column is

$$M_h = A_h(h) = 0.045wL^2 \tag{4.3a}$$

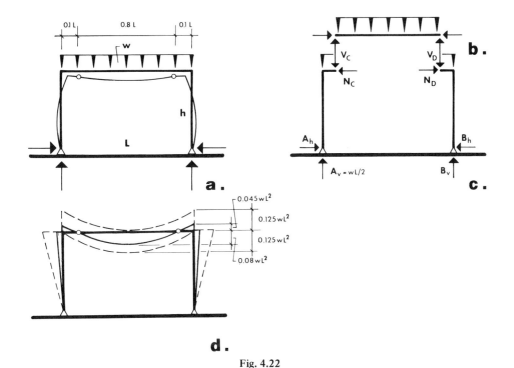

Fig. 4.22

This moment must be equal to the moment at the end of the beam since the two moments have to balance each other at the joint. The force flow along the beam portion of the frame can easily be derived by considering the portion of the beam between the assumed inflection points as a simply supported beam for which shear and moment diagrams are known. Remember that the length of this beam is $l = 0.8L$

$$M_{max} = \frac{wl^2}{8} = \frac{w(0.8L)^2}{8} = 0.08wL^2 \qquad (4.3b)$$

The field moment can also be derived by subtracting from the maximum moment of a simply supported beam the support moment transferred from the column

$$M_{max} = 0.125\ wl^2 - 0.045\ wl^2 = 0.08\ wl^2$$

The axial compressive force in the beam is constant:

$$H = 0 = A_h - N_C \qquad N_C = N_D = \frac{0.045wL^2}{h}$$

The shear flow is analogous to a simply supported beam. In Fig. 4.22d the moment diagrams for the three frames (post-beam, three-hinge, and two-hinge) are compared. One notices that the two-hinge frame is more efficient from a materials point of view (not necessarily from a cost or ease of construction point of view), since two-thirds of the total moment $0.125wL^2$ is carried by the beam while the remaining one-third is carried across the continuous corner joints into the columns

■ *Lateral Loading*

Since the location of the inflection point is assumed to be at $L/2$ this case is identical with the lateral loading of the three-hinge portal. Therefore, refer to the lateral force analysis for the three-hinge portal frame for the approximate behavior of the two-hinge frame.

### The Continuous Rigid Frame: An Approximate Solution

■ *Uniform Gravity Loading*

The continuous frame is three times indeterminate. In this specific case, due to symmetry, only two more conditions have to be known besides the three equations of static equilibrium. As the frame deflects under the gravity loading, inflection points form within the beam and column ranges. The location of these points of zero moment will be assumed so that the approximate force flow along the frame can be determined.

By fixing the two-hinge frame to the base, more moment is attracted to the stiffer columns, thereby decreasing the field moment in the beam. The beam inflection points, for the given uniform loading, will move further away from the columns as compared to the location of 0.1L. Their location may be assumed at 0.13L measured from each column (Fig. 4.23a) as based on equal column and beam stiffnesses.

The maximum moment at midspan for an equivalent simply supported beam of a length equal to $l = 0.74L$, is

$$M_{\max} = \frac{wl^2}{8} = \frac{w(0.74L)^2}{8} = 0.069wL^2 \qquad (4.4)$$

The beam support moment at the column intersection is the difference between the moment for a simply supported beam and the actual beam moment at midspan

$$M_h = 0.125wL^2 - 0.069wL^2 = 0.056wL^2 \qquad (4.5)$$

The inflection points in the columns form at one-third of the column height measured from the base as caused by equal column and beam stiffnesses. At this location the moment is zero and increases linearly to its maximum value $M_h$ at the beam column intersection and decreases to one-half of that maximum moment at the base

$$M_A = M_B = \frac{0.056wL^2}{2} = 0.028wL^2 \qquad (4.6)$$

The continuous frame can be visualized as a two-hinge frame sitting on column stubs $h/3$ high. Hence a similar approach may be used for its solution as already described for the two-hinge portal frame.

The thrust forces at the reactions, which must be equal and opposite to each other since no other horizontal forces are acting, may be determined from the free body of the column stub in Fig. 4.23c. Rotational equilibrium about the inflection point yields

$$M_c = 0 = A_h \left(\frac{h}{3}\right) - 0.028wL^2$$

$$A_h = 0.028wL^2 \frac{3}{h} = \frac{0.084wL^2}{h} = B_h$$

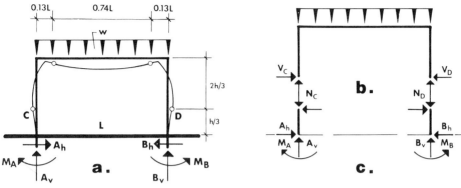

Fig. 4.23

The shear along the columns is constant and equal to the horizontal reaction forces and the axial compression force in the beam. The constant axial forces in the columns are obviously equal to the vertical reactions. The shear flow along the beam is the same as for a simply supported beam.

■ *Lateral Loading (Fig. 4.24)*

The wracking of the frame by the lateral force $P$ causes inflection points to form at mid-height of the columns and at midspan of the beam as based on the simplifying assumptions discussed. One may visualize a two-hinge frame of height $h/2$ sitting on column stubs as shown in free bodies $b$ and $c$.

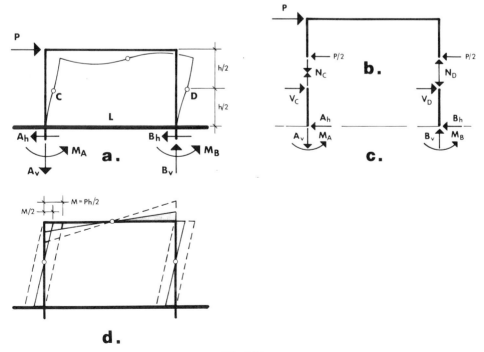

Fig. 4.24

The reaction forces (or axial column forces or beam shear at beam column intersection) are found by rotational equilibrium

$$\Sigma M_A = 0 = P\left(\frac{h}{2}\right) - N_D\,(L)$$

$$N_D = \frac{Ph}{2L} = B_V = A_V$$

The horizontal reaction forces are determined by taking moments about the inflection point at midspan beam

$$B_h\left(\frac{h}{2}\right) = N_D\left(\frac{L}{2}\right)$$

$$B_h = \frac{N_D L}{h} = \frac{P}{2} = A_h$$

From the column stub free body the support moment is obtained

$$M_A = \frac{P}{2}\,\frac{h}{2} = \frac{Ph}{4}$$

This moment is equal in magnitude to the one at the top of the column and the one at the end of the beam (Fig. 4.24d).

In comparison with the two-hinge frame, the rigid frame carries moments, axial column forces, and maximum beam shear of one-half the magnitude. While the two-hinge frame attracts the total moment to the beam column intersection and the post-beam structure to the column–foundation–earth intersection, the continuous frame, being between the two systems, distributes the moment equally to top and bottom (Fig. 4.24d).

### Frame Design

In Fig. 4.25 different framing systems are investigated. The typical procedure for the preliminary design of a steel frame is exemplified by sizing the members of the two-hinge frame [case (d)]. First the loading and then the force flow along the frame, as reflected by shear, moment and axial force diagrams, are determined. The design of the frame can now be based on the maximum force action.

**Example 4.2**   Refer to Problem 4.9 for description.

A typical interior frame must support a roof area of one-half of a bay on each side, that is, the joists on each side of the frame transmit to the frame one-half of the total roof gravity load that they are carrying

$$w = 40(0.025 + 0.030) = 2.2 \ \text{k/ft}$$

Similarly, the curtain panels transmit the lateral wind load to the spandrel beams and roof diaphragm, which in turn apply a single load $P$ to the frame at the beam-column intersection

$$P = 40(15/2)0.020 = 6 \ \text{k}$$

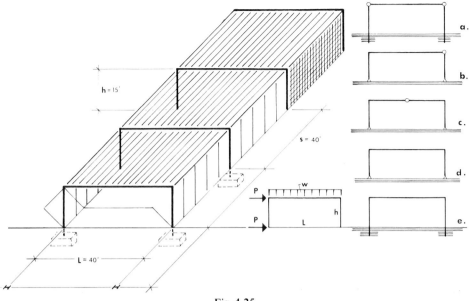

**Fig. 4.25**

## Analysis

The responses of the frame to uniform gravity loading and lateral force action are considered separately. Both loading cases have already been investigated. The general solutions are used for this specific problem.

■ *Beam Range*

$$\text{Gravity:} \quad +M = 0.08wL^2 \tag{4.3b}$$

$$= 0.08(2.2)40^2 = 281.6 \text{ ft-k}$$

$$-M = 0.045wL^2 \tag{4.3a}$$

$$= 0.045(2.2)40^2 = 158.4 \text{ ft-k}$$

$$N = \frac{0.045wL^2}{h} = \frac{M_h}{h}$$

$$= \frac{158.4}{15} = 10.56 \text{ k}$$

$$\text{Wind:} \quad \pm M = \frac{Ph}{2}$$

$$= \frac{6(15)}{2} = 45 \text{ ft-k}$$

$$N = \frac{P}{2} = \frac{6}{2} = 3 \text{ k}$$

■ *Column Range*

$$\text{Gravity:} \quad -M = 0.045wL^2 = 158.4 \text{ ft-k}$$

$$N = \frac{wL}{2}$$

$$= \frac{2.2(40)}{2} = 44 \text{ k}$$

$$\text{Wind:} \quad \pm M = \frac{Ph}{2} = 45 \text{ ft-k}$$

$$\pm N = \frac{Ph}{L}$$

$$= \frac{6(15)}{40} = 2.25 \text{ k}$$

The magnitude of shear forces along the frame has not been determined because shear will not influence the preliminary design of the steel frame.

*Design*

First the beam size will be determined. Three possible loading conditions are investigated:

■ The maximum member forces as controlled by gravity only

$$M_{max} = 281.6 \text{ ft-k}$$

$$N = 10.56 \text{ k}$$

■ The maximum member forces as controlled by full gravity acting together with wind keeping in mind that this load combination can be reduced by 25%

$$M_{max} = (158.4 + 45)0.75$$

$$= 152.55 \text{ ft-k} \ll 281.6 \text{ ft-k}$$

$$N = (10.56 + 3)0.75$$

$$= 10.17 \text{ k} < 10.56 \text{ k}$$

■ The maximum member forces as controlled by dead load and wind

$$M_{max} = 158.4(25/55) + 45$$

$$= 117 \text{ ft-k} \ll 281.6 \text{ ft-k}$$

$$N = 10.56(25/55) + 3$$

$$= 7.8 \text{ k} < 10.56 \text{ k}$$

It is quite apparent that the gravity case controls the preliminary design of the beam. Since the axial force $N$ is relatively small it may be neglected for the preliminary sizing of the member. The required section modulus for a compact beam section is

$$S = \frac{M}{F_b} = \frac{281.6(12)}{24} = 140.8 \text{ in.}^3$$

The most economical wide-flange section is obtained from Table A.8. Try $W24 \times 68$, $F_y'$ $> F_y$, $A = 20.1$ in.$^2$, $S_x = 154$ in.$^3$, $r_x = 9.55$ in., $L_c = 9.5$ ft $> L_b$. The section is compact because the theoretical yield stresses at which the flange becomes unstable is larger than the yield stress of the steel and because the compression flange of the beam is assumed to be laterally supported by the joists at a spacing of less than 9.5 ft. It can easily be shown that the column action of the beam is very small. The controlling slenderness ratio of the beam is:

$$\left(\frac{KL}{r}\right)_x = \frac{1(40)12}{9.55} = 50.26 \quad \text{say } 51$$

The allowable axial stress for this slenderness ratio (Table A.9) is:

$$F_a = 18.26 \text{ ksi}$$

Since the beam is predominately a bending member, the following interaction equation can be used to predict its beam-column behavior

$$\frac{f_a}{F_a} + \frac{f_b}{F_b} \leqslant 1 \tag{1.47}$$

$$\frac{N/A}{F_a} + \frac{M/S}{F_b} = \frac{10.56/20.1}{18.26} + \frac{281.6(12)/154}{24}$$

$$= 0.03 + 0.91 = 0.94 < 1$$

Only about 3% of the beam section is being used in axial action, which can obviously be neglected in a preliminary study.

In general, the preliminary design of the beam portion for any of the single-story, low-rise frames in Problem 4.9 can be based on the maximum moment as caused by uniform gravity loading.

To design the column, the controlling loading case has to be determined.

Gravity action:     $M = 158.4$ ft-k

$N = 44.0$ k

$$H = \frac{158.4}{15} = 10.56 \text{ k}$$

Full gravity and wind:     $M = (158.4 + 45)0.75$

$$= 152.55 \text{ ft-k} < 158.4 \text{ ft-k}$$

$N = (44 + 2.25)0.75$

$$= 34.69 \text{ k} < 44 \text{ k}$$

Dead load and wind:        $M = 158.4\left(\dfrac{25}{55}\right) + 45$

$$= 117 \text{ ft-k} < 158.4 \text{ ft-k}$$

$$N = 44\left(\frac{25}{55}\right) + 2.25$$

$$= 22.25 < 44 \text{ k}$$

The gravity case controls the design of the column as it did for the beam (Fig. 4.26). But note if the height increases slightly more, the full gravity and wind case will govern the design of the column. In comparison with the beam the axial action in the column is much larger relative to the moment. Hence axial force action cannot be neglected for the preliminary design of the column. Use the following procedure to determine the column size:

Select a preliminary section as based on bending only, however, keep in mind that the compression flange of the column is laterally supported only at its ends, hence a partially compact section is assumed with $F_b = 0.6F_y$

$$S = \frac{M}{F_b} = \frac{158(12)}{22} = 86.18 \text{ in.}^3 \qquad L_u \geqslant 15 \text{ ft}$$

Try $W14 \times 61$

$$S_x = 92.2 \text{ in.}^3 \qquad L_u = 21.5 > 15 \text{ ft} \qquad L_c = 10.6 < 15 \text{ ft}$$

$$r_x = 5.98 \text{ in.} \qquad r_y = 2.45 \text{ in.} \qquad A = 17.9 \text{ in.}^2 \qquad F_y' > F_y$$

Check this trial section as based on beam-column action.

Since the moment action is still predominant, as shown in the following equation, it is reasonable to use the simple beam-column interaction equation for this approximate investigation. Furthermore, for the preliminary design of an unbraced column one may assume that the column action is based on the weak axis about which the column in general does not sway ($K \leqslant 1$) rather than about the strong axis about which it sways laterally ($K \geqslant 2$) as indicated in Fig. 1.19.

The column slenderness about the weak axis, in this example, is

$$\left(\frac{KL}{r}\right)_y = \frac{1(15)12}{2.45} = 73.47 \quad \text{say } 74$$

To get the same slenderness about the strong axis requires a stiffness factor of

$$\frac{K_x(15)12}{5.98} = 73.47 \qquad K_x = 2.44$$

In comparison, it should be noted that for rigid beams that do not allow column rotation, the stiffness factor is 2.0; obviously in this example the beam will permit rotation of the column. However, it was found that for hinged base conditions, ordinary foundation anchorage details provide some restraining, resulting in a lower $K$ value of 1.5 for rigid beam conditions, which is considered conservative. In general, it is quite reasonable to assume

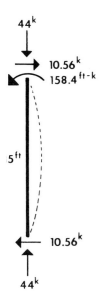

Fig. 4.26

the weak axis to control the design of the column. Should the column be laterally braced along its height about its weak axis then the strong axis may control the design. However, for the sake of preliminary design purposes neglect, conservatively, the lateral bracing about the weak axis. The allowable axial stress for the slenderness about the weak axis, $KL/r_y = 74$, is

$$F_a = 16.01 \text{ ksi} \quad \text{(Table A.9)}$$

Since the section is partially compact $(L_u > L_b > L_c)$ the allowable bending stress is $F_b = 0.6F_y = 22$ ksi. The beam-column interaction equation yields

$$\frac{f_a}{F_a} + \frac{f_b}{F_b} \leqslant 1 \tag{1.47}$$

$$\frac{N/A}{F_a} + \frac{M/S}{F_b} = \frac{44/17.9}{16.01} + \frac{158.4(12)/92.2}{22}$$

$$= 0.15 + 0.94 = 1.09 > 1$$

The section is not satisfactory, the next larger size should be investigated. However, if the column is laterally braced at midheight, the column will be sufficiently strong, assuming the strong axis $(KL/r)_x$ does not control, because the allowable bending stress $F_b$ increases to 24 ksi (i.e., the section is now compact as $L_c = 10.6$ ft $\geqslant L_b = 7.5$ ft). In addition, the allowable axial stress increases to $F_a = 19.42$ ksi for one-half of the slenderness ratio: $(KL/2r)_y = 74/2 = 37$.

In general, the preliminary design of any of the single-story low-rise frames in Problem 4.9 can be based on the uniform gravity loading case; the only exception are the post-beam structure [case (a)] and the L-frame [case (b)] in Fig. 4.25, where the moments in the columns are caused only by lateral force action. In this case, the dead + wind loading case controls the design of the column.

### Stiffness Considerations

In Section 2.3, The Lateral Force Resisting Structure, we stated that a rigid roof diaphragm distributes lateral forces in proportion to the relative rigidity R of the supporting structural elements. This rigidity $R$ for walls or stiffness $k$ for structures in general is a measurement of the resistance of the structure to lateral deformation. The stiffness is measured by a spring constant $k$ as a function of the lateral deformation caused by a unit force $P$

$$k = \frac{P}{\Delta} = \frac{1}{\Delta} \tag{4.7}$$

Stiffness is considered to be the reciprocal of lateral deformation or of the flexibility for a unit force. The lateral deflections of some typical structural systems are shown in Fig. 4.27. For cases (a) and (b) the lateral sway of the frames is analogous to the maximum deflection of a vertical cantilever supporting a single load of $P/2$ at its end. The deflection as caused by bending is equal to

$$\Delta = \frac{\frac{1}{2}Ph^3}{3EI} = \frac{Ph^3}{6EI} = \frac{P}{k_t}$$

where $E$ = modulus of elasticity of the column; $I$ = moment of inertia of the column; and $k$ = stiffness of one column, $3EI/h^3$.

In general, for single-story multibay frame systems the total frame stiffness $k_t$ is equal to the sum of the individual column stiffnesses. For the case where either the top or bottom joint is rotationally restrained, it is

$$k_t = \sum \frac{3EI}{h^3} \tag{4.8}$$

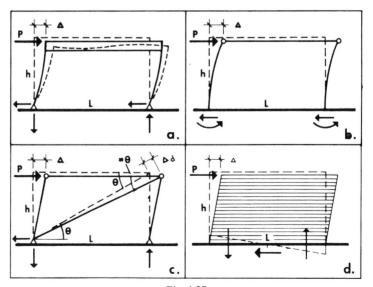

Fig. 4.27

For the condition where top and bottom are restrained the building stiffness is

$$k_t = \sum \frac{12EI}{h^3} \tag{4.9}$$

The girder of the two-hinge frame of case $a$ can rarely be considered to be infinitely rigid and to provide a truly fixed boundary condition for the column. More often the column will rotate the girder resulting in an increase of frame sway and reduction of the stiffness as is shown in dashed lines. The evaluation of the effect of beam flexibility will not be further discussed here, for an approximate solution refer to Problem 4.16.

The lateral sway of a hinged truss [case (c)] or a bay cross-braced with rods, where the compression diagonal is ignored, can be evaluated approximately by superimposing the deformations caused by the beam and the diagonal tension members, thus only considering the web drift. The axial deformation of the top chord is

$$\Delta_1 = \frac{PL}{AE} = \frac{f_t L}{E} \tag{c}$$

The axial tension in the diagonal is found from geometry, to be $P_d = P/\cos\theta$. This force causes an increase of the diagonal member length $L_d = L/\cos\theta$, and is equal to

$$\Delta_d = \left(\frac{PL}{AE}\right)_d = \frac{f_d L}{E \cos\theta} \tag{d}$$

The horizontal component of the elastic elongation of the diagonal is approximately equal to

$$\Delta_2 = \frac{\Delta_d}{\cos\theta} = \frac{f_d L}{E \cos^2\theta} \tag{e}$$

The total lateral sway of the truss is obtained by adding Eqs. (c) and (e)

$$\Delta = \Delta_1 + \Delta_2 = \frac{L}{E}\left(f_t + \frac{f_d}{\cos^2\theta}\right) \tag{4.10}$$

where $f_t$ = the axial stress in the top chord, $P/A_t$; and $f_d$ = the tension stress in the diagonal, $P_d/A_d = P/A_d\cos\theta$.

This equation can now be expressed in terms of the cross-sectional areas of the two members:

$$\Delta = \frac{PL}{E}\left(\frac{1}{A_t} + \frac{1}{A_d\cos^3\theta}\right) \tag{4.11}$$

The equation clearly shows that the cross-sectional area $A_d$ of the diagonal controls the lateral sway of the truss.

The lateral deformation of a wall [case (d)] is caused primarily by shear. The effect of bending can be ignored for very deep beams, whose depth is greater than their span that is up to about where the span $L$ is larger than roughly $2h/3$, as is the case for a single-story shear wall. In other words, tall walls that are much higher than wide behave as cantilevers in bending, while low walls which are wider than high act as simple shear panels.

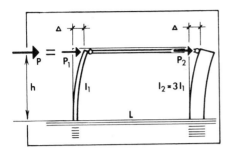

Fig. 4.28

The lateral shear deflection for a cantilever beam of rectangular cross-section, as is typical for walls that support an in-plane lateral point load at the top [see Eq. (1.26)], is

$$\Delta = \frac{1.2Ph}{AG} \tag{4.12}$$

For a preliminary estimate of stiffness for concrete or masonry walls, the modulus of rigidity (shear modulus) $G$ is assumed to be 40% of the modulus of elasticity $E$

$$G = 0.40E$$

Hence, the approximate lateral deformation of a concrete or masonry wall can be determined by

$$\Delta = \frac{3Ph}{AE} \tag{4.13}$$

where $A$ = the cross-sectional area of the wall; and $E$ = the modulus of elasticity of the wall material.

In general, for fixed base conditions the stiffness of a shear wall is dependent on both shear and moment when the wall height $h$ is more than roughly 1.5 times its width $L$, but less than about $6L$ where only flexure may be considered (i.e., $6L > h > 1.5L$)

$$\frac{1}{k} = \frac{3h}{AE} + \frac{h^3}{3EI} \tag{4.14}$$

For the condition where the wall is rotationally restrained at top and bottom, the stiffness is

$$\frac{1}{k} = \frac{3h}{AE} + \frac{h^3}{12EI} \tag{4.15}$$

In the section on building stability we stated that for rigid diaphragm action the horizontal forces are distributed to the vertical supporting structures in proportion to their relative rigidities. This statement is explained by using the simple example of a post-beam structure having one column with an inertia three times larger than the other (Fig. 4.28). Each of the columns carries a certain portion of the total lateral load $P$,

$$P = P_1 + P_2 \tag{f}$$

Both columns sway by the same amount, assuming rigid diaphragm action of the beam (i.e., no bending of beam)

$$\Delta = \frac{P_1 h^3}{3EI_1} = \frac{P_2 h^3}{3EI_2}$$

$$P_2 = \frac{I_2}{I_1} P_1 = 3P_1 \qquad (g)$$

Substituting Eq. (g) into (f) results in the magnitude of the force carried by each column

$$P = P_1 + P_2 = P_1 + \frac{I_2}{I_1} P_1 = 4P_1$$

$$P_1 = \frac{PI_1}{I_1 + I_2} = P/4$$

$$P_2 = \frac{PI_2}{I_1 + I_2} = 3P/4 \qquad (h)$$

The larger column resists 75% of the total load, while the smaller column resists only 25%. This result shows that the force $P$ is distributed in proportion to the stiffness $k$ of the columns, or in proportion to the column inertias if column heights and materials are the same. Generalizing Eq. (h) yields

$$P_i = P \left( \frac{I_i}{\sum\limits_1^n I} \right) \qquad (4.16)$$

In the case of shear wall systems under the same conditions as above, the stiffness $k$ of the bending elements is replaced by the rigidity $R$ of the walls, and the inertia $I$ is replaced by the cross-sectional wall area $A$ of the shear-resisting elements

$$P_i = P \left( \frac{A_i}{\sum\limits_1^n A} \right) \qquad (4.17)$$

Evaluating lateral deformation is important not only from the point of view of stiffness, but also for cases where the deformation of one member induces stresses in adjoining members. Such conditions result from such factors as elastic deformations, environmental changes in temperature and humidity, shrinkage, constant loading (creep), loss of prestress forces, and support movement such as spreading and settling of the foundation. In statically determinate structures, externally induced deformations cause no additional stresses, because the members are free to rotate and translate in response (Fig. 4.29). In indeterminate structures, however, the continuity between members does not allow for movement without causing additional stresses. For preliminary designs of frames and walls, the effect of material volume changes can usually be ignored, and small foundation movements can be tolerated. In order to develop an awareness of the effects of some typical external forces, several frame examples, with their response to different

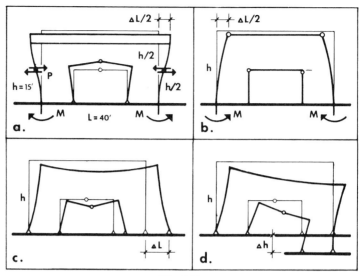

**Fig. 4.29**

types of deformations, as shown in Fig. 4.29, cases (c) and (d) indicate how horizontal and vertical support displacement causes bending in a two-hinge frame, while no bending stresses are imposed on the statically determinate three-hinge frame.

**Example 4.3**  For the rigid frame of case (a), the maximum column stress as caused by expansion of the roof steel beam is determined. The beam had a length of 40 ft when the building was built at a temperature of around 40°F. When the temperature has risen in and outside the building to 120°F, the temperature change ($\Delta T$) will be 80°F. A $W14 \times 68$ steel column is being used (see Example 4.2) with following properties:

$$S_x = 103 \text{ in.}^3 \qquad I_x = 723 \text{ in.}^4$$

The coefficient of expansion for steel is $\alpha = 0.0000065$ in./in./°F. The beam expansion is

$$\Delta L = \alpha L(\Delta T) = 6.5 \times 10^{-6}\,(40 \times 12)80 = 0.25 \text{ in.} \qquad (1.2)$$

Each column resists the force caused by one-half of the total expansion

$$\frac{\frac{1}{2}\Delta L}{2} = \frac{P(h/2)^3}{3EI} \qquad\qquad P = \frac{6\Delta LEI}{h^3}$$

but $M = P(h/2)$

$$M = \frac{3\Delta LEI}{h^2} \qquad\qquad (4.18)$$

The induced moment in the column is equal to

$$M = \frac{3(0.25)29000(723)}{(15 \times 12)^2} = 485.35 \text{ k-in.} = 40.45 \text{ k-ft}$$

The moment causes a bending stress equal to

$$f = \frac{M}{S} = \frac{485.35}{103} = 4.71 \text{ ksi}$$

In cases where the temperature stress is added to the stresses caused by gravity action, the allowable stresses can be increased by 33%. A similar approach can be used for the post-beam structure in Fig. 4.29b or for a two-hinge frame with a rigid girder. Here the beam shortens due to temperature drop and/or due to shrinkage and creep for a pre-stressed concrete beam

$$\frac{\Delta L}{2} = \frac{Ph^3}{3EI} \qquad P = \frac{1.5\Delta LEI}{h^3}$$

but

$$M = Ph$$

$$M = \frac{1.5(\Delta L)EI}{h^2} \tag{4.19}$$

Note that the maximum moment is twice as much for the rigid frame because of its higher degree of indeterminacy.

## Problems

**4.1** For the statically determinate frames shown in Fig. 4.8, draw shear, moment, and axial force diagrams and give numerical values at critical locations. Further, show how the frames deform under the external loading. Compare the different frame types and their response to the force action. Where the magnitude of the loading is not given, assume a unit load of 1 k/ft. Indicate clearly the process which you used to get the results.

**4.2** Investigate the effect of hinge location along the beam portion of a rectangular bent, pinned at the supports and carrying a uniform load $w$. Be systematic in your approach; explain by using moment diagrams. Give the best location of the hinge as based on moment flow. Show how each frame deforms under the loading.

**4.3** Show the loading cases you will investigate for the preliminary design of the simple shelter in Fig. 4.8j. Show moment diagrams for each loading case.

**4.4** Study the behavior of a three-hinge portal as one column is shortened (Fig. 4.8f), as a cantilever is added (g), and as the location of the hinge is moved (k).

**4.5** If the form of the frame members of simple rectangular bents is to respond to the magnitude of the force flow (tectonics), how would you shape the frames? Discuss at least four different bent types.

**4.6** Compare the response of the three-hinge frame to the various loading cases identified in Fig. 4.8p,q, and r. Draw your conclusions.

**4.7** Compare the force flow of a three-hinge frame with constant beam and column inertia under uniform loading with the one under asymmetrical live loading (Fig. 4.8n). Verify that the asymmetrical loading case does not influence the preliminary design of the frame. Do you know of any condition where the asymmetrical loading case may have an influence upon the design?

**4.8**  The frames, cases (a) and (c) of Fig. 4.8, are considered as support structures for an addition to an existing building. Which of the two proposals do you select if the deciding factor is economy of materials and gravity loading is assumed to control this preliminary design? Determine the preliminary member sizes ($A36$) for the case you select. The roof joists are spaced 5 ft on center. The columns do not sway laterally.

**4.9**  Different framing systems are investigated for enclosing the building volume shown in Fig. 4.25. The following roof loads must be supported: 25 psf dead load, 30 psf live load, and 20 psf wind load. The columns do not sway about their weak axes, because the building is laterally braced in the long direction. Draw shear, moment, and axial force diagrams with numerical values for the gravity and lateral loading cases. Show also frame deformations. Find the preliminary beam and column sizes using $A36$ steel as based on the critical loading cases. Compare the solutions for the different systems by taking the least weight as design criterion.

**4.10**  The foundations of a continuous portal frame fixed at the base rotate slightly under lateral force action because of weak soil conditions, generating a partially fixed joint with assumed inflection points in the column at $h/3$ measured from the base. Show the moment diagram for a unit load action and the deformation of the frame.

**4.11**  Assume the footing of the frame in Example 4.2 with $W14 \times 68$ columns, to spread $\frac{1}{2}$ in. horizontally due to tie elongation. Determine the bending stresses in the columns assuming rigid beam action.

**4.12**  A diagonally braced, hinged steel frame ($A36$), spanning 25 ft and being 12 ft high, must support at the roof level a lateral load of 5 k. Determine the approximate horizontal displacement of the frame. The lateral sway shall not exceed $\frac{1}{200}$ of the building height.

**4.13**  Determine the moments in $16 \times 16$ in. concrete columns (5000 psi concrete, normal weight) of a post-beam structure 12 ft high, as caused by shortening of a prestressed, prefab beam due to shrinkage and creep; assume the beam shortening as 0.24 in.

**4.14**  One of the foundations of a rigid frame (single bent), fixed at the base, settles vertically. It does not form any inflection points in the columns, only at midspan of the beam. Show deformation of frame and moment diagram.

**4.15**  If the frame of Problem 4.14 is pinned to its base, how does the frame deform as one support settles vertically? Show also the moment diagram.

**4.16**  Derive the approximate lateral sway of a single bent, pinned at the base, as caused by a horizontal load $P$ at the beam-column intersection, by taking into account the beam flexibility.

## 4.3  THE PITCHED FRAME

The potential occurrence of inclined structural members for various forms of roof enclosures is shown in Fig. 4.30. The application of the structural principle to actual building cases is exemplified in Fig. 4.31. It is shown that the concept ranges from the typical usage as the primary structure for roofs, to the special case of a single A-shaped steel

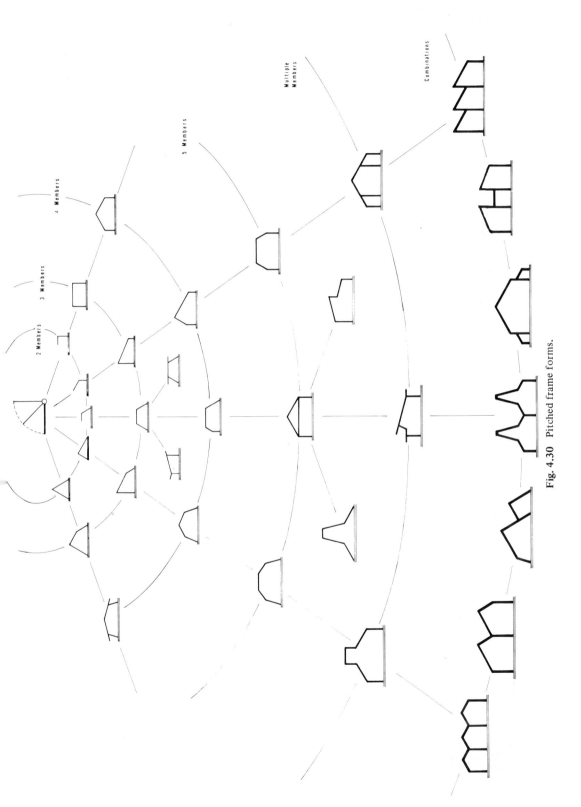

2 Members

3 Members

4 Members

5 Members

Multiple Members

Combinations

**Fig. 4.30** Pitched frame forms.

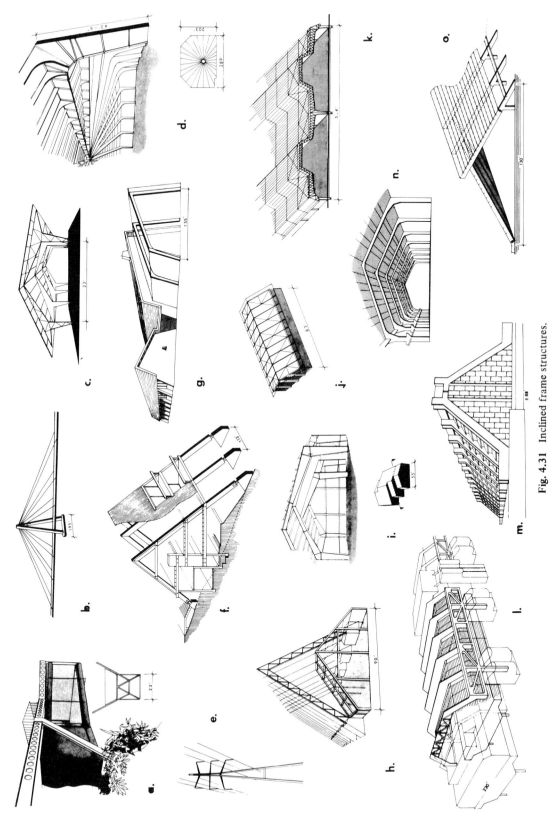

Fig. 4.31  Inclined frame structures.

230

tower from which the bridge roadway is hung (b), the free-standing transmission tower with its slender cantilevering arms (e), and finally the unique application as a support for a structure that cantilevers daringly from a cliff (a).

As a support structure for the exterior envelope, the folded frame concept occurs on the large scale of a congress center (1), where the 230-ft span transverse frame-trusses are sitting on the longitudinal facade trusses, which in turn rest on the concrete pillars incorporated in the stair towers. On a smaller scale, one finds the precast concrete A-frames (m) that are hinged at the top and supported by columns. The ribs are laterally stabilized by the inclined concrete slabs which provide for the necessary shading as louvers.

Standardized rigid steel gable frames were employed for a theater (i). Other typical prefabricated systems include the concrete frame (n) and the trussed three-hinge gable frame of case (c) consisting of tubular steel. The lateral thrust of the laminated wood rafters (o) is resisted by the exposed reinforced concrete buttresses.

In case (k) truss frames are spaced 20 feet apart; they act in combination with the overall roof as a folded plate. The simple gable roof of case (j) acts like a folded plate with two trusses leaning against each other.

Steel trusses in (h) form a three-hinge A-frame; the roof deck spanning between the trusses acts as a diaphragm. The entire building on the hillside (f) is a pitched roof consisting of parallel, asymmetrical A-frames. The building envelope with sloped surfaces in case (g) is supported by parallel glue-laminated frames 12 feet on center. Radially arranged welded steel gable frames were used for the polyhedral half-octagon dome of case (d).

To develop some understanding about the behavior of sloped members, the nature of the inclined beam is studied first.

## The Simply Supported Inclined Beam

The beam to be investigated is pin-supported at the reaction $A$, and roller-supported at the reaction $B$. The reaction conditions at $A$ are considered to be constant, while three different orientations of the roller support $B$ are investigated. Furthermore, the effect of different types of loading on the beam behavior are studied.

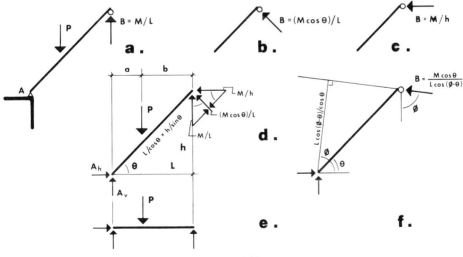

Fig. 4.32

Visualize a single load $P$, the resultant of some type of loading, to act as shown in Fig. 4.32. To find the reaction at support $B$, moments are taken about point $A$. The acting moment at this point is $M = P(a)$. This moment is balanced by the counteracting moment provided by the reaction at support $B$.

■ *Case a: Reaction* B *is Vertical*

$$M = B(L) \qquad B = \frac{M}{L}$$

The components of the reaction parallel and perpendicular to the beam are:

$$B_N = B \sin \theta = \frac{M}{L} \sin \theta$$

$$B_V = B \cos \theta = \frac{M}{L} \cos \theta$$

Let the maximum moment occur at the point of application of the load

$$M_{\max} = B(b) = \frac{M}{L}(b)$$

■ *Case b: Reaction* B *is Perpendicular to the Beam*

$$M = B\frac{L}{\cos \theta} \qquad B = \frac{M}{L} \cos \theta = B_V$$

Since the reaction acts perpendicular to the beam there is no axial force component at $B$

$$M_{\max} = B\frac{b}{\cos \theta} = \frac{M}{L} \cos \theta \frac{b}{\cos \theta} = \frac{M}{L} b$$

■ *Case c: Reaction* B *is Horizontal*

$$M = B(h) \qquad B = M/h$$

The force components of the reaction are

$$B_V = B \sin \theta = \frac{M}{h} \sin \theta = \frac{M}{L} \cos \theta$$

$$B_N = B \cos \theta = \frac{M}{h} \cos \theta = \frac{M}{L} \sin \theta$$

The maximum moment is

$$M_{\max} = B_V \frac{b}{\cos \theta} = \frac{M}{L} b$$

Comparing the three cases, it is clear that only the axial force flow is dependent on the orientation of the support at $B$, while shear and moment flow are independent of the reaction conditions. Furthermore, notice that the moment is

$$M_{max} = \frac{M}{L} b \qquad M = Pa$$

or

$$M_{max} = \frac{Pab}{L}$$

Hence, the moment is equal to that for an equivalent beam on the horizontal projection carrying the same loading as the inclined beam (Fig. 4.32e). The findings above are exemplified for the following loading cases.

### Uniform Gravity Loading

The weight $w'$ acts along the structure while the live load $w$, such as a snow load, is most often assumed to act on the horizontal projection. In general, it is convenient to transform $w'$ into an equivalent load as shown in Fig. 4.33a. To determine shear and moment flow in an inclined, simply supported beam, an equivalent beam on the horizontal projection is used, as shown in Fig. 4.33b. The shear must be translated from the horizontal projection back into a position perpendicular to the inclined beam to obtain its true value. The value of the maximum moment remains the same, whether it is obtained from the projection or from the beam itself. The axial force flow is dependent on the beam's angle of inclination and on the support condition at $B$ (Fig. 4.33c).

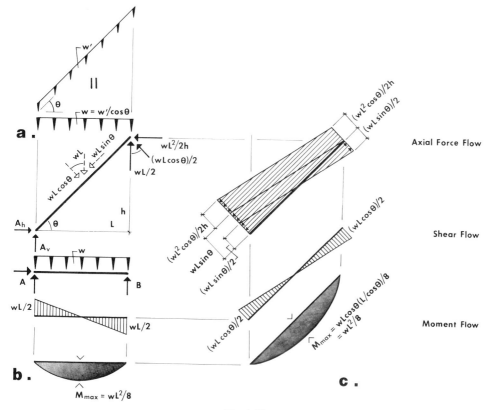

Fig. 4.33

The most efficient support condition in this context is the vertical one, since the total external axial force component, $wL \sin \theta$, is carried equally at $A$ in compression and at $B$ in tension. For the perpendicular support case the whole force component $wL \sin \theta$ must be resisted at the reaction $A$. In the horizontal reaction case the axial forces are very much increased. Not only does the axial load component due to the external loads have to be resisted, but also an additional force component due to the orientation of the reaction $B$.

In general, as the reaction $B$ rotates away from the vertical position, the axial force flow in the beam increases, especially when it has rotated through an angle larger than the angle of inclination $\theta$ of the beam.

### Uniform Lateral Loading

This case is analogous to the uniform gravity loading case just discussed. Visualize span $L$ and height $h$ to be exchanged, besides the exchange of the reactions.

### Uniform Loads Acting Perpendicular to the Beam

This case is well known, if the reactions are considered to act parallel to the loads (Fig. 4.34a). The transformation of these reactions to their real position yields the axial forces in the beam. Sometimes, however, it is more convenient to deal with the load compon-

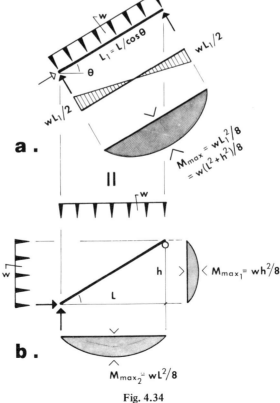

Fig. 4.34

ents on the horizontal and vertical beam projections. Resolving the load $w$ into its vertical load component $w_y$ yields

$$w_y = w \frac{L}{\cos\theta} \cos\theta \frac{1}{L} = w$$

Similarly, for the horizontal load components

$$w_x = w \frac{h}{\sin\theta} \sin\theta \frac{1}{h} = w$$

Hence, the load components on the projections are equal to the load acting on the inclined beam. The maximum moment is

$$M_{max} = \frac{wL_1^2}{8} = \frac{wL^2}{8} + \frac{wh^2}{8} = \frac{w(L^2 + h^2)}{8} \qquad (4.20)$$

where $L_1^2 = L^2 + h^2$.

Thus, the maximum beam moment may be obtained from equivalent beams on the horizontal and vertical projections carrying the same loading as the inclined beam.

### Conclusions

For inclined, simply supported beams:

- The moment flow is independent of beam inclination and support conditions.
- The shear flow is dependent on the inclination of the beam only.
- The axial force flow is dependent on the inclination of the beam and on the support conditions.

### Pitched Roof Structures in Residential Construction

The traditional inclined roof forms in residential construction are the shed roof, gable roof, and gambrel roof; from these three basic types are derived the hip and Mansard roofs (Fig. 4.36). Other shapes, in turn, can be developed from these five major forms either by transformation or by allowing them to intersect with each other as a result of irregular plan layout.

Basic principles of roof construction have already been briefly reviewed in Chapter 2 and are not further dealt with in this context.

The sloped roof may be chosen for aesthetic reasons, as an environmental protection against heavy rains, for the purpose of integrating a solar collector, or for functional reasons to utilize the interior space more efficiently. Whatever the reason for its choice, structure must be provided to support the form.

The typical structural skeletal systems including some detailing are defined in Fig. 4.35. The most common residential roof structures are generally in timber. They are:

- Joist roofs, including post-beam roofs (e.g., plank-beam, purlin-beam)
- Rafter roofs

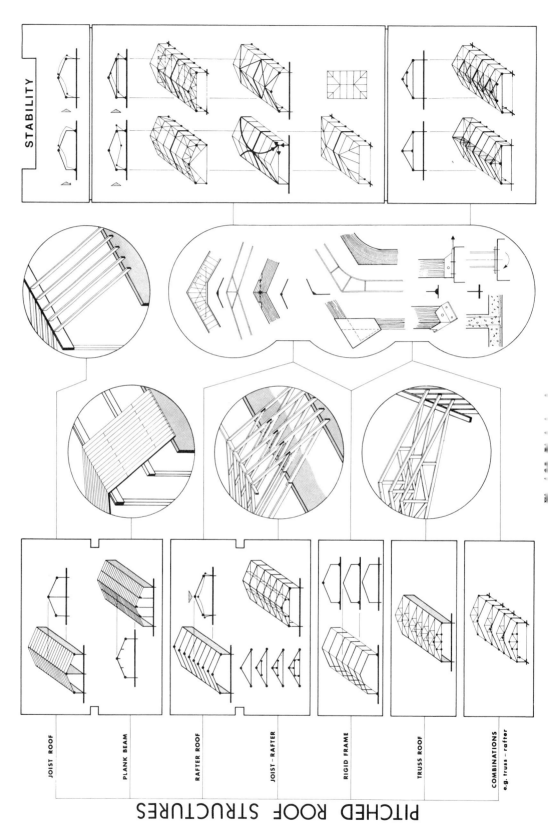

PITCHED ROOF STRUCTURES

JOIST ROOF

PLANK BEAM

RAFTER ROOF

JOIST – RAFTER

RIGID FRAME

TRUSS ROOF

COMBINATIONS
e.g. truss – rafter

- Truss roofs (see Section 4.5)
- Any combination of the above (e.g., truss-rafter)

Some less frequent construction systems used in the housing field are:

- Rigid frame (see Gable Frame Structures), pole-type construction
- Panelized roofs (see Chapter 6)

### The Joist and Post-Beam Roofs (Fig. 4.36)

In contrast to the rafter roof, where the rafters support each other at the crown to form a continuous frame unit, the joists function independently as inclined simple bending members, supported by beams spanning in the perpendicular direction. The concept of joist construction can be applied to any roof shape as indicated in Fig. 4.36, for traditional as well as free forms.

The typical wood joist in residential construction is of nominal 2-in dimension spaced 12, 16, or 24 in. on center. The spacing of the joists depends on the deck capacity (e.g., thickness and strength of plywood sheathing). The joist may just be a simply supported member bearing on the exterior wall and the center ridge beam, or it may be a continuous beam being supported at intermediate points on walls or beams.

In post-beam construction visualize the joists to be spaced further apart, such as 6–8 ft for timber plank construction, and to directly support the deck or if too far apart the purlins. From a structural point of view the two frameworks are quite similar; in both systems simple inclined beams support the roof deck. The difference is one of scale, where the closely spaced joists are of comparatively small size, while the beams must be much larger because of the higher loads they receive, since they are spaced further apart.

Closely spaced joists (or rafters, studs, trusses, etc.), not spaced more than 2 ft apart and joined adequately, distribute loads in bending to adjacent members. For this condition of repetitive member use, a 15% increase of the bending stresses for single members is permitted.

The uniform gravity loading generally controls the design of the joist, which behaves like a simple inclined beam with only vertical reaction forces (Figs. 4.33 and 4.36d) causing no lateral thrust at the base. Since the joist does not resist any axial forces at the location of maximum moment, one may conclude that it is basically equivalent in behavior to a simple horizontal beam which can be designed rather easily.

### The Rafter Roof (Fig. 4.37)

In the simplest form of residential application, a continuous three-hinge A-frame is formed by the inclined beams, called rafters, which act together with the floor joists. Here the rafters support each other and are often joined by a ridge board unlike the independent roof joists which are carried by the ridge beam. The lateral thrust which is absent from roof joists, but typical for frames, is resisted conveniently by the floor joists that behave like tie rods across the width of the building. For steeper roofs more intricate rafter framing systems may be necessary, such as the three statically indeterminate collar frames in Fig. 4.37g–i.

By placing a collar strut into the A-frame (Fig. 4.37b) to reduce the bending in the rafters, the lateral thrust at the base is increased by the amount of compression induced

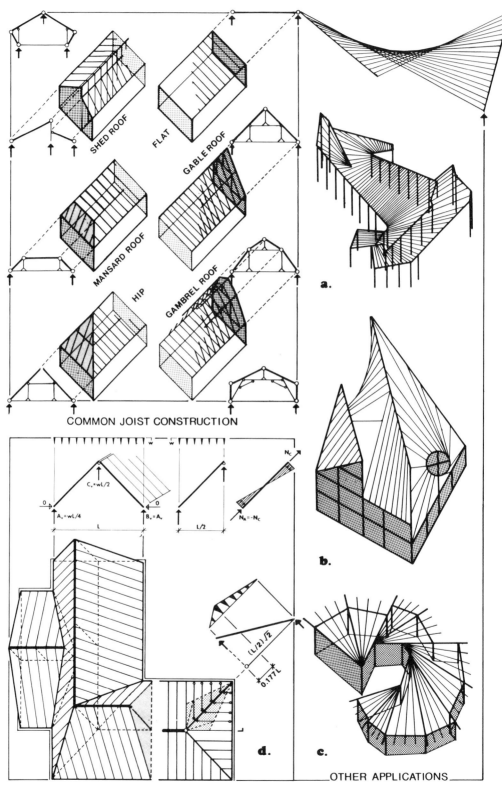

SHED ROOF

FLAT

GABLE ROOF

MANSARD ROOF

HIP

GAMBREL ROOF

COMMON JOIST CONSTRUCTION

$C_v = wL/2$

$A_v = wL/4$

$B_v = A_v$

$L$

$L/2$

$N_C$

$N_A = -N_C$

$(L/2)/2$

0.177L

a.

b.

c.

d.

OTHER APPLICATIONS

**Fig. 4.36** Joist roof construction.

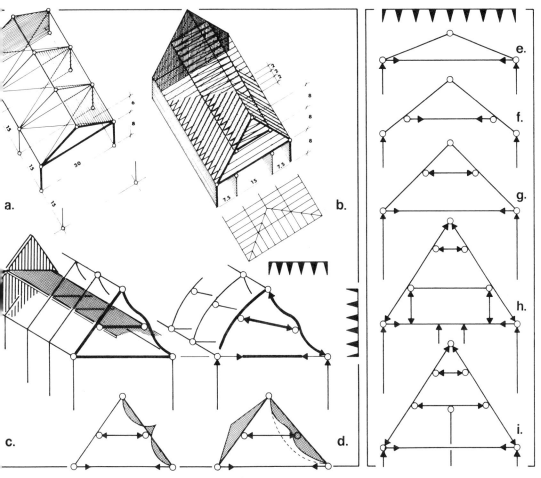

**Fig. 4.37** Rafter roof construction.

into the collar tie; the frame is now statically indeterminate to the first degree. For the strut to be truly effective, floor decking or horizontal bracing should connect the various collar ties together, to form a deep, relatively stiff, horizontal beam which must be supported by some shear walls (c). For this method of construction the collar strut provides a rigid support to the rafters; otherwise a flexible support (d) would only be available under unsymmetrical load action, requiring much larger rafter sizes.

As for joist construction, the rafters may be spaced closely at 12, 16, or 24 in. on center (Fig. 4.37b) supporting the deck directly, or they may be spaced farther apart, so that purlins are needed to span between them (Fig. 4.37a). The four sloped surfaces of the simple hip roof support each other laterally and thus provide a natural stability (Fig. 4.36). Hip roofs can be of joist or rafter construction. In joist construction the diagonal hip members along the junction of the surfaces (similar to the valley members along the junction of two pitched roofs) perform as inclined beams supported by a column, which for instance may be located at the intersection of the hip and ridge; the loading diagram for a typical hip beam is shown in Fig. 4.36d. Note that without the column supports the hip and ridge members must act as a spatial rafter framework. In rafter construction the shortened rafters (called jack rafters) that meet along the hip rafters support each other structurally, thereby placing the hip rafters in tension.

The behavior of a typical three-hinge A-frame, which includes the simple rafter roof, is investigated now for the most common loading conditions as based on parallel frame arrangement.

■ *Single Load Applied to the Joint at the Crown* (*Fig. 4.38*)

The reactions for the lateral and gravity loading cases are found in the same manner as for the three-hinge portal frame. Since the loads are applied to the joint at the crown, the A-frame represents the simplest form of a truss, where the members carry axial forces only. As based on the isolated crown joint, horizontal equilibrium for the gravity load case, and vertical equilibrium for the lateral load case, show that the two members share the load resistance equally. The member forces are found by summing up the force components at the apex

Gravity load case:     $\Sigma V = 0 = W - 2N \sin \theta$         $N = \dfrac{W}{2 \sin \theta}$

Lateral load case:     $\Sigma H = 0 = P - 2N \cos \theta$         $N = \dfrac{P}{2 \cos \theta}$

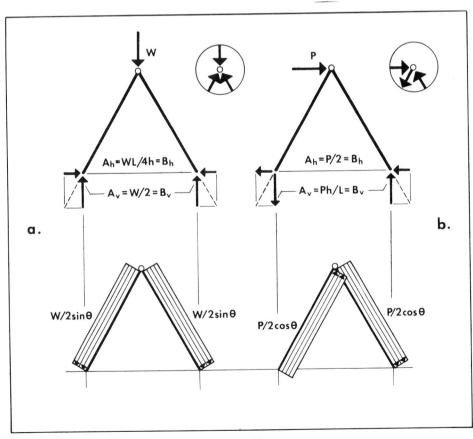

Fig. 4.38

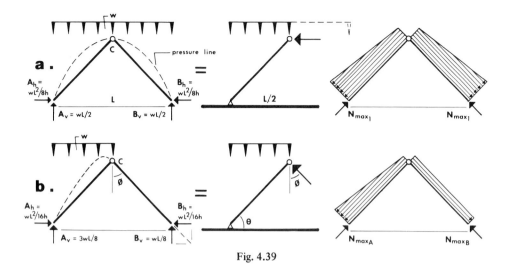

Fig. 4.39

■ *Uniform Gravity Loading*

Full uniform loading and loading of the A-frame on one side only are shown in Fig. 4.39. The reactions are found first. The free-bodies of the loaded frame clearly show that they are simply supported inclined beams, the behavior of which has been investigated. It was shown that the shear and moment flow for both free-bodies are the same. The maximum moment is

$$M_{max} = \frac{w(L/2)^2}{8} = \frac{wL^2}{32} \tag{4.21}$$

The maximum shear is

$$V_{max} = \frac{w(L/2)\cos\theta}{2} = \frac{wL\cos\theta}{4}$$

Only the axial force flow for the two cases is different. For the full loading case it was shown in Fig. 4.6 that the maximum axial force at the reaction is

$$N_{max\,1} = A_v \sin\theta + A_h \cos\theta$$
$$= w\frac{L}{2}\sin\theta + \frac{w(L/2)^2 \cos\theta}{2h}$$
$$= \frac{wL\sin\theta}{2} + \frac{wL^2 \cos\theta}{8h}$$

The maximum axial force for the asymmetrical loading case is

$$N_{max\,A} = A_v \sin\theta + A_h \cos\theta$$
$$= \frac{3wL\sin\theta}{8} + \frac{wL^2 \cos\theta}{16h} < N_{max\,1}$$

$$N_{max\,B} = B_v \sin\theta + B_h \cos\theta$$
$$= \frac{wL\sin\theta}{8} + \frac{wL^2 \cos\theta}{16h}$$

241

Since the nonloaded member in this case acts as a simple column, with a constant axial force, the normal force can also be determined from Fig. 4.32f

$$N_{\max B} = \frac{M \cos \theta}{L \cos (\phi - \theta)} = \frac{wL}{8} \frac{\cos \theta}{\cos (\phi - \theta)}$$

Comparing the two loading cases shows that for preliminary design purposes only uniform gravity loading acting across the full length of the frame has to be considered, since this case yields the maximum shear, moment, and axial forces.

■ *Uniform Lateral Loading (Fig. 4.40)*

For the discussion of this case refer to Fig. 4.34. The maximum moment is

$$M_{\max} = \frac{qh^2}{8} \tag{4.22}$$

It is interesting to compare the maximum wind load moment with the maximum live load moment, so as to get an approximate idea of the proportion $h/L$ at which wind loading becomes a determinant for preliminary design purposes. Setting the two moments equal to each other and neglecting the effect of combined action, yields

$$\frac{qh^2}{8} = \frac{wL^2}{32}$$

$$\frac{h}{L} = 0.5 \sqrt{\frac{w}{q}} \tag{4.23}$$

For the condition where the wind load is equal to one-half of the snow load ($w/q = 2$), the height-to-span ratio is $h/L = 0.707$, or the angle of inclination is $\theta = 54.73°$.

As based on this oversimplified approach and for the given loading conditions, one may conclude that if the frame height should be more than about 70% of the frame span or the roof slope steeper than about 54°, wind loading may control the preliminary design. Should the snow load be equal to the wind load ($w/q = 1$), then $h/L = 0.5$, or the angle of inclination is $\theta = 26.57°$. For this case, the frame height should be less than one-half of the span so that the wind case does not control.

In conclusion it may be stated that the uniform gravity loading usually controls the design of roof joists as well as rafters. While the shear and moment flow is the same in both construction systems, the axial force distribution is different. Since the joist does

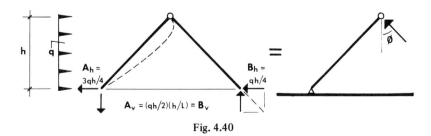

Fig. 4.40

not carry any axial force at the point of maximum moment, one may conclude that the joist is basically a simple beam, while the rafter is a beam-column.

The true structural behavior of closely spaced rafters or joists in residential construction, and the effect of the connection types upon the member behavior is highly indeterminate. Obviously the method of analysis presented here cannot be precise. However, it is conservative to treat the roof members individually and independent of each other, thus ignoring the spatial interaction. The member sizes obtained by analysis predict the results which used to be based on empirical rules that were employed until recently.

## Gable Frame Structures

There are infinitely many types of frames incorporating inclined members, including the A-frame and post-beam systems just discussed. Some typical cases are shown in Fig. 4.41; they only can give an indication of the potential occurrence. These frames are investigated in Problem 4.17 for the various loading conditions shown. Here, only the most common symmetrical gable frames (Fig. 4.42) are studied further.

Gable frames are either of two-hinge or three-hinge type. While the two-hinge frame is once indeterminate, the three-hinge frame is statically determinate and can be analyzed by using the three-equations of equilibrium.

The design of the members depends on the critical loading conditions, which have already been discussed for portal frames and A-frames. For preliminary design purposes, only the uniform gravity load case has to be considered. The reader may refer to Problem 4.17(s), (t), and (u), and compare the force flow for the typical gable frame acted upon by different types of loading.

Keep in mind that as the frame gets taller the wind will become a primary design determinant as was shown for the A-frame. Further, the asymmetrical gravity loading case yields the larger field moment and larger center-span shear for the gable beam; this, obviously has to be considered in the final structural design. However, for the preliminary sizing of a typical gable frame, it is reasonable to investigate only the full uniform gravity case.

### The Three-Hinge Gable Frame (Fig. 4.42)

It was shown that the reactions for the three-hinge frames are independent of the frame shape. The reactions are

$$A_v = B_v = \frac{wL}{2} \qquad A_h = B_h = \frac{wL^2}{8h}$$

The internal axial and shear force flow along the range of the vertical column is equivalent to the reactions in magnitude. The column moment varies with height and is maximum at the knee

$$M_e = A_h(h_c) = \frac{wL^2 h_c}{8h}$$

$$M_d = B_h(h_c) = \frac{wL^2 h_c}{8h}$$

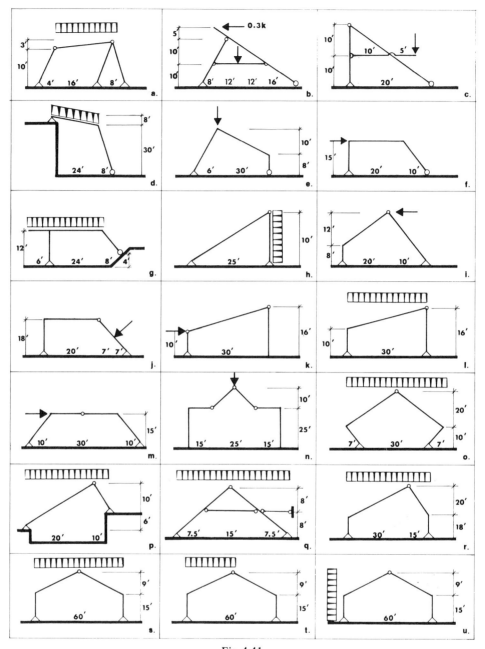

**Fig. 4.41**

The force flow is shown in Fig. 4.42. The internal force flow along the gable beam is found by using the equations derived in Fig. 4.6. In general, the magnitude of the axial forces is

$$-N_x = (A_v - W_y) \sin \theta + (A_h + W_x) \cos \theta$$

$$x = 0: \qquad -N_0 = A_v \sin \theta + A_h \cos \theta$$

$$= \frac{wL}{2} \sin \theta + \frac{wL^2}{8h} \cos \theta$$

$$x = L/2: \quad -N_{L/2} = \left(A_v - \frac{wL}{2}\right) \sin \theta + A_h \cos \theta$$

$$= A_h \cos \theta = \frac{wL^2}{8h} \cos \theta \qquad (4.24)$$

In general, the magnitude of the shear force is

$$V_x = (A_v - W_y) \cos \theta - (A_h + W_x) \sin \theta$$

$$x = 0: \quad V_0 = A_v \cos \theta - A_h \sin \theta$$

$$= \frac{wL}{2} \cos \theta - \frac{wL^2}{8h} \sin \theta$$

$$x = L/2: \quad V_{L/2} = \left(A_v - \frac{wL}{2}\right) \cos \theta - A_h \sin \theta$$

$$= -A_h \sin \theta = -\frac{wL^2}{8h} \sin \theta \qquad (4.25)$$

$$x = ?: \quad V_x = 0 = \left(\frac{wL}{2} - wx\right) \cos \theta - \frac{wL^2}{8h} \sin \theta$$

$$0 = \frac{L}{2} - x - \frac{L^2}{8h} \tan \theta$$

where

$$\tan \theta = \frac{f}{L/2} = \frac{y}{x}$$

$$x = \frac{L}{2} \left(1 - \frac{f}{2h}\right)$$

$$= \frac{L}{4} \left(1 + \frac{h_c}{h}\right) \qquad (4.26)$$

The maximum field moment in the beam appears at the distance $x$, where the shear is zero

$$M_{max} = A_v(x) - wx \frac{x}{2} - A_h(h + y)$$

$$M_{max} = A_v(x) - \frac{wx^2}{2} - A_h(h + x \tan \theta)$$

The field moment $M_{max}$, in comparison to the knee moment $M_d$ (i.e., $M_{min}$) is rather small and does not have to be considered for preliminary design purposes.

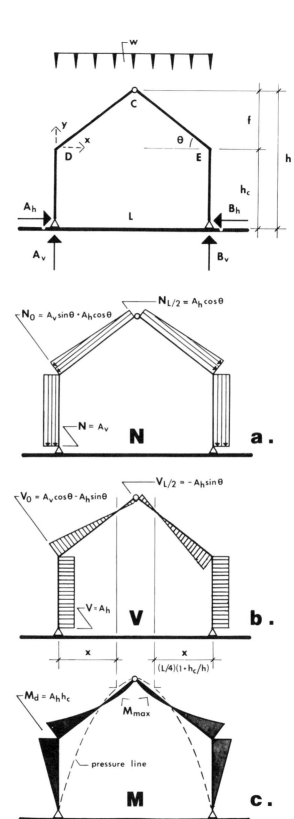

Fig. 4.42

246

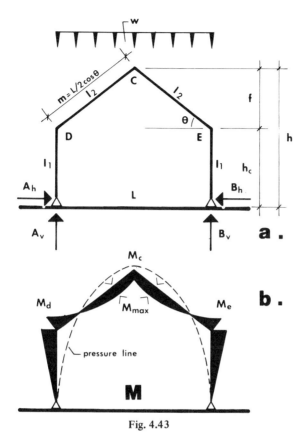

Fig. 4.43

### The Two-Hinge Frame (Fig. 4.43)

The frame is once indeterminate; one additional known condition is needed. The relative sizes of the frame members influence the force flow along the frame. For instance, replace the pin at support $B$ with a roller. Now the frame is statically determinate and the column will roll outwards under the load action. The amount of lateral displacement depends on the stiffness of the frame members. It can be shown that the horizontal base force necessary to push the column back to its original position (i.e., to have a two-hinge frame again) is approximately

$$A_h = B_h = \frac{wL^2}{8h_cN} (8 + 5Q)$$ 

(4.27)

where

$$Q = \frac{f}{h_c}$$

$$k = \frac{I_2/m}{I_1/h_c} = \frac{I_2h_c}{I_1m}$$

$$N = 4(k + 3 + 3Q + Q^2)$$

$$m = \frac{L}{2} \cos \theta$$

Note that for rectangular portal frames $Q = 0$.

The relative member sizes can be estimated as the ratio of rafter inertia to column inertia $I_2/I_1$. Once the reactions are known, the force flow along the frame can be obtained by statics.

The moment at the knee is

$$M_d = M_e = A_h(h_c)$$

The moment at the ridge is

$$M_c = A_v\left(\frac{L}{2}\right) - \frac{wL}{2}\frac{L}{4} - A_h(h)$$

or

$$M_c = \frac{wL^2}{8} - A_h(h)$$

The maximum field moment can be found in the same way as for the three-hinge frame.

### Conclusion

As a conclusion to the investigation of the various pitched frames, note that some systems are compared in Fig. 4.44 for a typical gable roof enclosure. The maximum moment of $M = wL^2/8$ for the bent beam is taken as the basis for this comparison. It appears that the A-frame (d) with a maximum rafter moment of only 25% of $M$ and pure axial action in the columns is the most efficient solution if one accepts the tie rod (or buttress). This tie, however, is not necessary for the frames (c), (f) which are continuous across the rafter–column intersection and resist the thrust as maximum bending at the junction thereby throwing a large moment into the columns. Obviously, the ideal solution from the force flow point of view is the parabolic arch in pure compression, reflecting the funicular response to the loading.

### Preliminary Design of a Laminated-Wood Gable Frame

**Example 4.4**  The frame shown in Fig. 4.45 spans 80 ft and is 30 ft high at the crown; the eave height is 20 ft. The frames are spaced 16 ft on center. Dead and snow load are 15 and 35 psf, respectively, and assumed to act on the horizontal projection of the roof. The effect of wind does not have to be considered for preliminary design purposes. Glued laminated Douglas Fir 22F will be used with the following allowable stresses under normal duration of loads:

$$F_b = 2200 \text{ psi} \qquad F_c = 1500 \text{ psi}$$

$$F_v = 165 \text{ psi} \qquad E = 1.8 \times 10^6 \text{ psi}$$

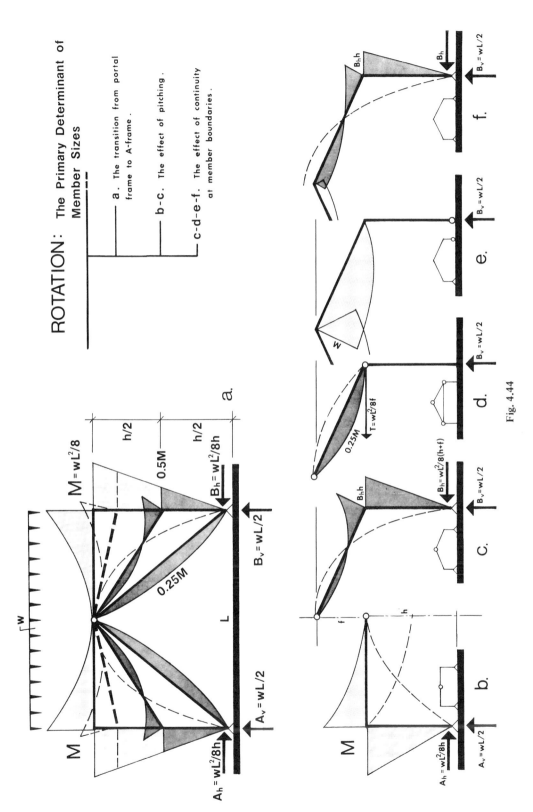

ROTATION: The Primary Determinant of Member Sizes

a. The transition from portal frame to A-frame.

b-c. The effect of pitching.

c-d-e-f. The effect of continuity at member boundaries.

Fig. 4.44

249

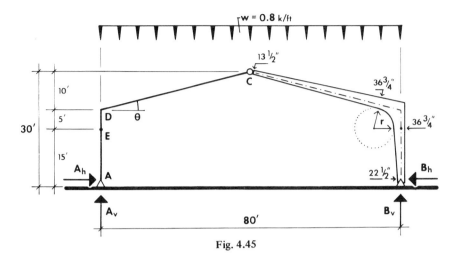

**Fig. 4.45**

The allowable stresses will not be adjusted for such variables as load duration, section size, section curvature, moisture content, temperature, treatment of timber, etc. To ignore load duration is conservative in this case, since the given allowable stresses are based on a normal duration (about 10 years). Allowable stresses are usually increased by 15% for snow loads, which are assumed to have a duration of two months.

The roof slope is

$$\tan \theta = \frac{10}{40} = 0.25 \quad \theta = 14°$$

$$\sin \theta = 0.243 \quad \quad \cos \theta = 0.970$$

The uniform loads acting on the horizontal projection of the rafter are

$$w = (15 + 35)16 = 800 \text{ lb/ft} = 0.8 \text{ k/ft}$$

The reactions are

$$A_v = B_v = \frac{wL}{2} = \frac{0.8(80)}{2} = 32 \text{ k}$$

$$A_h = B_h = \frac{wL^2}{8h} = \frac{0.8(80)^2}{8(30)} = 21.33 \text{ k}$$

The moment at the frame knee is

$$M_D = A_h h_c = 21.33(20) = 426.6 \text{ ft-k}$$

The required section modulus at the knee is

$$S = \frac{M}{F_b} = \frac{426.6(12)}{2.2} = 2326.91 \text{ in.}^3$$

Adding about 10% to the section modulus, because axial force action is neglected, yields

$$S = 1.1(2326.91) = 2559.60 \text{ in.}^3$$

For a width of 8.75 in. the required depth is

$$S = \frac{bd^2}{6}$$

$$d = \sqrt{\frac{6S}{b}} = \sqrt{\frac{6(2559.60)}{8.75}} = 41.90 \text{ in.}$$

or, from the Section Properties Table A.7 for a .75 in. lamination thickness, select a trial cross-section of

$$8.75 \times 42.0 \text{ in.}$$

$$S = 2572.5 \text{ in.}^3 \quad A = 367.5 \text{ in.}^2$$

Refer to Problem 4.23 for consideration of combined beam-column action. The curved portion at the knee is subject to radial stresses perpendicular to the grain; these stresses are not checked in this preliminary investigation. The required section modulus at point $E$, where the curve transforms into a straight line, is

$$M_E = 21.33(15) = 319.95 \text{ ft-k}$$

$$S = \frac{M}{F_b} = \frac{319.95(12)}{2.2} = 1745.18 \text{ in.}^3$$

Adding about 10% to the section modulus, because axial force action is neglected, yields

$$S = 1.1(1745.18) = 1919.7 \text{ in.}^3$$

For a width of 8.75 in. the depth of the section is:

$$S = \frac{bd^2}{6}$$

$$d = \sqrt{\frac{1919.7(6)}{8.75}} = 36.28 \text{ in.}$$

This yields a trial section (Table A.7) of

$$8.75 \times 36.75 \text{ in.}$$

$$S = 1969.6 \text{ in.}^3 \quad A = 321.6 \text{ in.}^2$$

The size of the column at the base is controlled by shear:

$$F_v \geqslant \frac{3V}{2A} \quad \text{where } A = bd = 8.75d$$

$$0.165 = \frac{3(21.33)}{2(8.75)d}$$

$$d = 22.16 \text{ in.}$$

Select $8.75 \times 22.5$ in., $A = 196.9$ in.$^2$.

The axial stresses at the column base are

$$f = \frac{P}{A} = \frac{32000}{196.9} = 162.52 \text{ psi}$$

The allowable compressive stresses parallel to the grain, as determined by elastic buckling, are

$$F_a = \frac{0.3E}{(h_c/d)^2} \leqslant F_c \tag{1.45}$$

$$= \frac{0.3(1.8 \times 10^6)}{[20(12)/8.75]^2} = 717.77 \text{ psi} > 162.52 \text{ psi}$$

This clearly shows that the axial stresses are not critical, even if conservatively assuming that the full height of the column is laterally unsupported.

The depth of the frame at the crown is rarely determined by the magnitude of the force action at that point; most often it is dependent on detail considerations, such as the depth of the purlins, and considerations of appearance. As a first trial, the depth of the section at the crown may be considered 50% larger than the width

$$d = 1.5b = 1.5(8.75) = 13.125 \text{ in.}$$

Select $8.75 \times 13.5$ in., $A = 118.1$ in.$^2$.

It was shown that the shear and axial forces at the crown are

$$V_c = -A_h \sin \theta = -21.33(0.243) = -5.18 \text{ k} \tag{4.25}$$

$$N_c = A_h \cos \theta = 21.33(0.970) = 21.12 \text{ k} \tag{4.24}$$

The axial and shear stresses are

$$f_c = \frac{P}{A} = \frac{21120}{118.1} = 178.83 \text{ psi}$$

$$f_v = \frac{1.5V}{A} = \frac{1.5(5180)}{118.1} = 65.79 \text{ psi} < 165 \text{ psi}$$

Taking into account the fact that the roof sheathing prevents the buckling of the rafter about the weak axis, and using conservatively the depth of the section at the crown as its depth along the entire length, results in the following compressive buckling strength:

$$F_a = \frac{0.3E}{(L/d)^2} \leqslant F_c \tag{1.45}$$

$$= \frac{0.3(1.8 \times 10^6)}{\{[40(12)/\cos \theta]/13.5\}^2} = 401.9 \text{ psi} > 178.83 \text{ psi}$$

The stresses are far below the allowable ones. It shows clearly that the member size at the crown is not derived from force action. The size of the gable frame, as determined by preliminary design, is shown in Fig. 4.45.

## Problems

**4.17** For the statically determinate frames shown in Fig. 4.41, draw shear, moment, and axial force diagrams and show numerical values; indicate clearly how these values are obtained. Further, show how the frames deform under loading. Where numerical values for the loads are not given assume a unit load.

**4.18** Determine the approximate size of the purlins and roof rafters (Fig. 4.37a). The roof framing is spaced at 15 ft, and supports the purlins running perpendicularly to it. The building is laterally stabilized by a horizontal, rigid plane, such as a trussed floor level, and by vertical, rigid diaphragms in the end bays, which act as shear walls. Assume 10 psf for sheathing, roofing, and purlins and 2 psf for rafters. Consider a snow load of 20 psf on the horizontal roof projection, and a wind load of 20 psf on the vertical roof projection. Use Douglas Fir South Select structural with the following properties: $F_b$ = 1550 psi, $F_v$ = 85 psi, $F_c$ = 1000 psi, $E$ = 1,200,000 psi.

(a) Design the simply supported timber purlins, spanning between the rafters, by arranging them in eight equal spaces across the full width of the roof. First, assume that the thrust component parallel to the roof plane is carried by the skin, such as planking to the rafters. Then, design the purlins by considering that the skin, such as plywood sheathing, is only able to resist the twisting and not the lateral movement parallel to the roof slope (Fig. 1.15). For the purlin design, assume conservatively that the horizontal wind pressure acts normal to the roof skin. For this preliminary design, consider only bending.

(b) Select the rafter size as based on gravity bending only. Verify that the full gravity loading case controls the design. Check the rafter for combined force action (i.e. beam-column); assume that the weak axis of the rafter is laterally supported by the roof skin. Check shear stresses. Check deflection of rafter for an allowable live load deflection of $L/240$ and a total load deflection of $L/180$.

**4.19** Design the building in Fig. 4.37a and Problem 4.18 as a joist roof. Assume the joist to be spaced at 16 in. on center.

**4.20** For a preliminary estimate, determine the size of a typical rafter (Fig. 4.37b) spaced at 2 ft on center. Notice that this case has already been analyzed in Problem 4.17, case (q). Use the following loads: 13 psf for roof tiles and laths, 2 psf for rafter weight, 20 psf for snow load on the horizontal projection, and 15 psf for wind load on the vertical projection. Use Douglas Fir South with the properties given in Problem 4.18, the only difference being that the rafters are assumed to have a plaster ceiling, which results in an allowable live load deflection of $L/360$ and an allowable total load deflection of $L/240$.

Neglect the 15% increase of allowable stresses, due to load duration as caused by snow loading. Also, the increase of the allowable bending stress $F_b$ due to the repetitive member use is ignored.

**4.21** In an industrial building, three-hinge gable frames of $A$ 36 steel are spaced 20 ft apart. The frames must support the following loads:

| dead load: | | | live load: | snow | 20 psf |
|---|---|---|---|---|---|
| | roofing | 4 psf | | | |
| | metal deck | 2 psf | | | |
| | insulation | 3 psf | wind load: | is neglected for | |
| | purlins | 4 psf | | this preliminary | |
| | other | 2 psf | | design. | |
| | | 15 psf | | | |
| | frame | 5 psf | | | |
| | total | 20 psf | | | |

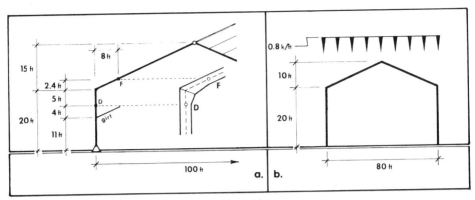

Fig. 4.46

(a) Determine the preliminary sizes of column and rafter by considering only bending. The critical moment locations at the haunch are identified as points D and F in Fig. 4.46a for column and beam design. The haunch itself will not be designed at this initial stage. The rafter is laterally stabilized by the purlins which are spaced at 5.8 ft on center, and the column is laterally supported about its weak axis by the girts.

(b) Check the beam section and the column section by considering axial action as well as bending (i.e., beam-column action).

(c) Verify that the full gravity case controls the preliminary design by assuming a wind pressure of 20 psf on the vertical roof projection.

**4.22** For the building in Fig. 4.46b, the following structural systems are investigated: joist–rafter, rafter only, bent beam, three-hinge frame, and two-hinge frame. Show deformation of frames and moment diagrams with numerical values for the given uniform gravity case.

**4.23** Do a preliminary check of the beam-column action for the frame in Example 4.4.

## 4.4  THE ARCH

The most common funicular cable shapes are shown in Fig. 3.1a; they are the catenary and parabola for typical gravity loading conditions. When these shapes are "frozen" and inverted, they become funicular arches responding in pure compression. However, the assumed loads do not remain constant. When they change, the rigid arch cannot readjust its shape, hence is subject to flexure. One may conclude that although the arch is primarily a compressive structural system, it also must resist bending which for roof structures generally controls its design.

In addition, the boundary conditions of the arch are to be considered, since large thrust forces may have to be resisted with the necessary capacity being provided by the soil, tie rods, or buttresses. Light, steep arches cause less thrust than corresponding heavy, flat arches!

In the past, the arch, together with the arch-like vault, was one of the few structural systems which made it possible to span larger distances by using masonry with its low tensile capacity. As early as several centuries B.C. the Assyrians and Babylonians included arches in their architecture (e.g., Ishtar Gate in Babylon, circa 575 B.C.). Although the Egyptians and Greeks were familiar with the arch concept, they did not make it part of their building design language. Only the Romans developed the arch as an important element of their architecture as expressed by triumphal arches, amphitheaters, aqueducts, etc.; they not only used its engineering potential but gave it a special meaning.

One of the most famous arch vaults of the ancient world is the audience hall of the Palace of Ctesiphon near modern Baghdad, built at about 550 A.D. by the Sassanians. The 83-ft span vault has a nearly catenary shape 120-ft in height; this funicular form was necessary because of the low tensile capacity of the mudbrick material. The Romans used mostly semicircular arches, which are efficient from a construction point of view but not in terms of force flow; but they also used much stronger masonry material and concrete.

The Gothic pointed arch, which is composed of circular arcs, is a good approximation of the funicular shape for the given loading conditions, although the medieval master builders did not know the concept of force flow, at least not on a scientific basis; their primary concern was structure as geometry and construction.

The ingenious Rennaissance engineers replaced in their bridge design the semicircular arch forms of the Romans by the segmental curves, as so clearly illustrated by the extremely shallow Ponte Vecchio in Florence and the Rialto Bridge in Venice.

Probably Robert Hooke, in 1670, was the first to realize, from a scientific point of view, that the catenary is the funicular response of the arch weight. Antonio Gaudi, in his search for the true nature of form, revived the idea of the funicular curves of the loads by deriving them from suspended scale models, as to achieve purity of form or, from an economical point of view, maximum efficiency of materials. It was around the turn of this century, when he used parabolic arches as an approximation for the catenary.

At about the same time concrete arches were rediscovered, exciting new forms were developed especially in bridge construction by the great designers Francois Hennebique and Robert Maillart. Maillart's funicular arch forms seem to control perfectly the force flow with a minimum of effort through correct placement of mass and to be in full harmony with nature (e.g., Fig. 4.49a). In 1916 Eugene Freyssinnet started to build his famous 262-ft span parabolic, thin shell folded concrete vaults for the Orly hangars near Paris.

While the correct arch shape is of utmost importance for materials weak in tension or where weight is an important consideration, the strong new materials iron and then steel, which developed through the nineteenth century, did not have to place that much emphasis on this aspect, as they can easily resist bending. The continuous (fixed) trussed, wrought iron arches for St. Pancras Station in London (1869) span the enormous distance of 244 ft. About 20 years later, a new era in scale was established with the 375-ft span of the three-hinged arch-like trussed steel gable frames for the Galerie des Machines of the 1889 Paris Exhibition.

The rapid progress in the sciences, material strength, and construction techniques is expressed by the world's currently largest steel arch span of 1700 ft of the New River Gorge Bridge in West Virginia (1978), and the world's longest concrete arch of 1280 ft of the Krk Bridge in Yugoslavia (1979).

Today, because of the formability of the major materials steel, reinforced concrete, and timber, there is hardly any limit set to the formal potential as the various arch systems derived in Fig. 4.47 clearly express.

The arch principle can be employed in many different ways within the building context (Fig. 4.49). For instance, arches may form the building enclosure or roof: a typical

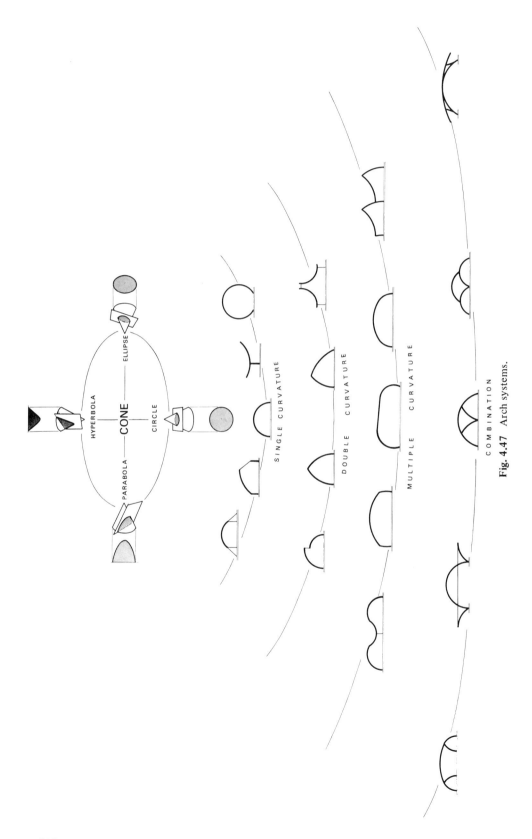

**Fig. 4.47** Arch systems.

256

parallel arrangement yields a cylindrical shape, while a radial one results in a dome. The arch may provide the support for another structure such as for a roof or a roadway as is typical for bridges; or it may be the compression ring for a stadium roof.

Besides these typical, familiar applications, arches can be stimulating to design. The examples in Fig. 4.48 can only suggest ways of how arches may define building space. The reader may also refer to Chapter 2, where the richness of the curvilinear grids are experienced in Fig. 2.2.

Following, some typical examples of arches in architecture as shown in Fig. 4.49 are briefly discussed.

The hollow triangular legs of the catenary Gateway Arch in St. Louis (f) each contain stairs, a train, and an elevator which rises to about two-thirds of the way. The sandwich walls are composed of the inner and outer steel skins connected to the core concrete by shear connectors to obtain a stressed-skin-type of action.

The various bridges (a)–(e) exemplify the many ways the arch can be used to support the roadway. Arch and roadway can be one and the same along the central portion of the bridge (a); the deck can sit on top of the arch (b); it can hang from the arch (d); it can be used as the tie for the arch (c), (d); it can be the arch (e), in this case using the cantilevering ramps as counterbalance for the main arch. The bridge principle is applied to the grandstand roof of the San Mames Stadium, Bilbao, Spain (r), which consists of two two-hinged steel arches tied together by diagonal bracing and horizontal ties. The roof framing is suspended by hanger rods from the arches; the size of the welded arch box section is nearly $20 \times 70$ in. with $\frac{1}{2}$-in. flanges and (internally braced) $\frac{3}{8}$-in. webs.

For all the other cases in Fig. 4.49, the arches are used to enclose the building and are mostly arranged in a parallel fashion.

The glued-laminated, three-hinged wood arches for a field house in Paris (p) are spaced at 20.5 ft apart and span the enormous distance of 307 ft. The size of the arch at the crown is $5.5 \times 25.5$ in. and, at the base, $5.5 \times 60$ in. The flat cylindrical roof of the Convention Center in Niagara Falls, N.Y. (o), is supported by parallel 10-ft deep trussed steel arches spanning 355 ft. The 63-ft space between the arches is bridged by butterfly trusses at 10 ft on center; the light-gauge metal roof deck acts compositely with the trusses. The two-hinged vault roof of the stadium at the University of Idaho, Moscow (m), a continuous composite steel web and wood chord structure, spans the large distance of 400 ft! The $7\frac{1}{2}$-ft deep trussed arches are composed of $1\frac{7}{8}$-in. thick laminated wood deck chords and 2 in. diameter tubular steel web members.

For the underground convention hall in San Francisco (1981), eight pairs of 275-ft concrete arches were used to obtain the column-free space. The arches were post-tensioned by tying their abutments together with tendons through the mat foundation; they will support not only the roof surface with its loading but also the future three-story buildings.

The precast, three-hinged concrete arches ($21 \times 36$ in.) in case (k) are spaced 18 ft on center, and their lateral thrust is directly resisted by the inclined footings. The tension ties for the parabolic concrete arches of a one-family house (n) are hidden under the floor.

The Activity Center in Aabenraa, Denmark (q), consists of parallel suspended, three-hinged laminated wood arches. The lateral thrust is resisted by the concrete wall buttresses. The shape of the curved bents for the pagoda-like shelter (h) and, even more, the detail of case (g) express the formal potential of glued laminated wood construction.

The 180-ft dome (i) consists of radially arranged laminated bow-string trusses inclined

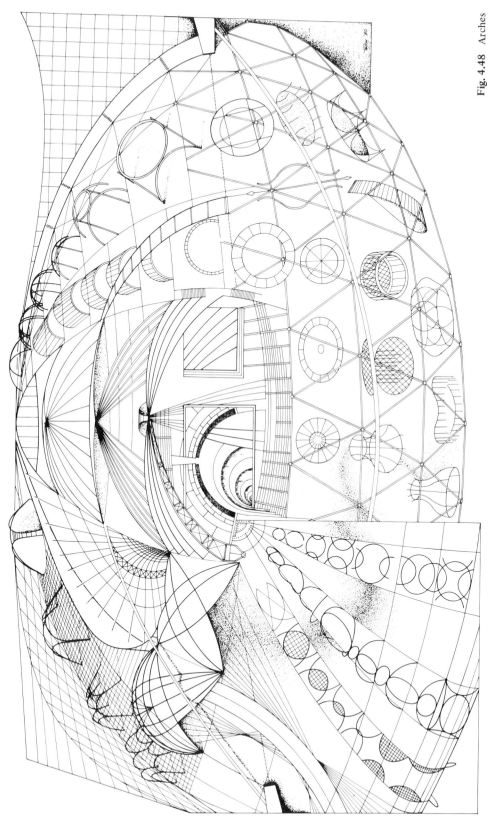

Fig. 4.48 Arches

at 45° and joined to the compression ring at the crown. The glued laminated arches (7 × 26 in.) for the ribbed dome in case (j) span 144 ft.

A rather complex arrangement of arches is used for the spherical roof segment of the velodrome in Montreal (l) which rests on four abutments. The primary roof framing consists of three pairs of prestressed concrete arches and two edge arches. The arch pairs, in turn, are tied together transversely by prestressed beams and slabs. The precast concrete arch elements were glued together before they were post-tensioned so that the roof can act as a true monolithic surface structure.

## The Response of the Arch to Loading

An arch must be connected to its base so that any lateral displacement is prevented. Should one of the supports be equivalent to a roller, then the arch degenerates to a curved beam and loses its identity. This fact clearly shows that much care must be taken with the design of the anchorage system which must resist the lateral thrust.

Here, the determinate three-hinged arch is investigated. It finds wide application especially in glued-laminated timber construction, but is also used in precast concrete and steel construction. Some of the advantages of its application not only lie in the simpler structural analysis and in its adaptability to any movement without being stressed, but also lies in easier transportation, erection, and assemblage procedures. Further, the indeterminate two-hinged arch can be treated as a three-hinged one for preliminary design purposes.

The analysis of the three-hinged arch is approached in the same manner as for the frame. The reactions do not change under constant loading, they are independent of the frame shape which bridges the given space. However, the intensity of force flow, obviously, varies with the form of the structure. In the introduction to frames it was shown that for a given loading condition, the difference between the ideal funicular form and the actual frame shape constitutes rotation (bending) which is the primary determinant of member size.

For the case, where an arch is loaded only by a single external force $P$ such as a concentrated vertical or horizontal load or a moment (Fig. 4.50 a–c), the reactions can be found directly by balancing the three forces $R_A$, $R_B$, and $P$ about the point of concurrency $d$, where all the three forces meet when translated along their line of action. The reaction $R_B$ must pass through the hinge at the crown since there is no external force interference along this side of the arch and the moment is zero at the hinge; the reaction force is colinear and in equilibrium with the resultant force at the crown (Fig. 4.50a). Hence, where $R_B$ intersects with the force $P$ is the location of the point of concurrency; this point connected to the other support establishes the direction of the reaction $R_A$. The lines of force flow for $R_A$ and $R_B$ directly balancing the external load are analogous to an imaginary cable supported at the reactions which has adjusted its shape to the force action so that it can resist in axial manner. This cable is "frozen" and inverted as to form the funicular shape also called the pressure line. The axial forces along the funicular lines must be relocated to the real structure. In general, the displacement of a translational force to any other place in space must cause in addition rotation about this new force location. Furthermore, the translational force must be resolved into components perpendicular and parallel to the member curvature resulting in shear and axial action, respectively. From this discussion one may conclude that the moment at any given arch section can be deter-

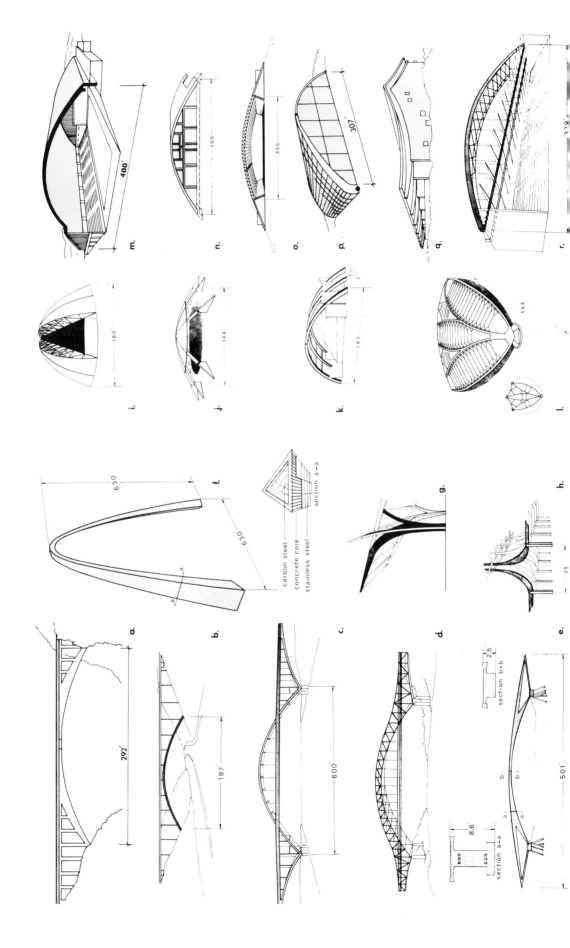

a.

b.

c.

d.

e.

f.

g.

h.

i.

j.

k.

l.

m.

n.

o.

p.

q.

r.

292'

197'

600'

501'

630'

630'

section a-a

carbon steel
concrete core
stainless steel

section a-a

section b-b

8.6

2.5

180

144

147

564

400'

105

355

307'

379'

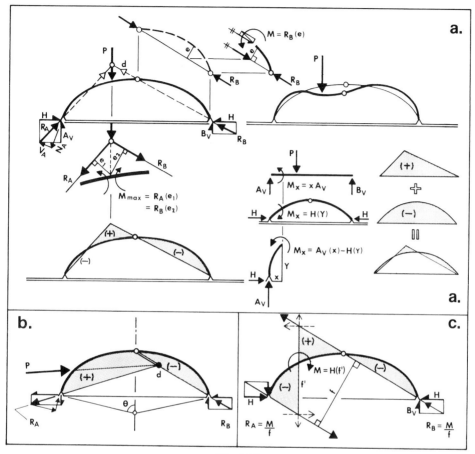

Fig. 4.50

mined by the product of the axial funicular force and the corresponding perpendicular distance to the location of the section. For instance, the maximum moment at load $P$ (Fig. 4.50a), causing tension along the inside face of the member, is

$$M_{max} = R_A (e_1) = R_B (e_2)$$

It is quite apparent that the largest moment appears at an arch section which is furthest away from the pressure line $(e_{max})$, if the small effect in change of magnitude of the funicular force is ignored; notice that for the investigated case the funicular forces are constant.

Though the moments at any location along the arch can be found as just discussed, it is considered simpler to determine them in the known manner, by cutting the member at the point to be investigated and then establishing equilibrium of all the forces acting on the free body. For example, for the special case in Fig. 4.50a, the arch moment at a distance $x$ is equal to

$$M_x = A_v(x) - H(y)$$

$$= M_{beam} - M_{geometry} = M_{arch}$$

This expression shows that the moment of a simply supported beam, $M_{beam} = A_v(x)$, with the same span and the same loading as the arch, is reduced by the effect of geometry or thrust, $M_{geometry} = H(y)$. Since the bending moment diagram of the simply supported beam has the same form as the pressure line and the moment diagram of the thrust has the shape of the arch, one may conclude that the deviation of the arch geometry from the funicular form is defining and equivalent to the arch moment diagram.

The maximum shear and axial forces, for the case of investigation, act at the left support and can be determined by using the general equations of Fig. 4.6

$$V_A = A_v \cos \theta - A_h \sin \theta$$
$$-N_A = A_v \sin \theta + A_h \cos \theta$$

Again, notice that not only the moment of an equivalent simply supported beam but even more, the beam shear is reduced. On the other hand, an axial force is introduced due to arch action; now buckling criteria must be considered. Axial forces may be beneficial for materials weak in tension such as masonry and concrete, since they act as natural prestress agents trying to overcome the cracking (tension) of the section as caused by bending. Though the arch is primarily an axial system, assuming that its shape is funicular to the predominant loading in contrast to the beam which is primarily a bending system, the relative small arch moments still determine the size of the arch as shown later.

From a material point of view the arch should have a funicular shape, however, arches are rigid and cannot adjust their geometry under variable load action as flexible cables do in order to stay in tension. True funicular arches do not exist, they are only funicular for one loading condition. There are rare situations where the nonchanging dead weight comprises the largest portion of the total load such as for underground structures and possibly the medieval gothic vaults. For these cases the arch geometry can be selected so that the pressure line can be kept within the middle third of the member cross-section resulting in no tension along the entire arch length. In general, an optimal geometrical arch form with a minimum of moment action can be derived by superimposing the influence of the various loading conditions and by developing a critical loading envelope. Rather than going through this complex optimization process, often the pressure line due to the constant dead load is used as the arch form so that moments are only generated by live load action. For building types where the superimposed dead load acts along the arches in a uniform manner the funicular response is the catenary. Because of the complex mathematical nature of this form it is often approximated by a second degree parabola as discussed in the section on cables. This parabola represents the funicular response to uniform load action on the horizontal roof projection. Hence, dead load action may be approximated as a horizontal uniform load and considered similar to snow loading. The selection of the height-to-span ratio of the arch is an important consideration. As the height increases for a given span, the lateral thrust decreases but the arch length increases, in other words, with increase of height the support costs decrease while the arch costs increase. It is apparent that there is some optimal height-to-span ratio from a material efficiency point of view.

The arch is part of the frame family, but it distinguishes itself from the other members by providing a continuous one-member enclosure without having any kink points along its geometry. The forces flow smoothly along the arch and are not concentrated at points of sudden change of form assuming the external loads evenly distributed and not concentrated either.

In the following discussion, the arches are considered to carry uniformly distributed loads such as for cylindrical roofs where parallel arches provide the support of the roof skin. The same loading cases which have been investigated for the frame design will also be analyzed for the arches (Fig. 4.51). The force flow is determined for uniform gravity loading across the full arch span and one-half span, and it is found for uniform lateral loading against the vertical arch projection. These loading cases represent dead, live and wind loads; their proper combination will yield the critical loading conditions necessary for the preliminary design of the arch. Here, only parabolic and circular arches are investigated. Other arch geometries can be treated as parabolas for preliminary design purposes, if their height-to-span ratio is less than one-to-five. Other types of arches under different

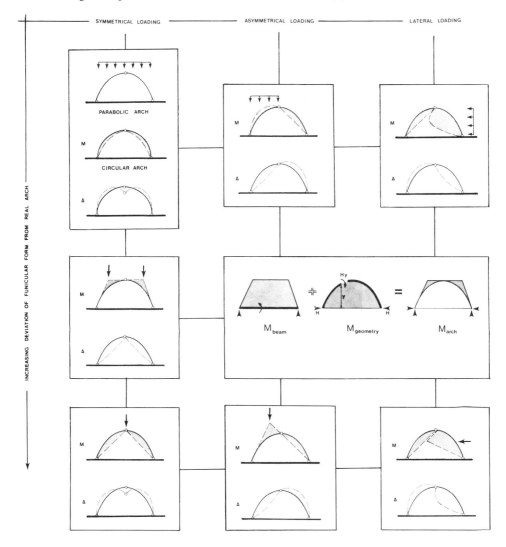

ARCH  RESPONSE  TO  LOADING

Fig. 4.51

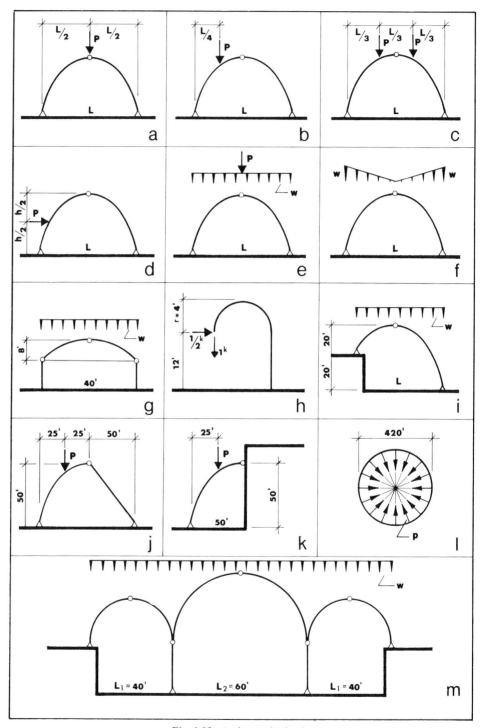

**Fig. 4.52** Arches under load.

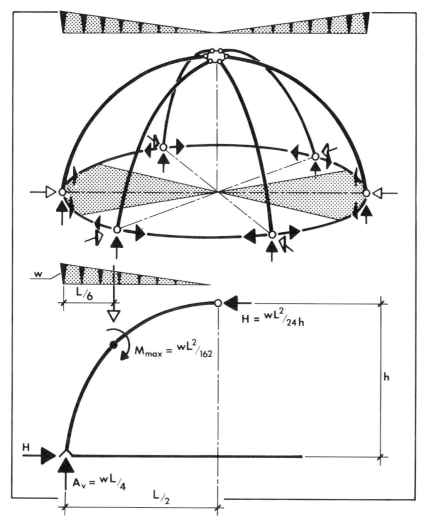

$$H = {}^{wL^2}\!/_{24h}$$

$$M_{max} = {}^{wL^2}\!/_{162}$$

$$A_v = {}^{wL}\!/_4$$

**Fig. 4.53**   Ribbed dome.

kind of loading are studied in Problem 4.24 (Fig. 4.52); the response of the arch to different loading cases is shown in Fig. 4.51.

Ribbed domes consist of radially arranged arches which are laterally supported by a
tension ring at the base and a compression ring at the crown. For preliminary design purposes, these arches can be treated as three-hinge ribs carrying a triangular gravity loading
as shown in Fig. 4.53. For further discussion the reader may refer to braced domes (Section 8.3) and to Problem 4.35.

*The Parabolic Arch (Fig. 4.54)*

Under uniform, vertical load action (Fig. 4.54a), the pressure line coincides with the center line of the arch or the parabolic arch is the funicular shape for the given loading.
There is no bending and no shear along the arch, the forces are resisted in purely axial

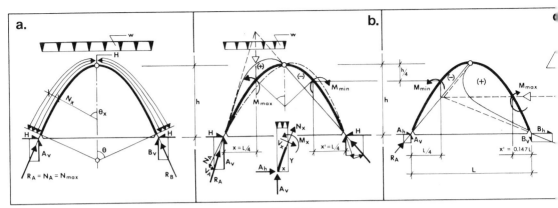

Fig. 4.54

manner; this momentless arch is often called a funicular arch. For a more detailed discussion on the funicular behavior, the reader may refer to the section dealing with the parabolic cable.

The reactions are obtained in the same manner as for the three-hinged portal and the A-frame and are equal to these cases

$$A_v = B_v = \frac{wL}{2}, \qquad A_h = B_h = H = \frac{wL^2}{8h}$$

For this special case, the resultant reaction and the axial force at the support are equal to each other because of the absence of shear

$$N_{max} = N_A = R_A = \sqrt{A_v^2 + A_h^2} = \frac{A_h}{\cos \theta} = \frac{A_v}{\sin \theta} \qquad (4.28)$$

where

$$\tan \theta = \frac{A_v}{A_h} = \frac{4h}{L}. \qquad (4.29)$$

Under uniform load action across one-half of the arch (Fig. 4.54b) the reactions have been shown to be equal to

$$A_v = \frac{3wL}{8} \qquad B_v = \frac{wL}{8} \qquad (4.30)$$

$$A_h = B_h = H = \frac{wL^2}{16h} \qquad (4.31)$$

The deviation of the arch from the funicular line indicates the magnitude of the moment flow. While the moment is positive along the loaded side where it causes tension along the inside face of the arch section, as the member deformation also shows, it is negative along the nonloaded portion. The position of the critical moments on each side must be found so that $M_{max}$ and $M_{min}$ can be determined. For cases where an arch must support single loads, the location of the critical moment may be at one of the concentrated loads and hence relatively easy to find. This is not the case for uniform loading, where first the point of zero shear has to be determined.

Using the general shear expression of Fig. 4.6 and setting it equal to zero first for the left and then for the right arch portion, yields the respective locations for the critical moments

$$V_x = (A_v - W_y) \cos \theta_x - A_h \sin \theta_x = 0$$

$$\tan \theta_x = \frac{A_v - W_y}{A_h} \tag{i}$$

Or, as based on geometrical considerations

$$\tan \theta_x = \frac{4h(L - 2x)}{L^2} \tag{3.33}$$

Equating the two expressions yields the location of the maximum moment

$$\frac{A_v - W_y}{A_h} = \frac{4h(L - 2x)}{L^2} \tag{j}$$

■ For the loaded arch portion from (j)

$$\frac{3wL/8 - wx}{wL^2/16h} = \frac{4h(L - 2x)}{L^2}$$

$$\frac{3L}{2} - 4x = L - 2x$$

$$x = \frac{L}{4}$$

as measured from the left support.

■ For the nonloaded arch portion from (j)

$$\frac{wL/8 - 0}{wL^2/16h} = \frac{4h(L - 2x')}{L^2}$$

$$x' = \frac{L}{4}$$

as measured from the right support.

The vertical distance to the maximum moment point according to the equation for the parabola, is

$$y = 4h\left[\frac{x}{L} - \left(\frac{x}{L}\right)^2\right] \tag{3.32}$$

$$= 4h\left[\frac{L}{4L} - \left(\frac{1}{4}\right)^2\right] = \frac{3h}{4} \tag{4.32}$$

The slope of the curvature at this location is

$$\tan \theta_x = \frac{4h(L - 2x)}{L^2} \tag{3.33}$$

$$\tan \theta_{L/4} = 4h\left[L - 2\left(\frac{L}{4}\right)\right] = \frac{2h}{L} \tag{4.33}$$

Hence, the location of the critical moments is at the same positions as measured from the respective supports.

The maximum moment at the loaded side is

$$M_{max} = \frac{3wL}{8} \frac{L}{4} - w\frac{L}{4} \frac{L}{8} - \frac{wL^2}{16h} \frac{3h}{4}$$

$$M_{max} = \frac{wL^2}{64} \tag{4.34}$$

The maximum moment at the non loaded side is

$$M_{min} = \frac{wL}{8} \frac{L}{4} - \frac{wL^2}{16h} \frac{3h}{4}$$

$$M_{min} = -\frac{wL^2}{64} \tag{4.35}$$

The axial force at $x = L/4$, the location of the maximum moment, according to Fig. 4.6 is

$$-N_x = (A_v - W_y) \sin \theta_x + A_h \cos \theta_x$$

$$-N_{L/4} = \left(\frac{3wL}{8} - \frac{wL}{4}\right) \sin \theta_{L/4} + \frac{wL^2}{16h} \cos \theta_{L/4}$$

$$-N_{L/4} = \frac{wL}{8} \sin \theta_{L/4} + \frac{wL^2}{16h} \cos \theta_{L/4} = R_B = -N_{3L/4}$$

Note the axial forces at the points of maximum moment are equal to each other in magnitude. It can be seen that the axial compressive force at the nonloaded side must be equal to the resultant reaction $R_B$ which acts along the funicular line and is moved parallel so that it is tangential to the arch at the maximum moment location where the shear is zero

$$N_{L/4} = N_{3L/4} = R_B = \sqrt{B_v^2 + B_h^2} \tag{4.36}$$

The maximum shear forces appear at either the crown hinge or at the support as was discussed for inclined beams. Vertical equilibrium of the forces along the free body of the nonloaded arch side clearly indicates that the shear at the crown must be equal in magnitude and opposite in direction to the vertical reaction $B_v$

$$V_c = -B_v = \frac{-wL}{8}$$

The shear at the left support is found by using the general shear equation

$$V_x = (A_v - W_y) \cos \theta_x - A_h \sin \theta_x$$

at $x = 0$, where $\tan \theta = 4h/L$

$$V_A = A_v \cos \theta - A_h \sin \theta$$

The parabolic arch responds to uniform lateral loading as indicated in Fig. 4.54c by the difference between the funicular line and the arch. The reactions were already determined for other frames and are equal to

$$A_v = -B_v = \frac{qh^2}{2L} \qquad A_h = \frac{qh}{4} \qquad B_h = \frac{3qh}{4}$$

The location of the maximum moment on the leeward side (nonloaded arch portion) is at $x = L/4$ and $y = 3h/4$ as has been derived. The magnitude of the moment is equal to

$$M_{min} = \frac{qh^2}{2L}\frac{L}{4} - \frac{qh}{4}\frac{3h}{4}$$

$$M_{min} = -\frac{qh^2}{16} \tag{4.37}$$

The location of the maximum moment on the windward side is assumed at midheight, $y = h/2$, similar to the asymmetrical gravity loading case just discussed, where the maximum moment appeared at midspan ($x = L/4$) of the curvilinear beam supported at the base and crown. The horizontal distance to the maximum moment point is obtained from the general equation of the parabola

$$y = 4h\left[\frac{x}{L} - \left(\frac{x}{L}\right)^2\right] \tag{3.32}$$

$$\frac{h}{2} = 4h\left[\frac{x'}{L} - \left(\frac{x'}{L}\right)^2\right]$$

$$(x')^2 - x'L + \frac{L^2}{8} = 0$$

$$x'_{1,2} = \frac{L}{2} \pm \sqrt{\left(\frac{L}{2}\right)^2 - \frac{L^2}{8}} = 0.5L \pm 0.353L$$

$$x' = 0.147L \tag{4.38}$$

The magnitude of the maximum moment is obtained by taking moments about this point

$$M_{max} = \frac{3qh}{4}\frac{h}{2} - \frac{qh}{2}\frac{h}{4} - \frac{qh^2}{2L}(0.147L)$$

$$M_{max} = \frac{qh^2}{5.66} \tag{4.39}$$

Note the moment is larger than for an inclined straight beam, where the maximum moment is

$$M_{max} = \frac{qh^2}{8} \tag{4.22}$$

Since the wind pressure distribution for an arch is considered less critical than for an A-frame, for preliminary design purposes, the curvilinear beam often is replaced by an imaginary straight beam and the lesser moment of $qh^2/8$ is used.

Just to get a rough first approximation for which height-to-span ratio, the lateral force action must be considered in the preliminary design of an arch under normal wind conditions, the critical moment due to live and dead loading is equated to the maximum moment due to wind and dead loading. It is assumed that the load combination of maximum wind and snow will probably not act at the same time, since the wind tends to blow the snow off the roof. Considering wind and snow loading of the same magnitude should be conservative for most situations.

$$\frac{wL^2}{64} = \frac{qh^2}{5.66} \quad \text{or} \quad \frac{h}{L} = 0.3$$

One may conclude that for preliminary design purposes as based on the assumptions above, wind may be neglected if $h/L \leqslant 0.3$, or as the arch height increases to more than about one-third of its span, wind should be looked into keeping in mind that the assumption of wind distribution may be rather conservative.

### The Circular Arch (Fig. 4.55)

Under uniform, vertical loading across the full width of the arch the parabolic pressure line does not coincide with the geometry of the circular arch. As indicated for the right arch portion in Fig. 4.55a, the funicular line is located inside, thus causing negative moments along the entire arch.

Before the location of the maximum moment is determined, some general geometrical relationships are derived from the free-body in Fig. 4.55a, where the origin of the coordinate system is located at the crown

$$\cos \theta_x = \frac{R - y}{R} = 1 - \frac{y}{R} \quad \text{or} \quad y = R(1 - \cos \theta_x) \tag{4.40}$$

$$\cos \theta = \frac{R - h}{R} = 1 - \frac{h}{R} \quad \text{or} \quad h = R(1 - \cos \theta) \tag{4.41}$$

$$\sin \theta_x = \frac{x}{R} \quad \text{or} \quad x = R \sin \theta_x \tag{4.42}$$

$$\sin \theta = \frac{L}{2R} \quad \text{or} \quad \frac{L}{2} = R \sin \theta \tag{4.43}$$

The reader may want to refer first to the section on the circular cable introducing the geometry of the circle.

The reactions for the full gravity loading case have already been determined for other frame cases, but are expressed here in terms of the angle $\theta$

$$A_v = B_v = \frac{wL}{2} = wR \sin \theta \tag{4.44}$$

$$A_h = B_h = \frac{wL^2}{8h} = \frac{w}{2} \frac{(R \sin \theta)^2}{R(1 - \cos \theta)}$$

but $\sin^2 \theta = 1 - \cos^2 \theta = (1 - \cos \theta)(1 + \cos \theta)$

$$A_h = B_h = H = \frac{wR}{2}(1 + \cos \theta) \tag{4.45}$$

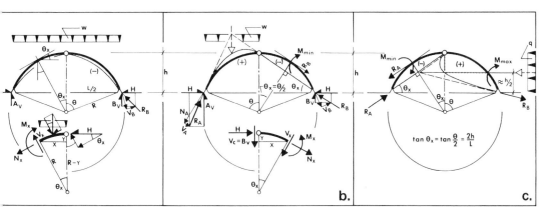

**Fig. 4.55**

The location of the maximum moment appears at the point where the shear is zero. Summing all the forces perpendicular to the curvature in the free body of Fig. 4.55a by setting them equal to zero, yields the general shear equation

$$V_x = wx \cos \theta_x - H \sin \theta_x \tag{4.46}$$

$$V_x = w(R \sin \theta_x) \cos \theta_x - \frac{wR}{2}(1 + \cos \theta) \sin \theta_x$$

$$V_x = -\frac{wR}{2} \sin \theta_x (1 + \cos \theta - 2 \cos \theta_x)$$

The location of the maximum moment is at $V_x = 0$

$$\cos \theta_x = 0.5(1 + \cos \theta) = 1 - \frac{h}{2R} \tag{4.47}$$

For a semicircle with $h = R$, $\cos \theta_x = 0.5$ or $x = R \sin \theta_x = 0.866R$ as measured from the midspan, which is equivalent to a distance from the support (Fig. 4.56)

$$\frac{L}{2} - x = R - R \sin \theta_x = R(1 - \sin \theta_x) = 0.134R = 0.067L \tag{4.48}$$

The general equation for the moment (Fig. 4.55a) is

$$M_x = H(y) - wx\frac{x}{2}$$

$$= \frac{wR}{2}(1 + \cos \theta)R(1 - \cos \theta_x) - \frac{w}{2}(R \sin \theta_x)^2$$

but $\sin^2 \theta_x = (1 - \cos \theta_x)(1 + \cos \theta_x)$

$$M_x = \frac{wR^2}{2}(1 - \cos \theta_x)(\cos \theta - \cos \theta_x) \tag{4.49}$$

The maximum moment at $\cos \theta_x = 1 - h/2R$, for $\cos \theta = 1 - h/R$, is

$$M_{\max} = -\frac{wh^2}{8} \tag{4.49a}$$

Note that the maximum moment is equal to the one for a simply supported beam of a span equal to the arch height, which in turn means that it must appear at midheight.

For a semicircle, the maximum moment at $y = h/2 = R/2$ and at a horizontal distance of $x = 0.067L$ from the support is

$$M_{\max} = -\frac{wR^2}{8} = -\frac{wL^2}{32} \tag{4.50}$$

The maximum moment for the semicircular arch is twice as large as for the parabolic arch by considering only live loading. Should the dead load be one-third of the total loading then the $M_{\max}$ for the semicircular arch is three times larger than for the parabolic arch! The maximum shear acts at the reactions since it is zero at the crown due to symmetry of loading

$$V_{\max} = V_A = A_v \cos \theta - A_h \sin \theta$$

The maximum axial forces also appear at the reactions and are equal to

$$N_{\max} = N_A = N_B = A_v \sin \theta + A_h \cos \theta$$

The axial force at the maximum moment location can be determined by using the general $N_x$-equation (Fig. 4.6).

The reactions for the uniform load action across one-half of the radial arch (Fig. 4.55b) have already been determined for the parabolic arch, only here they are expressed in terms of the angle $\theta$

$$A_v = \frac{3wL}{8} = \frac{3wR}{4} \sin \theta$$

$$B_v = \frac{wL}{8} = \frac{wR}{4} \sin \theta$$

$$A_h = B_h = H = \frac{wL^2}{16h} = \frac{wR}{4}(1 + \cos \theta)$$

The reactions for a semicircle with $R = L/2$, are

$$A_v = \frac{3wR}{4} \qquad B_v = \frac{wR}{4}$$

$$A_h = B_h = H = \frac{wR}{4}$$

The deviation of the pressure line from the arch geometry indicates the negative moment action along the nonloaded arch side and the positive moment action along the loaded portion. It can be shown that the absolute maximum moment appears on the nonloaded arch side. Further, for the loading condition where dead and one-half live load are superimposed, only the negative moments of the two cases act in the same direction. Therefore, here only the location of the maximum moment on the nonloaded arch portion is derived. The general shear equation is set up as based on the free body in Fig. 4.55b

$$-V_x = V_c \cos \theta_x - H \sin \theta_x$$

$$= \frac{wR}{4} \sin \theta \cos \theta_x - \frac{wR}{4}(1 + \cos \theta) \sin \theta_x$$

Setting this equation equal to zero yields the location where the moment is maximum

$$0 = \sin \theta \cos \theta_x - (1 + \cos \theta) \sin \theta_x$$

$$\tan \theta_x = \frac{\sin \theta}{1 + \cos \theta} = \frac{1 - \cos \theta}{\sin \theta} = \frac{2h}{L} \tag{4.51}$$

where

$$\sin^2 \theta = 1 - \cos^2 \theta = (1 - \cos \theta)(1 + \cos \theta).$$

This result could have been derived by inspection from Fig. 4.55b, as based on the symmetrical nature of the circular arch, where $\theta_x$ must be equal to $\theta/2$. For instance for a semicircle with $h = L/2 = R$

$$\tan \theta_x = 1 \quad \text{or} \quad \theta_x = \frac{\theta}{2} = \frac{90}{2} = 45°$$

The location of the critical moment for the semicircle as measured horizontally from the support (Fig. 4.56) is equal to

$$\frac{L}{2} - x = R - R \sin \theta_x = R(1 - \sin \theta_x)$$

$$= R(1 - \sin 45) = 0.293R = 0.147L \tag{4.52}$$

The location as measured vertically from the support is

$$h - y = R - R(1 - \cos \theta_x) = R \cos \theta_x$$

$$= R \cos 45 = 0.707R = 0.707h \tag{4.53}$$

Since the location of the maximum moment is known, its magnitude can easily be found. For the special case of a semicircle, the maximum moment is equal to

$$M_{min} = B_y(0.147L) - H(0.707h)$$

$$= \frac{wL}{8}(0.147L) - \frac{wL^2}{16h}(0.707h)$$

$$M_{min} = -\frac{wL^2}{38.63} = -\frac{wR^2}{9.66} \tag{4.54}$$

This moment is about 21% smaller than the one for full uniform loading ignoring the difference in magnitude between dead and live loads. However, as the circular arch becomes flatter the effect of the height $h$ as the moment determinant decreases and the effect of the span $L$ increases, the arch approaches the geometry of the parabola indicating that the design will be controlled by the asymmetrical, uniform loading case (Fig.

4.56). One may conclude that the steep circular arch, often roughly approximated as $h/L > 1/2.5$, is designed for full uniform gravity loading, while the shallow arch, say $h/L < 1/2.5$, is designed for dead and one-half live loading (see also Problem 3.39). Obviously, for the range in the neighborhood of $h/L = 1/2.5$ both loading cases must be checked.

It can be shown (Problem 3.33) that circular arches and other arch shapes with a height-to-span ratio of less than one-to-eight ($h/L \leq 1/8$) can be considered as parabolic arches. For preliminary approximation purposes already at a ratio of $h/L \leq 1/5$, the circular arch may be replaced by the parabolic arch, though the dead load moment should be considered which is not the case for the parabolic arch. This change in geometry simplifies the calculations very much, since the live load moment is a constant and equal to $-w_L L^2/64$ while the dead load moment is conservatively assumed as $-w_D h^2/8$, ignoring safely the difference in location between the two moments.

The axial force at the maximum moment location for the asymmetrical loading case (Fig. 4.55b) is equal to the resultant reaction $R_B$

$$N_{\text{at } M_{\min}} = R_B = \sqrt{B_v^2 + H^2} \tag{4.55}$$

The deviation of the pressure line from the arch geometry indicates the intensity of moment flow as caused by the uniform lateral loading case (Fig. 4.55c). The location of $M_{\max}$ on the windward side may be approximated to be at midheight or the moment of an inclined straight beam may be used as a first approximation. No derivation is given here because the wind does not control under normal conditions as was discussed before; further, the assumed wind pressure distribution is actually quite different having extensive suction in the upper arch portion (Fig. 1.4). The location of $M_{\min}$ on the leeward

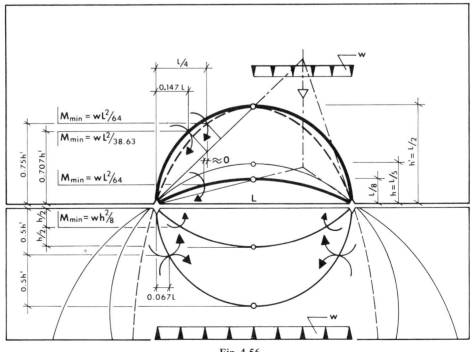

Fig. 4.56

side is defined by inspection at $\theta_x = \theta/2$ as was discussed already. The reactions for the wind laoding case are the same as for the parabolic arch.

## *Indeterminate Arches*

When the hinge at the crown of the three-hinged arch is eliminated, a once indeterminate, two-hinged arch, redundant to the first degree, is generated. When, in addition, the support hinges are made rigid, a three times indeterminate, hingeless or fixed arch is created. Many steel and some timber and prefab concrete arches are two-hinged, while most cast-in-place concrete arches are hingeless because of the process of continuous casting. As the degree of indeterminancy increases, the structure becomes increasingly more sensitive to boundary movements such as foundation settling and tie rod spreading, as well as to volume changes due to variations in temperature, creep, and shrinkage. While the determinate arch can respond to these types of actions by moving freely (i.e., ideal situations are assumed as defined in statics) so that it is not stressed, the two-hinged arch must resist some of these forces though it is much less vulnerable than the fixed arch.

The exact analysis of indeterminate arches cannot be treated here, however, some rough first approximations are given in Fig. 4.57 for parabolic and shallow circular arches by neglecting the effect of critical placement of live loading, elastic deformations, and other movement considerations. It is surprising that the continuity at the crown has hardly any effect on the lateral thrust of the two-hinged arch. For the asymmetrical loading case the point of contraflexure appears approximately at the crown so that the moment at this location is zero indicating that the thrust force has hardly changed. One may conclude, for preliminary design purposes, the two-hinged parabolic and flat circular

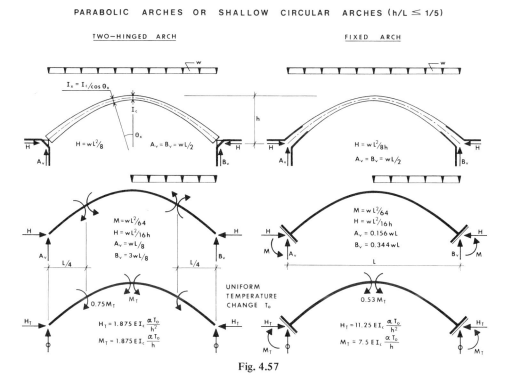

Fig. 4.57

arches can be treated as three-hinged ones. Even for the fixed arch the lateral thrust is not much larger and may be considered as equal to the three-hinged arch.


## Preliminary Design of Arches

**Example 4.5** A cylindrical roof is supported by parallel, three-hinged laminated wood arches of constant cross-section. The arches are 12 ft high, span 60 ft, and are spaced 16 ft apart. They are laterally braced by purlins spaced at 8-ft intervals measured along the arch. They must support a dead weight of 10 psf which includes the arch weight, a snow load of 30 psf, and a wind load of 20 psf assumed to act on the vertical roof projection.

For preliminary estimation purposes, the approximate size of a typical interior arch is determined. Douglas Fir under dry conditions is being used with following allowable properties: $F_b$ = 2400 psi, $F_c$ = 1500 psi, $F_v$ = 165 psi, $E$ = 1,800,000 psi.

Following uniform loads the arch must support:

$$w_D = 10(16) = 160 \text{ lb/ft} = 0.16 \text{ k/ft}$$

$$w_L = 30(16) = 480 \text{ lb/ft} = 0.48 \text{ k/ft}$$

$$w_W = 20(16) = 320 \text{ lb/ft} = 0.32 \text{ k/ft}$$

First, a parabolic arch will be investigated and then a circular one; both solutions are compared and evaluated.


### Parabolic Arch

Some general geometrical relationships are:

Slope at reactions:     $\tan \theta_A = \dfrac{4h}{L} = \dfrac{4(12)}{60} = 0.8$

$\sin \theta_A = 0.625 \qquad \cos \theta_A = 0.781$

Slope at one-quarter span:     $\tan \theta_{L/4} = \dfrac{2h}{L} = \dfrac{2(12)}{60} = 0.4$  (4.33)

$\sin \theta_{L/4} = 0.371 \qquad \cos \theta_{L/4} = 0.929$

Arch length:     $l = L \left[ 1 + \dfrac{8}{3} \left( \dfrac{h}{L} \right)^2 \right]$

$= 60 \left[ 1 + \dfrac{8}{3} \left( \dfrac{12}{60} \right)^2 \right] = 66.40 \text{ ft}$

The dead load is acting along the arch and not normal to the member axis as for horizontal beams. It is convenient to project this load onto the horizontal roof plane. As has been shown for the inclined beam, the transformed load is equal to $w = w'/\cos \theta_x$. Since $\cos \theta_x$ is a variable and dependent on the arch geometry, the dead load on the horizontal roof projection must be curvilinear. To simplify the calculations for the preliminary design, first the total dead weight is found by multiplying the load per foot by the arch length $l$ and then resolving the total load again into a uniform load on the horizontal roof projection by dividing it through the span $L$

$$w_D = w'_D \frac{l}{L} \tag{4.56}$$

$$= 0.16 \frac{66.40}{60} = 0.18 \text{ k/ft}$$

First, the arch is investigated under full gravity loading of $w = 0.18 + 0.48 = 0.66$ k/ft. The reactions for this loading case are equal to

$$A_v = B_v = \frac{wL}{2} = w \frac{60}{2} = 30w = 30(0.66) = 19.80 \text{ k}$$

$$A_h = B_h = H = \frac{wL^2}{8h} = \frac{w(60)^2}{8(12)} = 37.5w$$

$$= 37.5(0.66) = 24.75 \text{ k}$$

The maximum axial force is located at the reactions and, in this case, is equal to the resultant reaction

$$N_{max} = N_A = R_A = \sqrt{(30w)^2 + (37.5w)^2} = 48.02w$$

$$= 48.02(0.66) = 31.70 \text{ k}$$

or

$$N_{max} = \frac{A_h}{\cos \theta_A} = \frac{24.75}{0.781} = 31.69 \text{ k}$$

The axial force at quarter span as function of $w$, using the general $N_x$ equation, is equal to

$$-N_x = (A_v - W_y) \sin \theta_x + (A_h + W_x) \cos \theta_x$$
$$-N_{L/4} = (30w - 15w)0.371 + (37.5w)0.929 = 40.40w$$

Note this loading case provides the largest thrust and thus controls the preliminary design of the tie rod and the arch bearing at the reactions.

The arch is then investigated for one-half live loading. The reactions for this case were found to be

$$A_v = \frac{3wL}{8} = \frac{3(0.48)60}{8} \qquad = 10.80 \text{ k}$$

$$B_v = \frac{wL}{,8} = \frac{0.48(60)}{8} \qquad = 3.60 \text{ k}$$

$$A_h = B_h = H = \frac{wL^2}{16h} = \frac{0.48(60)^2}{16(12)} = 9.00 \text{ k}$$

The axial force at the point of maximum moment for each arch side, as was discussed before, is

$$N_{L/4} = N_{3L/4} = R_B = \sqrt{3.6^2 + 9^2} = 9.69 \text{ k}$$

Combining the axial force for the uniform dead load case and the one-half live loading case gives

$$N_{L/4} = N_{3L/4} = 9.69 + 40.40w = 9.69 + 40.40(0.18) = 16.96 \text{ k}$$

The maximum moment is only caused by the asymmetrical live load and is equal to

$$M_{max} = \frac{wL^2}{64} \tag{4.34}$$

$$= \frac{0.48(60)^2}{64} = 27.00 \text{ ft-k}$$

The maximum moment on the nonloaded side has the same magnitude but is opposite in direction.

The maximum shear appears at the crown due to one-half live loading

$$V_{max} = V_c = B_v = 3.60 \text{ k}$$

The maximum moment as caused by wind at midheight is equal to

$$M_{max} = \frac{qh^2}{5.66} \tag{4.39}$$

$$= \frac{0.32(12)^2}{5.66} = 8.14 \text{ ft-k}$$

The wind moment is clearly much smaller than the live load moment. Remember, it is improbable that wind and full live load appear at the same time, because the wind tends to blow the snow off the curvilinear roof; snow on one-half span produces the largest bending stresses on the shallow arch.

The moment is the primary determinant of the arch size for typical roof enclosures, so that the section can be selected as based on bending only by adding about 20% to the section modulus because the axial action is neglected. The percentage added is higher than for frames because the bending intensity is smaller in comparison to the frames

$$f = \frac{M}{S} \leqslant F_b \text{ or } S = 1.2 \frac{27(12)}{2.4} = 162 \text{ in.}^3$$

From Table A.7 for section properties for structural glued laminated timber a $5\frac{1}{8} \times 14\frac{1}{4}$ in. with nine $1\frac{1}{2}$ in. laminations is selected. This section provides the least area and has a depth-to-width ratio of less than $5/1$, $A = 73.00 \text{ in.}^2$, $S_x = 173.40 \text{ in.}^3$.

In this approximate approach the reduction of bending stresses due to arch curvature and member size is ignored as is the increase of allowable stresses due to load duration.

To check the selected section for beam-column action, the allowable axial stresses have to be determined; they may have to be reduced for buckling about either the strong or weak axis. While the effective length perpendicular to the bending plane is known and equal to the spacing of the purlins (i.e., points of lateral bracing), the effective length of the arch is unknown and quite difficult to determine. Buckling of arches depends on the type of curvature (flatness of curves besides geometry), material, type and location of loading, boundary conditions, and other criteria. An equivalent effective length may be roughly approximated by the straight-line distance between the hinges at the base and crown for three-hinged arches, or between hinge and inflection point or between inflection points for indeterminate arches.

Here, only the slenderness ratio about the weak member axis is considered; in a more precise analysis the critical buckling load for the arch should be determined and compared with the actual loading

$$\left(\frac{l}{d}\right)_y = \frac{8(12)}{5.125} = 18.73 \leqslant 50$$

The allowable axial stress as function of member slenderness is

$$F'_c = \frac{0.3E}{(l/d)^2} = \frac{0.3(1800000)}{(18.73)^2} = 1539.28 \text{ psi} \geqslant F_c = 1500 \text{ psi}$$

Beam column interaction yields

$$\frac{f_a}{F_a} + \frac{f_b}{F_b} = \frac{P/A}{F_c} + \frac{M/S}{F_b} = \frac{16.96/73.0}{1.50} + \frac{27(12)/173.4}{2.40}$$

$$= 0.155 + 0.779 = 0.933 < 1$$

The selected preliminary section is satisfactory. The axial stresses even for this relatively flat arch are low, as was assumed. For steeper arches their effect will further decrease, while for flatter arches the impact of the axial stresses will increase under similar loading conditions.

The shear stresses are

$$f_v = \frac{3V}{2A} = \frac{3(3600)}{2(73)} = 73.97 \text{ psi} \ll F_v = 165 \text{ psi}$$

Obviously, the shear stresses and also the maximum axial stresses at the reaction under full loading are negligible for the preliminary design because the cross-section is assumed to be constant along the curvature.

### Circular Arch

The needed geometrical relationships are:

Radius of curvature:    $R^2 = \left(\frac{L}{2}\right)^2 + (R - h)^2$

$$= 30^2 + (R - 12)^2 = 30^2 + R^2 + 12^2 - 24R$$

$$R = \frac{(L/2)^2 + h^2}{2h} = \frac{30^2 + 12^2}{2(12)} = 43.5 \text{ ft}$$

Curvature at the reactions:    $\sin \theta = \dfrac{L}{2R} = \dfrac{30}{43.5} = 0.690$                                    (4.43)

$$\cos \theta = 0.724, \qquad \theta = 43.60°$$

Arch length:    $\dfrac{1}{2}\theta = \dfrac{2\pi R}{360}$

$$l = \frac{\theta}{90} \pi R = \frac{43.60}{90} \pi (43.5) = 66.20 \text{ ft}$$

Note there is hardly any difference to the length of the parabolic arch, therefore the same dead load distribution will be assumed.

The radial arch because of its shallow character (i.e., $h/L \leqslant 1/5$) is first investigated under asymmetrical live loading (Fig. 4.55b). The reactions for this loading case are the same as for the parabolic arch

$$A_v = 10.80 \text{ k} \qquad B_v = 3.60 \text{ k}$$

$$R_b = 9.69 \text{ k} \qquad A_h = B_h = H = 9.00 \text{ k}$$

It was shown that the location of the maximum moment on the nonloaded side as measured from the support by $x$ and $y$ is at

$$\theta_x = \frac{\theta}{2} = \frac{43.60}{2} = 21.80° \qquad \sin \theta_x = 0.371 \qquad \cos \theta_x = 0.929$$

$$x = \frac{L}{2} - R \sin \theta_x = 30 - 43.5(0.371) = 13.86 \text{ ft}$$

$$y = h - R(1 - \cos \theta_x) = 12 - 43.5(1 - 0.929) = 8.91 \text{ ft}$$

The maximum moment at this location is

$$M_{min} = 3.6(13.86) - 9(8.91) = -30.29 \text{ ft-k}$$

The axial force at this maximum moment location is equal to the resultant reaction $R_B$

$$N \,(\text{at } M_{min}) = R_B = 9.69 \text{ k}$$

The maximum shear appears at the crown hinge and is equal to $B_v$

$$V_c = V_{max} = B_v = 3.6 \text{ k}$$

Next, the circular arch is investigated under full uniform loading. The reactions are analogous to the ones for the parabolic arch

$$A_v = B_v = 30w \qquad A_h = B_h = H = 37.5w$$

For dead load only, the reactions are

$$A_v = B_v = 30(0.18) \qquad = 5.40 \text{ k}$$

$$A_h = B_h = H = 37.5(0.18) = 6.75 \text{ k}$$

The reactions for dead and live loading are

$$A_v = B_v = 30(0.66) \qquad = 19.80 \text{ k}$$

$$A_h = B_h = H = 37.5(0.66) = 24.75 \text{ k}$$

The maximum compressive force is located at the supports and is equal to

$$N_{max} = N_A = A_v \sin \theta + A_h \cos \theta = 19.8(0.69) + 24.75(0.724)$$

$$= 31.58 \text{ k}$$

Note the axial force is slightly less than the resultant force $R_A = 31.70$ k because of the presence of the small shear force $V_A$.

The maximum moment for this full loading case at midheight is

$$M_{max} = -\frac{wh^2}{8} \tag{4.49}$$

$$= \frac{-0.66(12)^2}{8} = -11.88 \text{ ft-k}$$

The moment is much smaller than the live load moment of −30.29 ft-k even when the effect of dead weight is not added. This result is not surprising, since this arch is rather flat and the full gravity loading case does not control its design. It is quite apparent that dead load together with one-half live loading determines the arch size ignoring the wind loading case.

The dead load moment at the location of $M_{min}$, neglecting conservatively that by superimposing the two loading cases a new condition is generated that moves the location of the moment, is

$$M_{DL} = 5.4(13.86) - 0.18(13.86)13.86/2 - 6.75(8.91) = -2.59 \text{ ft-k}$$

The axial force due to the weight at the same location (Fig. 4.5), is

$$-N_x = (B_v - W_y) \sin \theta_x + (B_h) \cos \theta_x$$

$$= [5.4 - 0.18(13.86)]0.371 + 6.75(0.929) = 7.35 \text{ k}$$

The moments and axial forces due to dead and live loading are respectively,

$$M_{min} = -30.29 - 2.59 = -32.88 \text{ ft-k}$$

$$N \text{ (at } M_{min}) = 9.69 + 7.35 = 17.04 \text{ k}$$

Note there is not much difference between the results for the parabolic and circular arches. Since the height-to-span ratio of the circular arch is $h/L = 1/5$, the circular arch can be treated for live loading as a parabolic arch and because of the relative small magnitude of the dead load moment, the maximum moment due to uniform loading on the circular arch may be conservatively used

$$M_{min} = w_D \frac{h^2}{8} + w_L \frac{L^2}{64}$$

$$= \frac{-0.18(12)^2}{8} + \frac{-0.48(60)^2}{64} = -30.24 \text{ ft-k}$$

The moment is about 8% smaller as compared to the more precise solution, but the result should be still reasonable for preliminary approximation purposes.

The axial forces at the point of maximum moment can be approximated by using the resultant reaction $R_B$ at the side which is not loaded by live loading

$$B_v = w_D \frac{L}{2} + w_L \frac{L}{8} = \frac{0.18(60)}{2} + \frac{0.48(60)}{8} = 9.00 \text{ k}$$

$$B_h = w_D \frac{L^2}{8h} + w_L \frac{L^2}{16h}$$

$$= \frac{0.18(60)^2}{8(12)} + \frac{0.48(60)^2}{16(12)} = 15.75 \text{ k}$$

$$N \text{ (at } M_{min}) = R_B = \sqrt{9.00^2 + 15.75^2} = 18.14 \text{ k}$$

Remember, as the arch gets flatter and approaches h/L = 1/8, for all practical purposes, the circular arch can be considered a parabola, that is, the dead load moment becomes insignificant and the live load moment for both arch geometries is about the same.

## Problems

**4.24** Determine $M_{max}$, $V_{max}$, $N_{max}$, and $N$ at the location of $M_{max}$ for the arches in Fig. 4.52. All arches are parabolic with the exception of cases (g), (h), (l), and (m) which are circular. Show pressure lines, moment diagrams, and deformed shapes of arches. For the cases where dimensions and loads are not given assume following values: $P = 10$ k, $w = 1$ k/ft, $L = 100$ ft, $h = 20$ ft.

**4.25** Derive the maximum and minimum moments for case (g) (Problem 4.24) by considering the arch loaded uniformly only on one side.

**4.26** Consider the circular arch of case (g) (Problem 4.24) to be loaded by a uniform wind pressure acting on the vertical roof projection. Find the maximum moment on the windward side by assuming its location at midheight. Determine also the critical moment on the leeward side as based on the exact location.

**4.27** Assume a circular arch to carry the loading of case (f) (Problem 4.24). Derive the location of the maximum moment.

**4.28** Consider the arch of Problem 4.27 to be of semicircular shape. Show that the maximum moment is approximately equal to $-wL^2/138$.

**4.29** Show that the maximum moment for case (f) (Problem 4.24) is equal to $wL^2/162$.

**4.30** Design the three-hinged circular laminated wood arch of constant cross-section which was analyzed in Problems 4.24(g), 4.25, and 4.26. The arches are spaced 16 ft apart. The arch thrust is carried by steel tie rods (A36 steel). Consider the roof loads to be supported by closely spaced roof joists causing a uniform load. Assume following loading: 30 psf for snow, 20 psf for wind on the vertical roof projection, and the dead load of

| | |
|---|---|
| estimated weight of arch | 3.0 psf |
| roof joists | 2.0 psf |
| 1-in. sheathing | 2.5 psf |
| acoustical ceiling | 2.5 psf |
| three-ply built-up roofing | 4.0 psf |
| | 14.0 psf |

Use laminated Southern Pine with following allowable stresses for dry conditions: $F_b = 2600$ psi, $F_c = 2100$ psi, $F_v = 200$ psi, $E = 1,800,000$ psi.

**4.31** Select a steel wideflange section ($A36$) for the arch in Problem 4.30, by assuming the same loading conditions and the arches to be laterally supported by purlins spaced 4 ft apart.

**4.32** Three-hinged parabolic steel arches ($A36$), arranged in parallel are used as the primary structural elements for a factory building, similar in appearance to case (g) in Fig. 4.52. The arches are 40 ft high, span 200 ft, and are 40 ft apart. They are laterally braced by trusses spaced at 10 ft. Assume the buckling about the weak axis to control the allowable axial stresses. Use following loading:

| | |
|---|---|
| dead load: beams | 7 psf |
| cladding | 3 psf |
| | 10 psf |
| snow load on horizontal roof projection | 15 psf |
| wind load on vertical roof projection | 15 psf |

Determine the preliminary arch size by considering it to be of constant cross-section.

**4.33** Show that parallel, shallow, circular arches with a height-to-span ratio of less than one-to-eight ($h/L \leqslant 1/8$) can be considered as parabolic arches.

**4.34** Show that the maximum moment for a parabolic arch loaded at the crown by a single vertical load [Problem 4.24 (a)] is $M_{max} = PL/16$

**4.35** A ribbed parabolic dome has a diameter of 240 ft and is 40 ft high. It consists of 36 equally spaced radial steel ribs ($A36$) meeting at the compression ring at the crown which has a small torsional rigidity and thus can be considered equivalent to a spherical hinge. The ribs are tied together by 19 horizontal, equally spaced ring purlins. The spatial arch interaction as caused by ring purlins and roof skin is ignored; they are assumed to be individual members, acting as independent, three-hinged arches. Use as dead load 18 psf which is to change linearly from zero at the crown to a maximum at the base. The rather small constant dead load component due to the rib weight does not cause any moment and is conservatively included in the triangular load distribution. The live load (snow) is considered as 20 psf to act on the horizontal roof projection. Determine the approximate arch size.

**4.36** The dome in Problem 4.35 must carry at the apex an additional concentrated load of 20 k due to lighting and ventilating equipment. Determine the approximate member size by superimposing conservatively the maximum moments and axial forces of the two loading cases though they are not acting at the same location.

**4.37** Assume the ribbed dome of Problem 4.35 to be of spherical shape. Determine the critical force conditions for the arch design and compare the results with the ones for the parabolic dome.

**4.38** Determine the preliminary size of the circular concrete compression ring for the suspended cable roof of Problem 3.23. Approximate the individual radial cable force action by changing them to a uniform radial pressure $p$. Assume the vertical cable force component carried directly by the facade walls. Use 3000 psi concrete.

**3.39** Show that the critical moment caused by full uniform loading $w$ on a circular arch with a height-to-span ratio of $1/2.5$ is roughly equal to the critical moment caused by dead load and one-half live loading by assuming the dead load as one-third of the total load $w$.

## 4.5  THE FRAME TRUSS

### Review of Truss Characteristics

Trusses are rigid, planar structures composed of straight bars which are connected to one another to primarily transmit external loads in axial force action. The interpretation of the behavior of trusses, as expressed in their analysis, is based on following simplified assumptions.

- Hinged connections with frictionless pins: the partial rotational capacity of the connections, and the fact that the bars are bolted or welded to thin gusset plates of steel trusses is ignored.
- Weightless members: the weight of the members causes bending, which is small in comparison to the axial load therefore it can be neglected.
- Load application at joints: loads, such as purlins, are often applied to the members and thus cause bending. The bending stresses for typical conditions are in the range of 10–20% of the axial stresses.
- Members are assumed straight and of constant cross-section, thus their centroidal axes coincide with the centroid of the joint.
- Truss members are slender with a negligible bending capacity.
- Small deflection theory: the truss displacement is small and hardly influences the magnitude of the force flow.

In the ideal truss just described, members only resist forces in an axial fashion and not in bending. The small flexural stresses in the real truss are called secondary stresses.

A truss is generated by first connecting three members to form a base triangle. To this triangle other triangles are added that is two bars for each joint. Hence, the total number of truss members, $m$ is equal to the initial three of the base triangle with three joints, $j$ plus two members for each of the remaining $(j - 3)$ joints

$$m = 3 + 2(j - 3) = 2j - 3 \qquad \text{(k)}$$

The number of bars given in the equation must be provided for the truss to be internally stable and determinate. Should there not be enough bars, then the truss is unstable, but if there are more bars than needed, the truss analysis is indeterminate. Though this condition of the number of bars is necessary, it is not sufficient since the members must be properly arranged and, in most cases, form triangles. To prevent the collapse of the structure either members and sometimes reactions may be added or frame action (i.e., rigid joints) must be introduced.

For a planar structure to be externally stable and determinate, three reaction forces $(r = 3)$, which can be visualized as three equivalent axial members that should neither be parallel nor concurrent, must be provided. Should $r < 3$ the structure is externally unstable; if $r > 3$, the structure is externally indeterminate.

The term 3 in Eq (k) can be replaced by $r$ so that the equation takes into account not just internal, but external conditions as well

$$m + r = 2j \quad \text{determinate}$$

$$m + r < 2j \quad \text{unstable} \qquad (4.57)$$

$$m + r > 2j \quad \text{indeterminate}$$

Checking the conditions for the Pratt truss in Fig. 4.60,

$$41 + 3 = 2(22)$$

$$44 = 44$$

Since the number of bars and reactions are equal to twice the number of joints and since the members as well as reactions are properly arranged, the truss is stable and statically determinate internally and externally. Note that a truss, which is internally unstable ($m < 2j - 3$) but externally redundant ($r > 3$) may still be stable as a total system ($m + r = 2j$), since the additional reactive conditions may, but not necessarily do, prevent the collapse of the structure. Trusses, in general, are made of steel or timber, and sometimes of concrete. Members of steel trusses are standard rolled sections such as angles, channels, tees, wide flange sections and tubes.

In Fig. 4.58, some of the important truss characteristics are identified. They are organized according to geometry, application, and statical considerations. There is no limit to the geometrical layout of trusses; some common, simple trusses such as the familiar Pratt, Warren, and Howe trusses are shown. The application of the truss ranges from the small scale of a joist to the large scale of a deep truss supporting a stadium roof. Trusses may replace any solid elements such as beams, columns, arches, or frames. From a shape point of view, they may be classified as truss-cantilevers, truss-beams of various profiles (flat, tapered, pitched, curved, etc.), truss-arches, and truss frames forming single or multibay structures.

Trusses may be organized according to the arrangement of members and according to behavioral considerations:

- *Simple trusses:* they are formed by the addition of triangular member units and can be further subdivided as shown in Fig. 4.58.
- *Compound trusses:* they are formed by the addition of simple trusses. Again, different variations are identified according to the way in which the trusses are connected. Keep in mind that these compound trusses are not necessarily composed of only triangles, indicating that stable trusses can be generated by figures other than triangles.
- *Complex trusses:* they are neither simple nor compound. Special methods of analysis must be applied to these determinate trusses, since more than three members are attached to each joint, and sections cut through at least four members, resulting in more unknowns than available equations at the location to be investigated.

Trusses as structural elements have existed for a long time. According to Vitruvius in the first century B.C., the Romans already used inclined rafters for some of their roofs, tying them together at their base to eliminate the lateral thrust upon the wall supports. In

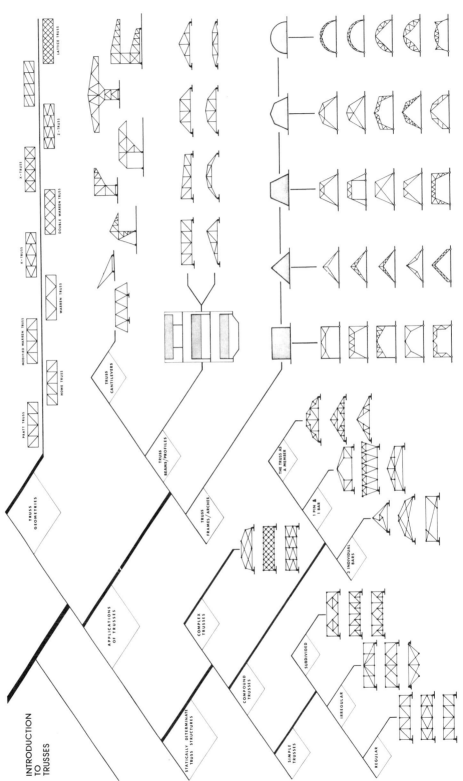

Fig. 4.58  Introduction to trusses.

the Middle Ages truss-like structures, sometimes lacking triangles, were used for steeply pitched roofs. While Leonardo da Vinci seems to be the first to actually propose a truly triangulated truss, Andrea Palladio about 100 years later is usually credited as the inventor of trusses. He described triangulated timber trusses for bridges in *The Four Books of Architecture* (1570).

The real evolution of trusses began in the first half of the nineteenth century, initiated primarily by the railway construction in the United States and Russia. Some of the pioneering design engineers were W. Howe (1840), T. Pratt (1844), A. Fink, and S. Whipple in North America as well as J. Warren in England, just to name few. The development of the truss theory follows closely and is credited to S. Whipple (1847) and D. Jourawski (1850) for the "method of joints," A. Ritter (1862) for the "method of sections," K. Culmann (1864), C. Maxwell (1864), L. Cremona (1872), and R. Bow (1873) for the graphical solution of trusses, and A Möbius (1837) and O. Mohr (1874) for the determination of the statical determinacy of trusses.

In the second half of the nineteenth century engineers employed iron and steel trussbeams and truss arches extensively. They were not only used on bridges but for other long-span structures such as market halls, exhibition buildings, and railway stations. The imaginative application of the truss principle probably reached its high point with Gustave Eiffel's Tower for the Paris Exhibition in 1889.

Some examples of innovative usage of trusses for buildings, which have recently been constructed, are shown in Fig. 4.59. The truss forms range from simple beams with flat or pitched profiles to complex framing systems (b), (c), and (j). They range from the relative small scale building (j) to the large scale stadium with a span of 440 ft (k); they range from standard geometries to individual designs (h). Though the truss for most of the buildings shown is an intricate part of the architectural design, in general, the aesthetical potential of trusses has rarely been challenged. The truss has been treated from a purely technological point of view, as a means of bridging space as is typical of floor joists and roof trusses for housing, industrial buildings, and gymnasiums.

The selection of truss geometry is not a simple undertaking, even from a purely functional point of view. It is closely related to economical considerations, where least weight does not necessarily yield the optimum solution, since with increase of span, fabrication, transportation and erection become controlling cost determinants. From the point of view of optimum weight, the shape of the truss should be funicular with respect to the critical external loading case so that the chords carry all the loads and the web members are zero and thus are primarily used for lateral bracing of the compression chord; this condition, is obviously only true for one loading case. The shape of the roof, in turn, influences the external load action; a lower pitch results in a larger snow load but less wind pressure as compared to a steep roof.

The average height of steel and timber trusses can be estimated from the typical depth-to-span ratios for trusses, which are in the range of about 1/5 to 1/12. As an approximation an average truss depth of $L/10$ is often used, resulting in a ratio of $L/5$ for the maximum height of a symmetrical, triangular truss. The depth for closely spaced, prefabricated open-web joists spanning up to 200 ft and spaced not further than 10 ft apart, is about $L/20$.

The arrangement of the members determines which ones are in tension and compression. For instance, for the simply supported truss beams (Fig. 4.58) under uniform gravity loading along the top chord, the diagonals of the Pratt truss are in tension and the verticals in compression, while for the Howe truss this situation is reversed and for the

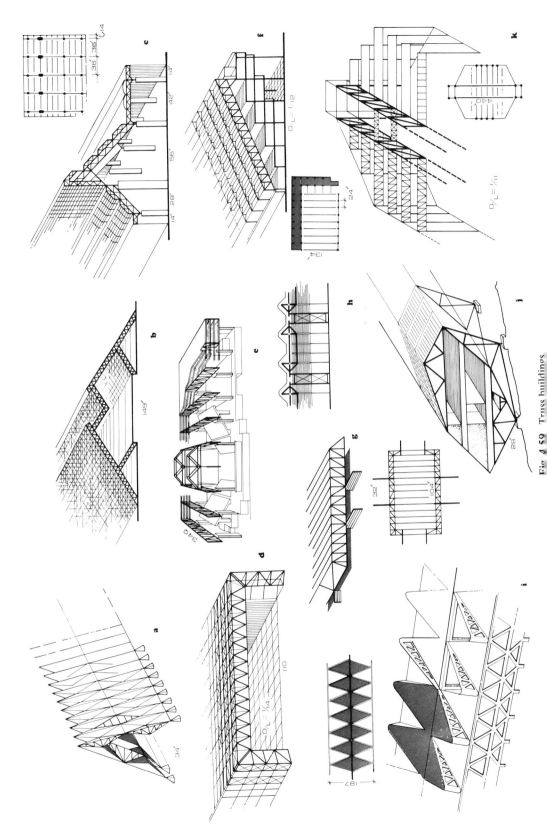

Fig. 4.59  Truss buildings

Warren truss the diagonals are alternately in tension and compression with the alternate verticals being omitted as they are zero members.

The proximity of the web members depends on the unsupported length of the compression bars, which should not be too slender because of buckling criteria. One may conclude that the shorter truss bars should be in compression, while the longer ones should be in tension. The bending stresses in the compression chord should be kept small in comparison to the axial stresses by reducing the member length or they should be eliminated by placing the purlins directly at the panel points. A deeper truss section will result in smaller chord forces and smaller bays will yield steeper diagonals carrying less force. Their slope is kept in the range of 40°–50° for flat trusses and 30°–60° for pitched trusses.

Should the compression chord not be laterally braced by the roof structure, then the chord must be laterally supported by transverse roof bracing, or space trusses (Fig. 5.16) may be used.

The spacing of the trusses depends on the span capacity of the roof skin and determines the magnitude of the loads the trusses must support. Under normal conditions lightweight materials should be taken to reduce the costs.

When continuous chord members are used, their sizes can easily be determined as based on the critical load action, as is shown in the following example. Should cables be used for tension members, care must be taken that under no loading condition will the members be in compression since the structure may collapse.

The intention is not to introduce the analysis of trusses, which has already been covered in a statics course. It has been shown that simple trusses can generally be solved by the methods of joints and/or sections, while graphical methods may be quicker for more complicated structural shapes such as arched trusses. The reader interested in a review of truss analysis may refer to the truss-enclosure systems (Fig. 4.62) proposed as an exercise. Here, the primary interest is in the quick sizing of critical members for estimation or preliminary design purposes.

### Preliminary Design of a Trussed Frame

**Example: 4.6** A gymnasium roof is supported by steel trusses spanning 80 ft and are arranged parallel (Fig. 4.60a). The trusses must carry a snow load load of 30 psf; the dead load of 20 psf includes the truss and bracing weight, which can be approximated roughly as 10% of the load it is supporting and is considered as 4 psf for this case. The wind pressure on the vertical surfaces is 20 psf. The preliminary, critical truss member sizes and column sections will be estimated in this example using $A36$ steel. For typical conditions, the spacing of the trusses is often considered roughly between a quarter to a fifth of the truss span, but not more than 20 ft. In this case, the spacing selected is $L/4 = 80/4 = 20$ ft. The depth of the trusses is estimated as $L/10 = 80/10 = 8$ ft. The small pitch of the trusses is neglected for this preliminary design.

The design of the critical truss members is based on the uniform gravity loading case for this flat roof structure. Remember, for steep roofs the combined wind and gravity loading case may be controlling as was discussed for A-frames.

The uniform load, the truss supports, is equal to

$$w = (0.030 + 0.020) \, 20 = 1 \text{ k/ft}$$

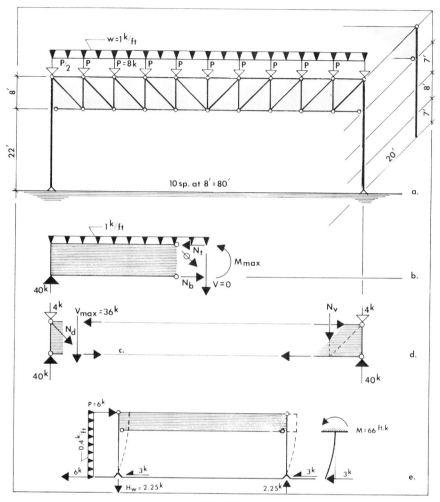

Fig. 4.60

This load causes single forces at the interior joints.

$$P = 1(8) = 8 \text{ k}$$

The truss, as a whole, is subject to beam action, while the individual truss members only respond as axial elements. Here, for fast approximation purposes, the truss is treated as a beam, where the chords, similar to the flanges of a girder, are assumed to resist the moments, while the web members carry the shear as the stirrups and bent up bars do in reinforced concrete beams.

The stiffness (depth) of the trussed beam is so high in comparison to the columns that its behavior is not restrained by the continuous columns and is allowed to rotate freely under gravity loading, hence it can be assumed to act as a simply supported beam with a maximum moment at midspan of

$$M_{\text{max}} = \frac{wL^2}{8} = \frac{1(80)^2}{8} = 800 \text{ ft-k}$$

It is conservative to assume that this moment is fully resisted by the chords and resolved into a force couple (Fig. 4.60b)

$$N_t(d) = N_b(d) = M \qquad N_t = N_b = \frac{M}{d} \qquad (4.58)$$

$$= \frac{800}{8} = 100 \text{ k}$$

Considering the top and bottom chord forces to be equal to one another ignores the effect of the web members or the fact that the loads are acting at the nodal points (see Problem 4.40).

Note that in this approach the layout of the web members does not have an effect on the magnitude of the chord forces at midspan where the shear is zero. Hence, even indeterminate multiple-web trusses can be analyzed by this approximate method.

The top chord, in addition to the axial force, must also resist local bending as caused by the roof skin. It acts as a continuous beam supported at the joints and carrying the uniform roof skin load to the joints. The maximum beam support moment is approximated as

$$M = \frac{wl^2}{10} = \frac{(0.030 + 0.016)20(8)^2}{10} = 5.89 \text{ ft-k}$$

The bending can be eliminated, if the purlins are placed directly at the truss joints, although this may be uneconomical because of the wide spacing.

Since the magnitude of the moment is relatively small as compared to the axial force, it is transformed by the bending factor into a fictitious axial load. The top chord is laterally supported about its weak axis by the roof skin and the small effect of buckling about its strong axis [i.e.; $(Kl)_{ye} = (Kl)_x (r_y/r_x) = 1(8)/2.77 = 2.89 \approx 0$] is neglected. Hence, the section can be assumed to fail in yielding rather than buckling

$$P + P' = P + B_x M_x \qquad (1.48)$$

$$= 100 + (0.339)5.89(12) = 123.96 \text{ k}$$

$$A = \frac{P + P'}{F_a} = \frac{123.96}{22} = 5.64 \text{ in.}^2$$

Try $W8 \times 21$, $A = 6.16 \text{ in.}^2$, $B_x = A/S_x = 6.16/18.2 = 0.339$.

In this case, the bottom chord does not have to be designed for bending, since it does not carry loads between panel points. As based on tension, the following net area is required:

$$A_{net} = \frac{N_b}{F_t} = \frac{100}{22} = 4.55 \text{ in.}^2$$

According to the AISC code, the net section shall not exceed 85% of the gross section. Since more information about the connection is not available at this time, the required gross area is assumed to be

$$A = \frac{A_{net}}{0.85} = \frac{4.55}{0.85} = 5.35 \text{ in.}^2$$

try $W8 \times 21$, $A = 6.16 \text{ in.}^2$.

The maximum shear adjacent to the supports is resisted fully by the web members. Its magnitude is equal to

$$V_{max} = 40 - 4 = 36 \text{ k}$$

This shear is carried by the diagonal and vertical web members. The vertical component of the diagonal force must be equal to the shear when using the beam approach (Fig. 4.60c)

$$N_d \frac{8}{8\sqrt{2}} = 36 \qquad N_d = 50.91 \text{ k } (T)$$

The approximate minimum gross area is

$$A = \frac{N_d}{0.85F_t} = \frac{50.91}{0.85(22)} = 2.72 \text{ in.}^2$$

Try $L3 \times 3 \times \frac{1}{2}$, $A = 2.75$ in.$^2$.

For indeterminate, multiple-web systems such as $x$ braced or lamella trusses, assume that each web member carries an equal portion of shear resulting in tension for some of the diagonal members and compression for others.

As based on the method of sections, the vertical web member carries directly the shear in compression (Fig. 4.60d).

$$\Sigma F_y = 0 = N_v - 40 + 4 \qquad N_v = 36 \text{ k } (C)$$

For a slenderness of $Kl = 1(8) = 8$, according to the AISC column tables try $2L3 \times 3 \times \frac{1}{4}$, $P_{all} = 36$ k.

At this stage some detailing should be done to see how the members fit together.

For the case where the trussed portal acts as a transverse bent resisting lateral forces, the preliminary design of the columns is based on the dead load case together with wind loading under normal loading conditions (i.e., no lateral thrust due to a crane, etc.). The typical structural unit (Fig. 4.60e) must resist a lateral wind force of

$$P = 0.020(20 \times 15) = 6 \text{ k}$$

The response of the column to this force depends on how it is connected to the trussed beam. Typical possibilities are illustrated in Fig. 4.61. The column is either a truss, a single solid, or a built-up member. In case (a), the column and beam form a continuous truss unit. The magnitude of the axial force flow can be determined by any of the known analytical or graphical methods of solution for trusses. In all the other cases of Fig. 4.61 the trussed beam is attached to single column members. To obtain an approximate solution for these cases, it is assumed that the trussed, deep beam is rigid and does not deform under lateral force action. It carries one-half of the wind or seismic load to the leeward column; in other words, the columns are considered equal in size and to share the loads equally. The lateral load $P$ wracks the columns (Fig. 4.60e) and generates a moment of

$$M = 22\frac{6}{2} = 66 \text{ ft-k}$$

This moment is resisted at the base by the cantilever columns of the post-beam structure [case (b)] or at the location where the bottom chord of the truss is attached to the con-

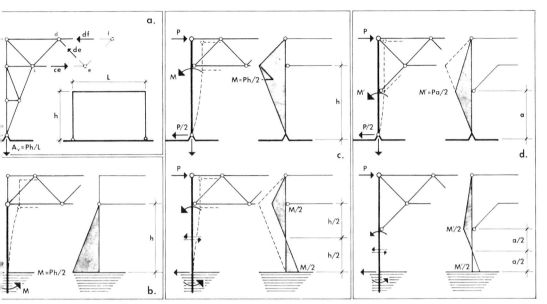

**Fig. 4.61** Trussed portals.

tinuous column of the two-hinge frame unit [case (c) top]. Should the column be fixed to the base and continuous up to the top, similar to a fixed portal unit [case (c) bottom], then the moment can be assumed to be shared approximately equally at the base and the point of intersection with the bottom chord, since rigid beam behavior causes inflection points at mid-way column base and bottom of truss

$$M = \frac{66}{2} = 33 \text{ ft-k}$$

The magnitude of the column moment can be further reduced by introducing knee braces [case (d)], which are diagonals extended from the truss to the column in order to decrease the column span or reduce the wracking distance of the column (i.e., its cantilever length). The points of contraflexure are approximated at midway between the column base and the bracing support.

The preliminary column size will be determined using $A36$ steel for the two-hinge portal unit [case (c) top]. The column must carry an axial dead load of

$$N_D = \frac{20(0.020)80}{2} = 16 \text{ k}$$

The dead load moment in the columns caused by the beam is small as compared to the wind load moment and is neglected. The axial column forces in tension and compression due to wind action are found by taking moments about one of the reactions

$$6(3) = N_W(80) \qquad N_W = 2.25 \text{ k}$$

The critical column is on the leeward side, where the axial forces due to wind and gravity add. The column has to support the following axial load and moment

$$N = 16 + 2.25 = 18.25 \text{ k} \qquad M = 66 \text{ ft-k}$$

It is assumed that the design of the column is controlled by bending and that the member is partially compact. In addition, the moment is increased by 10% to take into account axial force action

$$M = 66 \left(\frac{24}{22}\right)1.1 = 79.20 \text{ ft-k}$$

Try $W14 \times 30$, $M_R = 84$ ft-k

$$A = 8.85 \text{ in.}^2 \quad S = 42.0 \text{ in.}^3 \quad r_x = 5.73 \text{ in.}$$
$$r_y = 1.49 \text{ in.} \quad L_u = 8.7 \text{ ft} \quad L_c = 7.1 \text{ ft}, \quad L_b = 8 \text{ ft}$$
$$L_c < L_b < L_u \quad \text{or} \quad F_b = 22 \text{ ksi}$$

The governing slenderness ratio is checked to obtain the allowable axial stress. The column is laterally supported about its weak axis in the wall plane as shown in Fig. 4.60a.

$$\left(\frac{Kl}{r}\right)_y = \frac{1(8)12}{1.49} = 64.43 < 92$$

$$\left(\frac{Kl}{r}\right)_x = \frac{2(22)12}{5.73} = 92.15 \cong 92 \quad \text{or} \quad F_a = 13.97 \text{ ksi}$$

$$\frac{f_a}{F_a} + \frac{f_b}{F_b} = \frac{18.25/8.85}{13.97} + \frac{66(12)/42.0}{22}$$

$$= 0.148 + 0.857 = 1.005 > 1.0$$

The section is just barely overstressed, the next larger member is satisfactory. Notice the ratio $f_a/F_a < 0.15$, hence the axial force will not magnify the moment and the design approach is not an approximate one.

## Problems

**4.40** Determine the exact magnitude of the forces in the chord members at midspan for the uniform gravity loading case of Example 4.6.

**4.41** For the truss enclosure structures in Fig. 4.62, determine the forces in the members, which are identified by letters at their ends (i.e., at joints).

**4.42** Determine the critical column moments for cases (e), (f), and (l) in Fig. 4.62.

**4.43** Estimate the truss member sizes, if the two-way roof structure of Example 5.5a is replaced by a parallel, one-way truss system, using the same truss geometry and spacing and the same loading as for the two-way structure.

**4.44** See Problem 5.11a.

**4.45** Consider the columns of the trussed portal in Example 4.6 to be fixed at their base. Determine the axial column forces and critical moments and find the preliminary column section.

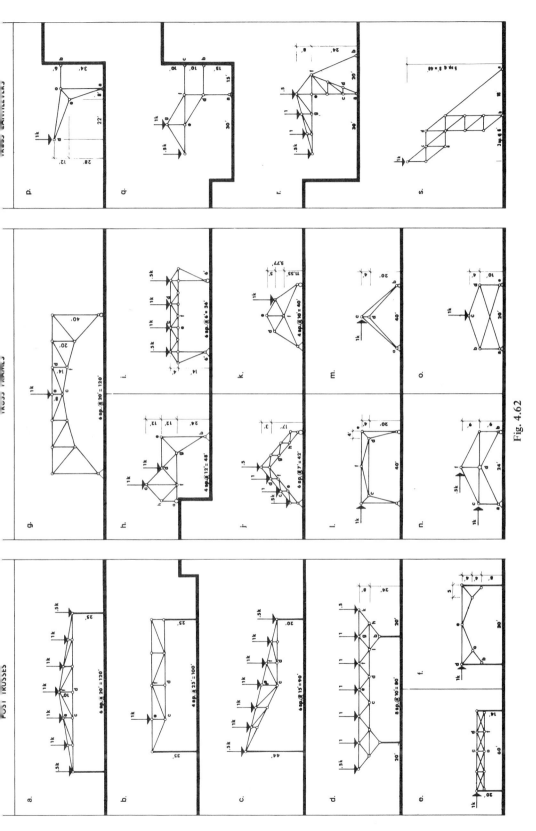

Fig. 4.62

295

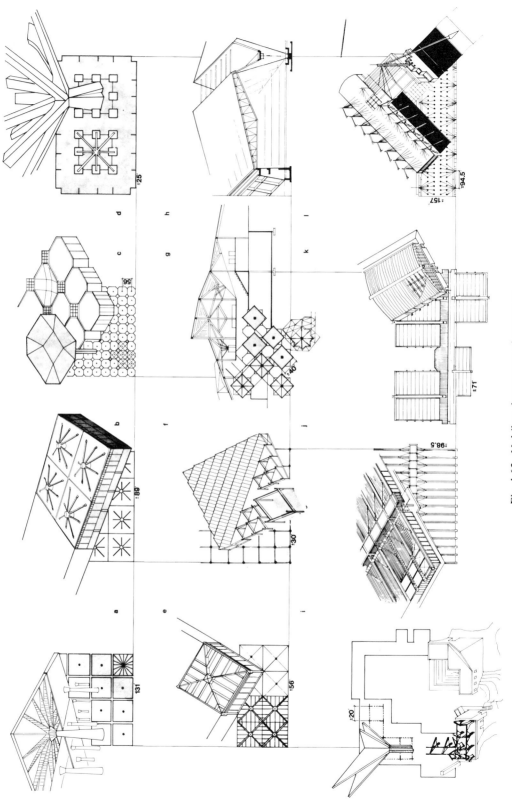

Fig. 4.63 Multibay, longspan roof structures.

## 4.6  MULTIBAY STRUCTURES

Large horizontal spaces are often needed for building types such as exhibition spaces, sports facilities, libraries, industrial buildings, factories, and so on. There are many structural systems that have already been or remain to be discussed which satisfy the spatial requirements. However, one should keep in mind that the structure should not be seen as an end in itself but as having evolved out of the synthesis of the various architectural determinants. The wide range and flexible character of the potential structural systems can only be suggested in Fig. 4.63.

For industrial buildings, mostly multibay column grid systems are employed, as the cases in Fig. 4.64 clearly express. Prefabrication construction methods are used for these modular structures that should be adaptable to future expansions. The column spacing should be wide enough so as to cause the least interference with the production or service process, that is, the placement of equipment and work stations, transportation requirements, and assembly areas; it should be adjustable towards future relocation and adaptable to new production methods about either building axis. The roof shape of these horizontally spread buildings depends a great deal on the treatment of ventilation and lighting (i.e., natural versus artificial); possible roof shape cross sections are shown in Fig. 4.65.

The reader may also refer back to Chapter 2, where various floor plans and their modularity together with floor/roof framing systems as related to support structures have already been conceptually investigated.

Following, the building structures in Fig. 4.63 will be identified and briefly described. Umbrella-type units were adopted to cases (a)–(c), (g) and (i) employing either cantilevering beams, the suspension principle, shells, or spreading columns. Post-beam systems are used in cases (h) and (k), while the suspension principle is taken in cases (j) and (l). The other buildings use either the flat slab or some roof framing for four-leg table units.

In case (a), independent steel umbrella plates are framed with welded steel girders that are radially arranged. They are supported at the center by tapering cruciform concrete columns. The space between the independent mushroom units is covered by skylight ribbons. Each roof unit in case (b) is suspended with eight concrete hangers from a central core column containing the ventilation and heating ducts. Inverted umbrella shells, each of which is supported by a central column containing drainage, are employed in case (c). The free space between the mushroom units is covered by fiberglass-reinforced plastic skylights. The complex roof in case (g) is developed from a series of squares, rotated squares, and octagonal modules. The roof units are radially framed and supported by central columns or clusters of inclined wood struts sitting on masonry piers. In case (i) the concrete columns flare out to form umbrella units.

The concrete waffle slab of case (d) is supported by the perimeter walls and by the two spreading interior columns which consist of eight large arms and four smaller ones along the diagonals, giving them the appearance of concrete trees. In case (e), tubular steel trusses span diagonally to the corner columns and, together with the edge beams, support the secondary trusses. Skylight ribbons are provided along the diagonal trusses and a ventilation shaft is located at the center intersection. The structural bays in case (f) are on a rectangular grid, while the sawtooth roof framing is placed diagonally to it to enable better lighting conditions.

The two-span roof structure of case (h) is composed of single-span steel trusses resting on the perimeter frames and central V-shaped concrete columns. The central post-beam

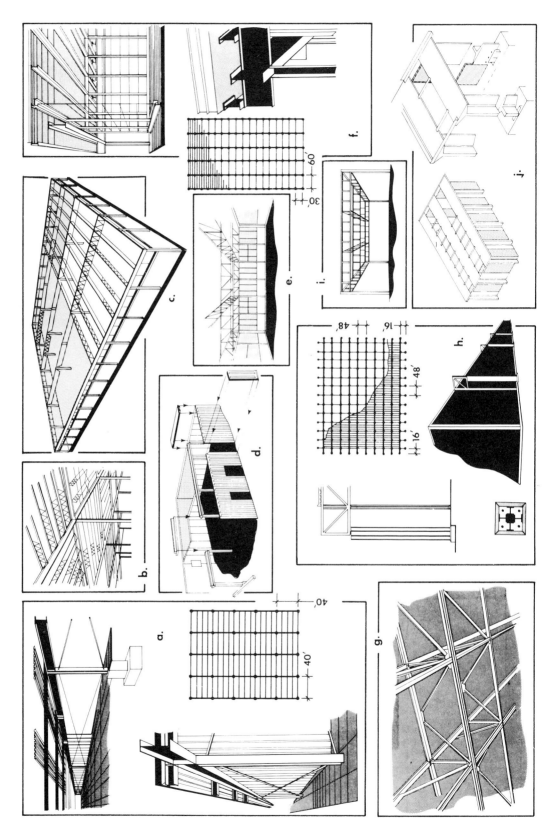

a.

b.

c.

d.

e.

f.

g.

h.

i.

j.

40'

40'

60'

30'

48'

16'

48'

16'

298

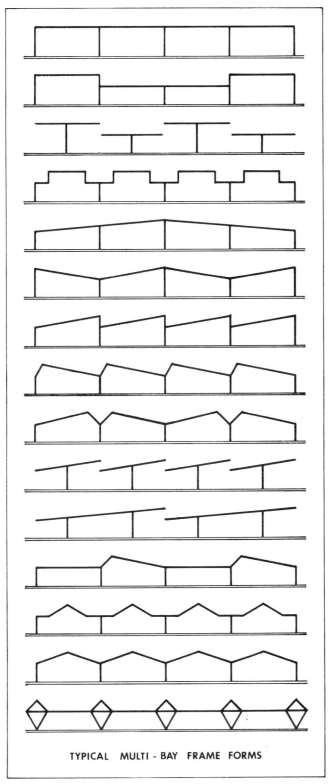

TYPICAL MULTI - BAY FRAME FORMS

Fig. 4.65

structure in case (k), consisting of a giant tubular steel beam which rests on cylindrical concrete columns at the building facade, supports the roof trusses. The stayed bridge principle is applied to the building of case (1). The rectangular roof modules are composed of four primary beams which are supported on the interior by the diagonal cables that are suspended from the tubular steel masts at the periphery and center of each module.

Along the central, longitudinal spine in case (j), two rows of columns carry a large concrete box girder which, in turn, supports the spatial steel trusses as well as the suspended steel tubes which give additional support to these cantilvering three-dimensional trusses.

The further discussion in this chapter will concentrate on the typical multispan frames as exemplified by the cases in Fig. 4.64 since the structural systems just discussed have been treated elsewhere in this book. In this figure, square or rectangular column grids are the basis for parallel multibay structure systems as further identified in Figs. 4.66 and 4.67. They form either post-beam systems (simply supported, cantilevered, or continuous beams) or frames, as well as any combination of the two. These parallel structural skeletons, which support the secondary beams, may have many different shapes, such as the ones proposed in Fig. 4.65, so that lighting requirements can be satisfied.

Notice the exposure of the structural order in the design of the building cases (a), (f), and (h) in Fig. 4.64, expressing and identifying the hierarchy of structural members so convincingly.

## Post-Beam Structures

In this type of construction the roof plane is hinged to the vertical structural planes, that is, the primary beams are pin-jointed to the columns, not continuous with them as is typical for frames. The analysis of these beams may be statically determinate with respect to gravity loading, if simple or cantilevered beams are employed as in Fig. 4.67a–d, or it may be statically indeterminate for continuous beams as in Fig. 4.67e.

With regard to lateral loading, the forces are carried by the cantilevering columns in proportion to their stiffness, or they are carried by braced bents or shear walls, in which case any unbraced columns are hinged to their bases, because they only resist gravity loading (Fig. 4.66a and b). Where cantilevering columns of equal size, length, and material are used, the lateral loads are shared equally among them. The distribution of the lateral forces depends on the nature of the exterior wall panels, as was discussed in Fig. 4.7. For the case where the loads are distributed horizontally, directly to the columns, a uniform load along the columns is generated. The column can be visualized as a vertical beam fixed at the base, with an elastic support at the top. The force flow is found by first assuming a rigid support at the top with no horizontal support movement (Fig. 4.68).

The horizontal reactions for this case are:

$$\text{at the top} \qquad P = \frac{3ph}{8}$$

$$\text{at the base} \qquad V_e{}' = \frac{5ph}{8}$$

The base moment is

$$M_e{}' = \frac{ph^2}{8}$$

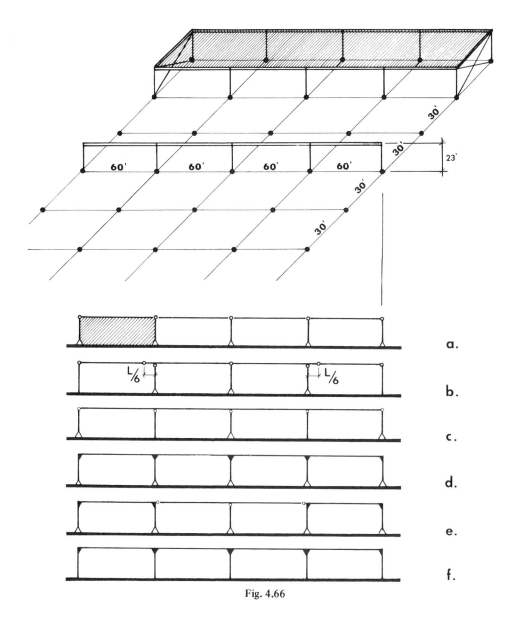

**Fig. 4.66**

The single load $P$ at the top is, in turn, shared equally by all columns including the exterior ones, ignoring the fact that the interior columns may be larger than the exterior ones. Hence, each column carries an equal portion of the lateral force $P$, which for the given condition of four columns yields

$$V_i = \frac{P}{4} = \frac{3ph}{32}$$

This force causes a maximum base moment of

$$M_i = V_i(h) = \frac{3ph^2}{32}$$

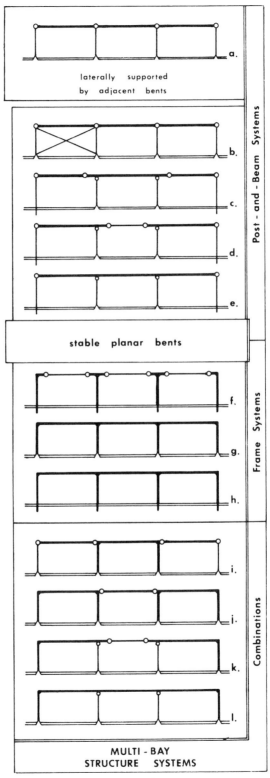

Fig. 4.67

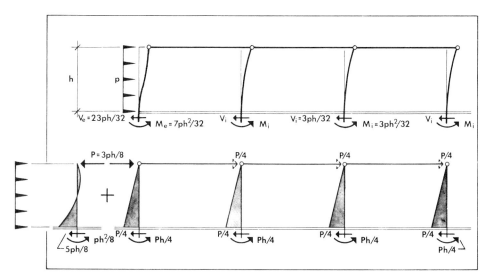

**Fig. 4.68**

For the exterior column, the results of the two loading cases are superimposed, yielding the following maximum shear and moment at its base (Fig. 4.68)

$$V_e = \frac{5ph}{8} + \frac{3ph}{32} = \frac{23ph}{32}$$

$$M_e = \frac{ph^2}{8} + \frac{3ph^2}{32} = \frac{7ph^2}{32}$$

Note that for the given condition and for lateral force action from either direction, the exterior columns must carry more than twice as much moment as the interior columns.

For the preliminary design of a multibay post-beam structure, one can assume that uniform gravity loading controls the design of the beams (i.e., the effect of live load arrangement for roofs, in general, can be ignored), while the lateral force case together with the dead loading governs the design of the cantilevering columns. Remember that the effective length factor of the column about the strong axis is $K_x = 2.1$ when a horizontal point load is applied to its top. The effective column length about the weak axis is $K_y = 1.0$, assuming no sidesway of the building in this direction.

## Portal Frames

In frame construction, beams and columns are connected by rigid joints; the members are continuous and not separated by hinges as in the post-beam construction. Any bending induced in one element causes bending in all other elements continuously connected to it. There are many types of frames, such as hinged column tree systems on the one hand (Fig. 4.67f), and truly rigid frames (Fig. 4.67h) on the other.

Briefly introduced here are the continuous frames with hinged and fixed column bases. The analysis of multibay rigid frames is highly indeterminate. To promote some understanding of the force distribution along the frame, gravity and lateral loading are investigated separately and then the critical moment values are combined, ignoring the magnification of the moment due to sidesway.

In the following discussion only the special case of rectangular bents of equal span and height, having at least four bays, is considered. The building is assumed to be of uniform strength where all columns are of nearly the same size.

### Approximate Analysis for Gravity Loading

It is rather difficult to develop an approximate method of solution for multibay frames under uniform gravity loading. It was shown in the discussion of single indeterminate portal frames that the force flow distribution depends on the stiffnesses of the beams and columns. In addition, for continuous multiunit systems, the placement of the live loads must be considered. In Chapter 1, the various loading arrangements for continuous beams were mentioned. It was indicated that the respective critical values due to the uniform dead load (placed across the full width of the frame) had to be superimposed on the respective values as caused by live loading (arranged in various patterns such as alternate spans or only adjacent spans) so as to yield critical moment or shear values. For flat roofs, however, it is quite questionable whether the snow load would ever place itself in the way just discussed. Furthermore, roof live loads are often relatively small in comparison to dead loads and the effect of their placement is less pronounced, assuming a constant building height and no parapets, that is, assuming areas which do not collect snow. One may conclude that under uniform gravity loading and symmetrical frame geometry, the interior columns will not resist much rotation, hence allow a continuous beam action with an absolute maximum moment at the interior supports of about $wL^2/10$. For other frame locations the approximate moment envelopes in Fig. 4.69a–c may be used for preliminary design purposes.

Because uniform gravity loads are the primary design determinant, that is because of the symmetrical arrangement of the loading and the symmetrical geometry of the frame, the interior columns may be assumed not to carry any gravity moments and thus are rather slender, since also the wind moments, in general, are rather small. This condition, obviously, is not true for unsymmetrical frames, where the columns must balance the difference in beam moments at the beam-column intersection, nor is it true for the exterior columns of the symmetrical frames which must resist the beam rotation of the end bay. Notice that the field moments in the end bays (Fig. 4.69b and c) are larger than the ones for a typical interior bay. For this approximate analysis the relatively small axial forces in the beams may be ignored.

### Approximate Analysis for Horizontal Loading

The response of the continuous and hinged frames to a lateral force $P$ at the beam-column intersection is shown in Fig. 4.69d and e. The approximate behavior of a multibay system is derived from the sum of the independent actions of the individual portal units. For a structure of $n$ equal bays, each frame unit carries an equal portion $P/n$ of

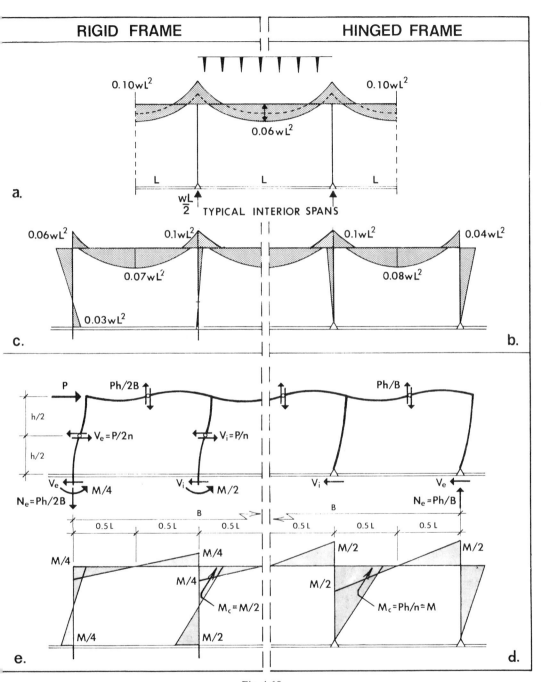

Fig. 4.69

the lateral force $P$. Based on this assumption and on the discussion of the individual portal frame units under lateral loading, one may draw the following conclusions:

(i) The total lateral shear $P$ is equally shared by the interior columns, while an exterior column only carries one-half the amount resisted by an interior one.

$$V_i = \frac{P}{n} \qquad V_e = \frac{V_i}{2} = \frac{P/2}{n} \qquad (4.59)$$

(ii) The rotation due to the lateral force $P$ is only carried by the exterior columns, that is, the force $P$ is resisted by a force couple composed of the axial forces in the exterior columns. For a hinged frame, these axial forces are

$$P(h) = N_e(B) \qquad N_e = \frac{Ph}{B} \qquad (4.60)$$

A continuous frame may be visualized as a hinged frame of height $h/2$ which sits on column stubs of the same height $h/2$ as is further clarified below. Hence, the axial forces in the exterior columns of the rigid frame are only one-half as large as those of the hinged frame

$$N_e = \frac{Ph}{2B} \qquad (4.61)$$

(iii) The frame deforms such that inflection points develop exactly at midspan of the beams, and at midheight of the columns for continuous frames with fixed bases.

The column moments can easily be derived by visualizing the shear forces racking the frame, or by visualizing the shears at the inflection points to cause cantilever action of the members as has already been discussed for the response of individual portal frame units (Fig. 4.24). For the hinged frame, the maximum interior column moments at the top are

$$M_c = V_i(h) = \frac{Ph}{n} \qquad (4.62)$$

Note that the interior columns carry twice as much moment as the exterior ones. For the continuous frame the maximum column moments at the top and bottom are only one-half as large as those for the equivalent hinged frame

$$M_c = \pm V_i \frac{h}{2} \qquad (4.63)$$

The maximum beam moments at the supports are caused by the racking of the vertical shear. This shear is equal to the axial forces in the exterior columns and thus is constant across the building width $B$. The constant shear at the assumed hinges at midspan cause the following maximum beam support moments

for hinged frames $\qquad M_B = \pm \dfrac{Ph}{B}\left(\dfrac{L}{2}\right) = \pm V_e(h) \qquad (4.64)$

for rigid frames $\qquad M_B = \pm \dfrac{Ph}{2B}\left(\dfrac{L}{2}\right) = \pm V_e\dfrac{h}{2} \qquad (4.65)$

Note that the beam moments can also be derived from the maximum exterior column moments, to which they are equal, as the beam and column moments must balance each other across the corner joint.

### Preliminary Design

For the preliminary design of single-story, multibay frames of normal height, one may assume that the full gravity loading case controls the design of beams and exterior columns, while the design of the interior columns is governed by the lateral force action together with gravity loading. For the column design, an effective length factor $K_y = 1.0$ may be used by assuming the weak column axis to control and by assuming that there is no sidesway about the weak axis (i.e., the building is laterally braced in this direction). The full column height should be used as the unbraced length, ignoring any lateral bracing about the weak axis. The gravity loads are considered to be distributed to the columns in the same manner as for a post-beam structure, where the columns carry simply supported beams.

### Problems

**4.46**  Show the moment and axial force diagrams with numerical values for the framing systems in Fig. 4.66, as caused by a lateral unit load acting at the roof level. Also draw the deflected frame. Compare the solutions and draw your conclusions.

**4.47**  Repeat Problem 4.46, but now consider uniform gravity loading, that is dead and live load, rather than lateral force action.

**4.48**  Determine the approximate sizes of the major structural members for the framing system shown in Fig. 4.66b. Assume the roof skin to consist of 2 X 6 in. tongue-and-groove wood planks 12 ft long, supported by timber beams spaced 6 ft apart. The beams are hinged to the girders. The roof skin consists of decking, insulation, and built-up roofing, altogether weighing 12 psf. Assume an equivalent weight for the beams of 4 psf and girders of 3 psf. Only gravity loading is needed, since the wind forces are carried by the roof diaphragm to braced shear walls along the facade. Use glued laminated Southern Pine 24F for the design of the beams and girders, which has the following properties: $F_b$ = 2.4 ksi, $F_v$ = 0.2 ksi, and $E$ = 1800 ksi. Design the girders as based on bending alone, while for the design of the beams also consider deflection. The allowable stresses for the interior column are $F_c$ = 1.5 ksi, and $E$ = 1800 ksi. Check the 2-in. deck which has the following properties: $F_b$ = 1.31 ksi for repetitive members, $F_v$ = 0.08 ksi, and $E$ = 1500 ksi. For the estimate of the member sizes, ignore the effect of load duration and member size.

**4.49**  Investigate the structural framing system in Fig. 4.66c. Use 8-in. hollow core slabs to span between the post-beam concrete structure. The roofing material weighs 10 psf and the precast slabs 57 psf. The snow load is 30 psf. Check if the prefab slab is satisfactory. Estimate the size of the girder by assuming the beam depth to be 2.5–3 times the beam width. Also check the required amount of steel reinforcement at the critical moment location. Determine the size of the central column. Use 4000 psi normal weight concrete and Grade 60 steel.

**4.50** Determine the approximate member sizes for the typical interior four-bay steel frame structure hinged to the foundations (Fig. 4.66d.). Use long-span steel joists (*LJ* series), which are spaced at 6 ft on center, to bridge the gap between the frames. The roof skin consists of roofing, metal deck, and insulation, which weighs a total of 12 psf. Assume an equivalent joist and frame girder weight of 3 psf each. The snow loading is 30 psf and the wind load on the vertical projection is 20 psf. Use $A36$ steel for the frame.

**4.51** Investigate whether it would be more efficient to have the interior columns act only as pendulumns carrying axial gravity loads, while letting the facade columns resist all the wind (Fig. 4.67l), rather than using the frame solution of Problem 4.50.

## Approximate Design of Frame and Wall Footings

Typical shallow foundations for multispan frames are shown in Fig. 4.70. While in the top case only one large footing stabilizes the entire vertical building plane laterally, in the second case the footings of the central rigid portal unit do so. These footings should be completely restrained from rotation so that the moments can be transmitted to the ground in a controlled manner, which in turn requires reliable soil conditions. Often the soil is poor and the more elaborate foundations required are not economically feasible, therefore it may be advantageous to have hinged connections between column base and footing. Further, from the discussion in Chapter 1 it is apparent that eccentrically loaded footings are of much larger size than the centrally loaded ones. Pin-connected conditions can be obtained, for instance, by bracing one bay, as indicated in Fig. 4.70 by the last two cases, or by stabilizing adjacent bays. In this way the footings carry primarily axial forces, if the relatively small rotational effect due to the lateral base forces is neglected.

In the following preliminary design of typical spread footings only centrally loaded wall footings and single column footings are investigated.

**Example 4.7** Design the concrete footing for the 12-in. exterior concrete wall of a one-story building. The footing is placed at a depth of 4 ft below the ground in order to avoid movement of the soil due either to heaving (uneven rise of the ground surface) or thawing of the frozen soil. The wall loads are shown in Fig. 4.71. The allowable soil bearing capacity at the footing base is $q_a = 3$ ksf. Consider the weight of concrete as 145 pcf and the weight of the earth on top of the footing (backfill material) to be 100 pcf.

(a) Use Grade 40 steel reinforcing to resist the tension as caused by bending. The concrete has a strength in compression of 3000 psi. The total load that the soil at the bottom of the footing must support is not known exactly, since the thickness of the foundation must be found first. Assuming the average weight of both concrete and backfill material to be 125 pcf should be conservative, as it is equivalent to saying that the depth of the footing for initial estimation purposes is equal to 2 ft.

The total pressure along the footing base area $A$ due to the wall loads and overburden must be less than the permissible soil bearing capacity $q_a$; for the loading conditions given in Fig. 4.71, it is

$$q = \frac{3.5 + 8.5}{A} + 4(0.125) \leqslant q_a = 3 \tag{1.51}$$

$$q_{a\ net} = 3 - 4(0.125) \geqslant \frac{3.5 + 8.5}{A}$$

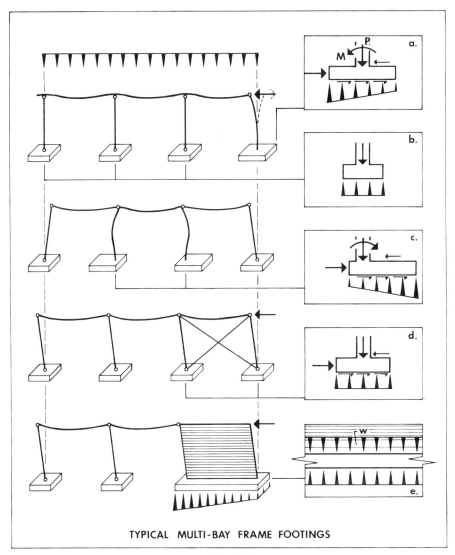

TYPICAL MULTI-BAY FRAME FOOTINGS

Fig. 4.70

Hence, the allowable net soil pressure available to resist the wall loads is equal to the full allowable soil pressure reduced by the 4 ft of 125 pcf uniform load

$$q_{a \text{ net}} = 3 - 4(.125) = 2.50 \text{ ksf}$$

The minimum required base area for the footing, or the minimum required width $L$ for a typical 1-ft long footing section is,

$$q = \frac{P}{A} \leqslant q_{a \text{ net}}$$

or

$$A = L(1) \geqslant \frac{P}{q_{a \text{ net}}} = \frac{3.5 + 8.5}{2.5} = 4.80 \text{ ft}$$

Select a footing width of $L = 5$ ft.

309

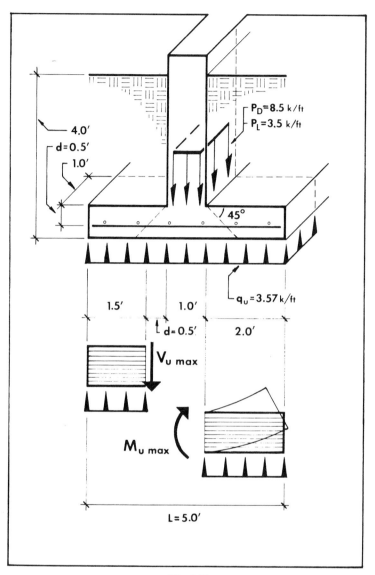

Fig. 4.71

The footing is subject to bending, as it transforms the wall loads concentrated at its center into a (theoretically) uniform contact pressure. On the other hand, foundation and soil overburden weights are already uniformly distributed over the footing and are directly resisted by the soil. Hence, only the net pressures as caused by the wall loads are used for finding the footing's thickness and amount of steel reinforcing, which together determine the footing's bending capacity.

The ultimate net base pressure for which the footing has to be designed, is

$$q_u = \frac{1.4\,P_D + 1.7\,P_L}{A} = \frac{1.4(8.5) + 1.7(3.5)}{5(1)} = 3.57 \text{ ksf}$$

The footing may be visualized as a one-way slab with two cantilevers projecting on both sides of the wall carrying the uniform, upwardacting ultimate load $q_u$ (Fig. 4.71). The effective length of the cantilever depends on the rigidity of the wall (or pedestal or column), as described by the *ACI Code*. For determining the moment arm length, the locations of the critical sections for following different cases according to *ACI 318-77* are:

(i) At the face of column, pedestal, or wall, for footings supporting a concrete column, pedestal, or wall.

(ii) Halfway between middle and edge of wall, for footings supporting a masonry wall.

(iii) Halfway between face of column and edge of steel base plate for footings supporting a column with steel base plates.

The location of the critical section for beam shear is at the distance $d$ measured from the face of column, pedestal, or wall for cases (i) and (ii) discussed above. For case (iii), the critical section for shear shall be measured from the critical location of the bending moment.

The depth of the footing is usually controlled by shear, when no shear reinforcing is being used. The shear strength of the concrete for beam action is

$$v_c = 2\sqrt{f_c'} = 2\sqrt{3000} = 109.55 \text{ psi}$$

Assuming a minimum footing depth $d = 6$ in. to the centroid of the reinforcement, the maximum ultimate shear force will be located 6 in. from the face of the wall. This force is equal to:

$$V_{u \text{ max}} = 3.57(1.5) = 5.36 \text{ k}$$

The ultimate shear stress at that location is:

$$v_{u \text{ max}} = \frac{V_{u \text{ max}}}{\phi bd} = \frac{5360}{0.85(12)6} = 87.58 \text{ psi} < 109.55 \text{ psi}$$

The minimum footing depth is satisfactory since the maximum shear is easily carried by the unreinforced concrete.

The maximum ultimate moment at the face of the wall is

$$M_{u \text{ max}} = 3.57(2)(1) = 7.14 \text{ ft-k}$$

The approximate steel area required to resist the tension at the footing base according to Eq. (1.39) is

$$A_s = \frac{M_u}{0.8 f_y d} = \frac{7.14(12)}{0.8(40)6} = 0.446 \text{ in.}^2/\text{ft}$$

Try #5 at 8 in., on center, $A_s = 0.46$ in.$^2$/ft.

The steel ratio selected must be larger than the minimum required

$$p = \frac{A_s}{bd} = \frac{0.46}{12(6)} = 0.00639$$

$$p_{\text{min}} = \frac{200}{F_y} = \frac{200}{40000} = 0.005 < p$$

It is apparent that the footing is underreinforced (i.e., $p \ll p_{max}$) since its steel ratio is barely larger than the minimum required: this is due to the fact that the selected footing depth is much larger than the depth needed only for bending.

According to the ACI Code, a minimum concrete cover of 3 in. must be provided for reinforcement if concrete is cast against and permanently exposed to earth. Thus, the minimum total footing depth is

$$t_{min} = 6 + \frac{0.625}{2} + 3 = 9.31 \text{ in.}$$

Select a 10-in. thick footing. Notice that the initially assumed 24-in. thick footing was very conservative and that a slightly smaller footing width $L$ could now be calculated.

The reinforcement for shrinkage and temperature effects, placed on top of and perpendicular to the main reinforcement, is

$$A_s = 0.002bt = 0.002(12)10 = 0.24 \text{ in.}^2/\text{ft}$$

Select #4 at 10 in. on center, $A_s = 0.24$ in.$^2$/ft.

(b) Design the wall footing using unreinforced 3000 psi concrete. The width of the plain concrete footing is equal to that of the reinforced footing of part (a) because of the initial conservative assumption of 24 in. depth. The ultimate net upward contact pressure does not change either. However, the depth of the footing will increase drastically because of the poor ability of the plain concrete to carry the tension loads due to bending.

The ultimate flexural tensile capacity of the concrete is equal to

$$F_{tu} = 5\sqrt{f'_c} = 5\sqrt{3000} = 273.86 \text{ psi}$$

The actual maximum ultimate tensile stress of the rectangular, *uncracked* section due to bending is

$$f_{tu} = \frac{M_u}{\phi S} \leqslant F_{tu} \tag{1.41}$$

or

$$S = \frac{bd^2}{6} = \frac{M_u}{\phi F_{tu}}$$

$$\frac{12d^2}{6} = \frac{7140(12)}{0.65(273.86)}$$

The minimum required effective thickness is: $d = 15.51$ in. Since the concrete in contact with the soil is considered of inferior quality, about 3-4 in. are added to the effective thickness. Select a depth for the plain footing of 19 in.

Note that the plain footing is about double as thick as the reinforced footing, while there is not much difference in footing width (assuming a precise analysis).

**Example 4.8** Design a single square, steel-reinforced concrete footing for the column of Example 4.2 as shown in Fig. 4.72.

The column is hinged to the foundation and thus transfers only the axial forces $P_D = 20$ k and $P_L = 24$ k (Fig. 4.72a). For the given loading condition, the lateral thrust is balanced by the tie rod connecting the column bases of the frame and does not influence

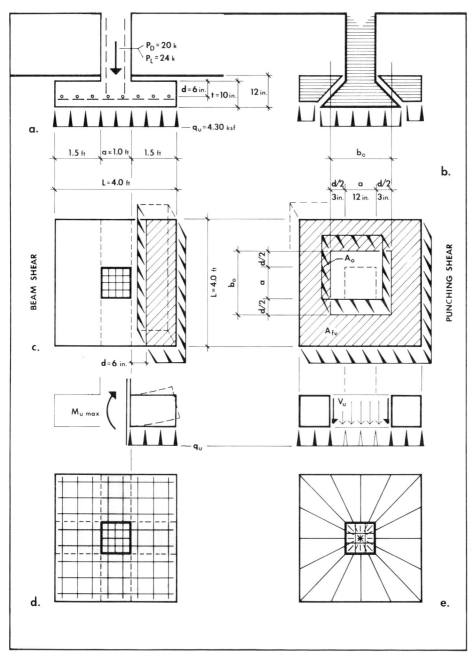

Fig. 4.72

313

this preliminary foundation design. The exterior curtain walls and interior walls are assumed to be carried by independent foundations.

Since this footing is located in the building's interior, it is not affected by frost, and is placed 1 ft below the ground surface, just deep enough to rest on undisturbed soil. For this exercise consider an equivalent square concrete column section of 12 in. The foundation materials are 4000 psi concrete and Grade 40 steel, and the bearing capacity of the soil $q_a$ is 3 ksf. The reasoning used for determining the footing size is analogous to the wall footing approach of the previous problem.

If the weight of both concrete and backfill is conservatively assumed as 145 pcf, then the net allowable soil pressure remaining to support the column loads is

$$q_{a \; net} = 3000 - 1(145) = 2855 \; \text{psf}$$

The minimum base area required, without overstressing the soil, is

$$q = \frac{P}{A} \leqslant q_a \tag{1.51}$$

or

$$A = L^2 = \frac{P}{q_a} = \frac{20 + 24}{2.855} = 15.41 \; \text{ft}^2$$

Try a 4-ft square footing, $A = 16 \; \text{ft}^2$.

The ultimate net base pressure $q_u$ acting upward to bend the foundation is

$$q_u = \frac{1.4P_D + 1.7P_L}{A} = \frac{1.4(20) + 1.7(24)}{16} = 4.30 \; \text{ksf}$$

While the wall footing bends in one direction like a one-way slab, the column foundation is subject to bending in two directions like a flat slab.

The column attempts to punch through the foundation but is resisted by the footing's shear capacity along a perimeter concrete area $A_0$ measured at a distance of $d/2$ from the column faces, according to the *ACI Code* (Fig. 4.72b). The punching shear stresses along the given critical perimeter area can only be considered nominal, as actual shear failure would not occur along that surface but along the surface of a truncated pyramid as shown in Fig. 4.72b.

The thickness of a single square footing is controlled in most cases by two-way "punching" shear, when no shear reinforcing is used. Assuming the minimum required thickness from the footing's top to the centroid of the upper steel layer of $d = 6$ in., the area $A_0$ will be equal to the perimeter $b_0$ times the depth $d$ as shown in Fig. 4.72b

$$A_0 = b_0 d = 4(a + d)d = 4(1 + 0.5)0.5 = 3.00 \; \text{ft}^2 = 432 \; \text{in.}^2$$

The upward ultimate force $V_u$ trying to punch through the footing is caused by the pressure $q_u$ acting on the area $A_{fv}$ (shown hatched in Fig. 4.72b) is

$$V_u = q_u A_{fv} = q_u [A - (a + d)^2] = 4.30[16 - (1 + 0.5)^2] = 59.13 \; \text{k}$$

The nominal circumferential shear stress is equal to the force $V_u$ increased by the capacity reduction factor $\phi = 0.85$, and divided by the resisting area $A_0$

$$v_u = \frac{V_u}{\phi A_0} = \frac{59130}{0.85(432)} = 161.03 \; \text{psi}$$

The shear strength of the concrete for two-way action according to the *ACI Code* is

$$4\sqrt{f_c'} = 4\sqrt{4000} = 252.98 \text{ psi} > 161.03 \text{ psi}$$

The minimum depth is clearly satisfactory.

The beam shear, or one-way shear (Fig. 4.72c), used to determine the depth of the wall footing is rarely significant as is shown for this example

$$v_u = \frac{V_u}{\phi b d} = \frac{4300(1.5 - 0.5)4}{0.85(48)6}$$

$$= 70.26 \text{ psi} < 2\sqrt{4000} = 126.48 \text{ psi}$$

In general, punching shear controls the depth of the reinforced single column footing.

To simplify the complex behavior of the flat slab type of foundation, visualize the slab to be cut into radial segments (Fig. 4.72e) so as to form cantilever beams projecting from the central located column. Based on this assumption, the main reinforcement could theoretically be placed in a similar radial manner. However, the design of single footings has been further simplified by the *ACI Code*, which treats such footings as two intersecting wall footings placed perpendicular to each other (Fig. 4.72d). Correspondingly, two identical layers of reinforcement are placed perpendicular to each other at the bottom of the foundation. Although there is one bar diameter difference between the effective depths of the two reinforcement layers, the steel area $A_S$ is conservatively determined, using the shorter dimension of the upper steel layer.

The maximum moment at the face of the column is

$$M_{u \text{ max}} = \frac{4.30(1.5)1.5}{2} = 4.84 \text{ ft-k/foot width}$$

The approximate required steel area is:

$$A_s = \frac{M_u}{0.80 f_y d} = \frac{4.84(12)}{0.80(40)6} = 0.303 \text{ in.}^2/\text{ft}$$

The total steel required for the full foundation width of 4 ft is

$$A_s = 4(0.303) = 1.21 \text{ in.}^2$$

The minimum steel area should be:

$$A_{s \text{ min}} = p_{\text{min}} b d = \frac{200}{F_y} b d = \frac{200}{40000} 48(6) = 1.44 \text{ in.}^2$$

The minimum steel ratio $p_{\text{min}}$ controls the design because the footing is much deeper than required by prior analysis, that is, the depth $d$ required for bending is much less than that needed for shear (the minimum depth in this case).

Try eight #4 bars, $A_s = 1.57$ in.$^2$ placed in each of two layers perpendicular to each other at the bottom of the foundation. The total thickness of the footing, assuming $d$ is measured to the center of the upper steel layer, is

$$t = 6 + \frac{0.5}{2} + 0.5 + 3 = 9.75 \text{ in.}$$

Select a 10-in. thick footing.

Note that the initial assumption of a 12-in. thick footing was conservative.

### Problems

**4.52**  Design the single square footing of Example 4.8 as a plain concrete footing.

**4.53**  Determine the size of a reinforced concrete footing to support a 12-in. masonry wall which transmits to its footing a dead load of 6 k/ft and a live load of 4 k/ft. Find also the approximate amount of steel and show the layout of the reinforcing. Use 3000 psi concrete and Grade 40 steel. The allowable soil pressure is 2500 psf. The depth from the ground surface to the base of the foundation is 12 in.

**4.54**  Design the wall footing of Problem 4.53 as a plain concrete footing.

**4.55**  Is the footing size in Problem 4.54 different if the wall is not made of masonry but concrete? If so, determine the dimensions.

**4.56**  A single reinforced concrete footing must carry a 15-in. square concrete column transferring a dead load of 200 k and a live load of 150 k. The column is located at the center of the square footing. Determine the size of the foundation and the approximate amount of reinforcement for an allowable soil pressure of 5 ksf, using 3500 psi concrete and 40 ksi steel. The height from foundation base to ground level is 4 ft; for this overburden use as a first approximation a load of 125 pcf.

## 4.7  OTHER LONG-SPAN STRUCTURES

Any of the frame systems which have been discussed in this chapter may be used for long spans; a long span is considered one of at least 100 ft—that however depends on the material and the structure system. Some special building types that employ the principle of the cantilever or the beam (bridge) are now investigated briefly.

It was already mentioned in the introduction to this chapter that long-span structures cannot be designed any more like any other building type because of their vulnerability to failure.

The larger scale may require unique building configurations quite different from traditional forms as well as other materials and nonconventional detailing techniques. It requires a more precise evaluation of loading conditions than just provided by codes, this includes the placement of expansion joints as well as the inclusion of secondary stresses due to the deformations of the members and their interaction, which cannot be ignored any more as for small-scale buildings or structures of high redundancy. Further, it requires a much more comprehensive field inspection to control the quality during the erection phase; post-construction building maintenance and periodic inspection is necessary to monitor the effects of loading and weather on member behavior in addition to the potential deterioration of the materials.

One may conclude that the potential consequences of failure to a large number of people makes it mandatory that special care be taken in the design of long-span structures. It must be realized that the linear increase of dimensions does not result merely in the linear increase of building form and in the corresponding methods of construction, but that the larger scale generates new, complex design determinants!

## Cantilever Structures

Some typical examples of buildings using the cantilever principle are shown in Fig. 4.73. These cases demonstrate that the concept is not only found on the smaller scale of overhanging eaves and cantilevered balconies, but also on the medium scale to support buildings because of unfavorable site conditions [(c), (e)], as well as on the large scale for roofs of stadiums and hangars because of functional necessity.

Frank Lloyd Wright considered the building as an integral part of nature, as an organism. He perceived the cantilever projecting out from the central building core as being similar to the branches of a tree. The continuity of the horizontal planes, so convincingly expressed in his Prairie architecture [e.g., Robie House (a)] made it possible to balance opposite loads in a natural manner. These overhanging horizontal surfaces generate an openness and lightness; they somehow allow the inner space to move outward. The integration of structure and space, or architecture and engineering, is most perfectly expressed in Wright's famous house "Fallingwater" (f). Here the cantilevered concrete slabs projecting over the waterfall seem to be part of nature; they seem to grow out of the earth.

In general, house construction on steep hills is not economical; it may require extensive site corrections (excavations, grading, retaining walls, etc.), and possibly impair the stability of the site. Often, however, the cantilever principle provides an efficient solution. In case (c) the cross-shaped cantilevering building rests on four central columns with inclined arms, while in case (e) each of the parallel double cantilever plywood box beams sits on the main central concrete foundation with a pipe column at the uphill side resisting unequal loading.

In case (j), each of the cantilevering masses is supported by its side walls, which in turn act as vertical cantilevers with respect to gravity action. The continuous wall-roof space truss envelope of case (k) is only edge supported at three locations; it allows a column-free interior space and flexibility in the placement of openings and large overhangs.

The single- or double-cantilevered roofs for the airline hangars eliminate supports, thus resulting in an unobstructed floor area necessary for the service of the airliners. Similar are the roofs of grandstand structures, where the column-free cantilever system is an apparent solution. In case (g) the thin shell sawtooth, hyperbolic paraboloid roof spans between the cantilevering frames, while in case (d) the cantilevering roof girders are supported from above by steel pipes in tension.

### Hangars (Fig. 4.74)

Currently, the cantilever type of construction is frequently used for large scale hangars. The structural concept permits maximum flexibility of operation since the interior space is free of any obstructions and since most of the columns along the perimeter are eliminated so as to provide the necessary freedom for movement. The facade doors are ground-supported on the base tracks while the runners at the roof spandrel give the lateral support; the free deflection of the cantilever roof must, obviously, be taken into account in the design of the sliding hangar doors.

Hangars are built as single- or double-cantilever systems. In the symmetrical double-cantilever design the dead load balances, which is not the case for a single-cantilever structure, where extensive anchorage must be provided to take care of the overturning moment. The central spine for double-cantilevers contains the shops, stores, office facilities, and so on; it supports the roof and acts as counterweight for any asymmetrical loading. Often,

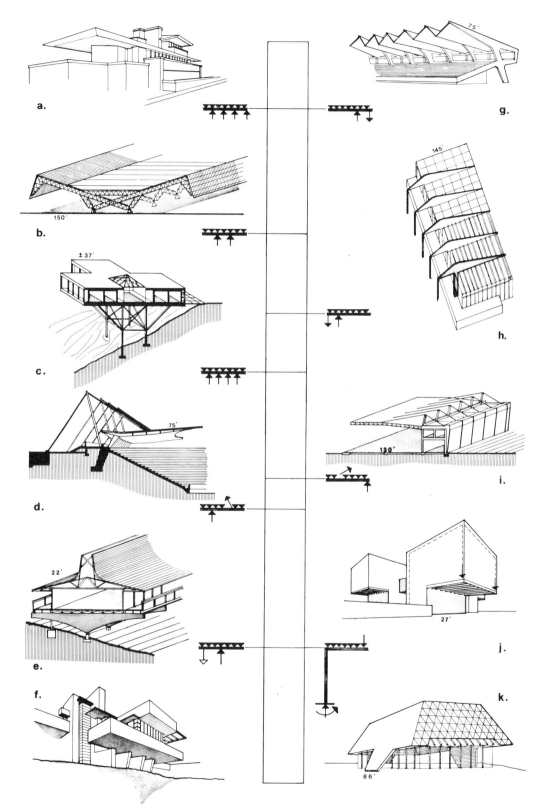

**Fig. 4.73** The cantilever in architecture.

the floors are suspended from the continuous roof structure, thereby relieving some of the stresses caused by the cantilever action.

The roof must not only resist the gravity and lateral loading, as well as effects due to temperature change, but also uplift pressure. Special care must be taken in suspended construction when the roof weight is less than the uplift forces, with the cables not being able to carry compression. This consideration is not a problem for pure cantilever beam structures; however, these systems require deep members resulting in much dead space.

There are basically two main groups for the typical cantilever systems shown in Fig. 4.74:

■ Pure cantilever structures, possibly prestressed, using as members (or roof skin) tapering trusses, girders, folded plates, and shells.
■ Cable-supported cantilevers supporting any of the members mentioned above.

In case (g), the cables support the corrugated shell roof near the outer edges and are anchored to deep concrete wall beams at the top of the central building portion. From these anchor walls are suspended the two floors below, thus causing the stresses due to the roof system to counteract. The corrugations give the thin-shell beam its necessary flexural rigidity.

The cantilevering steel girders spaced at 32.5 ft, of case (h), are pin-connected to the central steel frame core and supported by stayed cables at 50 ft from the outer edge. The roof was designed for 40 psf live load and 30 psf uplift pressure. A similar support principle is applied to the concrete structure of case (i), where curved cylindrical shell beams are employed.

The continuous welded plate girders of case (d) are spaced at 51.5 ft; they are pin-connected to the columns, which in turn are tied together and fixed to the ground. The form of the tapering columns corresponds to the moment variations under combined vertical and horizontal loading, similar to the tapering steel girders which change in depth from 14 to 5 ft at the perimeter.

The double-cantilever hangar of case (e) employs a nonprestressed folded plate concrete structure which is continuous over the central core portion.

The roof portion of case (a) forms nearly a semicircle in plan view. Its 52-ft deep radial cantilever steel trusses are anchored to the 11-story central circular core, which serves as counterweight to the huge projecting roof wings. Under hurricane conditions the hangar doors act as tie-down for the uplift forces.

Other examples of continuous double-cantilever trusses are given in cases (b) and (c). The trusses increase in depth from the perimeter to the inner column supports following the magnitude of the moment flow.

The folded plate roof of case (f) cantilevers the enormous distance of 230 ft, on each side, from the 100-ft wide central steel trussed core. It consists of flat corrugated steel decking twisted into hyperbolic paraboloid shapes and welded to the restraining rigid edge members along the valleys and ridges. The warped light-gauge metal acts as a shear membrane similar to the web of an I-beam, though keeping in mind that shell behavior is quite different from beam behavior; the unique geometry of the hyperbolic paraboloid (hypar) carries primarily the loads in pure shear action within its surface resulting in a much stronger and stiffer system. Furthermore, about 20% of the loads are resisted by prestressed cables running from the ridge at the core to various points of support along the valley members. The typical folded hypar module is of triangular cross-section that

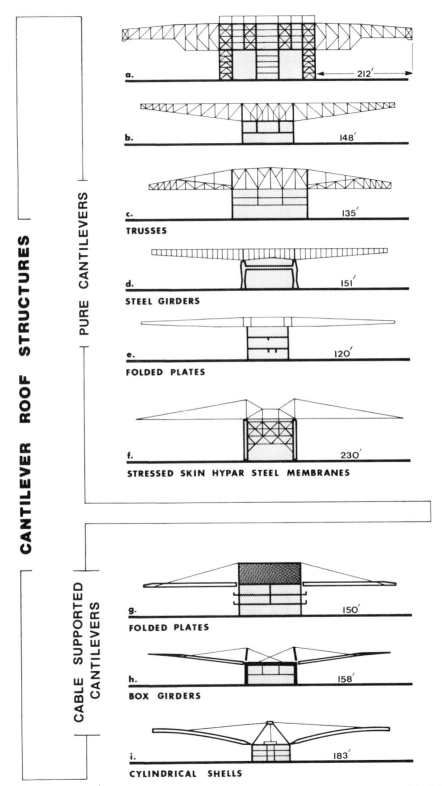

**CANTILEVER ROOF STRUCTURES**

**PURE CANTILEVERS**

a.                                   212′

b.                                   148′

c.          135′

**TRUSSES**

d.          151′

**STEEL GIRDERS**

e.          120′

**FOLDED PLATES**

f.          230′

**STRESSED SKIN HYPAR STEEL MEMBRANES**

**CABLE SUPPORTED CANTILEVERS**

g.          150′

**FOLDED PLATES**

h.          158′

**BOX GIRDERS**

i.          183′

**CYLINDRICAL SHELLS**

Fig. 4.74

tapers from a depth of 40–4 ft. This stressed-skin membrane type of construction yields a weight of about 17 psf, resulting in a saving of 40% over conventional truss systems.

### Grandstands

Grandstand structures must provide the necessary support for the roof and the seating, as well as the access and exit passages. The required unobstructed view makes the cantilever system an apparant solution. As open structures they are not just vulnerable to the static loading of downward gravity and upward wind pressure, but also to temperature changes and to the dynamic loading of wind gusting. For cable-stayed roofs the tensile forces must be anchored within the supporting structure, and the downward roof weight may have to be larger than the potential upward wind pressure. Some typical grandstand cantilever structures are shown in Fig. 4.75.

The cantilevering radial concrete ribs of the inverted L-shape for the Parc des Princes Stadium in Paris (c) are fixed to the ground and span the striking maximum distance of 150 ft; the stands and other facilities underneath are structurally independent. The columns of these bents are of variable parabolic profile arched outward and they are of a varying triangular cross-section. The entire bent rib is composed of precast segments epoxy-glued and post-tensioned together as based on the Freyssinet system.

The Olympic Stadium in Montreal (a) is derived from similar structural and construction principles. The difference lies in the larger scale, the heavier loads due to the wider spacing of the radial bents, and the rear cantilever with its hanging ramps that provide the counter ballast to the roof rotation. The precast ribs support the spectator seating as well as the roof steel beams with the metal deck. As in Paris, the two-story compression ring at the top which contains the lighting, sound, heating, and ventilation equipment, is not used as a lateral support for the cantilevering ribs; the large temperature differences in Montreal would have caused excessive stresses due to the continuity between the ring and cantilever arches. The ring, which eventually will support a retractable fabric roof, causes a point load of as high as 150 $t$ at the ends of the cantilevers.

Nervi planned the roof geometry for the Florence Stadium in Italy (e) so that the resultant of all the roof loads would fall between the primary support columns and thus not cause any tension in the rear columns, thereby eliminating costly foundation anchorages. Should the weight of the cantilevered roof portion be larger than the one of the back portion, then the rear support will be in tension causing the inner support to resist the entire weight and the tie load, thus requiring extensive, massive piers.

Also for the Flaminio Stadium in Rome (d), Nervi selected the dimensions of the cantilevering folded plate roof, tapered front to back, as well as the location and inclination of the concrete-filled steel pipe columns, such that the roof loads did not increase the stresses in the overhanging portion of the grandstand frame much.

Giant bent steel frames are formed by the cantilevering roof and the upper seating deck of cases (g) and (h); they are supported by the building below.

### Beam Buildings

Considering an entire building to span between vertical cores, thus behaving as a gigantic beam, immediately brings to one's mind the urban megastructures proposed by the futurists of the 1960s. Architectural groups such as the Metabolists and Archigram, or designers

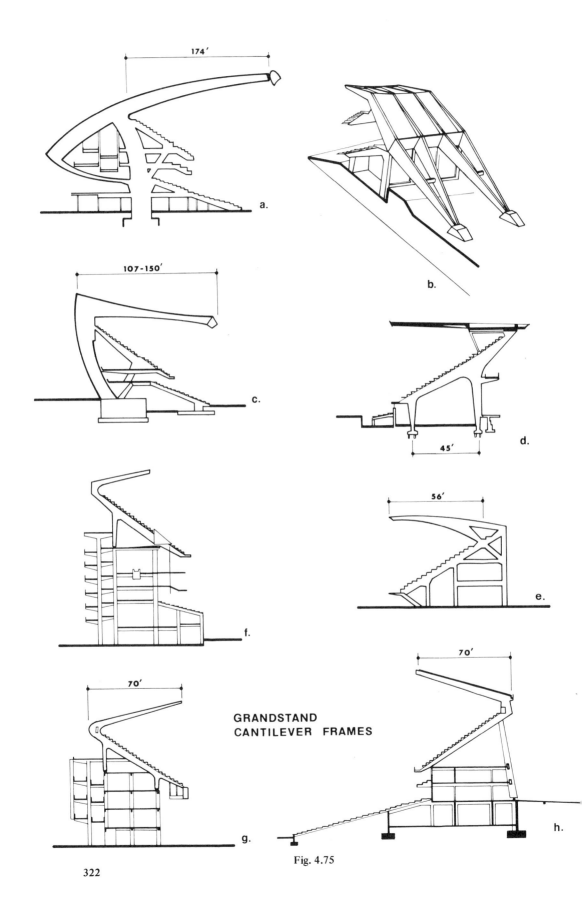

174'

a.

b.

107-150'

c.

45'

d.

e.

56'

f.

GRANDSTAND
CANTILEVER FRAMES

70'

g.

70'

h.

Fig. 4.75

322

such as Yona Friedman, E. Schulze-Fielitz, and Paolo Soleri, just to name a few, employed the principle of bridge building for the design of their multilayer cities. Some of their design concepts can be found, on a smaller scale, in the offshore oil-drilling towns and the interstitial systems in the hospital design.

The idea of using the bridge not only for traffic but also for buildings is not new. The Old London Bridge (1209, demolished in the nineteenth century) and the Ponte Vecchio (1340) in Florence are famous examples, where shops, housing, etc. were/are an integral part of the bridge. Present technology makes it possible that a bridge need not support the building, but, instead, that one beam building constitutes the bridge.

Bridge-type buildings are not necessarily only part of a macro scale, they may only house a restaurant or a corridor for pedestrian movement. Again, there is no limit set to the application of the concept.

There may be many reasons for designing a building or a portion of a building as a beam structure, such as:

- To preserve special site conditions, such as existing buildings, or to leave the terrain below undisturbed
- To allow space for other activities such as plazas, exhibition spaces, roads, railways, etc.
- To link other buildings or to bridge valleys and rivers
- Marine structures

The necessity for the bridge-type building may be due to intensive use of land because of high real estate costs, or because of the specific location, or the desire for a view and open spaces.

Beam buildings may be of various forms ranging from platforms to linear tubular forms. The major structural elements may be wall beams, trusses, girders, frames (Vierendeel trusses), monocoque shells, or any other structural systems. The beam buildings may be one- or multistory systems; they may be supported by a single core or many cores that may be arranged in many different ways; they may be continuous beams, cantilever beams, tree units, or simply supported individual beams. The supporting cores contain the vertical transportation and energy supply systems.

Some typical examples of beam buildings are shown in Fig. 4.76 and are discussed briefly below. The building in case (d) consists of two parallel facade frames, each being made up of two columns and 6-ft deep cantilevering floor and roof plate girders, which are tied together by the window mullions that serve as struts to equalize deflections between floor and roof level. The steel girders, in turn, carry the 90 ft trusses that are spaced 9 ft on center and support the concrete slabs. In case (a), the two huge cantilevering post-tensioned concrete box beams contain the corridors and support the roof and floor framing between them. The fenestration pattern in the box beam reflects the layout of the prestress cables. Two-story Vierendeel facade trusses that are laterally hinged to the columns support the floor and roof structures in case (c).

The bridge wing of the two-story building in (e) is carried by four parallel 16-ft deep steel trusses that span across the roadway and tie the adjacent buildings together. The building box (i) sits on only four trussed pylons. Its primary structure consists of four giant interior cantilevering trusses that support the outer facade trusses of the same 57-ft height. Three of the supporting towers contain the stairwells and the fourth one houses the elevator shaft. Soleri's organic, bone-like cantilevered bridge (g) has sculptural qualities; its depth and member density follow the intensity of the moment flow.

# Beam
# Buildings

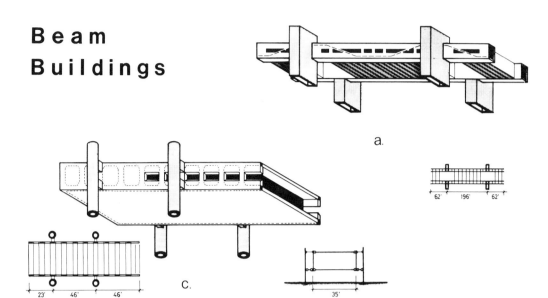

a.

c.

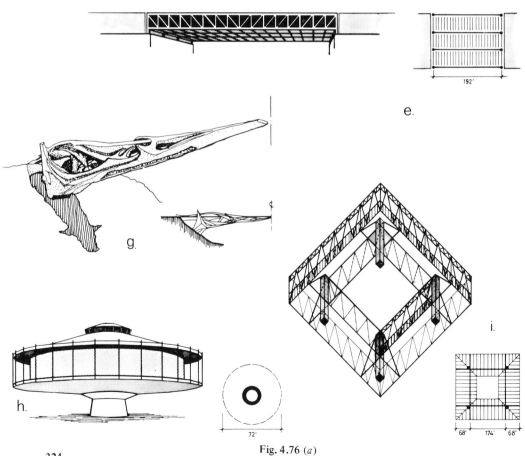

e.

g.

h.

i.

Fig. 4.76 (*a*)

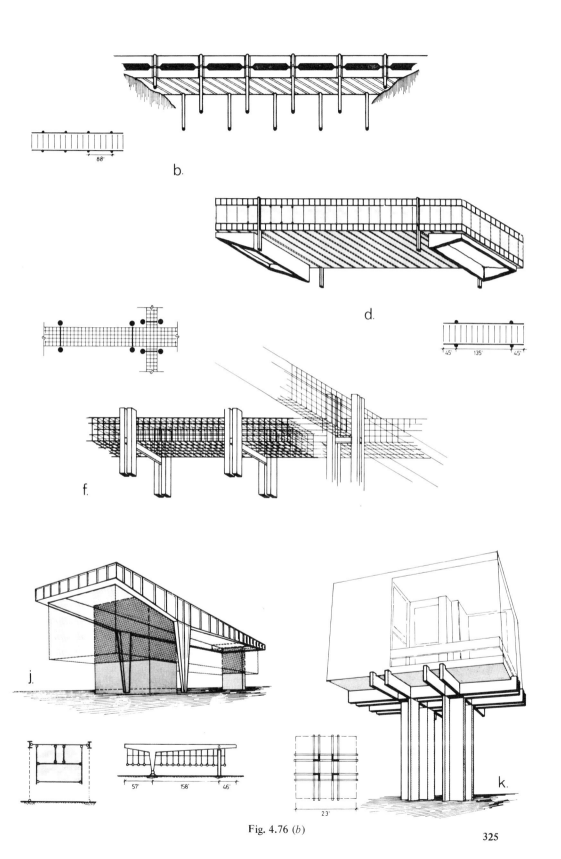

b.

d.

f.

j.

k.

Fig. 4.76 (b)

The circular, tree-like house of case (h) sits on a central concrete pedestal and revolves. While its cantilever action is achieved by hanging the floor framing from the radially arranged roof trusses, the building box in (k) sits on cantilevering frames. The two-story building in case (j) is hung from two huge cantilevering steel plate girder frames.

# 5 SPACE FRAMES

## 5.1 INTRODUCTION

Most buildings consist of cubical spaces, where the structure can be treated as an assemblage of planar systems. The horizontal floor planes are supported by the vertical wall planes; only forces parallel to the vertical planes can be transferred from the floor structure, if the planes are hinged to each other (Fig. 5.1a). However, should the vertical structure be inclined, then it also can carry forces parallel to the floor framing (Fig. 5.1b). In general, where hinged planes or spatial units are framing into each other at an angle not equal to 90°, the structure must be treated as a whole from a three-dimensional point of view.

The transformation of two-dimensional thinking in structural design to the spatial treatment of force flow is now possible due to rapidly advancing computer technology; computers can be programmed to deal with the complex interaction of physical phenomena. Similar to planar trusses, space frames are considered to be hinged, so that their members resist only axial forces and no moments are transferred across the joints. The loads are assumed to act directly at the hinges, and the member weight and truss deformation are considered negligible.

Space frames can be subdivided into single-layer and multilayer systems. Single-layer space trusses are of the envelope type, in other words three-dimensional surface structures. Like thin shells, they are axial systems that have no bending capacity normal to their latticed surface, and only the individual grid members spanning from joint to joint can behave as beams. Single-layer space frames obtain their strength through spatial geometry (i.e., their profile) by being either folded or bent. They may be organized according to the shape of their surfaces, which is discussed in the section introducing bent surfaces; or they may be organized as based on the pattern formed by the member network, which is further treated under the various shell topics. These bar grids may be acting independently or in composite action together with the skin. In this chapter, only the special, envelope-type structures of polyhedral, dome-like surface systems are briefly discussed (Fig. 5.2).

Multilayer space frames are generated by adding spatial, polyhedral units to form new three-dimensional building blocks. In contrast to single-layer systems, the multilayer structure has bending stiffness and does not need curvature; therefore, it can behave as a

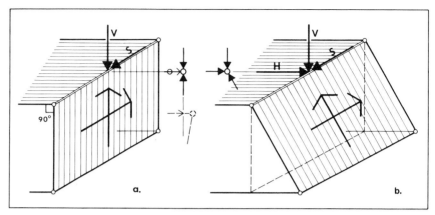

**Fig. 5.1**

plate. A familiar example of this is the flat space frame roof, where depth is a determinant of strength. It should be kept in mind that stability considerations may require a single-layer dome to become a double-layer system, as Buckminster Fuller did for some of his geodesic domes, where profile together with surface depth provide the strength and stiffness.

The source of space frame structures can be found on both the micro and macro scale in the organic and inorganic world around us, where the physical order is reflected in visible geometry. Nature is full of examples showing the principles of surface grids and spatial packing characteristics. The hexagonal prisms of the honeycomb, the cell structures of plant organisms, the porous structure of a sponge skeleton, and the uniform, repetitive order of crystals, just to name a few, all exemplify the packing of spatial units. The architecture of crystals such as the beautiful structures of snowflakes or the internal arrangement of the atoms which determine the external visible crystalline shapes are examples of that spatial geometrical order typical of space frame construction. Nature forms its structures over time thus allowing them to respond with a minimum of effort; hence, through principles of economy, nature can achieve an optimal strength in a light-weight skeletal structure. It is apparent that the designer should study the geometry in nature and learn, for instance, from the structural patterns in a leaf, where the network of veins branch out from the stem and interconnect the entire surface, or from the microscopically small grid surfaces of the radiolaria with their extremely delicate skeletal cell walls (see Fig. 7.1).

The concept of spatial construction has evolved out of the various framing systems for huts or houses of the nomadic tribes and agricultural societies; it has evolved out of planar truss construction. The medieval timber framing for walls and especially for steeply pitched church roofs was developed to a high degree of sophistication in their truss-like structural systems. Palladio, in 1570, was probably the first designer to actually build truly triangulated beam trusses for a bridge. The high point of truss design, from a geometrical point of view, was reached in the nineteenth century. The truss was not only imaginatively applied in bridge design, but also in architecture as support for roofs for functional spaces such as railway stations, exhibition halls, warehouses, winter gardens, and market halls. The trussed gable frames for the Galeries des Machines for the 1889 Paris Exhibition reached an unbelievable span of 375 ft, thereby setting up a new dimension for column-free, long-span enclosure systems. Engineers with bold new design con-

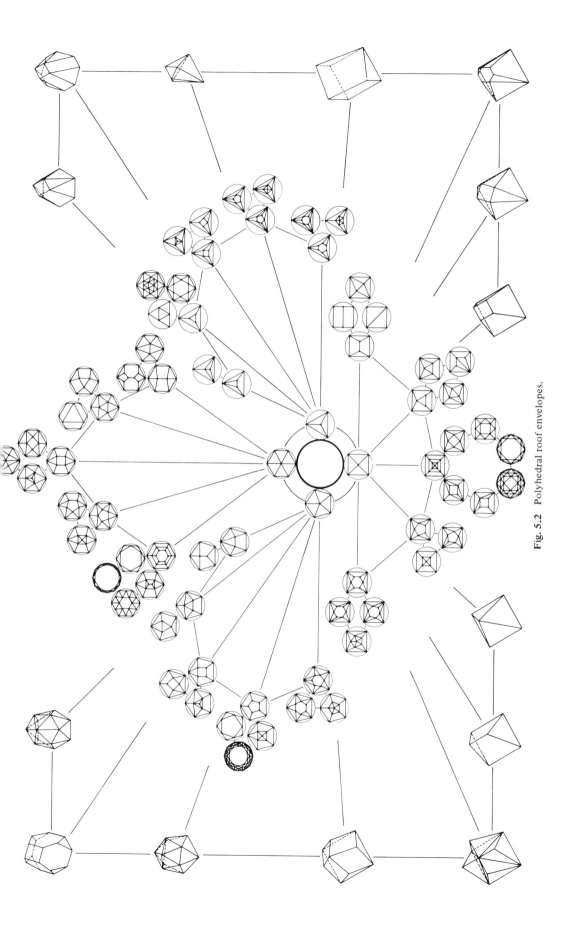

Fig. 5.2 Polyhedral roof envelopes.

cepts integrated the new materials of iron, glass, steel, and concrete with fabrication and construction considerations. Paxton's Crystal Palace (London, 1851) is often considered as a model. It established the independence of the frame by expressing the extreme lightness of the skeleton, thereby opening the new architectural dimension of antigravity. The geometrical layout of the building clearly reflects the repetitive use of standardized elements identifying the new concepts of prefabrication and mass production. These considerations of lightness, prefabrication, and repetitive member use are all basic design determinants of space frame construction.

The origin of space frames from a spatial or spiritual point of view may be traced back to classical Greece. Pythagorean and Platonic thinking interpreted the universe in terms of number and form of geometrical figures. Plato related the world of ideas to the material world, by proposing the five basic solids, the cube, the tetrahedron, the octahedron, the icosahedron, and the dodecahedron to correspond to earth, air, fire, water, and the cosmos. The Islamic geometric ornament evolved out of the interplay of Platonic figures and proportions and later influenced the geometric architecture of the Gothic period. The revival of Platonic thought in the Middle Ages resulted in a daring challenge to Euclidean geometry. The intricate ribbed vaulting of the late Gothic churches clearly predicts Nervi's hangars.

The development of the space frame is also related to dome construction. From the structure of the radially ribbed masonry domes of the Renaissance, developed a more elaborate expression of geometry and structure in the Baroque period. As in the Gothic epoch, Guarini expressed the skeleton construction in the intricate, intersecting arches that form the dome and lantern support of S. Lorenzo at Turin, Italy (1687). The development of concrete and steel in the nineteenth century allowed framed dome structures of much less weight and much larger spans to replace the traditional timber trusses and solid masonry vaulting. To the early forms of only radial ribs were added horizontal rings to tie the arches together; with advances in material and fabricating technology and methods of analysis, the dome slowly developed into a latticed shell structure. In 1863, J. W. Schwedler built in Berlin the first braced dome, and the structural system became known as the Schwedler dome (see Fig. 8.20). Other modified systems like the Zimmerman and cyclic network domes followed.

As mentioned previously, multilayer space frames evolved directly out of the planar trusses of the nineteenth century. The Eiffel Tower in Paris (1889) and the Forth Railway Bridge near Edinburgh (1890) are both famous examples indicating the trend towards spatial truss construction. In 1881, Föppl published his treatise on space frames, which was the basis for Gustave Eiffel's analysis of the tower. Often, Alexander Graham Bell, for his work around the turn of the century, is credited as the inventor of the space frame. He was preoccupied with tetrahedral forms to obtain strength with a minimum of material weight. His space frames were composed of tetrahedra and octahedra, and were used in his man-carrying kites and in an observation tower. Buckminster Fuller entered the limelight in the 1920s with his inventions of the first tensegrity structure (1927) and the Dymaxion House (1928). Max Mengeringhausen built his first space frame structure in Berlin in 1940 using his famous Mero joint, while in North America the idea of mass production of space frame structures was initiated in the early 1950s by A. E. Fentiman in Canada with his Triodetic system and by C. W. Attwood in the United States with the Unistrut system. Other engineers and architects who were important early contributors to the development of space trusses shortly after World War II, were Du Chateau, Friedman, Emmerich, Lederer, Le Ricolais, Makowski, Schulze-Fielitz, and Wachsmann, just to name some of the pioneers.

## 5.2 SIMPLE ENVELOPE SPACE FRAMES

Typical polyhedral buildings or roof units are shown in Fig. 5.2. The various forms are generated by transformation and trial and error. From the four basic pyramids at the center of the drawing with different regular, polygonal bases, the wealth of shapes is derived using rational processes such as translation, rotation, truncation, and member placement, and being intuitive about the selection of the shapes.

Some typical examples of architectural buildings are presented in Fig. 5.3. These cases clearly express the richness of the various spatial framing systems.

### Introduction to Space Statics

A typical Force $F$ can be resolved into $F_x$, $F_y$, and $F_z$ components as is shown in Fig. 5.4a. These force components form a box in which the diagonal is equal to the force resultant. Visualize these force components to be carried by simple axial members of length $x$, $y$, and $z$, as indicated by the smaller box contained in the larger one. Since the members act only axially, the magnitude of the forces must be proportional to their respective member length

$$\frac{F_y}{y} = \frac{F_x}{x} = \frac{F_z}{z} = \frac{F}{L} \tag{5.1}$$

or

$$F_y = F\frac{y}{L} = F_x\frac{y}{x} = F_z\frac{y}{z} \tag{5.2}$$

A similar relationship can be set up for the other force components.

The resultant force $F_{xy}$ of the forces $F_x$ and $F_y$ according to the Pythagorean theorem is equal to

$$F_{xy}^2 = F_y^2 + F_x^2 \tag{a}$$

The final resultant, in turn, is obtained by substituting Eq. (a)

$$F^2 = F_{xy}^2 + F_z^2 = F_x^2 + F_y^2 + F_z^2$$
$$F = \sqrt{F_x^2 + F_y^2 + F_z^2} \tag{5.3}$$

A similar relationship can be established between the member lengths

$$L^2 = x^2 + y^2 + z^2$$
$$L = \sqrt{x^2 + y^2 + z^2} \tag{5.4}$$

For the special case, where the spatial force system is concurrent (Fig. 5.4b), the forces at the point of concurrency must be in translational equilibrium. The sum of the $x$, $y$, and $z$ components of all the forces must be zero

$$\Sigma F_x = 0 \qquad \Sigma F_y = 0 \qquad \Sigma F_z = 0 \tag{5.5}$$

For this condition only three independent equations may be written, though the force equations can be replaced by moment equations. Only three unknowns should be present at the concurrent joint, since otherwise the solution is indeterminate.

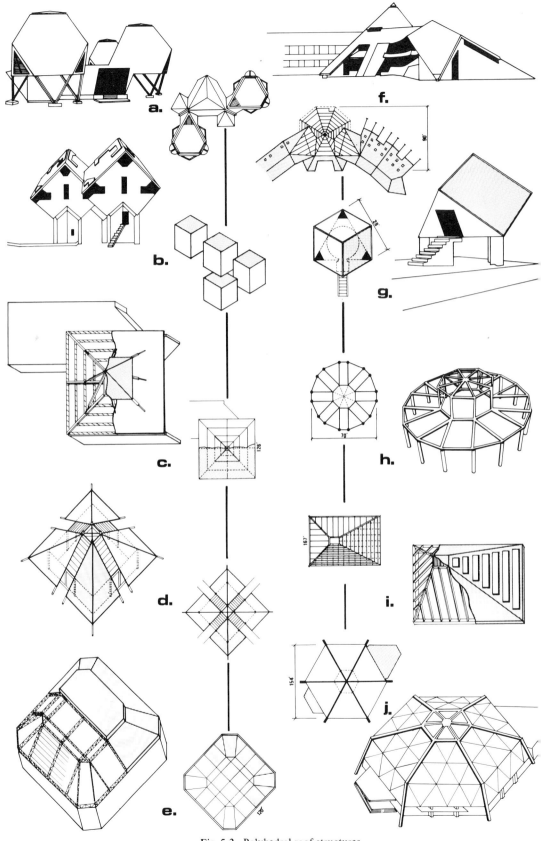

**a.**

**b.**

**c.**

**d.**

**e.**

**f.**

**g.**

**h.**

**i.**

**j.**

Fig. 5.3 Polyhedral roof structures.

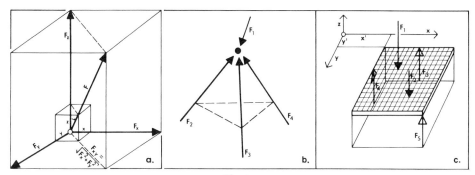

**Fig. 5.4**

For the special case, where the spatial force system consists only of parallel forces, such as the gravity loads acting on the roof supported by three vertical columns (Fig. 5.4c), the forces must be in translational and rotational equilibrium. The moments are taken about axes rather than about points as in planar systems. If, however, the spatial system is considered as consisting of side, front, and plan views, then the axes of rotation become points of rotation again. For the case shown, the forces can be solved by using following equations of equilibrium:

$$\Sigma F_z = 0 \qquad \Sigma M_x = 0 \qquad \Sigma M_y = 0 \qquad (5.6)$$

Obviously, these basic equations can be replaced by other equations of equilibrium, since rotation must be zero about any point in space.

$$\Sigma F_z = 0 \qquad \Sigma M_y = 0 \qquad \Sigma M_{y'} = 0$$

or

$$\Sigma F_z = 0 \qquad \Sigma M_x = 0 \qquad \Sigma M_{x'} = 0$$

or

$$\Sigma M_x = 0 \qquad \Sigma M_{x'} = 0 \qquad \Sigma M_y = 0$$

and so on.

Only three independent equations of equilibrium are available and necessary for a solution, as is apparent from Eq. (5.6), hence only three unknowns should be present for the structure to be determinate. Should, for instance, the roof be supported by four columns and the gravity loads not be arranged in a symmetrical manner, then the structure is indeterminate.

In general, when spatial force systems are neither concurrent nor parallel, the translational and rotational equilibrium along and about each axis, respectively, yields the following six independent equations necessary for solution

$$\Sigma F_x = 0 \qquad \Sigma F_y = 0 \qquad \Sigma F_z = 0$$
$$\Sigma M_x = 0 \qquad \Sigma M_y = 0 \qquad \Sigma M_z = 0 \qquad (5.7)$$

Note not more than six unknown forces should be present to have a determinate structure. Any of the force equations can be replaced by additional moment equations. The proper selection of the axes of rotation may save a great deal of calculation.

Examples of nonparallel, nonconcurrent force systems are shown in Fig. 5.5d–i, where

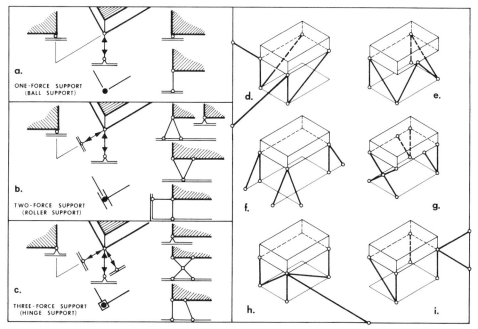

Fig. 5.5

a rigid building or roof is supported by a group of six columns ($r = 6$), each carrying only axial forces. Different support arrangements are given to establish stability under any type of load action. Rather than drawing a three-dimensional view of the structure to be investigated, it may sometimes be more convenient to take planar views from front, side, and top, by treating the spatial structure as a series of interacting planar systems. Forces are projected onto the planes and the ones normal to the planes which cannot produce reactions perpendicular to their line of action, are not shown. Now the force components in each plane can be treated in the familiar manner, remembering that the proper number of force components should be in each plane and that they should be arranged so they are neither parallel nor concurrent. In Problem 5.2 the cases in Fig. 5.5d–i are further investigated and the location of any members are corrected if their arrangement should not provide the necessary resistance.

In the discussion of concurrent force systems it was shown that at least three equations or three forces, that is, a minimum of three members $m$, not lying in the same plane, are necessary to prevent a point $P$ from moving in any direction under load action. This basic stable, three-dimensional structure is a tripod (Fig. 5.6a); space frames can be formed by simply adding tripods to one another. One may conclude that for each joint $j$ there must be at least three members $m$, not lying in the same plane, for a simple truss to be internally stable; more members result in redundancy while less than three members yield instability.

$$m = 3j \quad \text{determinate} \tag{b}$$

$$m < 3j \quad \text{unstable}$$

$$m > 3j \quad \text{indeterminate}$$

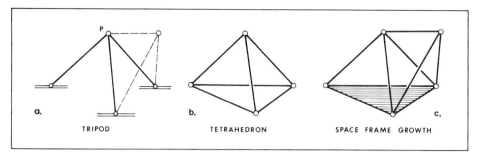

Fig. 5.6

Furthermore, it was shown that for nonconcurrent, nonparallel spatial force systems six independent equations of equilibrium are available. One may conclude for a space frame to be externally stable, at least six independent reaction components, properly arranged, must exist. Hence, for a structure to be externally stable and determinate the number of reactive conditions must be

$$r = 6 \qquad\qquad (c)$$

The reaction components can be visualized as equivalent to members. Then the total number of members, considering the space truss externally and internally, can be derived from Eqs. (b) and (c) as

$$m + r = 3j$$

or

$$m = 3j - r = 3j - 6 \qquad\qquad (5.8)$$

The same conclusion can also be found by studying the growth of a space truss as derived from its base unit, the tetrahedron (Fig. 5.6b). It is obtained by simply adding tripods resulting in a stable, self-contained unit with four joints and six members. The tetrahedron is the most fundamental, stable, spatial unit, similar to the triangle for planar structures. Its multidimensional stability and independence can easily be checked by squeezing a model of the structure between one's hands. The three base members in the tetrahedron can be visualized as equivalent to the external thrust reactions of the tripod. A space truss of $j$ joints can be formed by adding to the original six members of the tetrahedron with four joints, three members for each of the remaining $(j - 4)$ joints

$$m = 6 + 3(j - 4) = 3j - 6$$

It was shown before that the term $3j$ in the equation represents the internal stability, while the term 6 is equal to the necessary reaction conditions for external stability. The equation can be rewritten by letting $r = 6$, as was already derived

$$m + r = 3j \quad\text{determinate}$$

$$m + r < 3j \quad\text{unstable} \qquad\qquad (5.9)$$

$$m + r > 3j \quad\text{indeterminate}$$

In general, it is necessary that the total number of members and reaction components is equal to three times the number of joints so that the structure is externally and internally determinate and the forces can be found by statics. Though this condition is necessary, it is not sufficient, as was already discussed in relation to planar trusses; the members must be properly arranged. A more precise treatment of the spatial stability of compound and complex space trusses is beyond the scope of this work.

Some building or roof forms are shown in Fig. 5.7. It is quite apparent that the hinged cube can only be stable, if each of its rectangular faces is stabilized by a diagonal, while polyhedras with triangular faces such as the tetrahedron, octahedron, and icosahedron are self-contained stable units. Keep in mind that instability of the building unit does not necessarily mean that the whole structure is unstable, as additional external reaction components may correct this situation.

In the discussion of external supports only columns have been considered. A more general treatment of support organization is according to the number of translational forces, which can be transmitted from one structural system to another one (Fig. 5.5a–c):

- One-Force support: such as a single column or a spherical ball, which can only transfer forces perpendicular to the plane upon which it is sitting.
- Two-Force support: such as a two-member column support or a roller which cannot transfer forces in the direction it is allowed to roll.
- Three-Force support: such as a pin or ball-socket or a three-member support with the members not in the same plane.

Following are some simple polyhedral roof forms investigated mathematically. Framed domes (see Fig. 8.18) are not studied further here, because of the complexity of analysis necessary to solve for the member forces. Some of the braced domes may be treated as membranes as is discussed in the section on dome shells.

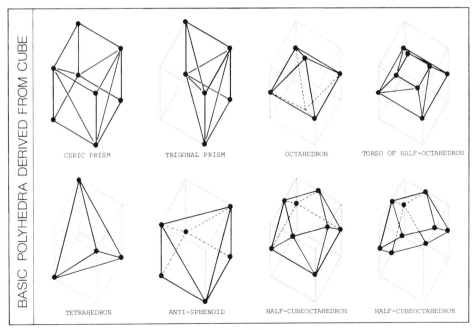

Fig. 5.7

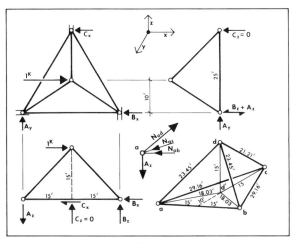

**Fig. 5.8**

**Example 5.1**  For a roof structure with the shape of a hinged tetrahedron with its geome-try identified in the isometric view of Fig. 5.8, the reactions and bar forces are found as caused by a lateral unit load.

First, the stability and determinacy of the structure is investigated. At each support, rollers are provided having an equivalent two-member force resistance (Fig. 5.5 b)

$$r = 3(2) = 6$$

One may conclude that the roof is externally stable and statically determinate because of the six reaction components, which are neither parallel nor concurrent in any of the three planes of plan, side, and front elevations.

Investigating the roof as a whole, externally and internally, the number of bars for the four joints should be at least equal to

$$m = 3j - 6 \tag{5.8}$$

$$= 3(4) - 6$$

$$6 = 6$$

Since the actual number of bars is also equal to six and since the members are properly arranged, the space truss is stable and statically determinate and can be further analyzed here.

The reaction forces are found by using the principles of statics. The vertical compon-ents are derived from the

side elevation: $\quad \Sigma M_{ab} = 0 = C_z (25) \qquad\qquad C_z = 0$

front elevation: $\quad \Sigma M_b = 0 = A_z (30) - 1(15) \qquad A_z = 0.5 \text{ k [tension (T)]}$

$\qquad\qquad\quad \Sigma F_z = 0 = 0.5 - B_z \qquad\qquad B_z = 0.5 \text{ k [compression (C)]}$

The horizontal reaction components are derived from the plan view of Fig. 5.8 as

$$\Sigma M_a = 0 = 1(10) - C_x(25) \qquad C_x = 0.4 \text{ k}$$

$$\Sigma F_x = 0 = 1 - 0.4 - B_x \qquad B_x = 0.6 \text{ k}$$

$$\Sigma F_y = 0 = A_y \qquad\qquad\qquad A_y = 0$$

The axial member forces can readily be solved by the method of joints. It was shown that the force components are proportional to their projected member lengths [Eq. (5.4)]. Hence, first the bar lengths together with their projections must be computed

$$L_{ad'} = L_{bd'} = \sqrt{15^2 + 10^2} \qquad\qquad = 18.03 \text{ ft}$$

$$L_{ad} = L_{bd} = \sqrt{15^2 + 10^2 + 15^2} \qquad = 23.45 \text{ ft}$$

$$L_{ac} = L_{bc} = \sqrt{15^2 + 25^2} \qquad\qquad = 29.16 \text{ ft}$$

$$L_{cd} = \qquad\qquad \sqrt{15^2 + 15^2} = 15\sqrt{2} \quad = 21.21 \text{ ft}$$

Since at each joint only three unknown forces act and three equations of translational equilibrium are available, it does not make any difference at which joint to start the analysis of the bar forces

Joint $a$:  $\Sigma F_z = 0 = N_{ad} \dfrac{15}{23.45} - 0.5$ $\qquad\qquad\qquad N_{ad} = 0.78 \text{ k (T)}$

$\qquad\qquad \Sigma F_y = 0 = 0.78 \dfrac{10}{23.45} - N_{ac} \dfrac{25}{29.16}$ $\qquad N_{ac} = 0.39 \text{ k (C)}$

$\qquad\qquad \Sigma F_x = 0 = 0.78 \dfrac{15}{23.45} - 0.39 \dfrac{15}{29.16} - N_{ab}$ $\qquad N_{ab} = 0.30 \text{ k (C)}$

Joint $c$:  $\Sigma F_z = 0 = N_{cd} \dfrac{15}{21.21} - 0$ $\qquad\qquad\qquad N_{cd} = 0$

$\qquad\qquad \Sigma F_y = 0 = 0.39 \dfrac{25}{29.16} - N_{cb} \dfrac{25}{29.16}$ $\qquad N_{cb} = 0.39 \text{ k (T)}$

$\qquad\qquad \Sigma F_x = 0 = 2 \dfrac{0.39}{29.16} 15 - 0.4$ $\qquad\qquad\qquad \text{O.K.}$

Joint $d$:  $\Sigma F_z = 0 = 0.78 \dfrac{15}{23.45} - N_{dc} \dfrac{15}{23.45}$ $\qquad N_{dc} = 0.78 \text{ k (C)}$

$\qquad\qquad \Sigma F_x = 0 = 2 \dfrac{0.78}{23.45} 15 - 1$ $\qquad\qquad\qquad \text{O.K.}$

Joint $b$:  $\Sigma F_x = 0 = 0.6 - 0.3 - 0.78 \dfrac{15}{23.45} + 0.39 \dfrac{15}{29.16}$ $\qquad \text{O.K.}$

**Example 5.2**  For the hinged, four-sided pyramid (Fig. 5.9) reactions and bar forces are found as caused by a vertical unit load.

There are two reactive force components at supports $a$, $b$, and $d$, and one at $c$. Hence, the total number of unknown external forces is seven, but only six equations of equilibrium are available

$$r = 3(2) + 1 = 7 > 6$$

The structure is once indeterminate externally!

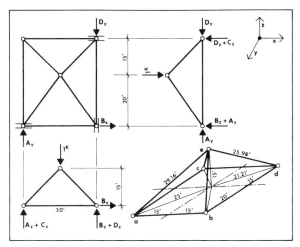

Fig. 5.9

Checking the truss as a whole for five joints with eight members and seven equivalent reaction members, yields

$$m + r = 3j \tag{5.9}$$

$$8 + 7 = 3(5)$$

$$15 = 15$$

The structure as a whole is determinate. Although the pyramid as a self-contained unit is unstable, the additional member it needs is provided by the extra external reaction. Because the structure is externally indeterminate, the reaction components cannot all be solved directly, but only in conjunction with the bar forces.

In this specific case, due to symmetry of geometry about the $y$ axis and due to the type of loading, the support forces can be obtained directly. The following vertical reactions must be equal to each other

$$A_z = B_z \qquad C_z = D_z$$

From the side elevation the vertical force components can now be computed

$$\Sigma M_{dc} = 0 = 1(15) - (B_z + A_z)35$$

$$A_z + B_z = 0.43 \text{ k} \qquad A_z = B_z \qquad A_z = B_z = \frac{0.43}{2}$$

$$\Sigma F_z = 0 = (D_z + C_z) + 0.43 - 1$$

$$D_z + C_z = 0.57 \text{ k} \qquad C_z = D_z \qquad D_z = C_z = \frac{0.57}{2}$$

From the plan view the $y$ and $x$ force components can be found

$$\Sigma F_x = 0 = B_x \qquad B_x = 0$$

$$\Sigma M_a = 0 = D_y(30) \qquad D_y = 0$$

$$\Sigma F_y = 0 = A_y \qquad A_y = 0$$

First, the lengths of the diagonal members are found so that the bar forces can then be computed

$$L_{ae} = L_{be} = \sqrt{15^2 + 20^2 + 15^2} \qquad = 29.16 \text{ ft}$$

$$L_{ce} = L_{de} = \sqrt{15^2 + 15^2 + 15^2} = 15\sqrt{3} = 25.98 \text{ ft}$$

For this case, the bar forces at any joint can be determined. Starting at support 'a' and using the method of joints, yields

$$\Sigma F_z = 0 = N_{ae} \frac{15}{29.16} - \frac{0.43}{2} \qquad N_{ae} = 0.42 \text{ k} \quad (C)$$

because of symmetry: $\qquad\qquad N_{ae} = N_{be}$

$$\Sigma F_x = 0 = 0.42 \frac{15}{29.16} - N_{ab} \qquad N_{ab} = 0.22 \text{ k} \quad (T)$$

$$\Sigma F_y = 0 = 0.42 \frac{20}{29.16} - N_{ac} \qquad N_{ac} = 0.29 \text{ k} \quad (T)$$

because of symmetry: $\qquad\qquad N_{ac} = N_{bd}$

At support $c$, bar forces are computed as follows

$$\Sigma F_z = 0 = N_{ce} \frac{15}{25.98} - \frac{0.57}{2} \qquad N_{ce} = 0.50 \text{ k} \quad (C)$$

because of symmetry: $\qquad\qquad N_{ce} = N_{de}$

$$\Sigma F_x = 0 = 0.50 \frac{15}{25.98} - N_{cd} \qquad N_{cd} = 0.29 \text{ k} \quad (T)$$

$$\Sigma F_y = 0 = 0.50 \frac{15}{25.98} - 0.29 \qquad \text{O.K.}$$

The results are checked at joint $e$

$$\Sigma F_z = 0 = 1 - 2\left(0.42 \frac{15}{29.16} + 0.50 \frac{15}{25.98}\right) \qquad \text{O.K.}$$

In the following examples, complex space trusses are investigated briefly. Here more than three members are attached to a joint and the bar forces cannot be solved directly anymore with the three equations of equilibrium available for a concurrent force system. A determinate complex space frame can still be analyzed by setting up the three equations of statics for every joint and then by solving these equations simultaneously by computer.

There are some approaches which may make it still possible to solve complex space trusses directly under certain conditions:

- Conditions of symmetry of building geometry and loading yield additional information about reactions and member forces.
- Before starting any analysis, zero members should be identified. The elimination of bars for a given loading case reduces the number of members at a joint.

■ Sometimes it may be helpful to sum the forces at a joint normal to or within the inclined trussed planes by rotating the coordinate system so that the $x$–$y$ plane is now
the inclined trussed plane. For instance, for the case where one of the three bars at a
joint does not act in the plane defined by the two others, this bar must be zero, if no
external force is applied to the point of concurrency.

The special considerations, just identified, are applicable to any spatial truss system; they
may reduce the computations and make solutions easier to obtain.

**Example 5.3** The reactions and bar forces are found for the square, truncated pyramid
(Fig. 5.10) under symmetrical gravity load action at the crown joints.
    At each of the supports two reaction components are present.

$$r = 4(2) = 8 > 6$$

As can be seen, the structure is externally twice indeterminate. However, the space
truss as a whole with eight joints, sixteen members and eight equivalent reaction bars
is determinate

$$m + r = 3j \tag{5.9}$$

$$16 + 8 = 3(8)$$

$$24 = 24$$

In general, the bars should be determined first, since there are too many support forces
but not enough equations available. In this specific case, due to the axisymmetric conditions of the roof geometry and the symmetrical arrangement of the loads, it is apparent
that each of the vertical reactions carries an equal share of the total loading

$$A_z = B_z = D_z = C_z = 1 \text{ k}$$

Because of the absence of any rotation in the $y$–$x$ plane, one can conclude that all reaction
forces in this plane must be zero. The lateral thrust due to gravity is self-contained and
carried by the tension ring at the base of the roof

$$A_x = D_x = 0 \qquad C_y = B_y = 0$$

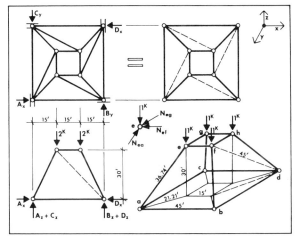

Fig. 5.10

For general loading conditions the solution of this structure is quite complicated, but for the given case causing no twisting, the funicular shape is defined by the edge members only (Fig. 5.10), so the diagonal members are not needed and equal to zero

$$N_{ag} = N_{be} = N_{df} = N_{ch} = 0$$

The lengths of the members are as follows:

$$L_{ae} = L_{bf} = L_{dh} = L_{cg} = \sqrt{15^2 + 15^2 + 30^2} = 36.74 \text{ ft}$$

$$L_{ag} = L_{be} = L_{df} = L_{ch} = \sqrt{15^2 + 30^2 + 30^2} = 45.00 \text{ ft}$$

Applying the method of joints, yields following member forces:

Joint e: $\quad \Sigma F_z = 0 = N_{ea} \dfrac{30}{36.74} - 1 \qquad\qquad N_{ea} = 1.23 \text{ k} \quad (C)$

because of symmetry: $\qquad\qquad N_{ea} = N_{fb} = N_{hd} = N_{gc} = 1.23 \text{ k} \quad (C)$

$\qquad \Sigma F_x = 0 = 1.23 \dfrac{15}{36.74} - N_{ef} \qquad N_{ef} = 0.5 \text{ k} \quad (C)$

because of symmetry: $\qquad\qquad N_{ef} = N_{fh} = N_{hg} = N_{ge} = 0.5 \text{ k} \quad (C)$

Joint a: $\quad \Sigma F_x = 0 = 1.23 \dfrac{15}{36.74} - N_{ab} \qquad N_{ab} = 0.5 \text{ k} \quad (T)$

because of symmetry: $\qquad\qquad N_{ab} = N_{bd} = N_{dc} = N_{ca} = 0.5 \text{ k} \quad (T)$

**Example 5.4**   The space frame roof (Fig. 5.11) consisting of a square base with a smaller square as top ring, which is rotated $45°$ with respect to the base ring, is investigated.

Again, there are eight reaction components. One at support $c$, three at $a$, and two each at both other supports

$$r = 1 + 3 + 2 + 2 = 8 > 6$$

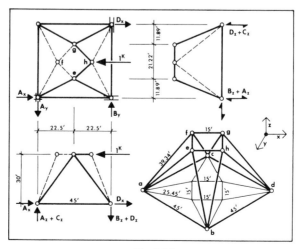

**Fig. 5.11**

Though the structure is externally twice indeterminate, the roof as a whole is determinate

$$m + r = 3j \tag{5.9}$$

$$16 + 8 = 3(8)$$

$$24 = 24$$

Also in this example, the reactions can be found directly from the symmetry of the roof geometry and the location of the load along the axis of symmetry

$$B_z = D_z \qquad A_z = C_z$$

The reactions can be determined, by first looking to the front elevation and then the plan view. For the front elevation (Fig. 5.11):

$$\Sigma M_{ac} = 0 = 1(30) - (B_z + D_z)45$$

$$B_z + D_z = 0.666 \text{ k} \qquad B_z = D_z = 0.33 \text{ k}$$

$$\Sigma F_z = 0 = (A_z + C_z) - (B_z + D_z)$$

$$A_z + C_z = 0.666 \text{ k} \qquad A_z = C_z = 0.33 \text{ k}$$

For the plan view (Fig. 5.11), because of symmetry,

$$A_x = D_x = \frac{1}{2} = 0.5 \text{ k}$$

Since there is no rotation, the forces in the $y$ direction must be zero

$$\Sigma M_a = 0 = 1(22.5) - 0.5(45) + B_y(45) \qquad B_y = 0$$

$$\Sigma F_y = 0 = A_y \qquad\qquad\qquad A_y = 0$$

The bar forces can now be derived by using the method of joints

Joint h:                                                $$\Sigma F_z = 0 = N_{hb} - N_{hd}$$

For joint $h$ to be in balance vertically requires one of the diagonal bars to be in tension and the other to be in compression. But this cannot be because of the symmetrical nature of the load action. Hence, the only solution possible is that both members are zero

$$N_{hb} = N_{hd} = 0$$

It is obvious from symmetry that:

$$\Sigma F_y = 0 = N_{hg} \frac{21.22/2}{15} - N_{he} \frac{21.22/2}{15} \qquad N_{hg} = N_{he}$$

$$\Sigma F_x = 0 = 1 - 2\left(N_{hg} \frac{21.22/2}{15}\right) \qquad N_{hg} = N_{he} = 0.71 \text{ k} \text{ (C)}$$

At joint $f$, the reasoning is similar to that for joint $h$. Vertical equilibrium requires that one of the diagonal members $N_{fa}$ or $N_{fc}$ is in tension and the other is in compression. But this is not possible because of symmetry, hence the members must be zero

$$N_{fa} = N_{fc} = 0$$

Since no load acts on the joint and since bars $N_{fg}$ and $N_{fe}$ cannot be in tension and compression, they must also be zero

$$N_{fg} = N_{fe} = 0$$

Now, only three unknown member forces act at each joint and can be solved directly (Problem 5.8).

## 5.3  PLANAR, MULTILAYER SPACE FRAMES

At present, space frame roofs are used extensively to cover large spans for buildings such as assembly halls, exhibition spaces, churches, gymnasiums, factories, swimming pools, and theaters.

To develop some understanding of multilayer space frames, the nature of spatial geometry must be investigated first. The order of the three-dimensional member network must be recognized and understood from a geometrical as well as behavioral point of view. The path of the force flow not only depends on the load action, the arrangement of the bars, and the stiffness of the entire plate structure, but also on the type and location of the support system. Aspects of mass production expressed in modularity such as repetition of members, details and assemblages, together with the easiness of fabrication, transportation, and erection procedures are essential criteria which must be considered in the design of space frames.

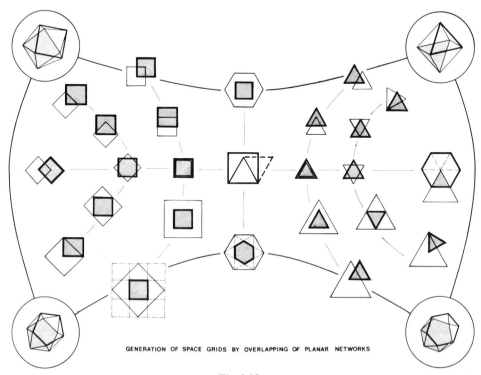

GENERATION OF SPACE GRIDS BY OVERLAPPING OF PLANAR NETWORKS

**Fig. 5.12**

## Geometrical Considerations

The geometry of space frames can be interpreted either from the closepacking of poly-hedra or from the interplay of surface tesselations.

For a double-layer space frame the top and bottom surface grids are connected at their nodes by web members to form an aggregate of polyhedra or a three-dimensional network. The web members are generally diagonals, however for cases where the nodes of the two layers are exactly above each other, vertical struts may be employed. There are infinite variations of overlapping planar tesselations and many ways of joining the two horizontal planes. The relationship of typical surface meshes is studied in Fig. 5.12 where, as an example, the square and the equilateral triangle are used as base units and processed through different transformations to indicate the unlimited possibilities of spatial net-work formation. Familiar are the antiprisms shown in the corners which have identical top and base figures like prisms, except that they are instead rotated against each other, thereby generating triangular faces for the vertical planes. The nature of two-dimensional tesselations was already introduced in Chapter 2 and is not further treated here.

Typical solutions for double-layer space frames are shown in Figs 5.13 and 5.14; keep in mind that there are infinite other possibilities.

### Direct Grids or Truss Grids (Fig. 5.13)

Top and bottom grids are identical and directly above each other, such as:

- Two-directional square grids either parallel (a) or diagonal (skew) to the boundaries
- Three-directional, triangular grids (b)
- Four-directional, quadruple grids generated by superimposing square and skew grids

### Space Grids (Figs. 5.13 and 5.14)

Two-directional square grids, not necessarily identical, are offset with respect to each other.

- Offset grids: top and bottom grids are identical, but offset with respect to each other such as square on square (e) generated by oblique translation, and modifications such as openings in top and bottom grids formed by process of elimination resulting in square grid on larger square grid (f).
- Differential grids: top and bottom square grids differ, such as diagonal square grid set on smaller square grid (g) and diagonal square grid set on larger square grid (h).

Three-directional, triangular network, or modifications generating offset or differential grids such as:

- Triangular grid on triangular grid offset generated by oblique translation (c)
- Modifications such as internal openings in top or bottom grid resulting in a combina-tion of hexagonal and triangular grid on triangular grid (d)

The horizontal grid layers are connected by web systems consisting of continuous or staggered, vertical, or inclined trusses such as that of the Pratt or Warren type.

TRIANGULAR GRID SURFACE PATTERNS-PRIMARY POLYHEDRAL UNIT: TETRAHEDRON

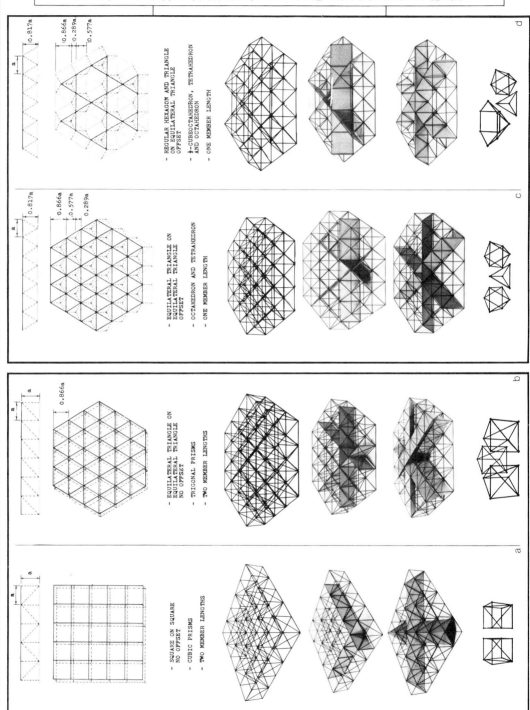

**d**

0.817a
0.866a 0.289a
0.577a

a

- REGULAR HEXAGON AND TRIANGLE ON EQUILATERAL TRIANGLE OFFSET
- ½-CUBEOCTAHEDRON, TETRAHEDRON AND OCTAHEDRON
- ONE MEMBER LENGTH

**c**

0.817a
0.866a 0.577a
0.289a

a

- EQUILATERAL TRIANGLE ON EQUILATERAL TRIANGLE OFFSET
- OCTAHEDRON AND TETRAHEDRON
- ONE MEMBER LENGTH

**b**

a

0.866a

a

- EQUILATERAL TRIANGLE ON EQUILATERAL TRIANGLE NO OFFSET
- TRIGONAL PRISMS
- TWO MEMBER LENGTHS

**a**

a

a

- SQUARE ON SQUARE NO OFFSET
- CUBIC PRISMS
- TWO MEMBER LENGTHS

## SQUARE GRID SURFACE PATTERNS − PRIMARY POLYHEDRAL UNIT: HALF-OCTAHEDRON

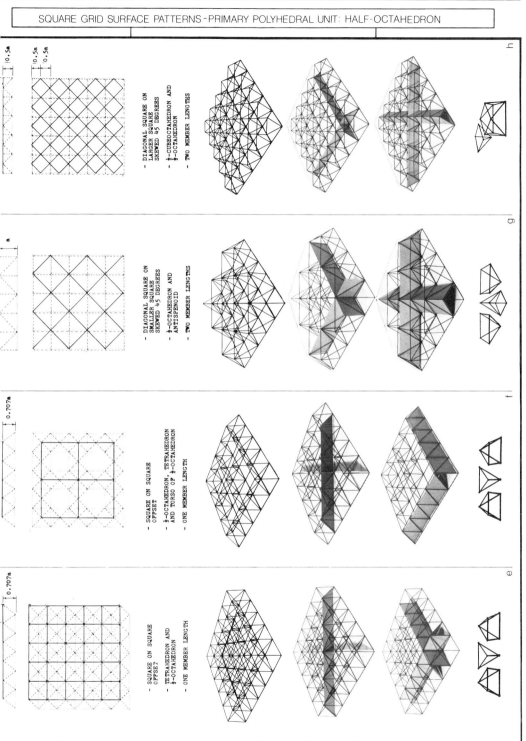

Fig. 5.14

347

The space frame geometry can be derived from the all-space filling polyhedra, where edges and vertices form a spatial network. The polyhedra are packed face to face, leaving no free space. Double-layer space trusses can either be produced by the additive process of packing or by the subtractive process of cutting the given spatial aggregate with two horizontal, parallel planes. Before continuing the discussion of closepacking systems, the nature of polyhedra is briefly reviewed in order to develop some understanding for the degree of regularity of these elements.

A polyhedron is defined as a three-dimensional figure, composed of at least four faces intersecting along the edges, which in turn intersect at the vertices. The angle formed by two faces along the common edge is called the dihedral angle. Leonard Euler (1707–1783) proved that the number of vertices, edges, and faces bear a constant relationship to each other. Polyhedra may be organized according to their degree of regularity as expressed by the number and type of polygonal surfaces, how the polygons meet at their common edges, the dihedral angles at the edges and the number of polygons meeting at a vertex. Of special interest are the so-called uniform polyhedra which have all their vertices touch a circumscribed sphere.

The regular polyhedra are known as the five Platonic solids. They are the tetrahedron, octahedron, and icosahedron all composed of equilateral triangles; the cube composed of squares; and the dodecahedron composed of pentagons. The concept of the regular polyhedron is important since it consists of regular polygons for all its faces, with vertices and dihedral angles identical. This feature of repetition is a fundamental consideration for the design of space frames as related to production, transportation, and erection.

There are two quasiregular polyhedra not having identical regular faces: the cubeoctahedron (dymaxion) and the icosidodecahedron. The semiregular polyhedra, often called the Archimedean solids, have neither identical faces nor identical dihedral angles. They consist of two or three different types of regular polygons (triangle, square, pentagon, hexagon, octagon, or decagon) with the same number of faces meeting at each corner. There are 11 Archimedean solids, though often taken as 13, if the quasiregular polyhedra are included, and there are an infinite number of regular prisms and antiprisms.

Only three of the Platonic solids (tetrahedron, octahedron, and cube) and six of the Archimedean solids (truncated tetrahedron, truncated octahedron, cubeoctahedron, truncated cubeoctahedron, rhombicubeoctahedron, and truncated dodecahedron) fill space either by themselves or in combination with each other.

Some of the more typical examples of interest to space frame construction as based on spatial equipartition or semiregular equipartition are:

- The eight single, self-closepacking polyhedra:
  - (a)   Cube
  - (b)   Hexagonal and trigonal prisms
  - (c)   Truncated octahedron
  - (d)   Others
- The ten dual, closepacking polyhedra:
  - (a)   Octahedron + tetrahedron
  - (b)   Octahedron + cubeoctahedron
  - (c)   Octahedron + truncated cube
  - (d)   Tetrahedron + truncated tetrahedron
  - (e)   Others

- The eight triple, closepacking polyhedra:
  (a)    Truncated tetrahedron + cubeoctahedron + truncated octahedron
  (b)    Truncated tetrahedron + truncated cube + truncated cubeoctahedron
  (c)    Others

Any of these space-filling polyhedra systems can be cut by parallel horizontal planes to form double-layer space frames such as the ones shown in Figs. 5.13 and 5.14. Notice that cases (c)–(f) only employ one member length $a$ with the truss depths adjusted accordingly, while the other cases use different member lengths. The space frames shown in the two figures can also be generated by packing the polyhedra identified in Fig. 5.7. All of the solids in this figure are derived from the cube, hence all dimensions such as height and member length are a multiple of $\sqrt{2}$.

Even though standardization is a basic requirement of mass production, the all-space filling systems just discussed are not necessarily the most useful; less regular ones may be more desirable, depending on the situation, because of function, availability of materials, or construction considerations, for example. Furthermore, the force flow along the space frame varies from a maximum to a minimum. Thus, the usage of identical member lengths and possibly sizes, together with the same connectors, may not be economical from a material point of view.

Double-layer space frames can also be visualized as consisting of a collection of pre-fabricated, skeletal pyramidal units with a square ($\frac{1}{2}$ octahedron), triangular (tetra-hedron), pentagonal, or hexagonal base. These pyramids can be connected in many different ways to produce the desired spatial network. For instance, the space frames based on square space grids (Fig. 5.14) consist of square pyramids joined along their top and bottom faces, while the one based on triangular space grids (Fig. 5.13c) is composed of triangular pyramids.

### Behavioral Considerations

The stability of single-layer, envelope-type space frames, such as those of the basic polyhedra units in Fig. 5.7, is checked by Eq. (5.9). While the stable, single-layer systems have triangulated surfaces for statically determinate boundary conditions, the multilayer space frames usually do not. Hence, in order to investigate the stability of multilayer aggregates, new mathematical expressions will have to be developed—a subject which is beyond the purpose of this work. However, certain conclusions can be drawn from the building blocks forming the space frames. Of the closepacking polyhedra in Fig. 5.7 only the trigonal prism, the octahedron, and the tetrahedron are stable, while the other units are unstable (see Problem 5.1).

It is apparent that if a double-layer space frame is composed of stable, polyhedral units, then the entire assemblage must also be internally stable such as the triangular lattice grid (5.13b) and the triangular grid on triangular grid offset (Fig. 5.13c).

Should the hinged space frames be composed of stable and unstable units, then the total structure may still be internally stable, if the stable units are connected to each other in a manner that new, stable assemblages are generated. This, however, is not the case for the space frame square on square offset (Fig. 5.14e), where the four tetrahedra do not join to form a new stable unit.

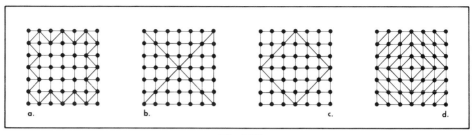

Fig. 5.15

For the condition where space frames are composed of unstable polyhedral units, such as the square lattice grid (Fig. 5.13a), or the diagonal on square cases (Fig. 5.14g, h), the entire structure must also be internally unstable. It was shown in the discussion of polyhedral domes that even for internally unstable structures, proper additional external supports may still result in a stable overall structure. The same reasoning, obviously, is applicable to space frames or any other structure. For larger scale structures, the spatial network is internally stabilized by adding members, usually in the compression plane (Fig. 5.15), rather than externally at the supports. A square grid may be stabilized by additional face diagonals causing torsional stability by either enclosing the structure along its periphery (a), by subdividing the structure plane into large-scale triangular units (b), (c), or by trussing each bay (d). If the roof decking is properly fastened to the frame, then it also can provide the necessary torsional rigidity in a stressed skin fashion.

From a behavioral point of view, space frames can be organized according to their response to loading (Fig. 5.16).

### Truss Grids (Figs. 5.13a, b; 5.16 a–c)

Vertical trusses arranged in a two-way or three-way fashion form truss grids. The two-way rectangular grids can be placed parallel/perpendicular or diagonal (skew) to the boundaries; the skew grids, often called diagrid structures, provide more rigidity, especially at the corners, thereby generating additional support in these areas and a reduction of span. While the load in case (a) of Fig. 5.16 is carried along one direction only, it is distributed by the truss grids of cases (b) and (c) in a two- and three-way manner. When the grid members are placed closer together and trusses are replaced by girders or beams, the system is called a beam grid and forms *a grillage-type* structure. For closely spaced concrete ribs acting compositely with the slab, the plate structure forms a slab grid, known as the *waffle slab*.

### Folded Plate Trusses (Fig. 6.5d)

This condition of one-way spatial surface action is not shown in Fig. 5.16, but is discussed in Chapter 6. Visualize the parallel trusses of case (a) to lean against each other to form a corrugated surface.

### Space Trusses (Fig. 5.16d)

Two folded plate trusses are tied together at their base to form a new linear spatial beam, which resists forces in all directions, including torsion.

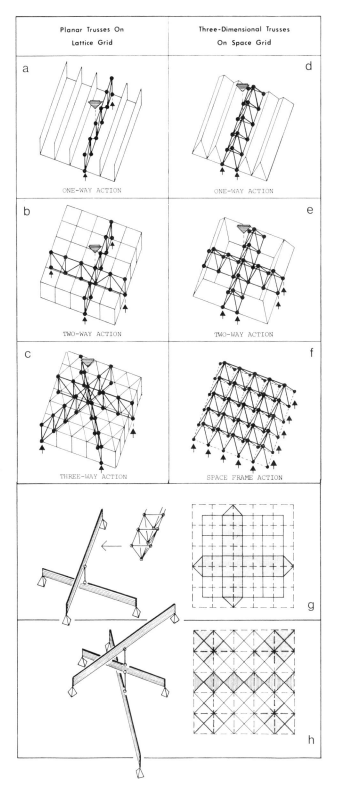

Fig. 5.16

*Space Grid Trusses (Figs. 5.16e-h)*

By letting the stiff space trusses intersect in a two-way grid fashion (e), (f), (g) a space frame of the square on square offset type is formed, providing considerably more torsional stiffness than the two-way truss grids. This structure can also be visualized as a two-way folded plate structure. The interaction of the linear space trusses is shown in (g); the compression member is assumed to consist of the two members so as to improve the buckling capacity of the top chord.

For the condition where one of the planar grids is diagonal, such as the diagonal square on smaller square (h), the force flow can be visualized along three directions, with one of the trusses being staggered. This surface structure is stiffer than case (g) and should come closer to the behavior of the two-way solid slab.

The stiffest double-layer space frame is the one formed by triangular grids offset with respect to each other (Fig. 5.13c). Here, three intersecting, continuous, inclined trusses distribute the loads truly in three directions.

## Planning Considerations

Space frames can be built from all kinds of materials, though the ones discussed here and used mostly in practice are made of steel and aluminum. They can behave as hinged skeletons (i.e., space truss), as rigid space frames, or as composite systems, where skin and skeleton act as a unit. In the following discussion space frames and space trusses are no longer differentiated. The typical depth-to-span ratio of horizontal, double layer space frames used as roofs for ordinary conditions, is in the range of

$$\frac{1}{18} \leqslant \frac{d}{L} \leqslant \frac{1}{25} \quad \text{or} \quad \frac{1}{9} \quad \text{for the cantilever span}$$

The bay size $a$ or modularity of the spatial structure can be derived directly, should one of the regular or partially regular frames of Figs. 5.13 and 5.14 be used, since for these structures truss depth and bay size are related and often approximated as equal to each other for preliminary design purposes. However, as mentioned before, other spatial geometries may be more economical for certain span and loading conditions. In this case, the bay size is dependent on considerations such as the location and type of supports, the building dimensions, the capacity of the deck or roof joists, the relationship of axial stresses to bending stresses in the compression chord, the density of members (number of members per unit area), repetition, orientation, inclination, and type of members, type of joints, integration of mechanical and electrical equipment, and other depth limitations. The maximum bay size is often assumed not larger than a fifth of the span or 30 ft

$$\frac{L}{5} \geqslant a \leqslant 30 \text{ ft}$$

An optimum bay size seems to be in the range of

$$1.2d \geqslant a \leqslant 2.5d$$

For the condition where the top chord is in compression, it may be advantageous to use a top grid smaller than the bottom grid to improve the buckling capacity of the compression chord members.

Soil conditions must be considered for the layout of space frame roof structures. A roof supported by only four columns transmits large forces to the ground, which is acceptable for high-capacity soils, but in the case of weak soils the cost of installing the large foundations that are required may make it economically unfeasible.

Another important design consideration relates to the process of construction. Depending on the scale and sequence of erection, temporary interior supports may be required, or the entire roof, or portions of it may be assembled on the ground and then jacked up or lifted into position, rather than constructing it in the air (i.e., in place). Individual pyramidal units can be stacked and thus easily shipped to the site. Frame assemblages not longer than 60 ft or wider than 15 ft can generally be transported by truck.

The economy of the space frame is closely related to the method of joining. The number of joints per square foot should be kept to a minimum. Larger modules with fewer members and nodes are generally more economical. The selection of the design of the connection depends on the scale of the structure and the joint capacity needed. It depends on whether or not it is assembled in the field or in the shop; it is a function of the shape and size of the bars as well as the geometry of the spatial member network, that is, the angle of intersection. In addition, it depends on requirements of accessibility and workability, easiness of construction, adaptability to attachments of other materials, dismantability, if so desired, and aesthetic criteria. Too many members joining at a node cause congestion, requiring the member ends to be tapered. A typical joint has approximately six to ten members attached to it. Connections should allow dimensional tolerances, so as to provide for the members to fit together properly.

Space frames are either designed for a specific job, or provided as systems by commercial outfits. Some of the better known standardized space frame structures currently available are the Nodus and Space Deck systems in Britain, the Unibat system in France, the Mero and Octaplatte systems in West Germany, and the Unistrut and Triodetic systems in North America.

It is not a simple task to organize space frames as based on the connection of their members, since there are infinitely many solutions possible. The members can either be directly attached to each other by welding or bolting, or special connectors can be used. The connectors may be flat, bent, or built-up gusset plates; they may be clamps as used for scaffolding, or they may have the shape of hubs, stars, or polyhedra internally threaded or with threaded projecting shanks. They may be a single piece or consist of several parts; they may have to be assembled or they may be a finished product. Any member types can be used, such as solid, tubular, or open (angles, channels, wideflanges, tees) sections, where the members may include special end pieces. The group of stressed skin type of space structures using thin metal sheets of steel or aluminum or skins of plywood, plastics, paper, ferrocement and so on, are still in an early stage of development and therefore not discussed further here.

Members can be connected by the familiar methods of bolting, welding, glueing, keying, and other special techniques. Some of the more typical connection types are shown in Fig. 5.17, with the patent joints currently available in the United States. Information with respect to the strength (capacity) of these systems is provided by the respective companies.

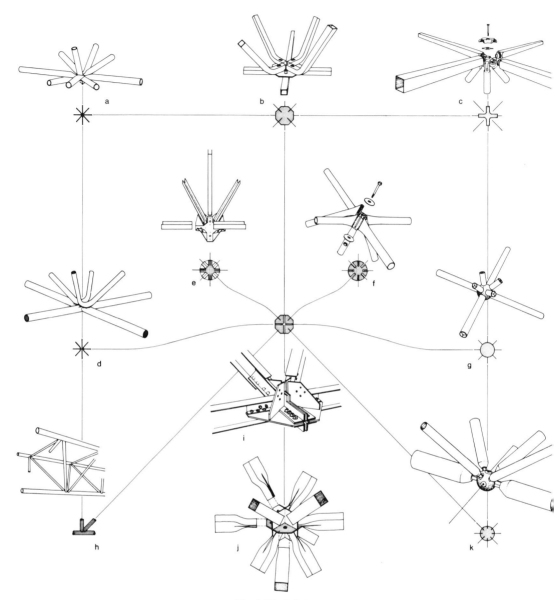

**Fig. 5.17**  Joint systems.

- *IBG System [Roper IBG International, Wheeling, Illinois, case (g)]*. The system consists of hollow ball nodes with openings for inserting fasteners into the round aluminum
  tubes.
- *Mero System [Unistrut Corp., Wayne, Michigan, case (k)]*. The system consists of solid
  forged steel spheres into which threaded holes are bored, and it consists of round tubular members with cone-shaped ends and protruding, threaded bolts fitting the tapped
  holes in the nodes.
- *Modu Span System [Unistrut Corp., Wayne, Michigan, case (e)]*. The system consists
  of bent connector plates with contact faces in the direction of the struts and cold-

formed, U-shaped members bolted to them. Reinforcing parts are added if a higher load-carrying capacity is required.

- ■ *Nodus System [British Steel Corp., case (c)]*. The system is comprised of tubular steel sections, where the chords are clamped into the joint, consisting of two half castings, by a single, high-strength center bolt. The web members have forked end connectors, which are secured to lugs on the joint by stainless steel pins.
- ■ *Power-Strut System [Van Huffel Tube Corp., Warren, Ohio, case (b)]*. The system consists of flat connector plates, to which the rectangular, tubular members can directly be bolted, while the web members are bent at their ends so that they can also be attached.
- ■ *Triodetic System [Butler Manufacturing Co., Grandview, Missouri, case (f)]*. The system consists of slotted hub connectors (aluminum extrusions) and usually aluminum tubing pressed at the ends, so that it can be force fitted into the slots.

No connector piece is necessary if the members are welded directly to each other, such as the bent diagonal rods or the tubular webs to the top and bottom chord members [cases (d), (h)], keeping in mind that welding does not allow for any member tolerances. For cases where pipe members intersect, additional joint pieces may be required, if enough weld length cannot be developed. Tubes may be pressed flat at their ends and bent so that a single bolt can hold the member assembly together [case (a)].

For large-scale structures, it may be necessary to design the space frame for the given condition, rather than using a commercial system which may not be strong enough or economically competitive. A typical solution [cases (i), (j)] consists of a welded multiplanar gusset unit, shop-fabricated, to which standard rolled sections are bolted in the field; or tubular shapes are necked down at the ends so that they may be connected to the plate-type joint.

## Approximate Design of Horizontal Double-Layer Space Frames

Double-layer space trusses, in general, are highly indeterminate, however should they be determinate, then the structure can be solved by statics using for each joint the three equations of equilibrium [Eq. (5.5)]. Since, usually, more than three members are attached to a node, the bar forces cannot be found directly from the joint to which they are connected. For instance, the space frame with triangle on triangle offset (Fig. 5.13c) has 74 joints with 9 members joined to each interior node. To determine the bar forces, 3(74) = 222 equations are needed, which obviously is not feasibly solved by hand; computers must be used. The situation is by far more complex for indeterminate space frames, where initial member sizes must first be assumed before a structural analysis can be performed. Even computers may sometimes have trouble handling extremely large structures, as was the case at the time for Buckminster Fuller's double-layer geodesic dome (see Fig. 8.21w) for the Expo 67 in Montreal, which had about 6000 nodes, 24,000 members, and about 27 miles of tubes.

However, in order to develop some intuitive feeling for double-layer space frame behavior and also to be able to estimate the preliminary member sizes, the plate analogy is briefly introduced here. The horizontal, double-layer space frame is assumed to behave like a solid plate, keeping in mind that the force flow must follow the grid prescribed by the bar layout and that it travels along the stiffest members to the respective supports;

this, however, is not the case for a solid homogeneous slab, where the direction of the force flow changes with loading. As the density of the spatial member network increases (i.e., for a high number of nodes), and also with the use of certain inherently strong geometries like the triangular grid on the offset triangular grid, the space frame approaches the behavior of the solid plate. The axial bar forces are obtained from the shear and moment values of the analogous slab multiplied by the respective member spacing. But one has to keep in mind that depending on the type of spatial grid, the maximum tension and compression in the chords do not necessarily appear at the same location as the maximum moment.

The behavior of flat space frame roofs, that is slabs, depends on the type and location of the support system. Typical slab structures are shown in Fig. 5.18a–i. The horizontal surface structures may form only a single bay (a)–(f) or they may be multibay systems (g)–(i). The roofs may be supported by walls or columns, which in turn may be arranged in various ways. If walls or closely spaced columns are placed parallel (b), the space frame can be considered to transfer loads directly from wall to wall like a one-way slab. However, if the supports are positioned along the periphery of a roof, the roof structure will respond similar to a two-way slab, if the ratio of the longer side to the shorter one is not larger than 2.

A square plate under uniform gravity loading is investigated in Fig. 5.18. The columns are arranged to provide symmetry about the x, y, and diagonal axes. The slabs of cases (e) and (f) are cantilevered to reduce the maximum field moment and deflection. The ideal location of the column is where the support moment is equal to the field moment, which is in the range 0.15–0.3L (Fig. 4.9), depending on the cantilever and midspan loading. The effect of cantilevering results in smaller chord sizes, but hardly influences the magnitude of the shear, that is, the web members.

The behavior of a truss grid, continuously supported along its circumference (a), depends on the spacing of the ribs. Should the two-way beams consist of relatively deep members of equal size, such as trusses, and should these members be spaced relatively far apart, then this highly indeterminate, intersecting grid structure may be replaced for approximation purposes by statically determinate vertical trusses, where each one carries one-half of the respective bay loading, assuming the joist layout as shown in Fig. 5.18a. The uniform load for a typical truss is $w(a/2)$ with a maximum moment at midspan of

$$M_{max} = \frac{(wa/2)L^2}{8} = \frac{wL^2}{16} a \qquad (5.10)$$

However, should the beams be much closer together, then the behavior of the roof structure is that of a grillage and may be roughly approximated by considering it as a solid slab, ignoring its lack of torsional rigidity. In true space frames this torsional strength is provided by the spatial diagonal web members; hence, a space frame roof continuously supported and hinged along its edges to the walls or the closely spaced columns (c) acts very much like a simply supported two-way slab which has its maximum moment at center span with a magnitude of

$$M_{max} = \frac{wL^2}{20} \qquad (5.11)$$

Notice this moment is 25% less than the one used for the truss grid due to the continuity of the solid slab providing twisting moments, thereby relieving the bending moments. There are diagonal, negative moments of smaller magnitude in the corner region which generate a clamping effect, as the principal moment contours in Fig. 2.11 indicate.

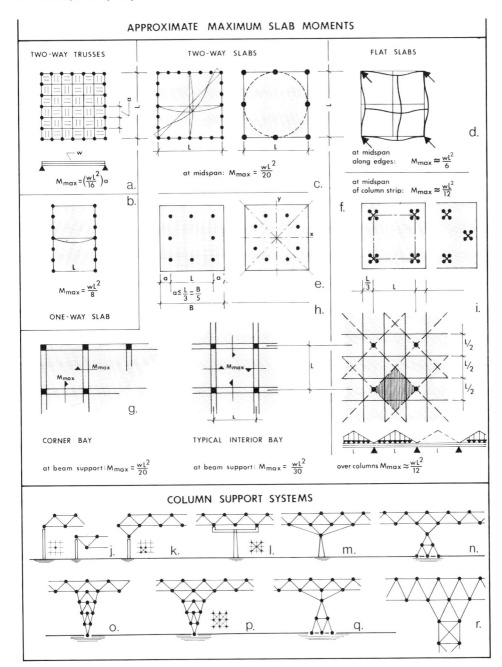

**Fig. 5.18**

The shear is not uniformly distributed along the periphery, it is maximum at the middle of the plate sides; in the corners the plate even has the tendency to lift up. The maximum shear can be approximated as

$$V_{max} = 0.34wL \qquad (5.12)$$

Hence, it is quite apparent that the reaction forces are not constant along the periphery, as this can only be true for a circular slab loaded uniformly.

For approximation purposes it can be assumed that as long as there is at least one support at midlength of the edges (c), the space frame can still be considered as a two-way slab simply supported along its perimeter. However, if these midspan columns along the edges are taken away, the behavior of the slab drastically changes, approaching that of a flat slab (d). The response of a slab, only supported at its corners, to uniform gravity loading is extremely complex. The slab must carry the loads directly to the columns, which is quite different than the condition where the two-way slab transmits the loads to the stiff edge beams, which in turn bring them to the columns. In a flat slab there are no beams, the slab itself must provide this additional task; hence the magnitude of the moments is in the same range as for one-way slabs and much larger than for equivalent two-way slabs. Here, the maximum moments occur at midspan along the edges and may be roughly approximated, conservatively, as

$$M_{max} = \frac{wL^2}{6} \qquad (5.13)$$

Notice the moment is $3\frac{1}{3}$ times larger than that of a two-way slab, but the increase in deflection is higher by far. In addition, the effect of shear in the flat slab is much more pronounced because of the punching effect at the columns, where a quarter of the total roof load must be resisted by the slab in shear. It is quite apparent that as the member sizes along the edges of the space frame, acting as a flat slab, increase and approach beam action, the stiffness as well as strength of the structure increases, eventually behaving as a two-way slab system.

The maximum moment for a typical interior bay of a two-way slab (h) is the negative moment at the beam supports (*ACI 318-63*, Method 2) and may be approximated as

$$M_{max} = \frac{wL^2}{30} \qquad (5.14)$$

The absolutely largest moment for a multibay system appears in the corner bay (g), where the support moments at the first interior beams are approximately equal to

$$M_{max} = \frac{wL^2}{20} \qquad (5.15)$$

The behavior of a multibay flat slab system is very complex, as was already mentioned. The maximum moment occurs over the columns and is roughly approximated as

$$M_{max} = \frac{wL^2}{12} \qquad (5.16)$$

The magnitude of this moment is not necessarily conservative. The effective width of the imaginary beam (column strip) is dependent on the size of the column head. The support width and the rigidity of the slab determine how the moments are distributed.

Similarly, it can be shown that the maximum moment for a cantilevering space frame roof on four supports (f) appears at the midspan of the column strips and may be estimated as

$$M_{max} = \frac{wL^2}{12} \qquad (5.17)$$

A space frame column must support gravity loads and possibly lateral forces. Typical column types are shown in Figs. 5.18j–r. They may either be simple one-point columns, two-point columns with one-way column arms, four-point columns with $x$ column arms, or pyramidal supports; or they may be multipoint support systems. For point supported flat slab-type space frames, punching shear around the supports, as for the familiar column footings, causes large forces in the web members. These forces may be reduced by providing shear heads, $x$ arms, or tree-like supports similar to the dropped panels or column capitals in concrete construction. Thus, a point-support may be changed to a four-point support (k), (l) or to a nine-point support (p) to increase the perimeter support area for resistance of punching shear, reduction of the positive field moments, and especially deflection. Columns are either separated from the roof plane by a pin, allowing free rotation of the much stiffer roof structure and only resisting axial and shear forces, or they may be an integral part of the space frame so as to form a two-hinge frame in cross-section with the roof plane being rigid and not deforming under lateral loading. The pin supports are either at the ground level (o), (p) or at some location along the column (k), (m), (n), (q). The roof can be supported at the top or bottom chord level.

The lateral loads must be carried by the columns or walls in either cantilever action or together with the roof in frame action, as was already discussed for trusses in Fig. 4.61. However, should there be an independent shear wall structure to resist the lateral forces, then the exterior columns can be constructed as pendulums supporting axial loads and allowing free expansion or contraction of the roof plane as caused by elastic behavior and temperature change. The upward acting wind can be ignored at least for preliminary design purposes, since in general the roof weight is larger than the suction force. For the design of the cladding, the wind must obviously be considered.

Typical examples of space frame roof structures are shown in Fig. 5.19. They are either supported along their edges or composed of a multibay system. The continuous perimeter support for the roof of the Omni Colisseum (D) is provided by wall trusses that cantilever at each end. The space frame roof of the Pauley Pavilion (E) has a varying depth with the maximum appearing at the center where the moments are the largest. The space frame geometries range from two-way Vierendeel trusses (J), two-way trusses diagonally braced (F) or not braced (C), and the girder grillage (G), to the hexagonal Vierendeel frame ($T$); they range from four-sided pyramids interconnected in single or double layers (B), (E), (A) to truncated pyramids arranged in a checkerboard pattern with diagonal rods connecting the pyramids in the upper chords (D). Denver's McNichols arena (300 $\times$ 400 ft) is covered with a two-way steel truss system that consists of rigid top chord and vertical members, while the diagonals and bottom chords are cables; the roof has the appearance of a tensegrity structure. One of the largest space frame roofs is the Reunion Arena in Dallas (opened in 1980). The 420-ft square roof spans 412 ft between the supporting eight columns, which must resist extremely large moments at their base. The structure is of the square on square offset type (Fig. 5.15e) with a module of 36 ft 5 in. and a depth of 18 ft 10 in. ($d/L = 1/22$). Another example of large-scale application of the space frame principle is the roof for an aircraft maintenance hangar in Singapore (1981) with a clear span of 720 $\times$ 300 ft. The roof structure is of the diagonal square grid type; it is supported on three sides leaving the 720-ft span column free.

The depth-to-span ratios of the roof structures range from $d/L = 1/10$ for the two-way truss grid (C) to 1/20 for the two-way Vierendeel truss (J) to 1/35 for the two-way girder roof of the Berlin Gallery (G) that reflects the character of a slab grid. The weights of some of the space frame roofs are about 13.2 psf for the Currigan Hall (A), 15 psf for the

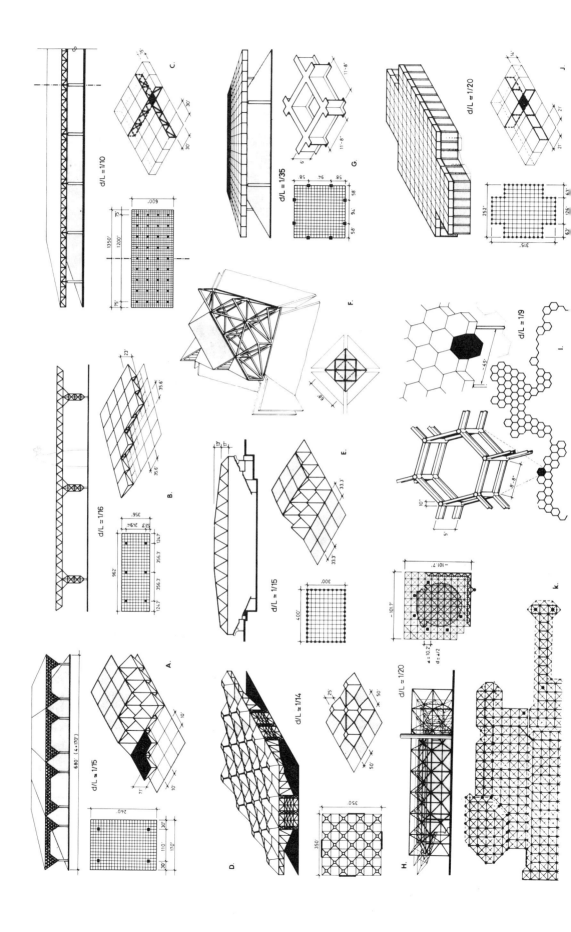

Pauley Pavilion (E), and 16 psf for the Omni Coliseum (D), thus clearly indicating the lightweight character of space frames.

Space frames easily adjust to multifunctional uses as convincingly reflected by case (K). The enormous New York Exposition and Convention Center by I. M. Pei, with its different levels and setbacks exemplifies the continuous character of the space frame fabric along the horizontal and vertical planes. The shell-like folded space frame surfaces on a stretched star plan, of the monumental Crystal Cathedral [see Fig. 6.2s, (415 ft long, 207 ft wide, 128 ft high)] in Garden Grove, California, by Johnson/Burgee also convincingly exposes the envelope quality of the space frame. The continuous space truss sloped roof planes can be visualized as diaphragms supported by the trussed shear walls; the structural envelope acts primarily in the short that is transverse direction.

**Example 5.5**  Different space frame roof systems ($A36$ steel) are investigated for a gymnasium. The two-way roof covers a column-free space of $100 \times 100$ ft and is simply supported along its four edges. The structure must support a live load of 20 psf; the weight of the roof skin consisting of joists, decking, roofing material, insulation, etc. is assumed as 10 psf and the self-weight of the space frame is considered as 15 psf. Ignored in this preliminary study is the change of weight for the different structural systems to be investigated.

*(a) Two-Way Truss Structure (Fig. 5.18a)*

The roof plane is subdivided in each direction into six equal spaces yielding a square grid of $100/6 = 16.67$ ft (Fig. 5.20a, b). For a depth-to-span ratio of $d/L = 1/15$, the typical truss depth is $d = L/15 = 100/15 = 6.67$ ft.

Because of the relatively wide spacing of the trusses, each one may be considered to individually carry the load of one-half bay

$$w = 0.045 \frac{16.67}{2} = 0.38 \text{ k/ft}$$

The maximum moment at midspan is

$$M_{max} = \frac{wL^2}{8}$$

$$= \frac{0.38(100)^2}{8} = 475 \text{ ft-k}$$

It is assumed that the shear is carried fully by the web members, while the moment is resisted by the chords. The influence of the small shear upon the force flow in the chords at midspan is ignored, that is, a uniform load is assumed rather than the single loads at the truss joints. Hence, the moment is resisted axially by the top, $N_t$, and bottom, $N_b$, chord members

$$M_{max} = N_t(d) = N_b(d) \qquad (4.58)$$

$$N_t = N_b = \frac{M_{max}}{d} = \frac{475}{6.67} = 71.21 \text{ k}$$

In addition to axial action, the top chord must also carry bending moments as caused by the decking. The top chord is considered a continuous beam supporting the weight of the

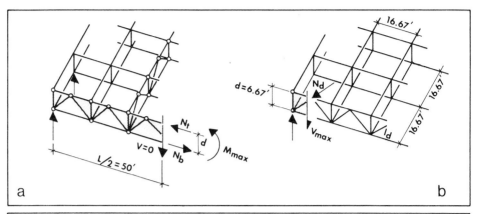

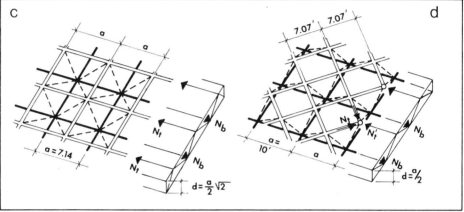

Fig. 5.20

roof skin and the live load, but its own small weight is neglected. The uniform gravity load is equal to

$$w = \frac{(10 + 20)16.67}{2} = 250 \text{ lb/ft} = 0.25 \text{ k/ft}$$

The maximum moment is approximated as

$$M_{\max} = \frac{wl^2}{10} = \frac{0.25(16.67/2)^2}{10} = 1.74 \text{ ft-k}$$

The roof decking is stiff enough to prevent buckling of the top chord about its weak axis. Since the effect of buckling about the strong axis is small, for approximation purposes the section can be assumed to fail in yielding rather than inelastic buckling. Further, notice that the effect of $K$-bracing results not only in a reduction of buckling length, but also in a reduction of beam span.

The moment is transformed by the bending factor into a fictitious axial load

$$P + P' = P + B_x M_x \tag{1.48}$$

$$= 71.21 + (0.456)1.74(12) = 71.21 + 9.52 = 80.73 \text{ k}$$

$$A = \frac{P + P'}{F_a} = \frac{80.73}{22} = 3.67 \text{ in.}^2$$

Try $W6 \times 15$, $A = 4.43$ in.$^2$. Note that bending due to transverse loading has only a minor effect on the design of the chord member.

The bottom chord is in tension and is assumed to carry no additional loads in bending. The required minimum net area is

$$A_{net} = \frac{N_b}{F_t} = \frac{71.21}{22} = 3.24 \text{ in.}^2$$

For bolted connections the net section shall not exceed 85% of the corresponding gross section, assuming that the capacity of the joint matches that of the members. Hence the required area can be approximated as

$$A = \frac{A_{net}}{0.85} = \frac{3.24}{0.85} = 3.81 \text{ in.}^2$$

Try $WT 8 \times 13$, $A = 3.84$ in.$^2$.

The largest compression diagonal resists the shear at the reactions, where the maximum shear is equal to

$$V_{max} = \frac{wL}{2} = 0.38 \frac{100}{2} = 19 \text{ k}$$

The length of the diagonal member is

$$l_d = \sqrt{\left(\frac{16.67}{2}\right)^2 + 6.67^2} = 10.68 \text{ ft}$$

The diagonal member must support the shear (Fig. 5.20b). The force is determined by setting its vertical component equal to the shear

$$\frac{N_d}{10.68}(6.67) = 19 \qquad N_d = 30.42 \text{ k} \qquad \text{(C)}$$

Using the column tables in the *AISC Manual* with $Kl = 1(10.68) \cong 11$ ft, gives the following section

$$2L\ 3 \times 3 \times \frac{3}{8}$$

At this stage, some detailing should be done to see if the members fit together at the joints.

### (b) Two-Way Beam Grid

The beams are spaced relatively closely so that this grillage structure may be considered analogous to a two-way slab simply supported along its periphery, ignoring the fact that its torsional rigidity is quite small. A square grid of 5 ft is selected. The slab moment is

$$M_{max} = \frac{wL^2}{20} \qquad (5.11)$$

$$= \frac{(0.045)100^2}{20} = 22.50 \text{ ft-k}$$

The critical beams along the center of the plate must resist the following moments as based on their spacing

$$M_{BM} = 5(22.5) = 112.50 \text{ ft-k}$$

The required section modulus, by considering the compression flange laterally supported, is

$$S = \frac{M}{F_b} = \frac{112.5(12)}{24} = 56.25 \text{ in.}^3$$

Try $W18 \times 35$, $S_x = 57.6$ in.$^3$.

The shear does not have to be checked since it will not be critical.

### (c) Diagonal Square on Square Space Frame (Fig. 5.14h)

A truss depth of $d = L/20 = 100/20 = 5$ ft is selected. Depth and bay size are related as $a = 2d$. Hence the bottom square module is $a = 2(5) = 10$ ft, subdividing the roof into 10 equal bays in each direction.

The top skewed square grid is

$$\frac{a}{2}\sqrt{2} = d\sqrt{2} = 5\sqrt{2} = 7.07 \text{ ft}$$

as identified in Fig. 5.20d. The maximum tensile force in the bottom chord at midspan is directly resisted, and equal to

$$N_b = \frac{M_{\max}}{d} a \tag{5.18}$$

$$= \frac{22.5}{5}(10) = 45 \text{ k}$$

The maximum compression force in the top chord at midspan is found by resolving the moment component $N'_t$ into the diagonal forces $N_t$ (Fig. 5.20d)

$$N'_t = 2\frac{N_t}{\sqrt{2}} = \frac{M_{\max}}{d} a$$

$$N_t = \frac{M_{\max}}{\sqrt{2}}\frac{a}{d} = \frac{N_b}{\sqrt{2}} \tag{5.19}$$

$$= \frac{45}{\sqrt{2}} = 31.82 \text{ k}$$

The top chord members are considered to act only axially, since the roof loads are assumed to be transferred directly to the joints.

Using the column tables of the *AISC Manual* for $Kl = 1(7.07)$ results in the following preliminary tubular section

$$\text{TS 3 OD} \times 0.216$$

The required net section for the bottom chord is

$$A_{net} = \frac{N_b}{F_t} = \frac{45}{22} = 2.05 \text{ in.}^2$$

Should the members be welded to each other, then there is no loss of cross-sectional area. In case of special connection types, it is assumed here that the tensile strength at any portion of the member, such as at the threaded end piece, and the strength of the connector are at least equal to the member capacity as based on its typical cross-section. This assumption must obviously be checked. Try TS 3 OD $\times$ 0.216, $A = 2.23$ in.$^2$.

The maximum shear appears at midlength of the sides and, according to the plate analogy is equal to

$$V_{max} = 0.34wL \qquad (5.12)$$
$$= 0.34 (0.045)100 = 1.53 \text{ k/ft}$$

The length of the diagonal members in plane with the bottom chords is equal to

$$l_d = \frac{a}{2}\sqrt{2} = d\sqrt{2} = 5\sqrt{2} = 7.07 \text{ ft}$$

The maximum compression in the diagonals is found by letting the vertical components of the two diagonals be equal to the bay shear.

$$2\frac{N_d}{l_d} d = \dot{V}_{max}(a) \qquad \text{where } d = \frac{a}{2}$$

$$N_d = V_{max}(l_d) \qquad (5.20)$$
$$= 1.53(7.07) = 10.82 \text{ k}$$

The section cannot be directly taken from the *AISC Manual*, hence try 2 OD $\times$ 0.154, $A = 1.07$ in.$^2$, $r = 0.787$ in.

For the slenderness ratio, the allowable axial stresses are

$$\frac{Kl}{r} = \frac{1(7.07)12}{0.787} = 107.80 \cong 108 \quad \text{or} \quad F_a = 11.94 \text{ ksi}$$

$$f = \frac{N_d}{A} = \frac{10.82}{1.07} = 10.11 \text{ ksi} \leqslant 11.94 \text{ ksi} \qquad \text{O.K.}$$

## Problems

**5.1** Determine the stability of the self-contained space trusses shown in Fig. 5.7. If necessary, add members at proper locations so that the structures are stable.

**5.2** Show conceptually how you obtain the reactions for the cases shown in Fig. 5.5d–i by first considering a resultant lateral load parallel to the short building side, and then a resultant gravity load to be acting somewhere on the rigid roof. Correct the location of support members if they are not properly placed.

**5.3** Change the orientation of the rollers at supports *a* and *c* of the hinged tetrahedron (Fig. 5.8) by placing the one at *a* parallel to the one at *b* and changing the one at *c* so that it is parallel to the original position of the roller at *a*. What can you say about this support structure?

**5.4**   If the horizontal unit load in Example 5.1 is relocated and placed parallel to the projection of member $\overline{dc}$ so that it acts towards joint $c$, what is the magnitude of the reaction forces for the tetrahedron due to this new loading condition?

**5.5**   Determine the reactions and bar forces for the hinged tetrahedron (Fig. 5.8), if the lateral load is replaced by a unit gravity load.

**5.6**   Determine the reactions and bar forces for the four-sided pyramid (Fig. 5.9) under a lateral unit load acting at joint $e$ towards $cd$, parallel to the long base sides.

**5.7**   Investigate the square, truncated pyramid in Fig. 5.10, by placing a unit gravity load at joint $f$. Find the member forces.

**5.8**   Determine the bar forces for the space truss in Example 5.4.

**5.9**   Consider the roof structure of Example 5.5c to consist of the space frame type "square on square offset" (Fig. 5.20c), using a 10 ft grid pattern. Estimate the critical tubular member sizes by letting the loads be applied at the joints (i.e., no bending in compression members).

**5.10** Is there any change of member sizes, if the roof of Example 5.5(c) is supported only at its four corners? If so, roughly estimate the critical chord and web member sizes.

**5.11** Relocate the columns in Problem 5.10 to form a $60 \times 60$ ft grid, similar to Fig. 5.18f, so that the space frame cantilevers 20 ft to each side. Determine the maximum chord forces and the force in the diagonal member at the column in the double-cantilever portion.

**5.12** Investigate different space frame roof structures to cover a space of $150 \times 150$ ft without the help of any interior columns. Use steel with $F_y = 36$ ksi. Consider as preliminary loading 10 psf for the roof deck, 9 psf for the weight of the structure, and 30 psf live load. Check the following systems:
  (a)   one-way trusses
  (b)   two-way trusses
  (c)   square on square offset space frame
  (d)   diagonal square on square space frame
  (e)   the effect of cantilevering

# 6 FOLDED PLATE STRUCTURES

## 6.1 INTRODUCTION

The capacity of a flat thin surface structure is rather limited in the scale range for which it can be used; however, its strength and stiffness is very much improved if it is folded or bent, which increases its depth and thus its moment of inertia. The effectiveness of a folded plate structure in terms of material requirements approaches that of shells; though not quite as efficient, it has the advantage of straight line construction.

Familiar examples of folded plate structures are concrete stairs, and on a small scale, corrugated light-gauge metal panels and sheet piling with their various cross-sections.

The richness of fold geometries have already preoccupied the Chinese and Japanese for many centuries; they consider paper folding, called *origami* by the Japanese, as a form of art. The recent fashion of folded lampshades are derived from their lantern designs.

There are basically two types of folded surface systems:

- Polyhedral surfaces: they form two-dimensional basic spatial surface units.
- True folded surfaces: they form three-dimensional basic surface units.

When these surfaces can be formed by a folding operation, they are called developable.

Some common polyhedral surfaces have already been discussed in Chapter 5 from a geometrical point of view and are not further treated here.

Folded plate structures can be organized from the following points of view as also indicated in Fig. 6.1.

- Geometry
  Types of folds: plane or curved; rectangular, triangular, pentagonal, etc. with straight or curvilinear edges (e.g., parabolic chords); regular and irregular prismatic, antiprismatic (Fig. 5.12), or nonprismatic folded surfaces.

  Fold arrangement: parallel, two-way, three-way, radial, circumferential, or any combination.

  Fold cross-section: V,W,M,Z,U types, northlight forms (saw-tooth roof), cellular, shell simulation (polyhedral), and infinitely more modifications.

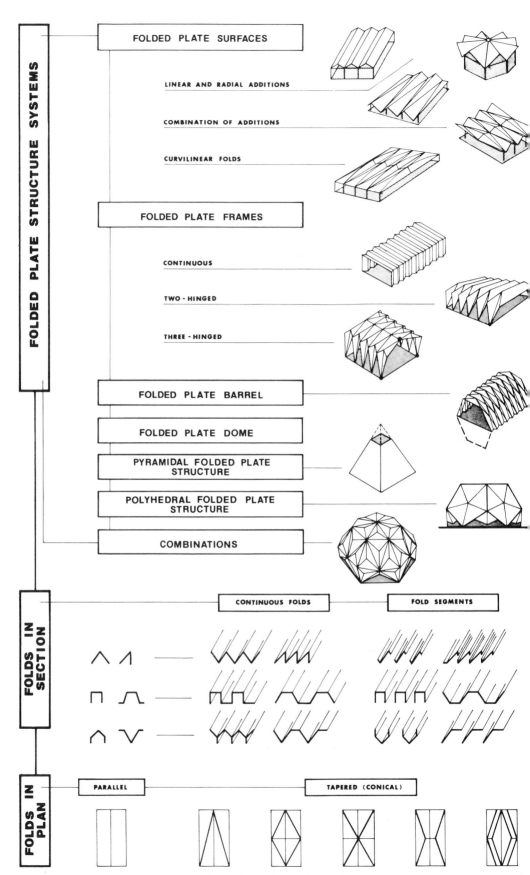

**Fig. 6.1** Folded plate structure systems.

- ■ Construction

  Plate structure: solid, framed, trussed, corrugated, composite, etc. (e.g., see Fig. 8.1).

  Construction process: cast-in-place, prefab components, folding operation.
- ■ Material: concrete, steel, timber, plastics, paperboard, composites (see Section 8.1).
- ■ Structural behavior: beams, arches, frames, surfaces, vaults, shells of various forms (e.g., domes, hyperbolic paraboloids), intersecting forms, etc.

The geometry of the folds greatly influences the behavior of the structure. This is apparent from Fig. 6.1 by comparing the folded plate frames and the barrel vault; the fold arrangement determines where hinges form and whether the structural action is predominantly linear or surface-like. The folds of cylindrical building forms are generally derived from antiprisms (Fig. 5.12); for instance, the geometry of the folded barrel in Fig. 6.1 is hexagon-based.

It is beyond the scope of this discussion to investigate the wealth and complexity of fold geometries. However, an appreciation for formal and technical possibilities is developed from the study of typical architectural buildings.

Complex ribless folded vaults have already been built by the late Gothic designers, especially along the Baltic coast, Bohemia, and Saxony. The Muslim architects of the fifteenth century employed also the folded vault principle. Among the first modern folded plate structures are Freyssinet's concrete hangars at Orly (See Fig. 8.9a) and the German coal bunkers of the early 1920s.

The few examples of folded plate structures in Fig. 6.2 express the limitless formal potential of the principle. The various fold shapes constitute either beams, slabs, or the entire enclosure.

First, some of the precast concrete systems are discussed. The 125-ft span roof with end cantilevers of case (a) indicates its strength by allowing the mezzanine floor to be suspended from it. The 3 in. thick trapezoidal folded plates of case (b) are 70 ft long and 9 ft wide. The T-sections in case (c) employ inclined flanges. The double-cantilever roof of case (d) is only supported on the walls along the central corridor. The 3 in. thick, 72-ft long folded plates of case (l) rest on double-legged Y-shaped concrete columns which effectively resist wind forces. Finally, the interlocking U- and M-shaped plate units of case (h) span 90 ft.

The roof of case (p) is composed of prefabricated triangular stressed-skin plywood panels. Similarly, for case (q) stressed-skin plywood panels of various sizes are combined to form a spatial polyhedral-type roof surface. The roof of the circular building in (m) consists of radially arranged steel beams supporting precast concrete slab elements.

Three sloping planes, which are framed with exposed steel members and the metal deck below, define the enclosure of the Miller Memorial Theater in Houston (r). The roof structure rests on the two primary 30-in. steel balls which are 195 ft apart, and the two secondary box columns. The balls are anchored to concrete pedestals and are encircled by claws which are attached to the roof frame so that uplift forces can be resisted. The space frame skin of the monumental Crystal Cathedral (s) forms a continuous envelope. Another striking example of the folding principle is the U.S. Air Force Academy Chapel in Colorado Springs (Fig. 4.59a).

Foldable, low-cost housing enclosures have been successfully developed by Hirshen and Van de Ryn in 1966 for migrant workers in California. The $\frac{3}{8}$-in. thick prefolded paperboard vaults (see Fig. 8.3c) consist of sandwich elements of coated kraftboard with polyurethane foam core.

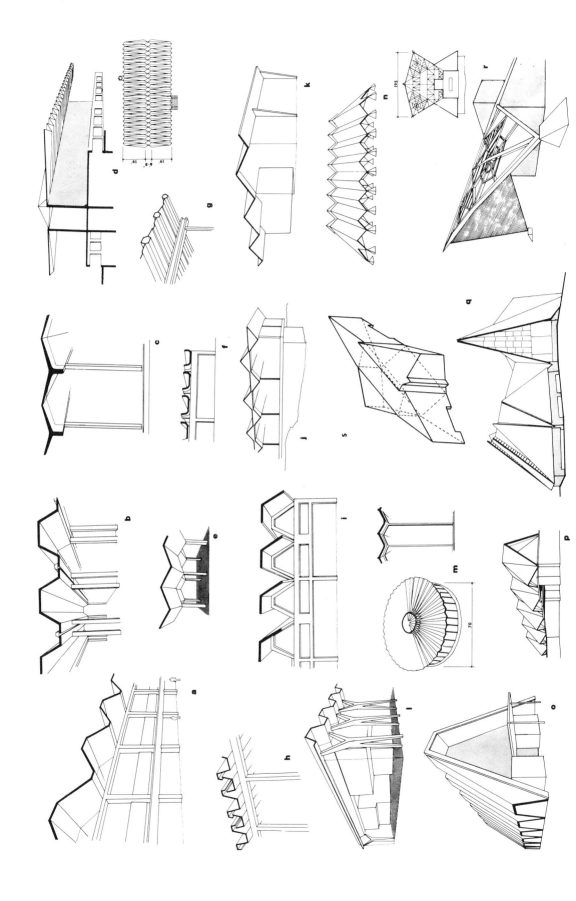

Though the folded plate principle in concrete is usually in the range 40–150 ft, it is found in much larger-scale buildings. Probably the world's longest clear span folded plate structure is the 14-ft deep prestressed Allegheny Airlines' hangar concrete roof (completed in 1971) at Boston's Logan International Airport with 252 ft.

Folded plate construction has also been applied to large scale cantilever structures (Fig. 4.74). Especially remarkable are the American Airlines hangars in San Francisco and Los Angeles with their enormous 230-ft stressed steel skin cantilevers on each side (see in Section 4.7, Cantilever Structures). A famous example of the application of the fold principle to shell construction is the concrete dome of the University of Illinois Assembly Hall at Urbana (Fig. 8.21h). The branching, triangular folds convincingly express the required buckling strength for this 400-ft span shell.

## 6.2  THE STRUCTURAL BEHAVIOR OF SURFACES WITH PARALLEL FOLDING

Here only the more common prismatic folded surfaces with triangular and trapezoidal cross-sections are investigated. The typical characteristics of folded plates are identified in Fig. 6.3 and should be referred to in the following discussion.

A folded plate roof structure may be formed by just one single folded plate unit, or it may consist of a multiple-bay system. Visualize a folded plate structure as a system of inclined beams leaning against each other. These tilted beams are carried by transverse supports such as frames, walls, and so on, at locations close to their ends. These supports transmit the vertical load components to the ground and also act as stiffeners, preventing the structure from unfolding or flattening out. The lateral thrust that causes this tendency to unfold is often carried by tie rods attached directly to the folded plates, in which case the support structure must resist only the vertical forces. Intermediate transverse diaphragms (i.e., panels above and/or below the folds, or ties) are sometimes used in order to reduce deformation, as well as to ensure that the folded surface is stiff enough to behave as a total unit. To increase the stiffness in beam action, longitudinal supports may be placed along the valley fold lines, that is, beams and trusses can be used to this effect. While the interior folded plates of a multiple-bay system can support each other laterally, the free longitudinal edge of the exterior plates are vulnerable to large displacements and, in general, need to be stiffened by edge beams.

To develop some understanding about the structural behavior of folded plates, the external load action is resolved into components perpendicular and parallel to the plates. The normal force components cause the plate to respond as a one-way slab with supports along the fold lines. These supports are critical since they are, to some degree, flexbible. For the purpose of approximate study, one may assume that the multibay roof is uniformly loaded, thus for a typical interior unit no differential displacements between the supports along the valley and ridge edges are caused; the supports along the fold lines can be considered rigid. In order to have true one-way slab action, using standard concrete construction, the plate span $L$ must be at least twice the plate width $b$ ($L \geqslant 2b$). The load components parallel to the plates, that is, the reactions of the transverse slab, cause the plates to act as deep beam structures resting on transverse supports; it is assumed that the inclination of the plates is steep enough to allow for this type of behavior.

The analysis can be assumed statically determinate for folded plates hinged along the

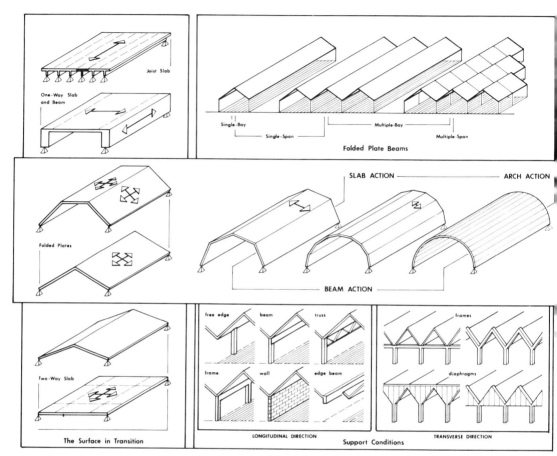

Fig. 6.3

fold lines such as steel and timber trusses or stressed-skin plates that lean against each other and are covered, for example, with light-gauge metal deck or plywood. In this case, the deck behaves similarly to the one-way slab, and the trusses or girders act as independent deep beams. However, the analysis is highly indeterminate for monolithic continuous folded plate structures such as cast-in-place concrete construction. Here, the plates act as both deep beams and slabs.

The following discussion attempts to develop some understanding about the behavior of monolithic folded plate structures. Previously, it was stated that the assumption of one-way slab action is justifiable only for plates having a proportion of $L \geqslant 2b$. As the plate span decreases and approaches the same dimension as its width, the plate begins to act more as a two-way slab. On the other hand, as the plate span increases ($L \gg b$), the slab action becomes less and less important. These conditions are encountered in such various examples as corrugated metal panels used as decking, monolithic concrete joist slabs, and wide-flange metal beams, where the flange width, in comparison to the beam span, is so small that only the beam action is considered.

The interplay of slab and beam action is investigated, from a geometrical point of view, in Fig. 6.3. The ribs in the concrete joist slab are so closely spaced that its primary behavior is its beam action; the slab behavior perpendicular to the joists is so small that usually only temperature reinforcing is required. As the ribs move further apart, slab action becomes more and more pronounced, resulting in a one-way slab system sitting on beams. The independent action of beam and slab is apparent not just from the location of the beams but also from the relative thickness of the slab as compared to the beam size. However, due to the continuity between slab and beam, part of the slab acts together with the beam, establishing the familiar concept of the effective flange width. Following, the widths of the edge beams are reduced to the same thickness as the slab and then inclined, thus decreasing the span of the slab. Now a new structural system is generated: a continuous folded surface. Here the horizontal and inclined plates both act as slabs and beams. The plate thickness depends on its width, that is, the magnitude of the transverse bending stresses depends upon the span of the slab. The total height of the folded beam is a function of the longitudinal span; the usual height-to-span ratio for folded plate structures is in the range $h/L = 1/10$–$1/15$. Further inclination of the plates eliminates the horizontal portions and results in V-shaped folding (Fig. 6.3). Now the direct slab action is decreased, since the force components normal to the surface, which only cause slab action, are reduced. But the overall effect may not cause a reduction in slab action because the slab span has been increased. As the fold height decreases, and the structure becomes flatter, the force components normal to the plate due to gravity action become larger, hence the slab action increases, approaching a two-way slab. Although the force components parallel to the plate decrease, the inertia of the folded plate beam decreases much faster, resulting in an increase in beam action and hence in longitudinal stresses. It is obvious from this discussion that the slope of the plates must be reasonable, so that the assumed behavior is possible and the material is efficiently used. For V- or W-shaped folding, the slope of the plates is typically in a range $25°$–$45°$.

It is of interest to note the changes in structural behavior in a given folded-plate system, as the number of folds is increased to the point where the structure becomes the equivalent of a single-curvature shell beam (Fig. 6.3). Although the effect of the number of folds on the beam behavior in the longitudinal direction is less pronounced, the slab behavior in the transverse direction is very much influenced by the change. As the number of folds increases, the slab width decreases, hence the slab moments decrease, keeping in mind that the slabs are considered to support each other along the fold lines. When the number of folds has become infinite, fold discontinuities and slab moments disappear. Now the forces normal to the curvilinear surface are carried in the transverse direction in arch action, that is, by axial forces and bending; the lack of curvature distinguishes folded plates from shells. Folded plates are much more vulnerable to bending stresses than shells and thus less efficient from a force resistance point of view.

### Approximate Design of Hinged Tilted Trusses and Continuous Folded Concrete Plates

A typical V-folded roof structure (Fig. 6.4a) will be examined by studying the approximate behavior of an interior bay unit. Two different construction systems are analyzed: first, hinged steel trusses and then continuous reinforced concrete plates. This folded plate roof is a single-span, multibay structure with the following dimensions:

longitudinal span: $L = 100$ ft
fold height: $h = 10$ ft
bay width: $2a = 30$ ft

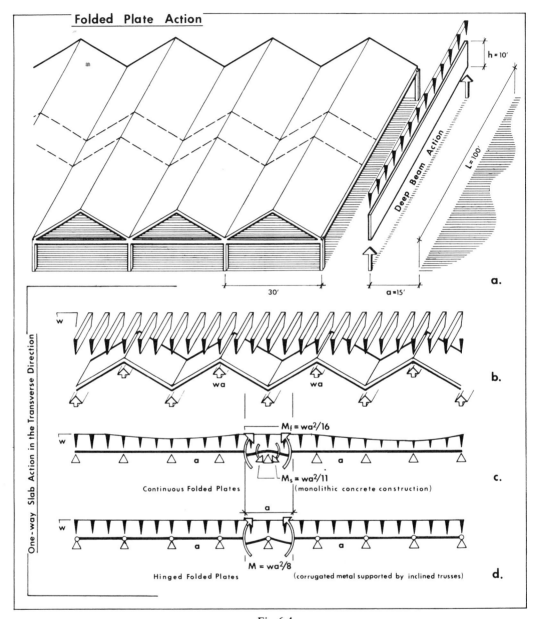

Fig. 6.4

The roof must support a snow load of 30 psf on the horizontal projection (keeping in mind that the true load distribution is quite different). The height-to-span ratio of the roof is typically in the range

$$\frac{h}{L} = \frac{10}{100} = \frac{1}{10}$$

The fold angle measured from the horizontal is

$$\theta = \arctan \frac{10}{15} = 33.69° \qquad \cos\theta = 0.832 \qquad \sin\theta = 0.555$$

The width of a typical plate is

$$b = \frac{15}{\cos\theta} = 18.03 \text{ ft}$$

The span-to-width ratio of the plate is

$$\frac{L}{b} = \frac{100}{18.03} = 5.55 > 2$$

Since the span-to-width ratio is greater than 2, the folded plate acts as a one-way slab in the transverse direction.

**Example 6.1** Assume the roof to be constructed of tilted steel Pratt trusses subdivided into ten equal bays of 10 ft width each (Fig. 6.5d). The dead loads are of the following magnitudes:

| | |
|---|---|
| built-up roofing and insulation | 5 psf |
| roof  decking  material | 5 psf |
| | 10 psf |
| truss weight | 10 psf |
| total weight | 20 psf |

### (a) Design of Roof Deck

The deck supports 30 psf of snow load on its horizontal projection and 10 psf of dead load along its own plane. By transforming the dead load onto the horizontal projection, the two loads may be added

$$w = 30 + \frac{10}{\cos\theta} = 42.02 \text{ psf}$$

The deck acts as a simply supported one-way slab, with a maximum moment of

$$M_{max} = \frac{wa^2}{8} = \frac{0.042(15)^2}{8} = 1.18 \text{ ft-k/foot width}$$

Using an allowable bending stress of $F_b = 22$ ksi, yields the required section modulus of

$$S = \frac{M}{F_b} = \frac{1.18(12)}{22} = 0.64 \text{ in.}^3/\text{foot width}$$

The steel decking may now be selected from manufacturers' catalogs, and then checked for resistance to deflection.

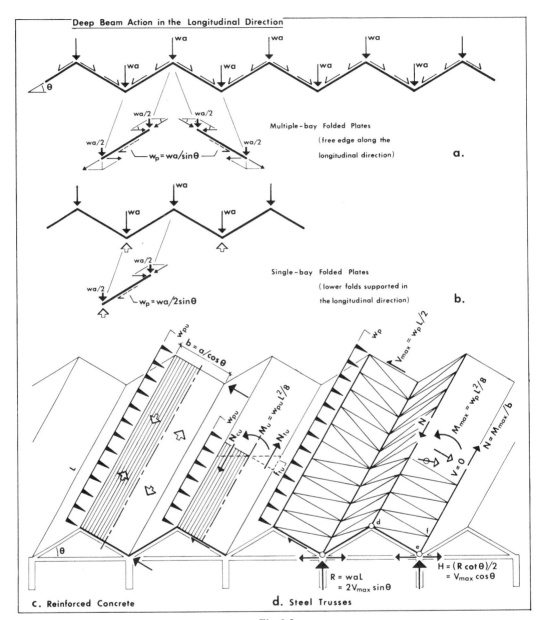

Fig. 6.5

## (b) Design of Inclined Trusses (A36 steel)

The trusses carry the reactions of the simply supported steel decking to the transverse supports located at both ends of the structure. Two typical interior trusses are isolated and separated from the remainder of the roof as shown in Fig. 6.5a. The deck reactions are resolved into two force components: horizontal components, which balance and cancel each other under symmetrical loading conditions, and forces parallel to the truss plane, which must be carried in bending to the end supports through axial member action. It is assumed that the trusses carry forces only parallel to their surface.

Resolving the reactions of the steel decking into linear loads parallel to the truss plane (Fig. 6.5a) yields

$$w_p = \frac{wa}{\sin \theta} \tag{6.1}$$

Should the trusses be supported longitudinally along the valley chords as in Fig. 6.5b, only one-half of the deck loads is carried by the trusses, while the other half is transferred by the deck directly to the longitudinal supports.

The uniform load on the horizontal roof projection, including the truss weight, is

$$w = 30 + \frac{20}{\cos \theta} = 54.04 \text{ psf}$$

The linear loads parallel to the truss plane are equal to

$$w_p = \frac{wa}{\sin \theta} = \frac{0.054(15)}{0.555} = 1.46 \text{ k/ft} \tag{6.1}$$

The maximum moment for the simply supported truss is

$$M_{max} = \frac{w_p L^2}{8} = \frac{1.46(100)^2}{8} = 1825 \text{ ft-k}$$

This moment occurs at midspan, and is considered to be resisted by the axial action of the top and bottom chords only, as shown in Fig. 6.5d; the effect of the steel decking in resisting bending in the longitudinal direction is conservatively neglected. The forces in the chords are

$$N = \frac{M_{max}}{b} = \frac{1825}{18.03} = 101.22 \text{ k}$$

In this approach it is assumed that the truss chords act independently of the one adjacent; should two adjacent trusses share a chord, then the axial force is twice as large.

In this preliminary design, local bending of the chord elements, caused by the continuous support of the decking along the length of the truss, is neglected and the loads are assumed to act only at the hinges. The allowable compressive stress for the top chord is equal to $0.6F_y$ or 22 ksi. This allowable stress is not reduced for buckling because adjacent trusses, as well as the steel decking, are assumed to provide enough lateral support. The required steel area, for one chord member only, is

$$A = \frac{N}{F_c} = \frac{101.22(2)}{22} = 9.20 \text{ in.}^2$$

For preliminary design purposes, select an angle section $L8 \times 8 \times \frac{5}{8}$, $A = 9.61$ in.$^2$. The detailing of the truss connections must be carefully considered, especially when inclination of the plates is some angle other than 45°.

The size of the bottom chord member depends on the net sectional area at the connection. Since no information is available at this stage, a reduction coefficient of 0.85 is used. Hence the minimum required gross member area is

$$A = \frac{N}{0.85F_t} = \frac{101.22(2)}{0.85(22)} = 10.83 \text{ in.}^2$$

Try $L8 \times 8 \times \frac{3}{4}, A = 11.4 \text{ in.}^2$.

The vertical reaction at the ends of the truss is carried by inclined columns such as column $\overline{de}$ (Fig. 6.5d). The axial compressive force in this member is equal to

$$N_{de} = 1.46(50) = 73.00 \text{ k} \quad \text{(C)}$$

For a slenderness about the strong axis (i.e., $L_y = 0$) of $(KL)r_y/r_x = 1(18.03)/1.77 = 10.19$, try $W6 \times 20$.

The largest shear force acts adjacent to the reactions, and is carried by the diagonal $\overline{df}$. Balancing the forces at joint $d$ yields the diagonal tension force

$$N_{df} = \frac{73}{18.03} 20.62 = 83.49 \text{ k}$$

where the length of the diagonal $\overline{df}$ is equal to $\sqrt{18.03^2 + 10^2} = 20.62 \text{ ft.}$

The required cross-sectional area for a reduction coefficient of 0.85 is

$$A = \frac{N}{0.85F_t} = \frac{83.49}{0.85(22)} = 4.47 \text{ in.}^2$$

Try $W6 \times 20, A = 5.87 \text{ in.}^2, r_y = 1.50 \text{ in.}$

$$\frac{l}{r_y} = \frac{20.62(12)}{1.50} = 164.96 < 240 \quad \text{O.K.}$$

The gravity loads acting on the roof cause a column load in the transverse support structure (Fig. 6.5d) of

$$R = w(2a)\frac{L}{2} \tag{6.2}$$

$$R = 0.054(15)100 = 81 \text{ k}$$

The transverse support structure must also resist the horizontal thrust of the end bays (and thrust due to asymmetrical loading) by means of tie rods or frame action

$$H = \frac{R}{2} \cot \theta = \frac{81}{2} \cot \theta = 60.75 \text{ k}$$

The required cross-sectional area for a reduction coefficient of 0.85 is

$$A = \frac{60.75}{0.85(22)} = 3.25 \text{ in.}^2$$

Try $L4 \times 3 \times \frac{1}{2}, A = 3.25 \text{ in.}^2$.

For shorter spans, stressed skin systems can be used instead of trusses. In this case the folded plate frames do not need diagonal elements to resist shear forces because the decking is constructed to act as a shear diaphragm, as well as to provide slab action along the folded surface. Plywood folded plates work in a similar manner (see Fig. 8.1). A typical plate consists of top and bottom chord members framed by intermediate rafters and covered with plywood, so that the structure essentially is an inclined box girder. The plywood web is fastened continuously to its framing, and must resist the shear caused by deep beam action and bending due to its function as sheathing. The magnitude of the stresses in the sheathing depends to a great extent on the spacing of the rafters (see Problems 6.4 and 6.5).

**Example 6.2**  The folded plate truss structure was considered to be a determinate system where the decking behaved independently as a slab in the transverse direction, while the truss acted as a plate or deep beam in the longitudinal direction. Reinforced concrete folded plates, however, are monolithic; the plates act not only as deep beams but also simultaneously as slabs. The approximate analysis and design of concrete folded plates may be carried out by the same methods as those for independently acting truss systems. The plates are first designed as continuous one-way slabs supported by the adjacent plates along the fold lines, and then as deep beams carried by the transverse supports. These two behavioral systems are superimposed upon each other, resulting in a structure that responds as a unit to both force actions.

## (a) Design of the Slab Action

Since the plates are continuous across the fold lines, the one-way slab action is also a continuous one (Fig. 6.4b). The ACI moment coefficients are used to approximate the magnitude of the moments at the supports (fold lines) and at midspan for a typical interior plate. The net span for such a plate is conservatively assumed to be the distance between the edges of the fold lines.

The thickness of the plate is primarily dependent on the slab action. For continuous one-way slabs, the thickness (in inches) is assumed to be one-third of the span (in feet) for this first rough approximation (i.e., $L/t = 36$), but at least 3 in. Using this rule of thumb, and considering the inclined slabs as equivalent slabs on the horizontal projection, results in a preliminary average slab thickness of

$$\frac{a}{3} = \frac{15}{3} = 5 \text{ in.}$$

The dead load of the 5 in. slab for normal weight concrete together with roofing and insulation materials is

$$W_D = 5 + \frac{150(5)}{12} = 67.50 \text{ psf}$$

The ultimate load on the horizontal roof projection is equal to

$$W_{nu} = 1.4 \frac{w_D}{\cos \theta} + 1.7 w_L$$

$$W_u = 1.4 \frac{67.50}{0.832} + 1.7(30) = 164.58 \text{ psf}$$

The ultimate slab moments are as follows: At the fold lines

$$M_{us} = \frac{w_u a^2}{11} = \frac{0.165(15)^2}{11} = 3.38 \text{ ft-k/ft}$$

At slab midspan

$$M_{uf} = \frac{w_u a^2}{16} = \frac{0.165(15)^2}{16} = 2.32 \text{ ft-k/ft}$$

Using 50 ksi steel and 4 ksi concrete yields the following approximate reinforcing for $d \approx h-1 = 5-1 = 4$ in.

$$A_s \cong \frac{M_u}{0.8 f_y d} \tag{1.39}$$

The required steel at the fold lines is:

$$A_s = \frac{3.38(12)}{0.8(50)4} = 0.254 \text{ in.}^2/\text{ft of slab}$$

Try #4 bars at 9 in. on center, $A_s = 0.26$ in.$^2$/ft.
The required steel at midspan is

$$A_s = \frac{0.254(2.32)}{3.38} = 0.174 \text{ in.}^2/\text{ft}$$

Try #4 bars at $13\frac{1}{2}$ in. on center, $A_s = 0.175$ in.$^2$/ft.
The required steel for temperature reinforcing is:

$$A_s = 0.002bt = 0.002(12)5 = 0.12 \text{ in.}^2/\text{ft} \tag{8.4}$$

Try #3 bars at $10\frac{1}{2}$ in. on center, $A_s = 0.12$ in.$^2$/ft.
Refer to Fig. 6.6 for the placement of the reinforcing bars in the slab. From a strength point of view, the assumed slab thickness is checked by comparing the steel ratio to the maximum allowable one; the steel ratio $p$ is expressed as the ratio of areas of reinforcing and concrete

$$p = \frac{A_s}{bd} = \frac{0.26}{12(4)} = 0.0054 \ll p_{max} = 0.0275 \quad \text{(Table A.5)}$$

The slab is clearly underreinforced and thus satisfactory.

### (b) Plate Design

The plate action in the longitudinal direction is highly indeterminate. In order to develop some understanding about the behavior, the plates are assumed to be hinged along the fold lines, and then the same process of analysis as for the inclined trusses of Example 6.1 is followed. The treatment of the panels as individual units causes incompatibility along the plate boundaries, since the stresses and deformations along the fold lines do not coincide as they should for continuous boundary conditions. The process of correcting these errors by the method of successive balance, for instance, is typical for the solution of

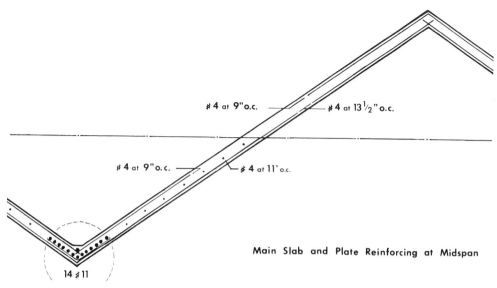

#4 at 9"o.c.

#4 at 13½"o.c.

#4 at 9"o.c.

#4 at 11" o.c.

**Main  Slab  and  Plate  Reinforcing  at  Midspan**

14 #11

**Fig. 6.6**

statically indeterminate structures. However, there is no correction necessary for the special condition of an interior plate of a multibay V-shaped folded plate structure where all the bays are identical and subject to the same uniform loading. For this condition the stresses of the individual plates along the fold lines are equal to each other, and the hinged boundary conditions are identical to the continuous ones. Rather than using the approach employed for the truss example, the beam method is taken by treating the folded plate structure as a series of parallel beams or as a corrugated slab. This statically determinate approach is more general for preliminary design purposes, since it is not restricted to just V-shaped folded structures, but can be applied to other systems such as the folded plate roof with a trapezoidal cross-section in Fig. 6.7, which is further investigated in Problem 6.7.

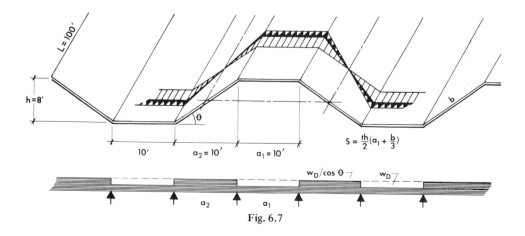

$$S = \frac{th}{2}\left(a_1 + \frac{b}{3}\right)$$

**Fig. 6.7**

Obviously, considering the cross-section of a folded plate structure as being equivalent to the cross-section of a beam can only be taken as a preliminary estimate and as an approximate structural analog, because any distortion of the section is neglected. In reality, the thin plate elements are much more susceptible to deformations than ordinary beam sections; the resulting stress pattern is not distributed linearly as assumed in the beam theory. However, if the folds are stiffened, the beam model becomes more realistic, especially as the span of the folded plate structure increases ($L \gg b$) as has already been discussed (Fig. 6.3). The beam method is used by structural engineers as a possible final design solution for interior plates of a multiple folded plate structure if the span-to-height ratio is greater than 10 ($L/h \geqslant 10$), which is the case for this problem.

In Fig. 6.8 a typical interior cross-section of the beam is shown. Because of symmetry of geometry and loading, only one inclined beam is considered. The equivalent ultimate line load on the horizontal roof projection is

$$w_u = 0.165(15) = 2.48 \text{ k/ft}$$

This yields a maximum ultimate moment at midspan of:

$$M_{u \text{ max}} = 2.48(100)^2/8 = 3100 \text{ ft-k}$$

It is assumed for folded plates and thin shells that the concrete is ideally elastic, homogeneous, and isotropic (see Section 8.1 A), hence the entire section modulus for the concrete cross-section can be used. The equivalent section modulus of a vertical beam placed parallel to the gravity loads (Fig. 6.8 and Problem 6.1) is

$$S_{CA} = \frac{(t/\sin \theta)h^2}{6} \tag{6.3}$$

$$S_{CA} = \frac{(5/0.555)(10 \times 12)^2}{6} = 21621.62 \text{ in.}^3$$

As based on the assumption of ideally homogeneous, isotropic behavior, the maximum stresses at the top and bottom fold lines (Fig. 6.8) are

$$\pm f_u = \frac{M_u}{S} = \frac{3100(12)}{21621.62} = 1.72 \text{ ksi}$$

The compressive strength of concrete is:

$$f_{c \text{ all}} = \phi(0.85f_c') = 0.7[0.85(4)] = 2.38 \text{ ksi} > 1.72 \text{ ksi}$$

The maximum compressive stress at the top is easily resisted by the strength of the concrete. The steel reinforcement will resist all tension; any tensile capacity of the concrete is neglected. The resultant total tensile force is:

$$N_{tu} = f_{tu}A = f_{tu}\frac{b}{2}\left(\frac{1}{2}\right)t = 1.72 \frac{18.03(12)}{2}\left(\frac{1}{2}\right)5 = 465.17 \text{ k}$$

The required steel area is

$$A_s = \frac{N_{tu}}{\phi F_y} = \frac{465.17}{(0.9)50} = 10.34 \text{ in.}^2$$

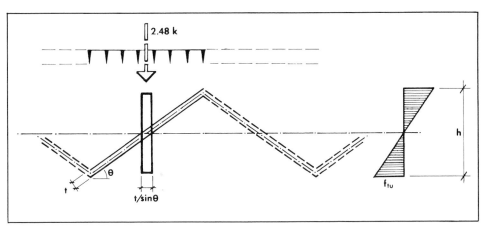

Fig. 6.8

According to ACI (see in Section 8.1, Reinforced Concrete Shells), where tensile stresses greatly vary it may be desirable to concentrate tension reinforcement in regions of maximum tensile stress rather than distributing it over the entire zone of the varying tensile stress. Try fourteen #11 bars, $A_s$ = 21.87 in.$^2$ > 2(10.34).

These bars are concentrated at midthickness of the plate in the valley fold region as indicated in Fig. 6.6. Since the major longitudinal reinforcing is concentrated in the valleys, the remaining portions of the tension area should, according to the *ACI Code*, have a minimum reinforcing of

$$A_s = 0.0035bt = 0.0035(12 \times 5) = 0.21 \text{ in.}^2/\text{ft} \qquad (8.3)$$

Try #4 bars at 11 in. on center, $A_s$ = 0.22 in.$^2$/ft.

The maximum shear stresses appear close to the supports as diagonal tension at 45° to the longitudinal axis. Shear reinforcing at 45° must be provided if the diagonal tension cannot be carried by the concrete itself. The approximate maximum ultimate shear at the supports due to the direct gravity loading only is

$$V_{u \text{ max}} = \frac{w_{pu}L}{2} = 2.48 \frac{100}{2} = 124 \text{ k}$$

The maximum nominal ultimate shear stress is

$$f_{vu} = \frac{V_u}{\phi h(t/\sin \theta)} = \frac{124\,000}{0.85(10 \times 12)5/0.555} = 134.94 \text{ psi}$$

The allowable shear stress for the concrete is

$$\nu_c = 2\sqrt{f_c'} = 2\sqrt{4000} = 126.49 \text{ psi} < 134.94 \text{ psi}$$

The shear stresses are larger than what the concrete is expected to be able to support. Therefore, diagonal reinforcing at the supporting ends must be provided. For a typical layout of such reinforcing, refer to the section on cylindrical shell beams (see Fig. 8.12).

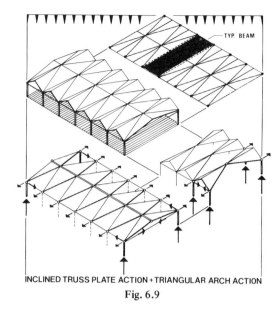

INCLINED TRUSS PLATE ACTION + TRIANGULAR ARCH ACTION

Fig. 6.9

## 6.3 INTRODUCTION TO STRUCTURAL BEHAVIOR OF TRIANGULAR FOLDED PLATE SURFACE STRUCTURES

The response of nonprismatic folded plate surface structures to loading is quite complex. For the special case shown in Fig. 6.9, the behavior of the roof under uniform gravity loading can be visualized as the combined action of:

■ Two *inclined trusses* spanning in the longitudinal direction with the ridge member serving as compression chord and the tie rods along the facades as bottom chords, while the inclined valley intersections form diagonal members; the thrust caused by the two trusses is resisted by ties across the building ends.

■ *Triangular (spatial) three-hinge arches* which cause lateral thrust in the transverse direction that must be carried by the trusses to the building ends.

A more general approach would be to subdivide the folded surface into a grid of beams. After the variable inertia of the typical beam has been determined critical stresses are found. This approach overestimates the magnitude of the stresses, since the real surface action in the transverse direction was ignored.

### Problems

**6.1** Show that the plate analysis using the equivalent vertical beam approach [Example 6.2b, Eq. (6.3)] does yield the same solution as the plate analysis in Example 6.1.

**6.2** Determine the longitudinal tensile stresses for a typical interior plate by considering the folded plates in Example 6.2 as hinged along the fold lines. Use the same approach as for the solution of the inclined trusses in Example 6.1.

**6.3**  Investigate a typical interior fold of a multibay, 120-ft span folded plate welded truss structure similar to the one shown in Fig. 6.5d. The Pratt truss is subdivided into eight spaces each at 15 ft; a typical bay width is $2a = 20$ ft, and the roof height is 10 ft. Assume a dead load of 11 psf for the roof deck, insulation and the built-up roof, as well as 10 psf for the truss. The snow load on the horizontal roof projection is 20 psf. Use $A36$ steel for the truss and an allowable bending stress of $F_b = 22$ ksi for the steel deck. Determine the approximate sizes for the critical truss members, the type of roof deck, and the size of the tie along the end supports.

**6.4**  Do a preliminary design of a folded plate plywood roof of a construction similar to the V-shaped single-skin plate structure shown in Fig. 8.1. The 64-ft simple span structure has a typical bay width of $2a = 40$ ft and a roof height of 10 ft. Assume a dead load of 10 psf and a live load of 15 psf, both to act on the horizontal roof projection. The allowable stresses for the standard plywood sheathing are $F_v = 185$ psi and $F_b = 1200$ psi. The allowable stresses for the other members are: $F_b = 1250$ psi, $F_c = 1100$ psi, and $F_t = 1050$ psi. Determine the approximate sizes of the sheathing, the rafters which are spaced at 32 in. on center and the eave and ridge chords.

**6.5**  Consider the folded plate plywood structure in Problem 6.4 to be a single-fold unit (or the outer plates of a multibay system) supported on longitudinal wall enclosures. Determine the preliminary member sizes for the sheathing, rafters, and chords.

**6.6**  Determine the approximate amount of the main reinforcing in the longitudinal and transverse directions for a typical $3\frac{1}{2}$-in. thick interior plate of a V-type folded plate roof of 4 ft height and a bay width of 10 ft (i.e., $a = 5$ ft) spanning 60 ft. Assume a dead load of 50 psf and a snow load of 30 psf. Use 50 ksi steel and 4 ksi concrete.

**6.7**  For the W-shaped folded concrete plate in Fig. 6.8 determine the main reinforcing at midspan in the transverse and longitudinal directions. The folded plate structure acts as a simply supported beam spanning 100 ft; the effect of the small cantilevers at the ends is neglected. Assume a plate thickness of 4 in. Use 50 ksi steel and 4 ksi concrete weighing 145 pcf.

# 7  INTRODUCTION TO BENT SURFACE STRUCTURES

To arrive at some initial understanding of bent surface structures an awareness of their origins in an architectural historical context is developed. Further appreciation is generated by pointing to examples in nature as analogs for curvilinear surface forms. Then the organization of various common surface geometries is presented. The last part of this chapter is most important; there the membrane forces for common surfaces under typical loading will be derived. They establish an essential basis for understanding the rigid and soft shells of the following chapters.

## 7.1  THE SHELL STRUCTURE IN NATURE

Living organisms are constantly changing and adjusting to new external pressures; they are transforming in time and space. Their formal response has always been intriguing to designers and a constant source for new discoveries, though they can never fully understand the forces and principles that shape the organism. Some mathematicians, architects, scientists, poets, and artists have fully concentrated on only the geometry in nature in order to recognize the conformity, and order of proportions defining space as expressed by lines, surfaces, and shapes; that is, they have tried to unveil the "Divine Order." For instance, the formal features of symmetry and regularity are always reflected by the beautiful snowflake crystals though they are never the same. Their patterns remind us of the minute skeletal shell structures of the diatoms (marine algae) and radiolaria (unicellular organisms). These skeletons reveal an extraordinary complexity and delicacy of geometry as well as a nearly endless variety of shapes and surface structures. They seem to correspond to architectural constructions and to illustrate basic building concepts such as least weight by employing a minimum solid ribbing, that is, accepting the structural engineering analog. Some of the radiolaria even encompass properties of triangulated, stressed-skin shells.

There is an abundance of surface structures in nature that are not just to be found on the microscopic scale; some typical examples are shown in Fig. 7.1. Common rigid shell forms are the shells of eggs, snails, turtles, mussels, skulls, hollow horns (e.g., goat, sheep), clay nests of ovenbirds, nests of the weaverbirds, etc.; all these shells express an un-

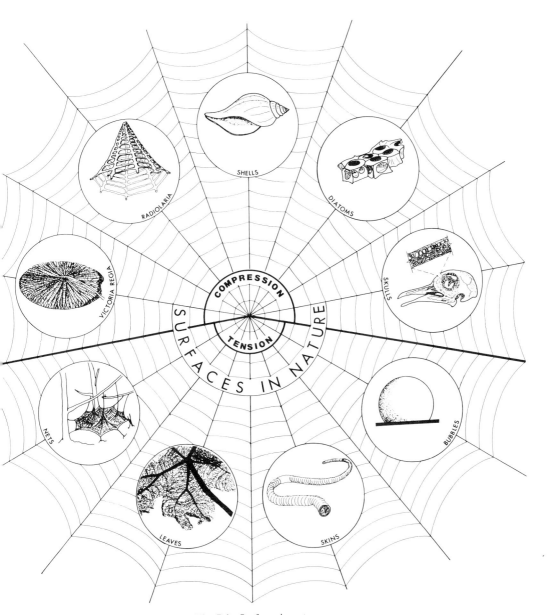

**Fig. 7.1**  Surfaces in nature.

believable richness of surface forms as well as the strength of the bent surface structure. The various spiral geometries of seashells, especially the beauty and perfectness of the nautilus, have always been inspiring. The dome-like shape of the skull uses minimum material to achieve maximum strength so that the most vital organs can be protected. The bone itself, on a microscopic scale, consists of an intricate three-dimensional rigid lattice network that contains the soft tissue elements. Depending on the type of skull capsule, the number of layers ranges from one to multilayer systems similar to sandwich construction.

There are many types of tensile membranes in nature. The lightweight wings of insects and bats respond to the necessary flexibility and mobility; they can be described as folding soft shell structures. They may be reinforced with a delicate network of ribbing, as for the much publicized dragonfly, reminding us of the branching grid structures of leaves.

Pneumatic forms are found in sea foam, soap bubbles, and organic flexible cells stabilized by fluids. The hydrostatic skeleton and the lack of stiff components, typical for some worms, clearly respond to flexibility.

There are infinitely many types of spider webs ranging from two-dimensional to three-dimensional net structures; they may be the familiar, vertical, sheet-like radial webs, or suspended tent-like membranes.

The radially stiffened membrane of Victoria, the giant water lily of the Amazon, has fascinated many architects. It probably started with Joseph Paxton who was intrigued by the beauty and strength of the branching rib pattern that supports the larger than 5 ft pad at the underside. Its structure influenced his design of the barrel vaulted iron/glass structure of London's Crystal Palace of 1851, which, in turn, had an extensive impact on subsequent architecture.

## 7.2 THE DEVELOPMENT OF BENT SURFACE STRUCTURES

The great dome structures of the past (Fig. 7.2), together with the cylindrical barrel vaults, are the forerunners of the present day soft and rigid shells, keeping in mind that the modern, thin membranes, with their formal flexibility, are actually of completely different nature. Still, the study of various construction methods for dome structures throughout Western history will strengthen the understanding and appreciation of current technology.

The structural design of the great domes of the past did not have a scientific origin. They were sized as based on empirical knowledge derived over time from material characteristics, construction processes, corrections of failures, geometric symbolism, and so on, and were contained in design rules as described, for instance, by the Roman Vitruvius in the first century B.C., and later in the Renaissance by Leone Battista Alberti (1485). Gothic master masons equated structure with geometry, possibly reflecting some intuitive feeling for force flow, though it was never formulated. The Renaissance architects, on the other hand, were absorbed by the geometry of form in general; they tried to reflect the harmony of nature in architectural proportions through mathematics. Structural concerns as reflected by the revived interest in Roman engineering hardly had any influence on the form-giving process of architecture. However, during this period of humanism, scholars began to search for an order in the universe separate from religion, thereby developing the basis for the modern sciences. Leonardo da Vinci (1452–1519) so clearly represented the ideals of this period; he had already recognized and defined several effects of theoretical mechanics. The evolution of structural mechanics started about 100 years later with Galileo Galilei and then progressed with the development of scientific thought through the Age of Reason, so that by the nineteenth century the basics of mechanics and elastic material behavior were clearly formulated. The necessary theory for the structural design of thin shells was then further developed at the beginning of this century.

The earliest dome forms probably are derived from the corbelling principle, where

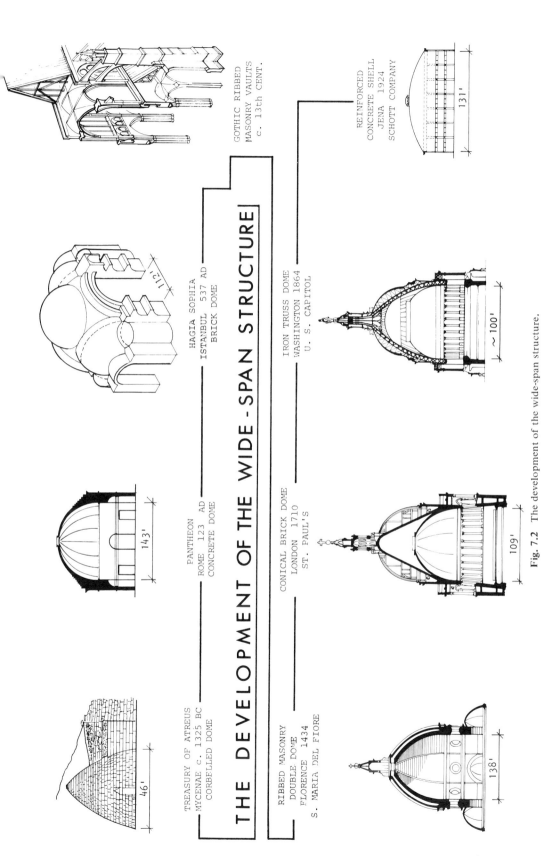

# THE DEVELOPMENT OF THE WIDE-SPAN STRUCTURE

TREASURY OF ATREUS
MYCENAE c. 1325 BC
CORBELLED DOME

PANTHEON
ROME 123 AD
CONCRETE DOME

HAGIA SOPHIA
ISTANBUL 537 AD
BRICK DOME

GOTHIC RIBBED
MASONRY VAULTS
c. 13th CENT.

RIBBED MASONRY
DOUBLE DOME
FLORENCE 1434
S. MARIA DEL FIORE

CONICAL BRICK DOME
LONDON 1710
ST. PAUL'S

IRON TRUSS DOME
WASHINGTON 1864
U. S. CAPITOL

REINFORCED
CONCRETE SHELL
JENA 1924
SCHOTT COMPANY

46'    143'    11'2"    131'

138'    109'    ~100'

**Fig. 7.2** The development of the wide-span structure.

389

rings of horizontal masonry layers project slightly beyond the ring of the previous layer, usually yielding conical outlines. The most famous example in the Western hemisphere is the Treasury of Atreus in Mycenae (circa 1325 B.C.).

Corbelled domes had not been used anymore in Europe for large scale enclosures, however in India the Islamic architecture continued to employ the principle. A sensational example is the great dome of Gol Gumbaz at Bijapur in southern India (1625–56 A.D.) which is 125 ft in diameter, thus larger than the Hagia Sofia. Astonishing is the fact that the dome uses much less thickness than the Pantheon to resist the tensile hoop forces.

The immense span of Hadrian's Pantheon in Rome (circa 123 A.D.) had been unequaled until the second half of the nineteenth century. The reactions of the hemispherical concrete dome due to gravity are tangential to the support and hence do not cause a horizontal thrust component, as do shallow domes. However, the familiar thrust due to the geometry of semicircular arches and vaults must be balanced in dome vaults internally by tensile hoop forces along the lower dome portion, as will be discussed later in much more detail. These tensile circumferential forces are resisted by the massive dome thickness, which increases towards the base, as well as by stronger material. To keep these forces to a minimum, the weight of the concrete is successively reduced towards the crown by employing lighter weight aggregates and reducing the vault's thickness, thereby also reflecting the magnitude of the force flow along the arches in the radial direction. The dome vault is further stiffened by eight relieving arches embedded in the concrete.

The series of domes of Justinian's Hagia Sofia in Constantinople, built by the master builders Anthemius of Tralles and Isodore of Miletus (537 A.D.), cause a rather dynamic flow of solid building elements together with an interior spaciousness that is quite different than the more static Pantheon. The shallow main brick dome is reinforced with ribs and is almost entirely in compression, if one considers it as a vault; thus, it evades the tensile stresses in semicircular domes and the necessary increase in shell thickness, which might not have been feasible because of the low tensile capacity of the brick and the lost art of the Roman concrete technology. The dome sits on four gigantic pendentives that convert the round base to the square space below. The pendentives, in turn, are vertically supported by four huge circular arches. The lateral thrust, which is large for shallow domes but not present for semicircular domes where it is transformed into circumferential tensile stress bands along the bottom part of the dome, is resisted by two semidomes in one direction and by massive corner buttresses in the other direction. The action of these buttresses had not been fully understood by the architects and thus could not prevent several collapses of the roof. Only in the cathedrals of the Middle Ages was the art of buttressing developed to a high level of sophistication.

About 1000 years later the Turkish architect Sinan abdur-Mennan (1489–1588), inspired by the Byzantine Hagia Sophia, transformed its architecture into the floating antigravity structures so typical for Ottoman mosques. In the Blue Mosque, he resisted the thrust of the dome by half-domes in both major directions, thus evading the support problem of the Hagia Sophia.

Gothic cathedrals are admired for their seemingly weightless interior spaces which are not achieved through record horizontal spans, but by span-to-height proportions (e.g., cathedral at Reims: 123-ft height to vault, 48-ft width for central aisle) with Amiens and Cologne cathedrals reaching about 1:3 and finally Beauvais the daring proportion of 1:3.33, quite a development from the typical ratio of 1:2 for the Romanesque churches! These proportions together with the effects of light and articulation of the slender skeleton structure convey a feeling of antigravity and dematerialization of space, in turn, resulting in a never ending upward surge as is so powerfully and daringly expressed in the French cathedrals of the High Gothic period.

The typical Gothic cross-vault is obtained by intersecting two pointed cylinders and by placing transverse ribs and diagonal ribs along the intersection lines (see Fig. 8.13). The ribs act together with the stone webbingg as a composite vault. In the late Gothic period the solid pointed vault is replaced by an intricate network of ribs. The vaults are supported vertically by interior piers, while their thrust and the thrust caused by the steep timber roof is usually transferred by two separate flying buttresses to the exterior massive vertical piers. These huge pier-buttresses are topped by pinnacles which can be visualized as a prestress agent adding weight, so that the resultant force due to thrust and weight is kept within the middle third of the horizontal pier cross-section so that no tension is generated. The high point and limit of the Gothic construction method was reached by Beauvais Cathedral (1347) with an incredible vault height of 158 ft.

The dome of S. Maria del Fiore in Florence (1434) can be considered the first modern dome structure and an important guideline for future domes. Visualize that it took nearly 900 years for a dome of the scale of the Hagia Sophia to be built. The geometry of the octagonal pointed dome is generated from the intersection of four circular cylinders. The primary supporting sandstone arches are placed along the four ridges, but in addition two intermediate secondary ribs are located in each of the cylindrical sectors. These radial ribs, together with horizontal circumferential stone rings, tie the inner and outer masonry shells of this double-layer dome together. In contrast to the previous domes which show predominantly vault (surface) action, here the radial steep arches can be assumed to be the primary structural components, they are not just the ribbing of a double vault. The arches cause lateral thrust even if their curvature is tangential to the supports; this thrust is further increased due to the weight of the heavy lantern but on the other hand reduced through the large dome height. Here the hoop tension is not resisted by the stronger and thicker vault portion along the lower part of the dome as for the comparatively flat Pantheon, nor by the buttressing as for the Hagia Sophia, but by hidden tension rings which consist of several layers of stone chains (sandstone blocks joined by iron clamps) and a timber chain. Fillippo Brunelleschi, the inventive designer of this polygonal dome, developed the method of composite action between ring and arches as well as the idea of double vault construction, which can be traced back to the thirteenth century Byzantine domes of St. Mark's in Venice; these domes employ outer timber framing. In addition, Brunelleschi's real invention lies in the erection of the dome. He did not use any central temporary shoring to support the dome, but employed the horizontal sandstone rings to prevent the arches from tilting inward during the construction.

Michelangelo's dome for St. Peter in Rome (1590), with nearly the same span, is based on similar construction principles, though its double brick vault is thinner, no horizontal circumferential stone rings are used, and less radial ribs are employed. Further, the entire dome thrust was resisted first by only three iron chains along the base, which proved to be insufficient so that five more tension rings had to be installed in 1743.

A revival of the idea of High Gothic ribbed vaulting is seen in Guarini's S. Lorenzo in Turin (1666–1687). Here, the solid domical surface is ingeniously resolved into eight intersecting arches, forming a star-like pattern in plan view.

Christopher Wren used a conical brick dome of only 18 in. thickness that is tied together at its base by a double iron chain to support the cupola of St. Paul's Cathedral in London (1710). This load-bearing dome is not visible, it is located between the inner, self-supporting brick dome and the hemispherical outer truss-like timber structure which is partly carried by the conical shell. The shape of the cone, only slightly curved along its inclined portions, comes very close to the funicular form responding to the single load due to the heavy 700 ton masonry lantern and the uniform roof loading, thus causing mainly compression and allowing this extremely light structure, the first of its kind, to be built.

The dome of the Church of the Invalides in Paris (1680–1691), built by Jules Hardouin-Mansart at about the same time, is constructed quite differently. It consists of an outer load-bearing, complex, trussed, timber framework and a self-supporting inner, elliptical brick dome which splits at about midheight into two vaults.

Jacques Germain Soufflot followed St. Paul's concept for the Pantheon in Paris (1755–1792) but replaced the trussed outer skin with a third masonry vault. His building marks the high point and the end of masonry vaulting. Now iron skeleton structures slowly start to gain in importance.

First iron and then steel were the materials for the large span structures of the nineteenth century. Thomas U. Walther's dome for the U.S. Capitol Building in Washington, D.C. (1864) can be seen as a typical example of the new material iron. The main structural elements for the ribbed dome are the inner trussed elliptical arches of nearly uniform depth. They support the crescent-shaped trusses on top, with the upper chords defining the elliptical profile of the cupola, and also carry the inner hemispherical plaster dome.

Johann W. A. Schwedler is credited as one of the first designers to have introduced true shell grid structures. He replaced the traditional ribbed dome with the braced dome concept. His largest steel dome was built in Vienna (1874) and spans 210 ft.

The cylindrical building of the Galerie des Machines for the 1889 Paris Exhibition reached an unprecedented and unheard span of 375 ft by employing parallel three-hinged, trussed gable frames made of steel.

The Spanish architect Antonio Gaudi, in the late nineteenth century, introduced important new concepts of design. He was fully absorbed in the relationship of form and structure. He searched for efficient structural shapes which exerted a minimum of bending and lateral thrust; he studied the intricacy of force and form from an experimental and empirical point of view. For instance, for the Colonia Guell Chapel (1898–1914) near Barcelona, he derived the funicular shape of the vaults and their inclined piers from a suspended string/sheet scale model with the proper weights hanging on it, to simulate the inverted rigid structure fully loaded. He may be considered the unacknowledged forerunner of modern shell construction; he employed the traditional Catalan thin-tile vaulting for the unusually complex curved surfaces that he developed. Though not widely recognized, Gaudi may be the first ever to have used hyperbolic paraboloids in building construction.

The tradition of the ribbed masonry domes was revived at the beginning of the twentieth century with reinforced concrete, obviously stimulated by the skeleton steel construction. It was much easier for the reinforced cast-in-place concrete, than for the masonry, to resist the critical hoop tension along the bottom portion of a steep dome. The most impressive concrete dome is the Centennial Hall in Wroclaw, Poland (formerly Breslau, Germany) designed by Max Berg (1912). The reinforced concrete skeletal dome has a span of 213 ft and thus was the first concrete dome to surpass the span of the Pantheon in Rome. Since the weight of concrete domes, which are based on traditional rib construction, increases rapidly with span, it was just a question of time for thin concrete shells to develop.

In 1916, Eugène Freyssinet began to build the two famous concrete airship hangars of parabolic cylindrical shape at Orly near Paris. These arched, 18-ft deep, undulating thin shell vaults had a span of 262 ft and were 184 ft high with a maximum shell thickness of only $3\frac{1}{2}$ in., thus yielding a very light structure. However, these arched vaults do not have a true shell form; the arch moment due to wind are just efficiently resisted by the depth of the folds thus allowing the thin concrete corrugations.

The first true concrete shell is the hemispherical, ribless, 53 ft dome of the Planetarium for the Zeiss Company in Jena, Germany (1922). It introduced the new era of rigid, thin shell structures and stimulated at first engineers, and then architects to become fully involved with the formal potential and the challenge of the bent surface.

Torroja's famous shallow dome for the Algeciras Market was built in 1933 and the cantilevering hyperbolic paraboloids for the Zarzuela Hippodrome in 1935. The first long-span shell structure in the United States are the short cylindrical shells for the Sports Arena in Hershey, Pennsylvania, designed by Anton Tedesco of Roberts & Schaefer Company in 1936. The development of shells was briefly interrupted during World War II, but then the 1950s reflected an explosion of concrete shell architecture as will be discussed later.

The skeletal shell continued the growth which Schwedler started. It was experimented with, in many new framing geometries, to increase the strength and stiffness of the surface while reducing its weight, as well as to keep member length variations to a minimum. Important historical turning points are the 384-ft stressed-skin, space grid, geodesic steel dome for the Union Tank Car Company in Baton Rouge, Louisiana, designed by Buckminster Fuller in 1958, as well as the lamella roof for the 642-ft Houston Astrodome (1964).

In the 1950s designers also started to experiment with tensile membranes, or soft shells. Prestressed cable network surfaces have the advantage that they can be built with prefabricated components and do not require much scaffolding. The Raleigh Arena, which opened in 1953, is regarded as the first important modern tensile roof structure. At about the same time, Frei Otto started his experiments in tent structures, reaching a formal as well as technical climax in the enclosures for the 1972 Olympic Games in Munich. In the 1970s, the further development of pneumatic structures was very much encouraged by the U.S. Pavilion at Expo 1970 in Osaka.

The change from the traditional dome structures of the past through the transition period of the second half of the nineteenth and first half of the twentieth centuries, and then to the present day bent surface structure with its limitless formal potential, is enormous, as will be shown in the following portions of this work.

From a technical point of view, span does not impose limits anymore upon architecture, at least not in the traditional sense; 350-ft spans are quite common today. Buckminster Fuller even proposed to cover Manhattan with a geodesic dome to produce a controlled climate. Differences between the heavy, traditional domes and the modern thin shells of stronger materials and more efficient stress distributions, as expressed in span and weight, become apparent from Table 7.1. The weight of the flat concrete shell for the Schott Co. (Fig. 7.2) has nearly the same span as St. Peter's but only about 2% of its weight. Some of the domes built later are much lighter in weight proportionally, though they have much larger spans. A pneumatic structure may be considered weightless; however, the rigidity of the soft shell must be provided by another energy source. Notice the span-to-thickness ratio of a hen's egg is five times larger than for St. Paul's, but only 10% as efficient as the shell for the CNIT Exhibition Hall! Remember, the span-to-depth ratios for beams are roughly in the range 20–24, that means about 20 times smaller than for concrete shells, indicating the material efficiency of the membrane system as compared to the flexural system ignoring other considerations of structural design such as the effect of scale.

Table 7.1

| DATE | NAME | SPAN (ft) | APPROX. AVER. THICKNESS (ft) | SPAN THICK | APPROX. WEIGHT (psf) | PER CENT |
|------|------|-----------|------------------------------|------------|----------------------|----------|
| 123  | Pantheon, Rome (concrete dome) | 143 | 13 | 11 | | |
| 1434 | S. Maria del Fiore, Florence (double shell masonry dome) | 138 | 7 | 20 | | |
| 1590 | St. Peter's, Rome (double shell brick dome) | 137 | | | 1389 | 100 |
| 1710 | St. Paul's, London (brick cone supporting outer and inner shells) | 109 | 3 | 36 | | |
| 1924 | Schott Co., Jena, DDR (reinforced concrete shell) | 131 | 0.2 | 655 | 31 | 2.23 |
| 1958 | CNIT Exhibition Hall, Paris (reinf. conc. double shell) | 720 | 0.4 | 1800 | 58 | 4.18 |
| 1969 | Conv. Center, Ohio U., Athens, Ohio (steel Schwedler dome) | 328 | | | 9 | 0.65 |
| 1973 | Louisiana Superdome, New Orleans (steel lamella dome) | 680 | | | 26 | 1.87 |
| 1975 | King County Stad., Seattle (reinf. conc., 5 in. shell between 6ft deep radial arches) | 661 | 0.6 | 1102 | 85 | 6.12 |
| 1977 | Stadium North. Arizona U., Flagstaff (triang. grid timber dome) | 502 | | | 17 | 1.22 |
| 1975 | Pontiac Stadium, Pontiac, MI (pneumatic dome) | 722 | | | 1 | 0.07 |
|      | Hen's egg | 0.13 | 0.001 | 180 | | |

The comparisons above are based purely on technical and not aesthetic considerations. The values of scale and engineering achievement as represented by the Houston Astrodome, for example, may not at all be superior to the spatial qualities of the dome architecture of the past! Further, bent surface structures should not be associated only with engineering technology and efficient long spans but should evolve as an integral part of the entire architecture.

## 7.3  SURFACE CLASSIFICATION

To predict the behavior of a membrane structure as well as to be able to construct it, not only must its geometry be known, but also the physical nature of the surface and other behavioral characteristics. These three basic considerations are defined in Figs. 7.3

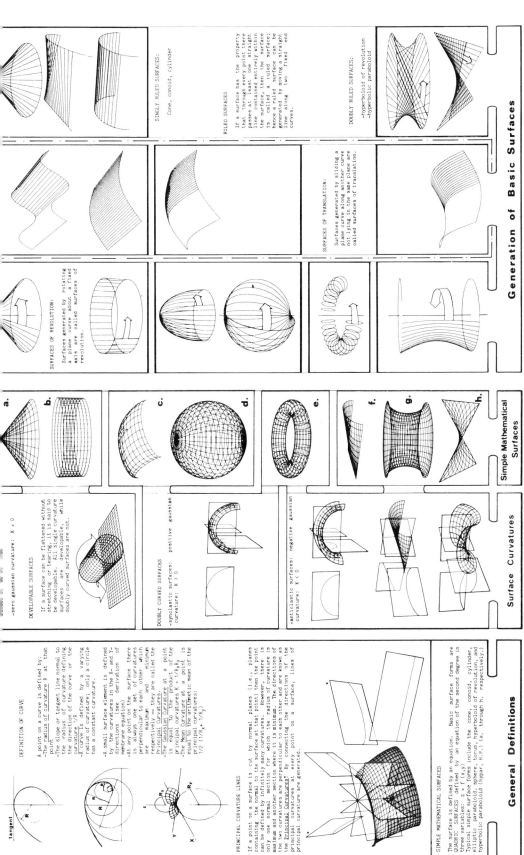

## General Definitions

### DEFINITION OF CURVE

A point on a curve is defined by:
- The radius of curvature R at that point.
- The slope or tangent line normal to the radius of curvature defining the direction of the curve or the curvature $1/R$.
- A curve is defined by a varying radius of curvature; only a circle has a constant curvature.
- A small surface element is defined by the curvatures in the X- and Y-directions (see derivation of membrane equation).
- At any point on the surface there is always one set of curvatures perpendicular to each other which are a maximum and minimum respectively, they are called the Principal Curvatures.
- The Gaussian Curvature at a point is equal to the product of the principal curvatures $K = 1/R_x R_y$.
- The Mean Curvature at a point is equal to the arithmetic mean of the principal curvatures: $1/2 \ (1/R_x + 1/R_y)$.

### PRINCIPAL CURVATURE LINES

If a point on a surface is cut by normal planes (i.e., planes containing the normal to the surface at that point) then the point can be defined by infinitely many curvatures. However, there is only one normal section for which the radius of curvature is maximum and another section where it is minimum. The directions of the two curvatures are perpendicular to each other and are known as the Principal Curvatures. By connecting the directions of the principal curvatures at every point on a surface, lines of principal curvature are generated.

### SIMPLE MATHEMATICAL SURFACES

The surface is defined by an equation. Basic surface forms are QUADRIC SURFACES defined by an equation of the second degree in three variables, $z = f(x,y)$.
(Typical simple surface forms include the cone, conoid, cylinder, elliptic paraboloid, sphere, torus, hyperboloid of revolution, and hyperbolic paraboloid (hypar, H.P.) (a. through h. respectively.)

---

## Surface Curvatures

-zero gaussian curvature: K = 0

### DEVELOPABLE SURFACES

If a surface can be flattened without stretching or tearing, it is said to be developable. All single curvature surfaces are developable, while doubly curved surfaces are not.

### DOUBLY CURVED SURFACES

-synclastic surfaces: positive gaussian curvature: K > 0

-anticlastic surfaces: negative gaussian curvature: K < 0

---

## Simple Mathematical Surfaces

a.

b.

c.

d.

e.

f.

g.

h.

---

## Generation of Basic Surfaces

### SURFACES OF REVOLUTION:

Surfaces generated by rotating a plane curve about a fixed axis are called surfaces of revolution.

### SURFACES OF TRANSLATION:

Surfaces generated by sliding a plane curve along another curve not lying in the same plane are called surfaces of translation.

### SINGLY RULED SURFACES:

Cone, conoid, cylinder

### RULED SURFACES

If a surface has the property that through every point there passes at least one straight line contained entirely within the surface, then the surface is called a ruled surface; hence a ruled surface can be generated by moving a straight line along two fixed end curves.

### DOUBLY RULED SURFACES:

-hyperboloid of revolution
-hyperbolic paraboloid

---

**Fig. 7.3**

## PRINCIPAL STRESS LINES (Isocontour Lines)

At every point on a surface the principal stress (i.e., maximum and minimum axial forces normal to each other) can be determined. The directions are identified at each point, and the connected form a pattern of lines reflecting the principal stress flow. Isocontour lines can be generated by computer, applying the finite element approach. Experimentally, photoelastic models can convincingly show the contour map of the stress flow, with colors identifying the different stress intensities.

## FUNICULAR SURFACES:

The geometry of funicular surfaces is a function of loading and ground plan; it may be partly synclastic and anticlastic.

## MINIMAL SURFACES:

Minimal surfaces have the following characteristics:

- least surface area for a given boundary
- constant skin stress
- constant mean curvature

Soap films can be used to produce minimal surfaces. When a wire framework such as a polyhedral wire skeleton of any other closed perimeter wire is dipped into a soap solution, then a particular minimal surface forms within the given framework. This simple experimental model helps to develop a first understanding about the nature of structural surface forms.

In the case of flying soap bubbles, the internal radial pressure is in balance with the constant surface tension. On the other hand, for a freely stretched film across some closed perimeter, the constant tensile surface forces a balance between the curvatures according to the geometry of the boundaries. Minimal surfaces may be organized according to the structural behavior of the film, or according to geometrical properties as follows:

SURFACES WITH CONSTANT ZERO MEAN CURVATURE (i.e., for every point on the surface, the sum of the radii of curvature is zero). Such as for anticlastic or saddle surfaces. Note that anticlastic surfaces are different from hyperbolic paraboloids, although they are similar in appearance. The discrepancy between them increases as the surface boundaries become steeper. A hyperbolic paraboloid with a regular square projection can be considered a reasonable substitute for a minimal surface bounded by the same perimeter.

SURFACES WITH CONSTANT POSITIVE MEAN CURVATURE
- such as for flying and floating soap bubbles

SURFACES WITH CONSTANT NEGATIVE MEAN CURVATURE
- such as for bubbles with negative inside gas pressure

## TYPE OF SURFACE:

    solid
    perforated
    ribbed
    network
    lattice

## STRUCTURAL ACTION:

VAULTS: -non-monolithic (e.g., brick, stone:) compression, some tension and bending
  -monolithic

SOFT SHELLS: Surface is so thin that it only carries tension and shear in the plane of the surface.

SUSPENDED MEMBRANE:
  hanging surface

PRESTRESSED MEMBRANE:
  Synclastic Pneumatic Structure

  Anticlastic Prestressed Cable Net: Downward cable prestresses upward cable, generating surface tension. Influence of membrane weight may be neglected for preliminary investigations.

RIGID SHELLS: -free standing shells
  -suspended shells

THIN SHELLS: The surface is so thin that it only carries tension, compression without buckling, and shear along the surface; the forces are often called the membrane forces.

THICK SHELLS: The surface is thick enough to carry bending moments and normal shears, in addition to the forces carried by thin shells.

**Surface Application**

**Behavioral Considerations**

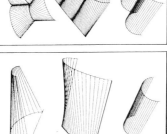

## CORRUGATED SURFACES

Either alternately anticlastic and synclastic, or purely anticlastic or synclastic.

## COMPLEX SURFACES

Using other fields as analog; e.g., catastrophe theory, nature, computer simulation, etc.

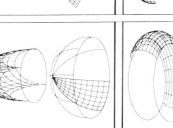
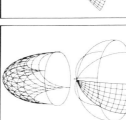
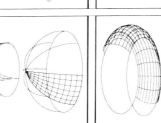
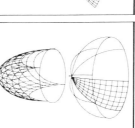
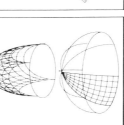
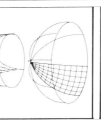
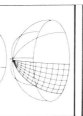
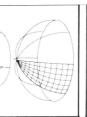
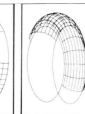
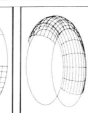
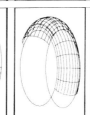
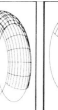
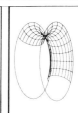
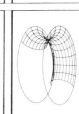
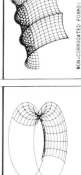

## SEGMENTAL FORMS

## NON-CORRUGATED FORMS:

Based on addition of elements.

**Generation of Surface Systems**

and 7.4 on an introductory level only, but then will be dealt with in more detail in the context of shell and tensile membrane discussion.

Basic features of geometry are identified first. The curve is the most fundamental property of the surface. Important characteristics of planar curves have already been discussed in the sections on cables and arches, such as the shape and the length of the curve, and the normals and tangents to the curve. In addition, the area, the location of the centroid, and the moment of inertia of the area below the curve are familiar characteristics.

However, surfaces can be defined by many different curves, therefore some special curvatures must be identified: the principal curvatures, the Gaussian curvature, and the mean curvature. These curvatures characterize the surface as a single- or double-curvature system, where the double-curvature surface is further subdivided into synclastic and anti-clastic surfaces.

The geometry of basic surfaces can be identified, according to the method of generation, as surfaces of translation and surfaces of rotation (revolution); they are defined mathematically by an equation. Common surface forms as found in books on analytical geometry are the cone, the cylinder, the sphere, the hyperbolic paraboloid (hypar, h.p.), the elliptic paraboloid (elpar), and the conoid. These shapes are discussed in more detail in the following section. Other important geometrical identifications are the ruled surface and the developable surface.

There is no limit set to the formal generation of surface systems; they are mostly made up of segments or of some combination of the basic surfaces. This aspect is treated later as part of the architectural context. In conclusion, one may organize the bent surfaces as generated from mathematical geometrical point of view as shown in Fig. 7.5.

Besides the mathematical form generators for bent surface structures there are many other methods for finding shapes as derived from considerations of behavior and experiments, construction process, art, as well from analogs in nature and other fields. Behavioral considerations of principal stress flow, and funicular and minimal surfaces are described in Fig. 7.4. Already Antonio Gaudi has experimented with the hanging reversed membrane concept as a source of generating form.

The behavior of the surface depends also on the nature of its physical composition. It can be flexible or rigid, it can be solid or ribbed, or it can be isotropic or anisotropic (see Fig. 9.1). The basic classification as used here and defined in Fig.7.4, is soft shells (tensile membranes), rigid thin shells, and vaults.

## 7.4  THE MEMBRANE FORCES

### The Tensile Membrane Under Normal Pressure

Flexible membranes respond to external force action in pure tension by adjusting their geometry, in a manner similar to single cable systems. The membrane's force reaction to a pressure applied normal to its surface, is investigated here. The free body of a surface element is shown in Fig.7.6. The element is cut along the principal curvatures, so that only axial membrane forces ($N_x$ and $N_y$) resist the external load $p$. There are no tangential shear forces along the membrane edges, because of the absence of skewed curva-

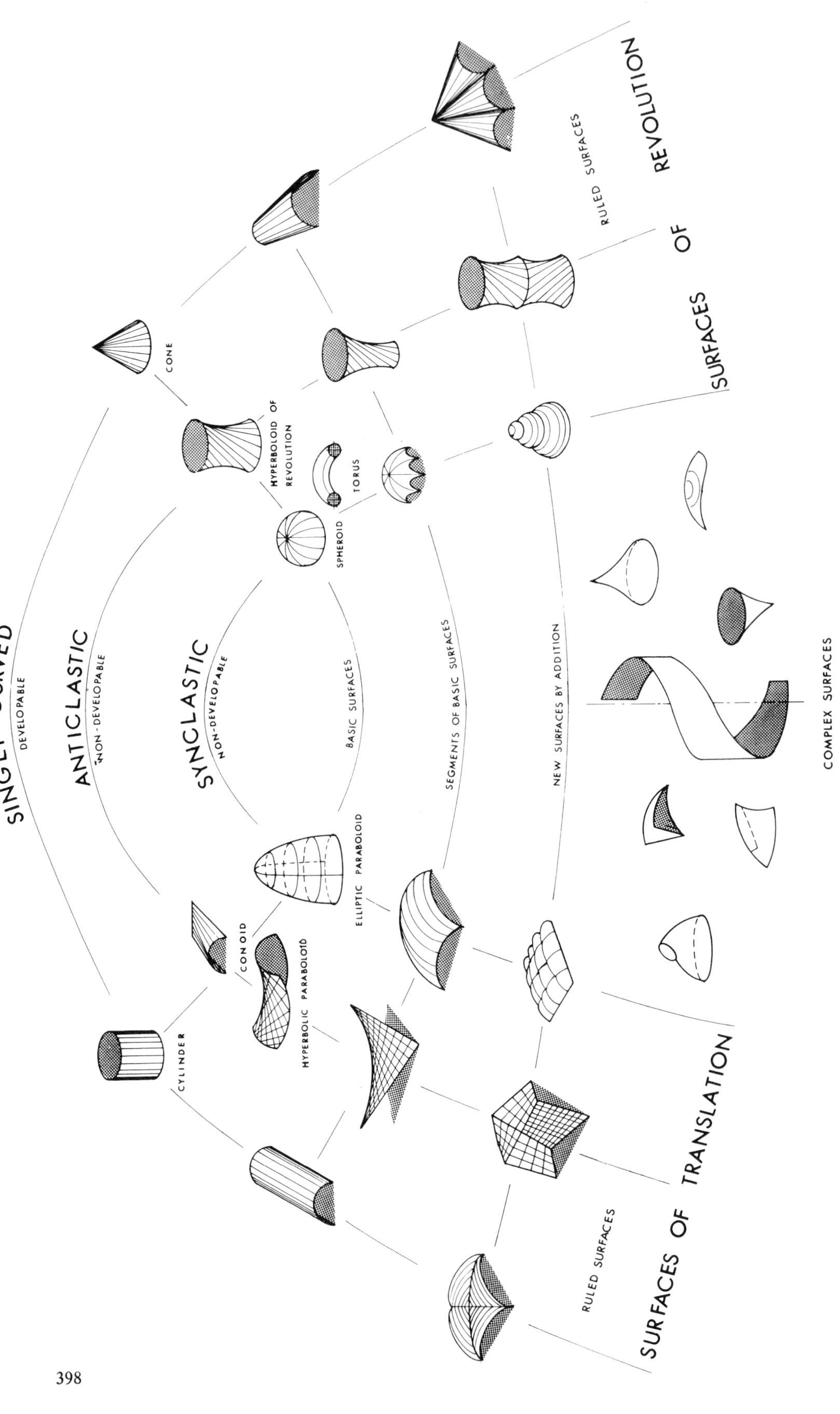

SINGLY CURVED
DEVELOPABLE

ANTICLASTIC
NON-DEVELOPABLE

SYNCLASTIC
NON-DEVELOPABLE

BASIC SURFACES

SEGMENTS OF BASIC SURFACES

NEW SURFACES BY ADDITION

CONE

HYPERBOLOID OF REVOLUTION

TORUS

SPHEROID

RULED SURFACES

SURFACES OF REVOLUTION

COMPLEX SURFACES

CYLINDER

CONOID

HYPERBOLIC PARABOLOID

ELLIPTIC PARABOLOID

RULED SURFACES

SURFACES OF TRANSLATION

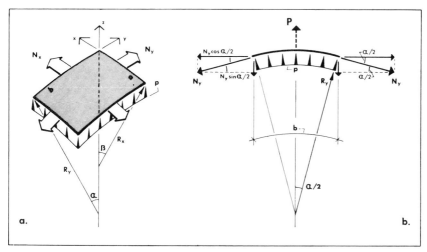

**Fig. 7.6**

tures. The membrane curvatures, along which the forces act, are equal to $1/R_x$ and $1/R_y$. It is assumed that the free-body is sufficiently small so that the curvatures are constant along the edges: they are considered to be circular arcs. The arc lengths of the edges are

$$a = \beta R_x \qquad b = \alpha R_y$$

Where $\alpha$ and $\beta$ are expressed in radians. The total resultant pressure $P$ acting on the surface is equal to

$$P = p(\alpha R_y)(\beta R_x) \tag{a}$$

The components of the membrane forces parallel to the resultant pressure $P$ (Fig. 7.6b) are

$$N_{yv} = N_y \sin \frac{\alpha}{2} \qquad N_{xv} = N_x \sin \frac{\beta}{2} \tag{b}$$

The resultant pressure $P$ must be resisted by the sum of the vertical force components acting along the perimeter of the free-body

$$\Sigma V = 0 = P - 2[N_{yv}(a) + N_{xv}(b)] \tag{c}$$

Substituting Eqs. (a) and (b) into (c), and considering that the angles $\alpha$ and $\beta$ are very small [$\sin(\alpha/2) \cong \alpha/2$] yields

$$pR_x R_y = R_x N_y + R_y N_x$$

$$p = \frac{N_y}{R_y} + \frac{N_x}{R_x} \tag{7.1}$$

This formula is known as the "membrane equation." It shows that under load pressure normal to the membrane's surface, the axial membrane forces are proportional to their curvatures.

The membrane equation can be simplified for the special case of an axisymmetrical form or surface of revolution. Axisymmetrical surfaces are formed by rotating a line, called the meridian, with a varying radius of curvature $R_1$, about a fixed axis. As the meridian rotates, each point along its length describes a circle or hoop having a radius $R_2$ about the fixed axis. The radii $R_1$ and $R_2$ are the principal radii of curvature (Fig. 7.7a, b, and c). Due to the symmetry of form of all axisymmetrical surfaces, the uniform pressure loading normal to the surface is resisted by axial forces only, and the principal force flow coincides with the principal curvatures. For clearer presentation purposes, the membrane and its surface element in Fig. 7.7a and b are not shown in the hanging position but standing as stabilized by the interior pressure $p$.

The membrane equation can be rewritten by using the expressions for the hoop forces $N_\theta$ and meridional forces $N_\phi$ as

$$p = \frac{N_\phi}{R_1} + \frac{N_\theta}{R_2} \tag{7.2}$$

Independent equations for the membrane forces can be derived from Fig. 7.7c and d. Visualize the membrane to be cut by a horizontal section perpendicular to the axis of rotation. The vertical components of the meridional membrane force along the circumference must resist the vertical components of the pressure normal to the surface. The vertical pressure components are equal to the pressure acting on an imaginary circular plate at the level to be investigated

$$\Sigma V = 0 = 2\pi R_0 (N_\phi \sin \phi) - p(\pi R_0{}^2)$$

$$N_\phi = \frac{pR_0}{2 \sin \phi} = \frac{pR_2}{2} \tag{7.3}$$

The meridional membrane forces at a given level are constant and are proportional to the radius defining the hoop curve at that level. Substituting $N_\phi$ into Eq. (7.2) and solving for the hoop force yields

$$N_\theta = pR_2 \left(1 - \frac{R_2}{2R_1}\right) = R_2 \left(p - \frac{N_\phi}{R_1}\right) \tag{7.4}$$

The membrane forces for some common surface forms are investigated in the following sections. The membrane, however, will not be seen anymore as an ideal system that is always in pure tension by adjusting its suspended, flexible surface to the various loading conditions to form a funicular membrane. Now it will be seen as a thin rigid surface, either standing or hanging, that is just thick enough so it does not buckle. Since the membrane cannot change its shape anymore, it has to resist uniform loading not just in tension but also in compression and possibly in shear.

The response of the following membranes to typical loading conditions is discussed.

- *Surfaces of revolution:* the spherical segment (dome), the cone, and the circular cylinder
- *Surfaces of translation:* the hyperbolic paraboloid, the elliptic paraboloid, and the conoid

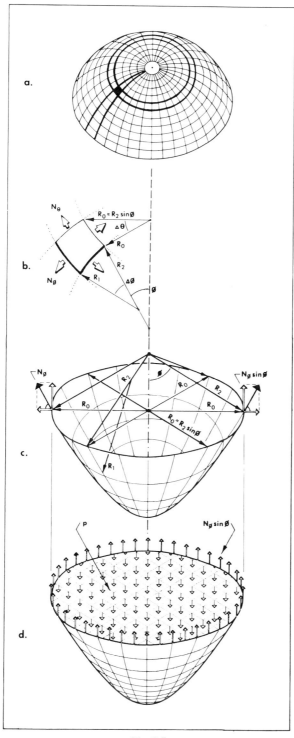

Fig. 7.7

## The Spherical Membrane

The spherical membrane is a special case of the group of axisymmetrical forms, its surface being defined by a constant radius of curvature.

$$R_1 = R_2 = R$$

The meridional forces according to Eq. (7.3) due to normal pressure are

$$N_\phi = \frac{pR}{2}$$

Substituting this expression into Eq. (7.4) yields the hoop or circumferential forces

$$N_\theta = pR\left(1 - \frac{R}{2R}\right) = \frac{pR}{2}$$

thus

$$N_\phi = N_\theta = \frac{pR}{2}$$

Hence, the axial forces in a spherical membrane as caused by uniform force action normal to the surface are constant at any point on the surface (e.g., a balloon).

The response of the membrane to forces acting normal to its surface constitutes one specific loading condition as encountered, for instance, by the internal pressure stabilizing pneumatic structures. However, roof structures have to carry other types of loads, such as snow and the weight of the surface itself. Wind forces are considered to be of secondary importance and are neglected in this introductory discussion.

First, the force flow along the membrane as caused by distributed uniform loading acting on the horizontal projection of the roof, as given by codes and other sources for snow and live loads, is derived below.

Visualize a spherical membrane (Fig. 7.8a, c, and d) cut horizontally in order to be investigated for two ranges: $\phi \leqslant 90°$ and $\phi \geqslant 90°$. For the range $\phi \leqslant 90°$ (Fig. 7.8c), vertical equilibrium necessitates that the external load acting on the projected area must be balanced by the vertical components of the meridional membrane forces acting along the circumference

$$\Sigma V = 0 = N_\phi \sin\phi \, (2\pi R \sin\phi) - q\pi(R\sin\phi)^2$$

$$N_\phi = \frac{qR}{2} \qquad (0° \leqslant \phi \leqslant 90°) \tag{7.6}$$

For the range $\phi \geqslant 90°$ (Fig. 7.8d), the vertical equilibrium of forces yields

$$\Sigma V = 0 = N_\phi \sin(180° - \phi)\,[2\pi R \sin(180° - \phi)] - q\pi R^2$$

but $\sin(180° - \phi) = \sin\phi$

$$N_\phi = \frac{qR}{2\sin^2\phi} \qquad (90° \leqslant \phi \leqslant 180°) \tag{7.7}$$

One may conclude that for a spherical segment smaller or equal to a hemisphere, the meridional membrane forces are constant under horizontally projected loading. However,

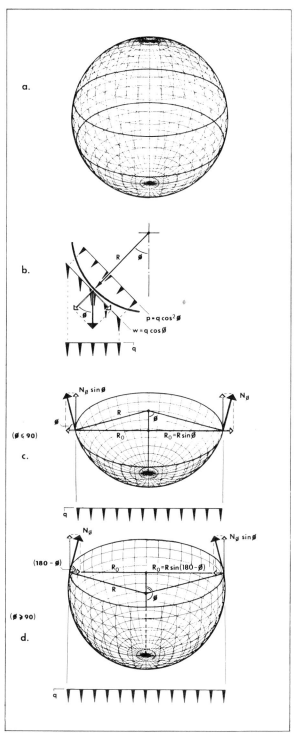

Fig. 7.8

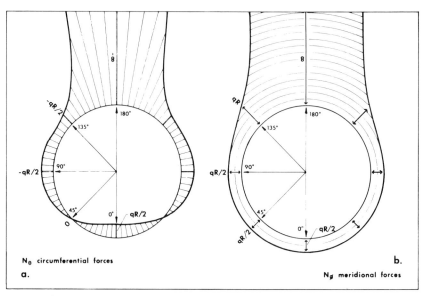

$N_\theta$ circumferential forces

a.

b.

$N_\phi$ meridional forces

Fig. 7.9

as the spherical segment increases beyond the hemisphere, the meridional forces increase, approaching infinity as $\phi$ nears $180°$ (Fig. 7.9b and Problem 7.1).

The hoop or circumferential forces $N_\theta$ for this loading case can be derived from the membrane equation as follows:

$$p = \frac{N_\phi}{R_1} + \frac{N_\theta}{R_2} \qquad R_1 = R_2 = R$$

$$N_\theta = pR - N_\phi \tag{7.8}$$

The horizontally projected load $q$ must be expressed as a load $p$ acting normal to the surface (Fig. 7.8b). First, project the load $q$ onto the surface, which results in an equivalent load $q \cos \phi$, and then resolve this load into a component normal to the surface (refer also to the treatment of loading for inclined beams)

$$p = q \cos \phi \, (\cos \phi) = q \cos^2 \phi$$

Substituting this expression, as well as the previously derived equations for the meridional forces $N_\phi$, into the general membrane equation (Eq. 7.8) yields for $0° \leqslant \phi \leqslant 90°$:

$$N_\theta = (q \cos^2 \phi)R - \frac{qR}{2}$$

$$= \frac{qR}{2}(2 \cos^2 \phi - 1)$$

but $2 \cos^2 \phi - 1 = \cos 2\phi$

$$N_\theta = \frac{qR}{2} \cos 2\phi \tag{7.9}$$

For $90° \leqslant \phi \leqslant 180°$

$$N_\theta = qR \cos^2 \phi - \frac{qR}{2 \sin^2 \phi}$$

$$N_\theta = \frac{qR}{2} \left( 2 \cos^2 \phi - \frac{1}{\sin^2 \phi} \right) \tag{7.10}$$

The distribution of the hoop forces is shown in Fig. 7.9a. (refer also to Problem 7.2 for discussion). It is clear from these equations that the hoop forces are in tension when $\phi < 45°$, changing at that point into compression that approaches infinity as $\phi$ increases towards $180°$.

The membrane forces caused by uniform loads acting along the membrane surface, such as the weight of the membrane, are now investigated. The derivation of the membrane forces is done similarly to the case of uniform loads on the horizontal roof projection just discussed.

Vertical equilibrium (Fig. 7.10c) requires that the uniform load along the spherical surface is balanced by the vertical components of the meridional forces along the circumference

$$\Sigma V = 0 = w[2\pi R^2(1 - \cos \phi)] - N_\phi \sin \phi (2\pi R \sin \phi)$$

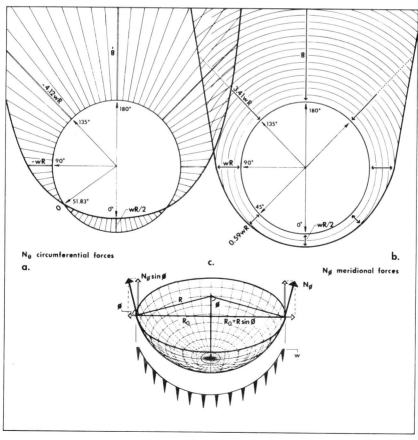

$N_\theta$ circumferential forces

**a.**

**c.**

$N_\phi$ meridional forces

**b.**

Fig. 7.10

Where the surface area $A$ of a spherical segment (Problem 7.6) is

$$A = 2\pi R^2(1 - \cos \phi)$$

$$N_\phi = \frac{wR(1 - \cos \phi)}{\sin^2 \phi}$$

but $\sin^2 \phi = 1 - \cos^2 \phi = (1 - \cos \phi)(1 + \cos \phi)$

$$N_\phi = \frac{wR}{1 + \cos \phi} \qquad (7.11)$$

This equation is applicable for any spherical segment (i.e., $0° \leqslant \phi \leqslant 180°$, refer to Problem 7.3 for discussion). The distribution of the meridional forces is shown in Fig. 7.10b. With the increase of the spherical segment, the maximum meridional forces increase; when $\phi = 90°$, $N_\phi$ is equal to $wR$.

The hoop forces $N_\theta$ are derived from the membrane equation. The derivation is similar to the one used to obtain Eq. (7.9). In this case, however, the load $w$ is already projected onto the surface, and its component normal to the surface is $w \cos \phi$

$$N_\theta = pR - N_\phi$$

but $p = w \cos \phi$

$$N_\theta = (w \cos \phi)R - \frac{wR}{1 + \cos \phi}$$

$$N_\theta = wR\left(\cos \phi - \frac{1}{1 + \cos \phi}\right) \qquad (0° \leqslant \phi \leqslant 180°) \qquad (7.12)$$

This equation also is applicable to the full range of the sphere. The distribution of the hoop forces is shown in Fig. 7.10a. The hoop forces are in tension in the range $0^0 \leqslant \phi < 51.83°$ (see Problem 7.5). After that point, they change into compression. Notice that the maximum forces increase rapidly as the spherical segment becomes larger than a hemisphere.

## The Conical Membrane

The conical membrane is generated by rotating the meridian, in this case a straight line with a radius of curvature $R_1 = \infty$, about the $z$ axis. Any horizontal section (i.e., parallel to the $yx$ plane) is a circle defined by the radius of curvature $R_2$. It is convenient to replace $R_2$ by the radius $R_0$ lying in the circular plane. (Fig. 7.11b)

$$R_0 = R_2 \cos \alpha = f \tan \alpha = f\frac{\sin \alpha}{\cos \alpha}$$

or

$$R_2 = \frac{R_0}{\cos \alpha} = f\frac{\sin \alpha}{\cos^2 \alpha} \qquad (d)$$

Substituting Eq. (d) into Eq. (7.3) yields the meridional forces due to uniform loading

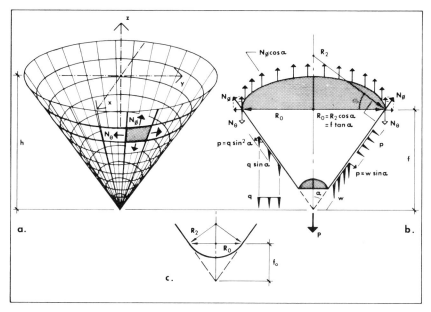

**Fig. 7.11**

normal to the surface

$$N_\phi = \frac{pR_2}{2} = \frac{pR_0}{2\cos\alpha} = \frac{pf\sin\alpha}{2\cos^2\alpha} \qquad (7.13)$$

The hoop forces are derived from the membrane equation by substitution, remembering that $R_1 = \infty$

$$p = \frac{N_\phi}{R_1} + \frac{N_\theta}{R_2} = \frac{N_\theta}{R_2}$$

$$N_\theta = pR_2 = 2N_\phi \qquad (7.14)$$

Notice that the hoop forces are always twice as large as the meridional forces at any given location.

Membrane forces in a truncated cone do not change, they are the same as for the regular cone. Should the truncated cone have a spherical cap, the membrane forces at the juncture of cone and cap can be derived from (d) by letting $f = f_0$

$$R_2 = \frac{R_0}{\cos\alpha} = \frac{f_0\sin\alpha}{\cos^2\alpha}$$

The membrane forces as based on the cone portion are

$$N_\theta = 2N_\phi = pR_2$$

The membrane forces as based on the spherical segment are

$$N_\theta = N_\phi = \frac{pR_2}{2}$$

Notice that the hoop forces $N_\theta$ for the truncated cone are twice as large as the ones in the cap, thus causing differential displacement at the junction (e.g., folding in a pneumatic structure).

In the following section, the membrane forces for common loading cases are investigated. Should the cone carry only a single load $P$ at its apex, then vertical equilibrium requires that the load $P$ be balanced by the vertical components of the meridional forces (Fig. 7.11b)

$$\Sigma V = 0 = N_\phi \cos \alpha(2\pi f \tan \alpha) - P$$

$$N_\phi = \frac{P}{2\pi f \sin \alpha} \tag{7.15}$$

The hoop forces are derived from Eq. (7.14) by considering that $p = 0$, that is, there are no loads acting along the surface

$$N_\theta = pR_2 = 0 \tag{7.16}$$

The meridional forces directly carry the single load in a linear, funicular manner, and there are no circumferential forces, as they are not needed to provide equilibrium.

The membrane forces for uniform loading (e.g., weight) along the conical surface is derived as follows.

The vertical components of the meridional forces balance the uniform loading along the membrane surface

$$V = 0 = N_\phi \cos \alpha(2\pi f \tan \alpha) - \frac{2\pi(f \tan \alpha)}{2} \frac{f}{\cos \alpha} w$$

$$N_\phi = \frac{wf}{2 \cos^2 \alpha} \tag{7.17}$$

The corresponding hoop forces are derived by considering

$$p = w \sin \alpha \qquad R_2 = \frac{f \sin \alpha}{\cos^2 \alpha}$$

$$N_\theta = pR_2 = wf \tan^2 \alpha \tag{7.18}$$

The membrane responds to uniform loading acting on a horizontal plane (e.g., snow) as follows. The vertical components of the meridional forces must balance the loads acting on the horizontal plane.

$$\Sigma V = 0 = N_\phi \cos \alpha(2\pi f \tan \alpha) - \pi(f \tan \alpha)^2 q$$

$$N_\phi = \frac{qR_0}{2 \cos \alpha} = \frac{qf \sin \alpha}{2 \cos^2 \alpha} \tag{7.19}$$

The corresponding hoop forces are derived by considering the equivalent load $p = q \sin^2 \alpha$ (see Fig. 7.11b)

$$N_\theta = pR_2 = qf(\tan^2 \alpha) \sin \alpha \tag{7.20}$$

**The Circular Cylindrical Membrane**

A cylindrical surface can be generated by translating a straight line, the meridian with $R_1 = \infty$, along a fixed curve having a variable radius of curvature $R_2$. For a circular cylindrical membrane the radius of curvature is constant, that is, $R_2 = R$ (Fig. 7.12a). There is no force action in the longitudinal direction of the open-ended cylinder, the meridional forces are zero, since the loads acting on the single curvature membrane must be resisted along the circumferential direction (Fig. 7.12b). The circumferential or hoop forces due to the radial force action normal to the surface are derived from the membrane equation by substituting $R_1 = \infty$ and $R_2 = R$

$$p = \frac{N_\phi}{R_1} + \frac{N_\theta}{R} = \frac{N_\theta}{R}$$

$$N_\theta = pR \tag{7.21}$$

Note that the hoop forces are constant along the surface, and are twice as large as for the spherical membrane, which uses two equal curvatures to resist the same loading. This result was already obtained in Eq. (3.12).

The hoop forces as caused by the weight of the membrane, when $0° \leqslant \theta \leqslant 90°$, are found by expressing $w$ in terms of $p$ (Fig. 7.8b)

$$p = w \cos \theta$$

Substituting $p$ into Eq. (7.4) yields

$$N_\theta = wR \cos \theta \tag{7.22}$$

The hoop forces due to uniform loads on the horizontal roof projection are found by substituting $p = q \cos^2 \theta$ (see Fig. 7.8b) into Eq. (7.4)

$$N_\theta = qR \cos^2 \theta \tag{7.23}$$

The flow of the hoop forces along the membrane is discussed in Problems 7.7 and 7.8; refer also to Fig. 8.11 which shows the arch action of cylindrical shells with the neutral plane at $\theta = 90°$.

Note that the maximum hoop force appears for both loading cases at the crown of a standing membrane where $\theta = 0$. Hence

$$N_{\theta\ max} = (w + q)R \tag{7.24}$$

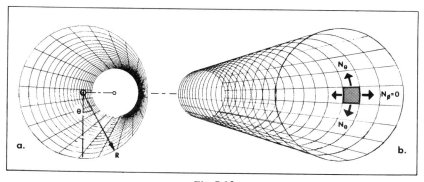

Fig. 7.12

### The Hyperbolic Paraboloid Membrane

The hyperbolic paraboloid, often called hypar or h-p (HP), is a translational surface not a surface of revolution; cutting the surface vertically gives parabolas while horizontal sections result in hyperbolas (see Fig. 8.27). It can be generated by sliding a concave parabola or suspended cable called generatrix parallel to itself along a convex parabola or arch called directrix which is located perpendicular to it or vice versa. The parabolas follow the principal curvature lines and are called principal parabolas. They establish a rectangular coordinate system at the saddle point as shown in Fig. 7.13f.

The parabolic generatrices can be defined at the origin of the coordinate system as has been shown for parabolic cables letting $R_0$ equal to $R_{x'}$ and $R_{y'}$, respectively [Eq. (3.30)]

$$y' = 0: \quad z = \frac{(x')^2}{2R_{x'}} \tag{e}$$

$$x' = 0: \quad z = \frac{-(y')^2}{2R_{y'}} \tag{f}$$

The equation defining the surface of the hyperbolic paraboloid is

$$z = \frac{(x')^2}{2R_{x'}} - \frac{(y')^2}{2R_{y'}} \tag{7.25}$$

In this equation $R_{x'}$ and $R_{y'}$ are the principal radii of curvature at the saddle point.

The plan projection of the parabolic generatrices form a rectangular grid. For the condition, where the convex and concave parabolas are identical or $R_{x'} = R_{y'} = R$, the generatrices form a square grid in plan projection and the hyperbolas are equilateral. For this special case, the membrane forces as caused by load action normal to the surface can be derived from the general membrane Eq. (7.1) by substituting the following relationships

$$R_x = -R_y = R \qquad N_x = -N_y = N$$

$$p = \frac{N_y}{R_y} + \frac{N_x}{R_x} = \frac{2N}{R} \tag{g}$$

The membrane forces $N$ are equal in magnitude but opposite in direction; they are in tension along the suspended parabolas and in compression along the parabolic arches. Hence, according to Eq. (g)

$$\pm N = \frac{pR}{2} \tag{h}$$

Visualize a rectangular hypar element of size $2a \times 2b$ to be cut from the saddle surface of the membrane as shown in Fig. 7.13a. This surface element can be considered shallow if the rise f is less than the ratio of the shorter side to five ($f \leqslant a/5$, if $a \leqslant b$). For these very shallow membranes the external, uniform loads w and q do not have to be considered separate, both dead and live loads can be treated as one load w to act on the horizontal roof projection. Further, the uniform gravity loads w may be considered as equal to the loads p acting normal to the surface, remembering that for shallow membranes the radius of curvature R changes very little. Hence, Eq. (h) may be expressed as

$$\pm N = \frac{wR}{2} \tag{i}$$

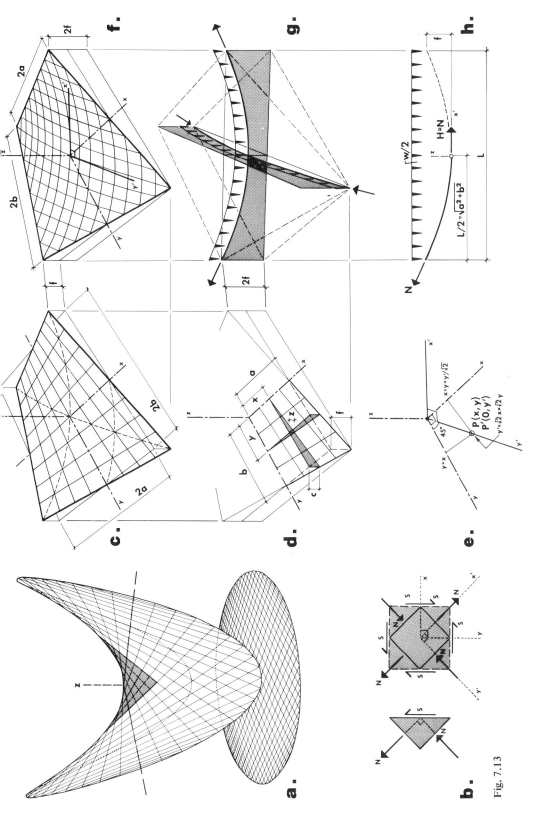

Fig. 7.13

411

Note the similarity of this equation to the one defining the axial force flow in a spherical membrane (Eq. 7.6) with a constant radius of curvature. For approximation purposes, one may consider the shallow parabolas to have a circular curvature since their radius hardly changes.

The radius of curvature for the parabola at its apex was derived as

$$R_0 = \frac{L^2}{8f} \tag{3.29}$$

Considering this radius to be constant along the flat surface and also remembering that for shallow cables (arches) the maximum force $T_{max}$ at the support is approximately equal to the cable force $H$ occurring at the low point, then one may substitute $R_0$ into Eq. (i)

$$\pm N = \frac{wR_0}{2} = \frac{wL^2}{16f} \tag{g}$$

This expression can also be derived using a different approach as based on Fig. 7.13f, g, and h, by considering the load to be shared equally by the arched membrane in compression and the suspended membrane in tension. One should keep in mind that the parabola is the funicular shape of uniform loading on the horizontal roof projection only; the effect of dead load located along the surface geometry can only be neglected for flat surfaces!

As based on Fig. 7.13h, rotational equilibrium yields

$$N(f) = \frac{(w/2)L^2}{8} \quad \text{or} \quad N = \frac{wL^2}{16f}$$

The hyperbolic paraboloid is a doubly ruled surface; it can be defined by two families of intersecting straight lines which form in plan projection a rhombic grid if related to the principal parabolas as surface generators (generatrices), in other words, they are the asymptotes of the hyperbolas. Here, the particular case is investigated, where straight lines perpendicular to each other, analogous to identical parabolas, are the generators. These straight lines form a rectangular grid as seen in plan view; the surfaces are called rectangular hyperbolic paraboloids. In Fig. 7.13d, the warped surface may be generated by dropping one corner below the plane described by the remaining three or by a straight line slid along two other straight lines slightly skewed with respect to each other or vice versa. The following geometrical relationship is derived for a rectangular, warped surface as based on Fig. 7.13d.

$$\frac{a}{x} = \frac{f}{c} \quad \text{or} \quad c = \frac{fx}{a} \tag{k}$$

$$\frac{b}{y} = \frac{c}{z} \quad \text{or} \quad z = \frac{cy}{b} \tag{l}$$

Substituting Eq. (k) into (l) gives

$$z = \frac{f}{ab} xy = kxy \tag{7.26}$$

Hence, any point on the h-p surface can be defined by the linear equation just derived. In this expression, $k = f/ab$ is the twist factor representing the warping or sloping of the surface, it also defines the curvature along the $y'$ and $x'$ directions as explored below.

It can be shown that the two surface generating systems are related to each other such that the straight line generators in plan projection bisect the rectangular grid formed by the parabolic generators. Hence, the axes of the coordinate system $xy$ are simply transformed by rotating the system through $45°$ in the case of a rectangular hypar to form the new coordinate system $x'y'$.

It is shown in Fig. 7.13e that any point $P$ on the $y'$ axis is defined as

$$x = y = \frac{y'}{\sqrt{2}} \tag{m}$$

Substituting Eq. (m) into Eq. (7.26) yields

$$z = \frac{k(y')^2}{2} \tag{n}$$

For the special condition of $z = f$ and $y' = x' = L/2$, this equation becomes

$$f = \frac{kL^2}{8} \quad \text{or} \quad \frac{1}{k} = \frac{L^2}{8f} = R_0 = \frac{ab}{f} \tag{7.27}$$

This expression shows that $k$ not only defines the curvature of the parabola but also the geometry of the warped surface. Substituting this equation into Eq. (g) yields

$$\pm N = \frac{wR}{2} = \frac{wL^2}{16f} = \frac{w}{2k} = \frac{wab}{2f} \tag{7.28}$$

This is the general equation for the axial membrane forces along a shallow hyperbolic paraboloid supporting uniform gravity loading, where the terms are defined in Fig. 7.13. The forces are in compression along the arched parabolas and in tension along the suspended parabolas. The equation reflects the important characteristics of shallow membranes in that it shows the axial forces as constant along the entire surface. Remember, there is no shear in the direction of the parabolas because they are funicular for the assumed symmetrical, uniform loading condition.

The principal axial forces, in turn, can be resolved into pure shear forces at $45°$ to them as shown in Fig. 7.13b. Hence, one can visualize the uniform loading to be balanced either by the principal axial forces in tension and compression, or by their equivalent, the pure shear along the straight line generators; that is the reason why hypar surfaces are often called shear systems. The diagonal tension or compression, which acts on a typical surface element $1 \times 1$ as shown in Fig. 7.13b, is balanced by the shear forces along the straight line generators without the help of any axial forces along this direction. The shear force $\bar{S}$ that acts along the length $2(1) \sin 45°$ replaces the equal normal forces in the diagonal direction along the parabolic generators, which act along the unit sides

$$\bar{S} = 2N \sin 45° \qquad N_x = N_y = 0$$

The stress due to the shear force is

$$f_s = \frac{\bar{S}}{A_s} = \frac{2N \sin 45°}{A(2 \sin 45°)} = \frac{N}{A}$$

This expression shows that the shear stresses in the membrane are equal to the normal stresses, or the shear forces are equal to the axial forces

$$S = N = \pm \frac{wab}{2f} \qquad (7.29)$$

Along the straight line generators there are no axial forces, the shallow membrane is in the state of pure shear. One may conclude that the surface of a shallow hyperbolic paraboloid responds to uniform gravity loading by developing uniform stresses over its entire surface, clearly reflecting its perfect efficiency from a force intensity point of view.

**The Elliptic Paraboloid Membrane**

Elliptic paraboloids, also called elpars, can be generated in the same fashion as hyperbolic paraboloids by letting a convex, principal parabola slide parallel to itself along another convex parabola perpendicular to it. The double curvature surface is synclastic and not ruled; it does not have any straight line generators. Vertical sections yield parabolas while horizontal sections give ellipses. The general equation defining the surface is equal to the one for the hypar with the origin of the coordinate system at the crown, by only changing signs and letters. Let $x' = x$ and $-y' = +y$, then from Eq. (7.25) the following result can be obtained

$$z = \frac{x^2}{2R_x} + \frac{y^2}{2R_y} \qquad (7.30)$$

For the special case where $R_x = R_y = R$, the translational elliptic paraboloid can also be generated as a paraboloid of revolution, where the general equation for this parabolic dome can be derived from Eq. (7.30)

$$z = \frac{x^2 + y^2}{2R} \qquad (7.31)$$

The radius of curvature $R$ can be obtained for the special condition in Fig. 7.14 where $z = \bar{f} = f_x + f_y$, at $x = a$ and $y = b$ [see also Eq. (7.33)]

$$R = \frac{a^2 + b^2}{2\bar{f}} \qquad (7.32)$$

Equation (7.30) can further be simplified for rectangular plan conditions (Fig. 7.14) rather than elliptic ones, by replacing the principal radii with

$$R_x = \frac{L_x^2}{8f_x} = \frac{a^2}{2f_x} \qquad R_y = \frac{L_y^2}{8f_y} = \frac{b^2}{2f_y} \qquad (7.32a)$$

In this equation the plan dimensions are defined as $L_x = 2a$ and $L_y = 2b$. It should be kept in mind that the definition of $a$ and $b$ for the hyperbolic paraboloid is measured diagonally and not parallel to the principal parabolas as in the case here.

The surface equation can now be defined as

$$z = 4f_x \left(\frac{x}{L_x}\right)^2 + 4f_y \left(\frac{y}{L_y}\right)^2 = f_x \left(\frac{x}{a}\right)^2 + f_y \left(\frac{y}{b}\right)^2 \qquad (7.33)$$

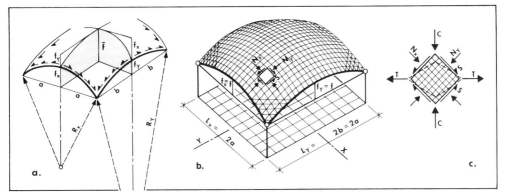

Fig. 7.14

The membrane analysis for the elliptic paraboloid is quite complex. For the special condition of symmetry, that is for a parabolic dome on a round plan resisting uniform loading across the horizontal projection of the roof, where $a = b$ and $f_x = f_y = f$, the axial
membrane forces at the crown in the direction of the principal arches share the load resistance equally without the help of shear. Since the loads at the crown (or low point of a
dish) act truly perpendicular to the surface, the membrane forces at that point according
to the general membrane equation, or according to the membrane equation for the hypar
as based on a shallow funicular arch, must be equal to

$$N_{x0} = N_{y0} = \frac{wR}{2} = \frac{wa^2}{4f} = \frac{wL^2}{16f} \tag{7.34}$$

$$N_{xy} = N_{yx} = S = 0$$

For the magnitude of the membrane forces due to uniform live loading, in general, refer
to Problem 8.12.

The membrane force flow for a parabolic dome on a rectangular plan (Fig. 7.14), however, is much more complex. In the hypar the axial arch forces are balanced by the cable
curvatures in tensile action. This function of the internal balance of arch action in the elpar
must be provided by the shear mechanism since opposite curvatures are not available to
respond in a direct manner. Hence along the principal parabolic curvatures not only axial
compression forces $N_x$ and $N_y$ but also shear forces $S$ must act. These shear forces, in
turn, cause tension and compression in the diagonal direction. (Fig. 7.14c).

Along the boundaries, the elpar membrane on a rectangular plan can only respond in
one direction like a single-curvature system (cylindrical membrane), since there is no
other curvature available to carry part of the load. Hence, the maximum compressive
membrane forces must appear along the perimeter edges. If the membrane is shallow,
then the boundary arch can be considered funicular and the thrust at midspan is equal to
the maximum axial compression force, yielding the familiar expression

$$N_{x\,max} = wR_x = \frac{wL_x^2}{8f_x} = \frac{wa^2}{2f_x}$$

$$N_{y\,max} = wR_y = \frac{wL_y^2}{8f_y} = \frac{wb^2}{2f_y} \tag{7.35}$$

Keep in mind that the thrust cannot be considered anymore as equivalent to the maximum axial forces as the membrane becomes steeper. Sometimes it may be helpful for rather shallow membrane conditions ($f/L \leqslant 1/5$, as discussed for circular arches), to treat the parabolic curvature as a circular arc.

The membrane shear forces in the principal directions are zero along the $x$ and $y$ axes because of symmetry of geometry and loading. As has been stated before, the shear balances the arch action in a diagonal manner so that no forces act perpendicular to the boundary edges. The shear flow along the principal curvatures increases toward the edges because of having to resist more and more axial arch action. Along the outside perimeter edges, the shear increases from zero at midspan to a maximum at the corners, similar to the shear flow along the edges of a warped, rectangular surface (hypar). The maximum shear at the corners of a shallow elpar on rectangular plan can be shown as approximately equal to

$$S_{max} = \frac{wab}{\sqrt{f_x f_y}} \tag{7.36}$$

This maximum shear force may be taken as roughly equal to the maximum diagonal tension ($T_{max}$) assuming ideal membrane conditions at the corners with zero axial forces, which obviously is not the case for a real dome structure supported along the perimeter or only at the corners.

For a shallow parabolic dome on square plan ($a = b$, $f_x = f_y = f$), the critical compression and shear forces are

$$N_{x0} = N_{y0} = \frac{wa^2}{4f} \qquad N_{max} = \frac{wa^2}{2f} \qquad S_{max} = \frac{wa^2}{f} \tag{7.37}$$

Note the maximum compressive stresses are twice as large as at the crown, assuming constant membrane thickness, but only half as large as the maximum shear or diagonal tensile stresses in the corners.

## The Conoidal Membrane

The conoid is generated in a manner similar to that of the cylinder, cone, and hyperbolic paraboloid; in each case a straight line is translated along two parallel vertical plane curves called directrices thus forming ruled surfaces. When a horizontal line slides along two identical curved directrices, a cylinder is generated; when the line is inclined and its one end rotated about one point while the other end moves along a curved directrix, a cone is formed. In the case of a hyperbolic paraboloid the directrices are straight lines having each a different slope. Should one of the directrices be a curve and the other a horizontal, straight line, or a different curve, a conoid or truncated conoid is generated. The hyperbolic paraboloid can be considered as a special case of the conoidal family where one of the directrices is changed from a curve to a straight line. While the doubly ruled hypar may be defined by the linear equation $z = kxy$, the equation of the singly ruled parabolic conoid with a parabola as the curved directrix can be shown as equal to

$$z = kxy^2 \tag{7.38}$$

The conoidal surface is anticlastic with a negative Gauss curvature. As shown in Fig.

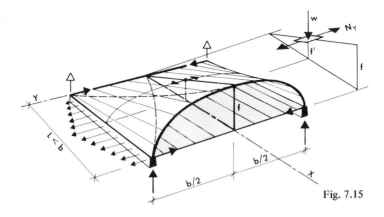

Fig. 7.15

7.15, the principal curvature lines in the diagonal direction are curves of opposite curvature. The conoid is nondevelopable because it is a doubly curved surface.

For the condition, where the shell width $b$ is larger than the span $L$, it is reasonable to assume for rough approximation purposes that most of the loads are carried primarily in arch action like a single curvature system (vault) by visualizing the wide shell to be cut into parallel independent arch strips. This phenomenon is discussed in some more detail in the section on short cylindrical shells. Furthermore, for uniform load action on the horizontal roof projection, which is reasonable for shallow membranes (see also hypars and elpars) the parabolic arches represent the funicular shape and thus will carry all the loads directly in axial compression so there will be neither axial nor shear action in the $x$ direction. Hence, for shallow conoids the membrane or arch forces can be roughly approximated with the familiar expression

$$N_y = w R_y = \frac{w b^2}{8f'} \tag{o}$$

The variable arch height $f'$ at $x$ distance can be replaced by $f(x/L)$

$$N_y = w R_y = \frac{wLb^2}{8fx} \tag{7.39}$$

$$\text{at } x = L: \quad N_y = \frac{wb^2}{8f} \tag{7.40}$$

$$\text{at } x = 0: \quad N_y = \infty$$

The magnitude of the membrane forces increases as they approach the flatter shell portion and are infinitely large along the straight line base. Obviously, the membrane theory is not applicable in the shallow region of the surface, where curvature loses its influence and plate behavior replaces membrane behavior. A bending theory, which is beyond the scope of this introductory discussion, must be developed.

At the boundaries, the arch reactions are carried by walls or, in this case, by beams (Fig. 7.15) which, in turn, will transfer the vertical force components to the columns and the lateral thrust to the horizontal edge beam and the tie rod along the edge arch. Notice the thrust distribution along the beam, which increases with decrease of arch height, however, at a certain location it decreases again when arch behavior is slowly replaced by slab action. For boundary disturbances, as caused by the incompatibility between the supporting edge members and the thin shell refer to the discussion on the structural behavior of dome shells.

## Problems

7.1   Show how the meridional membrane forces $N_\phi$ change as $\phi$ changes from 0 to $\infty$ or as the spherical segment approaches the full sphere (Fig. 7.9b), as caused by the uniform loading $q$ acting on the horizontal projection of the membrane.

7.2   Investigate the spherical segment for the same range as in Problem 7.1 but with respect to the circumferential forces $N_\theta$ (Fig. 7.9a).

7.3   Show that Eq. (7.11) for the meridional forces due to uniform loads $w$ acting along the membrane is also applicable in the range $90° \leqslant \phi \leqslant 180°$.

7.4   Show the distribution of the meridional membrane forces (Fig. 7.10b) as defined by Eq. (7.11).

7.5   Show the distribution of the hoop forces due to the uniform loading $w$ acting along the spherical membrane (Fig. 7.10a).

7.6   Derive the equation defining the surface area of a spherical segment $A = 2\pi R^2(1 - \cos \phi_1)$.

7.7   Show the distribution of the hoop forces for a semicircular cylindrical membrane as caused by a uniform load acting along the surface.

7.8   Show the distribution of the hoop forces for a semicircular cylindrical membrane as caused by a uniform load acting on the horizontal projection of the roof.

# 8 RIGID SHELL STRUCTURES

The plasticity of the shell and the potential uninterrupted flow of the bent surface has opened a new dimension in architectural design. Shells, as the name suggests, are closely related to nature and thus express the dynamism of change that characterize living organisms. In the past, emphasis in shell design has often been only on scale and geometry and the techniques of structural design, rather than the integration of other design determinants and response to a much broader scope of cultural needs.

The behavior and some of the characteristics of the shell can be best visualized by first observing a suspended flexible membrane. This membrane is under pure tension in response to the loads. When it is frozen and inverted, it becomes a thin shell in pure compression. However, as the live loads change, the flexible membrane adjusts its shape so as to remain in tension. The shell, on the other hand, cannot do so; it is rigid. It not only has to react in compression but also in tension and in tangential shear. The shell must be very thin, as exemplified by an eggshell, and thus does not resist any bending, normal shear, or twisting, but still must be thick enough so that it does not buckle. It is clear then that the thin shell, because of its double curvature, can resist uniform loading in direct force action within its surface plane. Since skeletal shells also resist loads primarily by in-plane forces, and not in bending, they are treated in this chapter as part of shells.

The membrane theory derived in the previous chapter is taken as the basis for the design of shells, but it does not necessarily reflect the true force distribution, because it only assumes statically determinate conditions. However, the simple mathematical expressions make it possible to develop a feeling for the overall magnitude of the force flow. The approach here can be considered a crude approximation, but it is a valid introduction to a field of structures otherwise not accessible to the general designer. The actual analysis of shells is extremely complex and can only be dealt with by a selected group of structural engineers specializing in this field.

In the derivation of the membrane theory it was assumed that symmetrical uniform loads act upon a continuously curved surface, since concentrated loads can only be reacted in bending, assuming that the shell curvature does not have a kink point at the location of the load. It was further assumed that the forces along the membrane edges are compatible with the support conditions, which is rarely the case. This incompatibility along the boundaries between the thin shell and the rigid support causes bending in the shell, which fortunately is only significant near the edges in most cases; in this area the shell thickness is increased.

Concrete shells of large span may have to be prestressed to reduce tensile cracks and control deflection. Prestressing may also be necessary if the shell is constructed from precast components.

The selection of the shell shape evolves out of a complex synthesis of many architectural design determinants. The shell form reflects the spirit that the designer wants to express, besides having to serve the function of the building. Its shape must provide the load capacity for the given scale with a minimum of bending and must respond to construction considerations. Its geometry may be derived from the standard mathematical forms (Fig. 7.3) or experimental methods like reversing hanging membranes or leaving them suspended (suspended rigid shells) as well as from pneumatic forms or methods of construction. The shell is not necessarily a continuous solid surface; it may consist of precast ribbed shell units with very thin slabs or be formed by a network of members. The shell material ranges from reinforced concrete, steel, aluminum, timber (plywood), and plastics to reinforced ceramic shells; common materials are discussed in more detail later in this section. The cost of the reinforced concrete shell is primarily in the formwork, since in many countries the cost of labor is more critical than the cost of materials. Hence, the shape of large-scale shells must lend itself to a mechanized construction process such as mobile scaffolding and possibly the utilization of prefab surface units, particularly where intricate forms are required. It is obviously advantageous if the shell is constructed from a series of self-supporting parts so that the formwork is repetitive and can be resued. Most of the great pioneers of concrete shell design were less theoreticians than builders. The designers Candela, Dischinger, Esquillan, Finsterwalder, Freyssinnet, Isler, Maillart, Nervi, Tedesko, Torraja, Taillibert, and Tsuboi, just to name a few, have all integrated structural design with the actual building of shells. Shells may be organized into three groups according to their static behavior.

*Shell beams,* or long shells, are singly curved (or folded) beams similar to corrugated panels with the beam span by far larger than the beam width. Here, bending is the primary feature, which is resisted for simple beam action by a tension zone along the bottom edges and a compression zone at the crown. The approximate design of shell beams is further discussed under cylindrical shells and folded plates.

*Shell arches* are singly or doubly curved shells; they are short shells and span primarily in the cross direction rather than the longitudinal direction, thus acting predominantly as arches and not as beams.

True *"shells"* are doubly curved surface structures, each one with particular geometrical characteristics. Common forms are discussed in Chapter 7 and typical applications to architecture are further investigated in this chapter. Double curvature shells are obviously stronger than single curvature ones, assuming proper support is provided so that full advantage can be taken of arch action in two directions. The shell transfers uniform symmetrical loading by tangential shear to the supporting edge ribs, which are assumed to be placed parallel to the form generators. Hence, the sum of the vertical components of the shear along the shell periphery is equal to the total load.

## 8.1  THE SHELL MATERIAL

### Reinforced Concrete Shells

For the design of shells and folded plate members, according to the *ACI Code* the reinforced concrete can be considered ideally elastic, homogeneous, and isotropic with identical stress–strain properties in all directions. In the context of this book, the stresses at
the elastic limit for this ideal material reinforced concrete are considered as ultimate
stresses. Hence the tensile stresses $f_{su}$ in the reinforcing steel $A_s$ must be less than the
steel yield strength $f_y$ reduced by the capacity reduction factor $\phi$

$$f_{su} = \frac{N_{tu}}{A_s} \leqslant \phi f_y$$

Or, the minimum required steel is

$$A_s = \frac{N_{tu}}{\phi f_y} = \frac{N_{tu}}{0.9 f_y} \tag{8.1}$$

Similarly, the compressive stress should be less than the material strength

$$f_{cu} = \frac{N_{cu}}{A_g} \leqslant 0.85 \, \phi f_c'$$

or

$$f_{cu} = \frac{N_{cu}}{0.7 A_g} \leqslant 0.85 f_c' \tag{8.2}$$

For the case where tensile stresses vary greatly in magnitude, reinforcement resisting the
total tension may be concentrated in the regions of maximum tensile stress. But, the
minimum reinforcement throughout the tensile zone should still be

$$A_{s \, min} = 0.0035 A_g = 0.0035 bt \tag{8.3}$$

The minimum reinforcing along the principal directions for shrinkage and temperature is

$$A_{s \, min} = 0.0020 A_g = 0.002 bt \tag{8.4}$$

for Grade 60 steel

$$A_{s \, min} = 0.0018 A_g = 0.0018 bt \tag{8.5}$$

The reinforcement shall not be spaced farther apart than five times the shell thickness,
nor shall the spacing exceed 18 in. It is assumed to act at the middle of the shell surface
and is placed either parallel to the line of principal stress (a deviation of up to 15° is
still permitted) or in two or three component directions by providing additional reinforcement.

The shell thickness is rarely dictated by strength requirements but rather by stability
considerations for large scale surfaces, by the required compatibility with stiff edge mem-

bers (i.e., bending), and most often by the minimum concrete cover for the reinforcement. Where the concrete is neither exposed to weather nor in contact with the ground, the minimum concrete cover for shells and folded plates for #5 bars and smaller should be $\frac{1}{2}$ in. for nonprestressed cast-in-place construction, and $\frac{3}{8}$ in. for precast concrete as well as prestressed concrete. The minimum shell thickness for three layers of reinforcement (e.g., transverse, longitudinal and diagonal), which is a typical condition, is

$$
\begin{array}{ll}
\text{Concrete cover: } 2 \times \frac{1}{2} & = 1.00 \text{ in.} \\
\text{Three layers of #4 bars: } 2 \times \frac{4}{8} & = 1.00 \text{ in.} \\
\text{Minimum spacing between top and bottom layer:} & \underline{= 1.00 \text{ in.}} \\
& t_{\min} = 3.00 \text{ in.}
\end{array}
$$

The typical shell thickness in the United States is in the range 3–4 in. Much thinner shells, however, have been built. The 52-ft dome of the Zeiss Planetarium at Jena, Germany (1922) is only $1\frac{3}{16}$ in. thick. It consists of a self-supporting triangular mesh of reinforcement similar to a high-frequency geodesic dome as based on the Dywidag System; here the concrete surface was formed by shotcreting the self-supporting mesh. Similar methods of construction have been used later by other builders to eliminate the cost of formwork. The Zeiss Planetarium may be considered the world's first *ferrocement* large-scale structure, though not exactly corresponding to the definition of ferrocement. This construction method yields extremely thin shells; here cement mortar is pressed, instead of sprayed under pressure as for the planetarium, into several layers of wire mesh (welded or woven as chicken wire, or expanded metal lath). Ferrocement consists of a much higher proportion of reinforcement and only fine aggregates (sand) in contrast to the conventional reinforced concrete with coarse aggregates and a low steel ratio.

Ferrocement shells are quite strong due to the relatively monolithic character of the composite material. Pier Luigi Nervi pioneered in the early 1940s the application of ferrocemento from which the word ferrocement is derived. He used the principle for the first time on a large scale for the corrugated roof of the 1948 Exposition Hall in Turin, where $1\frac{1}{2}$-in. thick prefab ferrocement panels are tied together by cast-in-place concrete ribs.

The advantage of ferrocement construction lies in the saving of material, equipment, formwork (only occasional shoring may be required), and skilled labor; it also lies in its design flexibility (formability), strength, and watertightness. On a large scale, a certain advantage may lie in its light weight which lends itself to prefabrication as demonstrated by Nervi. Thin, semirigid ferrocement ribbons are also used as suspended roof membranes especially for longspan structures. However, in general, the use of ferrocement in the United States is still in the developmental stage. This is due to the excessive construction time and that it is not easily adaptable to industrialized processes of mechanization. Presently, in this country, ferrocement seems to be mainly employed for boat building. For instance, 25–45-ft long boats have a shell thickness that varies from $\frac{1}{2}$ to $\frac{3}{4}$ in. depending on the strength and number of mesh layers.

A recent development in concrete shell design, though still in its experimental stage, is glassfiber-reinforced concrete. Since no conventional reinforcing steel is needed, the shell cannot only be reduced in weight, but also in thickness. These lightweight shells clearly lend themselves to prefabrication.

## Wood Shells

In Fig. 8.1, typical shell surfaces in timber are identified. There are three basic structural systems derived from the nature of the surface structure which resists the membrane forces.

### Skeletal Shells

Here the membrane forces are resisted by a member grid which makes up the skin (i.e., skin frame structure) rather than by a solid surface. The sheathing and purlins are not considered to act compositely with the member network comprising the shell, although they may be needed as diaphragms depending on the layout of the shell framing, especially if it is not triangulated. Various framework patterns are discussed later in this chapter. While for most framed surfaces the placement of the sheathing is apparent, for some grid shells it is placed according to the geometry of its member layout.

### Solid Laminated Wood Shells

Molded plywood is the simplest form of a solid shell on a small scale. Its technology was perfected during World War II in the aircraft industry (aircraft fuselages, wings, etc.) and the shipbuilding industry (laminated ship and boat parts such as boat hulls). Just after World War II, Charles Eames introduced his now classic molded plywood chairs.

Plywood is a composite material made up of several veneers with opposing grains, where the durability of the plywood is very much dependent on the quality of the adhesive. In the conventional roof construction, plywood sheathing (standard size 4 ft $\times$ 8 ft $\times$ $\frac{1}{4}$ - $1\frac{1}{4}$ in.) may span up to about 6 ft in bending.

Thin, solid laminated wood shells are constructed from layers of lumber sheathing or plywood. They are glue-nailed/stapled together to prevent buckling of the individual layers and are supported along their perimeters by edge beams. Since the membrane stresses are relatively low, high-grade material is not required. Boards or plywood are laid in various layers in different directions depending on the shape of the shell. For shallow surfaces, the tongue and groove boards can be easily bent or twisted, as the radii of curvature are generally much larger than the thickness of the membrane. Mostly, they are placed along the principal curvatures and/or at 45° to them. For instance, in a four-layer glue-stapled hypar shell, the boards in the bottom layer follow the first principal curvature and the second and third layers are placed parallel to the straight line generators but perpendicular to each other, while the fourth layer is positioned along the other principal direction.

For the condition where three layers of plywood are glue-stapled, the panels are arranged in a staggered fashion at a 45° angle to the layer beneath so that no joints are in line and on top of each other. Though plywood has a much higher shear capacity than lumber and is assembled faster, lumber sheathing has the advantage of narrow board width which adjusts more easily to the doubly curved hypar shape and thus has only a slight twist when placed along the straight line generators.

In a shallow cylindrical shell, the boards in the bottom layer may be placed along the principal curvature, while the second and third layers are laid at 45° and perpendicular to each other. For steeper slopes, curved members have to be prefabricated by applying

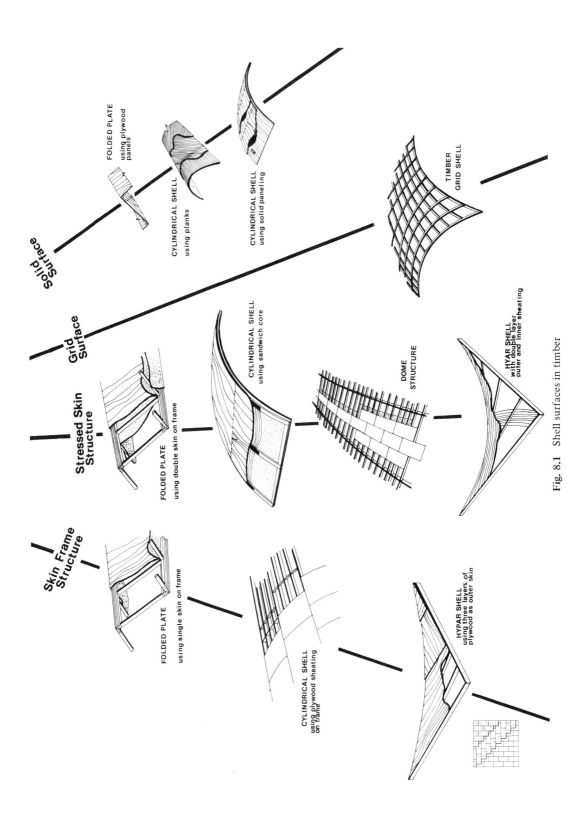

FOLDED PLATE
using plywood
panels

CYLINDRICAL SHELL
using planks

CYLINDRICAL SHELL
using solid paneling

Solid Surface

TIMBER
GRID SHELL

Grid Surface

Stressed Skin
Structure

FOLDED PLATE
using double skin on frame

CYLINDRICAL SHELL
using sandwich core

DOME
STRUCTURE

HYPAR SHELL
with double layer
outer and inner sheating

Skin Frame
Structure

FOLDED PLATE
using single skin on frame

CYLINDRICAL SHELL
using plywood sheating
on frame

HYPAR SHELL
using three layers of
plywood as outer skin

Fig. 8.1  Shell surfaces in timber

424

some type of softening or plasticizing treatment. Curved plywood can also be produced by bending and gluing the plies simultaneously similar to the production of curved laminated members.

Laminated wood shells are lightweight. Usually, two to three layers of sheathing of $1-1\frac{1}{2}$ in. thickness are adequate for the coverage of a square area of roughly 60 X 60 ft with a shell weight of about 5 psf.

One may approximately design solid wood shells, say for the condition where the sheathing is placed along the principal curvatures, as for a two-layer hypar shell for example, by assuming the unit tensile (or compressive) stress to be equal to the principal tension (or compression) force per inch divided by only the thickness of the sheathing along which the respective force acts. This approach of considering two independent layers is conservative since the capacity of the layer perpendicular to the force action is ignored. For the condition where the boards run parallel to the straight line generators, one may visualize that under uniform load action the principal axial forces are replaced by their equivalent, the pure shear at 45° to them (Fig. 7.13b). Hence, the membrane can be designed for pure shear only. The shear, however, must be transferred across the discontinuous adjacent boards (sheathing) through the adjacent layer; thus, the sheathing layers must be connected to each other to be able to transfer the shear. But should the sheathing not be placed parallel to the principal curvatures, then the principal forces do not act parallel to the grain but at some angle. Now, new elastic properties, such as allowable stresses, must be determined for the anisotropic material lumber.

## Composite Shell Systems

The concept of composite action of various structural elements is applicable to all materials on small or large scale. The principle is taken from the automotive and aircraft industry. In wood construction it is applied to glued plywood-lumber panels of the following types:

- Stressed-skin panel (double or single skin)
- Sandwich panel
- Solid core panel

In general, these panels are prefabricated similar to glued plywood I- or box-beams. They can take any form, such as flat panels (rectangular, triangular, trapezoidal, etc.) for folded plate structures, curved/warped panels for hypar shells, or arched panels as for cylindrical surfaces.

Conceptually, *stressed-skin* surfaces are obtained by bonding the sheathing to the frame or grid shell, hereby generating a composite surface structure that has a significantly higher strength and stiffness. The prefab panel approach as derived from aircraft fabrication techniques in the 1940s came only into commercial building application in the late 1950s. The panel component is produced by integrally connecting the plywood panels to the stringers so that it acts as a composite system where no slippage occurs between them as can be caused, for example, by horizontal shear due to flexure in arched systems. The structural action of a flat panel can be visualized similar to a series of adjoining built-up I-beams for double skin systems, or T-beams for single skin panels. Here, the flanges or the plywood facings carry the axial forces and the bending, while the webs or stringers resist the shear.

In *sandwich* or *solid core* construction the lumber stringers are replaced by some other core material, such as foamed plastic or paper honeycomb for sandwich panels as will be discussed further in the section Plastic Shells. The structural behavior of the surfaces is similar to the stressed-skin panels. The facings can be thinner because the core material provides continuous support to the skin and thus prevents buckling. The shear is carried by the core material.

## Steel Shells

Most large-scale steel shells, like domes, are of the skeleton type. Other steel shells may be composed of corrugated steel panels or they may be of the stressed-skin type of construction.

### Skeletal Shells

The various framing systems for different shell forms are discussed later in this section. In a trussed shell surface the metal decking together with the purlins are not needed as diaphragms. They are a separate load carrying system only acting as the roofing surface.

### Steel Sheet Shells

Water tanks, ship hulls, car bodies, pipelines, boilers, and containers clearly show the application of continuous metal sheets as developed into closed shell units.

In building construction, corrugated steel panels are frequently used because of their higher stiffness, especially against buckling, and because of their one-way bending capacity.

In barrel vaults the corrugations are generally placed along the arch action similar to folded plates where they provide the bending capacity due to transverse slab action. Should the corrugations extend longitudinally, transverse stiffeners and ribs must be provided to maintain the shape.

In hypar shells the formed steel decking is conveniently placed parallel to the straight line generators by only having to slightly warp them. Most long-span hyperbolic paraboloids are constructed from two layers of mutually perpendicular plates plug welded at the common intersections of the flat surfaces as the typical example in Fig. 8.2 indicates. Here, the four hypar surfaces, each one 33.5 ft square, are supported by four corner and one center column as well as by edge beams along the column lines.

For approximate design considerations refer to the discussion, Solid Laminated Wood Shells.

### Stressed-Skin Shells

The strength and stiffness of the skeleton-type shell is very much improved if the roof skin becomes an integral part of the shell membrane. The strength may further be increased by developing the flat or slightly bent skin into folded polyhedral shapes or into bent hypar panels. For this condition, the formed spatial panels may replace some of the members of the framed shell. One step further yields a shell surface composed of three-

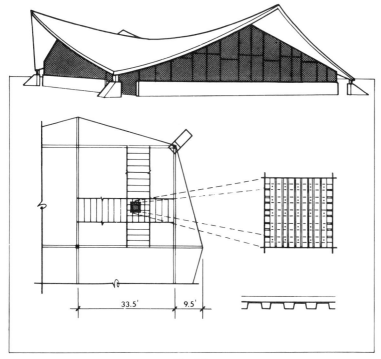

Fig. 8.2

dimensional panels attached to each other along their edges, which now form the member framework.

## Plastic Shells

Plastic shells immediately bring to one's mind the richness and the unprecedented expression of the continuously floating curved surfaces in furniture design, or they may remind one of the intricate, spatial shell shapes of car bodies or sculptured curtain walls. When in the early 1940s Charles Eames and Eero Saarinen invented the molded fiberglass shell technique and then mass produced their chairs, nobody could have predicted the explosion of the new era of the material plastics about 15 years later and the corresponding development of a wealth of innovative forms. In Italy, some architects converted to industrial design and created a new design aesthetics and art form so beautifully expressed in furniture which exposed the true nature and plasticity of the continuous shell. In 1955, I. Schein, Y. Magnant, and R. A. Coulon, in France, built the first all-plastics house in the shape of a snail's shell. Two years later, the famous Monsanto House (Fig. 8.3n) was developed by Hamilton and Goody and exhibited for many years in Disneyland. The cantilevering wings of the cross-shaped module clearly express the strength of the three-dimensional shell and the logic of the plastic form. Today, industrialized, cellular, container-like, intricate shell shapes for shelters, mobile units, building cores (kitchen and bathroom modules), etc., are quite common, as are the shell-shaped cladding panels for

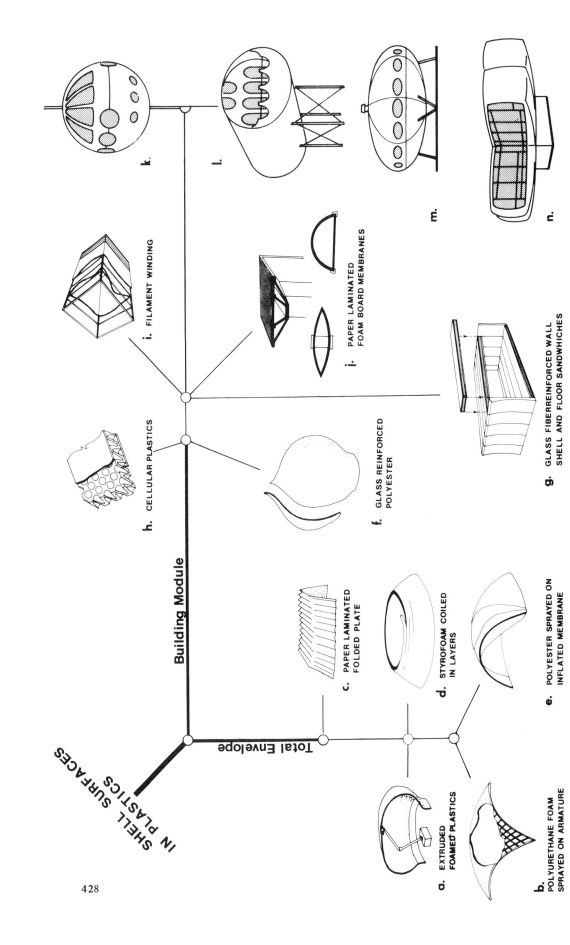

SHELL SURFACES IN PLASTICS

Building Module

Total Envelope

a. EXTRUDED FOAMED PLASTICS

b. POLYURETHANE FOAM SPRAYED ON ARMATURE

c. PAPER LAMINATED FOLDED PLATE

d. STYROFOAM COILED IN LAYERS

e. POLYESTER SPRAYED ON INFLATED MEMBRANE

f. GLASS REINFORCED POLYESTER

g. GLASS FIBERREINFORCED WALL SHELL AND FLOOR SANDWICHES

h. CELLULAR PLASTICS

i. FILAMENT WINDING

j. PAPER LAMINATED FOAM BOARD MEMBRANES

k.

l.

m.

n.

428

framed or trussed structures. Some of the early pioneers who developed an architecture of plastic shells are, besides Ionel Schein, Rudolf Doernach, and Wolfgang Döring in Germany, Renzo Piano and Angelo Mangiarotti in Italy, and Arthur Quarmby in England.

But plastic shells do not necessarily have to be factory produced; they can be constructed directly on the site using urethane foams. Architects Felix Drury and John M. Johansen in the United States have convincingly expressed how the process of construction may evolve into rather freeform shell structures that are in close contact with nature and its organic forms.

The major groups of modular panel construction, sandwich shells and foam shells, as identified in Fig. 8.3, are briefly discussed, in the following.

*Modular Plastic Panels*

These types of panels are factory produced and used primarily as secondary or contributing structural elements such as fill-ins for frames and trusses (e.g., corrugated roof panels, curtains, skylights). For larger-scale surfaces, they may be fabricated in segments and assembled on the site to form a complete folded plate or shell as in the twelve $\frac{3}{8}$ in. thick glassfiber reinforced polyester segments making up the 32 ft diameter onion dome (f).

Almost any shape can be generated by placing plastics, generally liquid epoxies or polyesters, or layered resin saturated reinforced material, usually fiberglass fabric, over a mold. Among the many processing techniques the more common ones for generation of shells are:

- Hand lay-up and spray-up (fiberglass boats, large unconventional components, etc.)
- Continuous process with conveyor belts (sheeting material, corrugated panels, etc.)
- Injection molding (e.g., shell-type furniture)
- Blow molding (e.g., skylight domes)
- Cold or hot press molding
- Matched-die molding (e.g., automotive applications)
- Filament winding (i) (aerospace components, room modules, etc.).

The actual method of production depends on the scale, shape, and number of components (custom-tailored versus mass production), cost, and other required properties. Some of the positive characteristics of reinforced plastics are their formability, light weight, strength, toughness, and light transmission. Their disadvantage lies in their relatively low stiffness and surface hardness, the high coefficient of expansion (Table 1.3), creep behavior, unknown durability, flammability, and cost. The stiffness of plastics is increased and deflection reduced by utilizing spatial forms, as was discussed in Chapter 1.

To develop some appreciation for the strength of acrylic shells, visualize spherical segment Plexiglas domes only $\frac{1}{4}$ in. thick as produced by Rohm and Haas for a design load of 20 psf, to cover a nearly 14-ft square area. Almost 4600 transparent acrylic skylights (about 7 × 3.3 ft) cover Houston's Astrodome. The U.S. Pavilion at "Expo 68," Montreal, was enclosed by more than 2000 acrylic domes varying from 8 × 10 ft to 10 × 12 ft in size. Translucent acrylic Plexiglas panels (9.5 × 9.5 ft × 0.16 in.) are covering the enormous roof area (808,000 ft$^2$) of the Munich Olympic tent-like net structures.

## Foam Shells

Foam shell enclosures may be generated on the site by one of the following methods.

### ■ *Spray Process*

Liquid foam, generally polyurethane, which is better known as an insulation material, is sprayed onto a flexible membrane [e.g., tent or inflated skin (e)] or onto an armature (b); it then produces gas and expands while, at the same time, quickly hardening. The shell may be weatherproofed by a rubber coating on the outside. This process of construction, in addition to using the foam shell as structure, generally is only applied to smaller-scale buildings.

### ■ *Extrusion Process*

In this method, a truck-mounted boom with a mold at its end extrudes layer after layer of foam which solidifies immediately (a).

### ■ *Spirogeneration*

In this process developed by Dow Chemical Co., thin shell domes are constructed from long blocks or strips of expanded polystyrene (styrofoam) similar to the building of Eskimo igloos (d). Successive layers are fused by employing a rotation boom anchored at the center of the dome, which carries the heat welding equipment. The foam shell is used as thermal insulation as well as formwork for the thin concrete shell that has a thickness of about $\frac{3}{4}$ in. for up to a 130-ft span and about $1\frac{3}{8}$ in. for up to a 200-ft span, with a foam shell thickness of 8 in. The structural concrete shell is a high bonding latex modified concrete, which is sprayed in three layers onto a wire mesh that is attached to the foam dome.

## Sandwich Shells

Laminated sandwiches consist of several layers of different materials. The rigid, *thin facing sheets* may be made of reinforced plastics, metal (steel, aluminum), plywood, hardboard, cement asbestos, reinforced concrete, etc. The *core*, which provides the thermal and acoustical insulation, may consist of plastic foams (PVC, polystyrene, polyurethane, phenolic plastic), honeycomb made of impregnated paper, or made of metal or plastics (h), particleboard, lumber core, plywood (e.g., 3 plies with grains at right angle to each other), member grids, etc.

Glass fiber reinforced polyester composites in sandwich form are most popular as self-supporting shell enclosures. Here, two glass laminates and foamed polyurethane, for instance, with localized stiffeners at points of load application are employed. Typical manufacturing processes are the simple open contact molding and the filament winding for shells under large stresses. One should keep in mind that the performance characteristics of the material (flammability, smoke release, durability, strength, cost, appearance, etc.) depend very much on the chemical and physical properties of the various polyester resins.

From a structural point of view, in sandwich construction the facing provides the strength and stiffness similar to the flanges of a W-section that resists primarily bending (axial action), while the core stabilizes the skin and carries the shear.

Sandwich shell construction is applied to panel systems (facade panels, roof cladding), mass-produced single unit containers (cabins, bus shelters, retail sales kiosks, telephone booths, kitchen and bathroom units, etc.), and to modular aggregates for housing [room modules, sectional units, wall and roof panels for mobile homes, individual components (g), etc.] .

The cantilevering shell buildings in Fig. 8.3, cases (k)–(n), clearly express their monocoque character, that is, the fact that the total structure participates in resisting the loading as already practiced in the automotive and space industries.

The shell of the Futuro II house (m), which has the shape of an ablate spheroid, that is roughly 26 ft in diameter and 12 ft high, consists of an only 2 in. thick stressed fiberglass sandwich with polyurethane foam insulation. The folded plate barrel-type structure (c) is a paperboard construction consisting of $\frac{3}{8}$-in. thick sandwich elements of polyethylene impregnated Kraftboard with polyurethane foam core.

The sandwich dome for the information center at the Hannover Fair, Hannover, Germany (1970), spans nearly 130 ft and weighs only 6.75 psf. For the sake of comparison, a Dow dome for the same span with an 8-in. foam shell and a $\frac{3}{4}$-in. reinforced concrete shell weighs about 10.40 psf.


## 8.2  THE CYLINDRICAL SHELL

Single-curvature cylindrical shells may be composed of many different types of curves, as shown in Fig. 8.4. The basic curves range from the defined geometries of the circular segment, parabola, ellipse, hyperbola, and cycloid to the responsive geometry of the funicular line. These basic shapes may be joined in innumerable ways to yield cross-sections of various forms, which may be identified as follows:

- Single shell constructed from single segment or multiple segments
- Single shell versus multiple shells (corrugated forms)
- Repeating versus nonrepeating units
- Convex versus concave versus undulating forms
- Continuous versus discontinuous (Y-shapes, tilted S-shapes, etc.) forms
- Symmetrical versus asymmetrical shells (e.g. north light shell), and so on.

The cylindrical shell units may be arranged in a parallel, radial, or intersecting manner; they may be straight, folded, or bent. Intersecting shells are discussed later in this chapter; here, only linear parallel cylindrical shells are briefly investigated.

The behavior of a simple linear cylindrical unit depends on its geometry, material, loading conditions, and the type and location of its supports. In the following discussion, uniform symmetrical gravity load action is assumed, as wind stresses are generally small and can be neglected for preliminary design purposes.

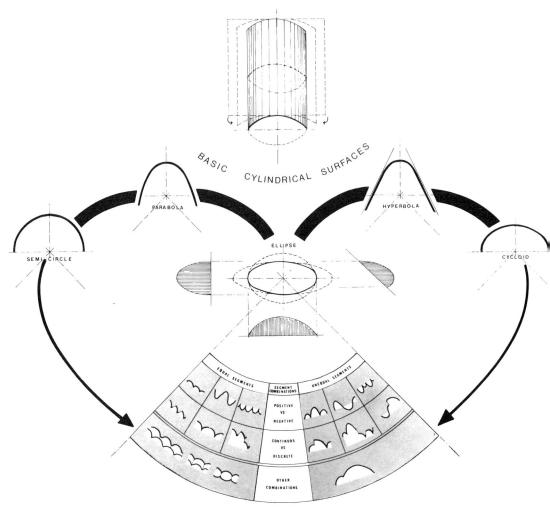

Fig. 8.4

The influence of support location is quite apparent from Fig. 8.5. Should the shell be continuously supported along its longitudinal edges by deep beams, frames, walls, or foundations, the forces are carried directly in the transverse direction to the supports. Its behavior may be visualized as the response of parallel arches, each 1 ft wide. These arches must be relatively thick, since they respond to forces by bending as well as axial force action. Since bending is a primary design consideration, these single-curvature surface structures are not considered shells, because their primary structural response is not membrane-type action. They are called vaults, and may be approximately designed as if they were arches.

On the other hand, if there are no supports in the longitudinal direction, but only in the transverse direction, the shell must behave as a beam spanning in the longitudinal direction; the forces can no longer be carried in arch action directly to longitudinal supports. For a cylindrical shell with a small chord width in comparison to its span, the primary response will be beam action. These types of shells are called long shells or shell beams; they can be visualized as beams with curvilinear cross-sections. They are assumed not to distort under load action so that linear stress distribution can be used. The shell carries the uniform loads in a purely axial manner in the longitudinal direction, and any bending stresses are neglected. The potential warping of the shell may be reduced by introducing longitudinal edge beams, transverse ribs, and adjacent shells. The usual height-to-span ratio for long shells varies from 1/10 to 1/15, although there is no precise point at which a cylindrical shell's shape can be considered "long". In general, the beam theory may be applied to long cylindrical shells that are of symmetrical cross-section and under uniform loading, and which meet the following span-to-radius of curvature conditions:

single shells without edge beams: $L/R > 5$
single shells with edge beams that are not too deep: $L/R > 3$
interior shells of a multiple system: $L/R > 2$
interior shells of a multiple system with edge beams: $L/R > 3$

One may conclude that with increase of $L/R$ (increase of span and/or decrease of radius of curvature) the beam theory becomes more realistic. Furthermore, the effect of preventing the shell from distorting under loads by using stiffening devices, permits the application of beam behavior for smaller $L/R$ ratios.

As $L/R$ decreases and the transverse supports move closer to each other, or as the dimension of the longitudinal span becomes smaller than the dimension of the shell width, the shell behavior changes from a primary action in the longitudinal direction

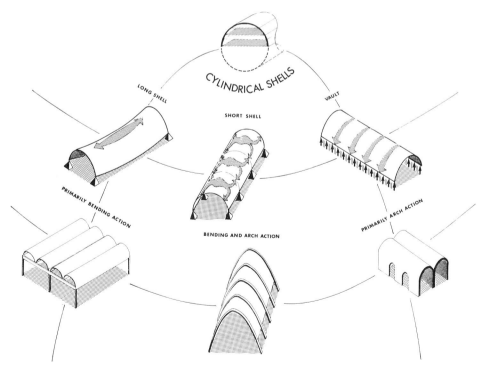

Fig. 8.5 Cylindrical shells.

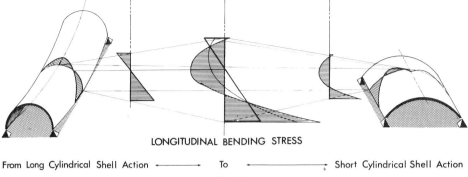

LONGITUDINAL BENDING STRESS

From Long Cylindrical Shell Action ⟶        To        ⟵⟶ Short Cylindrical Shell Action

Fig. 8.6

(beam action) to a primary action in the transverse direction (arch action). The type of cylindrical shells which are neither beams nor vaults are called short shells; their structural behavior is rather complex and very much dependent on their geometrical proportions. The forces in the longitudinal direction are not distributed anymore in a linear manner, but in a curvilinear one. The transition from a linear stress distribution (long shell) to a curvilinear one (short shell) is shown in Fig. 8.6. One notices that in the short shell more than one tensile zone exists, as the tension along the crown portion indicates.The stress flow in the transverse direction may be approximately evaluated by using membrane forces. The complex behavior of the short cylindrical shell can be visualized (Fig. 8.7) as consisting of slab action on the flat portion, where the loads are carried directly in bending to the transverse supports, and plate action in the steeper shell portion, which may be replaced by imaginary arches and cables.

The development of cylindrical shell forms originated in simple masonry barrel vaults and was perfected by the Romans as expressed so powerfully in the Maxentius Basilica in Rome (313 A.D.) where the vaults reached a span of 85 ft. Similarly, more than 200 years later, the parabolic brick vault of Ctesiphon achieved a span of 83 ft (see Section 4.4, Arches). The art of vaulting reappeared in the church architecture of the early Romanesque period. The evolution from heavy, tunnel-like masonry vaulting to groined vaulting, and finally to the elegant floating, intricate ribbed vaulting of the Gothic cathedral took

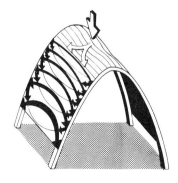

Behavior of
Short Cylindrical Shells

Fig. 8.7

more than three centuries; some of the beautiful rib patterns are shown in Fig. 8.13. However, the transformation from the vault to the shell is an achievement of the twentieth century. Franz Dischinger and Walter Bauersfeld developed the necessary theory for the design of cylindrical concrete shells and built, in 1924, the first reinforced cylindrical concrete shell for a factory building of the Zeiss company in Jena, Germany.

Cylindrical shells are not just characterized by the form of their cross-section, but also by the types of support in the longitudinal and transverse directions, by the kind of diaphragms and edge beam conditions, as well as by the continuity of the shells across several bays and spans. Because of the similarity of support conditions for the folded plate beam structure and the cylindrical shell beam, the reader may refer to Fig. 6.3 for further identification of these characteristics.

Some typical architectural cases exhibiting the shell beam principle are shown in Fig. 8.8. The usual span range of cylindrical concrete shell beams is in the range 80–160 ft with a chord width of 30–45 ft and a span-to-depth ratio of between 1/10 and 1/15. The shell thickness is usually 3 in. and may be increased near ribs and edge beams.

The cross-sections for the various cases range from the undulating concrete shells (f) to the north light shells (d), to the channel-like precast concrete units with bowed webs (b). Not only can the shells act as simple or continuous beams, but also as cantilevers, as reflected by the 50-ft cantilever shells (m) tapered from front to back, following the intensity of the moment flow.

The parallel concrete cycloid-shells for the Kimbell Art Museum (h) are separated by 7-ft wide channel-type beams. The 23-ft wide, 4-in. thick, post-tensioned shells span 104 ft and are supported at each end by arches and columns. The 3-ft skylight openings at the shell crowns are framed similarly to a Vierendeel truss to transfer the shell forces so that the shell can behave as a continuous unit.

In case (e), individual inverted plywood shell beams, $1\frac{1}{4}$-in. thick, span 30 ft and support arched glass fiber skylights.

The roof in case (j) consists of parallel 3 ft 3 in. deep plywood box girders, 11 ft 8 in. apart, to which are attached, on top and bottom, respectively, arched and suspended double layers of $\frac{1}{4}$-in. plywood sheets. The roof in case (l) has the appearance of an inverted cylindrical shell, where in reality corrugated steel sheeting is suspended from parallel trusses which are spaced at about 13 ft apart.

One of the largest shells covers the New Orleans' Rivergate Exhibition Center. The roof consists of six main, two-span, slightly arched shell beams that have spans of 139, 253, and 30 ft cantilevers at each end. A typical barrel is 18 ft deep ($d/L = 1/14$), 60 ft wide, and is post-tensioned along its full length of 452 ft.

Some examples that express the concept of short cylindrical shells and vaults are shown in Fig. 8.9. They range from the small scale of arched corrugated sheet metal (f) as found in industrial construction, and single-layer geodesic aluminum frame barrels with tension membranes as enclosure (d), to the large scale of parabolic barrel vaults consisting of parallel folded concrete arches (a) or prefabricated welded pipe space frames (i).

In case (b) the $2\frac{3}{4}$-in. thick cylindrical concrete shells are inclined for lighting purposes. The lateral thrust of the hipped lamella vaults (c), (e), of the arches supporting the short shells (h), (k), and of the vault (j), is resisted by inclined buttresses. This is quite powerfully expressed by the fan-shaped buttresses at the crossing of the supporting arch structure in (c). Nervi used his precast concrete system for the 219 ft clear span parabolic vault of the field house at Dartmouth College (1962). The double-layer trussed steel barrel of the Waldstadion Sports Complex, Frankfurt, Germany (1982), spans

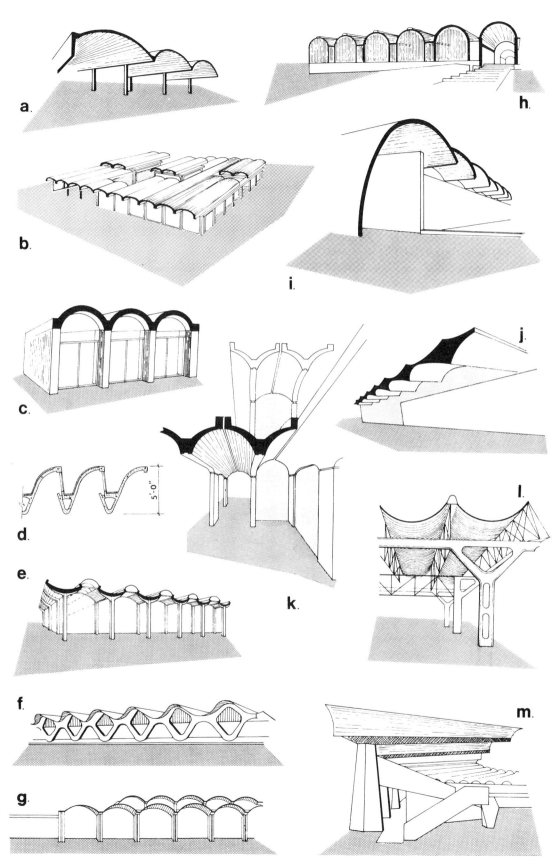

**Fig. 8.8** Cylindrical shell structures.

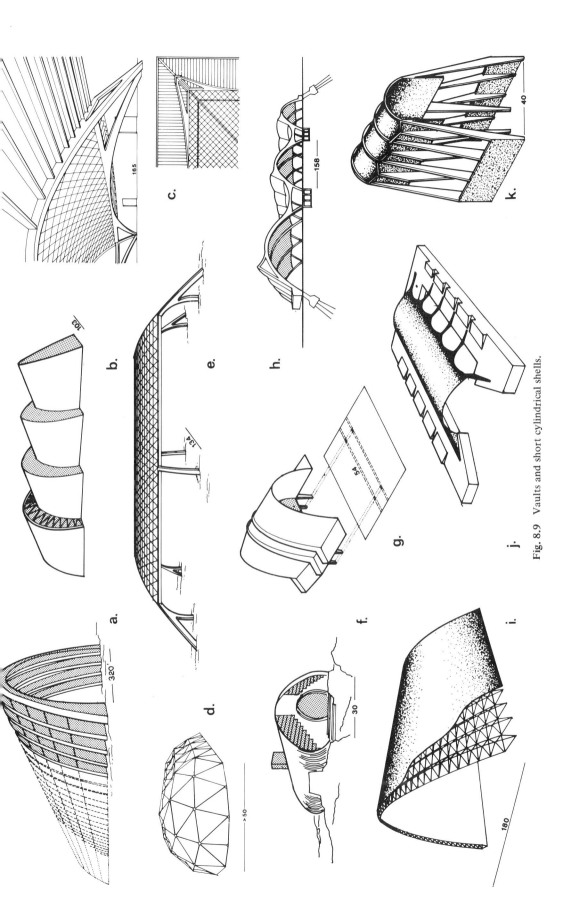

Fig. 8.9  Vaults and short cylindrical shells.

230 ft. The arched roof, consisting of triangular and hexagonal cells, transfers the loads directly to the ground through abutment frames.

### Approximate Design of Concrete Shell Beams

The three single-curvature linear surface structures—vault, short and long shells—can be further studied by investigating the transition of a one-way beam-supported slab to a shell beam (Fig. 8.10). For the case where the horizontal slab is supported by beams, the loads are first carried in slab action transversely and then in beam action longitudinally (see also Fig. 6.3). If the slab is bent, the slab action is replaced by arch action, assuming that the longitudinal edge beams are very stiff in comparison to the shell, so that the conditions are similar to a vault sitting on longitudinal supports. However, if the edge is relatively flexible, then edge beams and shell can act together as a total unit: the primary forces in this shell with edge beams are of axial nature, as caused by beam action in the longitudinal direction rather than bending due to arch action in the transverse direction.

The size of the edge beam depends on the ratio of shell height to shell span, among other considerations. In the longitudinal direction the shell acts as a beam; its cross-sectional height is the primary determinant of the moment of inertia, that is, the magnitude of the axial stresses. For a shallow long shell, large edge beams may be necessary to obtain the required inertia. As the shell height increases, the inertia also increases, thereby decreasing the size of the edge beam, which eventually will no longer be needed.

Similar reasoning is true for the behavior of the shell in the transverse direction. The flat shell causes large lateral thrust forces under vertical loading as caused by transverse arch action; this thrust must be carried by edge beams. As the height of the shell increases, the amount of transverse thrust decreases. Remember that the hoop forces due to membrane action for a semicircular cylindrical membrane are zero along the longitudinal edges (Fig. 8.11). One may conclude that as shell height increases, the size of the edge beams decreases, keeping in mind that the conditions for a single shell beam are quite different from those of a multiple shell grouping, where the shells support each other laterally.

For long cylindrical shells the edge beams are vertical, since their primary purpose is to resist longitudinal forces, while for short shells the edge beams can be placed horizontally, since they must resist the lateral thrust due to arch action.

The selection of the shell height, besides being dependent on functional and aesthetical considerations, is also a function of economical and practical aspects. The cost of a high shell with large surface area and low weight per unit area must be compared to the costs of a shallow shell with less surface area but higher weight per unit area. Further, the difference in costs among the varying construction procedures must be taken into account. Practical considerations, such as the casting of concrete onto steep slopes, may also determine the height of the shell. Typical maximum slopes of tangents at the edges of cylindrical concrete shells are $\theta_0 = 45°$ for shells without edge beams, and $\theta_0 = 30°$ for shells with edge beams.

The selection of the shell curvature should depend on the primary shell behavior, assuming that other criteria do not determine the shell form. Should arch behavior be the primary action, such as for vaults and very short cylindrical shells, then parabolic, catenary, or other funicular shapes derived from load action should be most efficient. Since dead load is, quite often, the primary load for short concrete shells, the catenary shape should be selected. These shapes are not, however, appropriate for long cylindrical shells,

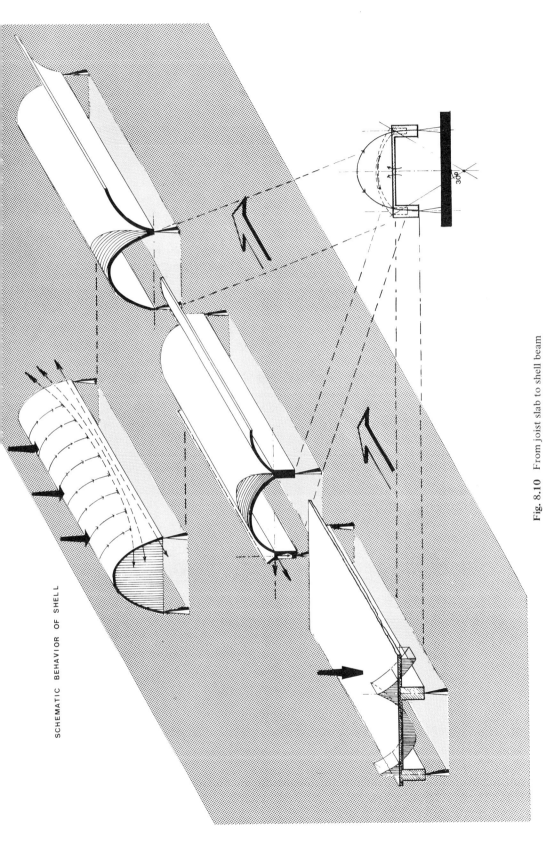

SCHEMATIC BEHAVIOR OF SHELL

Fig. 8.10  From joist slab to shell beam

439

since the arch forces are directly transferred along the funicular shape to the edges where the lateral thrust causes large deformations, especially if no edge beams are provided. These deformations make the use of the beam theory questionable, as it assumes that the beam cross-section does not warp under loading. Typical cylindrical shapes used, in general, are segments of circles, cycloids, and ellipses. Notice that the ellipse and cycloid provide a greater stiffness than the circle because of the larger curvature close to the edges. Further, the tangent to the curvature along the edges of the cycloid and ellipse are steeper and so reduce the effect of transverse bending along the edges as caused by arch action.

At the junction of the relatively rigid transverse support structure or the transverse ribs with the thin shell membrane, bending disturbances are generated in the shell. These disturbances are quite pronounced in the short shell, since they are propagated across the width of the shell, but have only a localized effect on the long shell, where the overall beam behavior is not influenced.

**Example 8.1**  A typical interior long cylindrical circular shell of a multiple shell group is investigated. It spans 70 ft and is considered to be simply supported, and not to have any edge beams. The chord width of the shells is 30 ft and the height is 6 ft. The shell must support a snow load of 30 psf on the horizontal projection of the roof, as well as a small load representing the roofing material. The wind load, in general, may be neglected for first design purposes. A preliminary shell thickness of 3 in. has been assumed. The thickness rarely depends on strength considerations, but is generally selected to ensure adequate coverage of the reinforcement. For very large shells, buckling may have to be considered as a determinant of shell thickness, although buckling of cylindrical shells is not as critical as it is for domes, because a relatively smaller portion of the shell surface is in compression. A concrete strength of 4000 psi and Grade 50 steel are used here.

The height-to-span ratio of the shell beam should be satisfactory since it is in the typical range 1/10–1/15

$$\frac{h}{L} = \frac{6}{70} = \frac{1}{11.67}$$

The radius of curvature for the given shell proportion (Fig. 8.11) is

$$R^2 = 15^2 + (R - 6)^2 \qquad R = 21.75 \text{ ft} \tag{9.7}$$

The semicentral angle, or the maximum shell slope along either edge, is

$$\tan \theta_0 = \frac{15}{21.75 - 6} = 0.952 \qquad \theta_0 = 43.60° = 43.60(\pi/180) = 0.761 \text{ rad}$$

$$\sin \theta = 0.690 \qquad \cos \theta_0 = 0.724$$

Considering buckling for long cylindrical shells in the crown zone, where longitudinal compressive stresses are high, it can be shown that elastic stability becomes critical at roughly $R/t > 200$

$$\frac{R}{t} = \frac{21.75(12)}{3} = 87 \ll 200$$

Buckling is not critical.

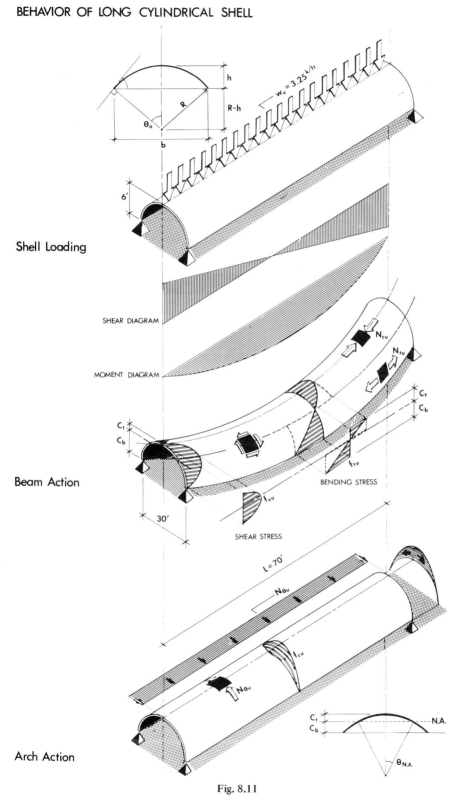

Shell Loading

Beam Action

Arch Action

Fig. 8.11

The maximum slope is less than $45°$, which is considered the maximum advisable slope for the placement of concrete. The span-to-radius ratio is

$$\frac{L}{R} = \frac{70}{21.75} = 3.22 > 2$$

As the $L/R$ ratio is greater than 2, the beam-shell approximation can be used. Remember that if this were to be a single-unit (isolated) shell, the beam theory could not be employed without the use of additional longitudinal beams.

In the following section, some basic geometrical properties of the circular shell segment are determined. The arc length is

$$l = \pi R \frac{\theta_0}{90} = \pi(21.75) \frac{43.60}{90} = 33.10 \text{ ft} \tag{3.14}$$

The location of the centroidal (neutral) axis, as measured from the crown and derived in Problem 8.1, is

$$c_t = R \left(1 - \frac{\sin \theta_0}{\theta_0}\right) = 21.75 \left(1 - \frac{0.690}{0.761}\right) = 2.03 \text{ ft} \tag{8.7}$$

The location of the centroidal axis, as measured from the bottom edge, is

$$c_b = 6.00 - 2.03 = 3.97 \text{ ft}$$

The location of the centroidal axis, as measured by the semicentral angle (Fig. 8.11) is

$$\cos \theta_{NA} = \frac{R - c_t}{R} = \frac{21.75 - 2.03}{21.75} = 0.907$$

$$\sin \theta_{NA} = 0.422 \qquad \theta_{NA} = 24.95° = 0.436 \text{ rad}$$

The moment about the centroidal axis, as caused by the total cross-sectional area above the centroidal axis and as derived in Problem 8.1, is

$$Q_{max} = 2tR^2 \left(\sin \theta_{NA} - \frac{\theta_{NA}}{\theta_0} \sin \theta_0\right) \tag{8.8}$$

$$= 2(0.25)21.75^2 \left(0.422 - \frac{24.95}{43.60} 0.690\right) = 6.42 \text{ ft}^3$$

The moment of inertia about the centroidal axis as derived in Problem 8.1, is

$$I_{ca} = tR^3 \left[\theta_0 + \sin \theta_0 \left(\cos \theta_0 - \frac{2 \sin \theta_0}{\theta_0}\right)\right] \tag{8.9}$$

$$= (0.25)21.75^3 \left[0.761 + 0.690 \left(0.724 - \frac{2(0.690)}{0.761}\right)\right] = 23.95 \text{ ft}^4$$

The shell weighs

| | |
|---|---|
| concrete $(150/12)3 =$ | 37.50 psf |
| roofing | 0.50 psf |
| total weight along the surface | 38.00 psf |

The snow load on the horizontal roof projection is 30 psf. The ultimate line load that the shell-beam must support is

$$w_u = 1.4(0.038 \times 33.10) + 1.7(0.030 \times 30) = 3.29 \text{ k/ft}$$

The maximum ultimate moment at midspan is

$$M_{u \text{ max}} = \frac{w_u L^2}{8} = \frac{3.29(70)^2}{8} = 2015.13 \text{ ft-k}$$

The maximum longitudinal compressive stresses in the crown portion at midspan are

$$f_{cu} = \frac{M_u c_t}{I} = \frac{2015.13(2.03)}{23.95} = 170.80 \text{ ksf} = 1.19 \text{ ksi}$$

The allowable compressive stress is

$$f_{c \text{ allow}} = \phi(0.85 f_c') = 0.7[0.85(4)] = 2.38 \text{ ksi} \tag{8.2}$$

As the actual compressive stress in the concrete is less than the allowable compressive stress, the selected thickness of the slab is more than adequate and not dependent on strength considerations. The maximum ultimate tensile stresses in the bottom edge at midspan are:

$$f_{tu} = \frac{M_u c_b}{I} = \frac{2015.13(3.97)}{23.95} = 334.03 \text{ ksf} = 2.32 \text{ ksi}$$

According to the *ACI Code*, the reinforcement to carry the total tension may be concentrated in the region of maximum tensile stress.

Here, however, an approximation is being used by considering a rectangular stress distribution over a height of 1 ft which is then assumed to decrease towards the neutral axis.

The maximum tensile force is

$$N_{tu} = f_{tu} A = 2.32(12)3 = 83.52 \text{ k/ft}$$

Now the corresponding steel area required to balance this tensile force may be calculated

$$A_s = \frac{N_{tu}}{\phi F_y} = \frac{83.52}{0.9 \times 50} = 1.86 \text{ in.}^2/\text{ft}$$

Select #6 bars at 2.75 in. on center, $A_s = 1.92 \text{ in.}^2/\text{ft}$.

These longitudinal bars are to be placed along the bottom shell portion over about a 1 ft range. Then the amount of reinforcement may be decreased towards the neutral axis keeping in mind that the minimum reinforcement in the tensile zone should be

$$A_{s \text{ min}} = 0.0035 A_g = 0.0035(12)3 = 0.126 \text{ in.}^2/\text{ft} \tag{8.3}$$

In the compression zone, only the minimum amount of steel needed to control temperature and shrinkage [Eq. (8.4)] must be provided.

Should longitudinal edge beams be used, then the neutral axis will be close to the junction of the shell and the beam, and the steel reinforcement carrying longitudinal tension forces may be concentrated in the beams, since primarily the beams will be carrying the tension.

Maximum diagonal tensile stresses, as caused by shear, will appear close to the transverse shell supports. The maximum ultimate shear, which is taken as equal to the support reaction, is

$$V_{u\ max} = 3.29\ \frac{70}{2} = 115.15\ k$$

This causes a maximum tangential diagonal tension stress at the neutral axis as derived in Problem 8.3, of

$$f_{vu} = \frac{V_u Q_{NA}}{I(2t)} = \frac{115.15(6.42)}{23.95(2)0.25} = 61.73\ ksf$$

$$= 429\ psi > 2\ \sqrt{f_c'} = 2\sqrt{4000} = 127\ psi$$

Diagonal reinforcement must be provided, since the shear capacity of the concrete is not sufficient. The diagonal tensile force is equal to

$$N_{vu} = f_{vu} A = 0.429(12)3 = 15.44\ k/ft$$

The diagonal reinforcement of the transverse support at the neutral (centroidal) axis, neglecting the shear capacity of the concrete, is

$$A_s = \frac{N_{vu}}{\phi F_y} = \frac{15.44}{0.9 \times 50} = 0.34\ in.^2/ft$$

select #5 bars at 11 in. on center, $A_s = 0.34\ in.^2/ft$.

For preliminary design purposes, the behavior in the transverse direction of the long shell beam of a multiple shell group may be neglected. However, to gain some insight into the so-called arch behavior, that is, the magnitude of the axial forces, the equation for maximum hoop forces at the crown, as derived for membrane action, may be used. Remember that the transverse bending, typical for arch behavior under nonfunicular loading, is neglected due to the many cumbersome calculations involved

$$N_{\theta\ max} = (w + q)R \tag{7.24}$$

$$= \frac{3.29}{30}\ 21.75 = 2.39\ k/ft$$

$$f_{cu} = \frac{2390}{12 \times 3} = 66.39\ psi \ll 2380\ psi$$

It is clearly shown that the transverse axial stresses are very small in comparison to the concrete's compressive capacity.

The typical layout of the reinforcing is shown in Fig. 8.12. The steel bars follow the tension trajectories of the principal stresses, with large bars at midspan, close to the bottom edges, to carry the longitudinal tension and smaller bars, placed at 45° diagonal to the transverse supports, which carry the shear (diagonal tension). Small bars are placed in the transverse direction in the crown portion to carry the tension caused by bending in arch action. At other places in the longitudinal and transverse directions, the minimum required temperature and shrinkage steel is provided.

Additional reinforcing steel, as well as the thickening of the shell, may be necessary at the continuous junction of the thin shell and the rigid end supports, due to local bending disturbances in the longitudinal direction. These types of secondary moments are always

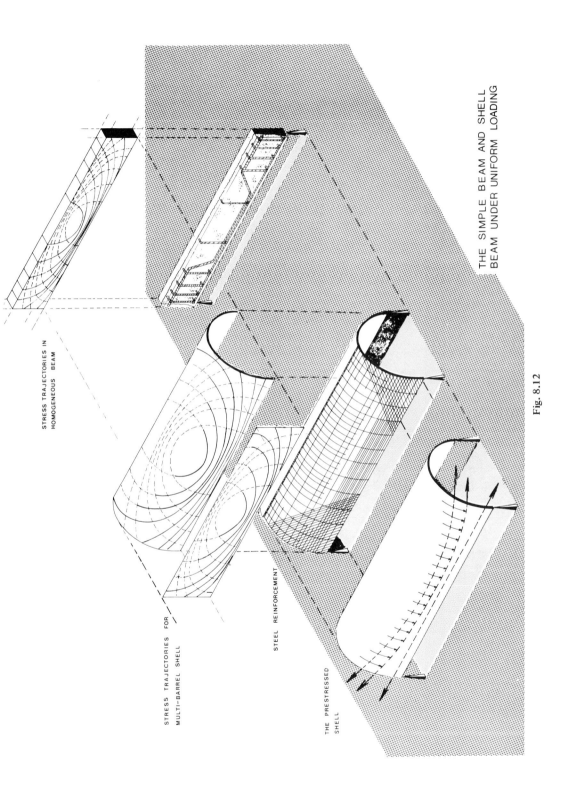

STRESS TRAJECTORIES IN
HOMOGENEOUS BEAM

STRESS TRAJECTORIES FOR
MULTI-BARREL SHELL

STEEL REINFORCEMENT

THE PRESTRESSED
SHELL

THE SIMPLE BEAM AND SHELL
BEAM UNDER UNIFORM LOADING

Fig. 8.12

445

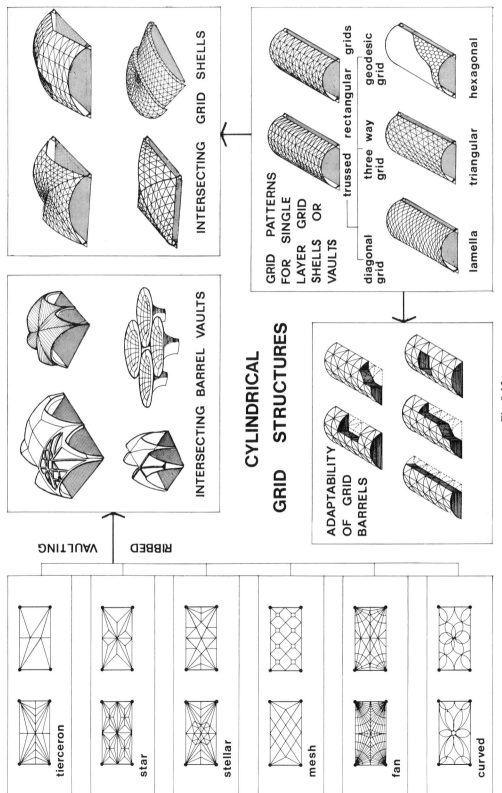

# CYLINDRICAL GRID STRUCTURES

INTERSECTING GRID SHELLS

GRID PATTERNS FOR SINGLE LAYER GRID SHELLS OR VAULTS

diagonal grid

trussed rectangular grids

three way grid

geodesic grid

lamella

triangular

hexagonal

INTERSECTING BARREL VAULTS

ADAPTABILITY OF GRID BARRELS

VAULTING

RIBBED

tierceron

star

stellar

mesh

fan

curved

Fig. 8.13

generated at the intersection of the shell membrane and stiffer structural elements such as ribs and edge beams, due to the incompatibility of edge conditions (displacements) along the shared boundaries of elements providing different types of structural action (see Fig. 8.23).

In prestressing of cylindrical shells, the cables follow the major tensile stresses; one can visualize the shell as sitting on the cables (Fig. 8.12).

The transverse supports of this problem must carry these ultimate loads

$$w_u = \frac{3.29}{30} \frac{70}{2} = 3.84 \text{ k/ft}$$

Hence, a typical interior column resists the following axial load due to gravity action

$$P_u = 3.84(30) = 115.20 \text{ k}$$

The horizontal thrust at the shell edge can be roughly evaluated by replacing the indeterminate two-hinge or fixed end support conditions by three-hinge ones. The approximate lateral thrust force is equal to

$$H_u = \frac{w_u b^2}{8h} = \frac{3.84(30)^2}{8(6)} = 72.00 \text{ k}$$

### Approximate Design of Cylindrical Grid Structures

The solid shell surface can be replaced by a grid structure; this aspect is discussed in more detail in Chapters 5 and 7, and in the next section Braced Domes. Some of the various tessellations possible for the cylindrical shell are simply trussed, rectangular, diagonal, three-way, or geodesic, as indicated in Fig. 8.13. From a formal point of view the grid shells have evolved from the ribbed vaulting of the late Gothic cathedrals; these ribbed vaults, in their simplest form, consist of diagonal ribs along groins, and the masonry webbing. The richness of various Gothic rib patterns are expressed in Fig. 8.13. The iron-glass vaults of the first half of the nineteenth century in England, used as winter gardens, may be considered the most recent forerunners of ribbed cylindrical shells.

The popular diamond-patterned lamella roof was developed in 1908 by Zollinger in Dessau, Germany, and was further advanced by G. Kiewitt in the United States. The roof structure may be visualized as a system of intersecting diagonal arches which are made up of short members of uniform length called lamellas. The diagonal member grid is indirectly triangulated by the roof decking or purlins, thus making the roof surface stable, even though the members may be hinged to each other. The predominant construction material is wood, but for larger span structures steel and concrete are used. Luigi Nervi's first hangars in Italy (1938, 1943) are famous first examples of the principle applied to concrete construction (Fig. 8.9e).

While in steel construction lamellas may be moment-connected, in wood structures only thrust and shear connections are used. Here, usually straight members of twice the length of the diamond sides are arranged in a staggered manner, as indicated in Fig. 8.14.

For preliminary design purposes, the lamella vault may be treated as a monolithic arched surface, which, in turn, can be considered as parallel three-hinge arches, rather than the actual two-hinge ones, spanning in the short direction of the building. The imaginary arches are first assumed as 1 ft wide and then corrected for the true lamella spacing.

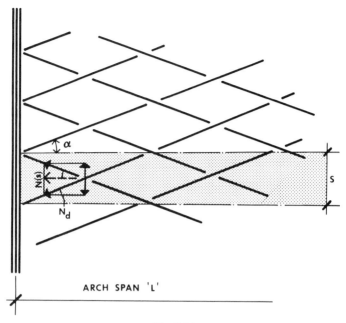

ARCH SPAN 'L'

**Fig. 8.14**

The actual axial forces $N_d$ which the diagonal arches must resist, for the given lamella spacing $s$ (Fig. 8.14), are

$$\cos \alpha = \frac{s(N/2)}{N_d}$$

$$N_d = \frac{N(s)}{2 \cos \alpha} \tag{8.14}$$

Under symmetrical loading, the horizontal thrust components balance each other. However, for asymmetrical loading the thrust components along the length of the roof must be resisted by the decking or ties in the longitudinal direction.

The moment action along the diagonal arches is found similarly, but considering only the continuous lamella as moment resistant.

$$M_d = \frac{M(s)}{\cos \alpha} \tag{8.15}$$

For the condition where the ribs form a continuous rigid grid, the moment is shared by both members.

$$M_d = \frac{M(s)}{2 \cos \alpha} \tag{8.16}$$

**Example 8.2** Design the roof in Example 4.5 as a lamella vault using the same structural lumber. Determine the approximate beam sizes for the given arch span of 60 ft and the rise of 12 ft. Assume the angle of inclination of the diagonal arches as $\alpha = 20°$ and the spacing of the lamellas, parallel to the length of the roof, as $s = 4$ ft.

Since the axial force and moment at the critical stress location of $L/4$ in Example 4.5 are based on a parallel spacing of 16 ft, the values are corrected for this problem to 1 ft spacing

$$N_{L/4} = \frac{16960}{16} = 1060 \text{ lb/ft}$$

$$M_{max} = \frac{27000}{16} = 1687.5 \text{ ft-lb/ft}$$

The actual stresses along the diagonal arches are

$$N_d = \frac{N(s)}{2 \cos \alpha} = \frac{1060(4)}{2 \cos 20°} = 2256.06 \text{ lb} \qquad (8.14)$$

$$M_d = \frac{M(s)}{\cos \alpha} = \frac{1687.5(4)}{\cos 20°} = 7183.2 \text{ ft-k} \qquad (8.15)$$

Try a 2 × 14 member with the following properties

$$A = 19.875 \text{ in.}^2 \qquad S_x = 43.891 \text{ in.}^3$$

$$\frac{f_a}{F_a} + \frac{f_b}{F_b} = \frac{2256.06/19.875}{1500} + \frac{7183.2(12)/43.891}{2400}$$

$$= 0.076 + 0.818 = 0.894 < 1$$

The 2 × 14 is satisfactory for preliminary design purposes.

**Example 8.3** The thin concrete shell of Example 8.1 is replaced by a three-way equilateral triangle network (Fig. 8.15). The purpose of this exercise is to determine the approximate member sizes needed to resist the maximum tension and compression forces using $A36$ steel.

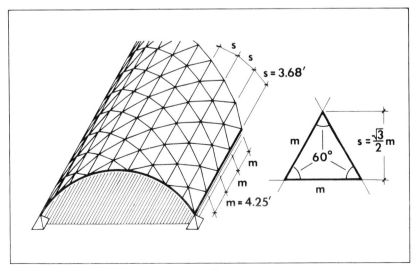

**Fig. 8.15**

The circumference or arc length of the shell has been found to be $l = 33.10$ ft. Subdividing the arc length into nine equal portions and ignoring the small difference in length between the arc and the straight chords, yields the spacing $s$ of the parallel longitudinal members

$$s = \frac{33.10}{9} = 3.68 \text{ ft}$$

Since the spacing is equal to the height of a typical equilateral triangle, the member lengths forming the grid (Fig. 8.15) is determined as

$$m = \frac{s}{\sin 60°} = \frac{2s}{\sqrt{3}} = 1.155s = 1.155(3.68) = 4.25 \text{ ft}$$

For an assumed dead load of 20 psf and horizontally projected snow load of 30 psf, the linear load that the grid shell must support is

$$w = (0.020 \times 33.10) + (0.030 \times 30) = 1.56 \text{ k/ft}$$

The maximum moment at midspan is

$$M_{max} = \frac{wL^2}{8} = \frac{1.56(70)^2}{8} = 955.50 \text{ ft-k}$$

The curved grid structure is treated here as a thin shell, assuming that the member sizes are large enough and the size of the triangular mesh small enough to approximate a continuous shell action. The maximum longitudinal forces appear at midspan; they are in compression at the crown and in tension at the bottom edge.

$$f_c = \frac{M(c_t)}{I} = \frac{N_c}{A} \qquad \text{or} \qquad \frac{M(c_t)}{I} = \frac{N_c}{t(1)}$$

The thickness $t$ in the expressions for the moment of inertia $I$ and the area $A$ cancel; or letting $t = 1$ yields the maximum compression force $N_c$.

$$N_c = \frac{M(c_t)}{I} \tag{8.17}$$

But, in this case the moment of inertia for the 3-in. concrete shell is used. Thus the axial force is

$$N_c = \frac{M(c_t)}{I/t} = \frac{955.50(2.03)}{23.95/0.25} = 20.25 \text{ k/ft}$$

The maximum tensile force is

$$N_t = \frac{M(c_b)}{I} \tag{8.18}$$

$$= \frac{955.50(3.97)}{23.95/0.25} = 39.60 \text{ k/ft}$$

The maximum compression forces at the crown in the transverse direction are:

$$N_\theta = (w + q)R = (0.020 + 0.030)\, 21.75 = 1.09 \text{ k/ft}$$

Visualize the cylindrical grid shell to be comprised of a series of differently inclined Warren trusses spanning to the transverse supports. In this structural system it can be assumed that under symmetrical gravity loading the diagonal truss members carry the longitudinal shear and the transverse axial forces, while the longitudinal members primarily carry the longitudinal axial forces and also transverse forces. The transverse forces, however, are very small in comparison to the longitudinal forces and thus are neglected in the following calculations. The longitudinal shear forces at the crown and at the bottom edge are zero. One may conclude that the maximum member forces are in the longitudinal members at midspan, and are caused primarily by beam action. The critical diagonal member forces appear at the transverse supports where the shear is largest.

The maximum compressive force in the longitudinal crown members, for a spacing of the bars of $s = 3.68$ ft, is

$$P_c = 20.25 \, (3.68) = 74.52 \text{ k}$$

Assuming an allowable axial stress of $F_a = 19$ ksi ($F_y = 36$ ksi), and neglecting the effect of bending by considering the loads to be applied directly to the joints, yields the following required steel

$$A_s = \frac{P_c}{F_a} = \frac{74.52}{19} = 3.92 \text{ in.}^2$$

Try circular structural tubing TS 4 OD × 0.337, $A = 4.41$ in.$^2$, $r = 1.48$ in.

The assumed axial stresses are checked

$$\frac{KL}{r} = \frac{1.0(4.25)12}{1.48} = 34.46 \quad \text{say 35}$$

This slenderness yields an allowable axial stress of $F_a = 19.58$ ksi, which is larger than the assumed value, thus the preliminary section choice is satisfactory.

The maximum tensile force in the bottom edge member for this condition of relative wide chord spacing $s$, is

$$P_t = 39.60 \, \frac{3.68}{2} = 72.86 \text{ k}$$

However, keep in mind that as the number of subdivisions for an arc length increases, the cord above, not the bottom one, will control (see Problem 8.6). For this condition it is conservative to just use the bottom member with the full chord spacing, that is $P_t = N_t(s)$

For an allowable tensile stress of $F_t = 22$ ksi, the required net steel area is

$$A_s = \frac{P_t}{F_t} = \frac{72.86}{22} = 3.31 \text{ in.}^2$$

The final member size depends on the type of connection; the area lost due to the connectors must be added to the net area to obtain the gross cross-sectional area. Assuming conservatively that the net area required above is equal to the gross area reduced by 25%, yields the following cross-sectional area

$$A_s = \frac{3.31}{0.75} = 4.41 \text{ in.}^2$$

Hence, the circular tubing selected for the crown will be satisfactory at the bottom edges.

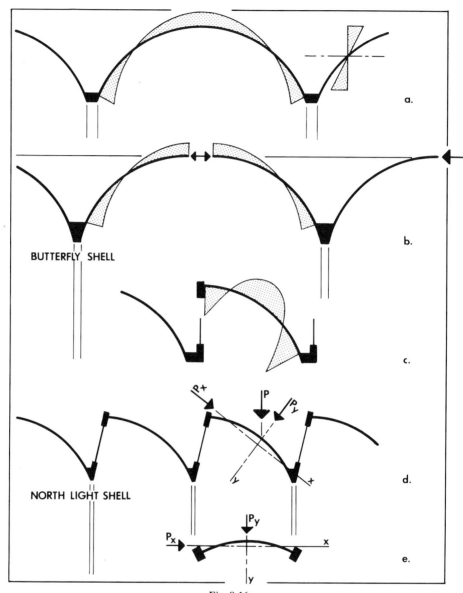

Fig. 8.16

## Asymmetrical Shell Beams

Asymmetrical shell beams, such as the north light cylindrical shell (Fig. 8.16), are much more intricate in behavior and complex to analyze as compared to symmetrical shell beams. The beam method, however, can still be used for rough, first approximation purposes by taking into account unsymmetrical bending.

First, imagine a series of cylindrical shells to be separated at their crown (Fig. 8.16a and b) and to support each other with struts. When these shell units act independent of each other, each unit is then a Y-shape with twin cantilevers, and often called a butterfly shell; these shell types are stiffened on top. Next, visualize the butterfly shells missing one of their balancing cantilevers, resulting in nonsymmetrical half-shells (c). At this stage the shell units can be seen as separate inclined cylindrical shells supported in the transverse direction by a small top beam and, at the bottom, a much larger gutter beam. These two beams are tied together by the mullion struts to form a slightly slanted frame (d). However, the frame is considered not to generate continuous transverse action; any potential continuity in this direction is conservatively neglected.

Since a typical shell unit is inclined, the gravity load $P$ must be resolved into components $P_x$ and $P_y$ parallel to the principal axes.

The bending stresses caused by the $P_y$ force about the $x$ axis are found in similar fashion as for a normal symmetrical beam (e), (a). Notice, the relatively low moment of inertia $I_x$ of a half-shell, as compared to that of the symmetrical shell composed of the two half-units (a). In other words, the effective depth of the north light shell is very flat and much less than the height of the full cylindrical shell unit, thus yielding much larger bending stresses.

The moment of inertia $I_y$ is by far larger than $I_x$, thus resulting in fewer critical stresses. The moment of inertia about the $y$ axis can be approximated by ignoring the effect of the shell and by assuming that the top and bottom beams (i.e., flanges) carry the entire moment as caused by the $P_x$ force.

The usual span range of north light cylindrical concrete shell beams is in the range 40–100 ft, and up to 150 ft if prestressed. Typical bay widths are 25–40 ft with a shell thickness of 3–3 $\frac{1}{2}$ in.

## Problems

**8.1** Derive the equations given below for a typical interior circular cylindrical shell without edge beams (Fig. 8.17a)

Area:
$$A = 2tR\theta_0 \tag{8.6}$$

Location of centroidal axis:
$$c_t = R\left(1 - \frac{\sin\theta_0}{\theta_0}\right) \tag{8.7}$$

First moment of the area about the centroidal axis:
$$Q = 2tR^2\left[\sin\theta - \frac{\theta}{\theta_0}\sin\theta_0\right] \tag{8.8}$$

where $Q_{max}$ is at $\theta = \theta_{NA}$.

Moment of inertia about the centroidal axis:
$$I_{ca} = tR^3\left[\theta_0 + \sin\theta_0\left(\cos\theta_0 - \frac{2\sin\theta_0}{\theta_0}\right)\right] \tag{8.9}$$

**8.2** Simplify the equations in Problem 8.1 by considering a semicircular cylindrical shell

Area:  $A = \pi R t$  (8.10)

Location of centroidal axis:  $c_t = 0.363R$  (8.11)

First moment of the area:  $Q_{max} = 0.42tR^2$  (8.12)

Moment of inertia:  $I_{ca} = 0.3tR^3$  (8.13)

**8.3** Set up the procedure for the derivation of the moment of inertia for a circular cylindrical shell, with edge beams, about its centroidal axis (Fig. 8.17b).

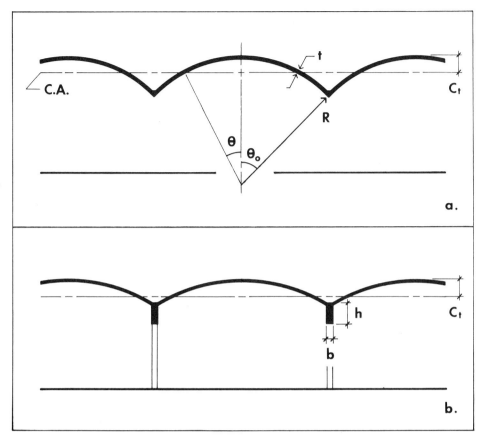

**Fig. 8.17**

**8.4**  A single long cylindrical shell with edge beams (Fig. 8.17b) spans 100 ft and has following properties
shell width = 30 ft, shell height = 5 ft, shell thickness = 3 in., edge beam height = 5
ft, edge beam width = 10 in. The shell must support a snow load of 30 psf. Check
the maximum compressive stresses and determine the reinforcement to resist the
tensile stresses caused by the moments; check also the tensile stresses at the bottom
edge of the shell. Further, investigate if diagonal reinforcing is required to cover the
shear stresses. Use Grade 50 steel and 4000 psi concrete.

**8.5**  A typical interior, 3-in. thick cylindrical semicircular shell of a multiple system
without edge beams is 20 ft wide and spans 100 ft. The shell loading consists of the
dead weight of 37 psf and the snow load of 30 psf. Check the critical compressive
stresses and find the tensile reinforcement at the maximum moment location of the
simple span beam. Check the shear stresses and determine if diagonal reinforcing is
necessary. Also investigate the transverse arch action. Use Grade 50 steel and 4000
psi concrete (see Problem 8.2).

**8.6**  A cylindrical grid shell beam of a triangular network composed of tubular members,
4.35 ft long (Fig. 8.15), spans 120 ft from support to support; it is 24 ft wide and

12 ft high. For a total load of 60 psf on the horizontal roof projection, determine the maximum tension and compression forces. Select the preliminary structural tubing ($A$36) assuming the loads directly applied to the joints. Check also the maximum tensile forces in the longitudinal chord above the bottom one.

8.7  Determine the approximate member sizes for a parabolic arch lamella roof with a span of $L = 60$ ft and a rise of $h = L/6 = 10$ ft. The angle of inclination of the members is $\alpha = 19°$ and the width of the diamond pattern equal to $s = 4$ ft. Assume a dead load and live load of 12 psf for each, on the horizontal roof projection. The allowable axial and bending stresses for the lumber are $F_a = 1450$ psi, $F_b = 1750$ psi.


## 8.3  THE DOME SHELL

Historically, domes represent an ideology of their own with a specific symbolic meaning. In the Roman, Christian, and Islamic worlds they were associated with temples, churches, mosques, memorials, baptistries, tombs, baths, and other meeting places; they were not just functional solutions for covering large spaces. This monumental architecture has derived from the domical shelters of the indigenous architecture that use primitive methods of construction, as is still found today in many regions of the world. They range from the stone trulli of Apulia in Italy, the yurts of the Mongol nomads of the central Asian steppe, the igloos of the Eskimos, the wealth of dome shapes of the African tribal architecture, to the geodesic domes of the hippie communes during the late 1960s in the United States.

The many construction methods for geodesic domes and other dome types used as houses are well documented in *Domebooks 1 and 2* (reference 90) and will not be further discussed here.

The modern, large-scale dome structures developed from the various skeletal iron domes of the second half of the nineteenth century, especially the Schwedler domes. Schwedler's 207-ft span dome in Vienna (1874) is often considered the milestone for dome development; it was among the first true domes based on surface behavior rather than on the concentrated arch action, as for the conventional ribbed domes. The 213-ft dome for the Breslau Centennial Hall (1912) is the most famous example of the early ribbed reinforced concrete dome construction. Finally, in 1924, the first large scale thin shell, only $2\frac{3}{8}$ in. thick, was introduced with the 131-ft dome for the Schott company in Jena, Germany. It was based on the Zeiss-Dywidag system, which consists of a triangular reinforcement network similar to a three-way grid dome.

Most domes are surfaces of revolution; typical synclastic forms are spherical, parabolic, elliptical, and conical, often covering circular or nearly circular areas. Other dome shapes, like the onion, melon, and bulbous domes, are to be found in Byzantine and Islamic architecture. Domes on polygonal bases may be segmental surfaces (see Fig. 8.22) with straight or curvilinear edges. To cover a rectangular floor plan, it may be more convenient to use a section of a torus or a translational surface, such as an elliptical paraboloid (Fig. 7.14); in the past, often pendentives (i.e., spherical triangles) were employed to make the transition from the circular dome to the rectangular base.

Dome surfaces may be continuous or pointed, as for conoidal and conical domes. They may consist of a single surface unit or intersecting surfaces, where several units are joined along valleys and ridges. In this section of the book only spherical domes are further investigated.

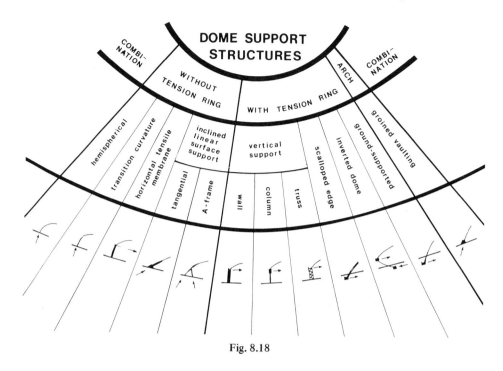

**Fig. 8.18**

Most of the early modern domes are of nearly hemisherical shape, thus not causing any lateral thrust; one should keep in mind that horizontal force action appears for ribbed domes, which are not true surface structures, as is discussed later. Needless to say, hemispherical domes use more surface area than shallow domes to cover the same space.

On the other hand, flat domes require a vertical support structure to increase the headroom, as well as large tension rings because of the extensive lateral thrust exerted by the dome (i.e., horizontal component of meridional force at support). Tension rings and other support systems are identified in Fig. 8.18. For instance, a transition curvature could be employed in order to smoothly adjust the dome curvature so that it is perpendicular to the base, such as for the synagogue of the Hebrew University in Jerusalem (see Fig. 8.21e), where the entire transition zone acts as a tension ring. Or, the meridional arch forces could be directly transferred by an inclined support structure in a tangential fashion to the ground, where the tension ring is located.

The plan form of the dome is often closely related to the number, location, and type of supports, as the various cases in Fig. 8.21 reflect.

Shell and skeletal domes may be organized according to the nature of their surface structure. Figure 8.19 attempts to indicate the infinite wealth of possibilities for braced dome patterns. From a conceptual point of view, the major framed domes are more clearly identified in Fig. 8.20, where all the systems are shown triangulated so that they can be more easily compared.

The primary dome structure types are:

Braced domes

- Ribbed domes, including polygonal domes
- Schwedler domes

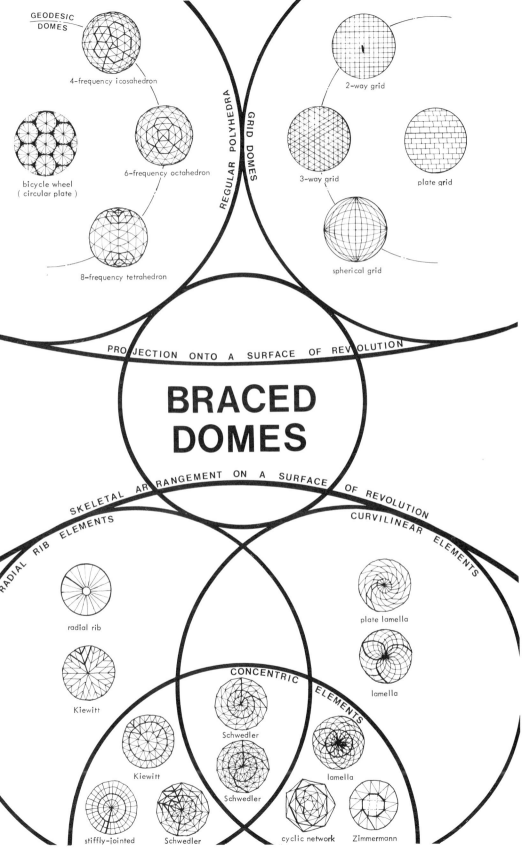

4-frequency icosahedron

bicycle wheel
( circular plate )

6-frequency octahedron

8-frequency tetrahedron

2-way grid

3-way grid

plate grid

spherical grid

REGULAR POLYHEDRA

GRID DOMES

PROJECTION ONTO A SURFACE OF REVOLUTION

# BRACED
# DOMES

SKELETAL ARRANGEMENT ON A SURFACE OF REVOLUTION

RADIAL RIB ELEMENTS

CURVILINEAR ELEMENTS

radial rib

Kiewitt

plate lamella

lamella

CONCENTRIC ELEMENTS

Kiewitt

Schwedler

lamella

stiffly-jointed

Schwedler

Schwedler

cyclic network

Zimmermann

Fig. 8.19

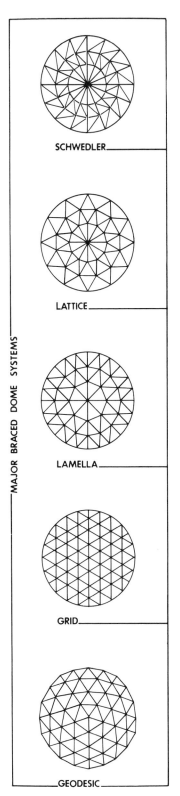

SCHWEDLER

LATTICE

LAMELLA

MAJOR BRACED DOME SYSTEMS

GRID

GEODESIC

Fig. 8.20 Braced dome systems.

458

- Polyhedral domes
- Lamella domes, including lattice domes (curved lamellas) and parallel lamella domes
- Grid domes including two-way grid domes and three-way grid domes
- Geodesic domes including single-layer framing, double-layer space trusses, and stressed-skin construction

Thin shell domes
- Ribbed shell domes
- Polygonal domes
- Corrugated shell domes
- Double (cellular) shell domes

These various dome types are now discussed, together with the cases in Fig. 8.21.

Ribbed domes are among the earliest and simplest types of bent surface structures (Fig. 8.21a). They are quite popular because of their easy fabrication and construction; the span range is around 150 ft. In these systems, arches are arranged in a radial fashion and laterally supported at the top by a compression ring, and at the base by a tension ring. For preliminary design purposes, the ribs may be treated as individual three-hinge arches with triangular gravity loading, as is discussed in Section 4.4 (Fig. 4.53).

One may conclude that, due to the individual behavior of their radial arches, rib domes are primarily direct thrust structures, which do not take advantage of the spatial spherical geometry of the surface. However, when circumferential or hoop rings are introduced, these ribs and rings form an interactive system. The two rings at the base and the crown for ribbed domes are now replaced by a series of concentric rings positioned along the surface and resisting the lateral thrust of the arches in a continuous manner. It is apparent that as the stiffness and homogeneous distribution of members and bar sizes increase, true membrane action is approached.

Bracing the radial ribs with concentric rings is the basic principle of the Schwedler dome. For the condition where the ribs and rings are hinged to each other, the roof skin may provide the necessary shear stiffness under asymmetrical loading for the quadrangular grid pattern. Diagonals may be introduced to stiffen the surface, or rings and ribs may be moment connected to form a rigid frame structure. There are many different layout patterns for the arrangement of the diagonal members.

The 328-ft Schwedler dome of the Convocation Center at Ohio University, Ohio (v) is one of the lightest dome structures in the United States; the roof steel framing weighs only 8.9 psf. The structure consists of 24 radial $W24$ steel ribs and three hoop beams supporting the 24-in. deep steel joists. The dome thrust is resisted by a concrete ring girder as well as a spider web of radial cables extending horizontally across the dome.

The Schwedler dome in case (b) is framed with 24 radial steel arches and 6 concentric ring beams which support the 5-in. lightweight concrete slab.

Polyhedral domes can be derived, as the name suggests, from the polyhedra; or the most simple dome forms may be generated by joining horizontal (or spatial) polygonal rings, which may have different shapes at the various layers, with meridional members to form linear or spatial radial arches; the resulting rectangular surfaces are braced with diagonals. Braced surfaces like the Schwedler dome, the Zimmermann dome, the plate-type dome, the cyclic network dome, as shown in Fig. 8.19, and infinite other domes can be generated this way. For further discussion of polyhedral types of braced domes, the reader may refer to Chapter 5, Fig. 5.2.

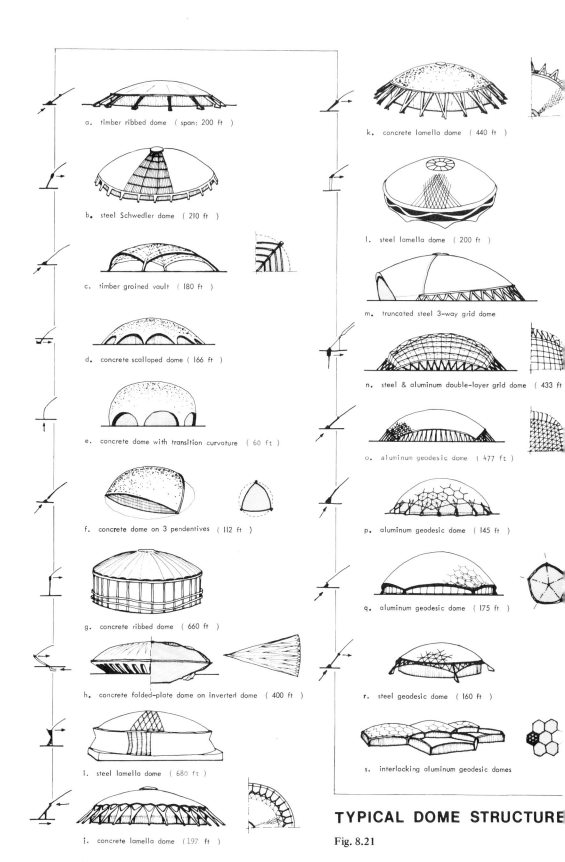

a. timber ribbed dome ( span: 200 ft )

b. steel Schwedler dome ( 210 ft )

c. timber groined vault ( 180 ft )

d. concrete scalloped dome ( 166 ft )

e. concrete dome with transition curvature ( 60 ft )

f. concrete dome on 3 pendentives ( 112 ft )

g. concrete ribbed dome ( 660 ft )

h. concrete folded-plate dome on inverted dome ( 400 ft )

i. steel lamella dome ( 680 ft )

j. concrete lamella dome (197 ft )

k. concrete lamella dome ( 440 ft )

l. steel lamella dome ( 200 ft )

m. truncated steel 3-way grid dome

n. steel & aluminum double-layer grid dome ( 433 ft )

o. aluminum geodesic dome ( 477 ft )

p. aluminum geodesic dome ( 145 ft )

q. aluminum geodesic dome ( 175 ft )

r. steel geodesic dome ( 160 ft )

s. interlocking aluminum geodesic domes

# TYPICAL DOME STRUCTURE

Fig. 8.21

460

For larger span domes, the lamella system is frequently used because of its even stress distribution and primarily axial member action. The system is a derivation of the Schwedler dome, where the major surface triangles defined by the radial ribs are further subdivided by parallel ribs, rather than radial ones, resulting in the so-called *straight* or *parallel lamella dome*. Should all radial ribs be omitted and replaced by pairs of diagonal struts forming diamond shapes along the radial lines, then the system is called a *curved lamella dome* or a *lattice dome*. When concentric rings are introduced, a triangular network is generated; however, the roof decking often takes the place of the ring members, leaving the lozenge-shaped member pattern intact.

The Louisiana Superdome in New Orleans (i), with a span of 680 ft, is the world's largest steel dome. The roof is a straight lamella structure (Fig. 8.20) constructed with 7 ft 3 in. deep welded steel trusses. The principal trussed framing consists of 12 main radial ribs connected by 5 concentric rings, about 56 ft apart, and the diagonal lamella members forming the diamond pattern. The roof is supported by a 8 ft 10 in. deep wide flange tension ring truss along its perimeter, which is mounted on rocker columns to allow for movement due to temperature changes. The dome also must support, at the center, a gondola for television screens with a total weight of 150 k. The roof system required 26 psf of structural steel.

Houston's Astrodome (u), with a span of 642 ft, is also of the parallel lamella type. It consists of twelve 5-ft deep main radial rib trusses, six hoop trusses, and diagonal lamella trusses. The roof was designed for a dead load of 30 psf, a live load of 15 psf, and an uplift pressure of 60 psf.

Nervi's famous Little Sports Palace (j) for the 1960 Olympic Games in Rome, Italy, uses a curved lamella dome consisting of diamond-shaped precast concrete panels of 13 different sizes, which acted as formwork for the cast-in-place concrete topping. The undulating dome edge is not a tension ring, it only collects the curved lamella ribs and redirects them to the column supports; thus, the dome surface is continuous with the 36 inclined forked buttresses with vertical legs. These buttresses are, in turn, carried by the tension ring below the ground, which also functions as their foundation. The dead weight of the dome surface is about 80 psf (i.e., about 60 psf taking shell and ribs together, and 20 psf for insulation and roofing). The dome must support the cupola besides the snow and wind loading.

The much larger dome of the Convention Center (k) in Norfolk, Va., is also a concrete lamella structure, but, in addition, has 14 ring beams. It consists of triangular precast units employed as formwork. The 440-ft dome rests on the tension ring which is supported by vertical columns and by the primary 24 V-shaped buttresses that sit on the foundations and tension ring below the ground.

The General Electric Pavilion dome (l) is also based on the curvilinear lamella concept. Five inch steel tubes which have $\frac{1}{8}$-in. thick walls comprise the three-layer framework, that is, the two arched layers and the inner suspended hoop layer, spaced 7 ft on centers, which carries the steel decking.

Grid domes are quite popular. Intersecting ribs form a network; most common are the two-way and three-way grids. The roof of the Sports Palace in Mexico City (n) for the 1968 Olympics consists of 22 intersecting trussed steel arches spanning 433 ft. These 16-ft deep arches, each one supported by buttresses, form a two-way frame on a nearly square grid ranging in size from 33 to 43 ft. The square spaces, in turn, are covered with a triangular mesh of aluminum tubes that form a hyperbolic paraboloid surface which is covered with two layers of $\frac{5}{8}$ in. plywood and a copper membrane. The dead weight of the roof is 19 psf, while the structural steel weighs 12.3 psf. The dome rests on vertical concrete walls and columns, as well as on inclined V-shaped struts. A tension ring at the base of the inclined columns resists the outward thrust due to the arches.

In appearance, geodesic domes are three-way grid structures where the primary radial ribs of the upper dome portion (see Fig. 8.26) lie on the great circles of a sphere. While in three-way grid domes only triangular surfaces along individual rings may be equal, in geodesic domes the sphere is subdivided into 20 identical equilateral, spherical triangles, which are then further subdivided. The resulting member network is nearly regular, that is, the members are virtually identical in length. These conditions are ideal with respect to ease of fabrication and construction, since most members and connectors are interchangeable. Other geodesic surface patterns, such as the rhombic and hexagonal ones, can be derived from the basic triangular network by process of elimination, or other patterns can be generated by projection of other regular polyhedra onto the spherical surface. The geometry of geodesic domes is discussed in more detail later in this section.

The U.S. Pavilion at Expo '67, Montreal, Canada (see Fig. 8.26), is the most famous example of a geodesic dome structure. It consists of a three-quarter sphere with a 250-ft diameter and a height of 200-ft. The shell is a 3 ft 6 in. thick double-layer space frame with the tubular members slotted at their ends so that they can be pin-connected to cast-steel spider connectors, which have central hubs and twelve radial arms for the outer layer (six exterior members and six web members), or six arms for the inner layer. The outer layer is triangulated, while the geometry of the inner layer is hexagonal. The varying lengths of the $3\frac{1}{2}$-in. tubes of the exterior skin does not exceed 10 ft, nor do the $2\frac{7}{8}$-in. dia. inner chord and web members exceed 6 ft. The wall thicknesses of the tubes vary, being greater in the exterior layer below the equator. The inner layer supports the 27-in. high $\frac{1}{4}$-in. thick Plexiglas domes, most of them measuring 10 × 12 ft, thereby causing the members to be also subject to bending besides their axial action.

The double-layer geodesic dome in Caracas, Venezuela (o), with a 477-ft span, is currently the largest aluminum dome on earth. Its two layers consist of the triangular exterior grid and the hexagonal interior one.

The 175-ft diameter Climatron (q) in St. Louis is another exciting geodesic dome consisting of two layers of hexagonal grids on top of each other, about 30 in. apart. The two layers of aluminum tubing are connected diagonally by aluminum rods to develop spatial truss action. A third, inner skin layer consisting of a triangular framework, which contains Plexiglas panels, is suspended from the double-layer aluminum dome structure.

The 502-ft diameter roof for the Northern Arizona University stadium, built in 1977, is currently the largest wood dome in the United States (t). The dome consists of a three-way grid of intermeshing great circle ribs, with steel tension rings at the base. The curved glue-laminated ribs are connected to hexagonal welded steel hubs to form triangles. The main members vary from 19.33 to 61.75 ft in length and $8\frac{3}{4}$ × 27 in. to $12\frac{1}{4}$ × 27 in. in section. Each triangle contains simple span purlins spaced at 8 ft on center. The system is known as the Varax dome and was developed by Western Wood Structures of Portland, Oregon. The roof was designed for a dead load of 17.4 psf, a snow load of 40 psf, and a 37.5 psf wind load, as well as hanging loads at the center.

For the Placer County Offices (s) in Auburn, California, five geodesic domes, with spans of 82 ft each, have been clustered. The dome surface structure consists of stressed-skin diamond-shaped aluminum panels. The panels are braced with tubular struts, so that each panel with its strut forms a tetrahedron; the struts, in turn, form a hexagonal grid pattern, which is derived from the basic triangular geodesic network, where six triangles produce a hexagon. Several concrete shell domes are briefly discussed now.

The concrete dome of the Kresge Auditorium at MIT (f) comprises a spherical triangle that is one-eighth of a sphere. It is supported by spherical bearings on three pendentives at the intersection of the great circles. The shell surface has a typical thickness of 3½ in., to which 2 in. of insulation and an outer nonstructural concrete shell of 2 in. are attached to reduce sound transmission. The total design dead load is 83 psf and the live load for wind and snow is 30 psf. A shell area of $4\pi R^2/8 = \pi(2 \times 112)^2/8 = 19{,}704$ ft$^2$ must be supported on less than 1 ft$^2$ of bearing area, which clearly indicates the tremendous stress concentration and special detailing required. Each support must carry a vertical force component of 19704(83 + 30)/1000(3) = 742.18 k. Considering the thrust component to be of the same magnitude yields, roughly, a resultant force of 742.18 $\sqrt{2}$ = 1049.60 k, causing an approximate stress of $1049.60/0.33(144) \approx 22$ ksi, which requires pure steel for resistance at the point of investigation.

The folded plate concrete dome of the University of Illinois Assembly Hall (h) sits on an inverted dome-like structure consisting of 48 radial buttresses, which, in turn, rest on a continuous ring footing. Here, the post-tensioned ring girder along the periphery must resist the horizontal thrust of both dome structures. The pattern of the branching roof folds resists buckling and absorbs the potential bending stresses efficiently. The maximum depth of the folds is 7.5 ft, with a typical depth of about 3.5 ft; the ribs at the valleys and ridges are connected by a $3\frac{1}{2}$-in. thick concrete web.

The King County Stadium, Seattle, Washington, is the world's largest concrete dome, with a span of 660 ft [720 ft CNIT Palace in Paris, France (see Fig. 8.33 f) is not considered a dome]. The roof consists of 40 identical wedge-shaped thin-shell segments which are doubly curved hyperbolic paraboloids of 5 in. thickness. The sections are stiffened by 2 × 6 ft ribs along their edges and are 55 ft wide at their base. The lateral thrust of the dome is carried by a 24-ft wide and 12-in. thick post-tensioned concrete ring beam which, in turn, is supported by channel-shaped columns.

### The Structural Behavior of Dome Shells

In the discussion of membrane forces it was shown how a spherical flexible membrane responded to the gravity loads $q$ and $w$. The meridian or arch forces $N_\phi$ along the lines of longitude are in compression while the circumferential or hoop forces $N_\theta$ along the parallels of latitude are in compression, or compression and tension depending on the height-to-span ratio of the dome. They are in compression if the angle $\phi$, which defines the shell boundaries, does not exceed a value between 45° and 51.83°. For the specific case where $\phi$ is equal to 51.83°, the dome edge is neither in compression nor tension. This plane of zero hoop stresses is called the neutral plane, similar to the neutral axis for beams.

The membrane behavior of a shell dome under uniform symmetrical loading can be visualized as the response of arches arranged in a continuous radial fashion but prevented from bending by the lateral support of the continuous ring or hoop bands. As the arches tend to displace, the rings prevent movement by resisting the forces in an axial manner.

Although the membrane forces were developed for uniform symmetrical loading, the shell is still in the direct stress state under unsymmetrical uniform load action as caused, for example, by snow and wind, because of the capability of the surface to distribute forces spatially. For this case, the shear capacity of the rigid shell enters, to resist the portion of the loads that the direct membrane forces cannot carry, similar to a suspended

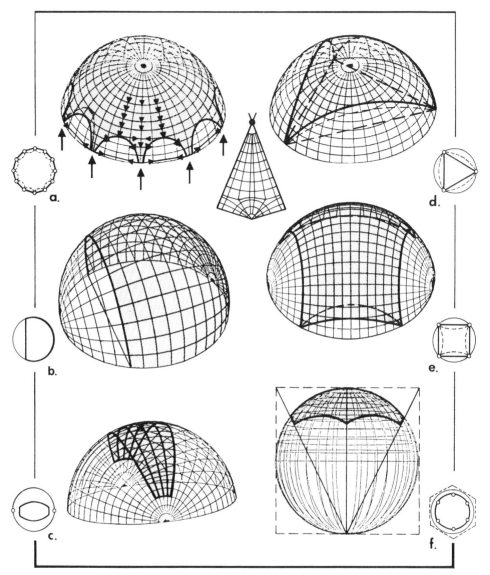

**Fig. 8.22**

membrane where the circumferential and meridional network is stiffened by diagonal members to resist shear.

The shell thickness for typical concrete domes is rarely selected as based on force action; construction considerations are, in general, the determinant of thickness. Because of this, the membrane stresses are low, hence additional loads such as those caused at the crown due to electrical and mechanical equipment, lanterns, or skylights can be supported easily. One must keep in mind that the surface loads must be continuous for the membrane theory to be valid. A concentrated load will cause a kink in the shell, in other words local bending. By way of analogy it can be shown that it does not take much effort to pierce an eggshell with a needle, but considerable force is required to break it by squeezing it lengthwise between the palms of one's hands, where uniform load action causes the shell to respond in membrane action. The collar load at the crown of a dome, due to such conditions as mentioned before, is not considered a concentrated point load if it is uniformly supported along a circle concentric with the dome's axis.

For the membrane theory to be truly applicable the dome should be continuously supported along its edges. Where the dome is carried at discrete points, the flow pattern of the membrane is significantly influenced since the forces must collect at the points of reaction. The isocontour lines in Fig. 7.4 for continuous and concentrated reactive conditions clearly indicate the impact of the number of supports upon the force flow pattern. The cases shown in Fig. 8.22 constitute segments of a surface of revolution with isolated (point) support conditions. For the scalloped shell (Fig. 8.22a), only the upper portion behaves according to the membrane theory, while in the lower portion the meridian forces must be carried by transverse transition arches. The concentration of forces at discrete points results in an increase of bending due to lateral thrust and the necessity of thickening the shell, as is discussed later. In general, the membrane forces in the central crown portion of dome segments do not vary significantly from the ones for the full dome from which they were cut; however, they do become much larger as they approach the point supports and as the number of supports decreases.

The membrane theory constitutes a true representation of shell behavior if the continuous flow of membrane forces across the shell boundaries is not disturbed or interrupted. The support forces along the shell edge should be collinear and equal in magnitude to the arch forces, and the circumferential shell displacement should be compatible with the displacement of the support structure. This compatibility at the junction of the thin shell and rigid support structure is rarely achieved. For it to occur, the shell should sit on frictionless rollers so that it is not prevented from free movement. For the special case of a shallow dome with its edge located on the neutral plane, the shell may be pinned to the base since loading will rarely affect a change in dome diameter. The geometry of a hemispherical dome (Fig. 8.23a) only requires its base structure to react vertically since there are no primary thrust forces at the edge of the shell; however, there are secondary ones. Under external force action, shrinkage, creep, and temperature change, the dome tends to displace laterally (Fig. 8.23a), but is not permitted to do so because of its fixed attachment to the boundary support structure.

This incompatibility causes bending in the thin shell. The effect of continuity between shell and beam, however, hardly influences the shell design as the meridional moments along the edges are relatively small. A similar situation exists for shallow domes of cycloidal, elliptical, or spherical shapes that use transition curves, where the tangent to the shell curvature along the edges is vertical; also here, no tension ring is required since the arch forces $N_\phi$ do not have any horizontal force components along the dome boundaries. The disadvantage of elliptical or cycloidal domes lies in the evaluation of the rather complex force distribution, the difficulty of constructing formwork and casting concrete along the steep portion, and in the relatively flat upper portion of the shell, which is vulnerable to bending and buckling. Domes can also be supported by inclined structures having a slope equal to the tangent to the curvature at the shell boundaries (Fig. 8.23b). For this case, the arch forces are directly transferred to the ground without having to be resolved into force components, as is required for vertical support structures.

The most common types of dome structures which are currently built are shallow spherical domes carried only by vertical support structures. They consist of large tension ring beams that resist the lateral thrust or horizontal force component of the arch forces, and a vertical cylindrical wall or frame which support the vertical components of the meridional forces $N_\phi$. Under the thrust the ring beam tends to expand while the shallow

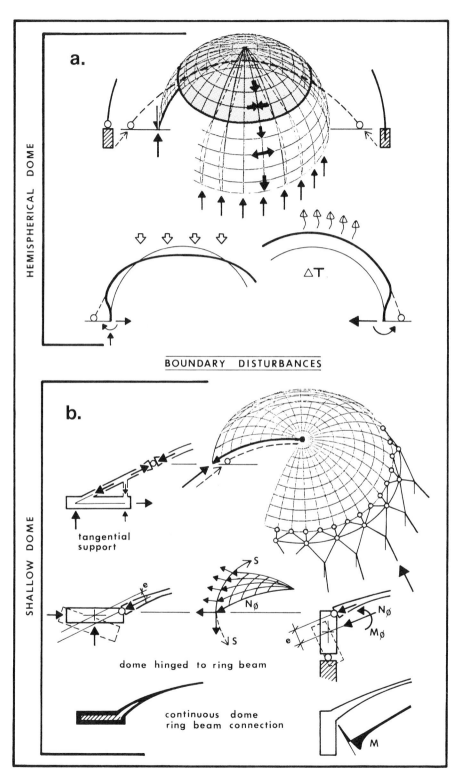

a.

HEMISPHERICAL DOME

BOUNDARY DISTURBANCES

$\triangle T$

b.

SHALLOW DOME

tangential
support

S

$N_\phi$

$\downarrow S$

e

$N_\phi$

$M_\phi$

e

dome hinged to ring beam

continuous dome
ring beam connection

M

Fig. 8.23

shell ($\phi < 45°$) contracts. This incompatibility in deformation will cause twisting of the beam and meridional bending in the shell. To reduce the difference in movement between shell and support structure, the ring beam may be prestressed so that it is in compression rather than tension; but the main purpose of the prestressing is the prevention of any excessive expansion in the concrete ring beam. The proper placement of prestress bars reduces the tension due to meridional and vertical bending. The incompatibility between thin shell and rigid beam can be further reduced by integrating the vertical beam into the shell, using transition curvatures and smooth changes of material thickness along the meridian, thereby nearly eliminating the lateral thrust force.

The shape of the ring beam and its location with respect to the shell determines the magnitude of the boundary disturbances (Fig. 8.23b). Visualize the shell to be hinged to the beam and hence free to rotate and slide. If the arch force $N_\phi$ does not pass through the centroid of the beam cross-section, rotation is generated. Since the shell, in reality, is not free to move because of the stiff ring beam to which it is fixed, this rotation due to the eccentric placement of the ring beam causes moments in addition to those caused by prevention of translational and rotational movements that is the fixed boundary conditions.

In general, the disturbance along the shallow shell boundaries initiated by the incompatibility between the stiffness of the thin shell and the beam/wall are confined to the edge zone and do not penetrate far into the shell. The meridional displacements at the edge are quickly dampened by the circumferential shell rings which tend to prevent expansion or contraction. The edge disturbances dissipate faster if the shell is thin in comparison to its overall dimensions.

### Approximate Design of Concrete Dome Shells

One may conclude that for preliminary design purposes of thin shell domes of spherical shape with continuous supports, the membrane equations may be used for a reasonable first approximation, keeping in mind that in the immediate vicinity of the supports the bending of the shallow shells may cause stresses by far larger than the ones due to membrane action. The analysis of secondary stresses in this area of transition from shell to beam is statically indeterminate and not treated further here; in this area additional reinforcement must be provided and the shell thickened. The effect of openings, such as for a lantern at the dome crown, introduces boundary disturbances similar to the ones along the base periphery.

As already mentioned, the concrete shell thickness rarely depends on the magnitude of the membrane forces but on the amount of concrete necessary for adequate coverage of two layers of reinforcement bars. Typical shell thicknesses range from 3 to $4\frac{1}{2}$ in. for concrete domes having a span range of 100–200 ft, with an increase of shell thickness of approximately 50%–75% near the periphery. For larger spans, however, the shell must be relatively thick, stiffened by concrete ribs, or designed as a double shell, in order to prevent buckling under compression. Nondevelopable, double-curvature surfaces are generally rather strong with respect to buckling. An approximate equation for the uniform load $p_{cr}$ under which a shallow ($h/L \lesssim 1/10$) concrete shell of thickness $t$, modulus of elasticity $E$, and radius of curvature $R$ will buckle, is

$$p_{cr} = 0.15E\left(\frac{t}{R}\right)^2 \qquad (8.19)$$

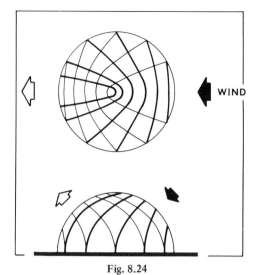

Fig. 8.24

For hemispherical domes, the critical buckling load $p_{cr}$ is about twice as high as for shallow domes.

As a first approximation for shell thickness, in which buckling problems are greatly reduced, the following expression is often used

$$t \geqslant \frac{R}{600} \tag{8.20}$$

The loading conditions for which the membrane forces were derived are a good approximation for preliminary shell design. In Fig. 8.24, the stress trajectories, due to wind loading perpendicular to the dome, express convincingly the compressive response of the inclined arches on the windward side and the tensile reaction of the cables on the leeward side. For typical conditions, wind force action is insignificant, as is explained in Problem 8.10.

**Example 8.4** A shallow concrete dome with a span of 200 ft is investigated. A concrete strength of 4000 psi and Grade 60 steel are used. The dome has the shape of a spherical segment, and for a typical height-to-span ratio for shallow domes of $h/L = 1/8$ a height of $h = 200/8 = 25$ ft is selected.

The radius of this dome is

$$R^2 = 100^2 + (R - 25)^2 \tag{8.21}$$

$$R^2 = 100^2 + R^2 + 25^2 - 50R$$

$$R\ \ = 212.5 \text{ ft}$$

The following geometrical relationships define the location of the shell edge

$$\cos \phi = \frac{R - h}{R} = \frac{212.5 - 25}{212.5} = 0.882$$

$$\phi = 28.07° \qquad \sin \phi = 0.471$$

The minimum shell thickness should not be less than about $R/600 = 212.5(12)/600 =$ 4.25 in., so that the shell does not buckle. For this dome a thickness of $4\frac{1}{2}$ in. is selected. This thickness will be increased in the boundary area close to the ring beam.

The shell weight is:

$$w = \frac{150(4.5)}{12} = 56.25 \text{ psf}$$

Adding the weight of roofing, interior finish, etc., results in a total area load of 60 psf. The assumed snow load of 30 psf is considered to act on the horizontal roof projection. Since the angle $\phi$ defining the shell edge is less than $45°$, the dome will be fully in compression according to the membrane theory; there will be no tension in the shell! The maximum compressive stresses appear along the meridians at the shell base (Figs. 7.9, 7.10). They are larger than the circumferential stresses at the crown and are, as caused by

shell weight: 
$$N_{\phi D} = \frac{wR}{1 + \cos \phi} \tag{7.11}$$

$$= \frac{60(212.5)}{1 + 0.882} = 6774.71 \text{ lb/ft}$$

live load: 
$$N_{\phi L} = \frac{qR}{2} = \frac{30(212.5)}{2} = 3187.5 \text{ lb/ft} \tag{7.6}$$

The ultimate membrane compression force is

$$N_{\phi u} = 1.4(6774.71) + 1.7(3187.5) = 14903.34 \text{ lb/ft}$$

The ultimate compressive stress, ignoring the capacity of the reinforcing, is

$$f_{cu} = \frac{N_{\phi u}}{\phi A_c} = \frac{14903.34}{0.7(4.5)12} \tag{8.2}$$

$$= 394.27 \text{ psi} \ll 0.85 f'_c = 0.85(4000) = 3400 \text{ psi}$$

The membrane stresses are quite small and it is apparent that the shell thickness is more than adequate to support the design loads.

The approximate load which will cause the shell to buckle is

$$p_{cr} = 0.15E\left(\frac{t}{R}\right)^2 \qquad \text{where } E = 57,000 \sqrt{f'_c} \tag{8.19}$$

$$p_{cr} = 0.15(57000 \sqrt{4000}) \left[\frac{4.5}{212.5(12)}\right]^2 = 1.68 \text{ psi} = 242.50 \text{ psf} \tag{1.24}$$

The safety factor against buckling for this dome, determined by dividing the approximate buckling load by the design loads, is:

$$SF = \frac{242.50}{60 + 30} = 2.69$$

This safety factor should be sufficient.

Since there is no tension in the shell, minimum reinforcing must be provided along both principal directions.

$$A_{s \, min} = 0.0018A_g = 0.0018(12)4.5 = 0.0972 \text{ in.}^2/\text{ft} \tag{8.5}$$

Select #3 bars at 13 in., $A_s = 0.10$ in.$^2$/ft, or use welded wire fabric.

The horizontal thrust components of the arch forces $N_{\phi u}$ ($\cos \phi$) in the shell are resisted by tension in the concrete ring beam. They act in a uniform radial fashion and thus cause the circular ring to respond in pure tension. It was shown that the constant tension in a circular cable under uniform radial pressure $p$ is

$$T = pR \qquad (3.12)$$

Thus, the ultimate tensile force in the ring is

$$S_u = (N_{\phi u} \cos \phi)\frac{L}{2} \qquad (8.22)$$

$$S_u = \frac{14903.34(100)0.882}{1000} = 1314.48 \text{ k}$$

To resist this force, the following reinforcement is necessary:

$$A_s = \frac{S_u}{\phi f_y} = \frac{1314.48}{0.9(60)} = 24.34 \text{ in.}^2$$

Select twenty #10 bars, $A_s = 25.32$ in.$^2$.

Rather than using this amount of steel to resist the side thrust of the shell, the edge beam may be designed as a prestressed element, so that the compression induced by the tensioned cables will be larger than the tension induced by the external loading. In addition, the post-tensioning of the edge beam overcomes some of the incompatibility between the beam and the shell. Usually the edge beam expands under gravity loading and temperature increase, while the diameter of the shell along the edges contracts (see Problem 8.14). Prestressing of the edge beam eliminates the expansion of the beam. It also increases the bending capacity of the beam, so that moments due to asymmetrical loading can be more effectively resisted.

It is assumed that there will be 20% loss of the prestress force due to creep, shrinkage, and other sources. Furthermore, as shown in Problem 8.14, the ring will expand about 25% more due to a temperature increase of 50° as compared to gravity loading. Hence, the post-tensioning force must be equal to the lateral thrust force increased by 25% for temperature effects and 20% for loss of prestressing

$$S_{up} = (1.25 S_u) 1.2 = 1.25(1314.48)1.2 = 1971.72 \text{ k}$$

Using high strength deformed alloy steel bars with a strength $f_y = 136$ ksi yields the following minimum required steel area for the prestress bars

$$A_s = \frac{S_{up}}{\phi f_y} = \frac{1971.72}{0.9(136)} = 16.11 \text{ in.}^2 \qquad (8.1)$$

Select thirteen #10 bars, $A_s = 16.45$ in.$^2$.

The concrete cross-sectional area required to resist the axial load due to post-tensioning is

$$A_g = \frac{P_u}{0.47 f'_c + 0.0056 f_y} \qquad (1.50)$$

$$= \frac{1971.72}{0.47(4) + 0.0056(60)} = 889.77 \text{ in.}^2 = 6.18 \text{ ft}^2$$

For a depth of 1.5 ft, the width $b$ is equal to $6.18/1.5 = 4.12$ ft. Select as a preliminary beam size 1 ft 6 in. $\times$ 4 ft 2 in., $A_g = 6.25$ ft$^2$. Additional reinforcement must be provided for torsion and beam action.

**Example 8.5** A hemispherical concrete dome is used to span the 200 ft of Example 8.4 with the same loads and materials. Keep in mind that the shell thickness could be reduced because of the higher buckling capacity of the dome.

The maximum compression along the meridian at the base is

$$N_\phi = R\left(\frac{q}{2} + w\right) \qquad (7.6/7.11)$$

Or, expressed as an ultimate load

$$N_{\phi u} = 100 \frac{[1.7(30/2) + 1.4(60)]}{1000} = 10.95 \text{ k/ft}$$

The ultimate compressive meridional stress is

$$f_{cu} = \frac{N_{\phi u}}{\phi A_c} = \frac{10.95}{0.7(4.5)12} = 0.29 \text{ ksi} < 0.85 f_c' = 3.40 \text{ ksi}$$

The compressive force action is no problem for the shell's allowable strength.

The maximum tension along the hoop at the base of the shell is equal in magnitude to the arch forces at this level (Figs. 7.9 and 7.10). The tensile stresses are very small and can be carried by the plain concrete, assuming an allowable tensile stress of $5\sqrt{f_c'}$ and a capacity reduction factor of $\phi = 0.65$ for flexure in plain concrete

$$f_{tu} = \frac{N_{\phi u}}{\phi A_c} = \frac{10950}{0.65(4.5)12}$$

$$f_{tu} = 311.97 \text{ psi} < 5\sqrt{f_c'} = 5\sqrt{4000} = 316.23 \text{ psi}$$

However, according to the *ACI Code,* tensile strength of concrete shall be neglected. Hence all the tension must be carried by the steel

$$A_s = \frac{N_{\phi u}}{\phi f_y} = \frac{10.95}{0.9(60)} = 0.203 \text{ in.}^2/\text{ft} > A_{s \text{ min}}$$

$$A_{s \text{ min}} = 0.0035 A_g = 0.0035(4.5)12 = 0.189 \text{ in.}^2/\text{ft} \qquad (8.3)$$

Select #4 bars at $11\frac{1}{2}$ in., $A_s = 0.21$ in.$^2$/ft, along the circumference up to the neutral plane, as there is not much difference between the required steel and $A_{s \text{ min}}$. The minimum reinforcing of #3 bars at 13 in. will be applicable above the neutral plane and should be placed along the lines of longitude (arch action) as well.

## Approximate Design of Braced Domes

The analysis of framed domes is quite complex and time consuming, but may be simplified by treating the braced dome as a continuous shell. The main difference between these two dome systems lies in the fact that the thin shell responds primarily in membrane action while the comparatively rigid individual members of the framed dome are

also subject to bending. As the number of equal-size members increases, the dome approaches the continuous material density of a shell surface. From a force flow point of
view, forces applied uniformly to the surface can distribute evenly within the surface of a
continuous shell, but may follow only specific pathways along the linear members in the
framework of a braced dome, even as the number of elements approaches infinity. The
material density of the framing should be uniform, in analogy to the constant thickness
of a shell. In their geometry, grid and geodesic domes reflect a uniform member distribution, in contrast with radially framed domes which have a higher member density at
their centers than at their peripheries. This disparity of density in radially framed domes
can be corrected by using smaller member sizes with less strength in order to obtain a
more uniform strength distribution. The geodesic dome comes closest to the uniform
force distribution of shell behavior, and responds primarily in axial (membrane) action
rather than with combined axial and bending forces.

In the design of dome shells with continuous supports, it was found that one of the
primary preliminary design determinants is the uniform gravity loading case. For this
condition, the membrane forces follow exactly the pattern of a Schwedler dome without
diagonals with the radially arranged arches tied together by horizontal rings, here the arch
forces $N_\phi$ are carried directly by the meridional rafters and the hoop forces $N_\theta$ by the
ring purlins. The joints at the intersections of rings and arches must be rigidly connected
to reduce distortion of the curvature. Under symmetrical gravity loading, this type of
framed structure is quite rigid and the shell analogy as a preliminary design approach is
quite reasonable if one assumes an appropriate density of members. However, under
asymmetrical loading, large deformations may appear which can be reduced by diagonal
bracing, such as trussing or tension tie-rod bracing and/or the roof skin. In this way the
shear is not carried by bending of the ribs and rings, but by axial forces in the diagonals,
hence the framed surface may be considered stiff enough to justify the use of the shell
analogy. Furthermore, frame members should be selected such that the material density
is uniform across the surface, as in a shell of constant thickness.

**Example 8.6** A Schwedler dome 40 ft high, with a span of 240 ft is investigated (Fig.
8.25). It is composed of 36 radial ribs and 20 rows of concentric rings, made of *A*36

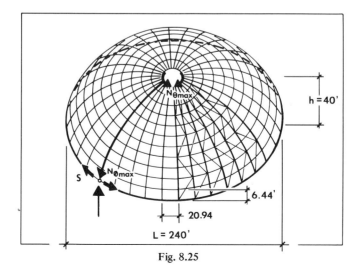

**Fig. 8.25**

steel. Diagonal bracing will be added to carry the panel shear as caused by asymmetrical loading. A dead load of 18 psf and a snow load of 20 psf are assumed. Because of the relatively flat profile of the dome, the entire roof is considered to be under wind suction; this loading condition will not influence the preliminary design of the members, only the design of the attachment of the skin to the framework.

The radius of the spherical cap is

$$R^2 = (R - 40)^2 + 120^2 \tag{8.21}$$

$$R^2 = R^2 + 40^2 - 80R + 120^2$$

$$R = 200 \text{ ft}$$

The angle $\phi$ defining the dome base is

$$\sin \phi = \frac{120}{200} = 0.6 \qquad \cos \phi = 0.8 \qquad \phi = 36.87°$$

The spacing of the 36 arches at the base is:

$$\frac{2\pi 120}{36} = 20.94 \text{ ft}$$

The length of one-half of the circumference of the dome is

$$\frac{\pi R}{180}\phi = \frac{\pi 200}{180} 36.87 = 128.70 \text{ ft}$$

The spacing of the 20 ring purlins is equal to:

$$\frac{128.70}{20} = 6.44 \text{ ft}$$

This spacing should be sufficient for the support of wood decking. The maximum compression forces along the meridians appear at the dome base and are found according to the membrane theory as follows

$$N_\phi = \frac{wR}{1 + \cos \phi} + \frac{qR}{2} \tag{7.11 and 7.6}$$

$$= \frac{18(200)}{1 + 0.8} + \frac{20(200)}{2} = 2000 + 2000 = 4000 \text{ lb/ft}$$

The rafters are spaced 20.94 ft apart at the base and must carry a maximum axial force of

$$N_{\phi r} = 4.00(20.94) = 83.76 \text{ k}$$

The deck acts in one-way action parallel to the arches; one may assume for this condition that the rafter does not have to resist any bending. However, for the case of two-way slab action or where the arch also must act as a joist which spans between the ring purlins, the rafter must also be designed for local bending; it is conservative to consider it as simply supported between the points of intersection of the parallel ring members.

Try as the preliminary maximum arch member size a $W10 \times 22$, A = 6.49 in.$^2$, $r_y$ =

1.33 in. The critical slenderness ratio for the section with the corresponding allowable axial stress is

$$\left(\frac{Kl}{r}\right)_y = \frac{1(6.44)12}{1.33} = 58.11, \quad \text{say } 59 \quad F_a = 17.53 \text{ ksi}$$

The actual stress is

$$f = \frac{N_{\phi}r}{A} = \frac{83.76}{6.49} = 12.91 \text{ ksi} < 17.53 \text{ ksi}$$

The trial section is stronger than necessary, but the next lower $W10$ section would not be sufficient.

Since $\phi = 36.87° \leqslant 45°$, the entire dome is in compression. The maximum hoop forces appear in the ring closest to the crown; the membrane forces at the crown are conservatively applied to the first ring

$$N_\theta = \frac{(q + w)R}{2} \tag{7.9 and 7.10}$$

$$= \frac{(20 + 18)200}{2} = 3800 \text{ lb/ft}$$

For a typical ring spacing of 6.44 ft the axial force that the purlin must resist is approximately

$$N_{\theta p} = 3.80(6.44) = 24.47 \text{ k}$$

The spacing of the meridian arches is so close at the crown that there is hardly any bending and no buckling in the purlin

$$A = \frac{N_{\theta p}}{F_a} = \frac{24.47}{22} = 1.11 \text{ in.}^2$$

Select $W6 \times 9$, $A = 2.68$ in.$^2$.

The axial compressive forces in the rings decrease as they approach the base, however, the effect of local bending increases because the length of the purlins increases. Again, one may conservatively consider the purlin as a simply supported beam spanning between the intersection of rings and arches, carrying the surface loads of the deck. Considering the snow to act together with the weight along the surface and using conservatively the span at the base, results in following maximum moment: $M = 6.44(20+18)(20.94)^2/8(1000) = 13.41$ ft-k. This moment can be resisted by a $W8 \times 10$, ignoring the small axial force and possible biaxial bending and torsion, which is considered to be controlled by the roof skin. Comparing the ring member sizes at the crown and base, one notices that they do not vary greatly.

The horizontal thrust components of the arch forces at the base are resisted by a tension ring. The tensile force the ring must support is

$$S = (N_\phi \cos \phi)\frac{L}{2} \tag{8.22}$$

$$S = 4.00(0.8)\frac{240}{2} = 384^k$$

The size of the base ring, based on tension alone and ignoring any effects due to the boundary conditions and asymmetrical loading that results in bending due to unsymmetrical radial forces, is

$$A = \frac{S}{F_t} = \frac{384}{22} = 17.46 \text{ in.}^2$$

try $W18 \times 60, A = 17.60$ in.$^2$.

Keep in mind that the tension ring may also be the beam portion of the vertical frame structure. In this case the vertical force components will cause torsion, which produces additional secondary bending on the W-section, but which may be ignored for closed rectangular beam cross-sections. Hence, curved beams of rectangular shape may be treated as straight beams with respect to bending; the torsional stresses may be ignored for preliminary design purposes because of the slight beam curvature and the relative close spacing of the columns.

For the braced dome just discussed, the frame members are in line with the membrane forces, and a typical member must support the membrane forces in a shell width that is equivalent to the center-to-center distance of member spacing at the point of investigation. For the case of grid domes, the framing does not coincide with the membrane force flow of the shell. Here, the membrane forces must be resolved into components according to the surface geometry and relative member sizes.

Triangular grids can be generated in many different ways, forming various patterns such as the geodesic, grid, lamella, and lattice domes as Fig. 8.20 indicates. The three-way geodesic grid has the advantage that the variations in member lengths is rather small resulting in a more or less uniform network of nearly equilateral triangles.

Three-way geodesic grids may be developed from the regular Platonic solids having triangular faces such as the tetrahedron, octahedron, icosahedron and their duals, or they may be generated from quasiregular polyhedra.

Buckminster Fuller, the famous inventor of geodesic domes, considers the triangulated icosahedron as the most efficient fundamental volume-controlling device of nature because it provides the most volume with the least surface; though not being the strongest (tetrahedron) it is a stable structure. Visualize this icosahedron projected onto a spherical surface (Fig. 8.26a), thereby subdividing the surface into 20 equilateral spherical triangles which constitute the maximum number of equal subdivisions possible. The extension of the icosa edges (Fig. 8.26b) form the 15 great circles, which are defined by a plane passing through the centroid of the sphere and cutting the sphere exactly in half. Buckminster Fuller showed that these 15 great circles are regularly arranged, and subdivide each of the 20 equilateral triangles of the icosahedron into 6 equal right-angled triangles, thus producing 120 identical right-angled triangles. This is the maximum number of identical triangles into which a spherical surface can be subdivided. Though this discovery is important, it does not solve the problem of equal member length. This can be approximately achieved by reducing the basic polyhedral face, in this case the 20 triangular icosahedral faces, into a larger number of components by further subdividing equally each of the equilateral triangles along their edges. The number of segments into which each of the principal sides is segmented is called the frequency $f$ as exemplified in Fig. 8.26d. The triangles formed by this subdivision are nearly equilateral. As the frequency or the number of components increases, the dome changes from a polyhedron, an icosahedron in this case, into a true spherical surface.

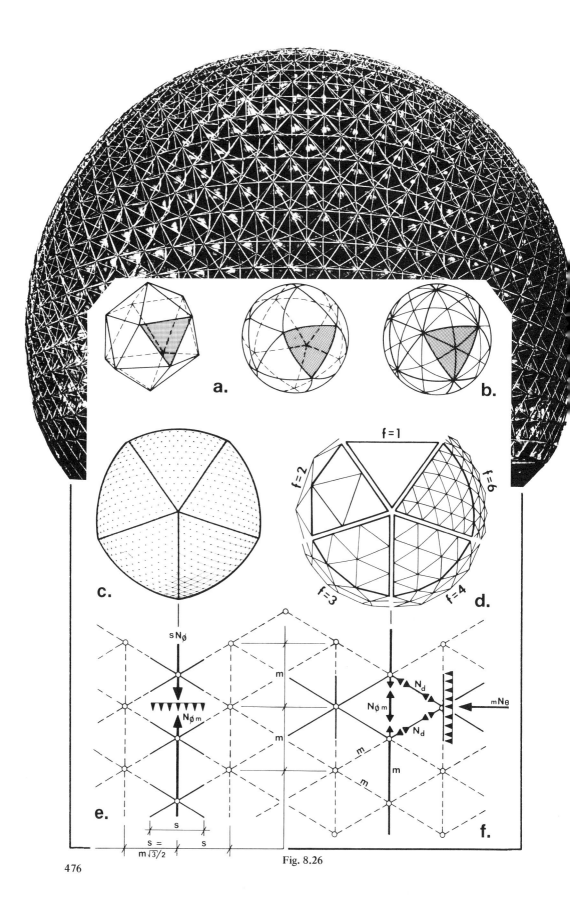

a.

b.

f = 1

f = 2

f = 6

f = 3

f = 4

c.

d.

$sN_\phi$

$N_{\phi m}$

m

m

$N_d$

$N_{\phi m}$

$N_d$

m

$_mN_\theta$

m

m

s

$s =$
$m\sqrt{3}/2$

s

e.

f.

476

Fig. 8.26

**Example 8.7** A three-way pin jointed grid dome is investigated instead of the Schwedler dome in Example 8.6 by keeping the loads and hence the membrane forces the same. Since the dome segment is shallow, it will be formed within the five spherical triangular faces of the icosahedron arranged around the vertex. For this approximation it is assumed that the triangles are truly equilateral and that the length of the straight members is equal to their respective arc length, that is, the members are considered curvilinear.

Subdividing the sides of the principal polyhedral triangle into $n = 15$ equal parts yields the member length $m$

$$m = \frac{\pi R}{180}(\phi)\left(\frac{1}{n}\right) = \frac{\pi(200)}{180}(36.87)\frac{1}{15} = 8.58 \text{ ft}$$

The maximum compressive member forces $N_{\phi m}$ due to symmetrical gravity loading appear along the sides of the principal polyhedral triangle. They can be approximately determined, assuming a truly repetitive grid, as follows.

The member must support the meridional membrane forces according to the spacing $s$ of the arch members (Fig. 8.26e)

$$N_{\phi m} = s N_\phi = \frac{m\sqrt{3}}{2}(N_\phi) \tag{a}$$

where $s = m\sqrt{3}/2$. The diagonal member forces $N_d$ resist the hoop forces (Fig. 8.26f)

$$2\left(\frac{N_d}{m}\right)s = m N_\theta$$

$$N_d = \frac{m\sqrt{3}}{3}(N_\theta) \tag{b}$$

The diagonal forces $N_d$, in turn, cause a tension force $N_{\phi m}$ in the arch member for a shallow dome where the ring forces are in compression

$$N_{\phi m} = \frac{N_d}{m}\left(\frac{m}{2}\right) = \frac{N_d}{2} \tag{c}$$

Subtracting Eq. (c) from (a) yields an approximate expression for the compressive forces along the arch members

$$N_{\phi m} = \frac{m\sqrt{3}}{2}(N_\phi) - \frac{N_d}{2}$$

$$N_{\phi m} = \frac{m\sqrt{3}}{2}\left(N_\phi - \frac{N_\theta}{3}\right) \tag{8.23}$$

Notice that the hoop forces $N_\theta$ for a shallow dome at the base are rather small and may be neglected.

For the magnitude of the membrane force at the base refer to Example 8.6

$$N_{\phi m} = \frac{m\sqrt{3}}{2}(N_\phi) = \frac{8.58\sqrt{3}(4.00)}{2} = 29.72 \text{ k}$$

Only axial action is considered for this preliminary design. The panels supporting the roof surface are assumed to transfer these loads directly to the joints or member intersection points. For a slenderness of $KL = 1$ (8.58), according to the AISC Manual column tables, try following circular structural tubing ($A$36)

$$\text{TS 3 OD} \times 0.216 \qquad P_{\text{all}} \cong 31 \text{ k}$$

However, it is quite unrealistic for large-span domes, as the one discussed above, to assume for the member design that the joints do not laterally displace ($K = 1$). Specially pin-connected, nearly spherical surface grids where the joints are approximately in the same plane, are very vulnerable to local instability under concentrated and unsymmetrical loading. Buckminster Fuller tried to overcome this problem of local instability by adding a partial inner dome or second structural layer, thereby increasing the local and overall buckling capacity of the surface.

## Problems

8.8   A spherical dome has a lantern opening of radius $R_0$ at the crown. A stiffening ring beam must be provided to carry the loads since the thin shell obviously cannot support the concentrated collar loads due to the lantern weight and due to other loads such as lighting and ventilating equipment. Consider the resultant of the uniformly distributed collar load around the opening to be $W_0$. Determine the ring forces at the crown and at the base, as well as the meridional and hoop forces at the shell edge along the base as caused by the shell weight and lantern load.

8.9   Determine the hoop and arch forces at the base of a pointed dome composed of spherical segments (i.e., conoidal dome) carrying a single load at its vertex. Also, give the thrust and vertical components of the arch force at the base.

8.10  Determine the maximum meridional membrane forces for a hemispherical shell as caused by a uniform wind load assumed to act on the vertical dome projection. Reason why the wind is insignificant in comparison to gravity loading for typical conditions.

8.11  Derive the membrane forces at the crown due to uniform load action on the horizontal roof projection for following dome shapes on circular plans with the radius of curvature $R_0$ at the vertex equal to

$$\text{elliptical dome:} \qquad R_0 = \frac{L^2}{4h} \qquad\qquad\qquad (8.24)$$

$$\text{parabolic dome:} \qquad R_0 = \frac{L^2}{8h} \qquad\qquad\qquad (3.29)$$

$$\text{spherical dome:} \qquad R_0 = R$$

8.12  Derive the membrane forces due to uniform load action on the horizontal roof projection for a paraboloid of revolution.

8.13  Determine the approximate change in radius for a shallow spherical dome at the base as caused by:

(a) The thrust component of the arch forces

$$\Delta R_0 = \frac{N_\phi R_0^2 \cos\phi}{AE} \qquad\qquad\qquad (8.25)$$

(b) The hoop forces

$$\Delta R_0 = \frac{N_\theta R_0}{Et} \tag{8.25a}$$

where cross-sectional area is $A = t$ (1 ft).

(c) Temperature change

$$\Delta R_0 = \alpha \Delta T R_0 \tag{8.25b}$$

**8.14** Determine the change in radius at the dome base in Example 8.4 as caused by:
  (a) Expansion of ring beam (not the prestressed case) due to gravity loading.
  (b) Temperature difference of 50°F and $\alpha = 0.0000065$ in./in./°F.
  (c) Hoop shortening due to gravity loads.

**8.15** Determine the maximum compressive membrane stresses in a concrete conical shell, which is $3\frac{1}{2}$ in. thick, is 10 ft high and has a span of 50 ft. The dome must support a snow load of 30 psf on the horizontal roof projection.

**8.16** A Schwedler dome made of $A36$ steel, spans 225 ft and is 40 ft high. It consists of 36 meridian rafters and 18 rows of concentric ring purlins. The dead and live load are each assumed as 20 psf. Determine the preliminary critical member sizes for the rafter, purlin, and tension ring.

**8.17** Design the dome in Problem 8.16 as a three-way, pin-jointed grid dome made of nearly equilateral triangles. What is the approximate maximum circular pipe size using $A36$ steel, if the member length should not be more than 8 ft.

**8.18** A $3\frac{1}{2}$-in. thick spherical concrete dome spans 150 ft and is 20 ft high. Investigate the shell for critical compression, tension and buckling, if 4000 psi concrete and 60 ksi steel will be used. Assume a snow load of 25 psf. Determine the typical steel reinforcement. Design the concrete ring beam by prestressing it to resist the lateral thrust due to the gravity loading and an assumed 20% loss of prestress force. Use Grade 136 prestress steel.

**8.19** The dome segment in Problem 8.18 is replaced by a 3-in. hemispherical concrete dome with the same material properties. Determine the critical tension stresses and select the necessary reinforcement.

See also Problems 8.27, 8.28, and 8.29.


## 8.4  THE HYPERBOLIC PARABOLOID

The hyperbolic paraboloid is an invention of this century. It has opened a new era for the building of continuous, adaptive surface forms; it has added a new dimension to the traditional rotational dome shapes by introducing the endless formal potential of translational surface generation and the relatively easy building of double curvature anticlastic surfaces using straight line elements. Although in 1669, Christopher Wren already discussed the hyperboloid from a mathematical point of view, and Antonio Gaudi around the turn of this century had used the hyperbolic paraboloid as part of his complex warped thin-tile surface vaulting, Bernard Lafaille in 1933 was the first to actually build the shape as a reinforced concrete shell. At about the same time the French engineer F. Aimond developed the membrane theory for this new surface geometry, and Giorgio Baroni applied the principle to the roof of the Alfa Romeo factory in Milan, Italy, in 1934. Finally, in 1935, Eduardo Torroja built the famous Zarzuela Hippodrome near Madrid, Spain. The real development, however, was initiated after World War II by Felix Candela in Mexico, who fully explored the visual richness and the potential of the hyperbolic paraboloid; through Candela the hypar became part of the architectural language as the examples in Fig. 8.29 clearly express.

The primary geometrical characteristics of the hypar were already identified in Section 7.4. It was shown that the general shape resembles a horse saddle or mountain pass where the hyperbolas in plan view look like a contour map. Keeping in mind that in this section only special conditions were considered—such as the vertical position of the $z$ axis which obviously can be tilted or the hypar was assumed to be rectangular, that is, to be made up of identical, principal parabolic generators with the straight line generators forming an orthogonal grid in plan projection. This network may be transformed by flattening into a rhombic tesselation, which in turn reflects unequal parabolic generators or a skewed hypar.

Some of the basic hypar features are shown in Fig. 8.27. Here, the central portion identifies the generating systems: the vertical parabolas, the horizontal hyperbolas, and the diagonal straight lines. An important characteristic of the hypar is its height-to-span ratio, which in the drawing is shown as a variable for a given rectangular plan. The progression of a typical unit from its flat to its steep stage is clearly presented. Similar is the transition from a horizontal slab to a shallow umbrella-type element to a steep dome-like shape as shown in the right portion of the drawing. In the left part the basic hypar unit is rotated to express the visual power of the form and the relation of the straight lines to the curve at different positions.

In the bottom part of Fig. 8.27a–d, some typical hypar elements and their location within the saddle are identified. It is quite apparent that these elements can have any geometrical configuration and can be cut from any location. A section through the saddle always generates, along the cut line, either a parabola, a hyperbola, or a straight line. Some common solutions, using only linear sections, are the following ones:

- To cut the hypar diagonally along the straight line generators to form straight edges [case (a)]
- To cut the hypar diagonally but skewed with respect to the straight line generators resulting in parabolic boundaries of concave or convex shape [case (a)]
- To cut the hypar vertically along the parabolas, parallel to the principal curvatures to form parabolic boundaries [case (c)]
- To cut the hypar horizontally to form hyperbolic boundaries [partially case (d)]

The curvilinear section in case (b) results in hyperbolic boundaries.

The shape of a hypar element depends on many architectural design determinants. It is a function of scale (span versus height), material, construction (process: in situ versus prefab, expertise), function and geometry of building plan, just to name some of the technical considerations. The shape of the building plan may be curvilinear (e.g., round, elliptic), lending itself to the use of a single hypar unit. For a polygonal plan (e.g., triangular, rectangular) an assemblage of units may be considered, though this obviously is not necessary, because a single hypar surface with linear or curvilinear edges

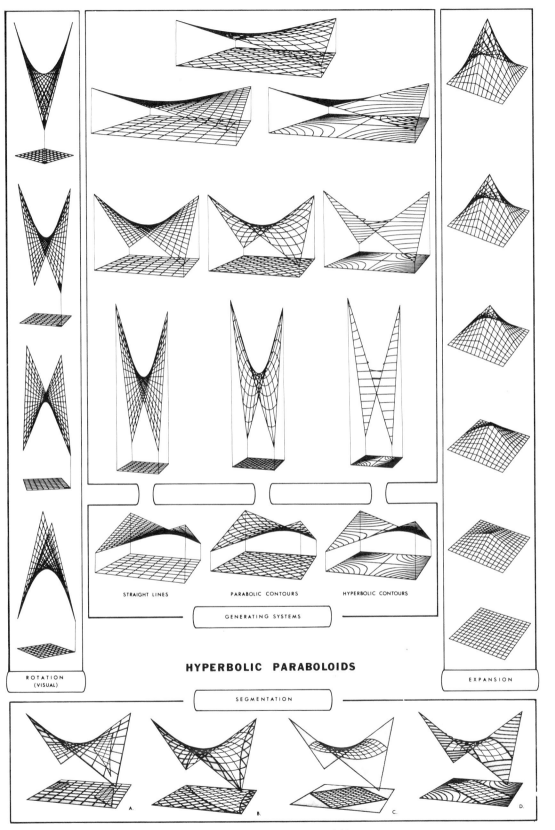

ROTATION
(VISUAL)

STRAIGHT LINES     PARABOLIC CONTOURS     HYPERBOLIC CONTOURS

GENERATING SYSTEMS

EXPANSION

**HYPERBOLIC PARABOLOIDS**

SEGMENTATION

A.     B.     C.     D.

**Fig. 8.27** Hyperbolic paraboloids.

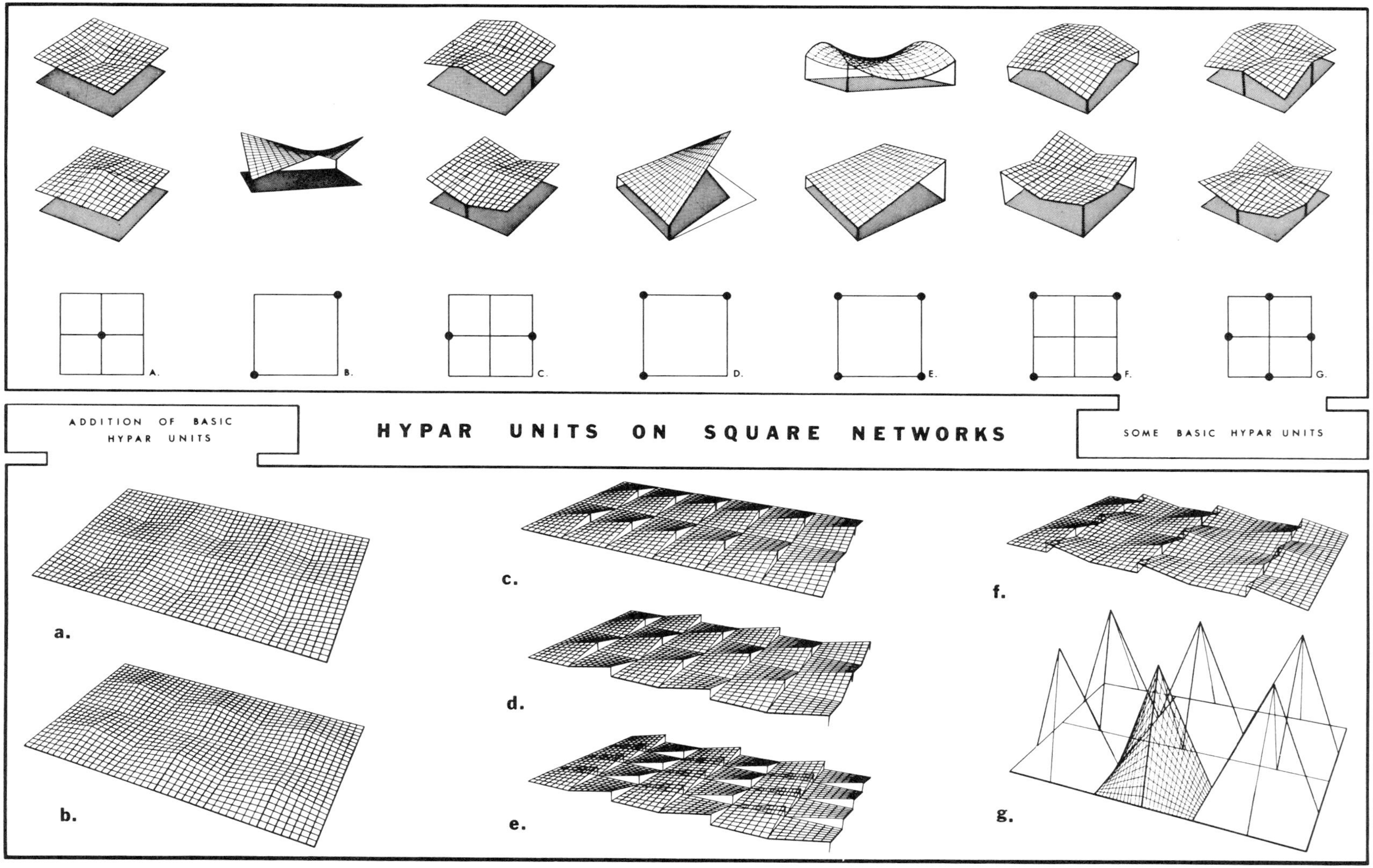

HYPAR UNITS ON SQUARE NETWORKS

ADDITION OF BASIC HYPAR UNITS

SOME BASIC HYPAR UNITS

Fig. 8.28

can cover a rectangular space for instance, as shown in Fig. 8.28e. From a purely geometrical point of view, there exist an infinite number of ways of combining hypar elements to enclose a given building space. The process of combining surface kits may be
based on addition (e.g., growth, superposition, penetration), subtraction (e.g., truncation,
dissection, subdivision), pressure (e.g., flattening) or rotation; it may be based on patterns
of arrangement such as linear ones (e.g., radial, orbital, nuclear, branching), planar ones
(regular and nonregular networks), or spatial ones (saddle polyhedra). Units of equal or
different shapes may be connected in a smooth or relatively continuous fashion, or they
may give the appearance of a folded-plate type structure. As can be seen, there is no
limitation to the generation of hypar forms; the buildings in Fig. 8.29 can only hint the
endless formal potential of architectural possibilities.

Different solutions for assembling warped rectangular surfaces to cover a square
building enclosure are shown in Fig. 8.28. While cases b, d, and e employ single saddle
surfaces with straight or curvilinear edges, the other solutions consist of a combination of
four equal hypar elements forming umbrella-type roofs with a central column, or gabled
roof types with supports along the outside perimeter. These basic building blocks, in turn,
can be added in various ways to form the multibay aggregates shown in the bottom
portion of the drawing.

Hyperbolic paraboloids, although double curvature systems, can be built by only using
linear structural members. Because of this important feature, the surface has been constructed not only with reinforced concrete and ceramics where formwork is an important
economical consideration, but also in steel, aluminum, and timber by employing multidirectional framing systems and, for smaller scale, two or more layers of decking placed in
opposite directions to act as two-way span systems.

Some of the abundant form potential of anticlastic surfaces can only be suggested by
the examples in Fig. 8.29. The scale of the structures ranges from one-family houses to
stadiums; there is no limit to the wealth of forms.

First, combinations of rectangular warped surface units assembled to relatively flat
roof structures are discussed.

Umbrella-type shells consist of four hypar units supported by a central column. Examples are the tilted inverted umbrellas (60 × 116 ft) of the grandstand at the Sciota Down
Raceway, Columbus, Ohio (J), with a typical concrete thickness of $4\frac{1}{2}$ in., and the 3-in.
concrete shells for the Berenplaat Water Treatment Plant, Rotterdam, Holland (L). The
roof of the Saier House near Deauville, France (C), consists of two square hypar surfaces
supported on three columns, while the Centre Le Corbusier, Zurich, Switzerland (B), has
a hipped and an inverted hipped roof, each composed of four square, steel panels. The
roof of the athletic facility for the Pratt Institute, Brooklyn, New York (O), is a multibay aggregate of twelve hipped roof units. The principal bays are 130 ft square and are
covered by 16 wooden square hypar units (32.5 × 32.5 ft) with the four central panels
forming a pyramid. The warped panels are supported along the fold lines by laminated
wood beams. The entire roof rests on sixteen buttresses, which are located along the
periphery in line with the A-frames, and at the four corners.

The roof of the Ponce Coliseum (D) consists of four straight-edge, nearly rectangular
hypar units and is supported by four abutments located at the center of each of the
exterior sides. The typically 4-in. thick concrete shell units rest on the interior gable
beams that span between the piers, and the 138-ft inclined cantilever edge beams. These
enormous cantilever beams had to be post-tensioned to control deflection and stresses;
the depth of the 30-in. wide edge beams varies from 18 in. at the corner to 94 in. at the

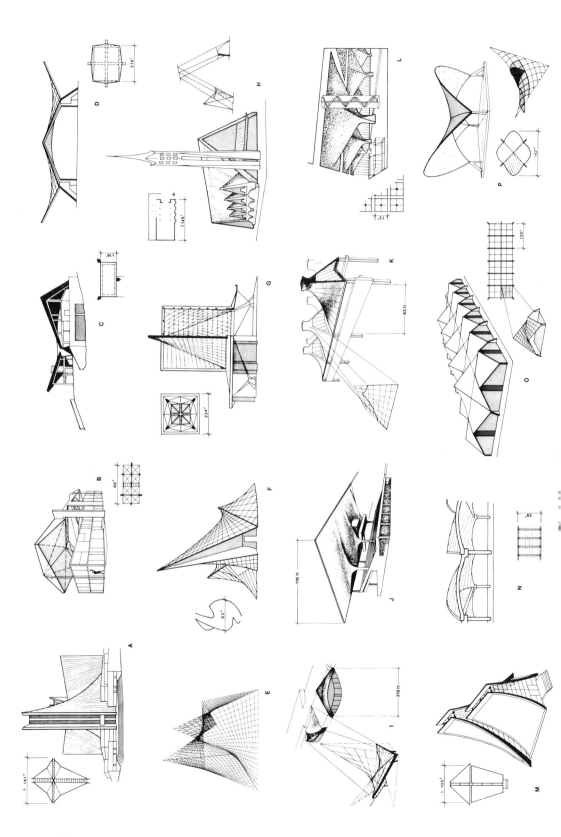

484

pier. The shell membrane is prestressed along the straight-line generators. The lateral thrust upon the abutments, due to asymmetrical loading as transfered by the interior beams, is balanced by prestressed tie beams between the abutments below ground.

The next group of buildings to be discussed uses thin vertical shells as inclined walls, arranged in such a way as to form pyramidal profiles.

The Virgen Milagrosa church (H) is composed entirely of deformed, inclined umbrella shaped units. Through this combination of the straight-edged hypar kits, none more than $1\frac{1}{2}$ in. thick, Candela achieved a powerful interior space of impressive quality.

The roof of St. Mary's Cathedral in San Francisco (G), is developed from eight identical hypar shells joined together to form a square base and a cross at the top level. In the diagonal direction, the shell intersections form an A-frame along which the thrust is directly transferred to the buttresses. The entire shell does not rest on the ground, but on 4 hollow, 140-ft arches along the periphery which, in turn, are supported by the four massive corner piers. The concrete shell surface consists of a triangular grid with a $5\frac{1}{2}$-in. shell thickness, and 8-in. wide ribs projecting $10\frac{1}{2}$ in.

St. Mary's Basilica in Tokyo (A) is composed of eight hypar surfaces of three different shapes which sit directly on the ground and form a cruciform. The lateral thrust developed in the valleys along the intersection of the shells (i.e., A-frame action) is resisted at the base by tie beams that span diagonally across the building.

The Philips Pavilion (F), in contrast, is much more of a freeform, organic structure, rather similar to the computer drawing shown adjacent to it (E). Also, the individual hypar units have straight edges above ground, whereas the edges along the ground are curvilinear.

The last building types to be investigated cannot be easily placed into one category, although the roof of the Madonna di Pompei Church, Montreal, Canada (P), is part of the larger group of intersecting saddle shapes similar to cross-vaults, as is discussed further in Fig. 8.32. The roof of this church is composed of four hypar units, where each pair of opposites is identical. The typical shell quadrant is cut from the general saddle to form parabolic curves along the two inside edges, and hyperbolic boundaries along the outside. Along the inside edges, the hypar units are supported by diagonal, nearly three-hinge, parabolic groin arches which, in turn, rest on the four abutments that carry the building. The concrete shell thickness varies from 6 in. at the crown to 10 in. near the supports. The primary structural behavior of the shell quadrant under gravity loading may be visualized as consisting of arch action between the supports in one direction, and cantilever action in the other direction.

The huge hypar concrete shells of the TWA Hangars of the Kansas City International Airport (I) are made up of two principal shell surfaces which, along their line of intersection—the central ridge—form a stiff 318-ft span arch. This arching shell is supported by abutments, and by additional column supports under the edge beams in the rear to resist asymmetrical loading. The typically 3-in. thick shell is post-tensioned to eliminate tensile stresses and is stiffened along the edges by hollow triangular beams defined by their own warped surface curvatures.

Each of the intricate domical roof units for a foundry at Lohr-am-Main, Germany (K), is composed of two hypar surfaces at opposite sides and a circular ventilating shaft.

Though conoidal shells are anticlastic surfaces and can be constructed from straight lines (Fig. 7.15), as is discussed in Chapter 7, they have rarely been built. A typical application is as north light shells (N), similar to the half-cylindrical shells in Fig. 8.16.

The thin vertical conoidal shell walls on the diamond-shaped plan of Memorial Chapel at Formosa's Tunghai University (M) express the sculptural quality of the building.

In the section on membrane behavior it was shown that the shallow hyperbolic paraboloid under uniform loading responds primarily as a shear system, where the shear forces, in turn, cause diagonal tension and compression. The behavior of the surface can be visualized as the interplay of thin compression arches in one direction and tension cables perpendicular to them. Here the spreading of the arches is prevented by the hanging cables or vice versa, resulting in a full internal equilibrium without the help of shear and bending along the principal curvatures. These axial forces cause pure shear with no normal forces in the diagonal direction. It was found that the stresses caused by axial and shear action were constant over the entire surface thus reflecting an optimal situation. This condition, however, is ideal and based on a rather shallow, rectangular warped surface under uniform loading, and undisturbed along its boundaries by edge beams and abutments. In reality, the loads are not uniform, nor is the membrane hinged to its boundaries or the stiffness of the edge members in the plane of the shell negligible, nor is the edge beam, possibly of variable cross-section, necessarily concentric with respect to the shell. This incompatibility between the thin shell and stiffer boundary members must cause additional shear and bending in the shell along the vicinity of the edges (Fig. 8.23). At corners, where beams intersect, the shell has hardly any double curvature and acts more like a slab. The span-to-height ratio of most hypars is in the range of nine ($f/L = 1/9$), or the slope of edge beams ($\tan \theta = f/a$) for rectangular units varies between 1/5 and 1/3. The membrane approach is reasonable for these typical conditions, however for steeper cases the shell weight cannot be considered anymore to act on the horizontal roof projection, but must be placed along the surface, which complicates the mathematical interpretation. Axial forces parallel to the straight line generators must now be taken into account; remember, they are zero for a shallow hypar surface. For the preliminary design of membranes these axial forces are not critical, but must be considered for the design of the edge beams, which resist the normal forces in beam action if they are linear or in arch action if they are curvilinear. The advantage of curved edge beams for steep hyperbolic paraboloids is apparent. The edge members for shallow hypars, if placed parallel to the straight line generators, only act as axially loaded columns resisting the sum of the tangential shear along the shell edges. Visualize the edge beams to form an independent structural system supporting the membrane units in an axial manner. This system must be properly supported and stable so it can resist the surface forces and guide them safely to the ground. At the intersection of shell segments, often ribs may be needed. For example, in the cross-vault formed by single-curvature cylindrical shells, arches are generated along the diagonal intersection of the shells (Fig. 8.13). Here, free edges may be used along the outside perimeter, since surface action will be primarily in compression, that is, arch action parallel to the free edges transfer the membrane loads directly to the diagonal ribs along the intersection of the shells (see Fig. 8.32).

The membrane approach assumes uniform load action which is only true for the weight of rather shallow membranes, live loads can take any position and edge beams exert a load concentration. The edge beams were found not to influence the overall membrane force flow along the shallow warped surface and hence their weight can be evenly distributed across the horizontal projection of the roof; they behave as a natural extension and coherent part of the membrane, if they are placed with their larger dimension parallel to the shell surface. As the weight or size of the boundary members increase with increase in span of the roof, they cannot be treated as part of the membrane any-more; to the contrary, they seem to hang from the membrane and tend to stretch it, which may be beneficial to a soft surface because of the prestressing effect. For large-scale rigid shell structures, however, the edge beams may have to be supported directly by walls or frames.

It should be quite apparent that the membrane approach presented here can only be considered as helpful for preliminary design purposes and for the developing of a first understanding of hypar shells. Though hyperbolic paraboloids all have common geo-metrical characteristics, their structural behavior is dependent on how the hypar elements are combined and where and how they are supported.

In the following examples and problems only simple but typical roof types, assembled from shallow warped surfaces, are investigated.

The shell thickness in reinforced concrete construction is usually not based on strength, but on construction process (spraying, casting), the necessary cover for the steel reinforce-ment, and leakage considerations, as has already been discussed. However, one should keep in mind that it does not have to be a minimum of three inches thick. This is clearly exemplified by the $\frac{5}{8}$-in. shell of the Cosmic Ray Pavilion at the University of Mexico, which spans about 39 ft and was built by Felix Candela in 1951. Buckling may deter-mine the shell thickness of hyperbolic paraboloids, but only for the flat portions or large spans. In general, stability considerations for anticlastic surfaces are not critical since the tensile curvatures tend to stabilize the arched curvatures.

The shell thickness for the typical application of a single concrete saddle unit (Example 8.8) is approximately 3 in. up to a projection (maximum cable span) of 100 ft and is 4 in. up to 200 ft.

**Example 8.8**   An inverted, reinforced concrete hypar umbrella shell is investigated. The unit is 50 $\times$ 50 ft in plan view and has a vertical rise of 8 ft (Fig. 8.30). A minimum shell thickness of 3 in. is selected. Grade 40 steel and 3000 psi concrete are used. The roof must support a snow load of 30 psf. Wind does not have any effect on the design of the flat membrane, however must be considered, if the umbrella unit is free-standing; for this case, the column is fixed to the ground and has to resist a maximum moment at the base, and the shell edge beams will also have to carry some rotation.

The dead load of the shell is

$$\text{shell weight } \left(\frac{3}{12}\right) 150: \qquad 37.50 \text{ psf}$$
$$\text{roof finish and edge beams:} \qquad \underline{3.75 \text{ psf}}$$
$$41.25 \text{ psf}$$

The ultimate surface loads are

$$w_u = 1.4\, w_L + 1.7\, w_L$$
$$= 1.4(41.25) + 1.7(30) = 57.75 + 51.00 = 108.75 \text{psf}$$

Uniform loading conditions are assumed so that the membrane equations can be used. Unbalanced live loading was found to have hardly any effect on the overall design of the shell, it only generated very small bending stresses.

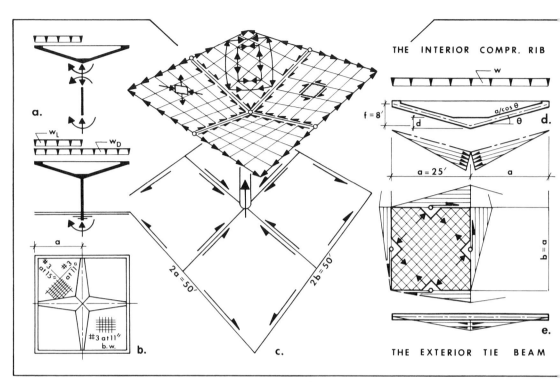

THE EXTERIOR TIE BEAM

**Fig. 8.30**

The ultimate membrane forces in tension, compression, and shear are based on one of the four warped surfaces

$$N_u = S_u = \pm \frac{w_u ab}{2f} = \frac{108.75(25)25}{2(8)1000} = 4.25 \text{ k/ft}$$

or

$$N_u = \frac{w_u L^2}{16f} = \frac{108.75(50\sqrt{2})^2}{16(8)1000} = 4.25 \text{ k/ft}$$

(7.28)

The compressive stress as caused by the ultimate axial force, ignoring the steel reinforcement, is

$$f_{cu} = \frac{N_u}{\phi A_c} = \frac{4.25}{0.7(3 \times 12)}$$

$$= 0.169 \text{ ksi} \ll 0.85 f_c' = 0.85(3) = 2.55 \text{ ksi}$$

As clearly shown, the membrane stresses are extremely small and the shell thickness is not dependent on strength.

Following reinforcing is required in the diagonal direction along the principal suspended parabolas by considering a cracked section (i.e., the tensile strength of concrete is neglected)

$$A_s = \frac{N_u}{\phi f_y} = \frac{4.25}{0.9(40)} = 0.118 \text{ in.}^2/\text{ft}$$

Select #3 at 11 in. on center, $A_s = 0.12 \text{ in.}^2/\text{ft}$.

Place shrinkage and temperature reinforcing perpendicular to the main bars along the parabolic arches

$$A_{s \text{ min}} = 0.002 \, A_g = 0.002 \, (3 \times 12) = 0.072 \text{ in.}^2/\text{ft}$$

with a maximum spacing of the bars equal to $5t = 5(3) = 15$ in.

Select #3 at 15 in. on center, $A_s = 0.09 \text{ in.}^2/\text{ft}$.

According to the *ACI Code*, the shell reinforcement shall be provided at the middle surface of the shell and be placed either parallel to the lines of principal tensile stress, as shown above, or in two or three component directions. For hypar shells it may be more convenient to lay the reinforcement parallel to the straight line generators rather than having to cut each bar in order to fit them along the principal parabolic curves. Hence, place #3 at 11 in. on center along each of the straight line generators (Fig. 8.30b).

The shear forces or the resultant of the principal parabolic forces cause axial action in the beams along the perimeter edges (Fig. 8.30c). Any eccentricity between edge beam and shell, and the effect of dead load ($f/a = 8/25 = 1/3.13 \leqslant 1/3$) causing bending is neglected. The exterior perimeter beam is in tension. Visualize a funicular cable along the circumference, responding to equal diagonal forces at the corners by taking a square shape. The maximum axial force appears at the intersection with the interior rib. Since a typical beam is parallel to the straight line generators, the maximum force is obtained by just summing up the tangential shear along the shell panel (Fig. 8.30e)

$$T_{B \text{ max}} = S(a) = \frac{w \, a^2 b}{2f}$$

$$T_{uB} = S_u(a) = 4.25 \, (25) = 106.25 \text{ k}$$

The required reinforcement in the edge beam at the intersection point with rib is

$$A_s = \frac{T_{uB}}{\phi f_y} = \frac{106.25}{0.9(40)} = 2.95 \text{ in.}^2$$

Select six #7, $A_s = 3.61 \text{ in.}^2$.

The interior inclined ribs are in compression. The maximum axial force at the column intersection is equal to the sum of all the shear along the edges of the adjacent warped panels accumulating linearly as they approach the support (Fig. 8.30d)

$$C_{R \text{ max}} = 2(S) \left( \frac{a}{\cos \theta} \right) = \frac{w \, b \, a^2}{f \cos \theta}$$

where

$$\tan \theta = \frac{f}{a} = \frac{8}{25} \quad \text{or} \quad \cos \theta = 0.952$$

The maximum ultimate compression force in the rib is

$$C_{uR} = 2(4.25) \frac{25}{0.952} = 223.21 \text{ k}$$

The required concrete area is based on axial action only by considering the rib as a short column fully laterally supported by the shell

$$A_g = \frac{P_u}{0.47f_c' + 0.0056f_y} \tag{1.50}$$

$$= \frac{223.12}{0.47(3) + 0.0056(40)} = 136.55 \text{ in.}^2$$

The rib cross-section is approximated as triangular (Fig. 8.30d)

$$A_g = \frac{d(2d \text{ ctg } \theta)}{2} = \frac{a d^2}{f}$$

$$136.55 = d^2 \frac{25}{8} \quad \text{or} \quad d = 6.61 \text{ in.}$$

A larger beam depth $d$ is selected so that the rib can resist the moment as caused by the cantilevering unsymmetrical live loading. This moment is larger than the one due to minimum eccentricity of axial forces as used in the formula above. The effective shell width, which helps to transfer the axial forces, is conservatively neglected.

The column must support the maximum axial load of

$$P_C = w(2a)(2b) = 4 \, wab$$

The maximum ultimate load is

$$P_{uC} = \frac{108.75 (50)(50)}{1000} = 271.88 \text{ k}$$

However, the governing loading condition is caused by unsymmetrical live load together with dead load (Fig. 8.30a).

The column must support a moment, if the rotation is not distributed to adjacent umbrella units similar to three-hinged portal frame action

$$M_C = w_L (2a)b \frac{b}{2} = w_L ab^2$$

The ultimate live load moment is equal to

$$M_{uC} = \frac{0.051(25 \times 50)25}{2} = 796.88 \text{ ft-k}$$

The corresponding ultimate axial dead and live load is

$$P_{uC} = \frac{4(57.75)25(25) + 2(51) \, 25(25)}{1000} = 208.13 \text{ k}$$

**Example 8.9**  A single, straight-edged hyperbolic paraboloid 100 × 100 ft in plan projection is 15 ft high at the center (Fig. 8.31), so that the slope of the edge member $f/a = 15/50 = 1/3.33$ is flat enough and the membrane theory can still be considered a reasonable first approximation. The reinforced concrete shell is $3\frac{1}{4}$ in. thick, the concrete's strength is 4000 psi and the yield stress of the reinforcing bars is 50 ksi. The roof must support a

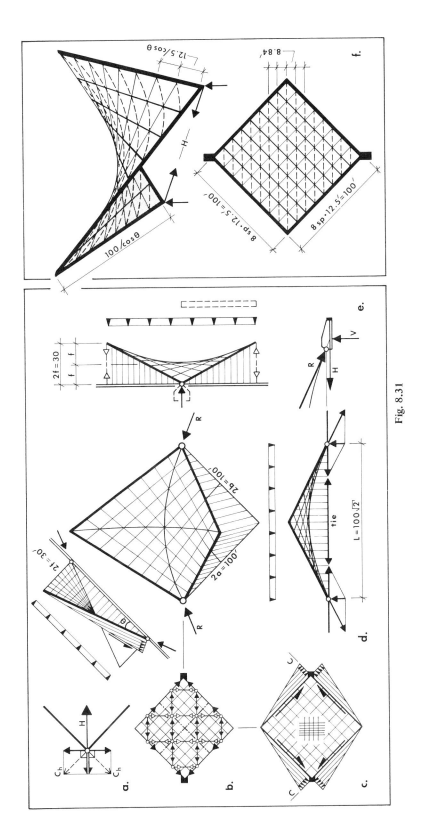

Fig. 8.31

491

snow load of 20 psf; wind forces are not critical for this preliminary design of the shell. The membrane is assumed hinged to its supports, hence can only be stable under symmetrical loading. To prevent the roof from tilting due to unsymmetrical gravity loading (in this case due to live load) and/or wind, the shell should be tied to the ground by tension or compression columns along the perimeter or only by single members at the high points similar to a tent structure. The shell may also be fixed to its support structure so that it can resist rotation, but this may only be reasonable for small-scale buildings; this type of solution influences the membrane behavior since the beams will bend as cantilevers to resist unsymmetrical loading thereby also bending the shell. The shell weighs

$$\frac{3.25}{12}\, 150 = 40.63 \text{ psf}$$

A dead weight of 43 psf will be assumed, taking into account the finish and edge beams.
The ultimate loads are equal to

$$w_u = 1.4(43) + 1.7(20) = 60.2 + 34.0 = 94.2 \text{ psf}$$

The force flow along the surface is composed of arch action straight across from support to support with the span of the compression parabola equal to L (Fig. 8.31b) and tension cables acting in the perpendicular direction; the arches act diagonally with respect to the plan view. Based on this interpretation of stress flow, the membrane forces may be determined as

$$\pm N = \frac{w L^2}{16f} \tag{7.28}$$

Or, the ultimate membrane forces are

$$\pm N_u = \frac{94.2(100\sqrt{2})^2}{16(15)1000} = 7.85 \text{ k/ft}$$

The single hypar shell may also be visualized as consisting of four equal rectangular warped surfaces as based on the surface subdivision by straight line generators (Fig. 8.31 b and d). From this interpretation the ultimate membrane forces may also be obtained

$$\pm N = \frac{wab}{2f} \tag{7.28}$$

$$\pm N_u = \frac{94.2(50)50}{2(15)1000} = 7.85 \text{ k/ft}$$

Obviously, both approaches must give the same solution. The compressive stress, neglecting the reinforcement, is

$$f_{cu} = \frac{N_u}{\phi A_c} = \frac{7.85}{0.7(3.25)12}$$

$$= 0.288 \text{ ksi} \ll 0.85\, f_c' = 0.85(4) = 3.40 \text{ ksi}$$

The thickness of the shell is clearly not dependent on the compressive stresses.
The reinforcing along the principal suspended parabolas is

$$A_s = \frac{N_u}{\phi f_y} = \frac{7.85}{0.9(50)} = 0.174 \text{ in.}^2/\text{ft}$$

Select #3 at $7\frac{1}{2}$ in. on center, $A_s = 0.18$ in.$^2$/ft.

The temperature and shrinkage steel perpendicular to the main reinforcement is

$$A_{s\,min} = 0.002\, A_g = 0.002\,(3.25)12 = 0.078 \text{ in.}^2/\text{ft}$$

with a maximum spacing of the bars equal to $5t = 5(3.25) = 16.25$ in.

Select #3 at 16 in. on center, $A_s = 0.085$ in.$^2$/ft.

The diagonal parabolas in tension and compression or the shear along the four warped surface elements (Fig. 8.31 b, c, and d) cause axial force flow along the edge beams, being zero at the highest points and increasing linearly to a maximum compression at the support.

The maximum ultimate axial force is equal to the sum of the shear along the shell edge

$$C_{max} = S\,\frac{2a}{\cos\theta} \quad \text{where} \quad \tan\theta = \frac{f}{a} = \frac{15}{50} \quad \text{or} \quad \cos\theta = 0.958$$

$$C_u = 7.85\,\frac{100}{0.958} = 819.42 \text{ k}$$

The required cross-sectional area for the edge beam, as based on a short column laterally supported by the shell, is

$$A_g = \frac{P_u}{0.47f_c' + 0.0056f_y} \tag{1.50}$$

$$= \frac{819.42}{0.47(4) + 0.0056(50)} = 379.36 \text{ in.}^2 = 2.64 \text{ ft}^2$$

try 2 ft 0 in. $\times$ 1 ft 4 in., $A_g = 2.67$ ft$^2$.

The beam depth is decreased towards the high point. Keep in mind that bending in edge beams increases as they approach the abutments; this intersection of edge members with support should be designed separately.

The ultimate horizontal thrust component of the maximum axial edge beam force is equal to

$$C_{uh} = S_u\,(2a) = 7.85(100) = 785 \text{ k}$$

The ultimate thrust $H_u$ to be resisted at the base by a tie rod or by the abutment (Fig. 8.31a) is

$$\frac{C_{uh}}{\sqrt{2}} = \frac{H_u}{2} \quad \text{or} \quad H_u = C_{uh}\,\sqrt{2}$$

$$H_u = C_{uh}\,\sqrt{2} = 785\sqrt{2} = 1110.16 \text{ k}$$

$$H_u' = \frac{H_u}{\phi} = \frac{1110.16}{0.9} = 1233.51 \text{ k}$$

Select $3\frac{1}{4}$ in. diameter single strand, $P_u = 1250$ k (Table 3.1). The total vertical ultimate force, acting upon the foundation, is

$$V_u = \frac{(\frac{1}{2})100(100)94.2}{1000} = 471 \text{ k}$$

This result checks with summing up the vertical components of the maximum edge beam force

$$V_u = 2\left(\frac{819.42}{100/\cos\theta}\right)30 = 471 \text{ k}$$

**Example 8.10**  Design the roof of Example 8.9 in steel by using a triangular surface network (Fig. 8.31f). W-sections are placed in two layers along the straight line generators to form a square grid which is 12.5 × 12.5 ft in plan view. This square grid must be stabilized against shear distortions by triangulating it with tie rods following the curvature of the concave tension parabolas. Consider dead and live load each equal to 20 psf along the horizontal roof projection. Use A36 steel.

The shell analogy is applied for this approximate design, in other words, the member grid is considered to behave as a solid surface (see also Approximate Design of Braced Domes). The membrane forces are equal to

$$N = S = \pm\frac{wab}{2f} \tag{7.28}$$

$$= \frac{(20+20)50(50)}{2(15)1000} = 3.33 \text{ k/ft}$$

Each of the parallel linear members must carry the load per foot multiplied by the spacing of the grid, which in turn varies depending on the slope or location of the member. Here, the maximum slope of the edge member is conservatively used

$$P = 3.33\frac{12.5}{\cos\theta} = 3.33\frac{12.5}{0.958} = 43.45 \text{ k}$$

The bottom member acts as a simple column laterally supported at the grid intersection points. For the given slenderness ratio a section can be selected from the column tables of the *AISC Manual*

$$(Kl)_y = 1(12.5/\cos\theta) = 1(12.5/0.958) = 13.05$$

try W6 × 15.

The perpendicular members in the top layer not only carry the axial membrane forces but also must support in bending the purlins, the corrugated steel deck and roofing. The maximum moment for the continuous beam is approximated as (see also discussion of inclined beams)

$$M_{max} = \frac{wl^2}{10} = \frac{0.04(12.5)12.5^2}{10} = 7.81 \text{ ft-k}$$

The roof skin is considered stiff enough to prevent buckling of the member about its weak axis.

The moment is transformed by the bending factor into a fictitious axial load so that the column tables in the *AISC Manual* can be used

$$(Kl)_x = (Kl)_y \frac{r_y}{r_x} = \frac{1(12.5/\cos \theta)}{1.77} = 7.37$$

The total axial load, the top member must carry, is equal to

$$P + P' = P + B_x M_X \qquad\qquad (1.48)$$
$$= 43.45 + 0.456(7.81)12 = 43.45 + 42.74 = 86.19 \text{ k}$$

try $W6 \times 15$, $A = 4.43$ in.$^2$.

Remember, this approximate design approach in general overestimates the member size, hence not the section required but the next smaller one is selected to be checked precisely.

Note the effect of buckling or unbraced length is so small that the member can be assumed to fail in yielding rather than in inelastic buckling. Hence, the required cross-sectional area can be determined fast

$$A = \frac{P}{0.6F_y} = \frac{86.19}{22} = 3.92 \text{ in.}^2$$

Try $W6 \times 15$.

Diagonal members prevent the shear distortions of the rectangular grid under asymmetrical loading. For their design it is conservatively assumed that the entire uniform load is carried not by the straight W-sections but by the diagonal bars. The membrane forces along the diagonal directions are also $N = 3.33$ k/ft; however, in this case no arched parabolas are provided to support one-half of the load, hence the suspended cables must carry double as much. Taking into account the tie spacing and considering the roof to be shallow (i.e., maximum cable slope is neglected) yields following axial force (Fig. 8.31f)

$$T = 2[3.33(8.84)] = 58.87 \text{ k}$$

The required cross-sectional area is

$$A = \frac{T}{F_t} = \frac{58.87}{22} = 2.68 \text{ in.}^2$$

Select a flat bar $2\frac{3}{4} \times 1$ in., $A = 2.75$ in.$^2$.

The maximum compression in the edge beam at the support is equal to the sum of the shear along the membrane

$$C_{max} = 3.33 \frac{100}{\cos \theta} = 347.60 \text{ k}$$

The member must also resist one-half of the moment a typical interior straight member of the top layer carries

$$M_{max} = \frac{7.81}{2} = 3.91 \text{ ft-k}$$

This moment causes such small stresses as compared to the axial force that it can be ignored. The edge beam can be assumed to fail in compression yielding, since it is restrained from buckling by the roof framing. The required cross-sectional area is

$$A = \frac{C}{0.6F_y} = \frac{347.60}{22} = 15.80 \text{ in.}^2$$

Select $W12 \times 58$, $A = 17.0$ in.$^2$.

The tie rod has to resist following force

$$H = 3.33(100)\sqrt{2} = 470.93\text{k}$$

The required cross-sectional net area for the welded connections, is

$$A = \frac{H}{F_t} = \frac{470.93}{22} = 21.41 \text{ in.}^2$$

Select $W14 \times 74$, $A = 21.8$ in.$^2$.

The magnitude of the vertical reaction forces is

$$V = \frac{0.04(100)100}{2} = 200 \text{ k}$$

## Problems

**8.20** If the inverted umbrella unit of Example 8.8 is turned upside down to form a true umbrella with the exact same dimensions, what does change with respect to force flow in the shell units and edge beams?

**8.21** For the following cases in Fig. 8.28 investigate the force action along the shell elements and beams. Show the position of the tie rods if needed for resistance of lateral thrust

   (a)  case (C) (bottom);

   (b)  case (F) (top)—then investigate this case by dropping the horizontal ridges inward;

   (c)  case (G) (bottom)—then investigate this case by letting the ridges be horizontal.

**8.22** A reinforced concrete hipped roof [Fig. 8.28F, (top)] consisting of four warped rectangular surfaces with horizontal ridge beams is supported by four corner columns. The roof covers an area of $120 \times 100$ ft and has a rise of 15 ft. It must support a live load of 20 psf and an equivalent uniform dead load for shell finish and edge beams of 5 psf. Use a minimum shell thickness of 3 in. and 4000 psi concrete together with Grade 50 steel. Determine the shell reinforcement and approximate sizes of beams and tie rods.

**8.23** A hypar concrete shell, 3 in. thick, consists of two single straight-edged hypar units, each $88 \times 88$ ft in plan projection with a height of $f = 11$ ft; in other words, an identical unit is added to the one shown in Fig. 8.31. The roof is supported by three piers, at the corners on one side and at midspan on the opposite side. The shell must support a 30 psf snow load and 41 psf dead load; check if the assumption for the shell weight is reasonable. Use 4000 psi concrete and Grade 50 steel. Determine for this preliminary investigation the shell reinforcement, approximate sizes of edge members and tie rod at base, and the vertical reaction forces.

**8.24** Design the roof of Problem 8.23 as a three-way surface grid structure similar to Example 8.10. The main straight lines are spaced at 11 ft in both directions. Consider the average uniform dead load to be 20 psf. Use $A36$ steel. Determine the preliminary member sizes.

**8.25** An identical roof assemblage is added to the structure of Problem 8.24 to form a new roof consisting of four, single straight-edged hypar units sitting on four abutments located at the middle of each outer face. Determine the critical forces in membrane and edge members, and reaction forces.

**8.26** Determine the minimum shell thickness [Eq. (8.2)] as based on strength considerations only for the shell in Problem 8.23.

**8.27** Determine the approximate maximum compression and tension stresses for a concrete shell, 3 in. thick, having the form of an elliptic paraboloid on a square plan of $100 \times 100$ ft with $f = 10$ ft at perimeter midspan. Ignore bending at the corners and consider the shell hinged to the edge beams. The shell is supported at its four corners, and boundary members carry the tangential membrane shear. The dome supports its own weight of 40 psf (check) and 20 psf snow load. Use 4000 psi concrete and Grade 50 steel. Find also the main shell reinforcement and the tie rods necessary to balance the dome thrust.

**8.28** Determine the maximum compression stresses for the dome in Problem 8.27 by treating the radius of curvature of the parabolic generators like circular arcs.

**8.29** Determine the maximum compression and shear forces in the membrane approximately, by letting the elliptic paraboloid of Problems 8.27 cover a rectangular plan of $80 \times 100$ ft with $f_x = 8$ ft (on 80 ft side) and $f_y = 10$ ft.

**8.30** Determine the membrane stresses in one of the 4 in. thick saddle shells of the Ponce Coliseum (Fig. 8.29D); a typical quadrant is $116 \times 138$ ft and has a rise of $f = 20$ ft. Check the stresses for the loading case of a wind pressure of 56 psf together with the shell dead weight ignoring the weight of the edge beams. Then, consider that the membrane was actually post-tensioned by 10–20 k/ft to minimize crack formation.

## 8.5 OTHER SURFACE FORMS

Of the infinite number of bent surface systems generated from the common basic shapes that were just discussed, the group of intersecting shells seems to appear quite frequently. The typical intersecting forms are single-curvature cylinders, as well as double-curvature elliptic and hyperbolic paraboloids. The crossing of two similar shells results in a rectangular plan, while three shells produce a hexagonal plan, hence the number of intersecting shells determines the plan form. The Romanesque cross-vault is the most familiar example of intersecting cylindrical surfaces. Also familiar is the cloister-vault constructed from four cylindrical sectors, yielding the polygonal dome (Fig. 8.13).

To develop some feeling for the behavior of these relatively simple forms, let two identical saddle surfaces intersect at right angles to cover a square plan (Fig. 8.32). First, visualize the four independent vault segments to be supported by diagonal arches. Each vault,

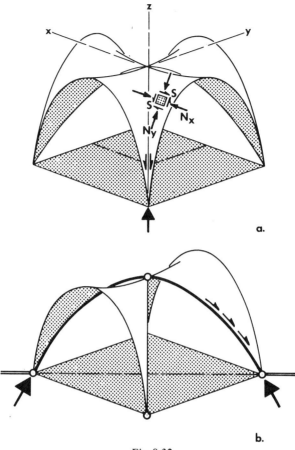

Fig. 8.32

in turn, consists of a series of adjacent parabolic arches parallel to the free edge, which transfer a uniform load, nearly in pure compression (i.e., no bending), to the diagonal ribs, or barrel intersections which, in turn, carry the resultant forces to the abutments. However, in reality, the structure is not a groined vault but a groined shell, which does not need diagonal arches as support, but possibly only stiffening edge members.

The primary shell action will be along the arches ($N_y$), since only little resistance can be provided perpendicular to the free edges (i.e., $N_x \cong 0$). While the arches in a vault are subject to bending, the arches in this thin shell cannot do so; here bending must be transformed into shear. Thus, no bending will be generated along the diagonal ribs, which will carry the resultant shell forces in purely axial manner to the abutments.

Some typical examples of building structures using the principle of intersecting shells are shown in Fig. 8.33.

The Good Hope Center at Cape Town, South Africa (a), is derived from two intersecting cylindrical shells, forming a cross-vault on a square base supported on four buttresses. The shell is composed of nearly equilateral triangular precast components varying in length from 11.5 to 13 ft, and in depth from 1.5 to 2.5 ft. The three intersecting, circular, cylindrical shell units for the Air Terminal at St. Louis (d) are based on the same geometri-

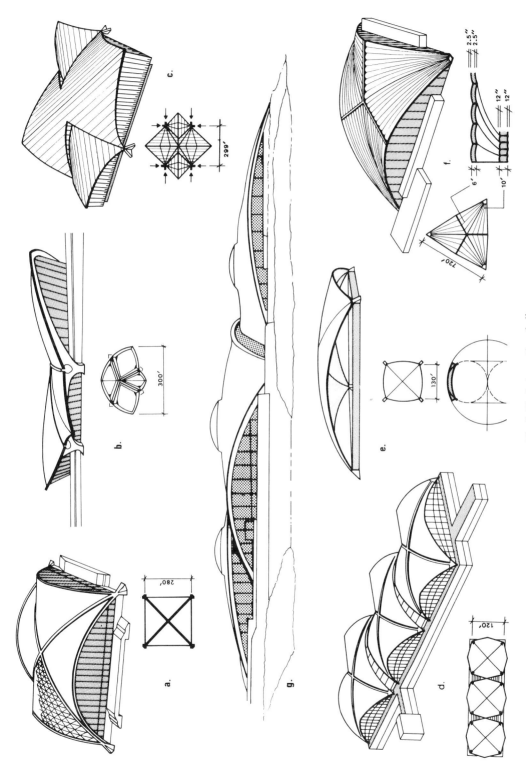

Fig. 8.33 Intersecting shells.

499

cal principles, though each shell cantilevers slightly beyond the square base to form an octagonal plan projection. The typical concrete shell thickness is $4\frac{1}{2}$ in. and increases to 8 in. at the edges.

The thin shell roof for a supermarket near Honolulu (e) is composed of equal double curvature torus segments. The shell does not employ any edge beams but instead requires the edges to be slightly thicker than the typical 3–4 in. thickness in the crown area.

The CNIT Exposition Hall, Paris, France (f), is the world's largest thin shell concrete roof. Because of the enormous span of 720 ft, and to avoid buckling, the roof had to be built as a double shell: 6 ft apart at the crown increasing to 10 ft at the abutments. The shells are tied together by a system of $2\frac{1}{2}$-in. thick longitudinal and transverse diaphragms. Each shell layer is corrugated and $2\frac{1}{2}$ in. thick, changing to about 12 in. at the supports. From a geometrical point of view, the roof is generated by three 720-ft wide, 152-ft high parabolic cylinders that intersect along lines that radiate from the abutments, thereby covering an equilateral triangular plan of about 5.5 acres! From a structural point of view, one may visualize the roof as three wide arches meeting at the crown line, where each of them, in turn, consists of a series of adjacent arches that fan out from the supports. Because of the asymmetrical shape of the arch forms as seen in plan, that is, the inclination of the adjacent arches, lateral thrust is generated along the crown line, which is balanced along the horizontal star-like rib system. These ribs divide the roof into three sections, in which corrugations fan out from the abutments towards the ribs at the crown, reflecting the intensity of force flow along the arches. The horizontal building thrust is resisted at the base by cables that tie the abutments together along the building edges.

The Olympic Ice Stadium at Grenoble, France (c), consists of two orthogonally intersecting cylindrical double shells. The large shell sits on four supports, while each of the two smaller ones is supported only by two abutments. A portal frame links the two small shells along the crown line across the large shell, so that, under asymmetrical loading, they can stabilize each other. The thickness of the double shell is 4.26 ft, where the upper and lower shells are each typically 2.4 in. thick. The concrete surfaces are tied together with webs which fan out from the abutments and also run parallel to the linear form generators. The roof structure can be visualized, similar to the CNIT Exposition Hall, as four arched shells, each of which consists of a series of adjacent arches, where the thrust caused by the inclined arches is balanced along the prestressed rib at the crown line. In addition to this arch action, however, there is cantilever action. The roof thrust is balanced partly by ties that connect the four abutments, and partly by inclined foundation piles.

Sculptural considerations, and not engineering criteria, were the basis for the design of the roof for the TWA Terminal Building at Kennedy Airport, New York (b). It consists of four independent spherical lightweight concrete shell segments, where each of these cantilevering, wing-like shells is bounded by edge beams and supported by two buttresses which are inclined along the direction of the resultant force action. Since each of the shell units only rests on two abutments, the units must stabilize each other. This is achieved by connecting the interior edge beams to a common plate at the intersection of the four units, located near the center of the roof. Continuous skylights span the 3-ft gap between the shells along the interior edge beams.

One of the recent impressive shell structures is the sports center in Chamonix (g) at the foot of Mont Blanc in the French Alps. It consists of intersecting shallow equilateral spherical triangles with heavy peripheral arched edge beams; the span range of the shells is from 98 to 196 ft for the largest one.

The wealth of other bent surface forms can only be suggested by the examples in Fig. 8.34. The shells range from forms derived from basic geometries (p), (o), (n), (s) to cate-

Fig. 8.34   Other surface structures.

nary shells that reflect the funicular shape of the shell's dead weight (r). They range from scalloped forms (e), and corrugated shells, such as beams or arches formed from a segment of the rotational hyperboloid (Figs. 7.3 and 7.4), to a habitable sculpture (q) or complex, so-called freeforms (b), which may be obtained by combing surfaces which have the parabola as a common geometrical generator. For instance, the elliptic paraboloid or parabolic dome is often used in combination with the circular conoid, which looks like a truncated, inverted parabolic dome, with the hyperbolic paraboloid as a transition system between the other shapes; the slopes between the various basic surfaces must be perfectly matched along their edges.

The shell forms may evolve out of considerations of minimum weight or construction process. They may just be derived as based on purely functional, economic, and engineering aspects, or the image of the building and its spiritual expression may be the essential issue.

Dynamic forms which seem to be fluid and in motion, such as the helix spiraling upward (g), (f), (i), the sprawling amoeba (r), the opening-up of the sail-like triangular shells (c), the flying wing shapes (h), and the unfolding of fan-shaped surfaces (k) stand quite in contrast to more static forms, such as the egg sitting on a stem (s), or a container with its opening at the top (m).

With respect to the development of freely shaped concrete shells, Heinz Isler of Switzerland must be considered as the most creative designer currently. His shells express such an elegant lightness with their edges free of beams often only stabilized by counter-curvatures; they seem to float in such a perfectly natural manner clearly expressing their derivation from funicular considerations rather than mathematical geometries (Fig. 8.34u). Isler determines the shell shapes primarily through experiments by reversing hanging membranes, by using pneumatic membranes as well as flowing forms. For shallow pneumatic bubble shapes the air pressure perpendicular to the tensile membrane is nearly equal to the uniform gravity loading, thus causing only compression in the corresponding rigid shells. In his "flow method" Isler uses the varied advancing velocity of viscous fluids inside a tube, where it is zero along the wall but maximum at the center, as the model for producing impressive shapes.

The shell forms range from surfaces derived from existing geometries as well as mathematical and behavioral formulations to the opposite, the antistructure. Kiesler called his endless house (d) "continuous tension." Here the free-modeled shell shape responds directly to the life of the interior of the organism; it is not derived from geometry. The chapel at Ronchamp (a) is not subject anymore to the laws of reasoning, such as structural interpretations or mathematical definitions. The suspended concrete double-shell roof resting on the tapered heavy walls, creates a mysterious interplay of masses and surfaces, exposing a deeply spiritual and timeless expression. The chapel does not seem a building in the usual sense; its structure is resolved in its form, reflecting poetry in sculptural art. Its perfect correctness cannot be interpreted anymore with the language used in this context.

Following, some of the buildings in Fig. 8.34 are discussed briefly. The bent surfaces of the Sydney Opera House (c) are segments of equivalent spheres ($R$ = 246 ft), which allowed a maximum use of repetitive elements. The largest shell rises 220 ft. The shell surface is built of a fan of adjacent pointed arches that are comprised of precast concrete segments post-tensioned together. The radiating, similar ribs lie on the great circles; they are hollow, wide open Y-tubes at the upper surface portion, and change to narrow solid T-sections as they approach the pedestal. The behavior of the shell-like surface is that of individual inclined arches supported at the base and ridge. The ridge beam in turn is tangentially supported by the side shell that acts similar to a tripod. It should be emphasized that the spherical surfaces of the Sydney Opera only give the appearance of the shell but are not true shells!

The wooden grid shell of the Mannheim Exhibition, Germany (r), is of enormous proportions, covering an area of 80,000 ft$^2$. The surface geometry of the catenary, two-way, double-layered lattice structure is derived by inverting a hanging chain model to a standing position (i.e., mirror image) and thus is primarily curved synclastically. The out-of-plane stiffness of the shell, necessary for buckling resistance, is obtained mainly by the double layer laths, while the in-plane stiffness of the two-way grid is increased by cross-cables connecting the joints. The Western Hemlock laths, nearly 2 × 2 in. in section, are bolted together to form an even 20 × 20 in. square mesh along the horizontal crown portion while, along the sides, the grid is an uneven, diamond-shaped mesh. The timber lattice is covered with translucent PVC skin reinforced with woven Trevira net.

The Meeting Center at Albany, New York (s), consists of an 80-ft deep, nearly ellipsoidal, inverted concrete shell (200 × 280 ft) placed eccentrically on a three-legged pedestal. A post-tensioned triangular tension ring stiffens the shell at about midheight, as does one prestressed interior slab. The thickness of the shell varies from 1.5 ft at the top to 5 ft at the pedestal. The radially arranged steel roof trusses, which carry the steel deck and concrete fill, are supported along the shell edge and the core.

The roof of the B'nai Jehudah in Kansas City (i) consists of two parts: the inner pipe-framed cone and the outer helix. The conical helix, which is formed by straight long-span steel joists, is supported along the exterior walls and on the inner cone, whereas the upper cone is framed with exposed 5-in. tubular steel pipes and supported by an eccentric concrete mast and prestressed tie-down cables anchored into the bedrock.

The fan-shaped roof of the Blossom Music Center at Akron (j) looks similar to a truncated cone. It consists of radially arranged steel pipe trusses that cantilever 28 ft beyond the girder support at one end and rest on a huge 560-ft span, peripheral, inclined steel box-girder arch at the other end. The arch, in turn, is supported by sloping tapered steel box columns.

The thrust of the fan-shaped half-dome in case (k) is supported by a single flying arched buttress. The thrust at the base due to the radial, folded sectors, which form the dome and the buttress, is balanced by a system of prestressed, subgrade concrete tie beams.

The saddle shell roof in case (e) is constructed from 2 × 6 in. rafters, 18 ft long, placed side-by-side to form a solid surface. The roof shape is generated by translating the 18-ft members along the straight line axis and the undulating outer edges.

The complex, spiral-like roof of the United Church of Rowayton, Connecticut (f), consists of intricately shaped, glued–laminated arches tied together by purlins with the sheathing forming a stressed-skin structure. Similarly, the spiral roof of case (g) is developed from inclined, glued–laminated rafters that are supported centrally by a compression ring at the top, and by brick walls along the periphery.

The St. Louis Planetarium (p) is formed by a rotational hyperboloid of one sheet, as commonly used for cooling towers (o). The thin concrete shell is generated by revolving a straight line (see Fig. 7.3).

The Sanctuary for the Dead Sea Scrolls in Jerusalem (m) is a double parabolic dome that is open at the top.

The Civic Center Synagogue in Lower Manhattan, New York (l), is enclosed by three concrete shells: the 7-in. thick front wall shell, the 4-in. thick rear wall shell, and the 5-in. suspended-like roof shell.

The Eastman Kodak Pavilion (b) is a self-supporting, freeform sculpture with arbitrary curvatures. The concrete shell supports itself primarily by giant tapered columns, with a clear span of 117 ft on one side and closely spaced spatial portal arches on the other side.

The slender, graceful shell for the Garden Center in Camorino (u), Switzerland, is $3\frac{1}{8}$ in. thick with the free edges in tension, and is supported at four spreading points on a square grid of 89 × 89 ft.

# 9 SOFT SHELL STRUCTURES

Membrane structures are extremely lightweight, quite contrary to the conventional rigid structures where weight resists the instability caused by lateral force action. The thin tensile surfaces are supported by air pressure or rigid members such as masts, arches, or frames. In traditional gravity-type buildings the inherent massiveness of material transmits a feeling of stability and protection. Tensile structures, on the other hand, seem to be weightless and to float in the air; their stability is dependent on an intricate, curved three-dimensional geometry in which the skin is prestretched. These antigravity structures require a new aesthetics, now the curve rather than the straight line is the generator of space. This aesthetics is closely related to biological structures such as spider webs, the wings of flies, bird and bat wings, and liquid skins like water drops, soap bubbles, and bubble conglomerations in sea foam. This close relationship of the tensile membranes to natural forms makes it possible to truly integrate them with the landscape.

Though membrane structures are presently being discovered and developed, the principle of employing fabrics and nets as structures has been known for thousands of years. They have been used as fishing nets, hunting nets, umbrellas, awnings, sails, kites, tents, and for many other purposes.

The Romans used inflated bags of animal skins to support bridges and rafts. They used sun awnings made of cloth to cover their amphitheaters. Similarly, in southern Spain awnings have been strung over streets since the sixteenth century. Also, umbrellas may be considered forerunners of tensile membrane structures having been known by Egyptians and Assyrians. In 1783, the Montgolfier brothers, in France, reinvented the hot-air balloon made of paper and linen. Today helium-filled balloons are also used for construction purposes and unloading of cargo ships.

Tents probably represent the closest relationship to the soft shell structures of today; they are civilization's earliest form of dwelling. To the nomads, the lightness, flexibility, portability, and ease of construction are all features necessary to their living style. The tent can be found in extremely diverse climates extending from the deserts of Saudi Arabia to the high altitudes of the Himalayan mountains, from the steppe of Mongolia and the taiga forest to the arctic tundra.

There are many forms of tent construction ranging from conical, dome, vaulted, box, and wedge, to pole tents or any other combination. The membranes may only be hung for shading purposes; they may be prestretched to provide the primary enclosure; or they may just cover the building frame. Familiar to the reader are the black tents of the Bedouins, Berbers, Kurds, and many other tribes. These tents are generally woven from goats' hair, and are primarily prestressed tensile structures, having only a few compression members as support. On the other hand the tepee of the Indians of the North American plains employs straight poles to form a conical frame which is covered with buffalo skin.

Covered circus tents were introduced last century, in the early 1820s. The Ringling Brothers tent of the 1940s could seat an audience of 13,000! The early development of the tensile membrane in modern architecture may be traced back to V. G. Shookhov's daring steel sheet tents for the Nijny-Novgorod Industrial Fair of 1896 (the circular tent had a diameter of 223 ft); the construction principle for the pavilions was far ahead of its time. An influence may be seen in the work of the Italian futurist Antonio Sant' Elia, who before World War I experimented with the dynamism of tension to express movement. After the Revolution, some of the Russian constructivists continued to experiment with spatial tensile forms, as did Naum Gabo in so many of his powerful constructivist sculptures of the 1930s. One of the first, real lasting tensile structures of these early years of development is Marcel Breuer's famous armchair of 1925, in which canvas was stretched between the metal-tube skeleton. The true application of the tensile membrane surface to architecture happened in the 1960s. Some of the important contributors to the recent development of suspension structures are Walter Bird, David Geiger, Fritz Leonhard, Frei Otto, Robert Le Ricolais, Eero Saarinen, Rene Sarger, Fred Severud, Peter Stromeyer, Lev Zetlin, and Kenzo Tange.

The Raleigh Arena (1953) responds clearly to the nature of the surface tension with its saddle roof; it is regarded as the first important modern tensile roof. Frei Otto is one of the most prominent pioneers of tensile architecture; he started his research in the early 1950s. He first explored the potential of the fabric membrane and then the cable net for the large-scale tent, climaxing in the roof for the Olympic Games at Munich, Germany, in 1972. The development of pneumatic structures began in the United States with Walter Bird's first radome which he built in 1946 for the military to house radar for defense and space communications. The U.S. Pavilion at the Expo 70 in Osaka, Japan (see Fig. 9.7a), designed by the architects Davis, Brody, Chermayeff, Geismar, de Harak, and the engineer David Geiger, together with the other pneumatic buildings at the exhibition started the enthusiasm, and made the public aware of the formal and large-scale potential of the pneumatic principle. The 80,638-seat Pontiac Stadium (see Fig. 9.7e), completed in 1975, is currently the largest air-supported roof in the world. The Teflon-coated fiberglass membrane has a projected life of at least 20 years. It clearly shows that this type of roof structure cannot be considered as temporary anymore; the penumatic principle is now in competition with traditional rigid building concepts.

The fabric of soft shell structures used to be made of cotton or other natural fibers; today it is fabricated from high strength synthetic fibers and then coated to last. Eventually, stronger fibers, like the heat resisting carbon fibers or even whisker fibers, will make much larger span structures possible. One can conclude that fabric structures should not just be regarded as circus or camping tents, but as potential permanent structures; in 1973, the first nontemporary fabric structure in the United States was completed for La Verne College in California. Fabric structures can resist extreme weather in zones ranging from Saudi Arabia to Alaska. They provide relatively low cost shelters, and can be prefabricated, easily transported anywhere, and quickly erected because they are lightweight. Membrane structures are also safe due to their lightness; nobody gets hurt if there is structural failure; but rarely will a local failure even result in the collapse of the entire membrane because of its continuous character. Fabric skins are presently used for sheltering sports arenas, tennis courts, pool enclosures, greenhouses, convention/exhibition and market halls, stores, storage and warehousing, construction shelters, production spaces, shopping streets, reservoir covers, and disaster shelters among others.

## 9.1 TENSILE MEMBRANES

From a structural point of view, tensile membranes may be classified according to their behavior as isotropic and anisotropic membranes (Fig. 9.1).

Woven fabrics must be considered anisotropic membranes since they exhibit different behavior in the warp and filling directions. The fabric consists of sets of twisted yarns interlaced at right angles, where the yarn is formed by twisting several filaments together, and is then woven into a fabric using one of many possible weaving patterns. The yarns running longitudinally down the loom are called warp yarns and the ones running crosswise are called filling yarns, weft yarns, or woof yarns. The tensile strength of the fabric is a function of the number of filaments in the twisted yarn, the number of yarns per inch of fabric, and the type of weaving pattern. The typical woven fabric consists of the straight warp yarn and the undulating filling yarn (Fig. 9.1). It is apparent that the springlike filler yarn elongates more than the straight length-wise yarn. From a structural point of view the weave pattern may be visualized as a very fine-meshed cable network of a rectangular grid where openings clearly indicate the lack of shear stiffness. The fact of the different behavioral characteristics along the warp and filling as well as in the diagonal directions makes the  membrane anisotropic. However, when the woven fabric is coated the rectangular meshes are filled, thus effectively reducing the difference in behavior along the orthogonal yarns so that the fabric may then be considered isotropic, similar to the cable network with the triangular meshes, plastic films, metal skins and other hanging semirigid or rigid shells.

The fabric must be coated not just from a stress point of view but also to make it airtight and waterproof, weatherproof (against effects of sunlight, acids, gas, etc.), and to make it resistant to ripping and abrasion. In addition, the coating facilitates the joining of the fabric pieces; the seams are bonded primarily by heat and pressure rather than by sewing or cementing.

The scale of the structure determines the selection of the tensile membrane type. For small-scale shelters, such as camping tents, awnings, canopies, outdoor curtains, sun and wind shields, etc., natural or synthetic canvas is used. The fabrics weigh between 1 and 2 oz/ft$^2$; they may be painted or coated, and have an average life of 5–10 years. The strength of vinyl-coated cotton fabric is about 160 lb/in. and, without coating, 120 lb/in. The common synthetic fabrics have a similar weight and strength to those of cotton fabrics. Plastic films have a relatively low tensile strength, such as, 16 lb/in. for a 20 mil vinyl film at low room temperature, which decreases with increase in temperature. For larger scale structures, stronger and thicker membranes are used. They are most often translucent nylon, polyester or fiberglass, coated with vinyl or Teflon.

Currently, the typical fabric for commercial, nonpermanent tent and pneumatic structures is polyester coated with polyvinyl chloride (PVC). It will not stretch as much as vinyl-coated nylon and is also much stronger, and can sustain its strength under proper treatment for 10–15 years, while nylon has an average life of only 5–7 years.

# TENSILE MEMBRANES

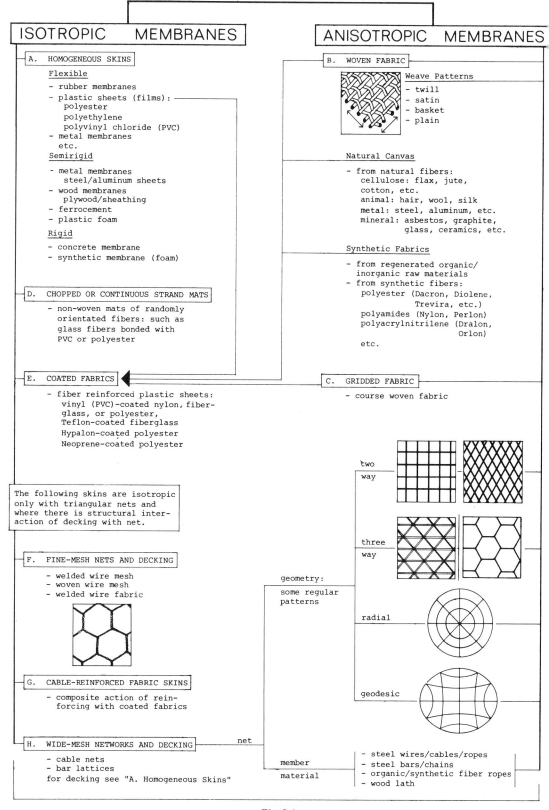

**ISOTROPIC MEMBRANES**

**A. HOMOGENEOUS SKINS**

Flexible

- rubber membranes
- plastic sheets (films):
  polyester
  polyethylene
  polyvinyl chloride (PVC)
- metal membranes
  etc.

Semirigid

- metal membranes
  steel/aluminum sheets
- wood membranes
  plywood/sheathing
- ferrocement
- plastic foam

Rigid

- concrete membrane
- synthetic membrane (foam)

**D. CHOPPED OR CONTINUOUS STRAND MATS**

- non-woven mats of randomly
  orientated fibers: such as
  glass fibers bonded with
  PVC or polyester

**E. COATED FABRICS**

- fiber reinforced plastic sheets:
  vinyl (PVC)-coated nylon, fiber-
  glass, or polyester,
  Teflon-coated fiberglass
  Hypalon-coated polyester
  Neoprene-coated polyester

The following skins are isotropic
only with triangular nets and
where there is structural interaction of decking with net.

**F. FINE-MESH NETS AND DECKING**

- welded wire mesh
- woven wire mesh
- welded wire fabric

**G. CABLE-REINFORCED FABRIC SKINS**

- composite action of reinforcing with coated fabrics

**H. WIDE-MESH NETWORKS AND DECKING**

- cable nets
- bar lattices
for decking see "A. Homogeneous Skins"

**ANISOTROPIC MEMBRANES**

**B. WOVEN FABRIC**

Weave Patterns

- twill
- satin
- basket
- plain

Natural Canvas

- from natural fibers:
  cellulose: flax, jute,
  cotton, etc.
  animal: hair, wool, silk
  metal: steel, aluminum, etc.
  mineral: asbestos, graphite,
           glass, ceramics, etc.

Synthetic Fabrics

- from regenerated organic/
  inorganic raw materials
- from synthetic fibers:
  polyester (Dacron, Diolene,
             Trevira, etc.)
  polyamides (Nylon, Perlon)
  polyacrylnitrilene (Dralon,
                      Orlon)
  etc.

**C. GRIDDED FABRIC**

- course woven fabric

two
way

three
way

radial

geodesic

geometry:

some regular
patterns

net

member

material

- steel wires/cables/ropes
- steel bars/chains
- organic/synthetic fiber ropes
- wood lath

Fig. 9.1

For permanent fabric structures, especially of the very large scale, such as stadiums, fiberglass coated with Teflon is being employed. Although it is about five times more expensive than vinyl-coated polyester, it is much stronger, stiffer, more permanent, incombustible and more reliable; its minimum life span is guaranteed as 20 years. While the prestressed polyester fabric creeps under constant loading over time, which makes it very difficult to predict its behavior, fiberglass coated with Teflon is much less susceptible to permanent elongations and hence more predictable. Vinyl-coated polyester produces black smoke under fire and must be regularly cleaned or painted. Fiberglass coated with Teflon, in contrast, is incombustible and does not contribute any fuel or smoke to a fire, and it is self-cleaning, that is, dirt does not stick to it, and hence needs no regular maintenance. The Teflon surface rejects approximately 75% of the sun's heat, and its translucent quality significantly cuts a building's daytime artificial lighting needs. It is claimed that the savings on lighting and cooling costs in summer, can outweigh the disadvantage of higher heating costs in winter due to larger heat loss.

The brittle character of the fiberglass fabric must be considered in the design and construction of a structure; prefabricated sheets are handled in rolls rather than folded as the much more flexible polyester fabric. The tensile strengths of the most common coated fabrics are given in Table 9.1.

#### Table 9.1   Tensile Strengths of Some Common Coated Fabrics

| Coated Fabric | Tensile Strength, lb/in. |
|---|---|
| Vinyl-coated nylon fabric | 200–400 lb/in. |
| Vinyl-coated polyester fabric | 300–700 lb/in. |
| Vinyl-coated fiberglass fabric | 300–800 lb/in. |
| Teflon-coated fiberglass fabric | 300–1000 lb/in. |

For example, the Owens-Corning Structo-Fab 450 fiberglass fabrics coated with Teflon is 0.038 in. thick and weighs 45 oz/yd$^2$. Its tensile strip strength along the dry warp is 800 lb/in. and 700 lb/in. along the dry fill.

Coated fabrics should have an ultimate strip tensile strength of not less than four times the maximum fabric stress in the warp and filling directions. This high safety factor takes into account that the strength of the fabric is lower under the permanent prestress.

The construction of a fabric structure involves true team interaction among the yarn producer (e.g., Owens-Corning Fiberglas Corp. for Beta fiberglass filament), the weaver (e.g., Chemfab for fiberglass fabric), the coater (e.g., DuPont Corp. for Teflon), the fabricator/contractor (e.g., Birdair Structures, Inc., Irwin Industries, Inc., for fabric structures coated with Teflon), and the designers.

As the scale of the structure increases, the fabric must be reinforced so that the skin is relieved of stresses which it may not be able to resist by itself; these forces are transferred and carried instead by a web of cables. The cables may be sewn into the edges of the prefab strips which are then clamped together at the site, or they may be attached to the fabrics by being covered with fabric strips; they may be heat-sealed directly into and across the fabric envelope for pneumatic structures. For larger tent structures the fabric is attached to the cable network.

The cable reinforcing may only appear at points of stress concentration, that is at specific locations, or it may form a regular pattern in one or two directions. Where the fabric strips are attached to each other, the overlapping and doubling of the material results in a reinforcing of the membrane that is equivalent to small cables.

For very large-scale structures, cable nets form the primary surface which supports the roof cladding as is further discussed on the following pages. Some typical network layouts are shown in Fig. 9.1; there are infinitely more net forms possible. Obviously, the nets with meshes of the same size and member length offer the advantage of repetitive infill panels, though one must keep in mind that under load the regular pattern will be distorted.

For hanging polygonal or synclastic dish-shaped roofs as well as for flat anticlastic surfaces, semirigid/rigid tensile members or surfaces may have to be used since the missing proper countercurvature cannot provide the necessary stability.

Typical roof details for tensile membranes are shown in Fig. 9.2. While simply suspended roofs need stiffness and/or weight as provided by concrete shells and continuous rigid members (Fig. 3.5), prestressed membranes should have light and flexible cladding so that the necessary pretensioning forces can be reduced to a minimum, since larger prestress forces require larger boundary structures. Further, the roof cladding should be flexible to allow for the large deflections of the cable network. Typical lightweight decking employed include wooden panels and corrugated sheeting made from steel, aluminum, plastics, asbestos-cement, and reinforced gypsum; insulation may be placed on top and covered with several layers of roofing felt. For large-scale penumatic roofs, fabric panels (e.g., Teflon-coated fiberglass) are clamped to the cable lattice.

The intersecting cables of the State Fair Arena in Raleigh (Fig. 9.2a) are fastened to each other at points of intersection and form a network. The corrugated metal sheets, in turn, are bolt-clipped to the cables (see also Fig. 9.17q).

The 2 X 8 in. wood plank roof deck of the Ingalls Hockey Rink at Yale University (b) is laid across and nailed to double 2 X 6 in. wood nailers which are bolted to the transverse cables spaced at 6 ft (see Fig. 9.17s).

The air supported low-profile cable roofs of larger scale (see Fig. 9.7) consist of a cable network of relatively large spacing to which the edges of the fabric panels are clamped. The fabric spans the distance between the cables. Typical connection details are shown for cases (d)–(g) of Fig. 9.2.

For the anticlastic membrane roofs of the Krylatskoe cycle track of the 1980 Moscow Olympic Games, not cable nets but 0.158-in. thick steel bands about 13 ft wide were used and connected in the transverse direction by continuous steel purlins.

The cables of the roof of the U.S. Pavilion at Osaka (see Fig. 9.7a) are clamped together at the intersection points and the skirts of the vinyl-coated fiberglass fabric are attached to the cables below [case (f)]. The joining of fabric to fabric was done by heat sealing with the same vinyl which covers the fabric.

The Pontiac Stadium roof (see Fig. 9.7e) consists of nine 3-in. diameter steel cables spanning in each of the diagonal directions. The edges of the Teflon-coated fiberglass panels are bordered with $\frac{1}{2}$-in. diameter nylon ropes. The adjoining fabric panels are covered with neoprene and then clamped between aluminum strips [case (e)]. The overlapping neoprene provides a waterproof seal for the bolted joint.

Using a second or multiple inner membranes called liners below the main roof skin (h) changes the ceiling geometry from concave to convex. A stagnant air space is created which, together with the coating, acts as a thermal insulation and reduces heat loss as well as improves acoustics and fire safety; in winter, hot air can be passed through the air space to melt snow.

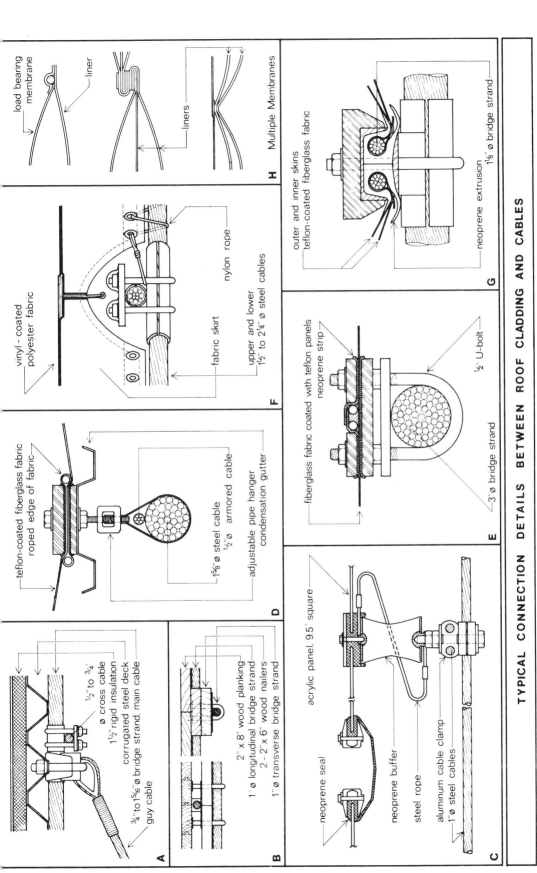

**TYPICAL CONNECTION DETAILS BETWEEN ROOF CLADDING AND CABLES**

Fig. 9.2

Many tent-type structures use arches and frames as major supports which usually directly support the fabric. Tents using masts as primary supports generally employ a radial cable network to carry and pretension the fabric membrane.

The Teflon-coated fiberglass fabric of La Verne College (see Fig. 9.18d) is factory fabricated; it was unrolled at the site and placed over the central mast to which a system of radial cables was already attached. This cable network supports and pretensions the membrane. Also the roof skin of the umbrella-like tent structures for the Jeddah International Airport in Saudi Arabia (see Fig. 9.18k) consists of a Teflon-coated fiberglass fabric stretched between the tension ring at the crown and the cables between the four steel pylons along the base. Radial cables were laced into sleeves in the fabric to stretch and strengthen the membrane.

Large-scale tent structures, such as the Munich Olympic Stadium (Fig. 9.2c and Fig. 9.18j), require special membrane detailing. The primary structure of the cable-net supports the separated secondary structure of acrylic panels on top of it. The panels are bolted to the network at cable intersection points. Neoprene buffers separate the panels from the steel cables. They act as shock absorbers to prevent the breakage of the plastic panels since the differential movement of the net cannot be transferred to the panels and since the temperature difference causes extensive change of panel sizes. A steel rope connecting the panel to the cable-net is provided as an additional safety precaution in case of buffer failure.

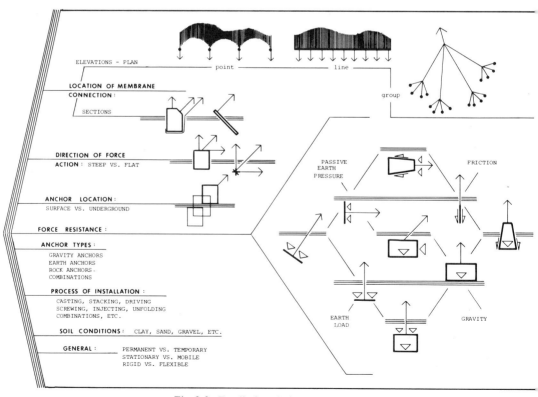

**Fig. 9.3** Tensile foundation principles.

## 9.2  TENSILE FOUNDATIONS

Tensile foundations must withstand the vertical uplift as well as the horizontal thrust forces due to external and prestress loading. The lift forces can be resisted by counteracting weight as well as by anchorage to the ground or to other building structures. The different ways in which foundations or ground anchorages can support tension is shown in Fig. 9.3. Vertical reactions can be provided by gravity, such as the weight of the foundation, ballast and earth loads as well as by friction of the anchorage along its contact surfaces, and any combination of the above. The horizontal thrust forces are either balanced by struts and/or slabs, which act as braces from one side to the other, or by compression rings; or they are resisted by passive earth pressure and/or skin friction. Some other considerations related to tension anchor design are identified in Fig. 9.3. Tensile membrane forces can be transferred to the foundations in a continuous uniform manner by employing, for example, strip footings, or they can be transferred with the help of edge cables to point supports, such as anchors or concrete piers. Tensile forces of large magnitude, as in guy cables, may be carried directly by one foundation or they may be broken down and resisted by a group of anchors.

The selection of the anchorage system depends, among other criteria, on the magnitude of the force action, the capacity of the soil, the strength of the membrane, the capacity and spacing of the anchors, the construction of the membrane along its base, and the nature of the structure (e.g., permanence).

Various tension foundations are identified in Fig. 9.4 and classified as

- Soil anchors
- Gravity anchors
- Rock anchors
- Compression rings
- Tensions rings
- Special foundations

Soil anchors can be easily transported, installed, and removed. Their capacity depends on the strength of both the anchor itself and the soil. There are many types of soil anchors; for more precise information the reader must refer to the literature provided by the producers. Earth anchors can be organized basically into two groups:

- Screw anchors for lighter soils
- Spread anchors

Since the soil capacity may be possibly reduced due to the process of installation, that is, due to the ramming or screwing of the anchor, a safety factor of 3.0 is generally applied to the maximum calculated loads for the selection of the soil anchors. The soil capacity around the anchor may be increased by injecting cement grout.

Gravity anchors prevent the vertical uplift simply by having enough counteracting weight which can be provided by some type of ballast (e.g., sand bags, water tanks) on top of or in the ground, by more permanent cast-in-place or precast concrete foundations, or by the soil burden above the anchor plates. Concrete foundations may be of the con-

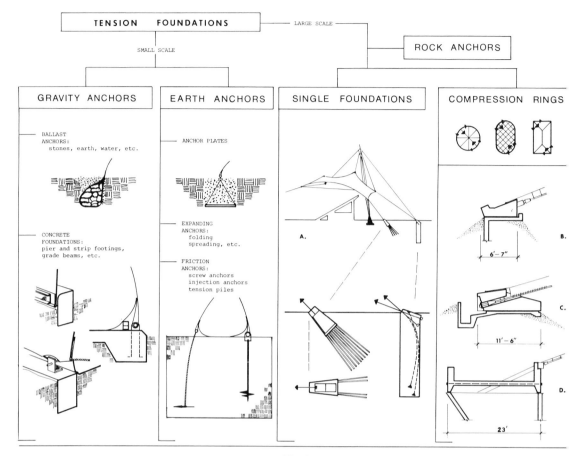

**Fig. 9.4**

tinuous strip type (i.e., grade beams) or they may be individual piers. A safety factor of 1.5 is generally applied to the design loads for concrete piers. While the vertical uplift component of the tension force is resisted by the weight of the foundation, ignoring any frictional resistance, the horizontal force component must be supported by the soil, the slab, or the struts (see Fig. 9.13).

In the case of curvilinear structures, closed ring beams replace the linear struts. Where membranes are relatively flat, such as pneumatic roofs for stadiums, the horizontal thrust forces are extremely large. The thrust is carried by compression rings (Fig. 9.4b-d) while the vertical uplift component due to internal air pressure and wind suction is resisted either by the ring alone or by the ring together with the walls/frames along the perimeter. For instance, the concrete ring for the U.S. Pavilion at Expo 70, Osaka, Japan (c) is 4 ft high and 11.5 ft wide. It is in pure compression under the uniform horizontal thrust as caused by the internal air pressure and its own weight; however, it will bend under the asymmetrical wind action. The ring alone also balances the upward lift. To prevent the transfer of horizontal forces to the supporting earth berm, the ring is separated from the berm by a slip joint which still provides enough frictional resistance to prevent the roof from sliding off its base.

Unlike the air-domes shown, the Hubert H. Humphrey Metrodome in Minneapolis

(1981) has a sloping compression ring tangential to the roof skin, thus much more effectively resisting the thrust forces. Further, the ring is not supported by the facade walls
or earth berms, but directly on the seating structure, to which it is hinged so that it is
allowed to float as an independent structure.

Individual or groups of tension piles (e.g., reinforced concrete piles) may support a
guy cable to transfer large forces to the ground. These piles are inclined so that the forces
are transferred directly in axial action; they resist the tensile forces primarily by their
mantle friction and possibly by their self-weight.

Special tensile foundations were designed for the Munich Olympics (Fig. 9.4a). The
ground anchor foundation directly resists the tension by the earth weight filled onto
the foundation as well as by its tension piles. The other anchorage system shown is
of the gravity type.

## 9.3  PNEUMATIC STRUCTURES

Pneumatic structures can be classified into two major groups (Fig. 9.5) as follows:

- Single membrane structures, such as domes and cylindrical forms, are supported by air
  pressure; they are often called low-pressure systems because only a small pressure is
  needed to hold the skin up. This pressure can be positive, causing a convex response
  of the tensile membrane, or it can be negative, resulting in a concave shape. Basic
  forms can be combined in infinitely many ways and subdivided by interior tensile
  point or line supports (i.e., columns or walls/beams).
- Air members such as high-pressure tubes and lower-pressure cellular mats are air-inflated
  structures. These air members act as columns, arches, beams, frames, and so on; they
  need a much higher internal pressure than air supported membranes.

Hybrid air structures are formed by a combination of the two systems above (e.g., air
cushion), or when one or both of the pneumatic systems are combined with any kind of
rigid support structure (e.g., arch supported). In double-walled air structures the internal
pressure of the main space supports the inner skin and must be larger than the pressure
between the skins, which, in turn, must be large enough to withstand the wind loads. This
type of construction allows a better insulation, it does not show the deformed state of
the outer membrane, and has a higher safety against deflation.

### Air-Supported Structures

The tensile membrane floats like a curtain on top of the enclosed air whose pressure ex-
ceeds that of the atmosphere; only a small air pressure differential is needed. The pneumatic shell must have a proper geometry and is prestressed by internal air pressure so that
it can support the external loads which act in compression on the tensile skin. The membrane must be anchored along its periphery to prevent its being lifted up; it is an antigravity structure quite in contrast to the heavy traditional building construction that we
are so used to. Air-supported skins cannot be completely airtight and therefore need a
continuous air supply to replace the air lost through leakage, thus maintaining internal

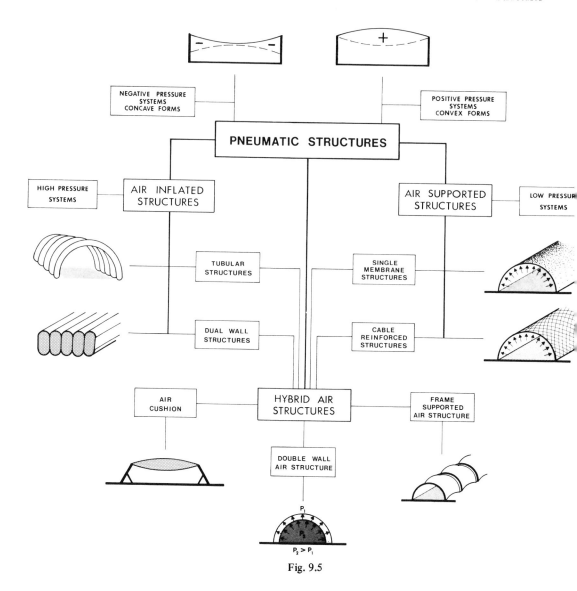

**Fig. 9.5**

pressure. At least two blowers are required, a primary blower and an auxiliary one as a back-up which, in case of an emergency, is activated automatically when the air pressure drops to an unsafe level. Each of the fans should be capable of supporting and prestressing the membrane to the desired value. The range in low pressure penumatic systems is roughly from 2 to 20 psf above atmospheric pressure. The magnitude of the design pressure depends on wind conditions, possibly snow loads, size of structure, and its tightness (i.e., leakage through skin and along its base, type and number of doors and windows, as well as size and number of vents and air venting requirements). The typical normal operating pressure for air-supported membranes in the United States is in the range 4.5–8 psf or roughly 1.0–1.5 in. water as read from a water pressure gauge.

To develop some feeling for the magnitude of this pressure, remember that the atmospheric pressure decreases with altitude. Near the sea level or the bottom of an ocean of air the atmospheric pressure is caused by the weight of all the air above; a column of air with a cross-section of 1 in.$^2$ extending through the atmosphere weighs 14.7 lb. The local effect of changing pressure due to moving air currents and altitude variations is in the range of 1 psi. The standard atmospheric pressure (atm) of 14.7 psi will support a mercury column of 29.92 in. at zero degree Celsius as measured by a barometer. The following relationships hold true:

$$1 \text{ atm} = 14.7 \text{ psi} = 2116.22 \text{ psf} = 29.92 \text{ in. Hg} \simeq 406.8 \text{ in. H}_2\text{O at } 4°\text{C}$$

Near sea level the air pressure decreases roughly 1 in. of mercury or 13.60 in. of water for each 1000 ft of altitude. Hence, one may conclude that 1 in. H$_2$O or 5.2 psf is approximately equivalent to 1/400 atm or 1000/13.60 = 74 ft height difference, which corresponds to the pressure difference between the seventh floor of a building and ground level. This small pressure variation is hardly noticeable, it is even caused inside a house when the wind blows.

At points of stress concentrations around openings (e.g., doors, windows, vent pipes, ducts) or where the membrane is attached to rigid structural elements (e.g., columns, arches, foundations) special reinforcement of the fabrics or isolation of the loads (e.g., transition shroud for entrance) is required. The joints (seams) are developed so they equal the capacity of the fabrics.

Air-supported structures may be organized as ground-mounted air structures (Fig. 9.6) and large scale, low-profile roof membranes (Fig. 9.7).

Typical conventional profiles for single membrane structures are shown in the upper portion of Fig. 9.6. The various cylindrical shapes can be distinguished by their different cutting patterns and by the layout of the reinforcement, as well as by the type of ends (round or nearly rectangular). They are commercially available with a width of more than 120 ft, a length of up to 500 ft, and a height of 42 ft.

Some examples of the infinite number of possible pneumatic shapes are shown in the bottom portion of the drawing. A group of architects called Chrysalis have concentrated on blending the art and technology of fabric structures. They are primarily concerned with the sculptural qualities of tensile architecture as expressed in the example for an exhibition structure [case (g)].

Large-scale air domes are discussed in Fig. 9.7. Because of their low profile, winds will only cause suction forces on the roofs. In case of deflation, the membranes can still hang free of the occupied space.

The U.S. Pavilion at Expo 70 in Osaka, Japan [case (f)], is the first air-supported clear span cable structure ever built of such large span. The membrane is a translucent vinyl-coated fiberglass fabric about $\frac{3}{32}$ in. thick with a strip strength of about 500 lb/in. It spans between the cables which form a diamond grid; the steel cables are 20 ft apart and vary in size from $1\frac{1}{2}$ to $2\frac{1}{4}$ in. in diameter (Fig. 9.2f). The cable network is anchored to the concrete compression ring which encloses the super-elliptical shape of the pavilion (Fig. 9.4c). The ring rests on top of the shallow earth berm which greatly deflects the wind upward to create suction on the flat dome which has a rise of only 23 ft. The skewed cable layout causes a funicular response of the ring under normal uniform loading; bending is only generated by unbalanced cable forces due primarily to wind action. The roof weighs 1.25 psf and is supported by an operating pressure of 5 psf; the membrane is designed to resist a wind suction of 30 psf.

The roof of the Pontiac Stadium in Michigan (1975) [case (e)] covers about ten acres, $\frac{1}{2}$ acre more than the Superdome in New Orleans, and covers about four times more area

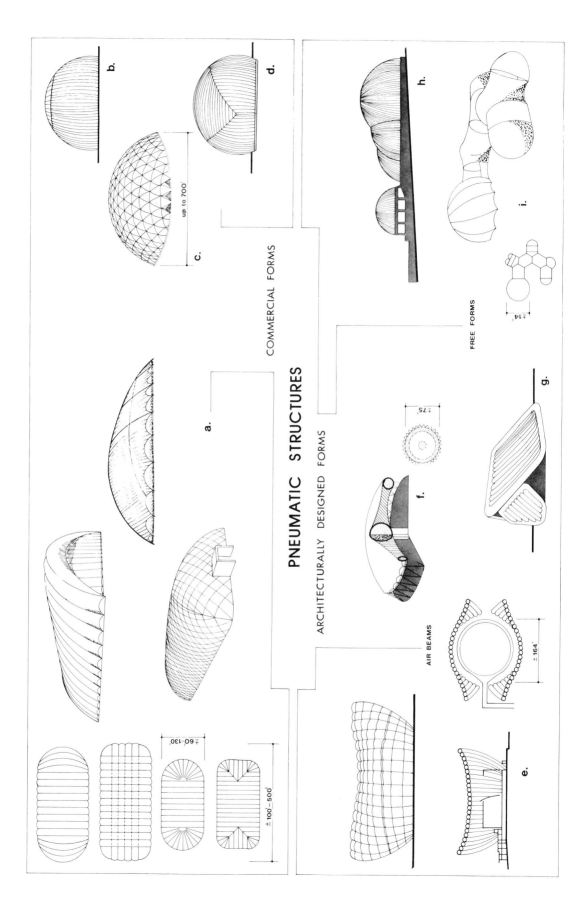

# PNEUMATIC STRUCTURES

COMMERCIAL FORMS

ARCHITECTURALLY DESIGNED FORMS

FREE FORMS

AIR BEAMS

a.

b.

c.

up to 700'

d.

e.

f.

±75'

g.

h.

i.

±14'

±164'

±60-130'

±100-500'

than the U.S. Pavilion in Osaka. Its span of 722 ft makes it currently the largest dome structure in the world. The octagonal dome is covered with 100 Teflon-coated fiberglass panels (32 nearly rectangular, 4 large triangular, and 64 diamond-shaped). The panels, with their edges bordered by $\frac{1}{2}$ in. diameter nylon ropes, are clamped to a network consisting of eighteen 3-in. diameter galvanized structural steel strands spaced at 41.63 ft intervals (Fig. 9.2e). The roof weighs only 1 psf; it is designed for a wind suction of 15 psf, and a snow load of 12 psf by increasing the internal air pressure.

The compression ring is a rectangle with the corners truncated parallel to the diagonals. This octagonal ring is not a funicular shape, although the moments are greatly reduced, and it is wide enough to keep the pressure line within the prestressed concrete plate girder under uniform loading (Fig. 9.4d).

There are 29 air blowers, but only 2 of them are used to support the roof with about a 3.5 psf normal operating pressure when the stadium is not occupied. The high fan capacity is needed to provide ventilation and heating; the number of fans in operation depends on the type of event, the outside temperature, and the magnitude of snow load.

The roof of the UNI-Dome at the University of Northern Iowa [case (g)] is similar in principle to the Pontiac Stadium but smaller in scale. It only needs 12 cables (2.875 in. diameter) spaced 42.43 ft apart to support the Teflon-coated fiberglass fabric roof. The roof weighs 1.0 psf and is designed for a wind suction of 15 psf and a snow load of 30 psf. The operating air pressure required to sustain the dome is approximately 5 psf. Sixty percent of the roof area is double-layered to allow for moving warm air so that heavy snow can be melted. The double layer also serves as an insulator and a sound absorber. The compression ring is supported by the exterior wall constructed from precast double tees.

The Leavey Center at the University of Santa Clara [case (b)] consists of two air-supported roof structures formed of super-ellipses. The larger of the two is covered with a Teflon-coated fiberglass fabric and the smaller one with a vinyl-coated polyester fabric which is retractable. The larger roof skin is supported by six $1\frac{7}{8}$-in. diameter steel cables spaced at 40 ft intervals and anchored to the compression ring cast atop earth berm walls (Fig. 9.4b).

The roof of the field house of Milligan College [case (c)] is an insulated membrane consisting of 4-in. thick blankets of fiberglass insulation sandwiched between two layers of coated fiberglass fabric. Lighting, with an equivalent weight of 0.5 psf, is hung from the roof cables. The cables ($1\frac{1}{2}$–$1\frac{1}{16}$ in. diameter) are spaced at 30 ft (Fig. 9.2g). The roof supports a wind suction of 15 psf, and a snow load of 20 psf through increased air pressure.

The fabric for the Metrodome in Minneapolis (completed in 1981) consists of two layers, the outer Teflon-coated fiberglass layer and the inner acoustical fabric layer. The dead air space between acts as an insulation layer. During winter warm air will be blown between the layers to melt the snow that may have accumulated.

The world's first air-supported stainless steel roof [case (a)] was recently built at Dalhousie University in Halifax, Nova Scotia, Canada; the concept was developed by Donald A. Sinoski. The low-profile roof consists of twenty-four $\frac{1}{16}$-in. thick trapezoidal steel sheet segments arranged radially around an oval center piece. The giant pie-shaped steel sheet slices are connected to special wave-shaped contraction joints that run between the sheet sections. The internal air pressure of 7.2 psf supports the roof weight of 2.6 psf and lights and other fixtures of 0.4 psf as well as 27 psf of snow load.

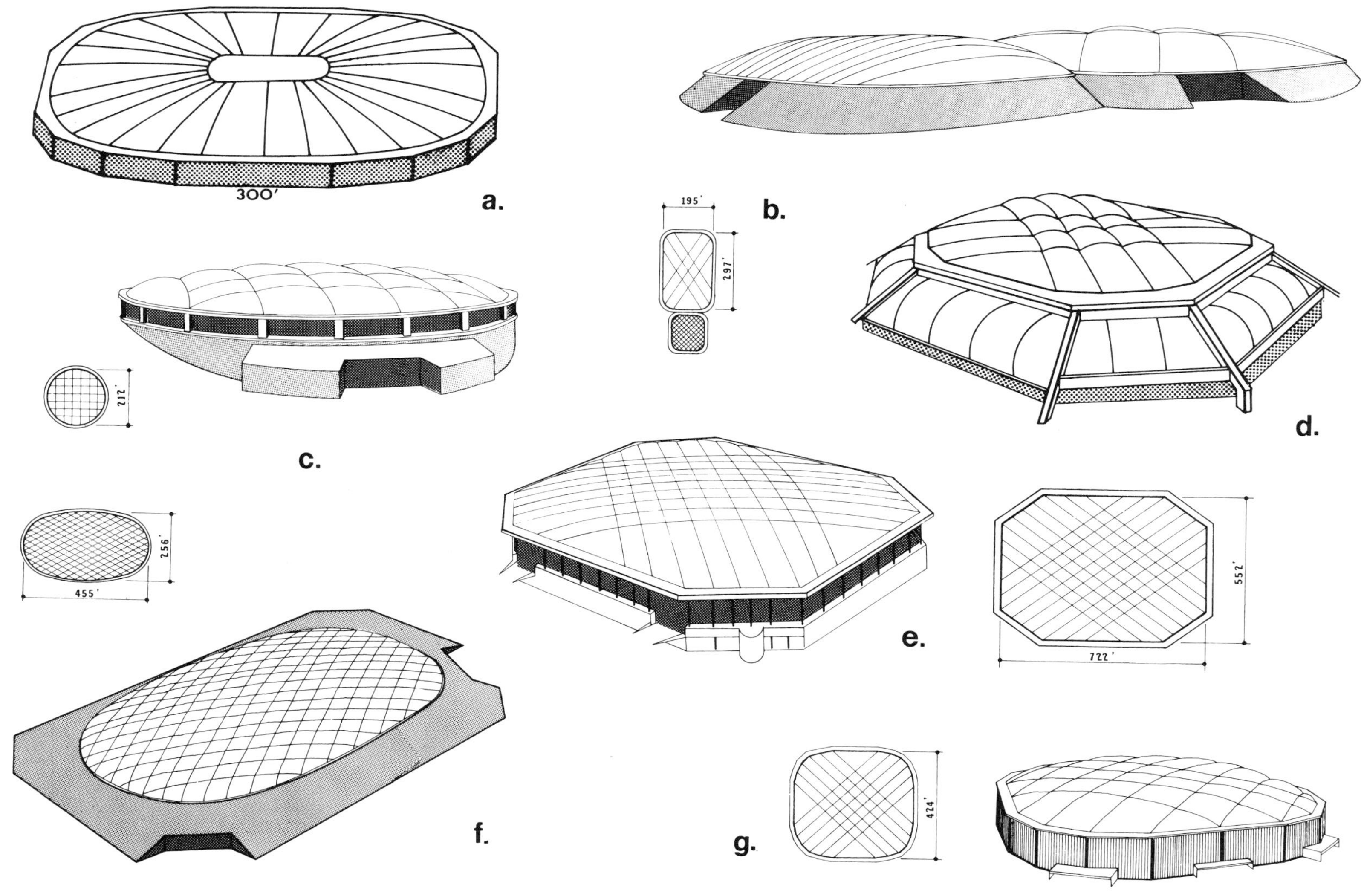

**Fig. 9.7** Low-profile, long-span pneumatic roof structures.

a.

b.

c.

d.

e.

f.

g.

300'

195'

297'

212'

256'

455'

424'

552'

722'

*The Effect of Internal Air Pressure on Geometry*

The stress condition for a spherical pneumatic structure loaded only by an inflation pressure $p_i$ has already been discussed in the section concerning the general treatment of a spherical membrane as it responds to a uniform load action normal to its surface [Eq. (7.5)]. There it was shown that the axial tension forces ($T$) along the membrane are optimal, as they are constant at any point. The forces are equal to

$$N = T = \frac{p_i R}{2} \tag{9.1}$$

These stresses do not vary for different spherical segments with the same curvature and internal pressure. The surface forces are independent of the profile of the pneumatic structure (Fig. 9.8a). Each of the cases in this figure however, covers a different ground surface area. For the condition where the same base area is to be enclosed by spherical

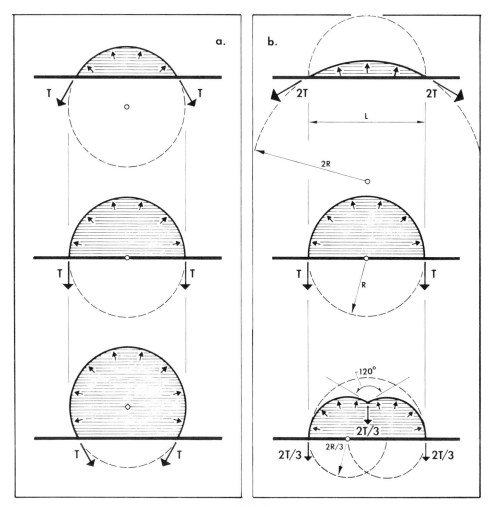

Fig. 9.8

membranes of varying radius (Fig. 9.8b), the decrease of height necessitates an increase of the radius of curvature and thus an increase of the membrane forces, if the internal pressure is to remain constant. A decrease in membrane forces may also be obtained by reducing the curvature of the membrane through usage of cable ribs (line supports) or tension columns (point supports). These systems relieve the membrane, similar to a beam or column added to support a floor structure [Fig. 9.8b (bottom)].

The spherical membrane represents a minimal surface under the action of radial pressure, since not only stresses and mean curvature are constant at any point on the surface, but also because the sphere by definition represents the smallest surface for the given volume. Some examples found readily in nature are the sea foam, soap bubbles floating on a surface forming hemispherical shapes, and flying soap bubbles. The small deviation from the spherical form, due to distortion caused by the soap film weight, will be ignored for this introductory approach.

The soap bubble is the result of an equilibrium reached between constant surface tension and the enclosed air pressure, the surface cannot withstand any shearing forces. Any decrease of internal pressure must increase the size of the bubble, because its surface is always under the same state of stress, that is, it cannot respond to force action in any other way, and must always be stretched with a constant force independent of the bubble size

$$T = \frac{p_1 R_1}{2} = \frac{p_2 R_2}{2} = \cdots = \frac{p_n R_n}{2} \tag{9.2}$$

This equation shows that the internal pressure $p$ is inversely proportional to the radius and directly proportional to the curvature of the bubble, when the surface tension is constant

$$p = \frac{2T}{R} \propto \frac{1}{R} \tag{9.3}$$

Large bubbles have a small internal pressure, while small bubbles have a large internal pressure. This phenomenon is exemplified when different-size bubbles are in contact with each other (Fig. 9.9), and a smaller bubble always tries to inflate the larger one.

In order to develop some understanding of the shapes of pneumatic structures, it is helpful to study the formal response of soap bubbles as they come in contact with each other. However, one must keep in mind that the shape of soap bubble conglomerations is not necessarily the most efficient one for pneumatic structures, which must respond to many other types of loading, snow and wind in particular. The spherical membrane no longer represents a minimal surface with respect to these loads, as the stresses along the surface are varying. Only for the one loading condition of inflation pressure does it represent a minimal structure. Since the live loads constantly change, it is impossible to develop a truly minimal structure to respond to them, though for given conditions an optimal geometry may be derived. For a more accurate determination of pneumatic forms, rubber models are better suited to experiments. They respond to any type of loading and are not limited, as soap bubbles are, to one type of force action or constant surface tension. For preliminary studies, however, it is reasonable to use soap bubbles as a first step for finding pneumatic forms.

Typical combinations of bubbles are shown in Fig. 9.9. No more than three ever come

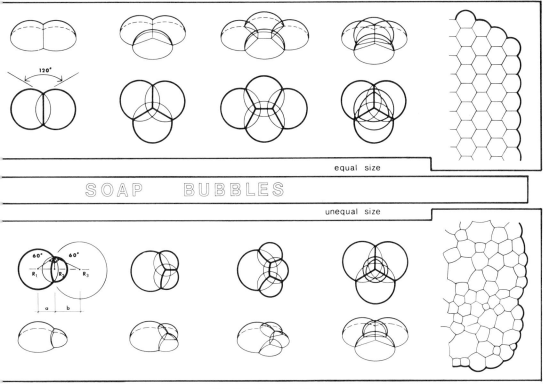

SOAP    BUBBLES

**Fig. 9.9**  Soap bubbles.

in contact with each other in two dimensional packing. The three soap film edges meeting at one point must form tangent angles of $120°$ so that the tensile forces balance at that point. In three-dimensional packing, not more than four bubbles will have a common contact point. The four edges meet each vertex at an angle of $109°\ 28'$ (the Maraldi angle) which appears as an angle of $120°$ in an orthogonal view.

When a free soap bubble falls on a flat surface it forms a hemispherical floating shape, that is, a sphere is transformed into a hemisphere without any change of contained volume, since the soap film is stretched to its limits

$$\tfrac{4}{3}\pi R_s^3 = \tfrac{1}{2}\left(\tfrac{4}{3}\pi R_h^3\right) \qquad R_h = 1.26 R_s$$

The radius of the floating bubble $(R_h)$ must be 26% larger than the radius of the flying bubble $(R_s)$ in order to enclose the same volume. With a change of radius the internal pressure must change, since the surface tension is always constant in a soap film

$$T = \frac{p_s R_s}{2} = \frac{p_h R_h}{2} = \frac{p_h (1.26 R_s)}{2}$$

$$p_h = 0.79 p_s \qquad p_s = 1.26 p_h \tag{9.4}$$

The pressure is proportional to the curvature $(1/R)$ or the pressure in the sphere is 26% larger than in the hemisphere.

When two bubbles of equal size meet, they must connect at an angle of $120°$ so that the equal tensile forces at the point of contact are in equilibrium (Fig. 9.9.)

$$\Sigma V = 0 = T - 2(T \sin 30°)$$

$$\Sigma H = 0 = T \cos 30° - T \cos 30°$$

Since the radii of both bubbles are the same, the internal pressure for both is equal as well, causing a straight intermediate partition.

This partition is curved for bubbles of different size, due to the fact that it must balance the internal pressure difference between the two or the larger pressure of the smaller bubble. The relationship of the radii for a twin bubble formed by two unequal soap bubbles can be derived as follows by considering that the internal pressures are inversely proportional to their radii (Fig. 9.9)

$$T = \frac{p_2 R_2}{2} = \frac{p_1 R_1}{2} = \frac{(p_2 - p_1) R_3}{2}$$

hence $\qquad \dfrac{R_3}{R_1} = \dfrac{p_1}{p_2 - p_1} = \dfrac{1}{p_2/p_1 - 1} \qquad$ but $\qquad \dfrac{p_2}{p_1} = \dfrac{R_1}{R_2}$

$$R_3 = \frac{R_1 R_2}{R_1 - R_2} \tag{9.5}$$

$$\frac{1}{R_2} = \frac{1}{R_1} + \frac{1}{R_3} \tag{9.6}$$

The geometrical relationship between the three surfaces is clearly governed by pressure adjustment as explained in the mathematical rules. Other arrangements of soap bubbles, as the ones shown in Fig. 9.9 are subject to the same geometrical laws just described.

Bubbles arrange themselves in different ways, mostly in a radial manner forming round (closed) shapes rather than linear (open) ones. As the spherical bubbles attach to each other, the interior enclosed ones change into polyhedral forms. Equal size bubbles form a hexagonal network in plan view. Bubbles of unequal size can form many different combinations, creating a great variety of polygonal arrangements as seen in plan.

### The Effect of Membrane Weight

For typical commercial pneumatic structures, the weight of the fabric can be neglected in structural calculations, because of its insignificance in comparison to the superimposed snow and wind loads. The membrane weight ranges from about 2 $oz/ft^2$ for canvas, to about 5 $oz/ft^2$ for coated fabric to 16 $oz/ft^2$ (1 psf) for a large stadium roof such as that of Pontiac Stadium in Michigan.

To develop some understanding of the effect of load action along a membrane, a spherical pneumatic structure, to be used as formwork for a lightweight concrete dome, will be investigated.

**Example 9.1** A 2-in. thick spherical segment of $L = 50$ ft span and $h = 15$ ft height is constructed by spraying lightweight concrete (100 pcf) on the outside of the pneumatic skin which is supporting the steel mesh reinforcing. This mesh also prevents the wet concrete from sliding off the pneumatic form. Inflation pressure and material strength of the membrane are to be determined.

The radius of curvature for the spherical membrane (Fig. 3.9a) is

$$R^2 = \frac{L^2}{2} + (R - h)^2 \tag{9.7}$$

$$R^2 = 25^2 + (R - 15)^2$$

$$R^2 = 25^2 + R^2 + 15^2 - 30R$$

$$R = 28.33 \text{ ft}$$

The cosine of the semicentral angle $\phi$ is

$$\cos \phi = \frac{R - h}{R} = \frac{28.33 - 15}{28.33} = 0.471$$

The concrete shell weighs

$$w = 2 \frac{100}{12} = 16.67 \text{ psf}$$

The tension in the skin as caused by air pressure $p_i$ must be at least as large as the maximum compression due to the concrete weight so as to preclude any folding of the skin. For this loading condition the maximum compression appears along the meridian at the base of the membrane [Eq. (7.11)]

$$\frac{p_i R}{2} = \frac{wR}{1 + \cos \phi}$$

$$p_i = \frac{2w}{1 + \cos \phi} \tag{9.8}$$

The inflation pressure is independent of the curvature, however it is a function of the profile: it increases rapidly as the spherical segment approaches the full sphere. The minimum air pressure for this example is

$$p_i = \frac{2(16.67)}{1 + 0.471} = 22.67 \text{ psf}$$

or a gauge pressure of $22.67(0.192) = 4.35$ in. of water. The maximum tensile force acts along the circumference at the base of the membrane (Fig. 7.10a), as caused by air pressure and shell weight [Eqs. (7.12) and (9.1)]

$$T_{\theta \max} = wR\left(\cos \phi - \frac{1}{1 + \cos \phi}\right) - \frac{p_i R}{2}$$

$$= 16.67(28.33)\left(0.471 - \frac{1}{1 + 0.471}\right) - \frac{22.67(28.33)}{2}$$

$$= -98.61 - 321.12 = -419.73 \text{ lb/ft} = -34.98 \text{ lb/in.}$$

The minimum required strip tensile strength is

$$T_u = SF(T_{\theta \max})$$

For the given conditions the safety factor can be neglected, since nobody is working underneath the shell during its construction.


*The Effect of Snow Loading*


Typical standard air-supported shapes, such as cylindrical and spherical structures of relatively high profile, are designed for wind loading only; snow is not considered critical. Not only does the wind blow the snow off the roof, but the heat loss through the skin melts the snow so that it easily slides off the smooth surface. Possible adhesion of snow to the skin, causing accumulation at the flat crown portion, can be broken by alternating changes of inflation pressure. The snow loading must be controlled in this manner since, from a static resistance point of view, it may require a higher inflation pressure than for wind. In cases where the enclosed space is not heated or where the skin has a high thermal insulation the membrane may have to be heated directly. In order for the snow not to cause any extensive skin deformations and thus allow for further snow accumulations, high inflation pressure should be kept to maintain the original shape.

The effect of snow on low-profile roofs is more critical. They can support additional loads up to a certain amount by increasing the internal air pressure, which will not increase the fabric tension if the snow loads are uniformly distributed ($p_i = q$, $\phi \leqslant 90°$). However, in reality, the snow is not evenly distributed, resulting in an increase in membrane tension together with an increase of inflation pressure. It is clear that some melting systems have to be employed. In case of failure the roof will slowly deflate and eventually act as a freely suspended membrane where the loads will be released through some new openings in the skin. For complex pneumatic forms designed by combining different shapes, snow can no longer be dispersed that easily and may gather at certain locations. For such cases snow must be considered in the structural analysis. The effect of snow loading upon structural design is investigated in the following example of an air-inflated cushion roof.


**Example 9.2** A lens-shaped pneumatic structure, 200 ft in diameter, is being used as a roof enclosure (Fig. 9.10). It consists of an upper and lower spherical membrane spaced 30 ft apart at center span and stabilized by internal air pressure causing equal tension in both surfaces. The membranes are not connected to each other by any webbing hence the bottom membrane only carries the inflation pressure, while the top membrane behaves like a prestressed dome resisting the internal air pressure and the superimposed loads. Since the building is closed the wind will only cause suction on the upper membrane, which will be ignored for this investigation. The air cushion is held in place along the perimeter by a concrete compression ring (4000 psi concrete, Grade 60 steel), which in turn is carried as a continuous beam by columns. For this example a snow load of 20 psf on the horizontal roof projection is assumed to control the preliminary design of the membrane. Conservatively, the ground snow load is used, it is not converted to a roof load. The weight of the membrane is considered negligible. The radius of curvature for the upper and lower spherical membranes (Fig. 9.10a) is

$$R^2 = \left(\frac{L}{2}\right)^2 + (R - h)^2 \tag{9.7}$$

$$R^2 = 100^2 + (R - 15)^2 = 100^2 + R^2 + 15^2 - 30R$$

$$R = 340.83 \text{ ft}$$

The semicentral angle is defined as:

$$\cos \phi = \frac{R - 15}{R} = \frac{340.83 - 15}{340.83} = 0.956$$

$$\sin \phi = 0.293 \quad \phi = 17.06°$$

To preclude any folding of the skin, the maximum compression in the upper membrane due to the snow loading must be balanced by a tension force caused by the internal air

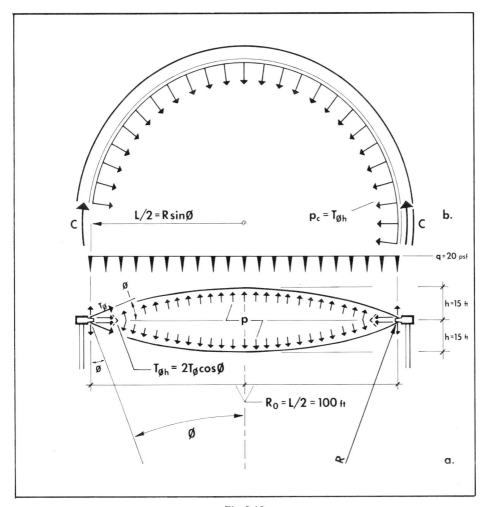

Fig. 9.10

pressure, which is at least equal in magnitude. The critical compression is generated by the constant meridional forces, and the circumferential forces at the crown (Fig. 7.9a and b)

$$\frac{p_i R}{2} = \frac{qR}{2}$$

$$p_i = q \tag{9.9}$$

Note that for spherical and cylindrical structures ($\phi \leqslant 90°$), the inflation pressure is only a function of snow loading and is independent of the profile and curvature. For this case, the required inflation pressure is

$$p_i = q = 20 \text{ psf}$$

or a gauge pressure of $0.192(20) = 3.84$ in. water. The maximum tensile stresses appear in the top and bottom membrane due to inflation pressure only. There will be no circumferential tension due to snow in the upper membrane since $\phi = 17.06° < 45°$ (Fig. 7.9a). Keep in mind that potential wind uplift forces, which have been considered as secondary in this example, may potentially increase the tensile forces in the top membrane.

$$T_{\phi \text{ max}} = \frac{p_i R}{2} = \frac{20(340.83)}{2} = 3408.30 \text{ lb/ft} = 284.03 \text{ lb/in.}$$

The minimum required strip tensile strength is

$$T_u = \text{SF } (T_{\phi \text{ max}}) = 4(284.03) = 1136.12 \text{ lb/in.}$$

The required tensile capacity is too high for common coated pure fabrics. The membrane has to be reinforced so that the fabric is relieved from carrying all the loads. The behavior of the cables and fabrics in composite action is rather complex. Steel cables have a high modulus of elasticity, while fabrics have a low one. This incompatibility in rigidity makes the design more difficult. For approximation purposes the strength of the fabric may be neglected, or the reader may refer to the manufacturer's literature on their patented reinforced membrane systems.

Stressed stainless steel membranes are, obviously, much stronger. For instance, a stainless steel skin $\frac{1}{16}$ in. thick with an allowable tensile stress of 20 ksi can support the following load

$$P = F_t A = 20\left(\frac{1}{16}\right)1 = 1.25 \text{ k/in.}$$

This load is by far larger than the 284.03 lb/in. to be covered in this example.

The maximum compressive forces in the concrete ring are caused by the maximum tensile membrane forces along the perimeter. For this case, the critical loading is due to inflation pressure only. Notice that the ring is funicular under the uniform loads causing equal radial forces $p_c$ (Fig. 9.10b). The horizontal inward acting thrust components $T_{\phi h}$ of the membrane forces $T_\phi$ along the perimeter are:

$$T_{\phi h} = 2(T_\phi \cos \phi) = p_c \tag{a}$$

This uniform radial pressure $p_c$ compresses the concrete ring with a constant axial force $C$ [see Eq. (3.12)]

$$C = p_c R_0 \tag{9.10}$$

$$= 2(T_\phi \cos \phi)\frac{L}{2}$$

$$C = T_\phi L \cos \phi \tag{9.11}$$

$$= \frac{3408.30(200)0.956}{1000} = 651.67 \text{ k}$$

The ultimate compression ring load, considering the constant inflation pressure as a dead load, is

$$C_u = \text{SF}(C) = 1.4(651.67) = 912.34 \text{ k}$$

The required concrete cross-section to resist this axial force is

$$A_G = \frac{P_u}{0.47f_c' + 0.0056f_y} \tag{1.50}$$

$$= \frac{912.34}{0.47(4) + 0.0056(60)} = 411.71 \text{ in.}^2$$

Try a cross section of $13 \times 32$ in., $A_G = 416$ in.$^2$

Additional reinforcement will be necessary besides the assumed 1% of the ring cross-section to carry the moments caused by asymmetrical roof loading. Further, the spacing of the columns determines the design of the ring as a beam with respect to the vertical plane.

### The Effect of Wind Loading

In general, air-supported structures are designed for wind loading, the condition in which they are subject to the greatest stresses. The wind pressure distribution, in contrast to the loading due to inflation or weight of the skin, is variable and quite complex. However, the critical wind forces must be known in order to determine the membrane stresses and the anchorage uplift forces. In this preliminary study, it is assumed that the wind response of rigid bodies is also applicable to pneumatic structures. This assumption constitutes only an approximation; it only would be true if the air structure under lateral pressure maintains its original shape, which is usually not the case for soft-shell structures, which, as they deform, further influence the wind pressure distribution. This deformation causes some benefit while, as the volume decreases, the internal pressure increases, which in turn increases the structure's rigidity. The building rigidity depends on the ratio of inflation pressure to wind velocity pressure $p_i/q$. As this ratio increases the rigidity of the building increases. It is shown in Chapter 1 that the equivalent static wind pressure $p$ (psf) acting perpendicular to the surface, is equal to the velocity pressure $q$ (psf) multiplied by the shape coefficient $c$

$$p = C_{pe}\, q_h = C_q \tag{1.8}$$

The velocity pressure $q_h$ for standard air density and a wind velocity $V$ (mph) at a height of 30 ft above ground is

$$q = 0.00256\, V^2 \tag{1.5}$$

This dynamic pressure is adjusted to the height of the building and the type of site. Here, only low-rise buildings are investigated, hence the increase of velocity with height is neglected. Further, the buildings are assumed to be located in an area of minimum obstructions.

The shape coefficients for the following building forms are defined as

- Cylindrical shapes (Fig. 1.4)
    maximum pressure:    $C = 1.4r = 1.4h/L$
    maximum suction:    $C = -0.7 - r$
- Spherical dome shapes (Fig. 9.11)
    maximum pressure                                          maximum suction
      hemisphere:           $C = 0.9$                           hemisphere:           $C = -1.0$
      three-quarter sphere  $C = 1.0$                         three-quarter sphere  $C = -1.25$

The difference in the distribution of the equivalent static wind pressure $p$ for structures of various profiles is quite apparent from Fig. 9.11.

The membrane of a low-profile structure is only stressed by suction forces. The compression at the base is carried by a rigid structure (e.g., earth berm, perimeter framing/walls). For this case, only a minimum inflation pressure is needed to carry the membrane weight, a possible snow load, and to stabilize the membrane against gusty winds. Under calm weather conditions, the membrane weight will, theoretically, already be supported by the buoyancy effect caused by the small temperature difference between outside temperatures and the warmer air generated within the enclosure. High-profile structures, on the other hand, must resist large wind forces. High wind pressure necessitates high inflation pressure to minimize deformation and folding of the skin.

One may conclude that with an increase of height, the external wind forces increase, causing higher inflation pressure and higher membrane forces, while at the same time, the radius of curvature decreases resulting in smaller membrane forces. These seemingly contradictory statements indicate that there must be some optimum solution with respect to material economy. According to Geiger (reference 164), the optimum rise of the dome is about 20% of the span if no rigid base structure is used and about 6% of the span where a solid base structure resists the positive wind pressure.

In the following, two air-supported buildings are investigated in order to study the effect of wind upon the preliminary structural design.

**Example 9.3** Design an air-supported hemispherical dome of 100 ft diameter to withstand a wind velocity of 80 mph. The structure is anchored to the ground by a continuous concrete grade beam. The small weight of the membrane is ignored.

The wind velocity pressure is

$$q = 0.00256V^2 \tag{1.5}$$

$$q = 0.00256(80)^2 = 16.38 \text{ psf}$$

The maximum equivalent static wind pressures perpendicular to the surface are

suction:     $p = qC = 16.38(-1.0) = -16.38 \text{ psf}$

pressure:    $p = qC = 16.38(0.9) = 14.74 \text{ psf}$

To maintain the shape and to prevent any folding of the envelope, the inflation pressure must be at least equal to the maximum positive pressure at the windward face at the base

$$p_i = p = 14.74 \text{ psf} = 2.83 \text{ in. water}$$

Some designers allow local folding of the membrane by using an internal pressure of 60-70% of the maximum equivalent wind load pressure but not less than a pressure of 1 in. water.

The maximum local membrane tension appears close to the crown as caused by wind suction and air pressure. It would be overconservative to design the fabric as based on this

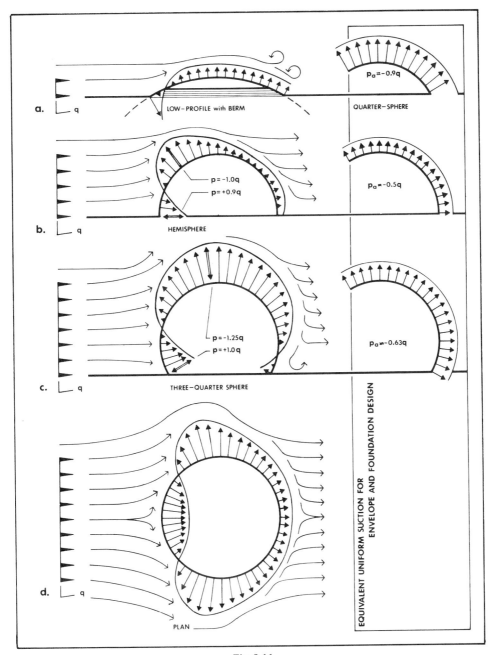

Fig. 9.11

critical stress location only, and to ignore the effect of the redistribution of forces along the skin. Here, an average or equivalent uniform suction $p_a$ equal to one-half of the maximum value (Fig. 9.11a, b, and c) is assumed. Hence, the maximum tension due to inflation and aerodynamic lift is

$$T_{\phi\ max} = (p_i + p_a)R/2 \tag{9.12}$$

$$= \frac{(14.74 + 16.38/2)50}{2} = 573.25 \text{ lb/ft} = 47.77 \text{ lb/in.}$$

The minimum required strip tensile strength is:

$$T_u = \text{SF}(T_{\phi\ max}) = 4(47.77) = 191.08 \text{ lb/in.}$$

The foundations anchor the envelope to the ground. They resist primarily uplift forces resulting from wind suction and inflation pressure, that is, the average maximum membrane tension along the base perimeter. In this case, the selfweight of a concrete grade beam (145 pcf) is employed as the anchorage system. The membrane is attached to the footing continuously, thus reducing stress concentrations in the fabric (Fig. 9.4) while at the same time providing an efficient air seal and drainage control. Since the membrane forces for the hemisphere along the base are vertical, they must be fully resisted by the weight of the foundation. The necessary self-weight to balance the uplift for a footing width of one foot and a concrete weight of $w_c$ = 145 pcf with $V_c$ equal to the concrete volume, and with a safety factor SF = 1.1 (reference 153), is

$$\Sigma V = 0 = T_{\phi\ max} - w_c(V_c)$$
$$= 1.1(573.25) - 145[1.0(d)\ 1.0]$$

$d$ = 4.35 ft, select a 1 $\times$ 4 ft 4 in. concrete footing.

Since the dome is hemispherical ($\theta = 90°$), there are no lateral thrust forces acting upon the ring foundation under the investigated loading conditions. However, should the dome be shallow ($\theta < 90°$) then the ring acts as an arch in compression, or for the condition where $\theta > 90°$ the foundation behaves like a tension ring.

**Example 9.4**  An air-supported cylindrical membrane, 70 ft wide and 30 ft high is investigated. The structure must resist a wind of 70 mph.

The radius of curvature is

$$R^2 = \left(\frac{L}{2}\right)^2 + (R - h)^2 \tag{9.7}$$

$$R^2 = 35^2 + (R - 30)^2 = 35^2 + R^2 + 30^2 - 60R$$

$$R = 35.42 \text{ ft}$$

The semicentral angle is defined as:

$$\cos\theta = \frac{R - h}{R} = \frac{35.42 - 30}{35.42} = 0.153$$

$$\sin\theta = 0.988 \qquad \theta = 81.20°$$

The wind velocity pressure is

$$q = 0.00256 V^2 \tag{1.5}$$

$$= 0.00256(70)^2 = 12.54 \text{ psf}$$

The maximum equivalent static wind pressures perpendicular to the membrane surface are:

pressure: $\quad p = qC = q(1.4r) = 12.54 \left(\dfrac{30}{70}\right)1.4 = 7.52 \text{ psf}$

suction: $\quad p = qC = q(-0.7 - r) = 12.54 \left(-0.7 - \dfrac{30}{70}\right) = -14.15 \text{ psf}$

The inflation pressure $p_i$ must balance the positive pressure $p$

$$p_i = p = 7.52 \text{ psf} = 1.44 \text{ in. water}$$

The maximum circumferential membrane forces due to the internal air pressure $p_i$ and the assumed average suction pressure $p_a$ are

$$T_{\theta \text{ max}} = (p_i + p_a)R \tag{9.13}$$

$$T_{\theta \text{ max}} = \left(7.52 + \dfrac{14.15}{2}\right)35.42 = 516.96 \text{ lb/ft} = 43.10 \text{ lb/in.}$$

The required minimum strip tensile strength is

$$T_u = \text{SF}(T_{\theta \text{ max}}) = 4(43.10) = 172.32 \text{ lb/in.}$$

The longitudinal membrane forces are zero for the condition where rigid end walls carry the wind independent of the air structure (Fig. 7.12b). However, should the end structure be part of the membrane and act together with the cylindrical portion as a total unit, then longitudinal membrane forces $T_x$ are generated. For this example, it is assumed that the cylindrical unit is capped at each end by spherical elements. Some structural designers approximate the magnitude of the longitudinal forces by considering the same load which is carried by the cylinder in one direction to be shared by the spherical end segment in two directions as based on uniform radial force action. The circumferential forces and, in particular, the meridional forces parallel to the cylinder must be supported by the longitudinal membrane forces in the cylinder (Fig. 9.12), which may then be approximated as

$$T_x = \frac{T_{\theta \text{ max}}}{2} \tag{9.14}$$

Laboratory tests, however, have obtained longitudinal forces by far larger than those suggested by the above approximation. Critical wind action against the end of the structure may generate longitudinal forces $T_x$ larger than the circumferential forces $T_\theta$. Special considerations have to be given to the juncture of cylinder and endpiece, where incompatibility of forces causes differential movement. The anchoring system for this structure will be provided at intermittent points along the perimeter. ASI (reference 153) suggests a safety factor of 3 for earth anchors and 1.5 for concrete pylons. The capacity of the anchorage system depends on the shear capacity of the soil as well as other soil characteristics. The uplift force to be resisted by each anchor, regularly spaced

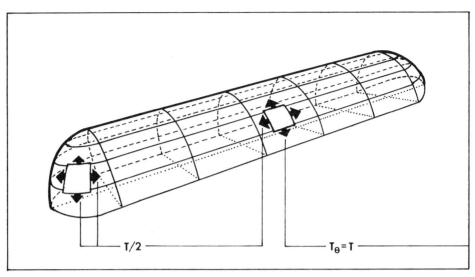

**Fig. 9.12**

at a distance $s = 5$ ft apart, is due to the vertical component of the maximum membrane tension, increased by a safety factor of 1.5 for concrete piers (Fig. 9.13).

$$V = \text{SF}(T_{\theta\ \max})\, (\sin \theta)s \qquad\qquad (9.15)$$

$$= \frac{1.5(516.96)\,(0.988)5}{1000} = 3.83 \text{ k}$$

This uplift force must be resisted by each pier in friction with the soil and its selfweight, similar to tension piles.

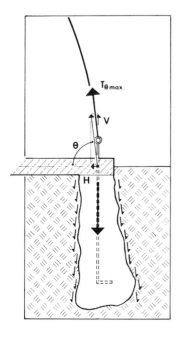

**Fig. 9.13**

The horizontal thrust component of the membrane force is resisted by the ground, or if too large, by the concrete floor acting as a compression strut. For this example, the thrust force acting at each pier (without safety factor) is equal to

$$H = (T_{\theta\ max})(\cos\theta)s \tag{9.16}$$
$$= 516.96(0.153)5 = 395.47\ lb$$

### Air-Inflated Structures

In air-supported structures, a single structural membrane is carried by a low internal pressure in excess of the atmospheric pressure, causing the membrane to float on top of the enclosed air space. Air-inflated structures, on the other hand, replace traditional rigid building members. Here, only the members are pressurized, and not the enclosed space. Air-inflated elements behave very much like rigid members, as they are subject to bending and buckling, while air-supported structures act truly as thin membranes. Because of their relatively small cross-section, air-inflated structures are high-pressure systems with an inflation pressure in the range 2-100 psi, or a difference in air pressure of about 0.2-7.0 atm. This pressure differential is about 100-1000 times higher than for an air-supported structure. A car tire is a typical example of an air-inflated element with an inflation pressure of about 30 psi or about 2 atm.

High air-pressure structures need high-strength materials. The performance of these materials is much more critical than for single-membrane systems, since they must contain the pressure over a greater time period, hence requiring higher safety factors against failure. In general, air tubes are made of coated fabric with some type of inner lining for air-tightness. While air-supported structures need continuous air supply, typical air-inflated members do not, although leakage and temperature variation cause a change in pressure and thus require adjustments from time to time. In structures with large air volumes, such as the Fuji Group Pavilion (Fig. 9.6e), air compressors are required to maintain a continuous flow of air.

Air-inflated structures can be organized in a way similar to rigid structures

- *Tubular systems* (line elements) have a strong curvature in one direction and much less or no curvature in the other direction: columns, beams, arches, and combinations such as grid structurers.
- *Dual-wall systems* or airmats (surface elements) are double-membrane envelopes which are joined to form walls, slabs, or shells. The webbing is made of threads or diaphragms. They can be arranged in many different ways forming many different types of cellular patterns. These cell compartments allow better control of leakage and failure.

There is no limit to the application of the principle of high-pressure systems with respect to intricate forms, however, from a practical point of view they are in an early stage of development with respect to broad application to the building field. Some typical examples are shown in Fig. 9.6. The Fuji Group Pavilion at Expo 70 in Osaka [case (e)] consists of air-beam arches 13 ft in diameter and inflated to about 16.2 psi. They are fastened to steel cylinders embedded in a concrete ring foundation. The arches are strapped together to cover a 164-ft diameter circular base area.

The Open-Air Restaurant, also at Expo 70 [case (f)], is composed of a high-pressure tubular perimeter ring about 10 ft in diameter and a central high-pressure sphere about 20 ft in diameter. Both are supporting a negative low-pressure double-membrane roof. Along the periphery, wire ropes anchor the roof to the foundations. The Events Structure for the Three Rivers Festival in Pittsburgh, Pennsylvania [case (g)] is composed of air mats along the perimeter enclosing about 2000 ft$^2$ of area; the structure is 35 ft high.

Many other experiments have been done with high-pressure structures. For instance, nylon-reinforced plastic air tubes have been connected to multidirectional air ball joints to form space frames or grid shells. The deflated nets can easily be shipped to the site and be inflated; the principle is applicable particularly as formwork for the construction of shells.

The structural behavior of high-pressure tubes is quite complex. Since there is no established design procedure, linear behavior is assumed for the very approximate design of the following simple structural elements, so that some basic understanding may be developed.

**Example 9.5** The membrane material and inflation pressure is to be determined for an air-inflated, 1-ft diameter tube closed at its ends with rigid plates. The behavior of the tube is first investigated as a column, and then as a beam. The equation for the membrane forces in the circular cylinder due to inflation pressure $p_i$ only, have already been determined. The circumferential membrane forces are

$$T_\theta = p_i R \qquad\qquad (7.21)$$

The longitudinal membrane forces are derived from the equilibrium of the internal pressure against the end plates and the longitudinal membrane forces along the circumference

$$\Sigma F = 0 = p_i(\pi R^2) - T_x(2\pi R)$$

$$T_x = \frac{p_i R}{2} = \frac{T_\theta}{2} \qquad\qquad (9.17)$$

This expression was already given as an approximation for the longitudinal forces in an air-supported cylindrical unit capped at each end with spherical segments.

(a) The high-pressure tube will first be designed as a column to carry an axial load of $P = 1000$ lb (Fig. 9.14). Visualize the rigid end plates to be separated from the membrane boundaries and to float on the internal air pressure. Vertical equlibrium yields

$$P = p_i \pi R^2$$

Hence the required mimimum inflation pressure is

$$p_i = \frac{P}{\pi R^2} = \frac{1000}{\pi (6)^2} = 8.84 \text{ psi}$$

One could have also reasoned that the compression exerted in the membrane by the external load must be balanced by the tension due to the air pressure

$$\frac{p_i R}{2} = \frac{P}{2\pi R} \qquad \text{or} \qquad p_i = \frac{P}{\pi R^2}$$

Though both approaches give the same result, each of the systems shows distinctly different behavior. The separation of the rigid end plates from the membrane similar to a

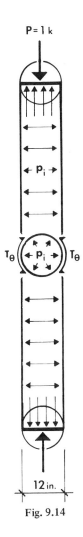

**Fig. 9.14**

piston, assuming this approach to be practically possible, makes it impossible for the skin to fold or buckle. Since the external load is supported solely by the fluid which, in turn, is supported by the circumferential membrane forces only, there will be no longitudinal forces in the membrane as is assumed for the other approach. The circumferential membrane forces are

$$T_\theta = p_i R = 8.84(6) = 53.04 \text{ lb/in.}$$

For the selection of membrane material, a safety factor of 6 is used. In general, they are larger for air-inflated structures than for air-supported skins, because of the sudden explosive-like nature of their failure. The required minimum tensile strength is

$$T_u = \text{SF}(T_{\theta \text{ max}})$$
$$= 6(53.04) = 318.24 \text{ lb/in.}$$

The capacity of the membrane in the longitudinal direction should be at least one-half of that in the circumferential direction as based on inflation pressure only.

(b) The high pressure tube, tied together by internal webs, is assumed to act as a simply supported beam spanning 12 ft and supporting a uniform snow load of 30 lb/ft. The weight of the fabric is neglected (Fig. 9.15). The beam must support a maximum moment of

$$M_{max} = \frac{wl^2}{8} = \frac{30(12)^2}{8} = 540 \text{ lb-ft}$$

Small deflection theory is assumed for this very approximate investigation, keeping in mind that the load/deflection relationship is not linear, due to local deformations and creep of the fabric. Hence the bending stresses can be defined as

$$f = \pm \frac{M}{S} \qquad \text{where } S_0 = \pi R^2 t$$

The axial forces at top and bottom face due to bending are

$$N = \pm \ tf = \frac{M}{\pi R^2}$$

The prestress force $T_x$ in the longitudinal direction due to inflation pressure must be at least as large as the critical compression force at midspan in order to prevent any folding of the membrane

$$\frac{p_i R}{2} = \frac{M}{\pi R^2}$$

$$p_i = \frac{2M}{\pi R^3} = \frac{2(540)\,12}{\pi(6)^3} = 19.10 \text{ psi}$$

A minimum air pressure of 19.10 psi is necessary for equilibrium, although it was found in experiments that local folding on the compression face does not cause collapse of the beam! The maximum tensile forces in the longitudinal direction appear at the bottom face at midspan due to air pressure and load action

$$T_{x \ max} = \frac{P_i R}{2} + \frac{M}{\pi R^2} = \frac{19.10(6)}{2} + \frac{540(12)}{\pi(6)^2} = 114.60 \text{ lb/in.}$$

The maximum tensile forces in the circumferential direction are

$$T_{\theta \ max} = p_i R = 19.10(6) = 114.60 \text{ lb/in.}$$

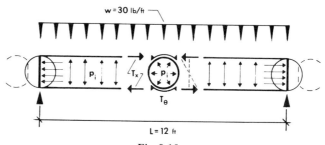

Fig. 9.15

The critical tensile stresses in the longitudinal and circumferential directions are equal to each other. Should the internal air pressure be increased by a safety factor, then the circumferential membrane forces will have a larger controlling value. The ultimate tensile strength of the membrane must be at least equal to

$$T_{u\ max} = SF(T_{\theta\ max}) = 6(114.60) = 687.60\ lb/in.$$

Shear must also be checked, since the fabric along the sides of the beam, close to the supports, may wrinkle before the top face at midspan folds due to bending.

Air-inflated elements are extremely flexible. The deformation of air beams is not controlled by bending, as for rigid beams, but by shear, because of the extremely low shear rigidity of the inflation pressure which takes the place of web material in rigid members. How the internal pressure affects the stiffness of the air beam is not yet exactly known.

## Problems

**9.1** Determine the increase in circumference and radius for a semicircular cylindrical structure as caused by inflation pressure only.

**9.2** For the combined spherical membranes (Fig. 9.16) determine the membrane forces for both domes as caused by an internal pressure of 5 psf. Find also the circumferential tension force for the ring at the juncture of the two domes.

**9.3** Determine the initial inflation pressure and the material strength to support a pneumatically stretched skin upon which is sprayed, from the inside, a heat insulating structural plastic which when stiffened, will support itself as a dome; at this first stage the shell weighs 5 psf. Once the plastic shell is rigid, further materials will be glued onto the surface to form a sandwich shell. Consider a spherical dome of 100 ft span and 30 ft height.

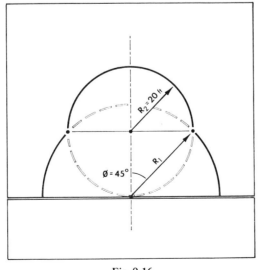

**Fig. 9.16**

**9.4**   An air cushion of 60 ft height, spans a stadium of 700 ft. It consists of equal spherical membranes made of nickel stainless steel with an allowable stress of 60 ksi. The roof membrane must carry a uniform 10 psf wind suction perpendicular to the surface, 25 psf snow load on the horizontal roof projection and 2 psf roof weight. First determine the internal air pressure and then the thickness of the membranes by neglecting their weight.

**9.5**   An open summer theater is covered with a lens-shaped roof which consists of an upper and lower spherical membrane of equal size, stabilized by internal air pressure producing tension in both surfaces. The roof has a diameter of 145 ft and a depth of 20 ft at the center. Both membrane layers only weigh about $\frac{1}{2}$ psf and will be neglected. Other live loads due to gravity are insignificant because the structure is only used during summer. Assume a uniform wind action of 3 psf perpendicular to the surface for this preliminary design. Determine the inflation pressure and the tensile capacity of the membrane.

**9.6**   Investigate the compression ring in Problem 9.5 by using $A36$ steel.

**9.7**   Do a preliminary investigation for a cylindrical membrane with quarter spheres as end pieces. The structure has a floor area 500 ft in length and 90 ft in width and a maximum height of 30 ft. Assume as the critical loading a wind velocity of 90 mph. Determine the internal air pressure, the tensile capacity of the membrane, and the depth of the 1.5-ft wide continuous concrete footing (145 pcf). Can the horizontal force components be carried by the 4-in. thick concrete slab of 4000 psi strength?

**9.8**   Investigate an air-supported three-quarter spherical dome structure with a base diameter of 100 ft. Design the dome approximately for a wind velocity of 75 mph. Determine the internal air pressure the tensile capacity of the membrane and the anchorage capacity of the foundation.

**9.9**   An air-inflated, 15-in. cylindrical column carries an axial load of 5 k. Determine the internal air pressure and the capacity as well as the type of membrane to be selected.

**9.10** Replace the gas medium air in Problem 9.9 with the liquid water ($w = 62.4$ pcf). Assume a column height of 12 ft. What material capacity do you select?

**9.11** A high-pressure cylindrical air beam spans a distance of 45 ft. If a working pressure of 100 psi is to be maintained, what minimum size tube must be selected to support 75 lb/ft? Determine also the tensile capacity of the membrane.

**9.12** A 10-in. pressurized tube of parabolic shape spans 40 ft and has a height of 20 ft. It must support an equivalent load of 100 lb/ft on the horizontal roof projection. Determine the internal air pressure and the capacity of the membrane material.

**9.13** Determine the inflation pressure and material strength for a truncated conical membrane which has a height of 30 ft and a diameter of 50 ft at the base and 12.5 ft at the top.

(a) Neglect material weight and assume a 20 psf snow load to act on the flat top portion.

(b) Consider the snow load to act on the horizontal projection of the cone.

## 9.4  PRESTRESSED TENSILE MEMBRANE STRUCTURES

Tensile membranes made of fabrics or cable nets can be classified either according to their surface form or according to the support conditions. Basic surface forms are either saddle-shaped and stretched between their boundaries or they are conical shaped and center supported at high or low points. The combination of these basic surface forms yields an infinite number of new forms. The classification of tensile membranes given in Fig. 9.17 is based on the type of support provided for the soft shell. The supports may be rigid or flexible; they may be point or line supports located either in the interior or along the exterior edges. Examples of small scale membrane skin structures (tents) with flexible boundaries are shown in the central portion of the drawing, while the cable net structures with rigid boundaries are identified along the outer ring. Other rigid exterior boundary forms have been already discussed in Fig. 4.48 under Arches.

In the following discussion of some of the cases, a further insight will be provided into the character of lightweight surface structures; first the cable net roofs in Fig. 9.17 are investigated briefly.

The North Carolina State Fair Building in Raleigh (i) has a nearly elliptical shape in plan view. Two inclined parabolic arches support in funicular action the uniform loading of the only slightly prestressed saddle-shaped cable roof which spans about 300 ft in both directions. The vertical arch loads are carried by columns around the perimeter. The steel strands form a net pattern of 6 × 6 ft squares which supports the corrugated metal sheets (Fig. 9.2a). The primary suspended cable sizes vary from $\frac{3}{4}$ to $1\frac{5}{16}$ in., while the arched cables range from $\frac{1}{2}$ to $\frac{3}{4}$ in. diameter. Actually, the roof is more of a one-way system, since the tension in the bracing direction is by far less. Therefore, guy wires are attached to the primary cables and tied down to the perimeter columns to reduce fluttering. Eero Saarinen's Hockey Rink at Yale University is probably the first true tensile surface architecture. In this sculpture-like building the dynamism of the surface is fully absorbed into the total architecture. The anticlastic cable roof [(g), 324 × 183 ft] is strung between a central vertical parabolic arch 70 ft high and two curved horizontal edge walls which act as curved vertical cantilevers to resist the lateral thrust. Concrete struts under the base of the rink prevent the sliding of the wall foundations. The central parabolic arch spans 240 ft and then cantilevers with reverse curvature at both ends to support the roof overhangs at the entrances. The main transverse suspended cables are $\frac{15}{16}$-in. in diameter and are spaced 6 ft apart. Nine lengthwise arched cables, also of $\frac{15}{16}$-in. diameter, are located on each side of the spine and stretch between four steel trusses at each end of the building. Additional direct transverse cables on the outside brace the central arch against unbalanced loading. A detail of the roof decking is shown in Fig. 9.2b.

The sculptural shapes of the two stadiums for the 1964 Olympics in Tokyo, Japan (d), (f), are without question masterpieces of modern architecture. The roof of the larger gymnasium [(d), 394 × 702 ft] is supported by heavy steel cables which are stretched between two towering concrete masts and tied down to anchorage blocks. One may visualize the main suspended roof as a net structure with hanging members of varying bending stiffness and the arched bracing members with zero stiffness. The hanging I-beams are hinged at one or two intermediate points along their spans; they provide the necessary stiffness because of the lack of curvature in the opposite direction, and are supported by the heavy central steel cables and boundary arches.

The smaller gymnasium (f) employs a quite different structural concept for its asymmetrical configuration. The radially arranged suspended members are not cables, but

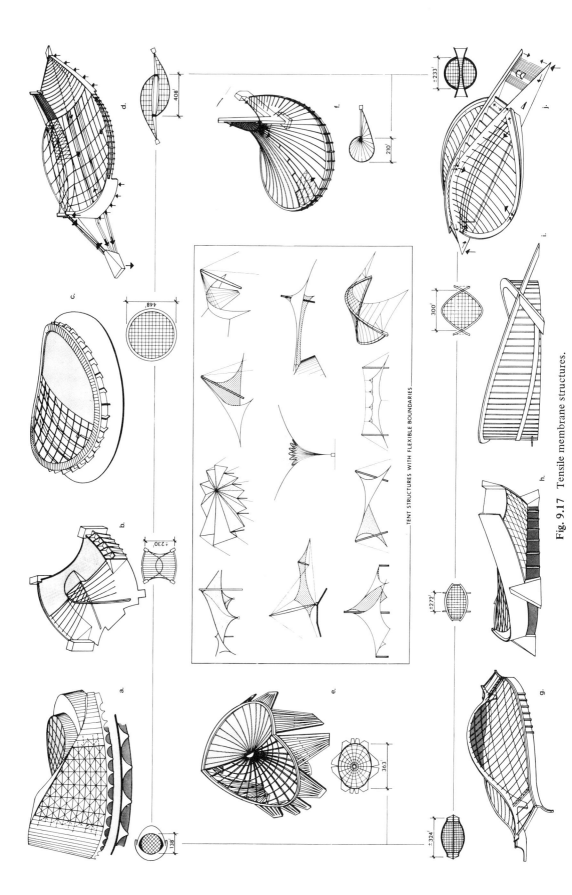

**Fig. 9.17** Tensile membrane structures.

trusts with some bending capacity. Since the flat portion of the roof did not allow any prestressing, the roof had to be treated as a one-way suspended structure requiring at least a minimum rigidity. The hanging trusses are supported along the circumference by columns that are part of the grandstand structure which forms a rigid closed cone (213 ft diameter) and, at the off-center by a hanging steel pipe. This suspended pipe forms a spatial spiral curve between the top of the concrete mast and the anchor block.

The El Paso Performing Arts Center (a) looks like two intersecting crescents in perspective. The roof membrane is anchored to the 138-ft diameter compression ring located between the crescents. The ring is three-dimensional and circular in plan view, which caused, in addition to the usual axial action and simple bending, biaxial bending and torsion. The cables ($1-2\frac{1}{8}$-in. diameter) are arranged at $45°$ to the roof's main axes and are spaced at 15 ft to form a square-gridded cable net which supports a precast concrete roof.

The roof membrane of the special events stadium of Indiana University (b) is not a cable net structure but a one-way suspended cable system which is stabilized by a precast concrete deck; the spaces between the planks are filled with concrete to create a stiff shell. The building is shown in this context because of the interesting way in which the cables are supported at the center by the intersecting inclined steel arches, and at the periphery by curved walls. The $1\frac{3}{8}$-in. diameter suspended cables are spaced 6 ft apart and span about 230 ft across the stadium.

The hyperbolic paraboloid roof of the Kagawa Prefectural Gymnasium (h) consists of a prestressed cable net forming approximately a 4-ft square grid which supports the nearly 2-in. thick precast concrete panels.

The roof of the circular, saucer-shaped Milan Sports Palace (c), is of roughly hyperbolic paraboloid form. It consists of zinc sheets resting on the prestressed cable net and is carried by the overhanging concrete "gantries" that also support the seating dish. Beautifully sculptured metal brackets are attached to the heads of these gantries; they serve as hinges to allow the steel box ring to behave independently of the base structure.

The deformed wheel-like roof of the main temple of Sho-Hondo at Taiseki-ji- (e) rests on fan-shaped, inclined column clusters of various configurations that form pyramid-like space truss supports. The roof is not a lightweight, prestressed cable-net surface, but a heavyweight semirigid tensile structure where the radial hanging members are not cables but steel beams which provide the necessary rigidity against wind and other loads. These curved beams are suspended between the inner circular tension and the outer elliptical compression rings; they are laterally braced by concentric ring beams. This beam grid, in turn, provides the support for the precast lightweight concrete panels.

For the 1980 Olympic Games in Moscow, the Russian designers built two tensile membrane structures of enormous scale. The roof of the main oval stadium has the shape of an elliptic paraboloid with $735 \times 610$ ft along its main axes and is supported by a suspended steel membrane consisting of the steel skin and the hanging radial trusses. The nearly elliptical Krylatskoe cycle track with $551 \times 453$ ft consists of two hyperbolic paraboloids joined along the center axis by two inclined parabolic arches similar in appearance to case (j). The anticlastic roof membranes of the bicycle track stadium are of particular interest since they were constructed not from cable nets but suspended steel sheets connected and stiffened in the transverse direction by continuous purlins.

The next cases to be discussed are of the tent type membrane structures as shown in Fig. 9.18. With the German Pavilion at Expo 67 in Montreal, Canada (a), large-scale tent construction had reached a certain level of maturity, its form and structure established direction and identity. The primary structure of the saddle-shaped roof consists of the

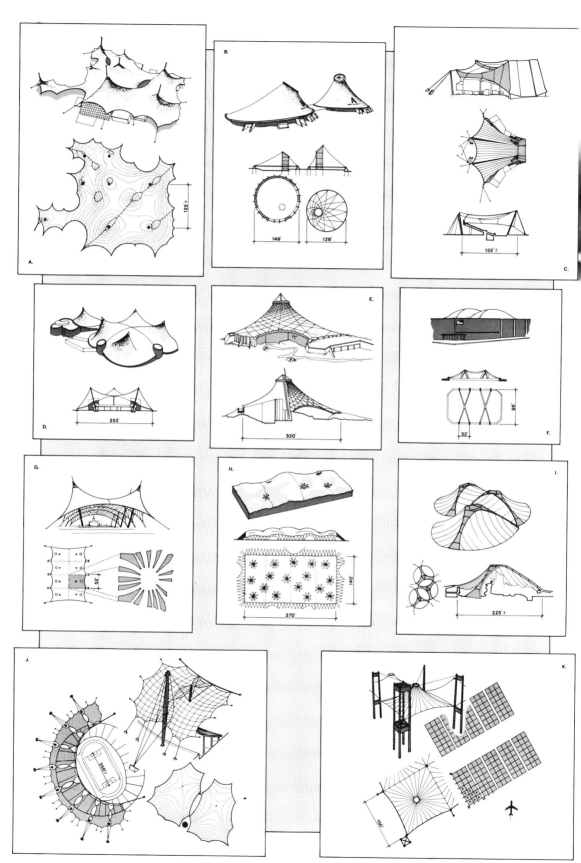

**Fig. 9.18** Tent architecture.

prestressed cable net supported by ridge and 2-in. diameter edge cables which in turn are carried by eight inclined tubular steel masts (largest mast is 125 ft high and 40 in. diameter), three interior restraint eyes, and thirty anchor points around the perimeter. The cable mesh consists of $\frac{1}{2}$-in. diameter steel cables that form in general a square net of 20 × 20 in. It is prestressed to an average uniform tension of 20–30 psf to resist the 20 psf snow load and the wind uplift forces. The cable eyes at the high and low points are covered with acrylic glass. The secondary structure is the translucent PVC-coated polyester fabric suspended from the steel cable mesh. The two structures are separated by adjustable turnbuckles to compensate for differential movement.

The tent-like roofs for the Munich Olympics in 1972, cover an area of about 808,000 ft$^2$ that is much more than the roughly 87,000 ft$^2$ for the German Pavilion at Expo 67. The covered space includes three stadiums, the main stadium, the swimming area, the sports arena, and the spaces linking the stadiums. The scale and method of construction of these roofs is a major achievement for Frei Otto; he proved that tensile membranes can be permanent architecture. The western grandstand of the main outdoor stadium is covered by nine saddle-shaped prestressed membrane units (j) which are supported along the outside by stayed cables hanging from masts (on average 230 ft high) and along the inside by a huge edge cable which runs along the inner edge of the grandstands. This main cable is 1440 ft long and not only ties the entire roof together, but also makes the span of the roof possible. It is composed of a bundle of ten 4.7-in. diameter cables which together must resist forces of up to 10,000 k. To provide additional height, each of the membrane units is also supported by a flying guyed mast. The cable net roof of 30-in. square meshes is composed of twin steel cables of 1-in. diameter spaced at 2 in. and clamped together at cable intersection points. The net, in turn, is connected to the edge cables. The roof covering is placed above the network. It consists of translucent acrylic glass (plexiglass) panels approximately $9\frac{1}{2}$ ft square, which are bolted to the network at each of the clamped cable intersections (Fig. 9.2c).

Each of the conical roofs of the Automobile Pavilion (b) of Expo 70 in Osaka, Japan, consists of a prestressed cable net supported at the top by an inner cylindrical shaft, and a Hypalon-coated vinyl fabric hung from the mesh points. The cables are supported from the upper ring and anchored to the lower ring. The crossing cable pattern results in opposing cable curvatures which counteract each other and thus give stability to the roof.

The student center of La Verne College (d), built in 1973, is considered the first permanent fabric structure in the United States. The four overlapping conical tent units enclose a space of 68,000 ft$^2$. Each unit is supported by an inclined central tubular steel column. The Teflon-coated fiberglass fabric, weighing only 45 oz/yd$^2$, is strengthened by a web of thirty-two 1-in. diameter radial cables which are suspended from the top of the mast to the compression ring on top of the perimeter wall and to the two $1\frac{7}{8}$-in. diameter main cables along the intersection of the four tent units that arch between the four 24-ft cylindrical stairwell towers. The fabric roof is insulated with a 2-in. thick fiberglass blanket and supported by supplementary $\frac{3}{16}$-in. diameter polypropylene-coated cables.

The cone-shaped U.S. Pavilion of Expo 74 in Spokane, Washington, consists of a steel cable network from which the vinyl-coated fiberglass fabric is hung; the roof covers an area of about 280 × 320 ft. The primary radial cables are suspended from a crown ring, which is supported by a 152 ft high center mast, and are anchored to the concrete piers along the perimeter. The primary cables are stabilized by the secondary arched cables placed on top of them.

The Mecca Auditorium roof (c) is not a true cable net structure but is discussed here because of the tent character of the building. The roof consists of simply suspended steel cables approximately 1-in. diameter supporting a heavyweight decking. The cable roof is hanging from a steel frame at one end and edge cables spanning between guyed masts at the other end.

The humped tent for the BP inauguration in London (h) consists simply of a flat rect-angular polyester/cotton canvas sheet which is prestressed by being pushed up with masts and pulled down, as based on some predetermined pattern.

A typical unit of the zoo pavilion for the Franklin Park Zoo (i) is formed by three in-clined parabolic arches that rise from a circular base ring and combine to a bent tripod; this tripod supports the tensile membranes. An internal negative air pressure (suction) pulls the skin inward and thus stabilizes it against fluttering.

The membrane roof of Bullock's department store in San Jose, California (f) is sup-ported by two pairs of crossed, laminated wood arches hinged at the top, as well as by edge cables. The Teflon-coated fiberglass membrane covers the $96 \times 160$ ft space without the assistance of cable reinforcement; the fabric is prestressed to a level of 35 lb/in. A second inner fabric layer is suspended from the arches to improve insulation, acoustics and fire safety. For a new department store in San Mateo, California (completed in 1981) Bullock is covering the entire building with a 70,000 ft² Teflon-coated fiberglass roof.

The Haj Terminal of the New Jeddah International Airport (k) is comprised of 210 identical quasiconical roof units, each 150-ft square, covering an area of 105 acres. The Teflon-coated fiberglass fabric of a typical unit is strengthened and pretensioned by a sys-tem of cables arranged in a radial pattern. The radial cables are supported by a 13-ft diam-eter steel tension ring at the top, and at the bottom by ridge cables/edge cables which span between pylons. The tension ring at the top is suspended by four pairs of $1\frac{5}{8}$-in. diameter cables from the 148 ft high steel pylons at the four corners. The tents are under a prestress force of 66 lb/in. and are designed to resist a wind pressure upward and down-ward of 35 psf.

### Approximate Behavior of Anticlastic Prestressed Membranes and Cable Nets

Soft membranes such as fabric, film, and network lack rigidity; they are flexible and in-herently unstable; they must adjust their shape to the loading so that they can respond in tension. It was discussed in the section introducing linear cable systems that there are sev-eral ways in which stability can be achieved. For membranes one obvious and most natural method is to use anticlastic surface geometry, where two opposing curvatures balance each other. The main (convex, suspended, lower, load-bearing, etc.) cable is prevented from moving by the secondary (concave, arched, upper, bracing, etc.) cable, which is pre-stressed and pulls the suspended layer down, thus stabilizing it. This interdependence of the two opposing systems is rather similar to the dual-cable beam, where the damping cable stabilizes the primary cable. Visualize the initial surface tension analogous to the one caused by internal air pressure in pneumatic structures. The prestress force must be large enough to keep the surface in tension under any loading condition, preventing any portion of the skin or any member to slack because of the compression being larger than the stored tension. In addition, the magnitude of the initial tension should be high enough to provide the necessary stiffness so that the membrane deflection is kept to a minimum. The type of response the skin takes to external loading depends on the magnitude of the prestress force. However, the amount of pretensioning not only is a function of superimposed loading but also is directly related to the roof shape and the boundary support conditions. An open tent-like structure with flexible cables as edge supports is obviously more vulnerable to large deformations than a membrane attached to a closed rigid compression ring, which in comparison hardly deforms.

It was already discussed that cables and fabric do not behave in a linear manner, but resist loads by going through large deformations and causing the magnitude of the membrane forces to depend on the final position in space. Other nonlinear aspects are due to creep of the surface material (canvas, coated fabric, cables) and due to slippage at clamps and fittings allowing a change of net geometry. Temperature change and shrinkage also influence the linear behavior. Membranes are rather vulnerable to dynamic loading causing material fatigue which, in turn, results in reduction of strength with time. This nonlinear feature makes the design of membranes extremely difficult, requiring structural engineers specialized in this rather sophisticated field.

The determination of the roof shape for given building boundaries is not a simple undertaking. While the architect presents the surface geometry as based on static form of mass and gravity, thinking in terms of solid, rigid material as the decisive factors, the structural engineer must correct this shape. The engineer has to take into account the non-material, weightless flexible character of a membrane surface, its relation to external loading and to the type and arrangement of the supports as the primary form determinants.

The surface geometry is directly dependent on the magnitude of the prestressing, which in turn makes it possible for the surface to be in equilibrium with varied external loading combinations. For preliminary design purposes the surface geometry can be derived from its initial loading stage of uniform, constant surface tension. For this condition, the form is a function of the given boundary configuration as was discussed for minimal surfaces (Fig. 7.4). They can be formed experimentally by dipping a closed spatial frame, having the shape of the roof boundaries, into a soap solution. The resulting liquid film surface is anticlastic and if shallow enough, can be approximated by the hyperbolic paraboloid. Keep in mind that the actual surface material must respond to environmental changes, hence is quite different from a soap film being supported by surface tension only and well protected from any outside influence. The membrane is never really under uniform tension, it is constantly subject to other external forces. Furthermore, boundaries are not necessarily predetermined; there is an optimal solution between support form and surface shape considering also the wind load distribution as a function of the roof form. One may conclude that the minimal surface, unfortunately, can only be considered as a first approximation of the real membrane shape.

From a structural design point of view, prestressed anticlastic membrane surfaces may be subdivided into three main groups:

- Saddle surfaces—supported along exterior boundaries. In addition, supported by interior line supports (arches and cables), generating undulating and corrugating surface forms.
- Anticlastic surfaces point-supported in the interior (stress concentrations).
- Combinations.

While saddle surfaces, in general, use nets with regular meshes, mostly triangular and rectangular, or fabric consisting of long narrow strips sewn or glued together acting along the overlapping edges similar to small suspended cables, the point-supported surfaces use radial net or fabric strip patterns. They have the appearance of cones and derive their net

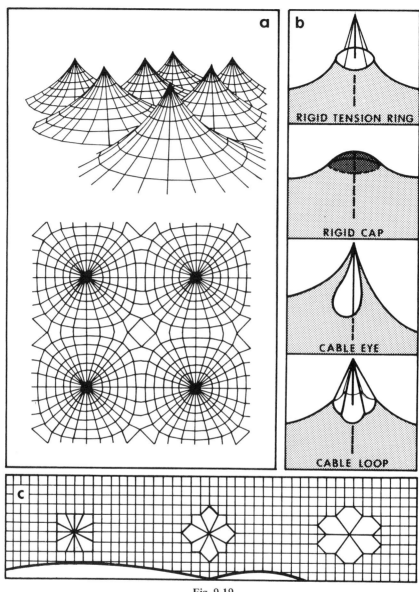

RIGID TENSION RING

RIGID CAP

CABLE EYE

CABLE LOOP

c

**Fig. 9.19**

pattern from the radial and circumferential stress flow, resulting in a regular radial/ring
type mesh, similar to a spider web if seen in plan view as in Fig. 9.19 a, for tents with rectangular bases. The cutting pattern of the fabric strips follows the radial stress flow or the
suspended cables. Possible combinations of the two surface systems are shown in Fig.
9.19c, where radial nets merge into orthogonal network. In the point-supported tent all
the tension forces are collected at the column head causing a stress intensity too high for
the membrane. To overcome this problem, either the membrane is reinforced with additional radial cables or relief is provided by one of the methods shown in Fig. 9.19b.

In the following discussion only simple saddle surfaces supported along their edges by
rigid or flexible members are further investigated (Fig. 9.20).

The stress state of the membrane for the ideal condition of pretension only, ignoring any other influences, can be derived from the general membrane equation for zero external loading conditions

$$p = \frac{T_y}{R_y} + \frac{T_x}{R_x} = 0 \tag{7.1}$$

$$-\frac{T_y}{R_y} = \frac{T_x}{R_x} \quad \text{or} \quad \frac{T_y}{T_x} = \frac{-R_y}{R_x} \tag{9.18}$$

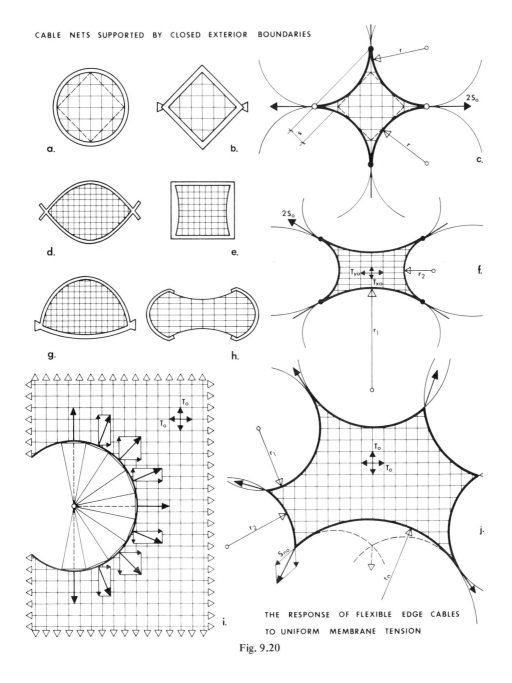

CABLE NETS SUPPORTED BY CLOSED EXTERIOR BOUNDARIES

THE RESPONSE OF FLEXIBLE EDGE CABLES
TO UNIFORM MEMBRANE TENSION

Fig. 9.20

As can be seen, the tensile forces along the principal curvatures must be proportional to their respective radii so they are in balance along the surface. Furthermore, the surface must be anticlastic to make equilibrium possible, as the negative sign indicates. Here, the special case of identical parabolas or equal radii of curvature is investigated. Obviously, for this condition the tensile forces must be equal to each other

$$T_{y0} = T_{x0} = T_0 \qquad (9.19)$$

The membrane is in a state of uniform tension; any effect of roof weight, temperature change, material creep and shrinkage, and flexible boundary supports, all of which will influence the ideal uniform stress distribution, is neglected. The stress state is obtained by assuming the cable network or net-like fabric to follow the principal parabolas forming a square grid in plan view; for this condition the mesh sizes vary, increasing from a minimum in the flat portion to a maximum in the steeper areas (Fig. 8.27). Prefabricated nets on the other hand, will have an equal square grid, where the deviation of its net pattern from the one based on the principal stress flow is only small for shallow surfaces. Hence, it is reasonable, for approximation purposes, to assume for shallow surfaces that the square mesh projects an equal square on the horizontal plan. However, one must keep in mind that for steeper surfaces the square mesh along the inclined surface portions wants to adjust its shape to coincide with the principal stress flow, thereby causing grid distortions and shearing forces at the cable cross points. In general, cables are clamped together at the points of intersection in order to get shear resistance and to prevent them from sliding. For a square mesh it can be shown from the equilibrium of forces at the cable intersection (Fig. 9.21) that the forces must be equal to each other. This was already concluded before as based on the membrane equation.

The surface is considered truly continuous and not as consisting of discrete points, as actually is the case for network surfaces.

In the following discussion, the square mesh net is not placed along the straight line generators of the hyperbolic paraboloid. The lack of curvature along the linear cables causes large deformations of the surface, which can only be overcome by increasing the prestress forces similar to the strings of a tennis racket. Further, it is assumed that the surface is not too flat so that deflection does not control.

The initial tension may be induced directly to the cables or by tensioning the boundary cables using prestress equipment; the tension can also be induced by an initial external overload $p$. Even if this approach should not be used, the load $p$ is helpful as a concept and can be seen as an imaginary or equivalent external load to express the prestress force.

According to the membrane equation for shallow hyperbolic paraboloids under uni-

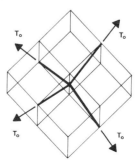

Fig. 9.21

form vertical load action, letting $w = p$, the membrane forces per unit width along each principal direction can be approximated as

$$T_{y0} = T_{x0} = T_0 = \frac{pR}{2} = \frac{pL^2}{16f} \qquad (9.20)$$

Or, the magnitude of the equivalent prestress load $p$ for a surface under constant tension is a function of the curvature

$$p = \frac{2T}{R} \qquad (9.21)$$

Note, that with a decrease of surface curvature or increase of radius less prestress force is needed!

A square-mesh net under uniform tension will cause a boundary cable to respond with the funicular shape of a circular segment. The cable forces cause radial resultants of equal magnitude along the edges, as is shown conceptually in Fig. 9.20i. Hence, a membrane under uniform tension causes its edge cables to take the shape of a circular segment (Fig. 9.20c and j) with a constant tension force $S_{n0}$ of

$$S_{n0} = T_0 r_n = \frac{pR r_n}{2} \qquad (9.22)$$

With the decrease in the radius of curvature along the edges, the cable force decreases yielding smaller cable sizes (Fig. 9.20j).

For the case where the cables are spaced differently in each principal direction, that is where a rectangular mesh net is being used, the radial force action upon the edge cable will no longer be constant as for the square grid, it will force the edge member to take the shape of an elliptical segment (Fig. 9.20f). For this condition, the axial force in the shallow edge cable can be shown as equal to

$$S_0 = T_{x0} r_1 = T_{y0} r_2 \qquad (9.23)$$

Rigid edge members may have a variety of forms. They may be planar such as horizontal circular rings, or spatial like warped rings, or inclined intersecting arches which may be straight or curved. While straight members have certain advantages from a constructional and functional point of view, they also must carry the membrane forces in bending, requiring large beam sections (Fig. 9.20b and e). The behavior of arched edge members may be interpreted as being the inverse of edge cables, though the flexible cable will adjust its shape to respond to the different loads (actual change is kept to a minimum by prestress force), which the rigid member cannot. The arches act primarily in compression, being possibly funicular for the controlling loading case, but otherwise must carry moments. The ring arch is stiffened significantly, as the membrane loads increase and, at the same time, increase the prestress effect on the ring, which is an important consideration in concrete design.

The magnitude of the prestress forces is not easy to determine; it depends on strength, stiffness, dynamic considerations, and for smaller structures often simply on experience. The pretension force should be large enough so that the membrane is always in tension and does not slack because of the compression caused by external loading. The critical stress stage for a suspended cable or an imaginary fabric strip is, in general, under full gravity loading. Yet, how are these loads distributed to the hanging and arched membrane portion? Is there any difference in response between the continuous fabric and the non-continuous network, where the cable intersection points may be considered hinged? In the discussion of the approximate load flow along a cable truss (Example 3.3), it is shown that a much higher portion of the load is carried by the suspended cable as compared to the damping cable. The true distribution of the loads is highly indeterminate. However, to develop some appreciation for prestressed membranes and some feeling for the importance of geometry, fabric and orthogonal nets are both treated in the same fashion as membranes. They are assumed to behave linearly, neglecting the effect of larger deformations in the flatter surface areas. Rigid boundaries are assumed, while the effect of flexible edge members on the membrane behavior is ignored thus allowing some slack. Furthermore, conditions of perfect symmetry of loading, geometry, and material are assumed. Not only are the boundary conditions symmetrical, but also the cables in each principal direction are considered identical in size and spacing. The membrane is positioned horizontally; for if it were inclined and wall-like, horizontal wind forces, obviously, become primary design determinants.

With respect to the superimposed loading, the membrane action of a rectangular hyperbolic paraboloid as applied for the design of thin shells, is assumed to reflect also the behavior of the flexible skin, ignoring the effect of prestressing. For this condition of symmetry, it is reasonable to consider the external loads to be equally shared by the suspended and arched cables. Keep in mind that perfect symmetry never exists, even for material symmetry environmental changes will cause asymmetry, developing a force flow quite different from the one assumed.

Under full gravity loading the lower, hanging cable or fabric strip $T_L$ is stressed to a maximum, while the arched membrane portion $T_T$ is stressed to a minimum, requiring only enough tension so that it does not slack. Hence, each cable system, taken as a membrane per unit width, carries an equal pretensioning force and an equal share of the superimposed loading

$$T_L = T_0 + \frac{wL^2}{16f} \qquad \qquad \text{(b)}$$

$$T_T = T_0 - \frac{wL^2}{16f} \geqslant 0 \qquad \qquad \text{(c)}$$

For first approximation purposes, under normal wind conditions where wind suction is less than snow loading, let the tensile force in the stabilizing cable [Eq. (c)] be equal to zero and do not consider any safety factor. The result is a prestress force generated by an imaginary load equivalent to one-half of the maximum superimposed loading

$$T_0 = \frac{wL^2}{16f} \qquad \qquad \text{(d)}$$

The magnitude of the prestress force is only a preliminary one; it may have to be changed to take into account membrane flexibility, surface flutter, and rigidity of boundaries. Substituting $T_0$ into Eq. (b) yields the following maximum membrane force per unit width

$$T_T = T_{max} = wR = \frac{wL^2}{8f} = \frac{wa^2}{f} \qquad \qquad \text{(9.24)}$$

The cable force is obtained by multiplying the unit force $T_{max}$ by the cable spacing. The terms in the equation have already been defined in the discussion of the membrane behavior of the hyperbolic paraboloid [Eq. (7.28)]. One may conclude that for the preliminary design of shallow membranes and cable nets all external loads are carried by the suspended portion of the surface similar to a single curvature system, while the arched portion only provides stability. Further, notice that at least one-half of the permitted tension in the cables is consumed by the initial stored tension.

The design of the arched cable system for lightweight roof structures is derived, in general, from the loading condition where maximum wind suction causes uplift and increases the stored prestress tension, which is considered here equal to one-half of the full gravity loading, minus the relatively small effect of membrane weight. For most cases it is conservative to consider the cable sizes in the arched direction as equal to the ones in the suspended direction.

Even for conditions of asymmetry, such as for different span ratios, sag ratios, or spacing and sizes of cables, one may still roughly approximate the forces in the shallow prestressed membrane in order to obtain a quick preliminary design estimate by using Eq. (9.24) and selecting mean values or the controlling values to be conservative. The radius of curvature in the equation may be treated as a constant, that is, the parabola may be replaced by the circle, and may be scaled off the drawing if necessary at the very initial design stage.

**Example 9.6** Determine the approximate cable size for a prestressed square mesh network 8 X 8 ft, covering a square plan of 128 X 128 ft (Fig. 9.22). The saddle-shaped roof has a typical sag-to-span ratio of 1/12, resulting in a sag and rise of 10.67 ft. The dead and live loads are 8 psf and 20 psf, respectively.

A typical suspended cable carries following load

$$w = (20 + 8)8 = 224 \text{ lb/ft} = 0.22 \text{ k/ft}$$

The maximum force according to Eq. (9.24) as based on full loading, for the primary cable is

$$T_{max} = w\,R = \frac{wL^2}{8f} = \frac{0.22(128)^2}{8(10.67)} = 42.23 \text{ k}$$

$$T_U = \text{LF}\,(T) = 2.2\,(42.23) = 92.91 \text{ k}$$

From Table 3.1 try a 1-in. diameter single-strand cable.

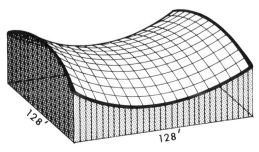

**Fig. 9.22**

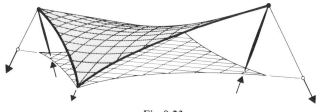

**Fig. 9.23**

**Example 9.7**  Replace the hypar shell of Example 8.31 with a tent structure, which is supported by columns at two opposite corners, while the two remaining corners are directly tied to the ground (Fig. 9.23). The membrane, consisting either of a coated fabric or orthogonal cables, is supported along its edges by diagonal cables.

The membrane forces due to live load and prestressing, ignoring the small weight, are according to Eq. (9.24) equal to

$$T_{max} = \frac{wL^2}{8f} = \frac{20(100\sqrt{2})^2}{8(15)} = 3333 \text{ lb/ft}$$

or

$$T_{max} = \frac{w\,a^2}{f} = \frac{20(50)^2}{15} = 3333 \text{ lb/ft}$$

The minimum required strip tensile strength for the coated fabric is

$$T_U = \text{LF}\,(T) = 4(3.33) = 13.32 \text{ K/ft} = 1.11 \text{ K/in.}$$

Since the maximum capacity of the strongest fabric, which at this time is Teflon-coated glass fabric, is about 1000 lb/in., a cable net must be selected.

For a mesh size of $4 \times 4$ ft, the cable force is

$$T_{max} = 4(3.33) = 13.33 \text{ k}$$

$$T_U = \text{LF}\,(T) = 2.2\,(13.33) = 29.33 \text{ k}$$

From Table 3.1 try a $\frac{1}{2}$-in. diameter single-strand cable.

At the initial stage of prestressing, the edge cable takes a circular shape due to radial net action as was discussed. The radial forces per foot are equal to one-half of the maximum membrane force

$$p_0 = \frac{T_{max}}{2} = \frac{3.33}{2}$$

This radial load causes a constant edge cable force of

$$S_0 = p_0\,r \qquad\qquad (9.22)$$

However, in this case the circular cable can be considered of parabolic shape, since its sag-to-span ratio is equal to $1/8$ or $\dfrac{\Delta}{L} = \dfrac{12.5}{100} = \dfrac{1}{8}$ (see also, The Circular Arch)

$$S_0 = p_0 r = \frac{p(2a)^2}{8s} = \frac{3.33(100)^2}{2(8)12.5} = 166.5 \text{ k}$$

Under full loading, only the suspended cable portion of the network applies a force to the edge member, while the forces in the secondary cables are zero according to the previous assumptions. Hence, the edge cable is only loaded diagonally from one direction. The evaluation of the maximum force for this loading condition is quite complex. In order still to be able to get a preliminary cable size, the shallow membrane is assumed, under full loading, to cause the shallow edge cable to respond as a parabola. Now the maximum cable force may be roughly approximated as:

$$S = p\,r = \frac{p(2a)^2}{8s} = \frac{3.33(100)^2}{8(12.5)} = 333 \text{ k}$$

$$S_U = \text{LF }(S) = 2.2\,(333) = 732.6 \text{ k}$$

From Table 3.1 try a $2\frac{1}{2}$-in. diameter single strand cable.

## 9.5  SOME OTHER SOFT SHELL STRUCTURES

Rather than using air as the primary support medium for columns and walls, water or sand may replace the gas and be contained in a tensile membrane. The liquid or soil carries the compression while the enclosing membrane prevents its lateral displacement in tensile action.

The principle of the sail or parachute with natural wind or a mechanically generated airflow produces a dynamic airborne roof structure. Additional support for the canvas may be provided by helium balloons anchored to the ground.

The ultimate minimum weight structure may be the massless air curtain enclosure (Fig. 9.24) proposed by the architect Peter Goering of Toronto; here the static material response is replaced by a dynamic energy system. He utilizes for this invisible architecture rapidly moving jets of air to protect the enclosed space from rain, snow, and wind.

### Problems

**9.14** Do a rough, preliminary design of the membrane, first by using a coated fabric and then a network $4\frac{1}{4} \times 4\frac{1}{4}$ ft and find also the edge cable size for a tent shown in Fig. 9.23. The tent covers a square base of 80 ft and has a maximum height at the

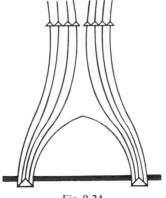

Fig. 9.24

masts of 20 ft; it must support a live load of 15 psf. The sag of the edge cables is 8 ft.

**9.15** Do a quick preliminary design for one of the nine saddle-like net surfaces of the Olympic Stadium in Munich (Fig. 9.18j). The membrane consists of a square mesh of about $2\frac{1}{2} \times 2\frac{1}{2}$ ft. The radii of curvature of the hanging cables vary between 164 ft and 230 ft. Assume the radius of curvature for the typical edge cable as 80 ft. The membrane must support its own weight of 4 psf and a snow load of 26 psf.

**9.16** A saddle-type canvas roof with negligible weight must support a snow load of 15 psf and a wind suction of 20 psf. If the mean radius of curvature of the membrane surface is 80 ft, what must be the capacity of the canvas?

**9.17** An elliptical paraboloid dish-type membrane roof with a sag of 17 ft at the center covers an elliptical area of $302 \times 382$ ft. The cables comprise a $10 \times 10$ ft grid and support the precast concrete ribs and slab panels. The tendons are post-tensioned so that the compression in the concrete shell is larger than the tension due to the design loads. Determine the magnitude of the prestress forces for the critical cables along the major and minor axes due to a dead load of 48 psf and a live load of 12 psf. Further, find the maximum compression force in the peripheral ring girder.

# APPENDIX

## 1. TABLES FOR REINFORCED CONCRETE

Table A.1

| ASTM Standard Reinforcing Bars | | | | |
|---|---|---|---|---|
| bar size | weight (#/ft) | nominal dimensions - round sections | | |
| | | diameter (in.) | cross sec.(in.$^2$) | perim. (in.) |
| #3 | .376 | .375 | .11 | 1.178 |
| #4 | .668 | .500 | .20 | 1.571 |
| #5 | 1.043 | .625 | .31 | 1.963 |
| #6 | 1.502 | .750 | .44 | 2.356 |
| #7 | 2.044 | .875 | .60 | 2.749 |
| #8 | 2.670 | 1.000 | .79 | 3.142 |
| #9 | 3.400 | 1.128 | 1.00 | 3.544 |
| #10 | 4.303 | 1.270 | 1.27 | 3.990 |
| #11 | 5.313 | 1.410 | 1.56 | 4.430 |
| #14 | 7.65 | 1.693 | 2.25 | 5.32 |
| #18 | 13.60 | 2.257 | 4.00 | 7.09 |

Table A.2

| Areas of Bar Combinations ( in.$^2$ ) | | | | | | | | | | | | | |
|---|---|---|---|---|---|---|---|---|---|---|---|---|---|
| number of bars | | | | | | | | | | | | | |
| bar size \ | 2 | 3 | 4 | 5 | 6 | 7 | 8 | 9 | 10 | 11 | 12 | 13 | 14 |
| 4 | 0.39 | 0.58 | 0.78 | 0.98 | 1.18 | 1.37 | 1.57 | 1.77 | 1.96 | 2.16 | 2.36 | 2.55 | 2.75 |
| 5 | 0.61 | 0.91 | 1.23 | 1.53 | 1.84 | 2.15 | 2.45 | 2.76 | 3.07 | 3.37 | 3.68 | 3.99 | 4.30 |
| 6 | 0.88 | 1.32 | 1.77 | 2.21 | 2.65 | 3.09 | 3.53 | 3.98 | 4.42 | 4.86 | 5.30 | 5.74 | 6.19 |
| 7 | 1.20 | 1.80 | 2.41 | 3.01 | 3.61 | 4.21 | 4.81 | 5.41 | 6.01 | 6.61 | 7.22 | 7.82 | 8.42 |
| 8 | 1.57 | 2.35 | 3.14 | 3.93 | 4.71 | 5.50 | 6.28 | 7.07 | 7.85 | 8.64 | 9.43 | 10.21 | 11.00 |
| 9 | 2.00 | 3.00 | 4.00 | 5.00 | 6.00 | 7.00 | 8.00 | 9.00 | 10.00 | 11.00 | 12.00 | 13.00 | 14.00 |
| 10 | 2.53 | 3.79 | 5.06 | 6.33 | 7.59 | 8.86 | 10.12 | 11.39 | 12.66 | 13.92 | 15.19 | 16.45 | 17.72 |
| 11 | 3.12 | 4.68 | 6.25 | 7.81 | 9.37 | 10.94 | 12.50 | 14.06 | 15.62 | 17.19 | 18.75 | 20.31 | 21.87 |
| 14 | 4.50 | 6.75 | 9.00 | 11.25 | 13.50 | 15.75 | 18.00 | 20.25 | 22.50 | 24.75 | 27.00 | 29.25 | 31.50 |
| 18 | 8.00 | 12.00 | 16.00 | 20.00 | 24.00 | 28.00 | 32.00 | 36.00 | 40.00 | 44.00 | 48.00 | 52.00 | 56.00 |

Table A.3

| Areas of Bars for One-foot Wide Slab (in.$^2$/ft) | | | | | | | | | |
|---|---|---|---|---|---|---|---|---|---|
| bar size | | | | | | | | | |
| | 3 | 4 | 5 | 6 | 7 | 8 | 9 | 10 | 11 |
| spacing (in.) 3 | 0.44 | 0.78 | 1.23 | 1.77 | 2.40 | 3.14 | 4.00 | 5.06 | 6.25 |
| 4 | 0.33 | 0.59 | 0.92 | 1.32 | 1.80 | 2.36 | 3.00 | 3.80 | 4.68 |
| 5 | 0.26 | 0.47 | 0.74 | 1.06 | 1.44 | 1.88 | 2.40 | 3.04 | 3.75 |
| 6 | 0.22 | 0.39 | 0.61 | 0.88 | 1.20 | 1.57 | 2.00 | 2.53 | 3.12 |
| 7 | 0.19 | 0.34 | 0.53 | 0.76 | 1.03 | 1.35 | 1.71 | 2.17 | 2.68 |
| 8 | 0.17 | 0.29 | 0.46 | 0.66 | 0.90 | 1.18 | 1.50 | 1.89 | 2.34 |
| 9 | 0.15 | 0.26 | 0.41 | 0.59 | 0.80 | 1.05 | 1.33 | 1.69 | 2.08 |
| 10 | 0.13 | 0.24 | 0.37 | 0.53 | 0.72 | 0.94 | 1.20 | 1.52 | 1.87 |

Table A.4

| Minimum Beam Widths | | | | | | | |
|---|---|---|---|---|---|---|---|
| bar size | number of bars in single layer | | | | | | |
| | 2 | 3 | 4 | 5 | 6 | 7 | 8 |
| #4 | 5 3/4 | 7 1/4 | 8 3/4 | 10 1/4 | 11 3/4 | 13 1/4 | 14 3/4 |
| #5 | 6 | 7 3/4 | 9 1/4 | 11 | 12 1/2 | 14 1/4 | 15 3/4 |
| #6 | 6 1/4 | 8 | 9 3/4 | 11 1/2 | 13 1/4 | 15 | 16 3/4 |
| #7 | 6 1/2 | 8 1/2 | 10 1/4 | 12 1/4 | 14 | 16 | 17 3/4 |
| #8 | 6 3/4 | 8 3/4 | 10 3/4 | 12 3/4 | 14 3/4 | 16 3/4 | 18 3/4 |
| #9 | 7 1/4 | 9 1/2 | 11 3/4 | 14 | 16 1/4 | 18 1/2 | 20 3/4 |
| #10 | 7 3/4 | 10 1/4 | 12 3/4 | 15 1/4 | 17 3/4 | 20 1/4 | 23 |
| #11 | 8 | 11 | 13 3/4 | 16 1/2 | 19 1/2 | 22 1/4 | 25 |
| #14 | 9 | 12 1/4 | 15 3/4 | 19 | 22 1/2 | 25 3/4 | 29 1/4 |
| #18 | 10 1/2 | 15 | 19 1/2 | 24 | 28 1/2 | 33 | 37 1/2 |

Table A.5   The Maximum Steel Ratio

| P max = 0.75 $P_b$ = 0.75( 0.85$\beta_1 f_c'/F_y$ )( 87000/( 87000 + $F_y$ ) ) | | | | |
|---|---|---|---|---|
| fc'(psi) | 3000 | 4000 | 5000 | 6000 |
| Fy        $\beta_1$ | 0.85 | 0.85 | 0.80 | 0.75 |
| Grade 40 | 0.0278 | 0.0371 | 0.0437 | 0.0492 |
| Grade 50 | 0.0206 | 0.0275 | 0.0324 | 0.0365 |
| Grade 60 | 0.0161 | 0.0214 | 0.0252 | 0.0283 |

Table A.6   Section Properties for Sawn Lumber and Timber

| Nominal Size b × d in. | Standard Dressed Size (S4S) b × d in. | Area of Section A in.² | X-X Axis Moment of Inertia I in.⁴ | X-X Axis Section Modulus S in.³ | Nominal Size b × d in. | Standard Dressed Size (S4S) b × d in. | Area of Section A in.² | X-X Axis Moment of Inertia I in.⁴ | X-X Axis Section Modulus S in.³ |
|---|---|---|---|---|---|---|---|---|---|
| 1 × 3 | 3/4 × 2 1/2 | 1.875 | 0.977 | 0.781 | 6 × 6 | 5 1/2 × 5 1/2 | 30.250 | 76.255 | 27.729 |
| 1 × 4 | 3/4 × 3 1/2 | 2.625 | 2.680 | 1.531 | 6 × 8 | 5 1/2 × 7 1/2 | 41.250 | 193.359 | 51.563 |
| 1 × 6 | 3/4 × 5 1/2 | 4.125 | 10.398 | 3.781 | 6 × 10 | 5 1/2 × 9 1/2 | 52.250 | 392.963 | 82.729 |
| 1 × 8 | 3/4 × 7 1/4 | 5.438 | 23.817 | 6.570 | 6 × 12 | 5 1/2 × 11 1/2 | 63.250 | 697.068 | 121.229 |
| 1 × 10 | 3/4 × 9 1/4 | 6.938 | 49.466 | 10.695 | 6 × 14 | 5 1/2 × 13 1/2 | 74.250 | 1,127.672 | 167.063 |
| 1 × 12 | 3/4 × 11 1/4 | 8.438 | 88.989 | 15.820 | 6 × 16 | 5 1/2 × 15 1/2 | 85.250 | 1,706.776 | 220.229 |
| 2 × 3 | 1 1/2 × 2 1/2 | 3.750 | 1.953 | 1.563 | 6 × 18 | 5 1/2 × 17 1/2 | 96.250 | 2,456.380 | 280.729 |
| 2 × 4 | 1 1/2 × 3 1/2 | 5.250 | 5.359 | 3.063 | 6 × 20 | 5 1/2 × 19 1/2 | 107.250 | 3,398.484 | 348.563 |
| 2 × 6 | 1 1/2 × 5 1/2 | 8.250 | 20.797 | 7.563 | 6 × 22 | 5 1/2 × 21 1/2 | 118.250 | 4,555.086 | 423.729 |
| 2 × 8 | 1 1/2 × 7 1/4 | 10.875 | 47.635 | 13.141 | 6 × 24 | 5 1/2 × 23 1/2 | 129.250 | 5,948.191 | 506.229 |
| 2 × 10 | 1 1/2 × 9 1/4 | 13.875 | 98.932 | 21.391 | 8 × 8 | 7 1/2 × 7 1/2 | 56.250 | 263.672 | 70.313 |
| 2 × 12 | 1 1/2 × 11 1/4 | 16.875 | 177.979 | 31.641 | 8 × 10 | 7 1/2 × 9 1/2 | 71.250 | 535.859 | 112.813 |
| 2 × 14 | 1 1/2 × 13 1/4 | 19.875 | 290.775 | 43.891 | 8 × 12 | 7 1/2 × 11 1/2 | 86.250 | 950.547 | 165.313 |
| 3 × 4 | 2 1/2 × 3 1/2 | 8.750 | 8.932 | 5.104 | 8 × 14 | 7 1/2 × 13 1/2 | 101.250 | 1,537.734 | 227.813 |
| 3 × 6 | 2 1/2 × 5 1/2 | 13.750 | 34.661 | 12.604 | 8 × 16 | 7 1/2 × 15 1/2 | 116.250 | 2,327.422 | 300.313 |
| 3 × 8 | 2 1/2 × 7 1/4 | 18.125 | 79.391 | 21.901 | 8 × 18 | 7 1/2 × 17 1/2 | 131.250 | 3,349.609 | 382.813 |
| 3 × 10 | 2 1/2 × 9 1/4 | 23.125 | 164.886 | 35.651 | 8 × 20 | 7 1/2 × 19 1/2 | 146.250 | 4,634.297 | 475.313 |
| 3 × 12 | 2 1/2 × 11 1/4 | 28.125 | 296.631 | 52.734 | 8 × 22 | 7 1/2 × 21 1/2 | 161.250 | 6,211.484 | 577.813 |
| 3 × 14 | 2 1/2 × 13 1/4 | 33.125 | 484.625 | 73.151 | 8 × 24 | 7 1/2 × 23 1/2 | 176.250 | 8,111.172 | 690.313 |
| 3 × 16 | 2 1/2 × 15 1/4 | 38.125 | 738.870 | 96.901 | 10 × 10 | 9 1/2 × 9 1/2 | 90.250 | 678.755 | 142.896 |
| 4 × 4 | 3 1/2 × 3 1/2 | 12.250 | 12.505 | 7.146 | 10 × 12 | 9 1/2 × 11 1/2 | 109.250 | 1,204.026 | 209.396 |
| 4 × 6 | 3 1/2 × 5 1/2 | 19.250 | 48.526 | 17.646 | 10 × 14 | 9 1/2 × 13 1/2 | 128.250 | 1,947.797 | 288.563 |
| 4 × 8 | 3 1/2 × 7 1/4 | 25.375 | 111.148 | 30.661 | 10 × 16 | 9 1/2 × 15 1/2 | 147.250 | 2,948.068 | 380.396 |
| 4 × 10 | 3 1/2 × 9 1/4 | 32.375 | 230.840 | 49.911 | 10 × 18 | 9 1/2 × 17 1/2 | 166.250 | 4,242.836 | 484.896 |
| 4 × 12 | 3 1/2 × 11 1/4 | 39.375 | 415.283 | 73.828 | 10 × 20 | 9 1/2 × 19 1/2 | 185.250 | 5,870.109 | 602.063 |
| 4 × 14 | 3 1/2 × 13 1/4 | 46.375 | 678.475 | 102.411 | 10 × 22 | 9 1/2 × 21 1/2 | 204.250 | 7,867.879 | 731.896 |
| 4 × 16 | 3 1/2 × 15 1/4 | 53.375 | 1,034.418 | 135.661 | 10 × 24 | 9 1/2 × 23 1/2 | 223.250 | 10,274.148 | 874.396 |

# Table A.7 Properties of Some Glulam Structural Sections

### 5 1/8 IN. WIDTH

| No. of Lams 1 1/2 in. | No. of Lams 3/4 in. | Depth, d (inches) | Size Factor $C_F$ | Area, A (inches²) | Section Modulus, S (inches³) | Moment of Inertia, I (inches⁴) |
|---|---|---|---|---|---|---|
| 3 | 6 | 4.50 | 1.00 | 23.1 | 17.3 | 38.9 |
|  | 7 | 5.25 | 1.00 | 26.9 | 23.5 | 61.8 |
| 4 | 8 | 6.00 | 1.00 | 30.8 | 30.8 | 92.3 |
|  | 9 | 6.75 | 1.00 | 34.6 | 38.9 | 131.3 |
| 5 | 10 | 7.50 | 1.00 | 38.4 | 48.0 | 180.2 |
|  | 11 | 8.25 | 1.00 | 42.3 | 58.1 | 239.8 |
| 6 | 12 | 9.00 | 1.00 | 46.1 | 69.2 | 311.3 |
|  | 13 | 9.75 | 1.00 | 50.0 | 81.2 | 395.8 |
| 7 | 14 | 10.50 | 1.00 | 53.8 | 94.2 | 494.4 |
|  | 15 | 11.25 | 1.00 | 57.7 | 108.1 | 608.1 |
| 8 | 16 | 12.00 | 1.00 | 61.5 | 123.0 | 738.0 |
|  | 17 | 12.75 | 0.99 | 65.3 | 138.9 | 885.2 |
| 9 | 18 | 13.50 | 0.99 | 69.2 | 155.7 | 1,050.8 |
|  | 19 | 14.25 | 0.98 | 73.0 | 173.4 | 1,235.8 |
| 10 | 20 | 15.00 | 0.98 | 76.9 | 192.2 | 1,441.4 |
|  | 21 | 15.75 | 0.97 | 80.7 | 211.9 | 1,668.6 |
| 11 | 22 | 16.50 | 0.97 | 84.6 | 232.5 | 1,918.5 |
|  | 23 | 17.25 | 0.96 | 88.4 | 254.2 | 2,192.2 |
| 12 | 24 | 18.00 | 0.96 | 92.3 | 276.8 | 2,490.8 |
|  | 25 | 18.75 | 0.95 | 96.1 | 300.3 | 2,815.2 |
| 13 | 26 | 19.50 | 0.95 | 99.9 | 324.8 | 3,166.8 |
|  | 27 | 20.25 | 0.94 | 103.8 | 350.3 | 3,546.4 |
| 14 | 28 | 21.00 | 0.94 | 107.6 | 376.7 | 3,955.2 |
|  | 29 | 21.75 | 0.94 | 111.5 | 404.1 | 4,394.3 |
| 15 | 30 | 22.50 | 0.93 | 115.3 | 432.4 | 4,864.7 |
|  | 31 | 23.25 | 0.93 | 119.2 | 461.7 | 5,367.6 |
| 16 | 32 | 24.00 | 0.93 | 123.0 | 492.0 | 5,904.0 |
|  | 33 | 24.75 | 0.92 | 126.8 | 523.2 | 6,475.0 |
| 17 | 34 | 25.50 | 0.92 | 130.7 | 555.4 | 7,081.6 |
|  | 35 | 26.25 | 0.92 | 134.5 | 588.6 | 7,725.0 |
| 18 | 36 | 27.00 | 0.91 | 138.4 | 622.7 | 8,406.3 |
|  | 37 | 27.75 | 0.91 | 142.2 | 657.8 | 9,126.4 |
| 19 | 38 | 28.50 | 0.91 | 146.1 | 693.8 | 9,886.6 |
|  | 39 | 29.25 | 0.91 | 149.9 | 730.8 | 10,687.8 |
| 20 | 40 | 30.00 | 0.90 | 153.8 | 768.8 | 11,531.3 |
|  | 41 | 30.75 | 0.90 | 157.6 | 807.7 | 12,417.9 |
| 21 | 42 | 31.50 | 0.90 | 161.4 | 847.5 | 13,348.9 |
|  | 43 | 32.25 | 0.90 | 165.3 | 888.4 | 14,325.2 |
| 22 | 44 | 33.00 | 0.89 | 169.1 | 930.2 | 15,348.1 |
|  | 45 | 33.75 | 0.89 | 173.0 | 972.9 | 16,418.5 |
| 23 | 46 | 34.50 | 0.89 | 176.8 | 1,016.7 | 17,537.6 |
|  | 47 | 35.25 | 0.89 | 180.7 | 1,061.4 | 18,706.4 |
| 24 | 48 | 36.00 | 0.88 | 184.5 | 1,107.0 | 19,926.0 |

### 6 3/4 IN. WIDTH

| No. of Lams 1 1/2 in. | No. of Lams 3/4 in. | Depth, d (inches) | Size Factor $C_F$ | Area, A (inches²) | Section Modulus, S (inches³) | Moment of Inertia, I (inches⁴) |
|---|---|---|---|---|---|---|
| 4 | 8 | 6.00 | 1.00 | 40.5 | 40.5 | 121.5 |
|  | 9 | 6.75 | 1.00 | 45.6 | 51.3 | 173.0 |
| 5 | 10 | 7.50 | 1.00 | 50.6 | 63.3 | 237.3 |
|  | 11 | 8.25 | 1.00 | 55.7 | 76.6 | 315.9 |
| 6 | 12 | 9.00 | 1.00 | 60.8 | 91.1 | 410.1 |
|  | 13 | 9.75 | 1.00 | 65.8 | 106.9 | 521.4 |
| 7 | 14 | 10.50 | 1.00 | 70.9 | 124.0 | 651.2 |
|  | 15 | 11.25 | 1.00 | 75.9 | 142.4 | 800.9 |
| 8 | 16 | 12.00 | 1.00 | 81.0 | 162.0 | 972.0 |
|  | 17 | 12.75 | 0.99 | 86.1 | 182.9 | 1,165.9 |
| 9 | 18 | 13.50 | 0.99 | 91.1 | 205.0 | 1,384.0 |
|  | 19 | 14.25 | 0.98 | 96.2 | 228.4 | 1,627.7 |
| 10 | 20 | 15.00 | 0.98 | 101.3 | 253.1 | 1,898.4 |
|  | 21 | 15.75 | 0.97 | 106.3 | 279.1 | 2,197.7 |
| 11 | 22 | 16.50 | 0.97 | 111.4 | 306.3 | 2,526.8 |
|  | 23 | 17.25 | 0.96 | 116.4 | 334.8 | 2,887.3 |
| 12 | 24 | 18.00 | 0.96 | 121.5 | 364.5 | 3,280.5 |
|  | 25 | 18.75 | 0.95 | 126.6 | 395.5 | 3,707.9 |
| 13 | 26 | 19.50 | 0.95 | 131.6 | 427.8 | 4,170.9 |
|  | 27 | 20.25 | 0.94 | 136.7 | 461.3 | 4,670.9 |
| 14 | 28 | 21.00 | 0.94 | 141.8 | 496.1 | 5,209.3 |
|  | 29 | 21.75 | 0.94 | 146.8 | 532.2 | 5,787.6 |
| 15 | 30 | 22.50 | 0.93 | 151.9 | 569.5 | 6,407.2 |
|  | 31 | 23.25 | 0.93 | 156.9 | 608.1 | 7,069.5 |
| 16 | 32 | 24.00 | 0.93 | 162.0 | 648.0 | 7,776.0 |
|  | 33 | 24.75 | 0.92 | 167.1 | 689.1 | 8,528.0 |
| 17 | 34 | 25.50 | 0.92 | 172.1 | 731.5 | 9,327.0 |
|  | 35 | 26.25 | 0.92 | 177.2 | 775.2 | 10,174.4 |
| 18 | 36 | 27.00 | 0.91 | 182.3 | 820.1 | 11,071.7 |
|  | 37 | 27.75 | 0.91 | 187.3 | 866.3 | 12,020.2 |
| 19 | 38 | 28.50 | 0.91 | 192.4 | 913.8 | 13,021.4 |
|  | 39 | 29.25 | 0.91 | 197.4 | 962.5 | 14,076.7 |
| 20 | 40 | 30.00 | 0.90 | 202.5 | 1,012.5 | 15,187.5 |
|  | 41 | 30.75 | 0.90 | 207.6 | 1,063.8 | 16,355.3 |
| 21 | 42 | 31.50 | 0.90 | 212.6 | 1,116.3 | 17,581.4 |
|  | 43 | 32.25 | 0.90 | 217.7 | 1,170.1 | 18,867.4 |
| 22 | 44 | 33.00 | 0.89 | 222.8 | 1,225.1 | 20,214.6 |
|  | 45 | 33.75 | 0.89 | 227.8 | 1,281.4 | 21,624.4 |
| 23 | 46 | 34.50 | 0.89 | 232.9 | 1,339.0 | 23,098.3 |
|  | 47 | 35.25 | 0.89 | 237.9 | 1,397.9 | 24,637.7 |
| 24 | 48 | 36.00 | 0.88 | 243.0 | 1,458.0 | 26,244.0 |
|  | 49 | 36.75 | 0.88 | 248.1 | 1,519.4 | 27,918.5 |
| 25 | 50 | 37.50 | 0.88 | 253.1 | 1,582.0 | 29,663.1 |
|  | 51 | 38.25 | 0.88 | 258.2 | 1,645.9 | 31,478.7 |
| 26 | 52 | 39.00 | 0.88 | 263.3 | 1,711.1 | 33,366.9 |
|  | 53 | 39.75 | 0.88 | 268.3 | 1,777.6 | 35,329.2 |
| 27 | 54 | 40.50 | 0.87 | 273.4 | 1,845.3 | 37,367.0 |
|  | 55 | 41.25 | 0.87 | 278.4 | 1,914.3 | 39,481.6 |
| 28 | 56 | 42.00 | 0.87 | 283.5 | 1,984.5 | 41,674.5 |
|  | 57 | 42.75 | 0.87 | 288.6 | 2,056.0 | 43,947.2 |
| 29 | 58 | 43.50 | 0.87 | 293.6 | 2,128.8 | 46,301.0 |
|  | 59 | 44.25 | 0.87 | 298.7 | 2,202.8 | 48,737.4 |
| 30 | 60 | 45.00 | 0.86 | 303.8 | 2,278.1 | 51,257.8 |
|  | 61 | 45.75 | 0.86 | 308.8 | 2,354.7 | 53,863.7 |
| 31 | 62 | 46.50 | 0.86 | 313.9 | 2,432.5 | 56,556.4 |
|  | 63 | 47.25 | 0.86 | 318.9 | 2,511.6 | 59,337.3 |
| 32 | 64 | 48.00 | 0.86 | 324.0 | 2,592.0 | 62,208.0 |

### 8 3/4 IN. WIDTH

| No. of Lams 1 1/2 in. | No. of Lams 3/4 in. | Depth, d (inches) | Size Factor $C_F$ | Area, A (inches²) | Section Modulus, S (inches³) | Moment of Inertia, I (inches⁴) |
|---|---|---|---|---|---|---|
| 6 | 12 | 9.00 | 1.00 | 78.8 | 118.1 | 531.6 |
|  | 13 | 9.75 | 1.00 | 85.3 | 138.6 | 675.8 |
| 7 | 14 | 10.50 | 1.00 | 91.9 | 160.8 | 844.1 |
|  | 15 | 11.25 | 1.00 | 98.4 | 184.6 | 1,038.2 |
| 8 | 16 | 12.00 | 1.00 | 105.0 | 210.0 | 1,260.0 |
|  | 17 | 12.75 | 0.99 | 111.6 | 237.1 | 1,511.3 |
| 9 | 18 | 13.50 | 0.99 | 118.1 | 265.8 | 1,794.0 |
|  | 19 | 14.25 | 0.98 | 124.7 | 296.1 | 2,109.9 |
| 10 | 20 | 15.00 | 0.98 | 131.3 | 328.1 | 2,460.9 |
|  | 21 | 15.75 | 0.97 | 137.8 | 361.8 | 2,848.8 |
| 11 | 22 | 16.50 | 0.97 | 144.4 | 397.0 | 3,275.5 |
|  | 23 | 17.25 | 0.96 | 150.9 | 433.9 | 3,742.8 |
| 12 | 24 | 18.00 | 0.96 | 157.5 | 472.5 | 4,252.5 |
|  | 25 | 18.75 | 0.95 | 164.1 | 512.7 | 4,806.5 |
| 13 | 26 | 19.50 | 0.95 | 170.6 | 554.5 | 5,406.7 |
|  | 27 | 20.25 | 0.94 | 177.2 | 598.0 | 6,054.8 |
| 14 | 28 | 21.00 | 0.94 | 183.8 | 643.1 | 6,752.8 |
|  | 29 | 21.75 | 0.94 | 190.3 | 689.9 | 7,502.5 |
| 15 | 30 | 22.50 | 0.93 | 196.9 | 738.3 | 8,305.7 |
|  | 31 | 23.25 | 0.93 | 203.4 | 788.3 | 9,164.2 |
| 16 | 32 | 24.00 | 0.93 | 210.0 | 840.0 | 10,080.0 |
|  | 33 | 24.75 | 0.92 | 216.6 | 893.3 | 11,054.8 |
| 17 | 34 | 25.50 | 0.92 | 223.1 | 948.3 | 12,090.6 |
|  | 35 | 26.25 | 0.92 | 229.7 | 1,004.9 | 13,189.1 |
| 18 | 36 | 27.00 | 0.91 | 236.3 | 1,063.1 | 14,352.2 |
|  | 37 | 27.75 | 0.91 | 242.8 | 1,123.0 | 15,581.7 |
| 19 | 38 | 28.50 | 0.91 | 249.4 | 1,184.5 | 16,879.6 |
|  | 39 | 29.25 | 0.91 | 255.9 | 1,247.7 | 18,247.5 |
| 20 | 40 | 30.00 | 0.90 | 262.5 | 1,312.5 | 19,687.5 |
|  | 41 | 30.75 | 0.90 | 269.1 | 1,378.9 | 21,201.3 |
| 21 | 42 | 31.50 | 0.90 | 275.6 | 1,447.0 | 22,790.7 |
|  | 43 | 32.25 | 0.90 | 282.2 | 1,516.8 | 24,457.7 |
| 22 | 44 | 33.00 | 0.89 | 288.8 | 1,588.1 | 26,204.1 |
|  | 45 | 33.75 | 0.89 | 295.3 | 1,661.1 | 28,031.6 |
| 23 | 46 | 34.50 | 0.89 | 301.9 | 1,735.8 | 29,942.2 |
|  | 47 | 35.25 | 0.89 | 308.4 | 1,812.1 | 31,937.7 |
| 24 | 48 | 36.00 | 0.88 | 315.0 | 1,890.0 | 34,020.0 |
|  | 49 | 36.75 | 0.88 | 321.6 | 1,969.6 | 36,190.9 |
| 25 | 50 | 37.50 | 0.88 | 328.1 | 2,050.8 | 38,452.2 |
|  | 51 | 38.25 | 0.88 | 334.7 | 2,133.6 | 40,805.7 |
| 26 | 52 | 39.00 | 0.88 | 341.3 | 2,218.1 | 43,253.4 |
|  | 53 | 39.75 | 0.88 | 347.8 | 2,304.3 | 45,797.1 |
| 27 | 54 | 40.50 | 0.87 | 354.4 | 2,392.0 | 48,438.6 |
|  | 55 | 41.25 | 0.87 | 360.9 | 2,481.4 | 51,179.8 |
| 28 | 56 | 42.00 | 0.87 | 367.5 | 2,572.5 | 54,022.5 |
|  | 57 | 42.75 | 0.87 | 374.1 | 2,665.2 | 56,968.6 |
| 29 | 58 | 43.50 | 0.87 | 380.6 | 2,759.5 | 60,019.8 |
|  | 59 | 44.25 | 0.87 | 387.2 | 2,855.5 | 63,178.1 |
| 30 | 60 | 45.00 | 0.86 | 393.8 | 2,953.1 | 66,445.3 |
|  | 61 | 45.75 | 0.86 | 400.3 | 3,052.4 | 69,823.3 |
| 31 | 62 | 46.50 | 0.86 | 406.9 | 3,153.3 | 73,313.8 |
|  | 63 | 47.25 | 0.86 | 413.4 | 3,255.8 | 76,918.8 |
| 32 | 64 | 48.00 | 0.86 | 420.0 | 3,360.0 | 80,640.0 |
|  | 65 | 48.75 | 0.86 | 426.6 | 3,465.8 | 84,479.4 |
| 33 | 66 | 49.50 | 0.85 | 433.1 | 3,573.3 | 88,438.7 |
|  | 67 | 50.25 | 0.85 | 439.7 | 3,682.4 | 92,519.9 |
| 34 | 68 | 51.00 | 0.85 | 446.3 | 3,793.1 | 96,724.7 |
|  | 69 | 51.75 | 0.85 | 452.8 | 3,905.5 | 101,055.0 |
| 35 | 70 | 52.50 | 0.85 | 459.4 | 4,019.5 | 105,512.7 |
|  | 71 | 53.25 | 0.85 | 465.9 | 4,135.2 | 110,099.6 |
| 36 | 72 | 54.00 | 0.85 | 472.5 | 4,252.5 | 114,817.5 |
|  | 73 | 54.75 | 0.85 | 479.1 | 4,371.4 | 119,668.3 |
| 37 | 74 | 55.50 | 0.84 | 485.6 | 4,492.0 | 124,653.9 |
|  | 75 | 56.25 | 0.84 | 492.2 | 4,614.3 | 129,776.0 |
| 38 | 76 | 57.00 | 0.84 | 498.8 | 4,738.1 | 135,036.6 |
|  | 77 | 57.75 | 0.84 | 505.3 | 4,863.6 | 140,437.4 |
| 39 | 78 | 58.50 | 0.84 | 511.9 | 4,990.8 | 145,980.4 |
|  | 79 | 59.25 | 0.84 | 518.4 | 5,119.6 | 151,667.3 |
| 40 | 80 | 60.00 | 0.84 | 525.0 | 5,250.0 | 157,500.0 |
|  | 81 | 60.75 | 0.84 | 531.6 | 5,382.1 | 163,480.4 |
| 41 | 82 | 61.50 | 0.83 | 538.1 | 5,515.8 | 169,610.3 |
|  | 83 | 62.25 | 0.83 | 544.7 | 5,651.1 | 175,891.5 |
| 42 | 84 | 63.00 | 0.83 | 551.3 | 5,788.1 | 182,326.0 |

# 3. TABLES FOR STEEL DESIGN

Table A.8  A Partial Selection of Weight Economy Sections

| $S_x$ (in.³) | Shape | $F_y'$ (ksi) | $F_y = 36$ ksi $L_c$(ft) | $L_u$(ft) | $S_x$ (in.³) | Shape | $F_y'$ (ksi) | $F_y = 36$ ksi $L_c$(ft) | $L_u$(ft) |
|---|---|---|---|---|---|---|---|---|---|
| 1110 | W 36 x 300 | - | 17.6 | 35.3 | 107 | W 12 x 79 | 62.6 | 12.8 | 33.3 |
| 1030 | W 36 x 280 | - | 17.5 | 33.1 | 103 | W 14 x 68 | - | 10.6 | 23.9 |
| 953 | W 36 x 260 | - | 17.5 | 30.5 | 98.3 | W 18 x 55 | - | 7.9 | 12.1 |
| 895 | W 36 x 245 | - | 17.4 | 28.6 | 97.4 | W 12 x 72 | 52.3 | 12.7 | 30.5 |
| 837 | W 36 x 230 | - | 17.4 | 26.8 | 94.5 | W 21 x 50 | - | 6.9 | 7.8 |
| 829 | W 33 x 241 | - | 16.7 | 30.1 | 92.2 | W 16 x 57 | - | 7.5 | 14.3 |
| 757 | W 33 x 221 | - | 16.7 | 27.6 | 92.2 | W 14 x 61 | - | 10.6 | 21.5 |
| 719 | W 36 x 210 | - | 12.9 | 20.9 | 88.9 | W 18 x 50 | - | 7.9 | 11.0 |
| 684 | W 33 x 201 | - | 16.6 | 24.9 | 87.9 | W 12 x 65 | 43.0 | 12.7 | 27.7 |
| 664 | W 36 x 194 | - | 12.8 | 19.4 | 81.6 | W 21 x 44 | - | 6.6 | 7.0 |
| 663 | W 30 x 211 | - | 15.9 | 29.7 | 81.0 | W 16 x 50 | - | 7.5 | 12.7 |
| 623 | W 36 x 182 | - | 12.7 | 18.2 | 70.6 | W 12 x 53 | 55.9 | 10.6 | 22.0 |
| 598 | W 30 x 191 | - | 15.9 | 26.9 | 70.3 | W 14 x 48 | - | 8.5 | 16.0 |
| 580 | W 36 x 170 | - | 12.7 | 17.0 | 68.4 | W 18 x 40 | - | 6.3 | 8.2 |
| 542 | W 36 x 160 | - | 12.7 | 15.7 | 66.7 | W 10 x 60 | - | 10.6 | 31.1 |
| 539 | W 30 x 173 | - | 15.8 | 24.2 | 64.7 | W 16 x 40 | - | 7.4 | 10.2 |
| 504 | W 36 x 150 | - | 12.6 | 14.6 | 62.7 | W 14 x 43 | - | 8.4 | 14.4 |
| 487 | W 33 x 152 | - | 12.2 | 16.9 | 60.0 | W 10 x 54 | 63.5 | 10.6 | 28.2 |
| 455 | W 27 x 161 | - | 14.8 | 25.4 | 58.1 | W 12 x 45 | - | 8.5 | 17.7 |
| 448 | W 33 x 141 | - | 12.2 | 15.4 | 57.6 | W 18 x 35 | - | 6.3 | 6.7 |
| 439 | W 36 x 135 | - | 12.3 | 13.0 | 54.6 | W 14 x 38 | - | 7.1 | 11.5 |
| 414 | W 24 x 162 | - | 13.7 | 29.3 | 51.9 | W 12 x 40 | - | 8.4 | 16.0 |
| 411 | W 27 x 146 | - | 14.7 | 23.0 | 49.1 | W 10 x 45 | - | 8.5 | 22.8 |
| 406 | W 33 x 130 | - | 12.1 | 13.8 | 48.6 | W 14 x 34 | - | 7.1 | 10.2 |
| 380 | W 30 x 132 | - | 11.1 | 16.1 | 47.2 | W 16 x 31 | - | 5.8 | 7.1 |
| 371 | W 24 x 146 | - | 13.6 | 26.3 | 45.6 | W 12 x 35 | - | 6.9 | 12.6 |
| 359 | W 33 x 118 | - | 12.0 | 12.6 | 42.1 | W 10 x 39 | - | 8.4 | 19.8 |
| 355 | W 30 x 124 | - | 11.1 | 15.0 | 42.0 | W 14 x 30 | 55.3 | 7.1 | 8.7 |
| 329 | W 30 x 116 | - | 11.1 | 13.8 | 38.6 | W 12 x 30 | - | 6.9 | 10.8 |
| 329 | W 24 x 131 | - | 13.6 | 23.4 | 38.4 | W 16 x 26 | - | 5.6 | 6.0 |
| 329 | W 21 x 147 | - | 13.2 | 30.3 | 35.3 | W 14 x 26 | - | 5.3 | 7.0 |
| 299 | W 30 x 108 | - | 11.1 | 12.3 | 35.0 | W 10 x 33 | 50.5 | 8.4 | 16.5 |
| 299 | W 27 x 114 | - | 10.6 | 15.9 | 33.4 | W 12 x 26 | 57.9 | 6.9 | 9.4 |
| 291 | W 24 x 117 | - | 13.5 | 20.8 | 32.4 | W 10 x 30 | - | 6.1 | 13.1 |
| 269 | W 30 x 99 | - | 10.9 | 11.4 | 31.2 | W 8 x 35 | 64.4 | 8.5 | 22.6 |
| 267 | W 27 x 102 | - | 10.6 | 14.2 | 29.0 | W 14 x 22 | - | 5.3 | 5.6 |
| 258 | W 24 x 104 | 58.5 | 13.5 | 18.4 | 27.9 | W 10 x 26 | - | 6.1 | 11.4 |
| 243 | W 27 x 94 | - | 10.5 | 12.8 | 27.5 | W 8 x 31 | 50.0 | 8.4 | 20.1 |
| 231 | W 18 x 119 | - | 11.9 | 29.1 | 25.4 | W 12 x 22 | - | 4.3 | 6.4 |
| 227 | W 21 x 101 | - | 13.0 | 21.3 | 24.3 | W 8 x 28 | - | 6.9 | 17.5 |
| 222 | W 24 x 94 | - | 9.6 | 15.1 | 23.2 | W 10 x 22 | - | 6.1 | 9.4 |
| 213 | W 27 x 84 | - | 10.5 | 11.0 | 21.3 | W 12 x 19 | - | 4.2 | 5.3 |
| 204 | W 18 x 106 | - | 11.8 | 26.0 | 21.1 | M 14 x 18 | - | 3.6 | 4.0 |
| 196 | W 24 x 84 | - | 9.5 | 13.3 | 20.9 | W 8 x 24 | 64.1 | 6.9 | 15.2 |
| 192 | W 21 x 93 | - | 8.9 | 16.8 | 18.8 | W 10 x 19 | - | 4.2 | 7.2 |
| 188 | W 18 x 97 | - | 11.8 | 24.1 | 17.1 | W 12 x 16 | - | 4.1 | 4.3 |
| 176 | W 24 x 76 | - | 9.5 | 11.8 | 16.7 | W 6 x 25 | - | 6.4 | 20.0 |
| 171 | W 21 x 83 | - | 8.8 | 15.1 | 15.2 | W 8 x 18 | - | 5.5 | 9.9 |
| 166 | W 18 x 86 | - | 11.7 | 21.5 | 14.9 | W 12 x 14 | 54.3 | 3.5 | 4.2 |
| 157 | W 14 x 99 | 48.5 | 15.4 | 37.0 | 13.8 | W 10 x 15 | - | 4.2 | 5.0 |
| 154 | W 24 x 68 | - | 9.5 | 10.2 | 13.4 | W 6 x 20 | 62.1 | 6.4 | 16.4 |
| 151 | W 21 x 73 | - | 8.8 | 13.4 | 12.0 | M 12 x 11.8 | - | 2.7 | 3.0 |
| 146 | W 18 x 76 | 64.2 | 11.6 | 19.1 | 10.9 | W 10 x 12 | 47.5 | 3.9 | 4.3 |
| 143 | W 14 x 90 | 40.4 | 15.3 | 34.0 | 10.2 | W 5 x 19 | - | 5.3 | 19.5 |
| 140 | W 21 x 68 | - | 8.7 | 12.4 | 9.72 | W 6 x 15 | 31.8 | 6.3 | 12.0 |
| 134 | W 16 x 77 | - | 10.9 | 21.9 | 8.51 | W 5 x 16 | - | 5.3 | 16.7 |
| 131 | W 24 x 62 | - | 7.4 | 8.1 | 7.81 | W 8 x 10 | 45.8 | 4.2 | 4.7 |
| 127 | W 21 x 62 | - | 8.7 | 11.2 | 7.76 | M 10 x 9 | - | 2.6 | 2.7 |
| 123 | W 14 x 82 | - | 10.7 | 28.1 | 7.31 | W 6 x 12 | - | 4.2 | 8.6 |
| 117 | W 18 x 65 | - | 8.0 | 14.4 | 5.56 | W 6 x 9 | 50.3 | 4.2 | 6.7 |
| 117 | W 16 x 67 | - | 10.8 | 19.3 | 5.46 | W 4 x 13 | - | 4.3 | 15.6 |
| 114 | W 24 x 55 | - | 7.0 | 7.5 | 4.62 | M 8 x 6.5 | - | 2.4 | 2.5 |
| 108 | W 18 x 60 | - | 8.0 | 13.3 | 2.40 | M 6 x 4.4 | - | 1.9 | 2.4 |

## Table A.9  Allowable Stresses for Columns of A36 Steel[a]

| Main and Secondary Members $Kl/r$ not over 120 | | | | | | Main Members $Kl/r$ 121 to 200 | | | | Secondary Members[a] $l/r$ 121 to 200 | | | |
| --- | --- | --- | --- | --- | --- | --- | --- | --- | --- | --- | --- | --- | --- |
| $\dfrac{Kl}{r}$ | $F_a$ (ksi) | $\dfrac{Kl}{r}$ | $F_a$ (ksi) | $\dfrac{Kl}{r}$ | $F_a$ (ksi) | $\dfrac{Kl}{r}$ | $F_a$ (ksi) | $\dfrac{Kl}{r}$ | $F_a$ (ksi) | $\dfrac{l}{r}$ | $F_{as}$ (ksi) | $\dfrac{l}{r}$ | $F_{as}$ (ksi) |
| 1 | 21.56 | 41 | 19.11 | 81 | 15.24 | 121 | 10.14 | 161 | 5.76 | 121 | 10.19 | 161 | 7.25 |
| 2 | 21.52 | 42 | 19.03 | 82 | 15.13 | 122 | 9.99 | 162 | 5.69 | 122 | 10.09 | 162 | 7.20 |
| 3 | 21.48 | 43 | 18.95 | 83 | 15.02 | 123 | 9.85 | 163 | 5.62 | 123 | 10.00 | 163 | 7.16 |
| 4 | 21.44 | 44 | 18.86 | 84 | 14.90 | 124 | 9.70 | 164 | 5.55 | 124 | 9.90 | 164 | 7.12 |
| 5 | 21.39 | 45 | 18.78 | 85 | 14.79 | 125 | 9.55 | 165 | 5.49 | 125 | 9.80 | 165 | 7.08 |
| 6 | 21.35 | 46 | 18.70 | 86 | 14.67 | 126 | 9.41 | 166 | 5.42 | 126 | 9.70 | 166 | 7.04 |
| 7 | 21.30 | 47 | 18.61 | 87 | 14.56 | 127 | 9.26 | 167 | 5.35 | 127 | 9.59 | 167 | 7.00 |
| 8 | 21.25 | 48 | 18.53 | 88 | 14.44 | 128 | 9.11 | 168 | 5.29 | 128 | 9.49 | 168 | 6.96 |
| 9 | 21.21 | 49 | 18.44 | 89 | 14.32 | 129 | 8.97 | 169 | 5.23 | 129 | 9.40 | 169 | 6.93 |
| 10 | 21.16 | 50 | 18.35 | 90 | 14.20 | 130 | 8.84 | 170 | 5.17 | 130 | 9.30 | 170 | 6.89 |
| 11 | 21.10 | 51 | 18.26 | 91 | 14.09 | 131 | 8.70 | 171 | 5.11 | 131 | 9.21 | 171 | 6.85 |
| 12 | 21.05 | 52 | 18.17 | 92 | 13.97 | 132 | 8.57 | 172 | 5.05 | 132 | 9.12 | 172 | 6.82 |
| 13 | 21.00 | 53 | 18.08 | 93 | 13.84 | 133 | 8.44 | 173 | 4.99 | 133 | 9.03 | 173 | 6.79 |
| 14 | 20.95 | 54 | 17.99 | 94 | 13.72 | 134 | 8.32 | 174 | 4.93 | 134 | 8.94 | 174 | 6.76 |
| 15 | 20.89 | 55 | 17.90 | 95 | 13.60 | 135 | 8.19 | 175 | 4.88 | 135 | 8.86 | 175 | 6.73 |
| 16 | 20.83 | 56 | 17.81 | 96 | 13.48 | 136 | 8.07 | 176 | 4.82 | 136 | 8.78 | 176 | 6.70 |
| 17 | 20.78 | 57 | 17.71 | 97 | 13.35 | 137 | 7.96 | 177 | 4.77 | 137 | 8.70 | 177 | 6.67 |
| 18 | 20.72 | 58 | 17.62 | 98 | 13.23 | 138 | 7.84 | 178 | 4.71 | 138 | 8.62 | 178 | 6.64 |
| 19 | 20.66 | 59 | 17.53 | 99 | 13.10 | 139 | 7.73 | 179 | 4.66 | 139 | 8.54 | 179 | 6.61 |
| 20 | 20.60 | 60 | 17.43 | 100 | 12.98 | 140 | 7.62 | 180 | 4.61 | 140 | 8.47 | 180 | 6.58 |
| 21 | 20.54 | 61 | 17.33 | 101 | 12.85 | 141 | 7.51 | 181 | 4.56 | 141 | 8.39 | 181 | 6.56 |
| 22 | 20.48 | 62 | 17.24 | 102 | 12.72 | 142 | 7.41 | 182 | 4.51 | 142 | 8.32 | 182 | 6.53 |
| 23 | 20.41 | 63 | 17.14 | 103 | 12.59 | 143 | 7.30 | 183 | 4.46 | 143 | 8.25 | 183 | 6.51 |
| 24 | 20.35 | 64 | 17.04 | 104 | 12.47 | 144 | 7.20 | 184 | 4.41 | 144 | 8.18 | 184 | 6.49 |
| 25 | 20.28 | 65 | 16.94 | 105 | 12.33 | 145 | 7.10 | 185 | 4.36 | 145 | 8.12 | 185 | 6.46 |
| 26 | 20.22 | 66 | 16.84 | 106 | 12.20 | 146 | 7.01 | 186 | 4.32 | 146 | 8.05 | 186 | 6.44 |
| 27 | 20.15 | 67 | 16.74 | 107 | 12.07 | 147 | 6.91 | 187 | 4.27 | 147 | 7.99 | 187 | 6.42 |
| 28 | 20.08 | 68 | 16.64 | 108 | 11.94 | 148 | 6.82 | 188 | 4.23 | 148 | 7.93 | 188 | 6.40 |
| 29 | 20.01 | 69 | 16.53 | 109 | 11.81 | 149 | 6.73 | 189 | 4.18 | 149 | 7.87 | 189 | 6.38 |
| 30 | 19.94 | 70 | 16.43 | 110 | 11.67 | 150 | 6.64 | 190 | 4.14 | 150 | 7.81 | 190 | 6.36 |
| 31 | 19.87 | 71 | 16.33 | 111 | 11.54 | 151 | 6.55 | 191 | 4.09 | 151 | 7.75 | 191 | 6.35 |
| 32 | 19.80 | 72 | 16.22 | 112 | 11.40 | 152 | 6.46 | 192 | 4.05 | 152 | 7.69 | 192 | 6.33 |
| 33 | 19.73 | 73 | 16.12 | 113 | 11.26 | 153 | 6.38 | 193 | 4.01 | 153 | 7.64 | 193 | 6.31 |
| 34 | 19.65 | 74 | 16.01 | 114 | 11.13 | 154 | 6.30 | 194 | 3.97 | 154 | 7.59 | 194 | 6.30 |
| 35 | 19.58 | 75 | 15.90 | 115 | 10.99 | 155 | 6.22 | 195 | 3.93 | 155 | 7.53 | 195 | 6.28 |
| 36 | 19.50 | 76 | 15.79 | 116 | 10.85 | 156 | 6.14 | 196 | 3.89 | 156 | 7.48 | 196 | 6.27 |
| 37 | 19.42 | 77 | 15.69 | 117 | 10.71 | 157 | 6.06 | 197 | 3.85 | 157 | 7.43 | 197 | 6.26 |
| 38 | 19.35 | 78 | 15.58 | 118 | 10.57 | 158 | 5.98 | 198 | 3.81 | 158 | 7.39 | 198 | 6.24 |
| 39 | 19.27 | 79 | 15.47 | 119 | 10.43 | 159 | 5.91 | 199 | 3.77 | 159 | 7.34 | 199 | 6.23 |
| 40 | 19.19 | 80 | 15.36 | 120 | 10.28 | 160 | 5.83 | 200 | 3.73 | 160 | 7.29 | 200 | 6.22 |

[a] $K$ taken as 1.0 for secondary members.

Note: $C_c = 126.1$

[a] Reproduced from the Manual of Steel Construction, 8th ed., courtesy of AISC.

# 4. METRIC CONVERSIONS   Table A.10

**Length :**

| | |
|---|---|
| 1 in. | = 25.40 mm |
| 1 ft | = 0.3048 m = 304.8 mm |
| 1 yd | = 0.9144 m |
| 1 mi | = 1.609 km |

**Area :**

| | |
|---|---|
| 1 in.$^2$ | = 645.16 mm$^2$ |
| 1 ft$^2$ | = 0.0929 m$^2$ |
| 1 yd$^2$ | = 0.8361 m$^2$ |
| 1 mi$^2$ | = 2.590 km$^2$ |
| 1 acre | = 4.047(10)$^3$ m$^2$ = 0.4047 hectare |

**Volume :**

| | |
|---|---|
| 1 ft$^3$ | = 0.0283 m$^3$ |
| 1 yd$^3$ | = 0.7646 m$^3$ |

**Section modulus :**

| | |
|---|---|
| 1 in.$^3$ | = 16.39(10)$^3$ mm$^3$ |

**Moment of inertia :**

| | |
|---|---|
| 1 in.$^4$ | = 416.2(10)$^3$ mm$^4$ |
| 1 ft$^4$ | = 8.63(10)$^{-3}$ m$^4$ |

**Mass :**

| | |
|---|---|
| 1 oz | = 28.35 g |
| 1 lb | = 0.4536 kg |

**Density :**

| | |
|---|---|
| 1 pcf | = 16.018 kg/m$^3$ |
| 1 lb/yd$^3$ | = 0.5933 kg/m$^3$ |

**Mass to force :**

One kilogram mass exerts a force (weight) of one newton as caused by an accelera-tion of one m/s$^2$ (i.e. force = mass times acceleration). For a standard accelera-tion of gravity $g_n$ = 9.807 m/s$^2$ = 32.174 ft/s$^2$, the weight of one kg mass is taken as 9.807 N :

| | |
|---|---|
| 1 N | = 1 kg(1 m/s$^2$) |
| 9.807 N | = 1 kg(9.807) m/s$^2$ = 1 kgf |
| 9.807 N | = 9.807 (kgm/s$^2$) = 1 kgf |

**Force :**

single load : 
| | |
|---|---|
| 1 oz | = 0.278 N |
| 1 lb | = 4.448 N |
| 1 k | = 4448 N = 4.448 kN |

line load : 
| | |
|---|---|
| 1 lb/ft | = 14.59 N/m |
| 1 k/ft | = 14.59 kN/m |

surface load : 
| | |
|---|---|
| 1 psf | = 47.88 N/m$^2$ (Pa) |
| | = 0.0479 kN/m$^2$ (kPa) |
| 1 ksf | = 47.88 kN/m$^2$ (kPa) |
| 1 oz/yd$^2$ | = 0.3325 N/m$^2$ |

density : 
| | |
|---|---|
| 1 pcf | = 0.1571 kN/m$^3$ |

**Moment :**

| | |
|---|---|
| 1 in.-lb | = 0.1130 Nm |
| 1 ft-lb | = 1.356 Nm |
| 1 ft-k | = 1.356 kNm |

**Stress (pressure) :**

| | |
|---|---|
| 1 pascal (Pa) | = 1 newton/meter$^2$ (N/m$^2$) |
| 1 kPa | = 1000 Pa(N/m$^2$) = 0.001 N/mm$^2$ |
| 1 MPa | = 1 N/mm$^2$ = 1000 kPa |
| | = 1 000 000 Pa(N/mm$^2$) |

| | |
|---|---|
| 1 psi | = 6.895 kPa |
| | = 6895 Pa(N/m$^2$) |
| | = 0.006895 MPa(N/mm$^2$) |
| 1 ksi | = 6.895 MPa(N/mm$^2$) |

at 4°C : 1 in.$H_2O$ = 0.249 kPa

at 0°C : 1 in. Hg = 3.387 kPa

**Velocity :**   1 mph = 1.609 km/h

**Temperature :**   $t_c$ = 5/9 ($t_F$ - 32)

**Coefficient of**
linear expansion: °F$^{-1}$ = 1.8 °C$^{-1}$

**Prefixes**

| | | |
|---|---|---|
| giga | G | 10$^9$ |
| mega | M | 10$^6$ |
| kilo | k | 10$^3$ |
| milli | m | 10$^{-3}$ |
| micro | μ | 10$^{-6}$ |

# LIST OF
# BUILDING ILLUSTRATIONS

## FIG. 1.1   THE LATERAL THRUST

The details are taken from the following buildings: The Olympic Stadium, Montreal, Canada (R. Taillibert); Convention Hall, Vatican, Italy (Nervi); St. Pius X Basilica, Lourdes, France, (P. Vago & E. Freyssinet); Stadthalle Bremen, Bremen, Germany, (R. Ranier); Tabriz Consulate, Tabriz, Iran (Edward Larrabee Barnes); Juan Ramon Loubriel Stadium, Bayamon, Puerto Rico (Reed, Torres, Beauchamp, Marvel, Hato, Rey Architects); Arcosanti (Paolo Soleri); Schwimmoper Hamburg, Hamburg, Germany (H. Niessen, R. Störmer); Dulles Airport, Chantilly, Virginia (E. Saarinen); Amiens Cathedral, Amiens, France.

## FIG. 1.13   BEAM VERSUS COLUMN

The details are taken from the following buildings: WIFI St. Pölten, Austria, (Schwanzer); New National Gallery, Berlin, Germany (Mies van der Rohe); Undergraduate Science Center, Harvard University, Cambridge, Massachusetts (Sert, Jackson); Boston Five Cents Savings Bank, Boston, Massachusetts (Kallmann & McKinnel); "Test Rig" House, England (Foster Associates); St. Franziscus, Brunau, Austria (Jodlbauer-Fonatti); Centre Pampidou, Paris, France (Piano & Rogers); Factory at Lissone, Italy, and structure S.A.C.I.E. (Angelo Mangiarotti); Book Storage Building, Harmondsworth, Britain (Ove Arup Associates); Professional Training Center for the Handicapped, Bremen, Germany (ME DI UM); Exhibition Hall for the Turin Motor Show 1958–60 (Ricardo Morandi); Doric System (M.D'Espouy, Ecole Des Beaux Arts, nineteenth century).

## FIG. 1.31   PRESTRESSING IN ARCHITECTURE

(f) Housing for the Elderly, Roxbury District, Boston, Massachusetts, I. Richmond and C. Goldberg Architects, A. R. June 1970; (h) Foundation, Olympic Cable Roof, Munich, Germany, Zodiac 21, 1972; (j) Foundation, CN Tower, Toronto, Canada, Nicolet, Carrier, Dressel and Associates, *Journal of PCI*, Vol. 21, No. 3, May–June 1976; (k) Sepp Firnkas structural system, *Journal of PCI*, July–August 1976; (l) Gulf Life Building, Jacksonville, Florida, Welton Beckett & Associates, *ENR*, July 7, 1966, A. R. January 1967.

## FIG. 1.32 PRESTRESSING: A CASE STUDY

(a) Tax Court Building, Washington, D.C., Victor A. Lundy Arch., *ENR,* Janaury 30, 1975, P/A, July 1976; (b) Rock Island parking structure, Rock Island, Illinois, Conrad Associates, *PCI Journal,* July–August 1977; (c) United Air Lines hangar, O'Hare International Airport, Chicago, Paul Rogers and Associates, *ENR,* September 17, 1959; (d) Lufthansa hangar, Frankfurt Airport, Frankfurt, Germany, Dyckerhoff & Widmann AG and Architects Beckertz Becker, *Civil Engineering,* December 1970, *ENR,* September 28, 1972; (e) Toronto City Hall, Toronto, Canada, Viljo Revell Architect, *Räumliche Dachtragwerke,* Vol. 1, H. Rühle, Verlag R. Müller, Köln, Germany; (f) Baltimore Convention Center, Baltimore, Maryland, Naramore Bain Brady & Johanson Architects, *ENR,* March 8, 1979; (g) Trade Group office building, Canberra, Australia, Harry Seidler Architects, P. L. Nervi, A+ February 1973, *Arch. Australia,* June/July 1976.

## FIG. 2.2 CURVILINEAR PATTERNS

The images are derived from the following buildings: Proposal for the Palazzo del Littorio in Rome, Italy, 1934 (Terragni); Ensemble Universitaire de la Croix-Rouge, Reims, France (A. and D. Dubard de Gaillarbois, 1972); Exhibition Hall, Turin, Italy (Nervi, 1948); Airplane Hangar, Rome, Italy (Nervi, 1936); Chiesa di Santa Maria Assunta, Riola, Italy (Alvar Aalto, 1978); Tokyo Metropolitan Yumenoshina Sports Center, Japan (Sakakura Associates, 1976); Niagara Falls Convention Center, New York (Johnson/Burgee, 1976); Fujimi Country Club, Japan (Isozaki, 1974); Great Flight Cage, National Zoo, Washington, D.C. (Daniel, Mann, Johnson & Mendenhall, 1964).

## FIG. 2.13

(s) Market Hall, Saint-Étienne, France, A. Ferraz and L. Seignol Architects, S. Du Chateau Engineer, *T.A.,* October 1973; (v) Cummins Engine Company Ltd., Lanashire, England, Ahrends Burton & Koralek Architects, Ove Arup & Partners Engineers, *RIBAJ,* January 1979, *Arch. Review,* January 1978.

## FIG. 2.15 STRUCTURE SYSTEMS IN RESIDENTIAL CONSTRUCTION

(a) Smith House, Darien, Connecticut, Richard Meier Architect, *Forum,* December 1967; (b) The Hilborn Residence, Preston, Ontario, Canada, Arthur Erickson Architect, A.R. May 1975; (c) Duncan House, Cobden, Illinois, 1965, Bruce Goff Architect, *Perspecta,* 13/14, 1971, *Arch. Design,* Vol. 48, No. 10, 1978; (d) Farnsworth House, Plano, Illinois, 1950, Mies van der Rohe; (e) The Kohler Centennial House, Kohler, Wisconsin, Booth & Nagle Architects, *Forum,* January/February 1974; (f) Villa Coupe, Myoukou, Japan, Kaisuke Yashido Architect, *AA* 163, August/September 1972; (g) The Capsuled Villa, 1972, Kisho Kurokawa Architect, *A+,* January/February 1974; (h) House Dissentshik (project), Tel Aviv, Israel, Zvi Hecker Architect, AA 163, August/September 1972; (i) Prototype Dwelling Units, Michigan City, Indiana, Ken Fryar Associates and R. Goodfellow, Arena/Interbuild, March 1968, *The New Building Block,* Center for Housing and Environmental Studies, Cornell University, 1968; (j) Lubetkin House, near Houston, Texas, Ant Farm (R. Jost and C. Lord, D. Michels) Architects, *P/A* 6, 1973, Stanley Abercrombie: *Ferrocement,* Schocken Books, New York, 1977.

## FIG. 3.4  CABLE STAYED STRUCTURES

(a) Proposal for a stadium roof, Madrid, Spain, Felix Candela, *Techniques and Architecture,* May 1976; (b) Burgo Paper Mill, Mantua, Italy, Luigi Nervi, P. L. Nervi: *Buildings Projects and Structures 1953-1963,* Praeger, New York, 1963. (c) Robin Hood Dell Amphitheater, Fairmont Park, Philadelphia, MacFayden/De Video, *ENR,* October 23, 1975, *A.R.,* November 1975, January 1977, *ASCE,* June 1977, *Bethlehem Steel Building Case History,* No. 48, 1976; (d) Wesleyan University Hockey Rink, Middletown, Connecticut, Warner Burns Toan and Lunde, P/A, April 1971. *ENR,* March 1969, July 1969; (e) Marché des Abattoirs, Saint Étienne, France, A. Ferraz & L. Seignol, *Techniques and Architecture,* October 1973. (f) Dymaxion House 1927, Buckminster Fuller, R. Buckminster Fuller and R. Marks: *The Dymaxion World of Buckminster Fuller,* Anchor Press/ Doubleday, New York, 1973; (g) Race Track Grandstand, near East Rutherford, New Jersey, Ewing Cole Erdman & Eubank, *A.R.,* November 1975; (h) Central elevator shaft with suspended floors, Housing Development, Rosebery, New South Wales, Australia, Harry Seidler & Associates, *Forum,* March 1968; (i) Olympic Ice Arena, Squaw Valley, California, Corlett Spackman and Kitchen & Hunt, *ENR,* July 1959; (j) Pan American Terminal, Kennedy Airport, New York, Tippets-Abbett-McCarthy-Stratton, *A.R.,* September 1961, *ENR,* March 1959; (k) Bridge across the Rhine, Bonn, Germany, H. Homberg; W. Podolny, Jr., "Cable-Stayed Bridges," *Engineering Journal,* AISC, 1st Quarter 1974, Fritz Leonhardt and Wilhelm Zellner: Cable-Stayed Bridges, The Canadian Steel Industries Construction Council, 1970, Morandi's Bridges, *Forum,* October 1971.

## FIG. 3.5  CABLE BEAMS

(a) Dulles International Airport Terminal, Chantilly, Virginia, Eero Saarinen & Associates, *P.A.,* August 1963, *ENR,* March 1962, *A.R.,* July 1963, *Forum,* April 1962; (b) John Deere Branch House, Baltimore, Maryland, Rogers, Taliaferro, Kostritsky, and Lamb, *Forum,* March 1968; (c) Hall in the "Estramed" Complex, Pomezia, Italy, Paolo Cercato, Acier-Stahl-Steel, March 1976, *L'a,* XXII, 487. (d) Johanneshov Stadium, Stockholm, Sweden, Paul Hedqvist; H. Rühle, *Räumliche Dachtragwerke,* Vol. 2, Verlag Rudolf Müller, Köln, Germany, 1970; (e) Special Events Center, Oral Roberts University, Tulsa, Oklahoma, Frank W. Wallace and Lloyd W. Abbot, *ENR,* January 1972; (f) Municipal Auditorium, Utica, New York, Gehron & Seltzer, Lev Zetlin Engineer, *A.R.,* August 1959, Bethlehem Steel Corp., "Cable Roof Structures," Booklet 2318-A, November 1968; (g) Salt Palace, Salt Lake City, Utah, Bonneville Architects, *ENR,* May 1969; (h) Villita Assembly Hall, San Antonio, Texas, O'Neil Ford and Associates, *P.A.,* February 1961, Bethlehem Steel Corp., "Cable Construction in Contemporary Architecture," Booklet 2264-A, 1968; (i) Forum, Inglewood, California, Charles Luckman & Associates, *ENR,* November 1967; (j) Hampton Roads Coliseum, Hampton, Virginia, Odell Associates, Bethlehem Steel Corp., "Building Case History No. 8," July 1971; (k) Madison Square Garden, New York, New York, Charles Luckman & Associates, *ENR,* December 1, 1966, *A & E News,* September 1966, Bethlehem Steel Corp., "A Spectacle in Steel," Booklet 2463, Civil Engineering, June 1967; (l) Oakland-Alameda County Coliseum, Oakland, California, SOM, *ENR,* July 14, 1966, AISI 70, Contemporary Structures.

## FIG 4.11  LONGSPAN PORTALS

(a) Crown Hall, IIT, Chicago, Ill., Mies van der Rohe, *A.R.,* August 1956, October 1963, etc.; (b) Reading Assembly Centre, Reading, England, R. Matthew, Johnson-Marshall & Partners, *Building Design,* September 9, 1977; (c) Athletic Facility, Phillips Exeter Academy, Exeter, New Hampshire, Kallman & McKinnel, Le Messurier Associates, Structural Engineers, *ENR,* January 1969, *A.R.,* June 1971, *Modern Steel Construction, AISC,* 1st Quarter 1969, Contemporary Structures, AISI; (d) Munson-Williams-Proctor Institute Art Gallery, Utica, New York, Philip Johnson Architect, Lev Zetlin Structural Engineer, *Building Construction,* March 1961, F. Wilson: *Emerging Form in Architecture,* Cahner Books, 1975. (e) Planetarium Stuttgart, Germany, Beck Architects, *Architektur und Wohnwelt,* December 1977, *Arch. Review,* March 1980; (f) R. Crosby Kemper Memorial Arena, Kansas

City, Missouri, C. F. Murphy Associates (Helmuth Jahn), *A.R.,* March 1976, *Domus,* October 1971, *T. A.,* May 1976, *Building Design and Construction,* November 1974, *Arch. Awards of Excellence,* AISC, 1975; (g) Athletic Center, Rutgers University, New Brunswick, New Jersey, J. R. Hillier and Eggers Group Architects, Lev Zetlin Structural Engineer, *ENR,* June 1977; (h) Jai-Alai Fronton, Hartford, Connecticut, Hirsch Associates, Fraioli-Blum-Yesselman Structurual Engineers, *Modern Steel Construction,* AISC, 1st/2nd Quarter 1977.

## FIG 4.31   INCLINED FRAME STRUCTURES

(a) Heineman Studio, Green Bay, Wisconsin, Harry Weese & Assoc., *Forum,* January/February 1971; (b) Severin Bridge Tower, Cologne, Germany, G. Lohmer Designer, *ENR,* February 1960; (c) Arcon Three-Pin Frame System, Taylor Woodrow, London, England; (d) W. D. Carmichael Jr. Auditorium, University of North Carolina, Chapel Hill, North Carolina, City Planning and Architectural Associates, *Modern Steel Construction,* AISC, 2nd Quarter, 1966; (e) Transmission Tower, Southern California Edison Co. and Henry Dreyfuss & Associates, *Contemporary Structures* 1970, AISI; (f) The Walther House, Menzlingen, Germany, Plück & Walther Architects, *Architektur + Wohnwelt,* June 1977; (g) Cedar Hill Community Center, Victoria, British Columbia, Canada, Peterson and Lester Architects, *The Canadian Architect,* February 1975; (h) St. Sebastian, North Hills, Pennsylvania, Gerard & McDonald Architects, *ENR,* February 18, 1960; (i) Theater, Phillips Exeter Academy, Exeter, New Hampshire, Hardy Holzman Pfeiffer Associates, *A. R.,* February 1975; (j) Laurel School, Menlo Park, California, Kingford Jones Architects, *ENR,* May 25, 1961; (k) Pan Am Hangar, Kennedy Airport, New York, Ammann & Whitney and Burns & McDonnell, *ENR,* April 23, 1970; (l) West Berlin Congress Center, Berlin, Germany, R. Schüler and Ursulina Schüler-Witte Architects, G. Bartels Structural Engineer, *DBZ,* July 1979, September 1979, *Domus* 597, August 1979, *ENR* November 24, 1977; (m) Glass Factory, Amberg, Germany, The Architects Collaborative (Walter Gropius), *Forum* April 1971; (n) Rye-Arc Ltd. Building, Silvertown, Great Britain, R. E. Eagan Ltd. Engineers; (o) Gymnasium, Connantre, France, J. D. Gouzien, Architect, *T. A.* 321, October 1978.

## FIG 4.36   JOIST ROOF CONSTRUCTION

(a) Tuskegee Chapel, Tuskegee Institute, Tuskegee, Alabama, Paul Rudolph Architect, *A. R.,* November 1969, *L'Architectura,* March 1970; (b) Episcopal Church of the Epiphany, Houston, Texas, Clovis Heimsath Associates, *A. R.,* September 1975; (c) Casa Chiocciola, Higashi Tadahito Architects, *L'Architectura,* March 1980.

## FIG 4.49   ARCH STRUCTURES

(a) Salginatobel Bridge near Schiers, Switzerland, Robert Maillart, 1930; (b) Bridge over the Autobahn, Aachen, Germany, *Modern Steel Construction,* 2nd Quarter, 1966; (c) Daniel Webster Hoan Memorial Bridge, Milwaukee, Wisconsin, Howard Needles Tammen & Bergendoff, Prize Bridges 1975, AISC, 1975; (d) Piscataqua River Bridge, Portsmouth, New Hampshire, Hardesty & Hanover, Prize Bridges 1973, AISC, 1973; (e) Pedestrian Bridge over the Rhine, Wiesbaden, Germany, Gerd Lohmer, *Arena/Interbuild,* January 1968; (f) Gateway Arch, St. Louis, Missouri, Eero Saarinen and Severud-Elstad-Krueger Associates, *A. R.,* May 1963; (h) Shelter, Austin Assoc. Inc., Seattle, Washington, *Building Construction,* April 1962; (i) Wyandotte Chemicals Corp. Wyandotte, Michigan, Weyerhaeuser Corp.; (j) Hunt Junior High School, Tecumseh, Washington, R. Billsbrough Price Architects, *Building Design,* July 1975; (k) Citrus Union High School, Azuza, California, Austin, Field & Fry Architects, *Southeast Builder and Contractor,* August 28, 1953; (l) Velodrome, Montreal, Canada, Roger Taillibert Architect, *ENR,* March 6, 1975, *Canadian Architect,* September 1976; (m) Idaho Stadium, Moscow, Idaho, Cline, Smull, Hamill & Associates, A. L. Troutner (Trus Joist Corp.), and KKBNA, *ENR,* October 16, 1975, *A. R.,* August 1975, *Building Design & Construction,* April 1976,

*Civil Engineering-ASCE,* June 1976; (n) Geller House II, Lawrence, New York, Marcel Breuer and Herbert Beckhard, *A. R.,* July 1970; (o) Niagara Falls Convention Center, Niagara Falls, New York, Philip Johnson and John Burgee, and Lev Zetlin, *ENR,* February 1976; (p) Institut National des Sports Fieldhouse, Joinville near Paris, France, Bovet, Berthelot and Cuzol Architects, *ENR,* September 12, 1963; (q) Agora in Aabenraa, Denmark, Arne Poulsen and Niels/Nielsen, *Architectur* DK 7, 1978; (r) Grandstand San Mames Stadium, Bilbao, Spain, J. Dominguez, R. Magdalena, and C. de Miguel, *ENR,* April 26, 1956.

### FIG. 4.59   TRUSS BUILDINGS

(a) Air Force Academy Chapel, Colorado Springs, SOM. *A.R.,* December 1962, *P/A,* September 1961, *Arch. Forum,* December 1962; (b) Gymnasium for the National Institute of Mexican Youth, Mexico, Manuel Gonzalez Rul Architects, *Techniques & Architecture,* June/July 1978; (c) Rainbow Center Mall and Winter Garden, Niagara Falls, New York, Gruen Associates, *P/A,* August 1978, *AIA Journal,* mid-May 1979; (d) Sainsbury Centre for Visual Arts, The University of East Anglia, Norwich, England, Foster Associates, *P/A,* February 1979, *A. Rev.* December 1978, *A.R.,* mid-August 1979; (e) The Veterans Memorial Coliseum, New Haven, Connecticut, Kevin Roche, John Dinkeloo & Associates, *Forum,* March 1974, *Domus,* 531, February 1974; (f) Gund Hall, Harvard University, Cambridge, Mass., John Andrews Architect, *ENR,* May, 1979; (g) Temple Sinai, Stamford, Connecticut, Sherwood, Mills & Smith Architects, *P/A,* June 1963; (h) Professional Training Center for the Handicapped, Bremen, Germany, Planungsgruppe ME DI UM, *Domus,* 596, July 1979, *Acier-Stahl-Steel,* 3/1979. *Forum* 12/1972, Modern Steel Construction, *AISC,* 1st Quarter 1973; (i) Port Authority Bus Terminal, New York City, New York, Pier Luigi Nervi, Pier L. Nervi, *Buildings, Projects, Structures 1953–1963,* Praeger, New York, 1963; (j) Simmons Company Jones Bridge Headquarters, Atlanta, Georgia, Thompson, Hancock, Witte & Associates, *A.R.,* December 1975, *Civil Engineering,* May 1977; (k) Joe Louis Sports Arena, Detroit, Michigan, Smith, Hinchman & Grylls Associates Architects, *ENR,* January 4, 1979 (the layout of the cross-trusses is shown only conceptually).

### FIG 4.63   MULTIBAY, LONGSPAN ROOF STRUCTURES

(a) Palace of Labour, Turin, Italy, P. L. and A. Nervi, *Arch. Forum,* September 1961, *ENR,* November 16, 1961, Pier Luigi Nervi: *Pier Luigi Nervi,* Praeger, New York, 1963; (b) Printing Plant for Weilin and Göös, Tapiola, Finland, Aarno Ruusuvuori, *A. R.,* November 1966; (c) Olivetti-Underwood Factory Building, Harrisburg, Pennsylvania, Louis Kahn Architect and August E. Komendant Engineer, *Forum,* April 1971, *A. E. Komendant: 18 Years with Architect Louis Kahn,* Aloray, 1975; (d) St. John's University Library, Collegeville, Minnesota, Marcel Breuer, *A. R.,* February 1964, *Forum,* May 1968; (e) Nitto Foods Co., Yamagata District, Japan, Noriaki Kurokawa and Associates, *Forum,* April 1968; (f) Michigan City Public Library, Michigan City, Indiana, C. F. Murphy, *Domus,* 581, April 1978, *P/A,* 7, 1978; (g) Wells Library, Aurora, New York, SOM (Walter Netsch) Architects, *P/A,* March 1969, *Interiors,* December 1969; (h) Cable Factory, Mudanya, Turkey, Hans Maurer Architect, Oswald W. Grube: *Industrial Buildings and Factories,* Praeger, New York, 1971; (i) Nobeyama Heights Center of the Tokyo YMCA, Japan, Shozo Uchii Architect, *J. A.,* May 1977; (j) Printing Plant at Haramachi, Shizuoka District, Japan, Kenzo Tange and the Urbanists and Architects Team, O. Grube: *Industrial Buildings and Factories,* Praeger, New York, 1971; (k) Prefectural Sports Center, Takaishi, Osaka, Japan, Maki and Associates, *J. A.,* March, 1973; (l) West Japan General Exhibition Center, Kitakyushu, Fukuota Prefecture, Japan, Arata Isozaki Atelier, *J. A.,* March 1978, *Building Design,* November 1977.

### Fig. 4.64   MULTIPLESPAN FRAME STRUCTURES

(a) Electronics Plant, Reliance Controls Ltd., Swindon, England, Norman Foster, Wendy Foster, Richard Rogers, *Forum,* April 1971; (c) Landmark Components, Butler Manufacturing Co., Kansas City, Missouri, 1975; (d) Versa-Space, Precast System, Inc., Chicago, Illinois, 1975; (f) Cummins

Engine Co., Ltd., Darlington, England, Kevin Roche John Dinkeloo & Associates, *Forum,* October 1966; (h) Scientific Data Systems, El Segundo, California, Craig Ellwood Associates, *Forum,* December 1967; (j) Building system, Lord & Den Hartog Associates, Boston, Massachusetts, *P/A,* October 1964.


## FIG 4.73   THE CANTILEVER IN ARCHITECTURE

(a) F. C. Robie House, Chicago, 1909, Frank Lloyd Wright; (b) Proposal for hangar, 1960, Konrad Wachsmann, K. Wachsmann: *The Turning Point of Building,* Reinhold, New York, 1961; (c) The Kent Sawyer House, Piedmont, California, W. K. Wong Architect, *Contemporary Structures,* 1970, AISI, *Modern Steel Construction,* 2nd Quarter, 1966; (d) London sports complex, England, Ove Arup & Partners, *ENR,* December 1964; (e) Residence, Marin County, California, R. R. Zahm Architect, *P/A,* June 1963; (f) E.J. Kaufmann House, Bear Run, Pennsylvania, 1936, Frank Lloyd Wright; (g) San Juan Stadium, Puerto Rico, P.A. Miranda & Associates, *ENR,* November 1962; (h) Airline Hangar Landsberg, Germany, Dyckerhoff & Widmann AG, Walter Meyer-Bohe: *Stahlbeton,* Verlag A. Koch GmbH, Stuttgart, 1974; (i) TWA Hangar, Philadelphia International Airport, The Ballinger Co, Ammann & Whitney Consulting Engineers, *ENR,* December 1956; (j) Everson Museum of Art, Syracuse, New York, I. M. Pei & Partners, Architects, *Arch. Forum,* June 1969, *P/A,* November 1962; (k) Frank C. Bishop Library, The York School, Monterey, California, Smith Barker Hanssen Architect, *ENR,* April 1969, *A. R.,* June 1974, *Modern Steel Construction,* 1971.


## FIG 4.74   CANTILEVER ROOF STRUCTURES

(a) National Airlines' Hangar, Miami, Florida, Greenleaf/Telescan Architects and Kellerman & Dragnett Inc., Engineers, *Modern Steel Construction,* AISI, 4th Quarter, 1971, *ENR,* April 1972; (b) American Airlines' Hangar, O'Hare Airport, Chicago, Illinois, *Building Construction,* November 1961; (c) Piedmont Airlines' Hangar, Winston-Salem, North Carolina, L. A. Redgate A.I.A. and Quinton-Budlong Engineers, *ENR,* October 1969; (d) United Airlines' Hangar, San Francisco International Airport, SOM (Myron Goldsmith), *ENR,* April 1959; (e) Mohawk Airlines' Hangar, Utica, New York, Ammann & Whitney Engineers, *ENR,* February 1958; (f) American Airlines' Hangar, San Francisco and Los Angeles International Airports, Lev Zetlin Associates, Engineers and Conklin & Rossant Architects, *Civil Engineering,* November 1970, *Forum,* January/February 1971, Bethlehem Steel Building Case History No. 11, September 1971; (g) TWA Kansas City Hangar, Kansas City, Missouri, Ammann & Whitney Engineers, *ENR,* January 1956 and February 1958; (h) Hangar 14, New York International Airport, New York, Port of New York Authority, *ENR,* May 1958; (i) Lufthansa Hangar, Rhein-Main Airport, Frankfurt a.M., Germany, Philipp Holzmann A.G., Engineers and Otto Apel Architect, 1959.


## FIG 4.75   GRANDSTAND CANTILEVER ROOFS

(a) The Olympic Stadium, Montreal, Canada, André Daoust and Roger Taillibert Architects, *ENR,* June 10, 1976, *The Canadian Architect,* September 1976; (b) Proposal for a stadium in Munich, Germany, Riccardo Morandi, *Architecture/Forms/Functions,* Vol. 13, 1967; (c) Parc des Princes Stadium, Paris, France, Roger Taillibert Architect, *L'Architecture D'Aujourd'hui,* June/July 1971 and October/November 1972, *ENR,* January 1971; (d) Flaminio Stadium, Rome, Italy, Pier Luigi Nervi, *A.R.,* December 1958, P. L. Nervi: *Aesthetics and Technology in Building,* Harvard University Press, Cambridge, Massachusetts, 1966; (e) Municipal Stadium, Florence, Italy, P. L. Nervi: *Aesthetics and Technology in Building,* Harvard University Press, Cambridge, Massachusettes, 1966; (f) Three Rivers Stadium, Pittsburgh, Pennsylvania, M. Baker, Jr. Engineer and Deeter Ritchey Sipple Architects, P C items #322, Prestressed Concrete Institute, 1974; (g) District of Columbia Stadium, Washington, D.C., Dahl-Erwin-Osborn Architects and Engineers; (h) Atlanta Stadium, Atlanta, Georgia, Heery and Heery, Finch, Alexander, Barnes, Rothschild and Paschal Architects, Prybylowski & Gravino Engineers, *Modern Steel Construction,* 1st Quarter 1965.

## FIG. 4.76   BEAM BUILDINGS

(a) Broome County Cultural Center, Binghamton, New York, B. Elbasani, Donn Logan, M. Severin, G. Freeman, *Arch. Forum,* December 1973; (b) Pedestrian Mall, Hokusetsu, Japan, Kenzo Tange, *J. A.,* August/September 1976; (c) Industrial Pavilion, Hannover Fair, Hannover, Germany, Hentrich and Petschnigg Associates, *Acier-Stahl-Steel,* 1/1972; (d) Abraham Lincoln Oasis, South Holland, Illinois, David Haid, *ENR,* July 13, 1967, Awards 68, The James F. Lincoln Arc Welding Foundation, 1969; (e) Art Center College of Design, Pasadena, California, Craig Ellwood Associates, *P/A,* January 1976, August 1977, *Domus,* 588, November 1978, *Modern Steel Construction,* Vol. XVIII, AISC, 1978; (f) Urban Bridge Structure, proposal, Metabolists, Japan, 1960s; (g) Bridge Proposal, Mesa City, Arizona, Paolo Soleri; (h) Foster House, Wilton, Connecticut, Richard Foster, *Architectural Record,* April 1969; (i) The U.S. Pavilion, New York, Harrison and Abramovitz: *World's Fair Preview,* Bethelem Steel Publication, 1963; (j) Highway Restaurant, Montepulciano, Italy, A. Bianchetti, *Acier-Stahl-Steel,* 4/1971; (k) Maison Girard, Plessis-Robinson, France, Pierre Sirvin, *L'Architecture d'Aujourd'hui,* 163, August/September 1972.

## FIG 5.3   POLYHEDRAL ROOF STRUCTURES

(a) Space Pack Motel, Biwa Lake, Japan, M. Osabe and R. Nakamura Architects, *AA,* 162, June/July 1972; (b) Tree Houses, experimental units, Helmond, Holland, Piet Blom Architect, *Building Design,* May 6, 1977, *P/A,* 3, 1980; (c) The Chappaqua Central School District Public Library, Chappaqua, New York, Kilham Beder & Chu Architects, "Building Case History No. 57," Bethlehem Steel Corp., 1979, *A. R.,* January 1980; (d) Hans Christian Andersen Memorial Museum, 1965, Kisho Kurokawa Architect, K. Kurokawa: *Metabolism in Architecture,* Westview Press, Boulder, Colorado; (e) Health, Physical Education and Recreation Complex, Morris Brown College, Atlanta, Georgia, J. W. Robinson Associates, *ENR,* September 30, 1976; (f) Hotel Le Cerf-Volant,Voglans-Savoie, France, Chanéac Architects, *Arch. Franc.,* December 1974; (g) The Buddhist Reliquary Hall at the Temple Unto-an/Minami-Uonuma, Niigata Prefecture, Makoto Suzuki Architect, *J.A.,* September 1979; (h) University City Hospital, Madrid, Spain, 1934, E. Torraja. *The Structures of Eduardo Torraja,* F. W. Dodge: New York, 1958; (i) Swimming Hall, Greve, Denmark, H. Nielsen & N. Pedersen Architects, *Architektur DK* 7, 1978; (j) Longshoremen's Building, San Francisco, California, H. Hill Architects, *P/A,* April 1960, *ENR,* May 15, 1958.

## FIG 5.19   HORIZONTAL-SPAN SPACE FRAME STRUCTURES

(a) Currigan Hall, Denver, Colorado, Muchow, Ream, and Larson, *A. R.,* December 1970, *Contemporary Structures,* AISI 1970; (b) Theme Pavilion, Expo 70, Osaka, Japan, Kenzo Tange, Forum April 1970, *ENR,* May 1978, *Tubular Structures,* 17, November 1970, *A.R.,* June 1970; (c) McCormick Place, Chicago, Illinois, C. F. Murphy, *Forum,* November 1971, *ENR,* October 1969, *A. R.,* May 1971, *P. A.,* October 1969; (d) Omni Colisseum, Atlanta, Georgia, Thompson, Ventulett, & Stainback, *A. R.,* August 1974, *Modern Steel Construction,* 1st Quarter 1975, *ENR,* November 1972; (e) Pauley Pavilion, UCLA, Los Angeles, California, Welton Becket, *A. R.,* March 1966, *Modern Steel Construction,* 2nd Quarter, 1967; (f) St. Benedict's Abbey Church, Benet Lake, Wisconsin, Stanley Tigerman, *A. R.,* January 1973, *AIA,* April 1978; (g) The New National Gallery, Berlin, Germany, Mies van der Rohe, *A. R.,* November 1968, *P. A.,* November 1968; (h) Centro Culturale, Maranello/Modena, Italy, R. Corradi, F. Lipparini, T. Lugli, *Domus,* 580 March 1978, *DBZ,* May 1979; (i) Uniform Tubes Plant, Trappe, Pennsylvania, Tofani & Fox, *Modern Steel Construction,* AISC, 4th Quarter 1966, *Modern Welded Structures,* The James F. Lincoln Arc Welding Foundation, Cleveland, Ohio, 1965; (j) Recreational Center, University of California, Davis, Parkin Architects, Engineers and Planners, *ENR,* April 1977, *Building Design and Construction,* May 1977; (k) City Center "Ballei" (partial plan view), Neckarsulm, Germany, Aichele-Bechler-Fiedler-Weinmann Arch., *DBZ,* 4/1981.

## FIG. 6.2  FOLDED PLATE STRUCTURES

(a) Sears Roebuck & Co., Tampa, Florida, Weed, Russel, Johnson & Associates, *A. R.,* June 1961; (b) Avocado Elementary School, Homestead, Florida, R. B. Browne Architects, *A. R.,* October 1963; (c) Student Union, Wilkes College, Wilkes-Barre, Pennsylvania, Lacy, Atherton and Davis Architects; (d) ACI Headquarters Building, Detroit, Michigan, Yamasaki, Leinweber & Associates, *ENR,* October 1957; (e) Regionalbad, Zurzach AG, Switzerland, Fritz Schwarz Architect, *Werk 2,* 1971; (f) Centre de Recherches Agricoles, St-Aubin FR, Switzerland, Jakob Zweifel and Heinrich Strickler, *Werk 1,* 1970; (g) Warehouse, Padua, Italy, Angelo Mangiarotti and Bruno Morassutti, Walter Henn: *Industriebau,* Vol. 3, Callwey, Munich, Germany, 1962; (h) Kiln Building, Ideal Cement Co., Castle Hayne, North Carolina, Ken R. White Co., *ENR,* August 1963; (i) Department of Art Building, University of Georgia, Athens, Georgia, Toombs, Amisano & Wells, *Architectural Forum,* February 1962; (j) Beckwith Residence, Franklin Hills, Michigan, Meathe, Kessler & Associates, *A. R.* Houses of 1961; (k) H. W. Moore Equipment Co. Building, Denver, Colorado, T. E. Moore Architect; (l) Vereen Residence, Miami, Florida, R. B. Browne Architect, *A. R.* Houses of 1961; (m) Wells Fargo Bank, San Francisco, California, SOM, *A. R.,* January 1961; (n) Open Air Tabernacle, Covington, Louisiana, Frey Associates, *A. R.,* April 1965; (o) Chapel for St. Josephs Hospital, Burbank, California, Welton Becket & Associates; (p) Trinity Lutheran Church, Lake Johanna, Minnesota, Buetow & Associates. *Plywood Components in Church Architecture,* American Plywood Association, 1964; (q) United Church of Christ, West Norwalk, Connecticut, Victor Christ-Janer Associates, *Plywood Components in Church Architecture,* American Plywood Association, 1964; (r) Miller Memorial Theater, Houston, Eugene Werlin & Associates and Walter P. Moore Associates, Engineers, *ASCE,* November 1969, *P/A,* October 1969; (s) Crystal Cathedral, Garden Grove, California, Johnson/Burgee Architects, Severud-Perrone-Szegezdy-Sturm Engineers, *A. R.,* November 1980, Modern Steel Construction, *AISC,* No. 4, 4th Quarter 1980, *P/A,* December 1980, *Arch. Rev.,* January 1981, *AIA Journal,* mid-May 1981, *Building Design & Construction,* December 1980.

## FIG. 8.2

Frisch's Restaurant, Cincinnati, Ohio, Woodie Garber and Associates, Architects, Truman P. Young & Associates, Engineers, *A. R.,* March 1962.

## FIG. 8.3  SHELL SURFACES IN PLASTICS

(c) Shelter for migrant farmworkers, California, Yates, Hirshen and Van der Ryn, 1966; (f) Orthodox Greek Catholic Church, New Haven, Connecticut, Carl Blanchard Architect, Henry A. Pfisterer Structural Engineer, *ENR,* February 1967; (g) The Plastic House 1968, Wolfgang Feierbach, Germany, *P/A,* October 1970; (k) The Sphere, Roland R. Hanselmann, Architect, Olten, Switzerland, *Werk,* October 1970; (l) The Cylinder, Architect Dutler, St. Gallen, Switzerland, Amtor Schwabe: *Kunststoffe im Bauwesen,* A. Koch GMBH, Stuttgart, Germany, 1971; (m) Futuro II, Matti Suuronen Architect, Finnland, Futuro Corp., Philadelphia, Pennsylvania; (n) Monsanto House, Disneyland (1957–1968), Albert G. H. Dietz: *Plastics for Architects and Builders,* The MIT Press, Cambridge, Massachusetts, 1969.

## FIG. 8.8  CYLINDRICAL SHELL STRUCTURES

(a) Signal Corps Hangar, U.S. Engineers and Roberts & Schaefer Co., Chicago; (b) Residence, Palm Springs, California, Rick Farber and Associates; (c) Slayton Residence, Washington, D.C., I. M. Pei, *A. R.,* 1964; (d) Library Institute for Advanced Study, Princeton, New Jersey, Harrison & Abramovitz, *P/A,* August 1966; (e) U.S. Plywood Warehouse & Sales Office Building, Seattle, Washington,

Gideon Kramer Architect, *Architectural Forum,* April 1963; (f) Dixie Form & Steel Co. Office Build-
ing, San Antonio, Texas, Marmon and Mok Architects, *ENR,* December 1963; (g) Maimonides School,
Brookline, Massachusetts, Hugh Stubbins, *P/A,* February 1967; (h) Kimbell Art Museum, Forth Worth,
Texas, Louis I. Kahn, *AIA Journal,* May 1975, A. E. Komendant: *18 years with Architect Louis Kahn,*
Aloray, 1975, *ENR,* November 1971; (i) American Embassy, Karachi, Pakistan, Richard J. Neutra,
Art & Architecture, March 1965; (j) Pine Lumber Co., Redford Township, Michigan, Hawthorne &
Schmiedeks Architects, Building Construction, November 1960, *A. R.,* May 1962; (k) Yukari Kinder-
garten, Tokyo, Japan, Kenzo Tange, *Arena/Interbuild,* March 1968; (l) Shopping Center Maxis,
Muiden, Holland, Choisy and van Embden Architects, *Werk,* 10/1974; (m) Honolulu Park Grandstand,
Hilo, Hawaii, R. S. Matsunaga & Associates, PCItems #326/1974.


## FIG. 8.9   VAULTS AND SHORT CYLINDRICAL SHELLS

(a) Air hangar, Orly, France, E. Freyssinet, 1915; (b) Production Hall, Goldzack Elastic Mill, Gossau,
Switzerland, H. Danzeisen, H. Voser, H. Hossdorf Architects, 1955; (c) Exhibition Hall Turin, Salone
C, Turin, Italy, Luigi Nervi, P. L. Nervi: *Aesthetics and Technology in Building,* Harvard University
Press, 1966. (d) Shelterdome, Dome East Corp., Hicksville, New York, (e) Airplane hangar, Italy,
1940, Pier Luigi Nervi, P. L. Nervi: *Aesthetics and Technology in Building,* Harvard University Press,
1966; (f) The Corrugated Tube House, Tokyo, Japan, Osamu Ishiyama Architect, *J. A.,* 7710/11; (g)
Cementhalle, Swiss National Exhibition, Zurich, 1939, Robert Maillart Architect, Max Bill: *Robert
Maillart,* Verlag für Architektur, Erlenbach-Zurich, Switzerland, 1949; (h) Wholesale Market Hall,
Hamburg, Germany, B. Hermkes, G. Becker, G. Schramm, and J. Elingius Architects, *Arch. Forum,*
June 1963; (i) Sugar Storage Shed, American Sugar Co., Baltimore, Philip Johnson Arch, W. Mouton
Struct. Engineer, *ENR,* June 1969, *P/A,* October 1969; (j) Mercato del Fiori, Pescia, Italy, E. Brizzi,
E. and G. Gori, L. Ricci, L. Savioli, *Domus,* 499, 1971; (k) St. Anselm's Abbey, Washington, D.C.,
Philip C. Johnson, *A. R.,* July 1962.


## FIG. 8.21   BRACED DOMES

(a) High school auditorium, College Station, Texas, Caudill, Rowlett, and Scott, *Consulting Engineer,*
December 1959; (b) Ice skating rink, Hicksville, N.Y., Wiedersum Associates, *ENR,* June 1966; (c)
Field house, North Dakota Teachers' College, Clark, Elken & Holmen, *Building Construction,* October
1961; (d) Australian Academy of Science, Canberra, Australia, Grounds, Romberg & Boyd, *A. R.,*
February 1960; (e) Synagogue, Hebrew University, Jerusalem, Israel, Ezra Rau, *Architectural Forum,*
July 1958; (f) Kresge Auditorium, MIT, Cambridge, Massachusetts, Ero Saarinen and Ammann &
Whitney, *A. R.,* July 1955, *RIBA Journal,* February 1955; (g) King County Stadium, Seattle, Wash-
ington, joint venture of Naramore, Skilling, Praeger, *ENR,* April 17, 1975, *ACI Journal,* April 1975;
(h) Assembly Hall, University of Illinois, Urbana, Illinois, Harrison & Abramovitz and Ammann &
Whitney, *Architectural Forum,* March 1963, *A. R.,* July 1963, *ENR,* June 1961; (i) Louisiana Super-
dome, New Orleans, Curtis & Davis and Sverdrup & Parcel, *Civil Engineering,* November 1974, *ENR,*
March 22, 1973, *Modern Steel Construction,* 1st/2nd Quarter 1976; (j) Palazzetto dello Sport, Rome,
Italy, Pier Luigi Nervi and Annibale Vitellozzi, H. S. Howard, Jr.: *Structure,* McGraw-Hill, New York,
1966; (k) Convention Center, Norfolk, Virginia, William & Tazewell and Nervi, *Architecture and
Engineering News,* November 1967; (l) General Electric Exhibition, New York World Fair 1964–1965,
Welton Becket and R. Bradshaw, *World's Fair Preview,* Bethlehem Steel Publication, October 1963,
(m) International Trade Center, Tokyo, Japan, Masachiko Murata, *A. R.,* April 1961; (n) Sports
Palace, Mexico City, Mexico, Candela, Peyri & Tamborrel and Praeger-Kavanagh-Waterbury, *Civil
Engineering-ASCE,* October 1969, *A. & E. News,* April 1968, *P/A,* November 1968, *AIA Journal,*
January 1968; (o) Aluminum geodesic dome, Caracas, Venezuela, Synergetics Inc., *Techniques et
Architecture,* March 1976; (p) Factory dome, Abilene, Kansas, Kaiser Aluminum, *Building Construc-
tion,* December 1959, *Consulting Engineer,* September 1961; (q) Missouri Botanical Garden Building,
St. Louis, Missouri, Murphy & Mackey and Synergetics Inc., *Building Construction,* September 1961;

(r) Walt Whitman High School Field House, Bethesda, Maryland, McLeod & Ferrara and Synergetics Inc., *Building Construction,* September 1962; (s) Offices for Placer County, Auburn, California, Liles & Co. using Temcor prefabricated domes developed by D. L. Richter, *P/A,* February 1968; (t) Northern Arizona University Stadium, Flagstaff, Arizona, Rossman & Partners and Western Wood Structures Inc., *ENR,* December 23, 1976, *Civil Engineering,* August 1977; (u) Harris County Stadium, Houston, Texas, Lloyd & Morgan and Praeger, Kavanagh and Waterman, and Kiewitt, *ENR,* February 27, 1964, *A. & E. News,* May 1964; (v) Convocation Center, Ohio University, Athens, Ohio, Brubaker & Brandt and Fling & Eeman, *Modern Steel Construction,* 2nd Quarter 1969.

## FIG. 8.26

U.S. Pavilion, Expo 67, Montreal, Canada, R. Buckminster Fuller and Shoji Sadao, *P/A,* June 1967, *Arch. Des.,* July 1967, *Japan Arch.,* August 1967, *Tubular Structures* 9, November 1967.

## FIG. 8.29   ANTICLASTIC SURFACE STRUCTURES

(a) St. Mary's Basilica of Tokyo Cathedral, Tokyo, Japan, Kenzo Tange & Urtec Team, *Japan Architect,* August 1965, *AIA Journal,* June 1966; (b) Centre Le Corbusier, Zurich, Switzerland, Le Corbusier, *Forum,* September 1967; (c) Saier House, near Deauville, France, Marcel Breuer and Mario Jossa, *A. R.,* August 1977; (d) Ponce Coliseum, Puerto Rico, Sanchez, Davila & Suarez, and T. Y. Lin, *PCI Journal,* September–October 1973; (f) Philips Pavilion, the Brussels World Fair, 1958, Brussels, Belgium, Le Corbusier, *Techniques + Architecture,* March 1958; (g) Saint Mary's Cathedral, San Francisco, McSweeney, Ryan & Lee, Pietro Belluschi, Robinson & Associates, and Pier Luigi Nervi, *A. R.,* September 1971; (h) Iglesia de la Virgen Miligrosa, Mexico City, Mexico, Felix Candela; C. Faber: *Candela—The Shell Builder,* The Architectural Press, London, England, 1963, *ENR,* May 16, 1957; (i) TWA Hangars, Kansas City International Airport, Biggs & Drummond, KKBNA, and Cooper-Carlson-Duy-Ritchie, *Civil Engineering* January 1975; (j) Grandstand of Scioto Downs Raceway, Columbus, Ohio, Kellam & Foley and Gensert, Williams & Associates; (k) Foundry Roof at Lohr-am-Main, Germany, Kurt Siegel Architect, K. Siegel: *Structure and Form,* Reinhold, New York, 1962; (l) Berenplaat Water Treatment Plant, Filtration Building, Rotterdam, Holland, A. M. Haas: *Design of Thin Concrete Shells,* Vol. 2, Wiley, New York, 1967; (m) The Luce Chapel, Tunghai University, Taichung, Taiwan, I. M. Pei, *Architectural Forum,* August–September 1964 (conoidal shells); (n) Conoidal shell roof in Bulgaria, J. Doganoff Architect, Sofia, Bulgaria, H. Rühle: *Räumliche Dachtragwerke Konstruktion und Ausführung,* Verlagsgesellschaft Rudolf Müller, Köln, Germany, 1969; (o) Pratt Institute Athletic Building, Brooklyn, New York, Daniel F. Tully Associates and Ezra D. Ehrenkrantz, *ENR,* September 19, 1974; (p) Madonna di Pompei Church, Montreal, Canada, F. A. Dawson and F. M. Kraus, *ACI Journal,* July 1967.

## FIG. 8.33   INTERSECTING SHELLS

(a) Good Hope Center, Cape Town, South Africa, Studio Nervi and Colyn & Meiring, *ENR,* February 1977; (b) TWA Terminal, Kennedy Airport, New York, Eero Saarinen & Associates, and Ammann & Whitney, *A. R.,* September 1961, *ENR,* May 1962, *World Conference on Shell Structures 1963,* National Academy of Science, 1964; (c) Olympic Ice Stadium, Grenoble, France, N. Esquillan of Enterprises Boussiron, and F. Levi, *The Structural Engineer,* May 1969; (d) Air Terminal, St. Louis, Missouri, Hellmuth, Yamasaki, & Leinweber, and Roberts & Schaefer Co., *Arch. Forum,* November 1952, May 1956; (e) Supermarket, Honolulu, Hawaii, R. R. Bradshaw and Wimberly & Cook, *A. R.,* August 1960; (f) CNIT Palace, Paris, France, N. Esquillan and Camelot, de Mailly and Zehrfuss, *ENR,* April 1958; (g) Sports Center, Chamonix, France, Roger Taillibert Architect, Heinz Isler Engineer, *B + W,* 11, 1976.

## FIG. 8.34  OTHER SURFACE STRUCTURES

(a) Notre Dame du Haut at Ronchamp, France, Le Corbusier Architect, G. E. Kidder Smith: *The New Churches of Europe,* Holt, Rinehart and Winston, New York, 1963; (b) Eastman Kodak Pavilion, New York World's Fair 1964–1965, W. Burtin, Kahn and Jacobs, and Lev Zetlin & Associates, *A. R.,* September 1963; (c) Sydney Opera House, Sydney, Australia, Jørn Utzon Architect and Ove Arup Partners, *A. R.,* January 1966, *Structural Engineer,* March 1969, *Arch +,* August 1973, *Time,* October 1973; (d) The "Endless House" project, Frederick Kiesler, F. Kiesler: *Inside the Endless House,* Simon and Schuster, New York, 1960; (e) House in Joplin, Missouri, G. K. Muenning, *P. A.,* June 1963; (f) United Church of Rowayton, Connecticut, J. Salerno and W. C. Wing, *Forum,* December 1962, *A. R.,* February 1963; (g) Precious Blood Roman Catholic Church, St. Boniface, Winnipeg, Canada, Gaboury Lussier Sigurdson, *Forum,* November 1969, *P/A,* September 1972; (h) Picnic Shelter, Cherry Creek Reservoir, Denver, Colorado, C. Childress and R. Behrens, and KKBNA, *A.R.,* August 1975; (i) Temple B'nai Jehudah, Kansas City, Missouri, Kivett & Myers, and R. Bradshaw, *A. R.,* July 1969, *Modern Steel Construction,* 4th Quarter 1967; (j) Blossum Music Center, Akron, Ohio, Schaefer, Flynn and Van Dijk Architects and R. M. Gensert Associates, *ENR,* July 1968, *A. R.,* June 1969, *Modern Steel Construction,* 3rd Quarter 1969; (k) Auditorium Robert Frost High School, Culver City, California, Flewelling & Moody and C. P. Johnson, *Art and Architecture,* May 1964, *ENR,* November 1964; (l) Civic Center Synagogue, New York, W. H. Breger Architect, and P. Gugliotta, *Forum,* October 1967; (m) Shrine of the Book, Jerusalem, Israel, Kiesler & Bartos Architects, and Strobel & Rongved, *AIA Journal,* July 1966, *P/A,* September 1965. *Forum,* September 1965; (n) Water Tower; (o) Cooling Tower; (p) St. Louis Planetarium, St. Louis, Missouri, Hellmuth, Obata and Kassabaum Architects, M. Ketchum and A. Alper, *P/A,* January 1960; (q) Charles Deaton House, Genesee Mountain, Colorado, C. Deaton Architect, *A. R.,* September 1965, *Concrete Construction,* April 1966; (r) Mannheim Exhibition Hall, Mannheim, Germany, Frei Otto and Mutschler, Lagner and Wessa, *ENR,* June 1975, *IL 10-Grid Shells,* Institute of Lightweight Structures, University of Stuttgart, Germany, 1974; (s) The Meeting Center, Rockefeller Plaza, Albany, New York, Harrison and Abramovitz Architects, and Ammann & Whitney, *Civil Engineering,* June 1979, *ENR,* September 1974; (t) *Marché* de Meubles, Chatillan de Michaille, near Genève, France, Chanéac Architect, *Architecture Français,* August 1974; (u) Garden Center, Camorino, Ticino, Switzerland, Heinz Isler, *B + W,* 11, 1976, IASS No. 71/72, September 1979.

## FIG. 9.2  TYPICAL CONNECTION DETAILS BETWEEN ROOF CLADDING AND CABLES

(a) State Fair Arena, Raleigh, North Carolina, M. Novicki and W. Dietrich, "Cable Roof Structures," Booklet 2318-A, Bethlehem Steel, November 1968; (b) Ingalls Hockey Rink, Yale University, New Haven, Connecticut, Eero Saarinen, *ENR,* April 1958; (c) Munich Olympic Stadium, Munich, Germany, Frei Otto, Behnisch & Partner; P. Krishna: *Cable-Suspended Roofs,* McGraw-Hill Book Company, New York, 1978; (d) Thomas A. Leavy Activities Center, University of Santa Clara, California, Caudill Rowlett Scott Architects, Geiger and Berger Structural Engineers, *P.A.,* May 1976, April 1978; (e) Pontiac Metropolitan Stadium, Pontiac, Michigan, O'Dell/Hewlett & Luckenbach Architects, Geiger Berger Associates, Structural Engineers, *Civil Engineering,* November 1975; (f) U.S. Pavilion, Expo 70, Osaka, Japan, Davis, Brody, Chermayeff, Geismar, deHarak Associates, Geiger Berger Associates, Consulting Engineers, *Civil Engineering* March 1970; (g) Steve Lacy Fieldhouse, Milligan College, Milligan, Tennessee, The Shaver Partnership Architects, Geiger Berger Associates, Structural Engineers, *Arch. Plus,* October 1973; (h) Multiple Membranes, *Air Structures Design and Standards Manual,* Air Structures Institute, St. Paul, Minnesota, 1977.

## FIG. 9.4  TENSION FOUNDATIONS

(a) Single foundations, Mick Eekhout: *Frei Otto and the Munich Olympic Games,* Zodiac 21, Milan, Italy, 1972; (b), (c), (d) Compression rings, David Geiger: *Single, Double, Dual Structures, Notes on the American Pavilion at the Osaka Exposition,* Zodiac 21, Milan, Italy, 1972; David Geiger: *Develop-*

*ments in Incombustible Fabrics and Low Profile Air Structures,* International Conference on the Practical Application for Air Supported Structures, 1974, Canvas Products Association, St. Paul, Minnesota, 1976; (b) University of Santa Clara, California; (c) U.S. Pavilion, Osaka, Japan; (d) Pontiac Stadium, Pontiac, Michigan.


### FIG. 9.6  PNEUMATIC STRUCTURES

(a) Commercial air supported structures as produced by following companies: Air-Tech, Birdair, Cidair, Taiyo Kogyo, Thermoflex, etc.; (b) Radome, Bochum, Germany, Krupp, Roger N. Dent: *Principles of Pneumatic Architecture,* Wiley, 1972; (c) Birdair Cable Dome, Birdair, *A. D.,* January 1973; (d) Airplane Maintenance Hangar, Taiyo Kogyo Co., Japan, *Arch. +,* October 1973; (e) Fuji Group Pavilion, Expo 1970, Osaka, Japan, Yutaka Murata: *Proceedings 1971, IASS Pacific Symposium Part II on Tension Structures and Space Frames,* Architectural Institute of Japan, Tokyo and Kyoto, 1972; (f) Open-Air Restaurant, Expo 1970, Osaka, Japan, Yutaka Murata, Proceedings *1971 IASS Pacific Symposium Part II on Tension Structures and Space Frames,* Architectural Institute of Japan, Tokyo and Kyoto, 1972; (g) Event Structure for Three River Festival, Pittsburgh, Pennsylvania, Chrysalis East, *P. A.,* February 1977; (h) Proposal for the French Pavilion, Expo 1970, Osaka, Japan, B. Quentin, Jean Le Couteur, D. Sloal, *AIA Journal,* March 1970, *Domus* #462; (i) Inflatable Kindergarten, Seminar on Pneumatic Structures, Institute für Umweltsplanung, Ulm, Germany, under the direction of Gernot Minke, Report: iup 9, 1972.


### FIG. 9.7  LOW-PROFILE, LONG-SPAN ROOF STRUCTURES

(a) Physical education complex, Dalhousie University, Halifax, Nova Scotia, Canada, Leslie R. Fairn & Associates, C. D. Carruthers & Wallace Engineers, Stainless Steel Membrane Roof, *AISI,* April 1980, *ENR,* November 8, 1979; (b) Thomas A. Leavy Activities Center, University of Santa Clara, California, Caudill Rowlett Scott Architects, Geiger-Berger & Associates, roof consultants, *P/A,* May 1976, *Building Design and Construction,* February 1976; (c) Steve Lacy Field House Milligan College, Milligan, Tennessee, The Shaver Partnership, Geiger-Berger Associates, Engineers, *Civil Engineering,* November 1975, *Building Design and Construction,* February 1976; (d) Stephen C. O'Connell Center, University of Florida, Gainesville, Florida, Caudill Rowlett Scott Architects, Geiger-Berger & Associates, roof consultants, *P/A,* 6, 1980; *P/A,* 8, 1981; (e) Pontiac Stadium, Pontiac, Michigan, O'Dell/Hewlett & Luckenbach Architects, Geiger-Berger Associates, Engineers for the roof structure, *A.R.,* January 1976, "Bethlehem Case History No. 45," 1976, *Civil Engineering,* November 1975, *Building Design and Construction,* February 1976; (f) U.S. Pavilion, Expo 70, Osaka, Japan, Davis Brody Chermayeff Geismar deHarak Architects, Geiger-Berger Associates, Structural Engineers, *Civil Engineering,* March 1970, *ENR,* November 1969, *Forum,* September 1970; (g) Uni Dome, University of Northern Iowa, Cedar Falls, Iowa, Thorson-Brom-Broshar-Snyder Arch., Geiger-Berger Associates, Structural Engineers, *A. R.,* January 1976, *Civil Engineering* November 1975, *Building Design and Construction,* November 1974, February 1976.


### FIG. 9.17  TENSILE MEMBRANE STRUCTURES

(a) El Paso Performing Arts Center, El Paso, Texas, Garland & Hilles, and Carroll, Daeuble, DuSang & Rand, and Izenour Associates, Architects, Severud-Perone-Sturm-Conlin-Bandel Structural Engineers, *ENR,* July 1972; (b) Indiana University Stadium, Bloomington, Indiana, Eggers and Higgins Architects, Severud-Perrone-Fisher-Sturm-Bandel Structural Engineers, *ENR,* May 1969, *Arch. & Eng. News,* August 1969; (c) Milan Sports Palace, Milan, Italy, Gilberto and Tammaso Valle Architects, O. Accossano Structural Engineer, *Domus,* August 1973, *Forum,* October 1973, *TA,* October 1973, *ENR,* May 17, 1973; (d) National Gymnasium, Tokyo, Japan, Kenzo Tange Architect, Tsuboi-Kawaguchi-Kawamata Structural Engineers, *P/A,* December 1964, *J. A.,* November 1964, *Arch. Des.,* May 1965, January 1964, November 1964; (e) Myoden, Buddhist temple of Sho Hondo complex, foot of Mount Fujiyama, Japan, Kimio Yokoyama Architect, Y. Tsuboi and S. Aoki Structural Engineers, *ENR*, August 1972, *A. R.*, July 1973, *Proceedings of the 1971 IASS Pacific Symposium*, Vol. 2, *Arch +*, February 1973; (f) Minor National Gymnasium, Tokyo, Japan, Kenzo Tange Architect, Tsuboi-Kawaguchi-Kawamata Structural Engineers, *P/A*, December 1964, *J. A.*, November 1964, *A. D.*, January 1964, November 1964, May 1965; (g) Ingalls Hockey Rink, Yale University, New Haven, Connecticut, Eero Saarinen Architect, Severud-Elstad-Krueger Structural Engineers, *A. R.*, August 1957, October 1958, *ENR*, April 1958; (h) The Kagawa Prefectural Gymnasium, Takamatsu City, Japan, Kenzo Tange Architect, T. Okamoto Structural Engineer, *J. A.*, August 1965; (i) North Carolina State Fair Building, Raleigh, North Carolina, W. H. Deitrick and M. Nowicki Architects, Severud-Perrone-Sturm-Conlin-Bandel Structural Engineers, Bethlehem Steel Corp., "Cable Roof Structures," Booklet 2318-A November 1968, *Arch. Forum*, June 1953, *AIA Journal*, September 1980; (j) Iwate Prefectural Gymnasium, Giappone, Japan, Yoshio Kabayaschi Architect, *L'Architectura*, 164, 1969, *J. A.*, April 1968.

## FIG. 9.18   TENT ARCHITECTURE

(a) German Pavilion, Expo 67, Montreal, Canada, Rolf Gutbrod Architect, Frei Otto Design Consultant, *Architectural Forum*, April 1967, *P. A.*, June, 1967; (b) Japan Automobile Industry Pavilion, Expo 1970, Osaka, Japan, Kunio Maekawa Associates, *Proceedings, 1971 IASS Pacific Symposium Part 2*, Paper No. 6-6, Architectural Institute of Japan, 1972; (c) Mecca Auditorium Conference Center, Mecca, Saudi Arabia, Rolf Gutbrod and Frei Otto, *Proceedings, 1971 IASS Pacific Symposium Part 2*, Paper No. 1–4, Architectural Institute of Japan, 1972, *P. A.*, 12, 1974; (d) Campus Center and Drama Lab, La Verne College, La Verne, California, Shaver Partnership, *ENR*, June 28, 1973, *Construction Methods & Equipment*, August 1973, *Arch. +*, October 1973; (e) U.S. Pavilion, Expo 1974, Spokane, Washington, Naramore, Bain, Brady & Johnson, *Civil Engineering*, June 1974, *P. A.*, 8, 1974; (f) Bullock's department store, San Jose, California, EPR Architects, Geiger-Berger Assoc., Engineers, *Arch. Rec.*, mid-August, 1979, *ENR*, June 8, 1978; (g) Independence Mall Pavilion, Bicentennial Structures, H2L2 Architects, Geiger-Berger Associates, Engineers and Design Consultants, *Arch. Rec.*, mid-August 1976; (h) BP Inauguration Tent, London, England, Ove Arup & Partners, Frei Otto, *Domus*, 503, October 1975, *B + W*, 11, 1976; (i) Proposal for Franklin Park Zoo, Roxbury, Massachusetts, Huygens and Tappé, Weidlinger Associates, 2nd International Conference on Space Structures, University of Surrey, Guildford, England, 1975, *P. A.*, June 1980, *Civil Engineering*, August 1977; (j) Olympic Stadium, Munich, Germany, Behnisch & Partners, Frei Otto, *Civil Engineering*, July 1972, *P. A.*, August 1972, *Zodiac 21*, September 1972, *Forum*, October 1972, *Design* 285, September 1972; (k) New Jeddah Airport, Jeddah, Saudi Arabia, SOM and Geiger Berger Associates, *Architectural Record*, mid-August 1979, 1980, and May 1980, *ENR*, January 18 and June 28, 1979, *P. A.*, June 1980.

# REFERENCES

## General

1 Acland, James H.: *Medieval Structure: The Gothic Vault,* University of Toronto Press, Toronto, 1972.

2 Ambrose, James: *Simplified Design of Building Structures,* Wiley, New York, 1979.

3 Ambrose, James and Vergun, Dimitri: *Simplified Building Design for Wind and Earthquake Forces,* Wiley, New York, 1980.

4 Architects and Earthquakes, AIA Research Corporation, Washington, NSF/RA – 770156, 1977.

5 Amrheim, James E.: *Reinforced Masonry Engineering Handbook,* 3rd ed., *Clay and Concrete Masonry,* Masonry Institute of America, Los Angeles, 1978.

6 Bill, Max: *Robert Maillart,* Verlag für Architektur AG, 1949.

7 Breuer, György: *Gyakorlati Szerkezettervezés,* Vols. 1 and 2, Müszaki Könyvkiadó, Budapest, Hungary, 1973.

8 Building Code Requirements for Reinforced Concrete (ACI 318–77), American Concrete Institute, Detroit, December 1977.

9 Burt, Michael: Spatial Arrangement and Polyhedra with Curved Surfaces and their Architectural Applications, M.S. Thesis, Technion, Haifa, Israel, 1966.

10 Büttner, Oskar and Hampe, Erhard: *Bauwerk, Tragwerk, Tragstruktur,* Vol. 1, Verlag Gerd Hatje, Stuttgart, Germany, 1976.

11 Cavallari-Murat, Augusto: Static Intuition and Formal Imagination in the Space Lattices of Ribbed Gothic Vaults, *The Student Publications of the School of Design,* Vol. 11, #2, North Carolina State College, 1963.

12 Cook, Peter: *Experimental Architecture,* Universe Books, New York, 1970.

13 Cowan, Henry J.: *Science and Building,* Wiley, New York, 1978.

14 Cowan, Henry J.: *The Master Builders,* Wiley, New York, 1977.

15 Dahinden, Justus: *Urban Structures for the Future,* Praeger, New York, 1972.

16 Degenkolb, Henry J. : Earthquake, Booklet 2717A, Bethlehem Steel, 1977.

17 Dietz, Albert G. H.: *Plastics for Architects and Builders,* The MIT Press, Cambridge, Massachusetts, 1969.

18 Faegre, Torvald: *Tents, Architecture of the Nomads,* Anchor Press/Doubleday, Garden City, New York 1979.

19 Foster, Jack Stroud, and Harrington, Raymond: *Structure and Fabric,* Part 2, B. T. Batsford Limited, London, England, 1976.

20 Gordon, J. E.: *The New Science of Strong Materials,* Walker and Company, New York, 1968.

21  Gordon, J. E.: *Structures,* Plenum, New York, 1978.

22  Green, Norman B.: *Earthquake Resistant Building Design and Construction,* Van Nostrand Reinhold Company, New York, 1978.

23  Grillo, Paul Jacques: *Form Function & Design,* Dover, New York, 1975.

24  Grube, Oswald W.: *Industrial Buildings and Factories,* Praeger, New York, 1971.

25  Grube, Oswald W., Pran, Peter C., and Schulze, Franz: *100 Years of Architecture in Chicago,* Follett, Chicago, 1977.

26  Hancocks, David: *Master Builders of the Animal World,* Harper & Row, New York, 1973.

27  Hart, Franz: *Kunst und Technik der Wölbung,* Verlag Georg D. W. Callwey, Munich, Germany, 1965.

28  Hodgkinson, Allan, Ed.: *AJ Handbook of Building Structure,* The Architectural Press, London, England, 1974.

29  Hollaway, Leonard: *Glass Reinforced Plastics in Construction,* Wiley, New York, 1978.

30  Howard, Seymour H., Jr.: *Structure An Architect's Approach,* McGraw-Hill, New York, 1966.

31  Kepes, Gyorgy, Ed.: *Structure in Art and in Science,* Studio Vista, London, England, 1965.

32  Kepes, Gyorgy, Ed.: *Module, Symmetry, Proportion,* Studio Vista, London, England, 1966.

33  *Long Span Steel Roof Structures,* American Iron and Steel Institute, Washington, D.C., 1978.

34  Mainstone, Rowland: *Developments in Structural Form,* The MIT Press, Cambridge, Massachusetts, 1975.

35  March, Lionel and Steadman, Philip: *The Geometry of Environment,* The MIT Press, Cambridge, Massachusetts, 1974.

36  Mark, Robert: The Structural Analysis of Gothic Cathedrals, *Scientific American,* November 1972, Structural Experimentation in Gothic Architecture, *American Scientist,* 10/11, 1978.

37  Metal Building Systems Manual, Metal Building Manufacturers Association, Cleveland, Ohio, 1981.

38  Nachtigall, Werner: *Biotechnik,* Quelle & Meyer, Heidelberg, Germany, 1971.

39  Nervi, Pier Luigi: *Aesthetics and Technology in Building,* Harvard University Press, Cambridge, Massachusetts, 1966.

40  Nervi, Pier Luigi: *Buildings, Projects, Structures, 1953–1963,* Praeger, New York, 1963.

41  Nilson, Arthur H.: *Design of Prestressed Concrete,* Wiley, New York, 1978.

42  Quarmby, Arthur: *The Plastics Architect,* Pall Mall Press, London, England, 1974.

43  Report of Summer Seismic Institute for Architectural Faculty, Stanford University, August 1977, AIA Research Corporation, Washington, D.C. 1977.

44  Rickenstorf, Günther: *Tragwerke für Hochbauten,* BSB B.G. Teubner Verlagsgesellschaft, Leipzig, German Democratic Republic, 1972.

45  Rickey, George: *Constructivism,* George Braziller, New York, 1967.

46  Salvadori, Mario: *Why Buildings Stand Up,* Norton, New York, 1980.

47  Shawcroft, Brian: Building Skeletons, *The Student Publications of the School of Design,* Vol. 17, #1, North Carolina State University, Raleigh, 1967.

48  Schaeffer, R. E.: *Building Structures,* Prentice-Hall, Englewood Cliffs, New Jersey, 1980.

49  Schmitt, Heinrich: *Hochbau Konstruktion,* 6th ed., Vieweg & Sohn, Braunschweig, Germany, 1977.

50  Schodek, Daniel L.: *Structures,* Prentice-Hall, Englewood Cliffs, New Jersey, 1980.

51  Siegel, Kurt: *Structure and Form in Modern Architecture,* Reinhold, New York, 1962.

52  Sontag, H., Hart, F. and Henn, W.: *Multi-Storey Buildings in Steel,* Wiley, New York, 1978.

53  Space Forms in Steel, *AISC Engineering Journal,* December 1965, American Institute of Steel Construction, New York.

54  Spiegel, Leonard and Limbrunner, G.F.: *Reinforced Concrete Design,* Prentice-Hall, Englewood Cliffs, New Jersey, 1980.

55   Stevens, Peter S.: *Patterns in Nature,* Little, Brown & Company, Boston, 1974.

56   Teng, Wayne C.: *Foundation Design,* Prentice-Hall, Englewood Cliffs, New Jersey, 1962.

57   The Underground Space Center, University of Minnesota: *Earth Sheltered Housing Design,* Van Nostrand Reinhold, New York, 1979.

58   Thompson, D'Arcy: *On Growth and Form,* Abridged Ed., John Tyler Bonner, Ed., Cambridge University Press, 1969.

59   Torroja, Eduardo: *The Structures of Eduardo Torroja,* F. W. Dodge Corporation, New York, 1958.

60   Torroja, Eduardo: *Philosophy of Structures,* University of California Press, Berkeley and Los Angeles, 1958.

61   Von Frisch, Karl: *Animal Architecture,* Harcourt, Brace Jovanovich, New York, 1974.

62   Wachsmann, Konrad: *The Turning Point of Building—Structure and Design,* Reinhold, New York, 1961.

63   Weidlinger, Paul: Visualizing the Effect of Earthquakes on the Behavior of Building Structures, *A. R.,* May 1977.

64   White, R. N., Gergely, P., and Sexsmith, R. G.: *Structural Engineering,* Vol. 1, Wiley, New York, 1972.

65   Whyte, Lancelot Law: *Aspects of Form,* Indiana University Press, Bloomington, Indiana, 1961.

66   Wilson, Forrest: *Emerging Form in Architecture: Conversations with Lev Zetlin,* Cahners Books, Boston, Massachusetts, 1975.

67   Wormuth, Rüdiger: *Grundlagen der Hochbaukonstruktion,* Werner Verlag, Düsseldorf, Germany, 1977.

68   Yanev, Peter: *Peace of Mind in Earthquake Country,* Chronicle Books, San Francisco, 1974.

## Frame Structures

69   American Institute of Timber Construction: *Timber Construction Manual,* 2nd Ed., Wiley, New York, 1974.

70   Andersen, Paul and Nordby, Gene, M.: *Introduction to Structural Mechanics,* Ronald Press, New York, 1960.

71   Gaylord, Edwin H. and Gaylord, Charles N., Eds.: *Structural Engineering Handbook,* 2nd Ed., McGraw-Hill, New York, 1979.

72   Gurfinkel, German: Wood Engineering, Southern Forest Products Association, New Orleans, Louisiana, 1973.

73   Henn, Walter: *Buildings for Industry,* London ILiffe Books Ltd, London, England, 1965.

74   Koncz, Tihamér: *Manual of Precast Concrete Construction,* Vols. 1–3, Bauverlag Wiesbaden and Berlin, Germany, 1968.

75   Marcus, Samuel H.: *Basics of Structural Steel Design,* Reston Publ., Reston, Virginia, 1977.

76   McCormac, Jack C.: *Structural Analysis,* 2nd Ed., International Textbook, Scranton, Pennsylvania, 1967.

77   Norris, Charles H. and Wilbur, John B.: *Elementary Structural Analysis,* 2nd Ed., McGraw-Hill, New York, 1960.

78   Salvadori, Mario: *Statics and Strength of Structures,* Prentice-Hall, Englewood Cliffs, New Jersey, 1971.

79   Salvadori, Mario and Levy, Matthys: *Structural Design in Architecture,* 2nd Ed., Prentice-Hall, Englewood Cliffs, New Jersey, 1981.

80   Tuma, Jan J.: *Theory and Problems of Structural Analysis,* Schaum's Outline Series, McGraw-Hill, New York, 1969.

81   Winter, George and Nilson, Arthur H., et al. *Design of Concrete Structures,* 8th Ed., McGraw-Hill, New York, 1972.

## Space Frame and Surface Grid Structures

82 Andersen, Paul and Nordby, Gene M.: *Introduction to Structural Mechanics,* Ronald Press, New York, 1960.

83 Baer, Steve: *Zome Primer,* Zomeworks Corp., Albuquerque, New Mexico, 1970.

84 Barr, Stephen: *Experiments in Topology,* Thomas Y. Crowell, New York, 1964.

85 Benjamin, B.S.: *The Analysis of Braced Domes,* Asia Publishing House, Bombay, India, 1963.

86 Borrego, John: *Space Grid Structures,* The MIT Press, Cambridge, Massachusetts, 1968.

87 Büttner, Oskar and Stenker, Horst: *Metalleichtbauten,* Deutsche Verlags-Anstalt, Stuttgart, Germany, 1970.

88 Critchlow, Keith: *Order in Space,* Viking, New York, 1970.

89 Davies, R. M., Ed.: *Space Structures,* Wiley, New York, 1967.

90 *Domebook 2,* Pacific Domes, Bolinas, California, 1971.

91 Engel, Heinrich: *Structure Systems,* Praeger, New York, 1968.

92 Fuller, Buckminster R.: *Synergetics,* Macmillan, New York, 1975.

93 Fuller, Buckminster R. and Marks, Robert: *The Dymaxion World of Buckminster Fuller,* Anchor Press/Doubleday, Garden City, New York, 1973.

94 Gheorghiu, Adrian and Dragomir, Virgil: *Geometry of Structural Forms,* Applied Science Publishers Ltd., London, England, 1978.

95 Ghyka, Matila: *The Geometry of Art and Life,* Dover, New York, 1977.

96 Kenner, Hugh: *Geodesic Math,* University of California Press, Berkeley, 1976.

97 Lee, Hung-gum and Makowski, Stanislaw: Study of Factors Affecting Stress Distribution in Double-Layer Grids of the Square and Diagonal Type, *Architectural Science Review,* December 1977.

98 Loeb, Arthur L.: *Space Structures,* Addison-Wesley, Reading, Massachusetts, 1976.

99 Makowski, Zygmunt S.: *Steel Space Structures,* Michel Joseph, London, England, 1965.

100 Mengeringhausen, M.: *Raumfachwerke aus Stäben und Knoten,* Bauverlag GmBH, Wiesbaden, BRD, 1975.

101 Naslund, Kenneth C.: Design Considerations for Horizontal Space Frames, *A.R.,* August 1964.

102 Norris, Charles H. and Wilbur, John B.: *Elementary Structural Analysis,* 2nd Ed., McGraw-Hill, New York, 1960.

103 Pearce, Peter: *Structure in Nature is a Strategy for Design,* MIT Press, Cambridge, Massachusetts, 1978.

104 Popko, Edward: Geodesics, School of Architecture, University of Detroit, Detroit, Michigan, 1968.

105 Pugh, Anthony: *Polyhedra,* University of California Press, Berkeley, 1976.

106 Pugh, Anthony: *Tensegrity,* University of California Press, Berkeley, 1976.

107 Richter, Don L.: Geodesic Domes, *Forum,* January/February 1972.

108 Rühle, Hermann: *Räumliche Dachtragwerke Konstruktion und Ausführung,* Vol. 2, Verlagsgesellschaft Rudolf Müller, Köln, BRD, 1970.

109 Salvadori, Mario and Levy, Matthys: *Structural Design in Architecture,* Prentice-Hall, Englewood Cliffs, New Jersey, 1967.

110 Second International Conference on Space Structures, Dept. of Civil Engineering, University of Surrey, Guildford, England, September 1975.

111 Sedlak, Vinzenz: Paper Shelters, *AD,* December 1973.

112 Space Forms in Steel, American Institute of Steel Construction, New York, 1965.

113 Stevens, David E. and Odom, Gerald S.: The Steel Framed Dome, *AISC Engineering Journal,* July 1964.

114 Williams, Robert: *Natural Structure,* Eudaemon Press, Moorpark, California, 1972.

## Shell and Folded Plate Structures

115 Abercrombie, Stanley: *Ferrocement,* Schocken Books, New York, 1977.

116 Angerer, Fred: *Surface Structures in Building,* Reinhold, 1961.

117 Billington, David P.: *Thin Shell Concrete Structures,* McGraw-Hill, New York, 1965.

118 Carney, J. M.: Plywood Folded Plates, Laboratory Report 121, American Plywood Association, Tacoma, Washington, 1971.

119 Catalano, Eduardo F.: Structures of Warped Surfaces, *The Student Publication of the School of Design,* Vol. 10, #1, Raleigh, N.C.

120 Chronowicz, Albin: *The Design of Shells,* 3rd ed., Crosby Lockwood & Son Ltd., London, England, 1968.

121 Concrete Thin Shells, Publication SP-28, American Concrete Institute, Detroit, Michigan, 1971.

122 Design of Circular Domes, Portland Cement Association, ST 55, Chicago, Illinois.

123 Design Examples: Space Forms in Steel, American Institute of Steel Construction, 1966.

124 Dome Structures, *Consulting Engineer,* December 1959.

125 Elementary Analysis of Hyperbolic Paraboloid Shells, Portland Cement Association, ST 85, Chicago, Illinois, 1960.

126 Engel, Heinrich: *Structure Systems,* Praeger, New York, 1968.

127 Faber, Colin: *Candela, The Shell Builder,* Reinhold, 1963.

128 Francis, A. J.: Domes, *Architectural Science Review,* November 1962.

129 Frostick, Peter: Antiprism Based Form Possibilities for Folded Surface Structures, *Architectural Science Review,* September 1978.

130 Haas, A. M.: *Design of Thin Concrete Shells,* Vols. 1 and 2, Wiley and Sons, New York, 1962, 1967.

131 Hyperbolic Paraboloid Shells, Western Wood Products Association, Portland, Oregon, Technical Guide TG-4.

132 Iffland, Jerome S.B.: Folded Plate Structures, *Journal of the Structural Division,* ASCE, Vol. 105, No. ST1, Proc. Paper 14300, 1979.

133 Joedicke, Jürgen: *Shell Architecture,* Reinhold, New York, 1963.

134 Ketchum, Milo: Design of Shell Structures: Barrel Vaults, *Consulting Engineer,* September 1961.

135 Nilson, Arthur H.: Steel Shell Roof Structures, *AISC Engineering Journal,* January 1966.

136 Pflüger, Alf: *Elementary Statics of Shells,* 2nd Ed., F. W. Dodge, New York, 1961.

137 Ramaswamy, G. S.: *Design and Construction of Concrete Shell Roofs,* McGraw-Hill, New York, 1968.

138 Rühle, Hermann: *Räumliche Dachtragwerke Konstruktion und Ausführung,* Vol. 1, Verlagsgesellschaft Rudolf Müller, Köln, BRD, 1969.

139 Salvadori, Mario and Heller, Robert: *Structure in Architecture,* 2nd Ed., Prentice-Hall, Englewood Cliffs, New Jersey, 1975.

140 Salvadori, Mario and Levy, Matthys: *Structural Design in Architecture,* Prentice-Hall, Englewood Cliffs, New Jersey, 1967.

141 Sedlak, Vinzenz: Paper Shelters; Folded Structural Forms in Paperboard, *A.D.,* December 1973.

142 Smith, Baldwin E.: *The Dome,* Princeton University Press, Princeton, New Jersey, 1971.

143 Torroja, Eduardo: *The Structures of Eduardo Torroja,* F. M. Dodge, New York, 1958.

144 Winter, George and Nilson, Arthur H.: *Design of Concrete Structures,* 8th Ed., McGraw-Hill, New York, 1972.

## Tensile Structures

145   Air Structures, *Engineering News-Record,* August 1974.

146   Air Structures Proceedings of the International Conference on the Practical Application for Air Supported Structures, 1974, Canvas Products Association, St. Paul, Minnesota, 1976.

147   Berger, Horst: The Engineering Discipline of Tent Structures, *AR,* February 1975.

148   Boys, C. V.: *Soap-Bubbles,* Dover, New York, 1959.

149   Bubner, Ewald: *Zum Problem der Formfindung vorgespannter Seilnetzflächen,* IGMA Dissertationen 2, University of Stuttgart, Karl Krämer Verlag Stuttgart/Bern, Germany, 1972.

150   Cable Construction in Contemporary Architecture, Booklet 2264A, Bethlehem Steel Corp., Bethlehem, Pennsylvania, 1966.

151   Cable Roof Structures, Booklet 2318A, Bethlehem Steel Corp., Bethlehem, Pennsylvania, 1968.

152   Dent, Roger N.: *Principles of Pneumatic Architecture,* Halsted Press, New York, 1972.

153   Design and Standards Manual, Publication ASI-77, Air Structures Institute (ASI), St. Paul, Minnesota, 1977.

154   Drew, Philip: *Frei Otto, Form and Structure,* Westview Press, Boulder, Colorado, 1976.

155   Engel, Heinrich: *Structure Systems,* Praeger, New York, 1968.

156   Fabric Structures Grow Up, *Arch. Plus,* October, 1973.

157   Geiger, David H.: Pneumatic Structures, *Progressive Architecture,* August, 1972.

158   Hanging Roofs, Booklet 2319, Bethlehem Steel Corp., Bethlehem, Pennsylvania, 1967.

159   Herzog, Thomas: *Pneumatic Structures,* Oxford University Press, New York, 1976.

160   Howard, Seymour H., Jr.: Suspended Structures Concepts, United States Steel, Pittsburgh, Pennsylvania, 1966.

161   Information of the Institute for Lightweight Structures (IL), University of Stuttgart, Germany:
      IL 1: The Experimental Determination of Minimal Nets, 1969.
      IL 5: Convertible Roofs, 1972.
      IL 8: Nets in Nature and Technics, 1975.
      IL 12: Convertible Pneus, 1975.
      IL 16: Tents, 1976.

162   International Conference on Tension Roof Structures, Polytechnic of Central London, England, 1974.

163   Joseph, Marjory L.: *Introductory Textile Science,* 2nd ed., Holt, Rinehart and Winston, Inc., New York, 1972.

164   Light Structures, *Zodiac* 21, Milan, Italy, 1972.

165   Krishna, Prem: *Cable-Suspended Roofs,* McGraw-Hill, New York, 1978.

166   Manual for Structural Applications of Steel Cables for Buildings, 1973 Ed., AISI.

167   Otto, Frei, Ed.: *Tensile Structures,* MIT Press, Cambridge, Massachusetts, 1973.

168   Proceedings of the First International Colloquium on Pneumatic Structures, IASS, University of Stuttgart, Germany, 1967.

169   Proceedings of the IASS Pacific Symposium—Part 2 on Tension Structures and Space Frames, Tokyo and Kyoto, 1971, Architectural Institute of Japan, Tokyo, 1972.

170   Proceedings, IASS World Congress on Space Enclosures, Vol. 2, Concordia University, Montreal, Canada, 1976.

171   Roland, Conrad and Frei, Otto: *Tension Structures,* Praeger, New York, 1970.

172   Rühle, Herrmann: *Räumliche Dachtragwerke Konstruktion und Ausführung,* Vol. 2, Verlagsgesellschaft Rudolf Müller, Köln, Germany, 1970.

173   Salvadori, Mario and Levy, Matthys: *Structural Design in Architecture,* 2nd ed., Prentice-Hall, Englewood Cliffs, New Jersey, 1981.

174   Schierle, Gotthilf Goetz, Ed.: *Lightweight Tension Structures,* Dept. of Architecture, University of California, Berkeley, 1968.

175  Stainless Steel Membrane Roof, Committee of Stainless Steel Producers, American Iron and Steel Institute, Washington, D.C., Booklet AISI SS 902-480-25M-GP, April 1980.

176  Tension Structures: Their Theory and Practice, *The Architects' Journal*, May, 1973.

177  The Era of Swoops and Billows, Fabric Structures, *Progressive Architecture*, June 1980.

178  Zetlin, Lev: Steel Cable Creates Novel Structural Space Systems, Space Forms in Steel, *AISC Engineering Journal*, 1965.

# ANSWERS TO
# SELECTED PROBLEMS

---

**1.3** (a) external pressure on frame: $p = 208$ psf. (b) the lower inside pressure may not be critical because of short time period and leakage

**1.4** $w_L = 42.72$ psf

**1.5** $f = 13.20$ ksi

**1.6** $L = 88.28$ ft

**1.10** $\Delta \propto 1/E$

**1.11** $\Delta \propto 1/EI$

**1.12** carbon steel: $L_u = 3.23$ mi, timber: $L_u = 5.46$ mi, etc.

**1.13** carbon steel: $E/\gamma = 8.52 \times 10^6$ ft, timber: $E/\gamma = 5.76 \times 10^6$ ft

**1.15** $\Delta_{St} = \Delta_{Al}/3$

**1.18** concrete: $\Delta_L = 0.066$ in., steel: $\Delta_L = 0.078$ in., aluminum: $\Delta_L = 0.157$ in.

**1.20** steel is about 75 times more ductile

**1.21** $f_{St} = 16.91$ ksi, $f_c = 2.16$ ksi

**1.23** use 6 × 24

**1.27** 75%

**1.28** use 8 × 12

**1.29** case (g, cantilever beam)

**1.37** $P = 110.71$ k

**1.38** TS 5 OD × 0.258

**1.39** TS 6 × 3 × $\frac{1}{4}$

**1.40** 16 in. on center

**1.41** use 4 × 8

**1.43** (a) $b = 2.32$ ft, (b) $b = 4.63$ ft, (c) $b = 3.47$ ft (d) $b = 7.25$ ft

**1.44** 28 ft 9 in. $\times$ 5 ft 3 in.

**1.46** $h = 2.54$ ft

**1.47** $M = 38.88$ ft-k/ft

**1.50** $M_{max} = 1.68$ ft-k/ft

**1.51** $M_{max} = 1.57$ ft-k/ft

**1.52** $M_{max} = 0.38$ ft-k/ft

**1.54** $\Delta_i = -1.01$ in. $= L/713$, O.K.

**1.56** $w_L = 0.29$ k/ft or 16 psf

**1.59** $w_{tot} = 2.53$ k/ft

**2.3** placement at third points

**2.4** $20LJ08$ @ $4\frac{1}{2}$ ft on center

**2.8** (a) $P_e = 12.50$ k, $P_i = 25$ k
(b) $P_e = 9.38$ k, $P_i = 15.63$ k

**2.9** 50.4 lb/ft

**2.10** two #6

**2.11** $P_{max} = 77.35$ k, $f_{v\ max} = 16.12$ psi

**2.12** $f_v = 20.52$ psi

**3.1** (a) two 2 in. diameter, (b) $\Delta l = 4.02$ in., $\Delta_y = 1.22$ in.

**3.2** $2\frac{1}{4}$-in diameter

**3.4** $2\frac{1}{4}$-in. diameter

**3.7** increase of cable force by 89%

**3.9** (a) $\frac{1}{2}$-in. diameter, (b) $y_{20} = 6.4$ ft, (c) $\tan \theta_{sup:} = 0.4$,
(d) $l = 102.67$ ft, (e) $\Delta l = 0.366$ ft, (f) $\Delta f = 0.686$ ft

**3.11** $f/L \cong 0.2$

**3.12** $\Delta l = 0.48$ in., $\Delta f = 0.9$ in.

**3.17** $1\frac{1}{2}$-in. diameter

**3.18** $3-3\frac{3}{4}$-in. diameter

**3.21** (a) $1\frac{5}{8}$ in. diameter

**3.22** $3-3\frac{1}{2}$ in. diameter

**3.23** $1\frac{3}{4}$-in. diameter

**3.27** $\Delta f = 1.92$ ft

**3.28** $\Delta f = 3.62$ ft

**3.30** 2-in. diameter

**4.0** (a) three times indeterminate, (b) five times indeterminate, (c) nine times indeterminate, (d) once indeterminate, (e) three times indeterminate, (f) three times indeterminate

**4.7** The asymmetrical loading case causes shear and positive bending within the midspan range, hence must be considered for the final design.

**4.8** case (a), beam: $W18 \times 35$, column: $W6 \times 16$

**4.11** $f = 4.71$ ksi

**4.12** $\Delta = 0.28$ in.

**4.13** $M = 32.13$ ft-k

**4.18** a) (a) use $3 \times 10$, (b) use $4 \times 10$
b) use $6 \times 14$

**4.19** use $2 \times 8$

**4.20** use $2 \times 6$

**4.21** column: $W27 \times 114$, beam: $W24 \times 84$

**4.25** $M_{min} = 27.83$ ft-k, $M_{max} = 22.33$ ft-k

**4.30** use $3\frac{1}{8} \times 13\frac{1}{2}$ in.

**4.31** $W10 \times 12$

**4.32** $W27 \times 94$

**4.36** $W33 \times 118$

**4.38** use $5 \times 2.75$ ft

**4.40** $N_t = 100$ k (C), $N_b = 96$ k (T)

**4.41** (a) $P_{cd} = 9.00$ k (T), $P_{ef} = 12.17$ k (C), $P_{cf} = 3.35$ k (T)
(b) $P_{cf} = 0.67$ k (T), $P_{ef} = 1.88$ k (C), $P_{cd} = 1.26$ k (T)
(f) $P_{ce} = 1.08$ k (C), $P_{de} = 1.43$ k (C)

**4.42** (e) $M_{max} = 3.5$ ft-k, (f) $M_{max} = 2.5$ ft-k, (e) $M = 0$

**4.45** $W10 \times 22$

**4.48** use $5\frac{1}{8} \times 15$ in. beams and $8\frac{3}{4} \times 39\frac{3}{4}$ in. girders

**4.49** use $16 \times 45$ in. girder with one #10 and 4 #9 in two layers

**4.50** (a) $18LJ03$ at 6 ft on center (b) $W30 \times 99$ girder
(c) $W14 \times 90$ ext. column, $W12 \times 50$ interior column

**4.51** The solution would be more efficient

**4.52** depth $t = 1$ ft 3 in.

**4.53** (a) use $L = 4$ ft 3 in. and $t = 10$ in. (b) use #5 at $9\frac{1}{2}$ in. on center

**4.54** $L = 4$ ft 5 in., $t = 1$ ft 5 in.

**4.55**  $L$ = 4 ft 4 in., $t$ = 1 ft 4 in.

**4.56**  (a)  use 8 ft 10 in. square footing with a depth of 23 in.
(b)  use sixteen #7 in both directions

**5.3**  The structure is externally unstable.

**5.4**  $B_x = -C_x$ = 0.6 k, $A_z = B_z$ = -0.3 k, $A_y$ = 1 k, $C_z$ = 0.6 k

**5.5**  $N_{ad} = N_{db}$ = 0.47 k (C), $N_{ac} = N_{bc}$ = 0.23 k (T),
$N_{ab}$ = 0.18 k (T), $N_{cd}$ = 0.57 k (C)

**5.9**  largest top chord members: TS $3\frac{1}{2}$ OD $\times$ 0.226
largest bottom chord and diagonal members: TS $2\frac{1}{2}$ OD $\times$ 0.203

**5.11**  chord members: $N_{top} = N_{bot}$ = 53.04 k

**6.2**  $f_{tu}$ = 1.72 ksi

**6.4**  4 $\times$ 8 rafters and 6 $\times$ 10 chord members

**6.6**  #3 at 16 in. in transverse direction and #3 at 9 in. in longitudinal direction together
with seven #8 along bottom fold

**8.5**  #6 at $3\frac{1}{4}$ in. on center in long. direction at midspan

**8.6**  TS 4 OD $\times$ 0.337

**8.7**  use 2 $\times$ 10

**8.14**  $\Delta R_1$ = 1.44 in., $\Delta R_2$ = 0.39 in., $\Delta R_3$ = 0.038 in.

**8.15**  $f_c$ = 104.41 psi

**8.16**  $W6 \times 15$ (rib), $W8 \times 10$ (purlin), $W14 \times 53$ (tension ring)

**8.17**  TS 3 OD $\times$ 0.216

**8.19**  #3 at 10 in. on center

**8.20**  The direction of the forces is opposite.

**8.22**  shell reinforcement: #4 at $11\frac{1}{2}$ in. on center and #3 at 15 in. on center
edge beam: 1 ft 3 in. $\times$ 1 ft 6 in.
interior ridge beam: 2 ft 5 in. $\times$ 1 ft 6 in.

**8.25**  $N = S$ = 44 k/ft, $C_{max}$ = 798.36 k (inside beam),
$C_{max}$ = 399.18 k (edge beam), $H$ = 774.4 k (tie rod)

**8.26**  $t = \frac{1}{2}$ in.

**8.29**  $N_{u\ max}$ = 11.25 k (long side), $N_{u\ max}$ = 9 k (short side),
$S_{u\ max}$ = 20.13 k (corners)

**9.3**  $p_i$ = 6.80 psf, $T_u$ = 83.95 lb/in.

**9.4**  $p_i$ = 27.02 psi, $t = \frac{1}{16}$ in.

**9.5**  $p_i$ = 3 psf, $T_u$ = 267.81 lb/in.

**9.7**  $p_i$ = 9.68 psf, $T_u$ = 331.42 lb/in., foundation: 1 ft 6 in. $\times$ 4 ft 3 in.

**9.8**   $p_i = 14.4$ psf, $T_u = 275.77$ lb/ft

**9.9**   $p_i = 28.29$ psi, $T_u = 1273.05$ lb/in.

**9.11**   $R = 12$ in., $T_u = 7200$ lb/in.

**9.12**   $p_i = 28.47$ psi, $T_u = 854.1$ lb/in.

**9.14**   (a)   $T_u = 0.8$ k/in.,   (b)   $\frac{1}{2}$ in. diameter structural steel wire rope

**9.16**   $T_u = 0.533$ k/in.

# INDEX

For names of designers, scientists, etc. as well as names and location of buildings refer to List of Building Illustrations and References.